Textbook on Administrative Law

First Edition	2015
Reprint	2020
Reprint	**2022**

Textbook on Administrative Law

Yashomati Ghosh
LLB, LLM, Ph.D
Assistant Professor of Law
National Law School of India University, Bangalore

LexisNexis

LexisNexis

This book is a publication of **LexisNexis**
(A Division of Reed Elsevier India Pvt Ltd)
14th floor, Building No 10, Tower–B, DLF Cyber City, Phase-II,
Gurgaon–122002, Haryana, India.
Tel: + 91 124 4774444 Fax: + 91 124 4774100
Website: www.lexisnexis.co.in / E-mail: help.in@lexisnexis.com

Yashomati Ghosh, *Administrative Law*, First Edition, 2016

ISBN: 978-93-5143-705-5

Printed at Replika Press Pvt. Ltd.

Printed and bound in India.

To
My Parents,
Anjana and Abhijit Ghosh,
for making me the person I am.

Preface

Administrative Law is that branch of public law which aims to control the abuse or misuse of governmental power, and keep the executive and its instrumentalities within the statutory limits. The substance of the law consists of various principles which have been evolved by the courts for the purpose of regulating the manner of administrative functioning so as to prevent arbitrary use of governmental powers and protect the rights of the citizens. These principles hold the key to establish accountability among the various functionaries of the state and to imbibe the values of good governance. The principles obligate the administrative functionaries to perform their administrative functions in a responsible and non-arbitrary manner.

In a modern welfare state, the functions of the government have increased manifold. The changing role of the state in the post-liberal era has further strengthened the dynamic role of the administration and has magnified the importance of study of administrative law.

Textbook on Administrative Law is an effort to introduce the social and legal importance of the principles of administrative law in the daytoday life of every ordinary citizen. The purpose is to orient them towards better understanding and appreciation of the functional role of the state and to equip them with the necessary administrative tool so as to not only protect their rights against arbitrary state actions but also discharge their obligations as informed citizens of this country in a more fulfilling manner.

The **key features** of the book are given below–

- It discusses some of the recent legislative and other initiatives undertaken for the purpose of promoting citizen-centric administration.
- It provides an insight into the core principles of administrative law, essential for the proper functioning of the administration.

- It explains the ever-increasing functions and powers of the administrative role of the state that have resulted in the growth of administrative law, including regulatory authorities and tribunals.

Contents and Structure

Chapter 1 discusses the importance of administrative accountability and establishes the linkage between administrative law and the notions of good governance and citizen-centric administration.

Chapter 2 deals with jurisprudential and constitutional foundations of administrative law. Chapter 3 classifies and differentiates between the different forms of administrative actions including administrative instructions.

Chapters 4 discusses various issues relating to growth of delegated legislation, its constitutionality and the different means of regulating the exercise of subordinate law-making powers.

Chapter 5 emphasizes the importance of quasi-judicial functions and the application of the principles of natural justice. The chapter discusses elaborately the cardinal principles of natural justices, including the various exceptions.

Chapter 6 involves the discussion relating to discretionary exercise of administrative powers. The chapter includes elaborate discussion on the different principles of judicial review developed for the purpose of preventing arbitrary exercise of power.

Chapter 7 demonstrates the importance of tribunals and highlights the different constitutional and legal challenges in the functioning of these administrative adjudicative bodies.

Chapter 8 brings forth a discussion on the emergence of independent regulatory authorities and discusses the importance of application of administrative law principles in their functioning.

Chapter 9 highlights the constitutional protection granted to the members of the civil service through the lenses of judicial decisions.

Chapter 10 identifies the different judicial processes in regulating and controlling administrative actions. It discusses the different forms of public law remedies and private law remedies available to the citizens.

Chapter 11 highlights some of the major legislative and administrative initiatives undertaken for the purpose of promoting good governance and citizen-centric administration.

Acknowledgement

I am grateful for the productive dialogue and discussions with my students, professors, and colleagues on various issues relating to administrative growth of power and the changing dynamics of accountability and governance in contemporary times which helped me in identifying the crucial issues and drafting the content of this book. I am thankful to all my students of National Law School of India University (NLSIU) for inspiring me to write this book.

I am in gratitude to Professor (Dr) Venkata Rao, Vice-Chancellor, NLSIU, for all his encouragement. He has been a pillar of support in all my endeavours and achievements.

This book has been enriched by my association and interaction with my senior professors and colleagues, particularly Dr O.V. Nandimath, Registrar NLSIU, for always emphasizing the importance of administrative law as a means to establish ethics and probity in governance and public life.

I express my gratitude to the staff members of NLSIU library for their kind assistance.

I shall remain grateful to the entire team of LexisNexis for their invaluable inputs and utmost cooperation.

I am extremely fortunate to have a kind and supporting family who have always stood by me. I am thankful to my parents, Anjana and Abhijit Ghosh, for always encouraging me to put in my best efforts. I am always indebted to them for their generous love, commitment, empathy, patience, and support. I am grateful to my parents-in-law, Jayshree and Sridev Chakrabarty, for their constant motivation and support. I appreciate the unconditional support extended by my husband, Anirban Chakraborty, in writing this book. Finally, I wish to thank my little Suryanshu for being a most wonderful son.

Yashomati Ghosh

Contents

I

Introduction to Adminisrative Law

LEARNING OBJECTIVES

After reading this chapter, you will be familiar with:

- Growth of Executive functions and the concept of Residuary powers
- Need of Administrative Law
- Definition of Administrative Law
- Nature, scope and objective of Administrative Law
- Linkage between principles of Administrative Law and the concept of Good Governance
- Characteristic features of the Eight Principles of Good Governance (United Nations)
- Emergence of Citizen-Centric Administration and its relevance to Administrative Law

1.1 INTRODUCTION

Administrative law as a branch of study emerged in the early parts of the 20th century. The idea of the State responsibility and the State being accountable to the people emerged in the 20th century. The economic principle of *laissez faire* of the earlier century had given rise to the principle of state non-interference in the affairs of the common people and greater autonomy to the people to determine their course of life. The *laissez faire* model propounded that the role of state will be minimal and confined to the maintenance of law and order, protecting the state against foreign aggressions and adjudicating disputes between the citizens. But the negative consequences of *laissez faire* economy soon caused hardships to the common people that made people realize that the free market policy will not necessarily give rise to optimal wealth and ensure well-being of all people. The profit making goals of the *laissez faire* economy caused hardship to a large section of the population like children, women, poor and old people who could not adequately fight for their interests in the unequal world and were forced to face lot of hardships. Conflicts arose between the have's and the have-nots, between members of the different economic strata like the factory owners and the workers. A realization came about in the minds of the educated people that the unregulated *laissez faire* policy was not conducive to the general well-being of society and required the positive intervention by the State. In addition, the rise of the democratic principles based on adult suffrage created new notions of State responsibility and the state representatives were required to uphold the interests of the common people in their functioning. When people acquired the right to vote, they started making the political system respond to their needs and the political parties and their leaders were compelled to adopt pro-people measures and ensure the well-being of the citizens.

The 20th century further witnessed the mass destruction of human lives during the two World Wars and also the independence of a large number of colonized nations of Asia and Africa created a conscious global community responsible towards the welfare of the people and protection of their rights. The Universal Declaration of Human Rights (UDHR) recognized a set of civil, political, economic, social and cultural rights as part of core human rights which are deemed inalienable for the purpose of promoting equality and development. The constitution of vast majority of these states incorporated these rights as fundamental in their governance and essential towards achieving their welfare goals. People expected their state to adopt welfare measures in the form of education, health, food, employment opportunities etc. Notions of socio-economic and political justice, rule of law and access to justice became the norms of the day. The consequence of all these actions was the increasing functions of the State. From the goals of minimal state intervention during the *laissez faire* period to the ever increasing responsibility of the state under the notions of a welfare state, 20th century witnessed a major transformation in the functioning of the state.

Traditionally there are three principle organs of the state – Legislature, Executive and Judiciary. These organs are entrusted with the performance of basic functions. The legislature is required to frame the policies and make the legislations for the welfare of the people. The primary task of the executive is to implement and execute the laws whereas the judicial function involves interpretation of laws, adjudication of disputes and administration of justice. The executive function of implementing the laws made by the legislature has always been categorised as 'administrative' functions generally.[1] The increase

1. Julius Stone, The Twentieth Century Administrative Explosion and After, California Law Review, Vol. 52, No. 3, (Aug., 1964), pp. 513-542, p. 513.

in state responsibility had imposed additional responsibilities on these three organs of the state. But the limited number of members and specific functional duties of the legislature and the judiciary had imposed inherent limitation on these organs to undertake the additional responsibilities. In this context the executive became responsible for the performance of various welfare activities like establishing schools, hospitals and colleges, construction of roads and other infrastructures etc. The executive was required to perform all the residuary state functions in exclusion of the legislative and the judicial functions. In the words of Professor Wade–

> If the state is to care for its citizens from the cradle to the grave, to protect the environment, to educate them at all stages, to provide them with employment, training, houses, medical services, pensions, and, in last resort, food, clothing, and shelter, it needs huge administrative apparatus. Relatively little can be done merely by passing Acts of Parliament. There are far too many problems of detail, and far too many matters that cannot be decided in advance.[2]

1.2 GROWTH OF EXECUTIVE FUNCTIONS-RESIDUARY FUNCTIONS

In the case of *In Re: Delhi Laws Act case*[3] the Supreme Court recognized that the Indian Constitution had broadly identified the separation of functions between the three principle organs of the state – legislature, executive and judiciary. These principle organs were required to perform their essential functions as part of their constitutional responsibility.

> Under the Constitution of India as adopted on the 26th of January, 1950, the executive government of the Union is vested in the President acting on the advice of the Ministers. A Parliament is established to make laws and a Supreme Court is established with the powers defined in different articles of the Constitution. The executive legislative and judicial functions of the Government, which have to be discharged, were thus distributed but the articles giving power to these bodies do not vest the legislative or judicial powers in these bodies expressly.[4]

Ram Jawaya Kapur v. State of Punjab[5] is the leading case dealing with the scope and extent of administrative functions in constitutional India. A writ petition under Article 32 of the Constitution was filed challenging the decision and the notifications issued by the Education Department (ED)

---

2. Wade and Forsyth, Administrative Law, Oxford University Press, 10th Ed. 2009, P. 4.
3. (1951) SCR 747.
4. Id, Para 11.
5. AIR 1955 SC 549 : (1955) 2 SCR 225.

of the Punjab Government as violative of the fundamental right of the petitioners to carry on their business of printing, publication and sale of school text books. After 1950 by several resolutions the government had introduced state monopoly in the publication of text books. The entire act of publishing, printing and selling of school text books were monopolized by the Government and private publishers were ousted from the business. The petitioners challenged these notifications on three fold grounds of–

Firstly the concept of modern state function enable the state to undertake any trade or business related activity, secondly whether the executive can undertake such activities without any specific legislative sanction, and thirdly whether the state can deprive the fundamental right of an individual without authority of law.

The Court defining the functions of a modern welfare state recognized that the functions of a modern State cannot be confined to mere police functions like collection of taxes, maintenance of law and order and protection of the state against external and internal aggression. *A modern State is certainly expected to engage in all activities necessary for the promotion of the social and economic welfare of the community.* Thus undertaking of a business or commercial activity by the state was held permissible under the multiplicity of functions which a welfare state is required to perform. Defining the scope of executive functions and responsibilities in the context of separation of power doctrine the Court observed–

> It may not be possible to frame an exhaustive definition of what executive function means and implies. Ordinarily the executive power connotes the residue of governmental functions that remain after legislative and judicial functions are taken away. The Indian Constitution has not indeed recognized the doctrine of separation of powers in its absolute rigidity but the functions of the different parts or branches of the Government have been sufficiently differentiated and consequently it can very well be said that our Constitution does not contemplate assumption, by one organ or part of the State, of functions that essentially belong to another. The executive indeed can exercise the powers of departmental or subordinate legislation when such powers are delegated to it by the legislature. It can also, when so empowered, exercise judicial functions in a limited way. The executive Government, however, can never go against the provisions of the Constitution or of any law. This is clear from the provisions of Article 154 of the Constitution but, as we have already stated, it does not follow from this that in order to enable the executive to function there must be a law already in existence and that the powers of executive are limited merely to the carrying out of these laws.

Thus the scope of the executive function is described as residuary in nature. Once the essential functions have been performed by the legislature and judiciary, the executive can be conferred with the power to make incidental or subordinate legislations as well as perform judicial functions in a limited manner, but the executive can never act contrary to the provisions of the Constitution or a statute. Justifying the role of the State Government it was emphasized that *in a written Constitution like ours the executive power may be such as is given to the executive or is implied, ancillary or inherent. It must include all powers that may be needed to carry out into effect the aims and objects of the Constitution. It must mean more than merely executing the laws.* It was further clarified that *an act would be within the executive power of the State if it is not an act which has been assigned by the Constitution of India to other authorities or bodies and is not contrary to the provisions of any law and does not encroach upon the legal rights of any member of the public.*[6]

Differentiating between the Australian Constitution and the Indian Constitution as regards the scope of executive powers, it was highlighted that the executive power in Australia was limited to the execution and maintenance of the Constitution and laws of the country[7] whereas Articles 73 and 162 of the Indian Constitution dealing with the executive powers of the Union and the States respectively categorically lay down that the executive power is co-extensive with the powers of the respective legislatures to make laws. Hence the executive authority of the Union Government is in respect of matters enumerated in List I of the Seventh Schedule whereas those of the State Government is restricted to areas specified in List II. It was further emphasized that it was not necessary under the provisions for the legislatures to make prior legislations for the purpose of the Executive to act in respect of those areas. *On the other hand the language of Article 162 of the Indian Constitution clearly indicates that the powers of the State executive to extend to matters upon which the state legislature is competent to legislate and are not confined to matters over which legislation has been passed already. The same principle underlies Article 73 of the Indian Constitution.*[8]

Highlighting the important role of the executive in formulating policies and enacting legislations in a parliamentary form of democracy the Court observed–

> The limits within which the executive Government can function under the Indian Constitution can be ascertained without much difficulty by reference to

6. Ibid, Para 13.
7. Australian Constitution Section 61 – The executive power of the Commonwealth is vested in the Queen and is exercised by the Governor-General as the Queen's representative and extends to the execution and maintenance of the Constitution and of the laws of the Commonwealth.
8. *Supra* note 5, Para 8.

the form of the executive which our Constitution has set up. Our Constitution, though federal in its structure, is modelled on the British Parliamentary system where the executive is deemed to have the primary responsibility for the formulation of governmental policy and its transmission into law though the condition precedent to the exercise of this responsibility is its retaining the confidence of the legislative branch of the State. The executive function comprises both the determination of the policy as well as carrying it into execution. This evidently includes the initiation of legislation, the maintenance of order, the promotion of social and economic welfare, the direction of foreign policy, in fact the carrying on or supervision of the general administration of the State.

In India, as in England, the executive has to act subject to the control of the legislature; but in what way is this control exercised by the legislature? Under Article 53(1) of our Constitution, the executive power of the Union is vested in the President but under Article 75 there is to be a Council of Ministers with the Prime Minister at the head to aid and advise the President in the exercise of his functions. The president has thus been made a formal or constitutional head of the executive and the real executive powers are vested in the Ministers or the Cabinet. The same provisions obtain in regard to the Government of States; the Governor or the Rajpramukh, as the case may be, occupies the position of the head of the executive in the State but it is virtually the Council of Ministers in each State that carries on the executive Government. In the Indian Constitution, therefore, we have the same system of parliamentary executive as in England and the Council of Ministers consisting, as it does, of the members of the legislature is, like the British Cabinet, "a hyphen which joins, a buckle which fastens the legislative part of the State to the executive part". The Cabinet enjoying, as it does, a majority in the legislature concentrates in itself the virtual control of both legislative and executive functions; and as the Ministers constituting the Cabinet are presumably agreed on fundamentals and act on the principle of collective responsibility, the most important questions of policy are all formulated by them.

Thus when the executive government formulates a particular policy in furtherance of their welfare activities it is not necessary to have a prior legislation in place. Subsequent parliamentary approval through authorization of expenditures will be deemed sufficient. However specific legislation may be necessary *if the Government require certain powers in addition to what they possess under ordinary law in order to carry on the particular trade or business.* For example specific legislation is required if the government action will give rise to encroachment of private rights. In this case no fundamental right of the petitioner to carry on their trade or commerce was infringed by state action, hence no legislation was necessary. *Ram Jawaya Kapoor* stands for the recognition of the growing administrative power in India which is indispensable in fulfilling the goals of a modern welfare state having multifarious obligations.

1.3 NEED OF ADMINISTRATIVE LAW

The Executive body and the various administrative bodies have been entrusted with the responsibility of carrying out the various welfare obligations of the state. The Constitution of India has adopted the welfare philosophy and through its various provisions it has attempted to attain the goals of socio-economic and political justice. Part III of the Constitution has secured equality, liberty, political justice and religious autonomy through the various fundamental rights whereas Part IV has directed the State to attain the higher objectives of social and economic justice by ensuring that the citizens have adequate means of livelihood, equal pay for equal work, decent standard of living, proper nutritional standards, access to social security and legal aid, protection of environment and many such goals. For the purpose of carrying out these additional responsibilities it became necessary to create a mammoth administration involving huge manpower and financial resources. A large number of ministerial departments and bureaucratic officers were created to perform the various state functions and obligations. The Indian Constitution has created and recognized a number of administrative bodies such as Election Commission (Article 324), Public Service Commission (Article 315), All India Services (Article 312), Finance Commission (Article280), Inter-State Water Dispute Authority (Article 262), Inter-State Council (Article 263), Administrative Tribunals (Article 323A), National Commission for Scheduled Castes (Article 338) and National Commission for Scheduled Tribes (Article 338A). These administrative authorities were granted lot of discretionary powers to make subordinate rules, decide quasi-judicial issues and to take administrative actions. In addition, the concept of ministerial responsibility backed by huge bureaucracy, laid the foundations for a massive administration. It was realised that mere dependency on the legislature for making laws on each and every issue or approaching the judiciary for resolving all disputes arising in the course of implementation of the laws was detrimental in the running of an efficient administrative system. Thus the modern day administration became the repository of huge authority and power.

Power corrupts and absolute power corrupts absolutely – This observation made by Edward Coke is of profound importance in the growth of administrative law. With the increase in the functions and powers of the administration it was felt necessary that there should be an adequate check on the workings of the administration so as to prevent abuse of powers which will be detrimental to the welfare of the people. It is essential that the various administrative bodies should carry out their functions and responsibilities in accordance with the constitutional goals and provisions. Adequate control should be exercised over the administration by means of political checks through the Parliament and legal control through the process of judicial review. The administrative bodies are required to adhere to a set of identified norms and rules in performance of their duties so as to prevent abuse of powers, arbitrariness, maladministration, non-performance of duties and breach of legal rights of the citizens. These norms and rules have been developed by the judiciary and are known as the principles of administrative law.

If discretionary power is to be tolerable, it must be kept under two kinds of control: political control through the Parliament, and legal control through the courts. Equally there must be control over the boundaries of legal power, beyond which there is normally no discretion.[9]

1.4 DEFINING ADMINISTRATIVE LAW

Administrative law is a judge-made law and comprises of various principles of state accountability and good governance which have been developed through different case laws. The essence of administrative law is to ensure that the multitude of functions which are performed by the different administrative authorities are in accordance with established legal principles of fairness and accountability and are within the fold of legality and propriety. Administrative law aims to prevent abuse of administrative powers and prescribes for remedial measures in case of breach of individual rights, liberties and privileges.

In light of the multifarious nature of administrative functions and the constantly evolving norms of accountability it has been difficult to lay down a single comprehensive definition of administrative law. Different scholars have described the nature and scope of administrative law based on the desired objectives. Some of the relevant definitions are–

Sir William Wade and Professor Christopher Forsyth in their book *Administrative Law* has defined administrative law as the law relating to the *control of governmental power.*[10] It is further described as "the primary purpose of administrative law, therefore, is to keep the powers of government within their legal bounds, so as to protect the citizen against their abuse.... It is also the concern of administrative law to see that public authorities can be compelled to perform their duties if they make default".

Professor Bernard Schwartz has defined the scope of Administrative law in the following words–

> Administrative law is that branch of the law that controls the administrative operations of government. Its primary purpose is to keep governmental powers

9. Wade and Forsyth, Administrative Law, Oxford University Press, 10th Ed. 2009
10. Id.

within their legal bounds and to protect individuals against the abuse of such powers. It sets forth the powers that may be exercised by administrative agencies, lays down the principles governing the exercise of those powers, and provides legal remedies to those aggrieved by administrative action.

This definition divides administrative law into three parts: (1) the powers vested in administrative agencies; (2) the requirements imposed by law upon the exercise of those powers; and (3) the remedies against unlawful administrative action.[11]

Professor I.P. Massey has defined Administrative Law as that "branch of public law which deals with the organisation and powers of administrative and quasi-administrative agencies and prescribes principles and rules by which an official action is reached and reviewed in relation to individual liberty and freedom".[12] He further describes the four foundational bricks of administrative law as–

1. Checking abuse or rerouting of administrative power;
2. Ensuring citizens an impartial determination of their disputes by officials;
3. Protecting citizens from unauthorised encroachment on their rights and interests;
4. Making those who exercise public power accountable to the people.

Professor M.P. Jain has described the scope, content and ambit of Administrative Law as–

> Administrative Law deals with the structure, powers and functions of the organs of administration; the limits of their powers; the methods and procedures followed by them in exercising their powers and functions; the methods by which their powers are controlled including the legal remedies available to a person against them when his rights are infringed by their operation.[13]

This statement has four limbs.

(a) The first limb deals with the composition and powers of organs of administration.

(b) The second limb refers to the limits on the powers of administrative authorities.

(c) The third limb refers to the procedures used in exercising those powers.

(d) The fourth limb refers to the control of the Administration through judicial and other means.

---

11. Bernard Schwartz, Administrative Law, Aspen Publishers, 3rd Ed. 1991.
12. IP Massey, Administrative Law, Eastern Book Company, 8th Ed. 2012.
13. MP Jain & SN Jain, Principles of Administrative Law, LexisNexis, 6th Ed. 2013.

An analysis of these various descriptions of administrative law clearly indicates that the primary objective is to ensure that the powers of the government are exercised in accordance with constitutional and legal principles so that certain limitations can be imposed on their functions for the purpose of preventing unfettered or arbitrary exercise of powers and ensuring that the rights of the citizens are protected from unauthorized administrative encroachment. Thus administrative law can be described as a body of principles dealing with the manner of exercise of governmental powers and duties and protecting citizen's rights.

1.5 LINKING THE PRINCIPLES OF ADMINISTRATIVE LAW TO THE CONCEPT OF GOOD GOVERNANCE

The emergence of Administrative law as a branch of public law was a phenomenon of the early 20th century. The essential norms of administrative law impose a negative obligation on the power of the various administrative authorities requiring that in the course of their functioning they should not misuse or abuse their powers and violate the rights of the common people. It fundamentally deals with limiting and regulating the powers of the administrative authorities. This theoretical understanding of administrative law did not impose any positive obligation on the state authorities to ensure that the working of the administration is towards achieving the welfare of the people. The goals of proper and effective governance were not reflected in the definitional scope of administrative law. The modern day understanding of the principles of good governance attempts to bridge that gap and introduces a positive obligation on the administration.

Santosh Hegde J. had recently observed that *Good governance is our fundamental right*[14] but the origin of the notions of good governance can be traced to ancient Indian literature. The popular ancient Indian text of Kautilya's *Arthashastra*[15] had emphasized that the traits of a king of a well governed State have been described as – "*in the happiness of his subjects lies his happiness, in their welfare his welfare, whatever pleases himself, he does not consider as good, but whatever pleases his subjects he considers as good*". The concept of good governance in ancient Indian implied that the immense power given to the king should be used for the common interest and welfare of the people. Kautilya's perception of the state was similar to a modern welfare state wherein the primary duty of the king was to protect his vulnerable and weak subjects like children, old people, women, disabled

14. Santosh Hegde delivered the 12th Nani Palkhivala Memorial Lecture on the topic 'Is Good Governance a Right of a Citizen in Democracy', The Hindu, September 3, 2015.
15. Arthashastra-Treatise on the art of Government and Administration.

and persons suffering from illness.[16] It was the responsibility of the king to maintain law and order as well as ensure proper administration of justice. In the ancient Indian system the bureaucratic accountability was considered an essential part of good governance and it was the responsibility of the chief officer of each state department to look after the performance of each person under their charge.

In modern day the goal of administration is to ensure *more governance and less government* by adhering to the norms of good governance. It is part of the present day demand that to bring in reforms in the traditional administrative structure and replacing the mammoth administrative structure of the last century with a lean but robust administration which will function on the ideals of good governance. The international community, under the auspices of the United Nations has taken a lead in promoting the goals of good governance as a mechanism to ensure the existence of stable, transparent and efficient state functioning.

The term 'good governance' assumed significance when the World Bank and the International Monetary Fund as part of their structural adjustment policy made adherence to the principles of good governance as a condition for providing financial aid to nations. The underlying rationale is that the applicability of good governance principles can help to combat corruption, nepotism, bureaucracy, mismanagement by means of transparency, accountability and proper procedures. The UN Economic and Social Commission for Asia and the Pacific in their leading paper *What is Good Governance?* had identified 8 major characteristics of good governance. These characteristics are – (i) Participatory, (ii) Consensus oriented, (iii) Accountable, (iv) Transparent, (v) Responsive, (vi) Effective and Efficient, (vii) Equitable and Inclusive, and (viii) Rule of Law. The objective behind application of these principles in the day to day governance is to make running of administration more democratic and accountable, and ensure the participation of the common people in the task policy formulation. In addition it is expected to minimize corruption and ensure inclusion of the minorities and the vulnerable sections into the decision making process and consequently make the administration more responsive to the present and future needs of the society.

The term 'governance' refers to *the process of decision-making and the process by which decisions are implemented (or not implemented).*[17] It includes both formal and informal actors who are involved in the decision

16. S.S. Ali, Kautilya and the Concept of Good Governance, The Indian Journal of Political Science, Vol. 67, No. 2 (Apr – June, 2006), pp. 375 – 380.
17. UN Economic and Social Commission for Asia and the Pacific, *What is Good Governance?* at http://www.unescap.org/sites/default/files/good-governance.pdf.

making process as well as in the implementation of the decisions made and the different formal and informal structures which have been created to arrive at and implement the decision.[18] In present day governance, the government is an important functionary along with other institutions and actors like media, lobbyists, international donors, multi-national corporations, financial institutions, political parties, research institutes, religious and caste leaders, NGOs etc. who play significant role in the decision-making process or in influencing such processes. In addition to formal process of policy making through the Parliament, in every modern society these actors participates and acts as advisors through informal processes. In such environment there is every possibility that government policy making will lack transparency and public welfare objective, and be vitiated by the motives of the several interest groups, including corrupt objectives.

In addition, there are traditional barriers to the emergence of Good Governance in society. The rigid structure of bureaucracy and the attitudinal problems of civil servants often act as impregnable to all reform measures. The Second Administrative Reforms Commission has described the bureaucracy as *wooden, inflexible, self-perpetuating and inward looking.* Rigid and formalistic procedural rules create obstacles for citizens' to access government institutions and thereby promoting corruption and red tapism. Lack of adequate administrative grievance redressal system poses serious difficulty in implementation of citizens' rights and timely enforcement of essential service. All these factors act as barriers in creating a citizen-centric and accountable administration. In these circumstances compliance with the principles of good governance becomes essential in creating an accountable, corruption-free, participatory and citizen-centric administration.

1.6 CHARACTERISTIC FEATURE OF THE EIGHT PRINCIPLES OF GOOD GOVERNANCE ACCORDING TO THE UNITED NATIONS[19]

1. Participation
   (a) Both men and women should participate.
   (b) Participation can be direct or indirectly through legitimate intermediate institutions or representatives.
   (c) Concerns of the vulnerable sections of the society should be taken into consideration.
   (d) Freedom of speech and expression and the right to form organizations and associations should be respected.

18. *Supra* note 17.
19. Id.

2. Transparency
   (a) Decisions and their enforcements should be in accordance with rules and regulations.
   (b) Information should be freely available and directly accessible by all those who are likely to be affected by it.
   (c) Information should be provided in easily understandable forms.
3. Rule of Law
   (a) Governance should be prescribed within a fair legal framework which is enforced impartially.
   (b) Protection of the human rights as well as the rights of the minorities.
   (c) Enforcement of laws through independent judiciary and an impartial and incorruptible police force.
4. Responsiveness
   (a) Decisions and their implementations should be within a reasonable framework.
5. Consensus oriented
   (a) Mediation between the different interest groups in society should be undertaken to reach a broad consensus about 'what is in the best interest of the whole community and how this can be achieved.'
   (b) Identification of broad and long-term goals based on principles of sustainable human development.
   (c) Preparing a proper plan of action for achieving the goals of such development.
6. Equity and Inclusiveness
   (a) All members of the society should feel that they have a stake in the developmental process.
   (b) No member or community should be excluded from the mainstream of society.
   (c) Adequate opportunities for all sections of the society, including the most vulnerable sections to improve and maintain their well-being.
7. Effectiveness and Efficiency
   (a) The state activities should work towards meeting the needs of the society by making the best use of resources at their disposal.
   (b) The concept of efficiency refers to sustainable use of natural resources and the protection of the environment.

8. Accountability
   (a) Key to good governance.
   (b) All formal and informal state actors like governmental institutions, private sectors, civil society groups must be accountable to the public and to their institutional stakeholders.
   (c) Accountability of an organization or an institution should be towards those members of the society who are likely to be affected by their decisions and actions.
   (d) Accountability is interlinked with transparency and the rule of law.

The notion of good governance is an ideal which is very difficult to achieve in totality by a nation. Very few states in the world have come to close adopting and adapting their mode of governance in accordance with the core principles of good governance but efforts should be every country to work towards achieving the character of a model state by restructuring their administration based on the above specified principles.

1.7 EMERGENCE OF CITIZEN-CENTRIC ADMINISTRATION

On a day to day basis a citizen is less concerned with politics and governance of the state. The primary involvement of the citizens with the state happens in relation timely access to various government services such as passport, LPG connection, ration card, land documents, proper medical services etc. But unfortunately in traditional administrative and governance studies citizens have conferred a very marginal and minimal role. Modern studies have tried to confer a more prominent role to citizens because of the conscious realization that the ultimate beneficiary of all state activities is the citizen. Hence the recent concept of citizen-centric administration demands that modern administration should place citizens at the center of all administrative functions. Thus the primary objective of principles of good governance is to promote citizen centric administration through the principles of transparency, efficiency, equity and stability. The fundamental goal of a constitutionally governed state is to promote the welfare of all its citizens and the Indian Constitution has tried to promote socio-economic and political justice for all the citizens.

According to Second Administrative Reforms Commission (ARC) *the concepts of good governance and citizen centric administration are intimately connected.* The four pillars of the concept of good governance are striving to achieve a pro-people model of governance through the values of – (i) Ethos implying service to the citizen; (ii) Ethics referring to character goals of administrative officers towards honesty, integrity and transparency;

(iii) Equity demanding treatment of all citizens alike, with particular empathy for the weaker sections, and (iv) Efficiency by speedy and effective delivery of essential service to the common people without harassment and making maximum use of Information and Communication Technologies.

The Second ARC was set up with the mandate to revamp the public administration into a *proactive, responsive, accountable, sustainable and efficient administration for the country at all levels of government.* It has identified the core constitutional and administrative law principles for making governance citizen-centric–

(i) Compliance with Rule of Law

(ii) Making government institutions vibrant, responsive and accountable towards citizen needs

(iii) Decentralization of government services

(iv) Transparency

(v) Civil Services Reforms

(vi) Ethics in Governance

(vii) Process Reforms

(viii) Periodic and independent evaluation of the quality of Governance

The ARC has further laid down the essential pre-requisites necessary for achieving citizen centric administration within the garb of good governance as–

(a) Sound legal framework

(b) Robust institutional mechanism for proper implementation of laws and their effective functioning.

(c) Competent personnel staffing these institutions; and sound personnel management policies

(d) Right policies for decentralization, delegation and accountability.

CONCLUSION

The principles of Administrative Law, Good Governance and Citizen-centric administration are inter-connected and intertwined with each other because of their common objective of creating an accountable state wherein the rights and liberties of common people are protected and enforced through recognized legal institutions by identified and structured legal process.

II Constitutional Foundations of Administrative Law

LEARNING OBJECTIVES

After reading this chapter, you will be familiar with:

- Relationship between Constitutional Law and Administrative Law
- Conceptual understanding of Rule of Law
- Importance of Rule of Law in the growth of Administrative Law
- Diceyan principles of Rule of Law
- Supreme Court's interpretative analysis of Rule of Law
- Understanding of Rule of Law in global context
- Modern Interpretation of Rule of Law
- Conceptual understanding of Separation of Power
- Importance of Separation of Power doctrine in the growth of Administrative Law
- Theoretical analysis of Checks and Balance theory and Essential Functions Theory
- Supreme Court's interpretative analysis of Separation of Power under the Indian Constitution

2.1 INTRODUCTION

The constitution is the grundnorm of India. It describes the primary organs of the State – Legislature, Executive and Judiciary and lays down their structure, composition, powers, functions and responsibilities and also describes the inter-relationship between these core organs. It highlights the relationship and responsibilities between the state and the citizens by prescribing the different fundamental rights, duties and the directive principles of state policy. The Constitution describes fundamental norms for the functioning of state based institutions on the defined aspirations of the people. It also deals with other issues like the federal structure of the state, liability of the state, conduct of elections etc. In addition, the concept of constitutional law includes various principles like rule of law, separation of power, independence of the judiciary and judicial review, essential functions theory and basic structure doctrine.

2.2 LINKING CONSTITUTIONAL LAW AND ADMINISTRATIVE LAW

Administrative law is an offshoot of constitutional law and is a branch of public law. It deals with the executive wing of the state and is involved with the conduct and performance of the core functions of execution and implementation of legislations and legislative policies, and conducting and governing the administration. Administrative law does not deal with the organizational structure and functional description of the various administrative departments of the state. The core purpose of the law is to describe the nature of the administrative functions, manner of performance of these functions by the administrative officers and to prescribe the procedures of administrative accountability so as to prevent arbitrariness and maladministration. The fundamental principles of administrative law is derived from different constitutional law principles such as rule of law, separation of power, sovereignty of the Constitution, independence of the judiciary, protection of the fundamental rights of the citizens etc. The power of judicial review of administrative actions is also derived from the Constitution.[1] It is the responsibility of the judiciary to ensure that the administration complies with constitutional norms and do not encroach upon the rights of the people. With the growing involvement of the administration in majority of the state activities, it has been deemed necessary to study the functioning of the administration through the independent branch of study of administrative law.

The objective of various constitutional law principles like rule of law, separation of powers, judicial review etc. is to establish a responsible and accountable administrative machinery in the governance of the state. Similarly the aim and objective of Administrative Law is to control governmental power and prevent all forms of maladministration. Historically the principles of Rule of Law and Separation of Powers were deemed detrimental to the growth of Administrative Law, but subsequently these constitutional principles became the foundations for the growth of administrative law in the common law countries. Today most administrative law principles developed by the judiciary are premised on the doctrine of rule of law and other constitutional law principles.

1. Articles 32 and 226 of the Indian Constitution.

2.3 RULE OF LAW

Rule of Law is one of the cardinal principles of constitutional law and is deemed to be a foundational stone for the growth of administrative law. The principle implies that law is the foundation of a civilized society and every act must be done in accordance with law. It implies that the law is supreme. *Everyone, whether individual or collectively, is unquestionably under the supremacy of law. Whoever he may be, however high he is, he is under the law. No matter how powerful he is and how rich he may be.*[2] The concept of Rule of Law is not of recent origin and was in application from time immemorial. In ancient India the notion of *Dharma* was based on the concept of abidance to one's own duty. The term *dharma* has been understood as law based duty which intrinsically refers to one's expected obligation and responsibility towards the members of the society. The dharma of a ruler was to protect the weak and ensure peace and prosperity in society. Aristotle in *Book IV* of his *Politics* had recognized law as the foundation of society. Law is a body of rules which are to be followed by every member of the society. In performance of their official duties, magistrates and other officers in ancient Greece were required to act in accordance with law. Sir Edward Coke, the modern day originator of the concept had asserted that the supremacy of the law should prevail over the Executive – *King is under no man, but under God and the law.* In Latin the principle is described as *quod rex non debet esse sub homine, sed sub deo et lege.*[3]

Discussing on the meaning of the term 'rule of law' Professor Goodhart has differentiated between various phrases of 'a rule of law', 'the rule of law', 'rule by law', 'rule under law' and 'rule of law'.[4] The phrase a rule of law refers to any rule of conduct which is binding on the citizens or on the public officials. Even in a tyrannical society citizens would be subjected to and regulated through laws. Unlike the phrase 'the rule of law' which governs and limits the powers and actions of all public officials, there is no inherent limit to the power of the ruling class by the interpretation of 'a rule of law'. Similarly differentiating between 'rule by law' and 'rule under law', the former is particularly applicable in a totalitarian state wherein laws are used as an instrument for enforcing tyrannical rule and curbing individual rights and freedoms through rule by law whereas the concept of rule under law emphasises that public officials are themselves bound by laws. The principle of rule of law applies the concept of *rule under the law which is the essential foundation of liberty.*

---

2. *T.N. Godavarman Thirumulpad v. Ashok Khot* (2006) 5 SCC 1.
3. As quoted in *T.N. Godavarman Thirumulpad v. Ashok Khot* (2006) 5 SCC 1.
4. Arthur L. Goodhart, The Rule of Law and Absolute Sovereignty, University of Pennsylvania Law Review, Vol. 106, No. 7, (May, 1958), pp 943-963.

Eminent British jurist and constitutional law theorist, Professor A.V. Dicey highlighted the importance of Rule of Law–

> When we speak of the rule of law as a characteristic of our country, not only that with us no man is above the law but that every man, whatever be his rank or condition, is subject to the ordinary law of the realm and amenable to the jurisdiction of the ordinary tribunals. In England the idea of legal equality, or the universal subjection of all classes to one law administered by the ordinary courts, has been pushed to its utmost limit. With us every official, from Prime Minister down to a constable or a collector of taxes, is under the same responsibility for every act done with legal justification as any other citizen. The reports abound with cases in which officials have been brought before the courts, and made, in their personal capacity, liable to punishment, or to the payment of damages, for acts done in their official character but in excess of their lawful authority. A colonial Governor, a Secretary of State, a military officer, and all subordinates, though carrying out the commands of their official superiors, are as responsible for any act which the law does not authorise as is a private and unofficial person.[5]

2.3.1 Conceptualization of Rule of Law

Justice Owen Roberts speaking on the issue of *The Rule of Law in the International Community* had emphasised that the idea of rule of law was a feature of the 'highly civilized nations' characterized by *first a country that has a representative form of government; second, a country where individual liberty and freedom are protected by law; and third where there are bounds and limits to what the government can do to an individual.* Of these three characteristics it is the last one which is considered as most essential for the application of rule of law and the other two conditions facilitate in its implementation. In the words of Goodhart *"These bounds and limits are marked by the control which is exercised over the public officers of the State by means of law. It is this which constitutes the rule of law or to use a more accurate phrase, government under law...A constitution may contain a most elaborate bill of rights, but if its terms can be disregarded at will by the public officers then these provisions will be of little effect".*[6] Accordingly every organ of the State is required to abide by rule of law by imposing or adhering to certain checks and limits. The legislative power is often regulated by the procedural norms of rule-making as well as the substantive provisions of the Constitution. The executive power is restricted to the implementation of the laws made by the Parliament. The exercise of discretionary power by the administrative officers is bound by the

5. A.V. Dicey, Introduction to the Study of the Law of the Constitution, 10th Ed. 1965.
6. *Supra* note 4 at p. 946.

provisions of the statute conferring the discretion, constitutional provisions and norms of fair procedure. The executive is accountable to the Parliament for its action and is also subject to judicial review. The judiciary has also imposed a number of checks on the exercise of their powers such as upholding constitutional principles and values, deciding disputes in accordance with the provisions of a validly enacted statute, adhering to established precedents, conforming with the norms of procedural fairness and exercising judicial discretion rationally and wisely.

2.3.2 Dicey on Rule of Law

Prof. Dicey conceptualized the doctrine of rule of law based on the following three propositions–

(i) Absence of discretionary power in the hands of the governmental officials;

(ii) No person should be made to suffer in body or deprived of his property except for a breach of law established in the ordinary legal manner before the ordinary courts of the land;

(iii) The rights of the people must flow from the customs and traditions of the people recognized by the courts in the administration of justice.

Dicey had advocated these propositions based on the political experiences in England. Rule of law is the foundation of the English legal system. In England the Parliament is the highest law-making body and enjoys absolute sovereignty. All laws were created by Parliament and there was no inherent limitation to the law-making power of the Parliament. All executive powers were required to be exercised in accordance with laws of the Parliament. The administrative officers were required to act in accordance with the Parliamentary laws and not act on their individual whims and fancies. There should be unanimity in the application of the laws so that every citizen of the country are equally governed by the same set of laws. Individual interpretation in the application of the laws by administrative officers would give rise to unpredictability and instead of being governed by the laws of the Parliament, citizens would be governed by laws as interpreted by individual officers. Hence Dicey advocated for absence of discretionary power in the hands of the governmental officers.

Under the common law system the rights and liabilities of the citizens are created by the laws made by the legislature, implemented by the administered officers and are determined by the judiciary in case of disputes. There is only one single hierarchy of courts in England which interprets the laws and determines all disputes, including administrative issues. All citizens as well as government officials are equally liable to be tried by the ordinary courts in England and there is no discrimination on the ground of being a public official. Hence Dicey had argued that under the notions of rule of law all people should be governed by same set of laws and should be subject to the same legal procedures.

In the absence of a written Constitution in England, Dicey had argued that the source of rights under the common law was from the customs and traditions existing in society. He believed that if the source of legal rights and liberties of the citizens were the written text of the Constitution, then by simply amending the Constitution the conferred rights and liberties could be curtailed or restricted. It is the faith and belief of the people along with the inherent values in society which acts as the strongest check against any form of abuse or arbitrary exercise of executive powers.

Dicey's concept of Rule of Law has been a subject of great analysis and criticisms. The principle point of criticism was that his rule of law proposition was made without taking into consideration the harsh realities of the growing administrative powers in England. His theory was a conscious attempt to distinguish the English common law system from other legal systems, particularly from the *droit administratif* system in France. Under the French legal system matters relating to State and administration are separately dealt by specific administrative tribunals known as *tribunal administratif* and not by the judiciary. Way back in 1790 the French Revolutionaries had made the proclamation that – *"Judicial functions are distinct and shall always remain separate from administrative functions. Judges will become guilty of misprision if they interfere in any manner with the activities of administrative bodies or summon before them the administrators on account of acts done in the course of the performance of their duties".*[7] As a consequence in 1799 Napolean established the administrative tribunals for exclusively dealing with the administrative disputes. In 1872 the *Conseil d'Etat* was constituted as the highest court of appeal for administrative matters. The ordinary courts are known as *Tribunal d'Instance* and the *Cour de Cassation* is the highest appellate court in France. The system of *droit administratif* has been largely appreciated by jurists across the world for creating a very liberal and progressive system of administrative law. In the words of Prof. Garner–

> It can now be said without possibility of contradiction that there is no other country where the rights of private individuals are so well protected against arbitrariness, the abuses and the illegal conduct of the administrative authorities and where they are so sure of receiving reparation for injuries sustained on account of such conduct. This is virtually the unanimous opinion of French jurists and writers on administrative law and it is entirely justified.

7. Justice David Annoussamy, French Legal System, Dr. Ambedkar Government Law College & NLSIU Bangalore, 2nd Ed., 2011.

> The council of state, which has come to be regarded as the principal guardian and protector of the rights and liberties of the people against a bureaucratic and highly centralized administration, occupies a place in the public esteem and confidence of the French which is higher even than that which the Supreme Court of the United States enjoys among the American people.[8]

Dicey had argued that in contradistinction to the political scenario of France, the English legal system was based on the notion of Parliamentary Sovereignty wherein the laws made by the Parliament were supreme and every government official was required to abide and implement those laws. There was no scope of arbitrary actions on the part of the executive. Scholars have criticised this singular focus of Dicey on the ground that the exercise of discretionary power by the administrative authorities had become a reality in England with the growing expansion of state activities. Legislations often granted certain choice making powers to the ministers and other officers. Similarly special courts like admiralty and ecclesiastical courts as well as administrative tribunals like Poor Law Boards were already in existence in England refuting his second proposition. His third proposition was based on distinguishing England from those countries having written constitution. He had asserted that in countries having a written Constitution, a despotic government could amend the Constitution at will and infringe on the rights of the citizens. In England no such abuse of rights could take place because the rights of the citizens are not based on a written text but flows from the customs and traditions. This proposition has been criticised on the ground of unsubstantiated presumptions because the common understanding among modern nations has been that a written constitution with specified rights of the citizens provides better protection against state abuses. As a consequence of Dicey's strong influence the recognition of the growth of Administrative Law was delayed by few years in England. Inspite of these criticisms it needs to be acknowledged that the aim of the common law concept of Rule of Law was similar to the goals of *droit administratif* in creating a responsible administration and protecting the rights and liberties of the citizens against executive infringement. In common law countries the principle of rule of law has been instrumental in negating administrative arbitrariness and promoting the principles of accountability by means of judicial review of administrative actions.

2.3.3 Supreme Court of India and Rule of Law

The constitutional principle of Rule of Law has been instrumental in the growth of Administrative Law in most common law countries, including

8. James W. Garner, French Administrative Law, The Yale Law Journal, Vol. 33, No. 6, (Apr., 1924), pp 597-627, 599.

India. It is considered to be the foundational stone for creating an accountable and responsible administration. The Supreme Court of India has recognized the principle as part of the basic structure doctrine of the Constitution. *The rule of law constitutes the core of our Constitution and it is the essence of the rule of law that the exercise of the power by the State whether it be the Legislature or the Executive or any other authority should be within the constitutional limitations.*[9] In numerous landmark judgments it has defined and described the changing dimensions of rule of law, including its multiple facets.

In *Bachan Singh v. State of Punjab*[10] the jurisprudence of rule of law was analysed by the Supreme Court–

> [T]he rule of law permeates the entire fabric of the Constitution and indeed forms one of its basic features. The rule of law excludes arbitrariness; its postulate is "intelligence without passion" and "reason freed from desire". Wherever we find arbitrariness or unreasonableness there is denial of the rule of law. That is why Aristotle preferred a government of laws rather than of men. "Law" in the context of the rule of law, does not mean any law enacted by the legislative authority, howsoever arbitrary or despotic it may be. Otherwise even under a dictatorship it would be possible to say that there is rule of law, because every law made by the dictator howsoever arbitrary and unreasonable has to be obeyed and every action has to be taken in conformity with such law. In such a case even where the political set up is dictatorial, it is law that governs the relationship between men and men and between men and the State. But still it is not rule of law as understood in modern jurisprudence, because in jurisprudential terms, the law itself in such a case being an emanation from the absolute will of the dictator it is in effect and substance the rule of man and not of law which prevails in such a situation. What is necessary element of the rule of law is that the law must not be arbitrary or irrational and it must satisfy the test of reason and the democratic form of polity seeks to ensure this element by making the framers of the law accountable to the people. Of course, in a country like the United Kingdom, where there is no written constitution imposing fetters on legislative power and providing for judicial review of legislation, it may be difficult to hold a law to be invalid on the ground that it is arbitrary and irrational and hence violative of an essential element of the rule of law and the only remedy if at all would be an appeal to the electorate at the time when a fresh mandate is sought at the election. But the situation is totally different in a country like India which has a written Constitution enacting fundamental rights and conferring power on the courts to enforce them not only against the executive but also against the legislature. The fundamental rights

9. *S.P. Gupta v. Union of India* MANU/SC/0080/1981.
10. (1982) 3 SCC 24 : AIR 1982 SC 1325.

erect a protective armour for the individual against arbitrary or unreasonable executive or legislative action.[11]

In the case of *ADM Jabalpur v. Shiv Kant Shukla*[12] the Court highlighted that the Constitution of India is the basic law of the land and the rule of law flows from the Constitution. In the recent judgment of *National Legal Services Authority v. Union of India*[13] the Supreme Court while upholding the right of the transgender community to seek gender identity alternate to the one assigned at the time of birth recognised it as a human right and necessary for protection under the rule of law. Rule of law is an important and pillar of the Indian Constitution and aims to fulfil the goals of social justice through public order. The Court recognizing the *substantive rule of law* observed that–

> It is the rule of proper law, which balances the needs of society and the individual. This is the rule of law that strikes a balance between society's need for political independence, social equality, economic development, and internal order, on the one hand, and the needs of the individual, his personal liberty, and his human dignity on the other. It is the duty of the Court to protect this rich concept of the rule of law.

In *DC Wadhwa v. State of Bihar*[14] the constitutional question before the Supreme Court was whether Governor under Article 213 of the Constitution had the power to re-promulgate ordinances from time to time without getting them replaced by Acts of the Legislature. Negating the act of the Governor the Court held that the power under Article 213 has been conferred for the purpose of enabling the Governor to take immediate action at a time when the legislative assembly was not in session and not for the purpose of re-promulgating ordinances for an indefinite period of time and thereby take over to himself the power of the legislature to legislate. Upholding the *locus standi* of the petitioner in filing the PIL under Article 32 the Court observed that *"it is a right of every citizen to insist that he should be governed by laws made in accordance with the Constitution and not laws made by the executive in violation of the constitutional provisions"*. Emphasising the relevant importance of determining the scope and limits of the power of the Governor to re-promulgate ordinances in chartering out the extent of Executive power the Court observed–

11. Ibid, Para 10.
12. AIR 1976 SC 1207.
13. (2014) 5 SCC 438.
14. AIR 1987 SC 579.

> The power conferred on the Governor to issue Ordinances is in the nature of an emergency power which is vested in the Governor for taking immediate action where such action may become necessary at a time when the Legislature is not in Session. The primary law making authority under the Constitution is the Legislature and not the Executive but it is possible that when the Legislature is not in Session circumstances may arise which render it necessary to take immediate action and in such a case in order that public interest may not suffer by reason of the inability of the Legislature to make law to deal with the emergent situation, the Governor is vested with the power to promulgate Ordinances. But every Ordinance promulgated by the Governor must be placed before the Legislature and it would cease to operate at the expiration of six weeks from the reassembly of the Legislature or if before the expiration of that period a resolution disapproving it is passed by the Legislative Assembly and agreed to by the Legislative Council, if any. .... The Executive cannot by taking resort to an emergency power exercisable by it only when the Legislature is not in Session, take over the law-making function of the Legislature. That would be clearly subverting the democratic process which lies at the core of our constitutional scheme, for then the people would be governed not the laws made by the Legislature as provided in the Constitution but by laws made by the Executive. The Government cannot by-pass the Legislature and without enacting the provisions of the Ordinance into an Act of the Legislature, re-promulgate the Ordinance as soon as the Legislature is prorogued. Of course, there may be a situation where it may not be possible for the Government to introduce and push through in the Legislature a Bill containing the same provisions as in the Ordinance, because the Legislature may have too much legislative business in a particular Session or the time at the disposal of the Legislature in a particular Session may be short, and in that event, the Governor may legitimately find that it is necessary to re-promulgate the Ordinance. Where such is the case, re-promulgation of the Ordinance may not be open to attack. But otherwise, it would be a colourable exercise of power on the part of the Executive to continue an Ordinance with substantially the same provisions beyond the period limited by the Constitution, by adopting the methodology of re-promulgation. It is settled law that a constitutional authority cannot do indirectly what it is not permitted to do directly. If there is a constitutional provision inhibiting the constitutional authority from doing an Act, such provision cannot be allowed to be defeated by adoption of any subterfuge. That would be clearly a fraud on the constitutional provision.

In this case the Court applied the rule of law test to invalidate the act of re-promulgation by the Governor. Even though the Constitution does not specifically prohibit re-promulgation of Ordinances but proper interpretation of the ordinance making powers under Article213 and Article123 clearly lays down the proposition that any executive effort to make an ordinance extend beyond the six months period will be misuse of power and give to *colourable exercise of power.* Legislature is the constitutional authority for the purpose of law making and if the Executive by means of Ordinances attempt to regulate the life and liberty of the citizens it would be contrary to the principles of rule of law. It is the constitutional right of the citizens to be governed by the laws made by the Parliament in the ordinary course of law making.

In *P. Sambamurthy v. State of Andhra Pradesh*[15] the Court emphasised the importance of the power of judicial review. It is an inherent constitutional power of the Supreme Court and the High Courts to review administrative actions, including the decisions of the tribunals. In this case the constitutionality of the proviso of Article371D(5) of the Constitution was challenged[16] on the ground that it was in violation of the rule of law principle as it negated the scope of judicial review. Upholding the contention that independent judiciary and the power of judicial review of executive actions are an integral part of rule of law, Supreme Court held that Article371D(5) was unconstitutional because under the provision the State Government was given the power to modify or annul any order of the Tribunal before it became effective. It observed–

> Invariably the State Government would be a party in every service dispute brought before the Administrative Tribunal and the effect of the Proviso is that the State Government which is a party to the proceeding before the Administrative Tribunal and which contests the claim of the public servant who comes before the Administrative Tribunal seeking redress of his grievance against the State Government would have the ultimate authority to uphold or reject the determination of the Administrative Tribunal. It would be open to the State Government, after it has lost before the Administrative Tribunal, to set at naught the decision given by the Administrative Tribunal against it. Such a provision is, to say the least, shocking and is clearly subversive of the principles of justice. A party to the litigation cannot be given the power to override the decision given by the Tribunal. It would be violating the basic concept of justice and make a mockery of the entire adjudicative process. Not only is the power conferred on the State Government to modify or annul the decision of the Administrative Tribunal starting and wholly repugnant to the notion of justice but it is also a power which can be abused or misused.

15. AIR 1987 SC 663 : (1987) 1 SCC 362.
16. Article 371D (5) – The order of the Administrative Tribunal finally disposing of any case shall become effective upon its confirmation by the State Government or on expiry of 3 months from the date on which the order is made; whichever is earlier.
Provided that the State Government may, by special order made in writing and for reasons to be specified therein, modify or annul any order of the Administrative Tribunal before it becomes effective and in such a case, the order of the Administrative Tribunal shall have effect only in such modified form or have no effect, as the case may be.

Emphasising that Article371D(5) was in violation of the principles of rule of law the Court observed–

> It is a basic principle of the rule of law that the exercise of power by the executive or any other authority must not only be conditioned by the Constitution but must also be in accordance with law and the power of judicial review is conferred by the Constitution with a view to ensuring that the law is observed and there is compliance with the requirement of law on the part of the executive and other authorities. It is through the power of judicial review conferred on an independent institutional authority such as the High Court that the rule of law is maintained and every organ of the State is kept within the limits of the law. If the exercise of the power of judicial review can be set at naught by the State Government by overriding the decision given against it, it would sound the death knell the rule of law. The rule of law would be meaningless as it would be open to the State Government to defy the law and yet to get away with it. The Proviso to cl (5) of Article 371-D is, therefore, violative of the basic structure doctrine.

In *T.N. Godavarman Thirumulpad v. Ashok Khot*[17] the Court further recognized that any disobedience of judicial orders would amount to violation of the rule of law principles. It observed–

> Disobedience of this Court's order strikes at the very root of the rule of law on which the judicial system rests. The rule of law is the foundation of a democratic society. Judiciary is the guardian of the rule of law. Hence, it is not only the third pillar but also the central pillar of the democratic State. If the judiciary is to perform its duties and functions effectively and remain true to the spirit with which they are sacredly entrusted to it, the dignity and authority of the courts have to be respected and protected at all costs. Otherwise, the very cornerstone of our constitutional scheme will give way and with it will disappear the rule of law and the civilised life in the society.

In *Veena Sethi v. State of Bihar*[18] Supreme Court recognized another facet of the rule of law principle. In this case a letter was written to the Supreme Court alleging illegal detention of 14 prisoners in the Hazaribagh Central Jail for almost two to three decades without due process of law. Treating the letter as a public interest litigation the Court recognized the gross human rights violation against the weaker sections of the society. Upholding access to justice and access to legal institutions as a legal right of the poor, downtrodden ignorant and illiterate sections of the community, the Court raised the pertinent question–

---

17. (2006) 5 SCC 1.
18. (1982) 2 SCC 583.

What meaning has the rule of law if the poor are allowed to languish in jails without the slightest justification as if they are the castaways of the society? The rule of law does not exist merely for those who have means to fight for their rights and very often for perpetuation of the status quo which protects and preserves their dominance and permits them to exploit large sections of the community but it exists also for the poor and the down trodden, the ignorant and the illiterate who constitute the large bulk of humanity in this country. It is the solemn duty of this Court to protect and uphold the basic human rights of the weaker sections of the society, and it is this duty we are trying to discharge in entertaining this public interest litigation.

The Supreme Court has emphasised the core principle of rule of law as anti-thesis of arbitrariness in numerous judgments. Bhagwati J., speaking for the Court, in *R.D. Shetty v. International Airport Authority of India*[19] had categorically stated that it is *"unthinkable that in a democracy governed by the Rule of Law, the executive Government or any of its officers should possess arbitrary power over the interest of the individual. Every action of the executive Government must be informed with reason and should be free from arbitrariness. That is the very essence of the Rule of Law and its bare minimal requirement"*. In *Dr. Subramanian Swamy v. Director, CBI*[20] the importance of the principle was re-emphasised with the observation that *'Absence of arbitrary power is the first essential of the rule of law upon which our whole constitutional system is based.'* Justice K.K. Mathew had observed in the article 'The Welfare State, Rule of Law and Natural Justice' that the modern day understanding of Rule of Law implies the *protection of the individual against arbitrary exercise of power wherever it is found.*[21] Linking arbitrariness as an antithesis of rule of law the Khanna J. speaking for the majority in *State of Punjab v. Khan Chand*[22] observed–

We may state that the vesting of discretion in authorities in the exercise of power under an enactment does not by itself entail contravention of Article 14. What is objectionable is the conferment of arbitrary and uncontrolled discretion without any guidelines whatsoever with regard to the exercise of that discretion. Considering the complex nature of problems which have to be faced by a modem State, it is but inevitable that the matter of details should be left to the authorities acting under an enactment. Discretion has, therefore, to be given to the authorities concerned for the exercise of the powers vested in them under an enactment. The enactment must, however, prescribe the guidelines for the furtherance of the objects of the enactment

19. (1979) II LLJ 217 SC; MANU/SC/0048/1979.
20. 2014 (6) SCALE 146; MANU/SC/0417/2014, para 4.
21. KK Mathew J., Democracy, Equality and Freedom Eastern Book Company (1978).
22. (1974) 1 SCC 549.

and it is within the framework of those guidelines that the authorities can use their discretion in the exercise of the powers conferred upon them. Discretion which is absolute, uncontrolled and without any guidelines in the exercise of the powers can easily degenerate into arbitrariness. When individuals act according to their sweet will, there is bound to be an element of 'pick and choose' according to the notion of the individuals. If a Legislature bestows such untrammelled discretion on the authorities acting under an enactment, it abdicates its essential function for such discretion is bound to result in discrimination which is the negation and antithesis of the ideal of equality before law as enshrined in Article 14 of the Constitution. It is the absence of any principle or policy for the guidance of the authority concerned in the exercise of discretion which vitiates an enactment and makes it vulnerable to the attack on the ground of violation of Article 14. It is no answer to the above that the executive officers are presumed to be reasonable men who do not stand to gain in the abuse of their power and can be trusted to use "discretion" with discretion. As mentioned on page 3 of Parliamentary Supervision of Delegated Legislation by John E. Kersell, 1960 Ed.

"The point is, however, that no one ought to be trusted with power without restraint. Power can be of an encroaching nature, and its encroachments are usually for the sake of what are sincerely believed to be good, and indeed necessary, objectives. Throughout history the most terrible form of tyranny has been the forcing on human beings of what someone believes to be good for them. The imposition of controls on the use of delegated legislative authority, therefore, does not imply a deep suspicion of malevolent intentions. Human nature, being what it is, has to be protected against itself, and where power is concerned the very existence of the possibility of restraint, as we shall see, is a safeguard against abuses in which ends may be used to justify means and the good in intent becomes the evil in effect".

Thus an analysis of the opinion of the Supreme Court in its numerous judgments clearly indicate that the principle of rule of law is part of the basic structure of our Constitution and has been integral in protecting the rights of the people from arbitrary exercise of administrative powers by giving recognition to newer dimensions of the principle. But mere legal recognition of rule of law is not adequate to bring a transformative change in the society. It is important to adhere to three essential requirements to ensure the application of rule of law in theory as well as in action.[23] Firstly there should be adequate mechanism for enforcement of laws, secondly public officials should recognize that they are bound by laws and their actions must be in accordance with the provisions of laws, and thirdly the society as a whole should have respect for rule of law in society and ensure that the legal rights of all men and women are equally protected and enforced.

23. Arthur L. Goodhart, The Rule of Law and Absolute Sovereignty, University of Pennsylvania Law Review, Vol. 106, No. 7, (May, 1958), pp 943-963, 961.

2.3.4 Rule of Law in Global Context

The International Commission of Jurists (ICJ) had organized an International Congress of Jurists in New Delhi 1959 on the theme of *The Rule of Law in a Free Society.* More than 185 judges, lawyers and law professors had participated in the Congress. The Congress attempted to 'define and describe within the context of modern constitutional and legal practice the Rule of Law, a notion familiar to lawyers of many different legal systems but too often viewed as a phrase of uncertain meaning'.

The Commission held that the term *"Rule of Law stands for a universally applicable set of principles, joined by respect for the individual and by abhorrence of any arbitrary rule withdrawn from effective control by the people over whom it is exercised".* It is deemed to be 'a living concept permeating several branches of the Law and having great practical importance in the life of every human being.' The outcome of the Congress is popularly referred to as the *Declaration of Delhi* wherein three important elements of Rule of Law were recognized–

> First, that the individual is possessed of certain rights and freedoms and that he is to protection of these rights and freedoms by the State; second, that there is an absolute need for an independent judiciary and bar as well as for effective machinery for the protection of fundamental rights and freedoms; and third, that the establishment of social, economic and cultural conditions would permit men to live in dignity and to fulfil their legitimate aspirations.[24]

A pledge was taken to promote rule of law in the area of legislative, executive, criminal process, and the judiciary and legal professionals. The conclusions of the Congress were summed up as–

1. Legislative and Rule of Law
   (i) Legislature should try to uphold the dignity of man by recognizing civil and political rights and by establishing social, economic, educational and cultural conditions.
   (ii) Minimum standards and principles regulating the individual within society were essential for RL. Such standards would imply certain limitations on the legislative power. The limitations on the legislative should be enshrined in a constitution and safeguarded by an independent judicial tribunal.
   (iii) Legislature had the responsibility to abstain from enacting retroactive penal legislation, not discriminate in its laws between one citizen and another; not interfere with freedom of religious belief; not deny

24. Lucian G. Weeramantry, The Pioneering Years, The International Commission of Jurists, p. 53.

members of society the right to responsible government; not place restrictions on the freedom of speech, assembly or association; not impair the exercise of fundamental rights and freedoms of the individual and provide the procedural mechanisms to protect the above mentioned freedoms.

2. Executive and Rule of Law
   (i) Granting of power by the legislative to the executive should be undertaken within the narrowest possible limits and that legislature should define the extent and purpose of such delegated powers, as well as the procedures by which such delegated power to be brought into effect.
   (ii) When the executive directly and adversely affected a person or the property rights of an individual, he or she should have the right to present his or her case before a court as well as the right to an adequate remedy.
   (iii) In the absence of a judicial review mechanism, antecedent procedures of hearing, enquiry and consultation should be established, through which parties whose rights or interests would be affected can have an adequate opportunity to make representation.
   (iv) RL would be strengthened if the executive were to be required to formulate its reasons when reaching its decisions, and at the request of a concerned party, to communicate them.
3. Criminal Process and Rule of Law
   (i) Prohibition of retrospective enactment of penal legislation.
   (ii) Principle of presumption of innocence would require that the burden of proof should only be shifted once facts creating a contrary presumption had been established.
   (iii) Power of arrest should be regulated and the arrested person should be told at once the grounds of his or her arrest.
   He/she should only be entitled to a legal advisor and be brought before a judicial authority within a short period of time.
   (iv) RL did not require any particular theory regarding punishment, but must necessarily condemn cruel, inhuman or excessive preventive measures or punishment – reformative measures should be adopted wherever possible.
4. Judiciary and Legal Profession under the Rule of Law
   (i) Independence of judiciary should be safeguarded.
   (ii) Legal profession should be free to manage its own affairs.
   (iii) Equal access to justice.

2.3.5 Modern Interpretation of Rule of Law

One of the recent interpretations of rule of law has been advocated by the World Justice Project. It has defined the concept of *Rule of Law* based on four universal principles which were derived from various internationally accepted standards.[25] The primary objective of the project is not to simply define the concept but to analyse the impact of rule of law on society specifically in terms of accountability, respect for fundamental rights and access to justice. The four universal principles of rule of law are–

1. The government and its officials and agents as well as individuals and private entities are accountable under the law.
2. The laws are clear, publicized, stable, and just; are applied evenly; and protect fundamental rights, including the security of persons and property.
3. The process by which the laws are enacted, administered, and enforced is accessible, fair and efficient.
4. Justice is delivered timely by competent, ethical, and independent representatives and neutrals who are of sufficient number, have adequate resources and reflect the makeup of the communities they serve.

These four principles has been further developed into nine practical factors which are essential for creating a Rule of Law index for nations adhering to the various norms of accountable and open governments.

According to the WJR the nine factors are– **Factor 1:** Constraints on Government Powers

1.1 Government powers are effectively limited by the legislature

1.2 Government powers are effectively limited by the judiciary

1.3 Government powers are effectively limited by independent auditing and review

1.4 Government officials are sanctioned for misconduct

1.5 Government powers are subject to non-governmental checks

1.6 Transition of power is subject to the law

Factor 2: Absence of Corruption

2.1 Government officials in the executive branch do not use public officials for private gain

2.2 Government officials in the judicial branch do not use public office for private gain

2.3 Government officials in the police and the military do not use public office for private gain

25. World Justice Project - Rule of Law Index 2014.

2.4 Government officials in the legislative branch do not use public office for private gain.

Factor 3: Open Government

3.1 The laws are publicized and accessible

3.2 The laws are stable

3.3 Right to petition the government and public participation

3.4 Official information is available on request

Factor 4: Fundamental Rights

4.1 Equal treatment and absence of discrimination

4.2 The right to life and security of the person is effectively guaranteed

4.3 Due process of law and rights of the accused

4.4 Freedom of opinion and expression is effectively guaranteed

4.5 Freedom of belief and religion is effectively guaranteed

4.6 Freedom from arbitrary interference with privacy is effectively guaranteed

4.7 Freedom of assembly and association is effectively guaranteed

4.8 Fundamental labour rights are effectively guaranteed

Factor 5: Order and Security

5.1 Crime is effectively controlled

5.2 Civil conflict is effectively limited

5.3 People do not resort to violence to redress personal grievances

Factor 6: Regulatory Enforcement

6.1 Government regulations are effectively enforced

6.2 Government regulations are applied and enforced without improper influence

6.3 Administrative proceedings are conducted without unreasonable delay

6.4 Due process is respected in administrative proceedings

6.5 The government does not expropriate without lawful process and adequate compensation

Factor 7: Civil Justice

7.1 People can access and afford civil justice

7.2 Civil justice is free of discrimination

7.3 Civil justice is free of corruption

7.4 Civil justice is free of improper government influence

7.5 Civil justice is not subject to unreasonable delay

7.6 Civil justice is effectively enforced
7.7 ADR is accessible, impartial, and effective

Factor 8: Criminal Justice
8.1 Criminal investigation system is effective
8.2 Criminal adjudication system is timely and effective
8.3 Correctional system is effective in reducing criminal behaviour
8.4 Criminal system is impartial
8.5 Criminal system is free of corruption
8.6 Criminal system is free of improper government influence
8.7 Due process of law and rights of the accused

Factor 9: Informal Justice
9.1 Informal justice is timely and effective
9.2 Informal justice is impartial and free of improper influence
9.3 Informal justice respects and protects fundamental rights

Based on the above factors the WJP has prepared the Rule of Law Index of 99 countries covering more than 90 percent of the world's population.

Today the doctrine of rule of law is an integral part of the universal notion of good governance. It has played a foundational role in extending the power of judicial review over administrative actions in common law countries and has consequently facilitated the growth of administrative law in these countries. The broad encompassing concept has branched out and is equally applicable to all organs of the state in every area of law.

2.4 SEPARATION OF POWERS

The doctrine of separation of power is the second constitutional principle which played an instrumental role in the growth of administrative law. The increased functions of the Executive organ of the state had given rise to few legal challenges relating to the functioning and accountability of the executive. One of the important issue was whether the increased functions of the executive was contrary to the principles of *separation of powers* and whether such increased powers would lead to executive dominance over other organs of the state.

The three core state functions of law making, execution of the law and judicial functions have been traditionally entrusted with the three organs of the State – Legislature, Executive and the Judiciary respectively. The doctrine of separation of power was founded on the premise that concentration of power in one or more organs of the state would give rise to unregulated and tyrannical exercise of power which would threaten the rights and liberties of the citizens. Lord Acton speaking on the issue of whether the Pope and the King should be treated in a manner different from other ordinary men and should be presumed that they can never do wrong observed – *If there is any presumption it is the other way against holder of power, increasing as the power increases. Historic responsibility has to make up for the want of legal responsibility. Power tends to corrupt and absolute power corrupts absolutely. Great men are almost always bad men, even when they exercise influence and not authority; still more when you super add the tendency or the certainty of corruption by authority.* If this principle is applied to state functionaries it would necessarily imply that if the legislature or the law makers are conferred with absolute power to administer the law made by them as well as determine all disputes involving the law then the common people would have no opportunity of a fair redressal of their claims and would have to suffer from injustice in the absence of alternative remedial mechanism. This point was reiterated by the Indian Supreme Court in its pertinent observation in the case of *Ashoka Kumar Thakur v. Union of India*[26] - *The Government cannot be trusted; that is precisely why we divide its powers into separate organs. If it could be trusted, there would be no need for co-equal branches in which power is shared. Separation of powers is an axiom of democracy.*[27]

Sir John Locke was one of the earliest scholar and philosopher to conceptually formalize the doctrine of separation of power in his *Second Treatise of Government (1689).* In a well-ordered society different powers of the state should be exercised by different institutions. He divided the state powers into three categories – legislative power, executive power and federative power. The legislative or law-making power was deemed supreme whereas the executive power was relating to the internal affairs of the state and the federative powers were maintaining the external affairs during war and peace, information of alliances and leagues. Locke advocated that for proper functioning of the state it was necessary that the legislative powers and executive powers, including the federative power should be exercised by different institutions so that the law making authority is also made subject to the same laws. However the credit for laying down the foundational stones of the doctrine is popularly conferred to Frenchman and lawyer Montesquieu.

Montesquieu was greatly inspired by the writings of Locke and the parliamentary form of governance in England, and was convinced that under a despotic rule where both the executive and the legislative powers were held in the same hands it would be detrimental for the protection of the rights and freedoms of the citizens. He advocated for the implementation

26. (2008) 6 SCC 1.
27. Id, para 509.

of the separation of power similar in the lines of which existed between the English Monarch and the Parliament as necessary for securing citizens' rights because Parliament being the representative of the people would not enact arbitrary laws similarly the denial of the legislative powers to the king would ensure that no unfair or arbitrary laws are made. In the 17th century England the legislative and tax imposing powers were exercised by the Parliament and the government headed by the king administered the laws passed by the Parliament. Judges were also assured of freedom through the Act of Settlement which secured them a tenure of service during their good behaviour differentiating from the earlier practice of tenure during the pleasure of his Majesty. Hence Montesquieu felt that the secret of Englishman's liberty was the separation of power and the functional independence of the three department of the state from one another.

Montesquieu laid down the underlying principle of the doctrine in his book *Espirit des Lois (The Spirit of Laws)* 1748. His fundamental propositions was that the legislature and executive powers should not be united in the same person or in the same body or magistrates as there will be no liberty secured to the common people. There will always be the possibility of tyrannical laws being enacted and similarly executed to the detriment of the people. Similarly there will be no liberty if the judicial power is not separated from the legislative and executive powers because the judiciary through the power of judicial review protects the rights of the citizens by exercising effective control against arbitrary exercise of power by administrative officers. If the judicial power is clubbed with the executive power then the judge might behave with violence and oppression. Thus the doctrine implies that one person or body of persons should not exercise all three types of powers. Legislative, executive and the judiciary should be separate and one organ must perform or interfere with the functions entrusted with the other bodies.

Blackstone in his Commentaries on the Laws of England (1765) had similarly observed that if the legislative, executive and the judicial functions were performed by one person then there would be no security of public liberty.

> [W]herever the right both of making and of enforcing the laws is vested in one and the same man, or one and the same body of men; and wherever these two powers are united together, there can be no public liberty. The magistrate may enact tyrannical laws, and execute them in a tyrannical manner, since he is possessed, in quality of dispenser of justice, with all the power which he, as legislator thinks proper to give himself....Were [the judicial power] joined with the legislative, the life, liberty, and property, of the subject would be in the hands of arbitrary judges, whose decisions would be then regulated

> only by their opinions, and not by any fundamental principles of law; which, though legislators may depart from, yet judges are bound to observe. Were it joined with the executive, this union might soon be an overbalance for the legislative.[28]

The practical rationality and importance of the doctrine has been appreciated by subsequent jurists as well as helped in the constitution making process of a large number of countries, including France and America. The growth of the *droit administratif* as a separate branch of law in France is a reflection of the ideology of separation of power. Madison while drafting the US Constitution consciously implemented the doctrine of separation of power between the three organs. According to Madison, *"the accumulation of all powers, legislative, executive, and judiciary, in the same hands, whether one, a few, or many, and whether hereditary, self-appointed, or elective, may justly be pronounced the very definition of tyranny".*[29] Article I of the US Constitution lays down that the Congress has been granted the power to make the laws. It is also entrusted with the functions of controlling the national budget, raising taxes, borrowing of money, authorization of the expenditures of the federal funds etc. Article II provides that the Executive branch will be headed by the President and his power will include the power to enforce the laws passed by Congress, to make treaties with other nations, to nominate judges, to appoint officers of the Government and to oversee federal agencies. Article III states that the judicial power is vested in the Supreme Court and such other inferior federal courts as established by the Congress. The judicial power includes the power to hear all cases and controversies arising under the Constitution, international treaties, federal statutes, as well as disputes between the States.

2.4.1 Checks and Balance

The objective of the separation of power doctrine is not simply to prevent usurpation of power and dominance by one organ over the other organs of the state. One of the cardinal objective of the doctrine is to ensure that every organ of the state should act within the confines of law and does not abuse their power. The wellbeing of the citizens is dependent on the efficient functioning of the three organs in accordance with the rule of law principles. Traditionally the legislature, executive and the judiciary are the three pillars of the state functioning, hence the separation of power doctrine further imposes the obligation on these organs to oversee the functioning of each other and exercise necessary checks in case of excessive exercise

28. Blackstone, Commentaries on the Laws (Dublin, 1771), vol. 1, pp. 146, 269.
29. The Federalist (Philadelphia, 1871), no. 47.

of power or abuse of power. Thus the separation of power theory is also recognized as a *theory of checks and balances.*

The implication of checks and balances necessities the prevention of water tight compartmentalization between the three organs of the state. Montesquieu in his conceptual framework had not specified about strict separation of power but had highlighted that all state powers should not be in the same hands and the departments should not have control over the acts of the other or exercise undue influence. The British Constitution which inspired Montesquieu to formulate the doctrine had never adhered to the strict concept of separation of power. In a parliamentary form of democracy strict separation between Executive and legislature is an impossibility. The Queen who is the executive head is an integral part of the legislature and all the ministers are also members of the either Houses of the Parliament. The House of Lords have been entrusted with both judicial and legislative functions. The Lord Chancellor is at the same time a member of the House of Lords, a member of the government, and the senior most member of the judiciary. Thus even though Montesquieu considered the English system of State as the ideal for governance, but England had never advocated strict separation of powers.

While working out the concept of separation of power Madison had recognized that even though the doctrine of separation of power is a political truth but the doctrine does not imply that the various departments should be completely and absolutely independent of each other. Hence the US Constitution, even though acknowledges the separation of power as an inherent principle of constitutional governance, has also incorporated the provisions of checks and balances. Thus the law making power has been conferred to the Congress, but the Executive has been given the power to exercise Presidential veto and may refuse to sign the legislation into law. The judiciary can also exercise a check on legislative power through the powers of judicial review and can declare a law as unconstitutional. Similarly the Congress can check the executive power as the right to remove the President from office *if he is guilty of bribery, treason or other high crimes or misdemeanours* has been bestowed on it. In addition the Congress can reject any treaty negotiated by the President, refuse to confirm the appointments made by the President to the judiciary or other government offices. The judiciary has the power to review all executive actions. The power of the judiciary is also curtailed by the process of impeachment of judges being conferred on the Congress for any misconduct in office. The appointments of the judges are made by the President on being ratified by the Senate. Thus the application of checks and balances are inherent in the framework of the US Constitution. In the words of Mr. Justice Miller–

> It is believed to be one of the chief merits of the American system of written constitutional law, that all the powers intrusted to government, whether state or national, are divided into the three grand departments, the executive, the legislative, and the judicial. That the functions appropriate to each of these branches of government shall be vested in a separate body of public servants, and that the perfection of the system requires that the lines which separate and divide these departments shall be broadly and clearly defined. It is also essential to the successful working of this system that the persons intrusted with power in any successful working of this system that the persons intrusted with power in any one of these branches shall not be permitted to encroach upon the powers confided to the others, but that each shall by the law of its creation be limited to the exercise of the powers appropriate to its own department and no other.[30]

The importance of the doctrine of separation of power has to be realised not from a philosophical or a theoretical perspective but as part of practical necessity. It is important to realize the need for functional separation of powers based on the concept of division of functions and as a system of checks and balances as modern day necessity in place of strict separation of powers.

2.4.2 Essential Functions Theory

The doctrine of separation of power was initially considered as an impediment to the growth of administrative powers under the modern welfare state functions. The increase of state responsibilities had imposed additional burden on the different organs of the state, but due to the various factors the legislature and the judiciary were often able to cope with the new responsibilities. The growth of residuary powers in the hands of the administrative organs was deemed to be in violation of the essence of the separation of power doctrine. In this context an adjustment was attempted to uphold the essential elements of the doctrine without compromising with the necessity to grant residuary powers to the executive organ by developing the *essential functions theory.*

In the landmark decision of the US Supreme Court in the case of *Panama Refining Co. v. Ryan*[31] wherein the legality of the Executive Order issued by the US President dealing with transportation in interstate and foreign commerce of petroleum and related products under the provisions of Section 9(c) of Title 1 of the National Industrial Recovery Act 1933 was challenged on the ground that the Congress had failed to lay down the necessary policy guidelines under the Section 9(c) as required under constitutional separation

30. The Federalist (Philadelphia, 1871), no. 47.
31. 293 US 388.

of power. Upholding the constitutional obligation of the Congress to make laws and lay down policy and necessary rules of conduct prior to the delegation of powers to the executive, the Court propounded the *essential functions theory.* It observed–

The Constitution provides that–

> "All legislative Powers herein granted shall be vested in a Congress of the United States, which shall consist of a Senate and House of Representatives".
>
> Article I, § 1. And the Congress is empowered "To make all Laws which shall be necessary and proper for carrying into Execution" its general powers. Article I, § 8, par. 18. The Congress manifestly is not permitted to abdicate or to transfer to others the essential legislative functions with which it is thus vested. Undoubtedly legislation must often be adapted to complex conditions involving a host of details with which the national Legislature cannot deal directly. The Constitution has never been regarded as denying to the Congress the necessary resources of flexibility and practicality which will enable it to perform its function in laying down policies and establishing standards, while leaving to selected instrumentalities the making of subordinate rules within prescribed limits and the determination of facts to which the policy as declared by the Legislature is to apply. Without capacity to give authorizations of that sort, we should have the anomaly of a legislative power which, in many circumstances calling for its exertion, would be but a futility. But the constant recognition of the necessity and validity of such provisions and the wide range of administrative authority which has been developed by means of them cannot be allowed to obscure the limitations of the authority to delegate, if our constitutional system is to be maintained.

The constitutionality of the essential functions theory was further reiterated by the US Supreme Court in the subsequent case of *Schechter Poultry Corp. v. United States.*[32] It was categorically held that–

> Extraordinary conditions do not create or enlarge constitutional power. The Constitution established a national government with powers deemed to be adequate, as they have proved to be both in war and peace, but these powers of the national government are limited by the constitutional grants. Those who act under these grants are not at liberty to transcend the imposed limits because they believe that more or different power is necessary.....The Congress is not permitted to abdicate or to transfer to others the essential legislative functions with which it is thus vested.

The essential functions theory advocates that under the constitutional scheme of separation of powers every organ of the state has been conferred with certain essential or core functions which the organ is required to perform

32. 295 US 495.

without delegating it to any other organ or department. Once the essential function has been performed the organ can delegate all other incidental, subordinate or ancillary functions to other organs and bodies. Accordingly the essential functions are–

(i) Essential Legislative Functions
- Monitoring and supervising the policy of the government
- Passing of budgets
- Ratification of treaties and international covenants
- Passing of laws and discussing various actions and policies of the government

(ii) Essential Executive Functions
- Maintaining law and order
- Administration of the state
- Dealing with foreign countries
- Ensuring implementation of the policies and programmes

(iii) Essential Judicial Functions
- Deciding disputes
- Interpretation of laws
- Determining the legality of government actions
- Determining civil and criminal liability of private persons and state officials.

2.4.3 Indian Constitution and Separation of Power

The text of the Indian Constitution has not included the phrase 'separation of power' in any of its part but the notion of separation of power between the three organs of the state are implicit in the various provisions of the Constitution. Article 53(1) specifies that the executive power of the Union is vested in the President of India and shall be exercised by him directly or through officers subordinate to him in accordance with the Constitution. The power of the executive shall be co-extensive with that of the legislature.[33] The executive power shall be exercised by the President under the aid and advice of the Council of Ministers.[34] Under Article 245 the law making power has been conferred to the Parliament for making laws for the whole or any part of India and on the State legislature to make laws for the whole or any part of the State. The subject-matter of the laws to be made by the Parliament and the Legislature has provided under List I, II and

33. Article 73.
34. Article 74.

III of the Seventh Schedule.[35] The need to separate the judiciary from the executive has been highlighted under Article.50 The jurisdiction of the Union Judiciary and the state judiciary has been specifically incorporated under Part V Chapter IV and Part VI Chapter V respectively. Thus the functional separation between the three organs of the state has been broadly identified in the Constitution.

The Constitutional framers have also incorporated the principle of checks and balances between the three organs to uphold the principles of accountability and rule of law. To uphold the norms of Executive dominated Parliamentary democracy the Constitution has empowered the President to summon each House of the Parliament as well as prorogue and dissolve them. He has the right to address and send messages to the Houses. The President has the power to promulgate ordinances during recess of the Parliament. The Council of Ministers are collectively responsible to the House of the People.[36] Similar powers have been conferred to the Governor of a State. In order to implement the norms of Parliamentary accountability the Council of Ministers are collectively responsible to the House of the People.[37] The Parliament has also been given the power to impeach the President under Aticle 61. Similarly to incorporate judicial accountability the President has been given the power to appoint judges of the Supreme Court as well as pass order for the removal of the judges.[38] The Governor has been given similar power of appointment and removal of judges of the High Court. The President has been conferred with the power to grant pardon and to suspend, remit or commute sentences of any person convicted of any offence by the highest court of India.[39] Similar power has been granted to the Governors of a State.[40] The judiciary by the means of judicial review can strike down any law made by the Parliament or any administrative actions on the grounds of *ultra vires* and violation of the Constitutional principles.[41] Under Article 145 the Supreme Court has been given some law making powers to make rules for the general practice and procedure of the Court. It has also been given executive powers of making appointments of officers and servants of the Court. Thus the principles of checks and balances have been indoctrinated in the Constitution.

35. Article 246.
36. Article 123.
37. Article 75(3).
38. Article 124.
39. Article 72.
40. Article 161.
41. Articles 32, 226 and 136.

Indian Constitution, unlike the Constitution of United States of America and Australia, does not have express provision of separation of powers. However, the structure provided in our Constitution leaves no manner of doubt that the doctrine of separation of powers runs through the Indian Constitution. It is for this reason that this Court has recognised separation of power as a basic feature of the Constitution and an essential constituent of the rule of law. The doctrine of separation of powers is, though, not expressly engrafted in the Constitution, its sweep, operation and visibility are apparent from the Constitution. Indian Constitution has made demarcation without drawing formal lines between the three organs — legislature, executive and judiciary.[42]

2.4.4 Supreme Court on Separation of Power

In *Ram Jawaya Kapur v. The State of Punjab*[43] the Supreme Court highlighted for the first time the concept of functional division between the three organs of the State in place of strict separation of power and also upheld the essential functions theory as the constitutional norm. It emphasised the concept of checks and balances when it categorically observed that *"The Indian Constitution has not indeed recognised the doctrine of separation of powers in its absolute rigidity but the functions of the different parts or branches of the Government have been sufficiently differentiated and consequently it can very well be said that our Constitution does not contemplate assumption, by one organ or part of the State, of functions that essentially belong to another".*

In *Kesavananda Bharati v. State of Kerala*[44] the doctrine of separation of power between the legislature, the executive and the judiciary was recognized as *basic structure* of the Constitution. The same view was expressed by the Court in several subsequent judgments.

In *Indira Nehru Gandhi v. Raj Narain*[45] the Court was required to interpret the validity of 39th Constitutional Amendment which inserted Article 329A in the Constitution. Appellant was found guilty of having committed corrupt practices under the Representation of the People Act.

In *I.R. Coelho v. State of Tamil Nadu*[46] the nine-Judge Constitution bench described the principles of equality, rule of law, judicial review and separation of powers as forming part of the basic structure.

42. *State of Tamil Nadu v. State of Kerala* (2014) 12 SCC 696, para 98.
43. AIR 1955 SC 549.
44. (1973) 4 SCC 225.
45. 1975 Supp SCC 1.
46. (2007) 2 SCC 1.

> Each of these concepts are intimately connected. There can be no rule of law, if there is no equality before the law. These would be meaningless if the violation was not subject to the judicial review. All these would be redundant if the legislative, executive and judicial powers are vested in one organ. Therefore, the duty to decide whether the limits have been transgressed has been placed on the judiciary.[47]

Explaining the scope of separation of power doctrine under the Indian Constitution the Supreme Court in *P. Kannadasan v. State of Tamil Nadu*[48] observed–

> It must be remembered that our Constitution recognises and incorporates the doctrine of separation of powers between the three organs of the State viz. the legislature, the executive and the judiciary. Even though the Constitution has adopted the parliamentary form of Government where the dividing line between the legislature and the executive becomes thin, the theory of separation of powers is still valid. Ours is also a federal form of Government. The subjects in respect of which the Union and the States can make laws are separately set out in List I and List II of the Seventh Schedule to the Constitution respectively. (List III is, of course, a concurrent list.) The Constitution has invested the Supreme Court and High Courts with the power to invalidate laws made by Parliament and the State Legislatures transgressing the constitutional limitations. Where an Act made by a State Legislature is invalidated by the courts on the ground that the State Legislature was not competent to enact it, the State Legislature cannot enact a law declaring that the judgment of the court shall not operate; it cannot overrule or annul the decision of the court. But this does not mean that the other legislature which is competent to enact that law cannot enact that law. It can. Similarly, it is open to a legislature to alter the basis of the judgment as pointed out by this Court in *Shri Prithvi Cotton Mills Ltd. v. Broach Borough Municipality* [(1969) 2 SCC 283] — all the while adhering to the constitutional limitations; in such a case, the decision of the court becomes ineffective in the sense that the basis upon which it is rendered, is changed. The new law or the amended law so made can be challenged on other grounds but not on the ground that it seeks to ineffectuate or circumvent the decision of the court. This is what is meant by 'checks and balances' inherent in a system of Government incorporating the concept of separation of powers. This aspect has been repeatedly emphasised by this Court in numerous decisions commencing from *Shri Prithvi Cotton Mills.* Under our Constitution, neither wing is superior to the other. Each wing derives its power and jurisdiction from the Constitution. Each must operate within the sphere allotted to it. Trying to make one wing superior to the other would be to introduce an imbalance in the system and a negation of the basic concept of separation of powers inherent in our system of Government.[49]

47. Id, para 129.
48. (1996) 5 SCC 670.
49. (1996) 5 SCC 670 Para 15.

In the case of *State of West Bengal v. Committee for Protection of Democratic Rights, West Bengal*[50] the issue raised was whether the High Court in exercise of their power under Article 226 could direct the Central Bureau of Investigation, established under the Delhi Special Police Establishment Act, 1946 to investigate a cognizable offence which has taken place within the territorial jurisdiction of a State, without the consent of the State Government. The argument of the appellant was largely premised on the doctrine of separation of power. It was argued that under the provisions of DSPA CBI investigation could not be initiated without the consent of the State Government and this would equally apply on the constitutional courts when exercising their power under Articles 32 and 226. Negating the contention the five-Judge Constitutional bench held that doctrine of separation of power could not be used as defence in case of violation of fundamental rights of the citizens. On the contrary the doctrine justifies the application of checks and balance theory and makes it obligatory for the judiciary to oversee the functioning of the administration in cases of government inaction. It was observed–

> [T]he moot question for consideration in the present case is that when the fundamental rights, as enshrined in Part III of the Constitution, which include the right to equality (Article 14); the freedom of speech [Article 19(1)(*a*)] and the right not to be deprived of life and liberty except by procedure established by law (Article 21), as alleged in the instant case, are violated, can their violation be immunised from judicial scrutiny on the touchstone of doctrine of separation of powers between the legislature, executive and the judiciary.
>
> To put it differently, can the doctrine of separation of powers curtail the power of judicial review, conferred on the constitutional courts even in situations where the fundamental rights are sought to be abrogated or abridged on the ground that exercise of such power would impinge upon the said doctrine?
>
> The Constitution is a living and organic document. It cannot remain static and must grow with the nation. The constitutional provisions have to be construed broadly and liberally having regard to the changed circumstances and the needs of time and polity.[51]

The importance of this judgment lies in implementing the doctrine of separation of power not to differentiate between the different organs of the state but rather to justify the obligation of one organ to oversee the functioning of the others in case of failure to adhere with their statutory and constitutional functions on the application of checks and balance theory. The Court in this case negated the opinion of Markandey Katju J. relating

50. (2010) 3 SCC 571, AIR 2010 SC 1476.

51. (2010) 3 SCC 571 Para 43-45, AIR 2010 SC 1476.

to judicial restraint based on narrow interpretation of separation of power doctrine as expressed in the earlier case of *State of U.P. v. Jeet S. Bisht*[52] and upheld the views expressed by S.B. Sinha J. wherein he justified the application of the theory of checks and balances as necessary obligation of one organ of the state to advise and recommend to other branches of the state in case of any inaction or failure to perform their functions. In the words of S.B. Sinha J.-

> Separation of powers is a favourite topic for some of us. Each organ of the State in terms of the constitutional scheme performs one or the other functions which have been assigned to the other organ. Although drafting of legislation and its implementation by and large are functions of the legislature and the executive respectively, it is too late in the day to say that the constitutional court's role in that behalf is non-existent. The judge-made law is now well recognised throughout the world. If one is to put the doctrine of separation of power to such a rigidity, it would not have been possible for any superior court of any country, whether developed or developing, to create new rights through interpretative process.
>
> Separation of powers in one sense is a limit on *active jurisdiction* of each organ. But it has another deeper and more relevant purpose: to act as *check and balance* over the activities of other organs. Thereby the *active jurisdiction* of the organ is not challenged; nevertheless there are *methods of prodding* to communicate the institution of its excesses and shortfall in duty. Constitutional mandate sets the dynamics of this communication between the organs of polity. Therefore, it is suggested to not understand separation of powers as operating in vacuum. Separation of powers doctrine has been reinvented in modern times.[53]
>
> ***
>
> The modern view, which is today gathering momentum in constitutional courts the world over, is not only to demarcate the *realm of functioning* in a negative sense, but also to define the *minimum* content of the demarcated *realm of functioning*. Objective definition of function and role entails executing the same, which however may be subject to the plea of *financial constraint* but only in exceptional cases. In event of any such shortcoming, it is the essential duty of the other organ to advise and recommend the *needful* to substitute inaction. To this extent we must be prepared to frame answers to these difficult questions.[54]
>
> ***
>
> If we notice the evolution of separation of powers doctrine, traditionally the *checks and balances* dimension was only associated with governmental excesses

52. (2007) 6 SCC 586.
53. Ibid, Para 77-78.
54. Id, Para 80.

> and violations. But in today's world of positive rights and justifiable *social and economic* entitlements, hybrid administrative bodies, private functionaries discharging public functions, we have to perform the oversight function with more urgency and enlarge the field of *checks and balances* to include governmental inaction. Otherwise we envisage the country getting transformed into a *state of repose*. Social engineering as well as institutional engineering therefore forms part of this obligation.[55]

In the recent of case of *State of Tamil Nadu v. State of Kerala*[56] while dealing with the validity of the Kerala Irrigation and Water Conservation (Amendment) Act, 2006 the five-Judge bench of the Supreme Court held the Act as unconstitutional and in violation of the separation of power doctrine as the Kerala State Legislature by enacting the Amendment had tried to disobey and disregard the decision of the Supreme Court in the earlier case of *Mullaperiyar Environmental Protection Forum v. Union of India*[57] wherein the Court had permitted the increase of height of the Mullaperiyar Dam to 142 ft. from 136 ft. After re-visiting the earlier judgments of the Supreme Court on the issue of separation of power the Court summarized the essential principles of separation of power doctrine under the Indian Constitution and laid down the test to determine if a legislative action violates the separation of power doctrine–

(1) Even without express provision of the separation of powers, the doctrine of separation of powers is an entrenched principle in the Constitution of India. The doctrine of separation of powers informs the Indian constitutional structure and it is an essential constituent of rule of law. In other words, the doctrine of separation of power though not expressly engrafted in the Constitution, its sweep, operation and visibility are apparent from the scheme of Indian Constitution. Constitution has made demarcation, without drawing formal lines between the three organs—legislature, executive and judiciary. In that sense, even in the absence of express provision for separation of powers, the separation of powers between the legislature, executive and judiciary is not different from the Constitutions of the countries which contain express provision for separation of powers.

(2) Independence of courts from the executive and legislature is fundamental to the rule of law and one of the basic tenets of Indian Constitution. Separation of judicial power is a significant constitutional principle under the Constitution of India.

55. Id, Para 83.
56. (2014) 12 SCC 696.
57. (2006) 3 SCC 643.

(3) Separation of powers between three organs—the legislature, executive and judiciary—is also nothing but a consequence of principles of equality enshrined in Article 14 of the Constitution of India. Accordingly, breach of separation of judicial power may amount to negation of equality under Article 14. Stated thus, a legislation can be invalidated on the basis of breach of the separation of powers since such breach is negation of equality under Article 14 of the Constitution.

(4) The superior judiciary (High Courts and Supreme Court) is empowered by the Constitution to declare a law made by the legislature (Parliament and State Legislatures) void if it is found to have transgressed the constitutional limitations or if it infringed the rights enshrined in Part III of the Constitution.

(5) The doctrine of separation of powers applies to the final judgments of the courts. The legislature cannot declare any decision of a court of law to be void or of no effect. It can, however, pass an amending Act to remedy the defects pointed out by a court of law or on coming to know of it aliunde. In other words, a court's decision must always bind unless the conditions on which it is based are so fundamentally altered that the decision could not have been given in the altered circumstances.

(6) If the legislature has the power over the subject-matter and competence to make a validating law, it can at any time make such a validating law and make it retrospective. The validity of a validating law, therefore, depends upon whether the legislature possesses the competence which it claims over the subject-matter and whether in making the validation law it removes the defect which the courts had found in the existing law.

(7) The law enacted by the legislature may apparently seem to be within its competence but yet in substance if it is shown as an attempt to interfere with the judicial process, such law may be invalidated being in breach of doctrine of separation of powers. In such situation, the legal effect of the law on a judgment or a judicial proceeding must be examined closely, having regard to legislative prescription or direction. The questions to be asked are:

  (*i*) Does the legislative prescription or legislative direction interfere with the judicial functions?

  (*ii*) Is the legislation targeted at the decided case or whether impugned law requires its application to a case already finally decided?

  (*iii*) What are the terms of law; the issues with which it deals and the nature of the judgment that has attained finality?

> If the answer to Questions (*i*) and (*ii*) is in the affirmative and the consideration of aspects noted in Question (*iii*) sufficiently establishes that the impugned law interferes with the judicial functions, the Court may declare the law unconstitutional.

Thus the importance of the doctrine of separation of power in modern day governance is manifold. It encourages functional differentiation between the organs of the state based on the objective of efficient government on the one hand and ensures preservation of individual liberty in society on the other hand. Hence modern constitutional law writers Wade and Phillips has prescribed the practical application of the doctrine of separation of power as–

(i) The same set of persons should not compose more than one department of the three governmental departments.

(ii) One department should not exercise the functions of the other two departments.

(iii) One department should not control, much less, interfere with the work of the other two departments.[58]

The doctrines of Rule of Law and Separation of Power are constitutional law principles which had a major impact on the growth of Administrative Law. The concepts of *ultra vires doctrine* and *essential functions theory* owe their origin to these constitutional doctrines and the judiciary by application of these principles under the broad umbrella of principles of administrative law have helped in establishing accountability among different organs of the state.

CONCLUSION

Since the fundamental principles of Administrative law are derived from different constitutional law principles such as rule of law, separation of power, sovereignty of the Constitution, independence of the judiciary, protection of the fundamental rights of the citizens etc., it can rightly be concluded that administrative law has its foundations in constitutional law.

58. E.C.S. Wade and G.G. Phillips, Constitutional and Administrative Law, (A.W. Bradely ed.) 9th Ed. 1979.

III Classification of Administrative Actions

LEARNING OBJECTIVES

After reading this chapter, you will be familiar with:

- Classification of Administrative functions
  - Delegated Legislation
  - Quasi-judicial action
  - Discretionary action
  - Ministerial action
- Difference between the various administrative actions
- Nature, scope and enforceability of Administrative Directions

3.1 INTRODUCTION

The growth of state functions in the last century imposed great functional responsibility on the executive authorities who were entrusted with the duties to undertake the *residuary functions* which could not be performed by the legislature and the judiciary because of their existing constitutional functions and responsibilities. The administrative functions have assumed a multi-dimensional character because of the varied nature of the responsibilities undertaken by them. Administrative law scholars have differentiated the administrative responsibilities based on the nature of the functions performed. Administrative actions are classified into – (i) Delegated Legislation, (ii) Quasi-Judicial functions, (iii) Administrative Discretionary functions and (iv) Ministerial functions.

These classifications of administrative actions have been deemed necessary because even though it is the executive organ of the state which is required to undertake these functions, but the nature of these functions and the manner of performance of these functions are vastly different from each other. Within the executive different departments and administrative officers are involved in the performance of the different administrative functions. The nature of the administrative functions differs based on the source from which the powers were derived, consequently, there is a difference in the rules and procedures applicable in the performance of these functions as well as the remedies available in case of any breach in the performance of these functions.

One of the major challenges in the area of administrative law has been in defining and distinguishing the nature and scope of the different administrative actions. The complexity in the performance of these functions has made the line of difference between these *vanish into an illusion*. In the words of Justice C.K. Thakker, *"No precise, perfect or scientific test has so far been evolved which distinguishes these functions from one another. A further difficulty arises where a single proceeding may combine more than one function. It is, therefore, not easy to classify them though several attempts have been made by jurists and authors on constitutional and administrative law".*[1] But from a citizen's perspective as well as legal perspective it is important to understand the different forms of administrative actions for the purpose of identifying the necessary procedural requirements in the conduct of the varied functions so as to ensure procedural propriety and the different remedies available in case of breach of these functions. As stated by Chinnappa Reddy J. in the *Cynamide India* case (*Union of India & Anr v. Cynamide India Ltd. & Anr* 1987 AIR 1802, 1987 SCR (2) 841) *though difficult, it is necessary that the line must sometimes be drawn as different legal rights and consequences may ensue.*[2]

3.2 DELEGATED LEGISLATION

Under the constitutional scheme law making is the primary responsibility of the legislature, wherein the members of the legislature are democratically elected and they act as representatives of the common people. It is the constitutional responsibility of the legislature to frame the laws of the land necessary for the governance of the state, based on the principles of rule of law and separation of power doctrine. *It is a right of every citizen to insist that he should be governed by laws made in accordance with the Constitution.*[3] But the practical exigencies of a modern welfare state makes it difficult for the legislature to devote necessary time for enacting a detailed

---

1. Justice C.K. Thakker, From Duty to Act Judicially to Duty to Act Fairly, (2003) 4 SCC J-1.
2. *Union of India & Anr v. Cynamide India Ltd. & Anr* AIR 1987 SC 1802.
3. *DC Wadhwa v. State of Bihar* (1987) 1 SCC 378.

legislation or the number of legislations necessary for the efficient working of the government, hence it becomes necessary for the legislature to transfer a part of their responsibilities to the Executive so as to bring in flexibility, expertise and expediency in the law making process. Exercise of law-making power by the executive as delegated to it by the legislature, is often described as the rule-making action of the administration or delegated legislation. But this grant of law making power is deemed to be of subordinate, ancillary or incidental in nature wherein the executive is required to fill in the necessary gaps in a law made by the Parliament in the course of implementation of the laws. In *Inter State Transport Commission v. P. Manjunath Kamath*[4] the Court held that *in the absence of any power to enact subordinate legislation by way of rules, the delegation of legislative power cannot be lightly inferred.* Thus delegated legislation is a process of making subordinate rules within prescribed limits and such limits are generally determined by the laws made by the legislature.

In *Prag Ice & Oil Mills v. Union of India*[5] the term 'legislation' was described as "A legislative measure does not concern itself with the facts of an individual case. It is meant to lay down a general rule applicable to all persons or objects or transactions of a particular kind or class." The characteristic features of a legislation determine the nature of a delegate legislation. A legislation is characterized by – (i) Generality, (ii) Prospectivity, (iii) Public Interest and (iv) Identification of rights and obligations. When the executive undertakes the responsibility of making rules, it is often deemed that the executive has stepped into the shoes of the legislature for the purpose of law making, hence the delegated legislations are bound by similar legislative and constitutional limitations as applicable to the legislations as well as their characteristic features. Some of the essential features of delegated legislation are–

Firstly, the legislature is required to enact a statute laying down the policy, essential rules of conduct and must contain provisions relating to conferring of rule-making powers on the executive.

Secondly the delegated legislation, like the laws made by the legislature, should not be exercised for the singular interest of an individual but should deal with public in general and their well-being.

Thirdly the delegated rules should be prospective in nature and should lay down a future course of action. The legislature in its law making capacity has the power to make retrospective legislations but similar power is not extended to subordinate law making authorities.

---

4. (1973) 3 SCC 733.
5. (1978) 3 SCC 459 para 37.

Fourthly by means of a delegated legislation the executive authority cannot expand or curtail the rights and obligations under a statute. The main objective of delegated legislation is to implement the provisions of a statute.

Fifthly principles of natural justice have no application in the rule-making process. Parliament is required to make laws in accordance with the rules of parliamentary procedure and is not bound by the norms of natural justice. Similarly in the making of delegated legislation, the executive is not bound by the principles of natural justice. The applicability of the procedural norms like consultation, pre-publication of rules etc. are to be determined by the parent statute. In *Indian Express Newspapers (Bombay) Pvt. Ltd. v. Union of India*[6] it was held that *subordinate legislation cannot be questioned on the ground of violation of principles of natural justice on which administrative action may be questioned.* Reiterating the same principle in *Union of India v. Cynamide India Ltd.*[7] the Supreme Court categorically observed that–

> [L]egislative action, plenary or subordinate, is not subject to rules of natural justice. In the case of Parliamentary legislation, the proposition is self-evident. In the case of subordinate legislation, it may happen that Parliament may itself provide for a notice and for a hearing — there are several instances of the legislature requiring the subordinate legislating authority to give public notice and a public hearing before say, for example, levying a municipal rate — in which case the substantial non-observance of the statutorily prescribed mode of observing natural justice may have the effect of invalidating the subordinate legislation. The right here given to rate payers or others is in the nature of a concession which is not to detract from the character of the activity as legislative and not quasi-judicial. But, where the legislature has not chosen to provide for any notice or hearing, no one can insist upon it and it will not be permissible to read natural justice into such legislative activity.

In *Shri Sitaram Sugar Co. Ltd. v. Union of India*[8] it was further observed–

> If a particular function is termed legislative rather than judicial, practical results may follow as far as the parties are concerned. When the function is treated as legislative, a party affected by the order has no right to notice and hearing, unless, of course, the statute so requires. It being of general application engulfing a wide sweep of powers, applicable to all persons and situations of a broadly identifiable class, the legislative order may not be vulnerable to challenge merely by reason of its omission to take into account individual peculiarities and differences amongst those falling within the class.[9]

6. (1985) 1 SCC 641.
7. (1987) 2 SCC 720 para 5.
8. (1990) 3 SCC 223.
9. Ibid Para 32.

Sixthly the laws made by the Parliament are subject to judicial review on the touchstone of constitutional provisions. Similarly the delegated legislations will also be subjected to judicial review on the basis of constitutional provisions and the parent statute. The judiciary will restrict its examination to the question whether the policy and the factors in the minds of the authorities were in accordance with the legislative policy and not contrary to the constitutional provisions.

Seventhly the applicability of writ remedies against the law making functions of the Parliament are limited, similarly the applicability of writ of mandamus is minimal in the case of delegated legislation.

3.3 QUASI-JUDICIAL ACTION

The increase in state functions had a consequent impact on the adjudication process. The traditional judicial system was already over-burdened with pending cases and disputes. In addition, various factors like inadequate number of judges, lack of specialization among the judges, long drawn judicial process, strict adherence to procedural norms made it necessary to create an alternative adjudication process to deal with the new challenges emerging out of new state laws and policies. In the course of implementation of various welfare statutes and other new areas of law the administrative authorities would require to be granted some elements of judicial powers so as to bring in flexibility and ensure quick disposal of matters.

The term 'quasi' refers to similar, but not exactly. The term quasi-judicial function refers to performance of functions similar to judicial in nature.

In *Indian National Congress (I) v. Institute of Social Welfare*[10] the Supreme Court while dealing with the issue of whether the Election Commission in exercise of power under Sec. 29-A of the Act is performing administrative or quasi-judicial functions analyzed the concept of quasi-judicial function. It observed–

> The dictionary meaning of the word quasi is "not exactly" and it is just in between a judicial and administrative function. It is true, in many cases, the statutory authorities were held to be quasi-judicial authorities and decisions rendered by them were regarded as quasi-judicial, where there was contest between the two contending parties and the statutory authority was required to adjudicate upon the rights of the parties. In *Cooper v. Wilson* [(1937) 2 KB 309] it is stated that "the definition of a quasi-judicial decision clearly suggests that there must be two or more contending parties and an outside authority to decide those disputes". In view of the aforesaid statement of law, where there are two or more parties contesting each other's claim and

10. (2002) 5 SCC 685.

the statutory authority is required to adjudicate the rival claims between the parties, such a statutory authority was held to be quasi-judicial and decision rendered by it as a quasi-judicial order. Thus, where there is a *lis* or two contesting parties making rival claims and the statutory authority under the statutory provision is required to decide such a dispute, in the absence of any other attributes of a quasi-judicial authority, such a statutory authority is quasi-judicial authority.

But there are cases where there is no *lis* or two contending parties before a statutory authority yet such a statutory authority has been held to be quasi-judicial and decision rendered by it as a quasi-judicial decision when such a statutory authority is required to act judicially. In *R. v. Dublin Corpn.* [(1878) 2 Ir R 371] it was held thus:

"In this connection the term judicial does not necessarily mean acts of a Judge or legal tribunal sitting for the determination of matters of law, but for purpose of this question, a judicial act seems to be an act done by competent authority upon consideration of facts and circumstances and imposing liability or affecting the rights. And if there be a body *empowered by law to enquire into facts*, makes estimates to impose a rate on a district, it would seem to me that the acts of such a body involving such consequence would be judicial acts".

Atkin, L.J. as he then was, in *R. v. Electricity Commrs.* [(1924) 1 KB 171] stated that when anybody of persons has legal authority to determine questions affecting the rights of subjects and having the duty to act judicially, such body of persons is a quasi-judicial body and decision given by them is a quasi-judicial decision. In the said decision, there was no contest or *lis* between the two contending parties before the Commissioner. The Commissioner, after making an enquiry and hearing the objections was required to pass order. In a nutshell, what was held in the aforesaid decision was, where a statutory authority is empowered to take a decision which affects the rights of persons and such an authority is under the relevant law required to make an enquiry and hear the parties, such authority is quasi-judicial and decision rendered by it is a quasi-judicial act.

In *Province of Bombay v. Khushaldas S. Advani* [AIR 1950 SC 222 p. 260, para 173] it was held thus:

"(*i*) that if a statute empowers an authority, not being a court in the ordinary sense, to decide disputes arising out of a claim made by one party under the statute which claim is opposed by another party and to determine the respective rights of the contesting parties who are opposed to each other there is a *lis* and prima facie, and in the absence of anything in the statute to the contrary it is the duty of the authority to act judicially and the decision of the authority is a quasi-judicial act; and (*ii*) that if a statutory authority has power to do any act which will prejudicially affect the subject, then, although there are not two parties apart from the authority and the contest is between the authority proposing to do the act and the subject opposing it, the final determination of the authority will yet be a quasi-judicial act provided the authority is required by the statute to act judicially.

In other words, while the presence of two parties besides the deciding authority will prima facie and in the absence of any other factor impose upon the authority the duty to act judicially, the absence of two such parties is not decisive in taking the act of the authority out of the category of quasi-judicial act if the authority is nevertheless required by the statute to act judicially."

The legal principles laying down when an act of a statutory authority would be a quasi-judicial act, which emerge from the aforestated decisions are these:

Where (*a*) a statutory authority empowered under a statute to do any act (*b*) which would prejudicially affect the subject (*c*) although there is no *lis* or two contending parties and the contest is between the authority and the subject and (*d*) the statutory authority is required to act judicially under the statute, the decision of the said authority is quasi-judicial.

.....

What distinguishes an administrative act from a quasi-judicial act is, in the case of quasi-judicial functions under the relevant law the statutory authority is required to act judicially. In other words, where law requires that an authority before arriving at a decision must make an enquiry, such a requirement of law makes the authority a quasi-judicial authority.

....

We do not find any merit in the submission. At the outset, it must be borne in mind that another test which distinguishes administrative function from quasi-judicial function is, the authority who acts quasi-judicially is required to act according to the rules, whereas the authority which acts administratively is dictated by the policy and expediency.[11]

Modern day governance had witnessed a growth of administrative tribunals performing quasi-judicial functions to provide efficacious remedies to the litigants on one hand and reducing the burden of the judiciary on the other hand. Some of the popular tribunals are consumer forum, administrative tribunal, competition commission, electricity commission, telecom regulatory commission etc. These administrative authorities are deemed to perform quasi-judicial functions. These authorities are statutory bodies and are empowered to do quasi-judicial functions under the provisions of a statute which would prejudicially affect the interest of the subject, even though there may be no *lis* or two contending parties and the contest is between the authority and the subject, and in these circumstances the statutory authority is required to act judicially by complying with the principles of natural justice. In performing the adjudicating function, the administrative

11. Id. Para 20-25, 27, 29.

authority is required to step into the shoes of the judicial authorities and in the course of their functions should be bound by ideals of fairness, independence and neutrality. The distinction between judicial decisions and quasi-judicial decisions have been described in *Shri Sitaram Sugar Co. Ltd. v. Union of India*[12] as *"Judicial decisions are made according to law while administrative decisions emanate from administrative policy. Quasi-judicial decisions are also administrative decisions, but they are subject to some measure of judicial procedure, such as rules of natural justice"*. The term 'administrative decision making' or quasi-judicial actions has been defined as 'a power to perform acts administrative in character, but requiring incidentally some characteristics of judicial traditions.'

A judicial function is described as interpretation of the law and its application by rule or discretion to the facts of particular cases. It involves ascertainment of facts in dispute according to the law of evidence. It is generally performed by courts of law or courts of justice. *Judicial function is exercised under legal authority to decide on the disputes, after hearing the parties, maybe after making an enquiry, and the decision affects the rights and obligations of the parties. There is a duty to act judicially. The Judge may construe the law and apply it to a particular state of facts presented for the determination of the controversy*[13]. Thus traditionally a judicial function involves a *lis* (dispute) between two or more parties and the following features–

(i) Presentation of the case by the parties to the dispute
(ii) If the dispute is a question of fact, the ascertainment of question of facts by means of evidence given by the parties and the arguments by or on behalf of the parties
(iii) If the dispute is a question of law, the ascertainment of questions of law will be made on the basis of submission of legal arguments.
(iv) A decision which disposes of the whole matter by applying the law to the facts, including a ruling upon a disputed question of law.

In contradistinction, when an administrative officer is required to perform a quasi-judicial function under the provisions of a statute then the process involves the first two determinants, may or may not involve the third determinants but never involves the fourth determinant. The fourth determinant is taken up by administrative action, the character of which is determined by the administrative officer's free choice involving expediency, discretion and policy consideration. In quasi-judicial functions the administrative authority is not required to follow elaborate judicial

12. (1990) 3 SCC 223.
13. *Jamal Uddin Ahmad v. Abu Saleh Najmuddin* (2003) 4 SCC 257.

procedures, but for the purpose of ensuring fairness in the administrative process the authorities are required to follow the principles of natural justice. Some examples of quasi-judicial functions are disciplinary proceedings, confiscation of goods, cancellation of licenses, determination of citizenship etc.

In *B. Prabhakara Rao v. Desari Panakala Rao*[14] Krishna Iyer J. observed–

> Administrative law — a growing branch of Indian jurisprudence — has a mission. Where the trelliswork of technical procedures and rules of evidence usually applicable to ordinary courts under the Code contains too many taboos regarding pleadings and too many proscriptions regarding trials, administrative bodies, manned by lay and legal men, charged with duties which are wider than decision of individual disputes between specific parties and operating quasi-judicially at the public interest level, have to enjoy more liberal powers and less formal and more flexible processes if they are to fulfil the statutory behest efficaciously. To over-judicialize is to undermine. In the construction of statutes establishing administrative agencies and defining their powers, there is little scope for the deep-rooted shibboleth that into the statute must be read, by lawyer's instinct, the requirements of the trial of a civil suit or the hearing of an appeal by the ordinary courts of the land. This may result in defeating their obvious purpose.

Thus the essential features of quasi-judicial functions are–

Firstly the administrative authority will be required to act judicially under the provisions of a statute in dealing with issues affecting the legal rights or having an adverse impact on the interests of the citizens.

Secondly in performance of the adjudicating function, the administrative authority is not required to follow the formal procedural norms, but is bound to comply with the principles of natural justice.

Thirdly, the quasi-judicial action will be based on application of the policy of the state within the norms of fairness.

Fourthly, the quasi-judicial action will always be subject to judicial review and will be bound by the writ remedies.

3.4 PURE ADMINISTRATIVE ACTION

Pure administrative action is the residuary action which is neither legislative nor judicial in character. It involves the core function of implementation and execution of the laws made by the legislature. The administrative action can be classified into two categories – (i) Discretionary functions and (ii) Ministerial functions.

14. (1976) 3 SCC 550.

(i) Discretionary Functions

Discretionary function involves exercise of a choice or judgment by an administrative officer. The discretionary power is granted under a provision of a statute and the officer is required to exercise his discretion or choice based on his wisdom, understanding and experience within the permissible statutory parameters in the course of implementation of the statute. Discretion deals with a particular situation and is devoid of generality. In performance of discretionary functions there is no procedural obligation for collecting evidences and weighing arguments, but there is an inherent duty to act fairly so that there shall be a minimum adherence with the norms of fairness. The action is based on subjective satisfaction of the administrative officer and the decisions are based on executive policy, fairness and expediency. In *U.P. State Road Transport Corpn. v. Mohd. Ismail*[15] speaking on the manner of exercising statutory discretion it was observed–

> The discretion allowed by the statute to the holder of an office, as Lord Halsbury observed in *Susannah Sharp v. Wakefield* [1891 AC 173] is intended to be exercised "according to the rules of reason and justice, not according to private opinion; ... according to law and not humour. It is to be, not arbitrary, vague, and fanciful, but legal and regular. And it must be exercised within the limit, to which an honest man competent to the discharge of his office ought to confine himself". Every discretion conferred by statute on a holder of public office must be exercised in furtherance of accomplishment of purpose of the power.[16]

Examples of discretionary functions are making reference to a tribunal, fact-finding action, entering names in the surveillance register, functions of a selection committee, decision to extend time during investigation etc.

The characteristic features of administrative discretionary functions are–

Firstly the legislature confers discretionary power on an administrative officer through statutory provisions and guidelines.

Secondly the exercise of discretionary is required to be made in accordance with the policy and provisions of the statute.

Thirdly there is no generality to the exercise of discretionary functions, the power is exercised in particular cases involving performing of particular acts.

Fourthly it involves making or issuing of specific directions; or the application of a general rule to a particular case in accordance with legislative policy.

15. (1991) 3 SCC 239.

16. Ibid Para 15.

Fifthly the administrative authority has a duty to act fairly in performance of his discretionary functions.

Sixthly the power of judicial review extends over administrative actions and the judiciary has developed various judicial principles to bring in administrative accountability.

Seventhly the discretionary functions are subject to writ remedies, barring the writ of mandamus.

(ii) Ministerial Functions

Ministerial functions are those functions which are routinely performed by an administrative agency without exercise of any discretion or judgment. It is described as a duty the discharge of which involves no element of discretion or independent judgment.[17] In *Edukanti Kistamma v. S. Venkatareddy*[18] it was held that once the rights and entitlements of the parties are determined by a judicial or quasi-judicial authority, then the issuance of an order based on such determination is characterized as a ministerial act. Ministerial functions are generally undertaken as a matter of duty imposed upon the agency. It is defined as an act "which a person performs in a given state of facts, in a prescribed manner, in obedience to the mandate of a legal authority, without regard to, or the exercise of, his own judgment upon the propriety of the act done. In ministerial duty nothing is left to discretion; it is a simple, definite duty".[19]

A writ of mandamus can be issued to compel the performance of a ministerial act.[20] Examples of ministerial functions are collection of revenue, preparation of annual report, presentation of an election petition to the High Court etc.

3.5 DIFFERENTIATING BETWEEN DELEGATED LEGISLATION, QUASI-JUDICIAL FUNCTION AND DISCRETIONARY FUNCTION

The Supreme Court while determining the nature of administrative action of 'price-fixation' in the case of *Union of India v. Cynamide India Ltd.*[21] made the pertinent observation that–

> It is true that, with the proliferation of delegated legislation, there is a tendency for the line between legislation and administration to vanish into an illusion.

17. *Sharif Ahmad v. Regional Transport Authority, Meerut* (1978) 1 SCC 1.
18. (2010) 1 SCC 756.
19. *Jamal Uddin Ahmad v. Abu Saleh Najmuddin* (2003) 4 SCC 257.
20. S.A. de Smith, Judicial Review of Administrative Action, 3rd Ed. P. 59.
21. AIR 1987 SC 1802.

> Administrative, quasi-judicial decisions tend to merge in legislative activity and, conversely, legislative activity tends to fade into and present an appearance of an administrative or quasi-judicial activity. Any attempt to draw a distinct line between legislative and administrative functions, it has been said, is 'difficult in theory and impossible in practice'.

The Court while dealing with the issue whether price-fixation of medicines was a legislative act or an act of administrative discretion or a quasi-judicial function elaborately discussed and defined the scope of the different categories of administrative actions.

> The distinction between the two has usually been expressed as "one between the general and the particular". "A legislative act is the creation and promulgation of a general rule of conduct without reference to particular cases; an administrative act is the making and issue of a specific direction or the application of a general rule to a particular case in accordance with the requirements of policy". "Legislation is the process of formulating a general rule of conduct without reference to particular cases and usually operating in future; administration is the process of performing particular acts, of issuing particular orders or of making decisions which apply general rules to particular cases". It has also been said: "Rule-making is normally directed toward the formulation of requirements having a general application to all members of a broadly identifiable class" while, "an adjudication, on the other hand, applies to specific individuals or situations". But, this is only a broad distinction, not necessarily always true. Administration and administrative adjudication may also be of general application and there may be legislation of particular application only. That is not ruled out. Again, adjudication determines past and present facts and declares rights and liabilities while legislation indicates the future course of action. Adjudication is determinative of the past and the present while legislation is indicative of the future. The object of the rule, the reach of its application, the rights and obligations arising out of it, its intended effect on past, present and future events, its form, the manner of its promulgation are some factors which may help in drawing the line between legislative and non-legislative acts. A price fixation measure does not concern itself with the interests of an individual manufacturer or producer. It is generally in relation to a particular commodity or class of commodities or transactions. It is a direction of a general character, not directed against a particular situation. It is intended to operate in the future. It is conceived in the interests of the general consumer public. The right of the citizen to obtain essential articles at fair prices and the duty of the State to so provide them are transformed into the power of the State to fix prices and the obligation of the producer to charge no more than the price fixed. Viewed from whatever angle, the angle of general application, the prospectiveness of its effect, the public interest served, and the rights and obligations flowing therefrom, there can be no question that price fixation is ordinarily a legislative activity. Price fixation may occasionally assume an administrative or quasi-judicial

> character when it relates to acquisition or requisition of goods or property from individuals and it becomes necessary to fix the price separately in relation to such individuals. Such situations may arise when the owner of property or goods is compelled to sell his property or goods to the Government or its nominee and the price to be paid is directed by the legislature to be determined according to the statutory guidelines laid down by it. In such situations the determination of price may acquire a quasi-judicial character. Otherwise, price fixation is generally a legislative activity. We also wish to clear a misapprehension which appears to prevail in certain circles that price fixation affects the manufacturer or producer primarily and therefore fairness requires that he be given an opportunity and that fair opportunity to the manufacturer or producer must be read into the procedure for price fixation. We do not agree with the basic premise that price fixation primarily affects manufacturers and producers. Those who are most vitally affected are the consumer public. It is for their protection that price fixation is resorted to and any increase in price affects them as seriously as any decrease does a manufacturer, if not more.[22]

In the earlier case of *Indian Express Newspapers (Bombay) Pvt. Ltd. v. Union of India*[23] the Supreme Court had emphasized the distinction between delegated legislation and discretionary functions as–

> A distinction must be made between delegation of a legislative function in the case of which the question of reasonableness cannot be enquired into and the investment by statute to exercise particular discretionary powers. In the latter case the question may be considered on all grounds on which administrative action may be questioned, such as, non-application of mind, taking irrelevant matters into consideration, failure to take relevant matters into consideration, etc. etc. On the facts and circumstances of a case, a subordinate legislation may be struck down as arbitrary or contrary to statute if it fails to take into account very vital facts which either expressly or by necessary implication are required to be taken into consideration by the statute or, say, the Constitution. This can only be done on the ground that it does not conform to the statutory or constitutional requirements or that it offends Article 14 or Article 19(1)(*a*) of the Constitution. It cannot, no doubt, be done merely on the ground that it is not reasonable or that it has not taken into account relevant circumstances which the Court considers relevant.

3.6 ADMINISTRATIVE DIRECTIONS

One important form of executive function is to issue orders, decisions, executive instructions, orders, circulars and guidelines. In the course of

22. Ibid Para 7.
23. (1985) 1 SCC 641.

Administrative law these are categorised as administrative instructions or directions. The core purpose of these directions is to fill in the necessary gaps in existing laws so as to prevent arbitrary exercise of power. Directions can be specific or have general application. It can be applicable to particular cases or instance. The exercise of power to issue directions comes within the general scope of administrative powers under Articles 73 and 162 of the Constitution.

Unlike delegated legislations, these instructions do not have the status of subordinate rules and can operate within the confines of legislation and rules. In addition, these instructions do not have the power to override a legislative policy nor cannot be contrary to the provisions of the Statute.[24] To distinguish delegated legislations from administrative directions, the latter is often referred to as 'administrative quasi-law' or 'administrative quasi-legislation'.[25]

In *P.H. Paul Manoj Pandian v. P. Veldurai*[26] Supreme Court highlighted the importance and legal effect of administrative directions. It observed–

> Departmental circulars are a common form of administrative document by which instructions are disseminated. Many such circulars are identified by serial numbers and published, and many of them contain general statement of policy. They are, therefore, of great importance to the public, giving much guidance about governmental organisation and the exercise of discretionary powers. In themselves they have no legal effect whatever, having no statutory authority. But they may be used as a vehicle in conveying instructions to which some statute gives legal force. It is now the practice to publish circulars which are of any importance to the public and for a long time there has been no judicial criticism of the use made of them.
>
> Once a law occupies the field, it will not be open to the State Government in exercise of its executive power under Article 162 of the Constitution to prescribe in the same field by an executive order. However, it is well recognised that in matters relating to a particular subject in absence of any parliamentary legislation on the said subject, the State Government has the jurisdiction to act and to make executive orders. The executive power of the State would, in the absence of legislation, extend to making rules or orders regulating the action of the executive. But, such orders cannot offend the provisions of the Constitution and should not be repugnant to any enactment of the appropriate legislature. Subject to these limitations, such rules or orders may relate to matters of policy, may make classification and may determine the conditions of eligibility for receiving any advantage, privilege or aid from the State.

24. *State of Rajasthan v. Jagdish Narain Chaturvedi* (2009) 12 SCC 49.
25. Megarry, Administrative Quasi-Legislation, 60 LQR 125 (1944).
26. (2011) 5 SCC 214.

The powers of the executive are not limited merely to the carrying out of the laws. In a welfare State the functions of the executive are ever widening, which cover within their ambit various aspects of social and economic activities. Therefore, the executive exercises power to fill gaps by issuing various departmental orders. The executive power of the State is coterminous with the legislative power of the State Legislature. In other words, if the State Legislature has jurisdiction to make law with respect to a subject, the State executive can make regulations and issue government orders with respect to it, subject, however, to the constitutional limitations. Such administrative rules and/or orders shall be inoperative if the legislature has enacted a law with respect to the subject. Thus, the High Court was not justified in brushing aside the Government Order dated 16-11-1951 on the ground that it contained administrative instructions.[27]

3.7 ENFORCEABILITY OF ADMINISTRATIVE INSTRUCTIONS

The general principle applicable is that administrative instructions are often deemed as not enforceable because they are not considered as law. But there are instances when the judiciary have recognized the importance of the administrative instructions and considered them as necessary for enforcement.

In *Sant Ram Sharma v. State of Rajasthan*[28] the Supreme Court had upheld the view that *"It is true that the Government cannot amend or supersede statutory rules by administrative instructions, but if the rules are silent on any particular point Government can fill up the gaps and supplement the rules and issue instructions not inconsistent with the rules already framed".*

In *Guman Singh v. State of Rajasthan*[29] the Supreme Court on appeal held that the implementation of the Rajasthan Administrative Service 1957 would be subject to the circular issued by the government prescribing the merit formula for the purpose of determining promotions. Based on the merits criteria the appellant officers were bypassed by junior officers, aggrieved by the action the appellants challenged the validity of the rules and instructions issued under the Circular. The Court recognized that the merit-based rules issued under the Circular were not violative of Articles 14 or 16 of the Constitution. The rules lay down the principle for assessing the merit of an officer and are made fundamentally to serve public interest. Justifying the rules, the Court held that - "the rule provides that the promotion based on merit in contra distinction to that based on seniority-cum-merit shall

27. Ibid.
28. (1968) 1 SCR 111.
29. (1971) 2 SCC 452.

strictly be on the basis of merit. The Selection Committee and the Promotion Committee consist of very responsible and senior officers of the State and being persons of experience they can be trusted to evaluate the merits of a particular officer. No doubt the term "merit" is not capable of an easy definition, but it can be safely said that merit is a sum total of various qualities and attributes of an employee such as his academic qualifications, his distinction in the University, his character, integrity, devotion to duty and the manner in which he discharges his official duties. Allied to this may be various other matters or factors such as his punctuality in work, quality and outturn of work done by him and the manner of his dealings with his superiors and subordinate officers and the general public and his rank in the service".

Upholding the legality of the Circular issued the Court held that–

> The Circular contains administrative instructions and it does not profess to lay down anything else. The Government have issued those instructions "for the guidance of all selection / promotion committee and appointing authorities mentioned in the Statutory Service Rules. These administrative instructions and the Statutory Service Rules should together be taken as a complete code on the subject". From the above extract it is clear that in the matter of selection or promotion the Committees concerned are enjoined not only to have regard to the statutory rules under which they function, but also to the administrative instructions given in the Circular. This makes it very clear that it is not open to the Committee concerned to ignore the instructions contained in the Circular or to act contrary to the directions contained therein. Therefore, it will be seen that if the Circular or any part of it gives instructions contrary to or opposed to any of the rules, the Circular or that part of the Circular to that extent will be invalid.

Highlighting the distinction between delegated legislation and administrative instruction, and the enforceability of the latter Jain & Jain has lucidly explained the position of law–

> In legal hierarchy, a rule is superior in authority to a direction.
>
> The basic distinguishing feature between a direction and delegated legislation is this: while delegated legislation is binding on both, the Administration and the individual, and is enforceable through a court of law at the instance of either the individual or the Administration, a direction, generally speaking, is not so binding and enforceable right on an individual, or impose an obligation of the Administration or the individual. Even if a direction is misapplied or ignored by the Administration, the affected individual and the Administration cannot enforce it against him.
>
> Although directions may not be enforceable legally, it does not follow from this that administrative authorities may disregard them with impunity. The

authorities are expected to follow the directions and their breach by them may lead to disciplinary or other appropriate action against them. There may be an administrative remedy available to an individual concerned for enforcing directions, e.g., he may go to a higher authority in the administrative hierarchy and plead for enforcing a direction in his favour issued by the concerned department. But the point still remains valid that the remedy available to the individual is intra-departmental or administrative in nature and not through a court of law. A breach of a direction by an officer is mostly a matter between him and his superiors and not for the courts to take cognisance of, barring some exceptional situations.[30]

CONCLUSION

Thus the growth of administrative functions has blurred the dividing line between the various forms of administrative actions. But it is equally important to identify and differentiate between the various forms of administrative actions and for the purpose it is important to look into several factors such as – nature of the power conferred, person or persons on whom it is conferred, framework of law concerning that power, consequences ensuing from the exercise of that power, manner in which the power is expected to be exercised and remedies available in case of breach of power – so that the rights and liabilities arising out of the different functions can be easily determined.

30. M.P. Jain & S.N.Jain, Principles of Administrative Law, LexisNexis, 6th Ed. 2010, pg. 170.

IV Delegated Legislation and Legal Issues

LEARNING OBJECTIVES

After reading this chapter, you will be familiar with:

- Reasons for the growth of Delegated Legislation
- Nature, meaning and scope of Delegated Legislation
- Constitutionality of Delegated Legislation under a written Constitution
  - United States
  - India
- Concept and application of the Essential Legislative Function Test
- Excessive Delegation of Legislative Power
- Scope of Sub-delegation of Legislative Power
- Types of Delegated Legislation
  - Power to Fill up the Details or Skeleton Legislation
  - Power of Inclusion and Exclusion
  - Power of Removal of Difficulty Clause (Henry VIII clause)
  - Power of By-passing
  - Power of Modification
- Difference between Rules, Regulations, Bye-laws and Orders
- Control of Delegated Legislation
  - Parliamentary Form of Control
    - Pre-enactment Control
    - Post-enactment Control
  - Procedural Form of Control
    - Drafting
    - Ante-natal publicity
    - Consultation
    - Publication
  - Judicial Review of Delegated Legislation
    - Parent Act is ultra vires the Constitution
    - Delegated Legislation is ultra vires the Constitution
    - Delegated Legislation is ultra vires the Parent Act

4.1 INTRODUCTION

The task of delegating the law making power by legislature to the executive is not a recent phenomenon, but is a regular feature in a democratic state where there is a separation between the Executive and the Legislature. Historically King Henry VIII of England by the Statute of Proclamations 1539 had been conferred with extensive powers to legislate by proclamations and executive laws. Statutes made by Parliament needs to confer authority on the Executive to make subordinate law making powers so as to give proper effect to the will of the Parliament. With the rise of welfare obligations, the intervention of State in multiple activities has increased the functional responsibility of the executive. The excessive pressure on the legislature for making laws on different areas of socio-economic and political nature has made it necessary for conferring subordinate legislative power on the executive authorities based on the theory of residuary powers.[1] In *Agricultural Market Committee v. Shalimar Chemical Works Ltd.*[2] the Supreme Court observed–

> Delegated legislation is not a new phenomenon. Ever since the statutes came to be made by Parliament, delegated legislation also came to be made by an authority to which the power was delegated by Parliament. It is no use going back into the pages of history or to look to the Statute of Proclamations, 1539 under which Henry VIII was given extensive powers to legislate by proclamations. What is intended to be emphasised is that there has always been, and continues to be, need for delegated legislation. The exigencies of the modern State, especially the social and economic reforms, have given rise to the making of delegated legislation on a large scale (by authorising the Government, almost in every statute passed by Parliament or the State Legislature to make rules) so much so that a reasonable fear could have arisen among the people that they were being ruled by the bureaucracy.[3]

The reasons for the growth of delegation of law making power have been generally identified as–

(i) Time constraint – Law making is a major task involving time and effort. Proper drafting of legislations and deliberation before passing of the legislation makes it necessary for the legislators to devote adequate time. But the legislators are often involved in various political activities during the working sessions of the Parliament which often denies them the opportunity to devote adequate time in the law making process. According to recent estimates almost 90 percent of Parliament's

1. *Ram Jawaya Kapur v. the State of Punjab* AIR 1955 SC 549 : (1955) 2 SCR 225.
2. AIR 1997 SC 2502.
3. (1997) 5 SCC 516, Para 22.

working time gets lost in the midst of political debates and protests, leaving very little time for consideration and passing of legislations.[4]

(ii) Technical complexity – The subject matter of law making may be technically complex and it is difficult to lay down in details all the complicated aspects of implementation of the law within the statute. Environmental laws, internet laws, taxing statutes, urban planning laws are few examples which requires expert knowledge and wisdom to lay down the intricate working of the laws in detail.

(iii) Experimentation – Many a times the executive requires time to carry out necessary experimentation for the purpose of bringing into effect the legislation. The executive faces many challenges in giving effect to social welfare legislations and often requires time to understand the working of the law and its impact on the people and implement effectively. It may need to bring the law into force in phases.

(iv) Fill up the details – The legislature often lays down the broad policy guidelines and the general rules of conduct and delegate the executive to fill up the details in the legislation through rules and regulations based on practical consideration and exigencies faced in the course of implementation at the ground level. The executive may require certain flexibility in working out the details of the legislation for the purposes of better implementation.

4.2 DEFINING 'DELEGATION'

The term delegation has been defined in Black's Law Dictionary as "the act of entrusting another with authority by empowering another to act as an agent or representative".[5] In P. Ramanatha Aiyar's The Law Lexicon it is described as "the act of making or commissioning a delegate. Delegation generally means parting of powers by the person who grants the delegation, but it also means conferring of an authority to do things which otherwise that person would have to do himself".[6]

In *Gwalior Rayon Silk Manufacturing (wvg.) Co. Ltd. v. The Assistant Commissioner of Sales Tax*[7] Supreme Court has described the concept of delegation as–

4. Economic Times, Washout of monsoon session of Parliament will lead to Rs 260 crore loss, July 25 2015, Available at: http://timesofindia.indiatimes.com/india/washout-of-monsoon-session-of-Parliament/listshow/48210376.cms (Accessed on, November 23, 2015).
5. Black's Law Dictionary 8th Ed.
6. 3rd Ed. 201.
7. (1974) 4SCC 98, MANU/SC/0361/1973.

> Delegation is not the complete handing over or transference of a power from one person or body of persons to another. Delegation may be defined as the entrusting, by a person or body of persons, of the exercise of a power residing in that person or body of persons, to another person or body of persons, with complete power of revocation or amendment remaining in the grantor or delegator. It is important to grasp the implications of this, for, much confusion of thought has unfortunately resulted from assuming that delegation involves or may involve, the complete abdication or abrogation of a power. This is precluded by the definition. Delegation often involves the granting of discretionary authority to another, but such authority is purely derivative. The ultimate power always remains in the delegator and is never renounced.[8]

Implementation of law is a complicated task and the members of the legislature do not often have the necessary time to work out the details of implementing the law, hence it is necessary to grant incidental or ancillary law making powers to a subordinate executive agency. The term delegated legislation has been defined by Salmond as *"that which proceeds from any authority other than the sovereign power and is therefore dependent for its continued existence and validity on some superior or supreme authority".*[9] In *St. Johns Teachers Training Institute v. Regional Director, National Council for Teacher Education*[10] the court further clarified and observed–

> A Regulation is a rule or order prescribed by a superior for the management of some business and implies a rule for general course of action. Rules and Regulations are all comprised in delegated legislations. The power to make subordinate legislation is derived from the enabling Act and it is fundamental that the delegate on whom such a power is conferred has to act within the limits of authority conferred by the Act. Rules cannot be made to supplant the provisions of the enabling Act but to supplement it. What is permitted is delegation of ancillary or subordinate legislative functions, or, what is fictionally called, a power to fill up details. The legislature may, after laying down the legislative policy confer discretion on an administrative agency as to the execution of the policy and leave it to the agency to work out the details within the frame work of policy. The need for delegated legislation is that they are framed with care and minuteness when the statutory authority making the Rule, after coming in to force of the Act, is in a better position to adapt the Act to special circumstances. Delegated legislation permits utilisation of experience and consultation with interests affected by the practical operation of statues. Rules and Regulations made by reason of the specific power conferred by the Statutes to make Rules and Regulations establish the pattern of conduct to be followed. Regulations are in aid of enforcement

8. Id at Para 37.
9. Salmond, Jurisprudence, 12th Ed. P. 116.
10. AIR 2003 SC 1533.

of the provisions of the Statute. The process of legislation by departmental Regulations saves time and is intended to deal with local variations and the power to legislate by statutory instrument in the form of Rules and Regulations is conferred by Parliament. The main justification for delegated legislation is that the legislature being over-burdened and the needs of the modern day society being complex it cannot possibly foresee every administrative difficulty that may arise after the Statute has begun to operate. Delegated legislation fills those needs. The Regulations made under power conferred by the Statute are supporting legislation and have the force and affect, if validly made, as the Act passed by the competent legislature.

4.3 LAW MAKING POWER OF THE LEGISLATURE

The primary function of the Parliament is to make laws for the people of India. Speaking on the scope of the Indian Parliament to make laws, the Supreme Court *In Re: Delhi Laws Act case*[11] observed that–

> Indian Parliament is the creature of the Constitution of India and its powers, rights, privileges and obligations have to be found in the relevant articles of the Constitution of India. It is not a sovereign body, uncontrolled with unlimited powers. The Constitution of India has conferred on the Indian Parliament powers to make laws in respect of matters specified in the appropriate places and Schedules, and curtailed its rights and powers under certain other articles and in particular by the articles found in Chapter III dealing with Fundamental Rights.

In *Agricultural Market Committee v. Shalimar Chemical Works Ltd*[12] it was further clarified that–

> The power of delegation is a constituent element of the legislative power as a whole under Article 245 of the Constitution and other relative articles and when the legislatures enact laws to meet the challenge of the complex socio-economic problems, they often find it convenient and necessary to delegate subsidiary or ancillary powers to delegates of their choice for carrying out the policy laid down by the Acts as part of the Administrative Law. The legislature has to lay down the legislative policy and principle to afford guidance for carrying out the said policy before it delegates its subsidiary powers in that behalf.

4.4 DELEGATION OF LEGISLATIVE POWERS UNDER A WRITTEN CONSTITUTION

In England the Parliament being supreme law making agency has the absolute power to make laws as well as to delegate its powers to other

11. [1951] 2 SCR 747.
12. (1997) 5 SCC 516.

instrumentalities of the state. In the absence of a written constitution, the Parliament enjoys sovereign law making powers without any restrictions or limitations. In contradistinction countries having a written constitution the organs of the state are bound by the constitutional norms and limitations. Delegation of legislative powers to the executive, even though a modern day necessity, had to face constitutional challenges on the ground of violation of the separation of power doctrine.

4.4.1 United States

The US Supreme Court was required to meet the challenge of upholding the constitutional requirement of separation of power between the three principle organs of the state and balance it with the growing demands for a proactive welfare state. In the leading case of *Panama Refining Co. v. Ryan*[13] the Court was required to deal with the constitutionality of legislations conferring broad delegation of law making powers to the Executive. The petitioners in this case were the owners of an oil refining company in Texas challenged an Executive Order issued by the US President for prohibiting 'the transportation in interstate and foreign commerce of petroleum and the products thereof produced or withdrawn from storage in excess of the amount permitted to be produced or withdrawn from storage by any State law or valid regulation or order prescribed thereunder, by any board, commission, officer, or other duly authorized agency of a State'. The executive order was issued under the provisions of Section 9(c) of title 1 of the National Industrial Recovery Act, 1933. The validity of the order was challenged on the ground of unconstitutionality of Section 9(c). It was argued that the provision made an unconstitutional delegation to the President of legislative power and transcended the authority of the Congress under the commerce clause. The US Supreme Court analyzed the scope of delegation of legislative power under Section 9(c) and held that the provision was unconstitutional because it failed to *lay down rules for the guidance of state Legislatures or state officers. It leaves to the states and to their constituted authorities the determination of what production shall be permitted.... It does not require any finding by the President as a condition of his action. The Congress in section 9(c) thus declares no policy as to the transportation of the excess production.* It was further observed that the fact that the delegation was made to the President and that he will act for what he believes to be public good is not a justification to validate the delegation of legislative powers in the absence of legislative policy. It is a constitutional imperative for the legislature to lay down the legislative policy and the

13. 293 U.S. 388.

same power cannot be conferred to the grantee (President) for determining the policy as he pleases. Speaking on the scope of delegation of legislative powers the Court observed–

> The Constitution provides that 'All legislative Powers herein granted shall be vested in a Congress of the United States, which shall consist of a Senate and House of Representatives'. Article 1, section 1. And the Congress is empowered 'To make all Laws which shall be necessary and proper for carrying into Execution' its general powers. Article 1, section 8, para. 18. The Congress manifestly is not permitted to abdicate or to transfer to others the essential legislative functions with which it is thus vested. Undoubtedly legislation must often be adapted to complex conditions involving a host of details with which the national Legislature cannot deal directly. The Constitution has never been regarded as denying to the Congress the necessary resources of flexibility and practicality, which will enable it to perform its function in laying down policies and establishing standards, while leaving to selected instrumentalities the making of subordinate rules within prescribed limits and the determination of facts to which the policy as declared by the Legislature is to apply. Without capacity to give authorizations of that sort we should have the anomaly of a legislative power which in many circumstances calling for its exertion would be but a futility. But the constant recognition of the necessity and validity of such provisions and the wide range of administrative authority which has been developed by means of them cannot be allowed to obscure the limitations of the authority to delegate, if our constitutional system is to be maintained.

Thus the US Supreme Court recognized the constitutional obligation of the legislature to perform their *essential legislative functions* of framing the legislative policy which cannot be abdicated or transferred. But for the purposes of granting flexibility and practicality it might be necessary to grant subordinate rule making powers to some other state agencies in a limited manner.

The view of the US Supreme Court was reiterated in the subsequent case of *Schechter Poultry Corp. v. United States.*[14] The appellants were arrested for violating the Code of Fair Competition for the Live Poultry Industry. The Code was enacted under Section 3 of the National Industrial Recovery Act which authorized the President to approve codes of fair competition for a trade or industry to prevent monopolies and monopolistic practices. The Code dealt with issues relating to hours of working, wages, general labour conditions, administration, trade practices etc. It was argued by the appellants that the delegation of legislative power was outside the permissible scope as laid in the *Panama case.* The Court upheld the contention of the appellant on the ground that the Congress had failed to lay down

14. 295 U.S. 495.

necessary legislative policy and instead had made a *sweeping delegation of legislative power.* It was held that Section 3 of the Recovery Act was unconstitutional as it did not lay down any standard nor did it *prescribe any rules of conduct to be applied to particular states of fact determined by appropriate administrative procedure.* In addition the discretion conferred on the President *in approving or prescribing codes, and thus enacting laws for the government of trade and industry throughout the country, is virtually unfettered.* The Code making authority was declared to be *unconstitutional delegation of legislative power.*

4.4.2 India

Post-independence the Indian Supreme Court was also required to deal with similar issues in the presidential reference of *In Re: Delhi Laws Act case.*[15] In this case a reference was made by the President of India under Article 143 of the Constitution to the seven-Judge Bench of the Supreme Court seeking the opinion on the three following issues–

(1) Was Section 7 of the Delhi Laws Act 1912 was ultra vires the Legislature passed the Act?

Section 7 – Provincial government may, by notification in the official gazette, extend with such restrictions and modification as it thinks fit to the Province of Delhi any enactment which is in force in any part of British India at the date of such notification.

(2) Was Section 2 of the Ajmer-Merwara (Extension of Laws) Act 1947 ultra vires the Legislature which passed the said Act?

Section 2 – The Central Government may, by notification in the official gazette, extend to the Province of Ajmer-Merwara with such restrictions and modifications as it thinks fit any enactment which is in force in any other Province at the date of such notification.

(3) Was Section 2 of the Part C States (Laws) Act 1950 ultra vires the Parliament?

Section 2 – The Central Government may, by notification in the Official Gazette extend to any Part C states (other than Coorg and Andaman and Nicobar Islands) or to any part of such State, with such restrictions and modifications as it thinks fit, any enactment which is in force in a Part A State at the date of the notification and provision may be made in any enactment so extended for the repeal or amendment so extended for the repeal or amendment of any corresponding law (other than a Central Act) which is for the time being applicable to that Part C State.

---

15. [1951] 2 SCR 747.

The point of reference for the Supreme Court was whether Indian Parliament and the State Legislatures had the power to delegate its legislative functions to an executive authority, and, if so, to what extent it can do so?

All the seven judges gave seven different judgments, however some major points of commonality can be identified in the opinions. On the issue of whether delegation of legislative powers is permissible under the Indian Constitution the Supreme Court based its rationality on three core arguments.

The first argument was based on the principle of *delegatus non potest delegare* which implies that a delegated authority cannot be further delegated i.e. one agent cannot lawfully appoint another agent to do the task. The Court after analyzing the legislative history of India observed that prior to independence even though the Indian legislature was bound by the Act of the Imperial Parliament which created and was incapable of going beyond the circumscribed powers but within those limits it was not an agent or delegate of the British Parliament. The plenary powers of law making of the Indian legislature were same as those of the British Parliament within such limits. Thus the doctrine was never applied against Indian legislature during the colonial regime, hence post-independence the same shall not be applicable against the Indian Parliament. On the related argument of whether the legislature can be deemed to be the delegate of the people or the electors. Negating the argument Kania C.J. observed – *"There can be no doubt that members of a legislature represent the majority of their electors, but the legislature as a body cannot be said to be an agency of the electorate as a whole. The individual members may and often do represent different parties and different shades of opinion, but the composite legislature which legislates, does so on its own authority or power which it derives from the Constitution, and its acts cannot be questioned by the electorate, nor can the latter withdraw its power to legislate on any particular matter"*. The second argument to invalidate delegation of legislative power was based on the doctrine of *separation of powers.* This argument was also negated on the ground the principle had not been applied in any country in absolute. Even in US wherein the doctrine has been incorporated in the Constitution but the delegation of legislative power to administrative agencies is considered to be a practical necessity. The last argument was based on the constitutional law argument of 'the power conferred upon the Legislature to make laws cannot be delegated by that department to any other body or authority because where the sovereign power of the State has located the authority, there it must remain'. The Supreme Court opined that the power to whose judgment, wisdom and patriotism the Constitution has entrusted the law making power, such authority cannot relieve itself of the responsibility of delegating it to other agencies. But in most other jurisdictions the courts have interpreted the proposition to imply that the legislature cannot abdicate its essential legislative functions and it cannot efface itself and set up a parallel legislature to discharge the primary duty with which it has been entrusted, similarly in India the parliament cannot delegate its essential law making functions. Thus by negating the three arguments put forth in favour of non-delegation of legislative powers, the Indian Supreme Court upheld the proposition that delegation of legislative powers is a permissible act.

On the issue of extent of delegation, the Court viewed since Indian Parliament were a creature of the Constitution and all its powers, rights, privileges and obligations are derived from different articles of the Constitution, the Parliament is not an uncontrolled body with unlimited powers. Subject to the limitations and controls imposed by the Constitution, the Legislature is supreme and its powers are plenary.

4.5 ESSENTIAL LEGISLATIVE FUNCTION TEST

After the opinion of the Supreme Court in *Delhi Laws Act case* the test of constitutionality of delegated legislation was analyzed by the five-Judge bench of the Court in the leading case of *Harishankar Bagla v. State of Madhya Pradesh.*[16] In this case the appellant and his wife were arrested for contravention of the provisions of the Cotton Textiles (Control of Movement) Order, 1948 which was framed under the provisions of the Essential Supplies (Temporary Powers) Act was challenged. It was alleged that Sections 3 and 4 of the Act were unconstitutional on the ground of excessive delegation of legislative power. The Court analyzed the preamble of the statute as well as Sections 3 and 4.

> Section 3. (1) The Central Government, so far as it appears to it to be necessary or expedient for maintaining or increasing supplies of any essential commodity, or for securing their equitable distribution and availability at fair prices, may by order provide for regulating or prohibiting the production, supply and distribution thereof and trade and commerce therein..........
>
> (2) Without prejudice to the generality of the power conferred by sub-section (1), an order made thereunder may provide-
>
> (a) for regulating by licences, permits or otherwise the production or manufacture of any essential commodity;..........
>
> (d) for regulating by licences, permits or otherwise the storage, transport, distribution, disposal, acquisition, use or consumption of any essential commodity;.........

16. AIR 1954 SC 465.

The Court negated the contention of excessive delegation of legislative power and laid down the principles governing the permissible limits of delegation by upholding the essential legislative function test. It observed–

> It was settled by the majority judgment in the Delhi Laws Act case ([1951] S.C.R. 747), that essential powers of legislation cannot be delegated. In other words, the legislature cannot delegate its function of laying down legislative policy in respect of a measure and its formulation as a rule of conduct. The Legislature must declare the policy of the law and the legal principles which are to control any given cases and must provide a standard to guide the officials or the body in power to execute the law. The essential legislative function consists in the determination or choice of the legislative policy and of formally enacting that policy into a binding rule no conduct. In the present case the legislature has laid down such a principle and that principle is the maintenance or increase in supply of essential commodities and of securing equitable distribution and availability at fair prices. The principle is clear and offers sufficient guidance to the Central Government in exercising its powers under section 3.

Thus the rule relating to delegation of legislative power was summarized that the legislature cannot delegate the essential legislative functions to an administrative body. It is the core function of the legislature to determine the legislative policy and formulate the binding rules of conduct. But the requirement to lay down the legislative policy and its determination often became a point of contention before the judiciary and in several cases the courts had to search for the legislative policy within the broad provisions of the statute, its preamble, title, legislative debates and even prior legislations. In *Bhatnagars & Co. Ltd. v. Union of India*[17] the Supreme Court stated *"if we can find a reasonably clear statement of policy underlying the provisions of the Act either in the provisions of the Act or in the preamble, then any part of the Act cannot be attacked on the ground of delegated legislation by suggesting that questions of policy have been left to the delegate". 18* While searching for the policy laid down in the Imports and Exports Act the Court referred to the predecessor enactment of Defence of India Act and the rules framed thereunder and Gajendragadkar J. observed *that the broad and main principle underlying the present Act, like its predecessor, was to maintain supplies essential to the life of the community.*

In this context K.K. Mathew J. in his minority opinion in *Gwalior Rayon Silk Mfg. (Wvg.) Co. Ltd. v. CST*[19] raised the concerns relating to the essential legislative functions theory. He observed–

17. *Bhatnagars & Co. Ltd. v. Union of India* 1957 SCR 701 : AIR 1957 SC 478.
18. *Id* at Para 11.
19. (1974) 4 SCC 98.

> Delegation of "law-making" power, it has been said, is the dynamo of modern Government. Delegation by the Legislature is necessary in order that the exertion of legislative power does not become a futility. Today, while theory still affirms legislative supremacy, we see power flowing back increasingly to the Executive. Departure from the traditional rationalization of the status quo arouses distrust. The Legislature comprises a broader cross-section of interests than any one administrative organ; it is less likely to be captured by particular interests. We must not, therefore, lightly say that there can be a transfer of legislative power under the guise of delegation which would tantamount to abdication. At the same time, we must be aware of the practical reality, and that is, that Parliament cannot go into the details of all legislative matters. The doctrine of abdication expresses a fundamental democratic concept but at the same time we should not insist that law-making as such is the exclusive province of the Legislature. The aim of Government is to gain acceptance for objectives demonstrated as desirable and to realise them as fully as possible. The making of law is only a means to achieve a purpose. It is not an end in itself. That end can be attained by the Legislature making the law. But many topics or subjects of legislation are such that they require expertise, technical knowledge and a degree of adaptability to changing situations which Parliament might not possess and, therefore, this end is better secured by extensive delegation of legislative power. The legislative process would frequently bog down if a Legislature were required to appraise beforehand the myriad situations to which it wishes a particular policy to be applied and to formulate specific rules for each situation. The presence of Henry VIII clause in many of the statutes is a pointer to the necessity of extensive delegation. The hunt by Court for legislative policy or guidance in the crevices of a statute or the nook and cranny of its preamble is not an edifying spectacle. It is not clear what difference does it make in principle by saying that since the delegation is to a representative body, that would be a guarantee that the delegate will not exercise the power unreasonably, for, if ex hypothesi the Legislature must perform the essential legislative function, it is certainly no consolation that the body to which the function has been delegated has a representative character. In other words, if, no guidance is provided or policy laid down, the fact that the delegate has a representative character could make no difference in principle.

In this context he advocated for the application of the 'abdication test' in place of the essential legislative function test. He advocated-*Delegation is not the complete handing over or transference of a power from one person or body of persons to another. Delegation may be defined as the entrusting, by a person or body of persons, of the exercise of a power residing in that person or body of persons, to another person or body of persons, with complete power of revocation or amendment remaining in the grantor or delegator.... Delegation often involves the granting of discretionary authority to another, but such authority is purely derivative. The ultimate power always remains in the delegator and is never renounced.*[20] Thus the theory of abdication implies that the legislature shall transfer legislative powers to the executive authority but such delegation shall not amount to abandonment, *since the executive in making the regulations is no more than an agent of the legislature which can always recall its authority.*[21]

However Khanna J. laying down the majority opinion rejected the abdication theory and upheld the longstanding essential functions theory. On the basis of constitutional limitations it was held that–

> [T]he power conferred upon the legislature to make laws cannot be delegated to any other authority does not preclude the legislature from delegating any power not legislative which it may itself rightfully exercise. It may confer an authority in relation to the execution of a law which may involve discretion, but such authority must be exercised under and in pursuance of the law. The Legislature must declare the policy of the law and fix the legal principles which are to control in given cases; but an administrative officer or body may be invested with the power to ascertain the facts and conditions to which the policy and principles apply. If this could not be done there would be infinite confusion in the laws, and in an effort to detail and to particularise, they would miss sufficiency both in provision and execution.[22]

It was further observed that conferring of blanket powers without any legislative policy, guidelines or standards in the statute would give rise to *startling* situation.

> Supposing the Parliament tomorrow enacts that as the crime situation in the country has deteriorated, criminal law to be enforced in the country from a particular date would be such as is framed by an officer mentioned in the enactment. Can it be said that there has been no excessive delegation of legislative power even though the Parliament omits to lay down in the statute any guideline or legislative policy for the making of such criminal law? The vice of such an enactment cannot, in our opinion, be ignored or lost sight of on the ground that if the Parliament does not approve the law made by the officer concerned, it can repeal the enactment by which that officer was authorised to make the law.[23]

In *Avinder Singh v. State of Punjab*[24] an attempt was made to balance the differing views as discussed in the *Gwalior Rayon case* and create a theoretical proposition to the concept of delegation of legislative power. It observed

20. Ibid.
21. Id.
22. (1974) 4 SCC 98 Para 23.
23. Id.
24. (1979) 1 SCC 137.

The Founding Document of the nation has created the three great instrumentalities and entrusted them with certain basic powers-legislative, judicative and executive. Abdication of these powers by the concerned instrumentalities, it is axiomatic, amounts to betrayal of the Constitution itself and it is intolerable in law. This means that the legislature cannot self-efface its personality and make over, in terms plenary, the essential legislative functions. The legislature is responsible and responsive to the people and its representatives, the delegate may not be and that is why excessive delegation and legislative *hara kiri* have been frowned upon by constitutional law. This is a trite proposition but the complexities of modern administration are so bafflingly intricate and bristle with details, urgencies, difficulties and need for flexibility that our massive legislatures may not get off to a start if they must directly and comprehensively handle legislative business in all their plenitude, proliferation and particularisation. Delegation of some part of legislative power becomes a compulsive necessity for viability. If the 500-odd parliamentarians are to focus on every minuscule of legislative detail leaving nothing to subordinate agencies the annual output may be both unsatisfactory and negligible. The Law-making is not a turnkey project, ready-made in all detail and once this situation is grasped the dynamics of delegation easily follow. Thus, we reach the second constitutional rule that the essentials of legislative functions shall not be delegated but the inessentials, however numerous and significant they be, may well be made over to appropriate agencies. Of course, every delegate is subject to the authority and control of the principal and exercise of delegated power can always be directed, corrected or cancelled by the principal. Therefore, the third principle that emerges is that even if there be delegation, parliamentary control over delegated legislation should be a living continuity as a constitutional necessity. Within these triple principles, Operation Delegation is at once expedient, exigent and even essential if the legislative process is not to get stuck up or bogged down or come to a grinding halt with a few complicated bills. It is apt to excerpt here an oft-quoted observation from Vasantlal Maganbhai Sanjanwala affirmed in *Devi Das Gopal Krishnan and Ors. v. State of Punjab and Ors.* [1967] 1 S.C.R. 557:

The Constitution confers a power and imposes a duty on the legislature to make laws. The essential legislative function is the determination of the legislative policy and its formulation as a rule of conduct. Obviously it cannot abdicate its functions in favour of another. But in view of the multifarious activities of a welfare State, it cannot presumably work out all the details to suit the varying aspects of a complex situation. It must necessarily delegate the working out of details to the executive or any other agency. But there is a danger inherent in such a process of delegation. An over burdened legislature or one controlled by a powerful executive may unduly overstep the limits of delegation. It may not lay down any policy at all; it may declare its policy in vague and general terms; it may not set down any standard for the guidance of the executive; it may confer an arbitrary power on the executive to change or modify the policy laid down by it without reserving for itself any control over subordinate legislation. This self-effacement of legislative power in favour

> of another agency either in whole or in part is beyond the permissible limits of delegation. It is for a Court to hold on a fair, generous and liberal construction of an impugned statute whether the legislature exceeded such limits. But the said liberal construction should not be carried by the Courts to the extent of always trying to discover a dormant or latent legislative policy to sustain an arbitrary power conferred on executive authorities. It is the duty of the Court to strike down without any hesitation any arbitrary power conferred on the executive by the legislature.

Thus the Supreme Court laid down the following propositions as the legal basis for upholding the constitutionality of delegated legislation.

(i) The legislature must perform their essential legislative function.

(ii) The incidental, ancillary or subordinate matters can be delegated.

(iii) After delegation the parliamentary control over the delegated legislation should be a continuing process.

(iv) Judiciary should exercise the power of review to ensure that excessive delegation does not take place and a legislation which fails to lay down the policy is struck down on the ground of unconstitutionality.

4.5.1 Test for Valid Delegation of Legislative Powers

In *Avinder Singh v. State of Punjab*[25] the Supreme Court applied the test for validity of delegated legislation while interpreting the provisions of Punjab Municipal Corporation Act, 1976.

> Such being the basics, accepted by precedential profusion of this Court, we have to examine whether any essential legislative function has been transplanted into the hands of Government or corporation by the Act. whether the delegation itself is an entrustment of overbroad power, so unguided that the delegate may run amok and do what is arbitrary, unreasonable and violative of Articles 14 and 19 of the Constitution. Taxation is exaction and even expropriation and, therefore, the right to property is in peril when a fiscal measure is afoot. Article 10 comes into play when law is made for purposes of taxation and that law must comply with Part III. Arbitrariness must be excluded in the law, for, if power is arbitrary it is potential inequality and Article 14 is fatally allergic to inequality before the law.

In this case Section 90 of the Punjab Municipal Corporation Act, 1976 was held to be *a text-book illustration of a valid delegation by the legislature.* The Court analysed the issue of whether the power to impose tax under Section 90 by the Corporation was ultra vires on the ground of absence of

---

25. (1979) 1 SCC 137.

any guiding principle to determine the *purpose of the Act*[26]. Negating the contention Krishna Iyer J. observed–

> While what constitutes an essential feature cannot be delineated in detail it certainly cannot include a change of policy. The legislature is the master of legislative policy and if the delegate is free to switch policy it may be usurpation of legislative power itself. So we have to investigate whether the policy of legislation has been indicated sufficiently or even change of policy has been left to the sweet will and pleasure of the delegate in this case.
>
> We are clearly of the view that there is fixation of the policy of the legislation in the matter of taxation, as a close study of Section 90 reveals; and exceeding that policy will invalidate the action of the delegate. What is that policy? The levy of the taxes shall be only for the purposes of the Act. Diversion for other purposes is illegal. Exactions beyond the requirements for the fulfilment of the purposes of the Act are also invalid. Like in Section 90(1), Section 90(2) also contains the words of limitation 'for the purposes of this Act' and that limiting factor governs Sub-sections (3), (4) and (5). Sub-section (3) vests nothing new beyond Sub-sections (1) and (2). Sub-section (4) does not authorise the government to direct the corporation to impose any tax falling outside Sub-section (1) or Sub-section (2). Sub-section (5) also is subject to a similar circumscription because the Government cannot issue an order to impose a tax outside the limitation of Sub-section (1) or Sub-section (2).

---

26. Section 90: Taxes to be imposed by Corporation under this Act and arrangement of certain taxes collected by Government (1) The Corporation shall, for the purposes of the Act, levy the following taxes:-
    (a) taxes on lands and buildings;
    (b) octroi;
    (c) a tax on vehicles and animals;
    (d) a tax on advertisements other than advertisements published in newspapers;
    (e) a development tax on the increase in urban land values caused by the execution of any development or improvement work.
    (2) Subject to the prior approval of the Government the Corporation may, for the purposes of this Act, in addition to the taxes specified in sub-section (1), levy,-
    (a) a tax on professions, trades, callings and employment; and
    (b) any other tax which the State Legislature has power to impose under the Constitution;
    Provided that no tax shall be imposed under this sub-section unless an opportunity has been given in the prescribed manner to the residents of the City to file objections and the objections, if any, thus received have been considered.
    ....
    (4) The Government may, by special or general order, direct a Corporation to impose any tax falling under sub-section (1) or sub-section (2) not already imposed, within such period as may be specified and the Corporation shall thereupon act accordingly.
    (5) If the Corporation fails to carry out any order passed under sub-section (4), the Government may by a suitable order notified in the Official Gazette impose the tax and the order so passed shall operate as if the tax had been duly imposed by the Corporation under sub-section (1) or sub-section (2), as the case may be.

> Thus, the impugned provision contains a severe restriction that the taxation leviable by the corporation, or by the Government acting for the corporation, shall be geared wholly to the goals of the Act. The fiscal policy of Section 90 is manifest. No tax under guise of Section 90(2)(b) can be charged if the purposes of the Act do not require or sanction it. The expression "purposes of this Act" is pregnant with meaning. It sets a ceiling on the total quantum that may be collected. It canalises the objects for which the fiscal levies may be spent. It brings into focus the functions, obligatory or optional, of the municipal bodies and the raising of resources necessary for discharging those functions-nothing more, nothing else.

In *Agricultural Market Committee v. Shalimar Chemical Works Ltd*[27] the Supreme Court referred to its earlier decisions and summarized the important principles of delegated legislation. It observed–

> The principle which, therefore, emerges out is that the essential legislative function consists of the determination of the legislative policy and the legislature cannot abdicate essential legislative function in favour of another. Power to make subsidiary legislation may be entrusted by the legislature to another body of its choice but the legislature should, before delegating, enunciate either expressly or by implication, the policy and the principles for the guidance of the delegates. These principles also apply to taxing statutes. The effect of these principles is that the delegate which has been authorised to make subsidiary rules and regulations has to work within the scope of its authority and cannot widen or constrict the scope of the Act or the policy laid down thereunder. It cannot, in the garb of making rules, legislate on the field covered by the Act and has to restrict itself to the mode of implementation of the policy and purpose of the Act.

Thus the tests for valid delegation of legislative power can be summarized into–

(1) The legislature cannot efface itself;

(2) it cannot delegate the plenary or the essential legislative function;

(3) even if there be delegation, parliamentary control over delegated legislation should be a living continuity as a constitutional necessity.[28]

4.6 EXCESSIVE DELEGATION OF LEGISLATIVE POWER

Post *In re Delhi Laws Act case* excessive delegation of legislative power on the executive authorities is deemed to be unconstitutional. Some of the examples of excessive delegation are – power to legislate on matters of policy, power to amend or repeal Acts of Parliament, power conferring wide

27. Id.
28. (1997) 5 SCC 516.

discretion without any limits specified, power to make rules without being challenged in a court of law etc.[29] The grant of excessive law making is popularly known as *Henry VIII clause.*[30]

The term Henry VIII clause has been commonly used to refer to delegated legislative powers contained in legislations which give "the delegate the power to amend the delegating Act in order to bring that Act into full operation or otherwise by Order to remove any difficulty, and at times giving power to modify the provisions of other Acts also".[31] Such provisions have been nicknamed as the 'Henry VIII clause' with regard to the English monarch Henry VIII as an impersonation of executive autocracy.[32]

Excessive delegation is also considered to be violation of Article 14 of the Constitution giving rise to arbitrary exercise of power. Article 14 has been used by the Indian judiciary in several cases to strike down conferment and exercise of arbitrary powers by the State or any of its instrumentalities. For the purpose of determining whether a legislation suffers from excessive delegation the Court is required to take into consideration the subject matter, the scheme, the provisions of the Statutes including its preamble and the facts and circumstances in the background of which the Statute is enacted. The judiciary generally starts with the presumption that a delegated legislation is intra vires and if it is open to two constructions, the courts generally adheres to that construction or interpretation which would make the law valid so as to avoid declaring it as ultra vires.[33]

In the leading case of *Hamdard Dawakhana v. Union of India*[34] the constitutionality of Drugs and Magical Remedies (Objectionable Advertisement) Act 1954 was challenged. It was alleged that the legislation was in violation of various fundamental rights under Articles 19(1)(a), (f) & (g), 14, 21 and 31 as the petitioners were facing difficulty in publicizing their products and were being unnecessarily harassed by the authorities in regard to their advertisements. It was further alleged that the clause (d) of Section 3 suffered from excessive delegation as it did not lay down *any certain criteria or proper standards and surrender unguided and uncanalised power to the executive to add to diseases in the Schedule.* Striking down the provision as unconstitutional the Court observed that Parliament has established no

29. IP Massey, Administrative Law, 6th Ed. 2005.
30. Detailed discussion on Henry VIII clause later in this chapter.
31. *Central Inland Water Transport Corporation Limited v. Brojo Nath Ganguly* MANU/SC/0439/1986, Para 100.
32. The constitutionality of *removal of difficulty clause* has been discussed under 'Power of Removal of Difficulty Clause'.
33. AIR 2003 SC 1533.
34. (1960) 2SCR 671 : AIR 1960 SC 554.

criteria, no standards and has not prescribed any principle on which a particular disease or condition is to be specified in the Schedule. It is not stated what facts or circumstances are to be taken into consideration to include a particular condition or disease. The power of specifying diseases and conditions as given in Section 3(*d*) must therefore be held to be going beyond permissible boundaries of valid delegation. As a consequence the Schedule in the rules must be struck down.

In *West Bengal Electricity Board v. Desh Bandhu Ghosh*[35] the Supreme Court dealt with the constitutionality of Regulation 34 of the Board's Regulation which was framed under the Electricity (Supply) Act, 1948. The respondent was a permanent employee of the WB Electricity Board and was dismissed from service without any assigned reasons on March 22, 1984 by an order of the Secretary of the Board applicable with immediate effect on payment of three month's salary in lieu of three months' notice. The termination of service was in accordance with Regulation 34 which provided that "in case of a permanent employee, his service may be terminated by serving three months, notice or on payment of salary for the corresponding period in lieu thereof". The Court compared Regulation 34 with Regulation 33 which dealt with termination of services of a permanent employee by the Board without notice. Regulation 33 states–

> 33(1) Unless otherwise specified in the appointment order in any particular case, the services of a permanent employee of the Board may be terminated without notice–
>
> (i) on his attaining the age of retirement or by reason of a declaration by the competent medical authority that he is unfit for further service; or
>
> (ii) as a result of disciplinary action;
>
> (iii) if he remains absent from duty, on leave or otherwise, for a continuous period exceeding 2 years.
>
> (2) In the case of a temporary employee, his service maybe terminated by serving of–
>
> (a) one month's notice on either side or on payment of a month's salary in lieu thereof; or
>
> (b) notice on either side for the period specified in the appointment order or contract or on payment of salary in lieu thereof, as the case may be;
>
> (c) the service of a temporary employee shall also be deemed to have been terminated automatically if the period of extraordinary leave without pay

35. (1985) 3 SCC 116.

and/or of unauthorised absence from duties exceeding (s) a maximum period of 90 days.

On comparison between the two Regulations the Court observed that the *Regulation 34 was arbitrary in nature and suffered from the vice of enabling discrimination* because unlike Regulation 33 it did not lay down any criteria or grounds for exercise of discretionary power. Negating the arguments of the appellant that the power under Regulation 34 was to be exercised by a high ranking officer and would be expected to be exercised in a reasonable manner the Court observed–

> On the face of it, the regulation is totally arbitrary and confers on the Board a power which is capable of vicious discrimination. It is a naked 'hire and fire' rule, the time for banishing which altogether from employer-employee relationship is fast approaching. Its only parallel is to be found in the Henry VIII class so familiar to administrative lawyers.[36]

The Supreme Court upheld that the power to dismiss an employee without the necessity to assign any-reason was not only an example of arbitrary, uncanalised and drastic power but also violative of principles of natural justice.

Similar rationale was applied by the Supreme Court in the case *Central Inland Water Transport Corporation Limited v. Brojo Nath Ganguly*[37] wherein Rule 9(i) of the Central Inland Water Transport Corporation Ltd. (Service, Discipline and Appeals) Rules 1979 conferred on the Corporation the power to terminate the service of a permanent employee by giving him three months' notice in writing or pay him the equivalent of three months' basic pay and clearness allowance in lieu thereof. The Court equated the provision to the *Henry VIII clause* as it conferred 'absolute and arbitrary power upon the Corporation' without any specific guidelines being laid down 'to indicate in what circumstances the power given by Rule 9(i) is to be exercised by the Corporation'. In addition no opportunity of being heard is provided to a permanent employee whose service was being terminated in the exercise of this power. On the issue of the power being exercised cautiously and not arbitrarily by the Board of Directors the Court negated the contention by observing *however highly placed a person may be, he must necessarily possess human frailties* based on Lord Acton's well-known saying "Power tends to corrupt, and absolute power corrupts absolutely".[38] Rule 9(i) was held to be an absolute, arbitrary and unguided power upon the Corporation which could even enable it to act in a discriminatory manner

36. MANU/SC/0374/1985, Para 4.
37. AIR 1986 SC 1571, MANU/SC/0439/1986.
38. Id at Para 101.

between employee and employee. It was further observed "A clause such as Clause (i) of Rule 9 is against right and reason. It is wholly unconscionable. It has been entered into between parties between whom there is gross inequality of bargaining power".[39] Other decisions applying similar rationale are *Delhi Transport Corporation v. D.T.C. Mazdoor Congress*[40] and *Daulat Sita Ram Kodone v. State of Maharashtra*[41]the Supreme Court equated the terms of an unfair contract with Henry VIII clause and held them as unconstitutional and arbitrary.

Gwalior Rayon Silk Mfg. (Wvg.) Co. Ltd. v. CST[42] is another leading case wherein the Supreme Court analyzed whether Section 8(2)(b) of the Central Sales Tax 1956 suffered from excessive delegation as the fixation of rate of tax is a legislative function and cannot be delegated to the executive. Section 8(2)(b) provided that 'the tax payable by any dealer on his turnover in so far as the turnover or any part of it relates to sale of goods in the of inter-state trade not falling within sub-section (1)... in the case of goods other than declared goods shall be calculated at the rate of 10% or at the rate applicable to the sale or purchase of such goods inside the appropriate State, whichever is higher'. It was argued by the appellants that the fixation of the rate of tax is a legislative function but the Parliament instead of fixing the rate of central sales tax had adopted the rates applicable to the sale or purchase of goods inside the appropriate state in cases where the rate exceeds 10% which amounted to abdication of its legislative function, hence Section 8(2)(b) amounted to excessive delegation of legislative power.

The Supreme Court upheld the constitutionality of Section 8(2)(b) and held that the provision does not suffer from any vice of excessive delegation of legislative power. Identifying the legislative policy it observed–

> The object of the law apparently is to deter inter-State sales to unregistered dealers as such inter-State sales would facilitate evasion of tax. It is also not possible to fix the maximum rate under Section 8(2)(b) because the rate of local sales tax varies from State to State. The rate of local sales tax can also be changed by the State legislatures from time to time. It is not within the competence of the Parliament to fix the maximum rate of local sales tax. The fixation of the rate of local sales tax is essentially a matter for the State Legislatures and the Parliament does not have any control in the matter The Parliament has therefore necessarily, if it wants to prevent evasion of payment of central sales tax, to tack the rate of such tax with that of local sales tax, in case the rate of local sales tax exceeds a particular limit.

---

39. Id at Para 103.
40. (1991) ILLJ 395 SC, MANU/SC/0031/1991.
41. 2013(10)SCALE 450, MANU/SC/0895/2013.
42. (1974) 4 SCC 98.

4.7 SUB-DELEGATION OF LAW-MAKING POWER

Subordinate legislations are in the nature of Rules and Regulations for the purpose of giving effect to the laws made by the Legislature. The task of making subordinate rules is conferred by the Legislature to a specified body. Such body cannot make further delegation of its rule-making responsibilities as it would be contrary to the principles of *delegatus non potest delegare* and would be contrary to the confidence reposed by the delegate.

In the case of *Harishankar Bagla v. State of Madhya Pradesh*[43] the issue of sub-delegation was analyzed by the Supreme Court. It was alleged that Section 4 of the Essential Supplies Act was unconstitutional on the ground of sub-delegation. Section 4 provided-

> Section 4. The Central Government may by notified order direct that the power to make orders under section 3 shall, in relation to such matters and subject to such conditions, if any, as may be specified in the direction, be exercisable also by-
>
> (a) such officer or authority subordinate to the Central Government, or
>
> (b) such State Government or such officer or authority subordinate to a State Government as may be specified in the direction.

The Court negated the argument that the Central Government has been empowered to delegate its own power to any officer or authority subordinate to it, on the contrary it held that the Parliament in Section 4 has specifically *enumerated the classes of persons to whom the power could be delegated or sub-delegated.* Thus the Parliament being the supreme law making power is empowered has the authority to make delegation of legislative powers to any persons or bodies it thinks suitable and also to identify such officials or authorities for the purpose of exercise such powers.

4.8 TYPES OF DELEGATED LEGISLATION

Ordinarily a classification is made between conditional legislation and delegated legislation. Conditional legislation refers to the power conferred to the delegate to determine when the rule of conduct declared under a statute becomes effective. In such kind of delegation the legislation will be complete in itself and the only conferring of discretion to the administrative body will be to determine the time and manner of carrying the legislation in to effect as well as to determine the area to which it is to be extended. Delegated legislation on the contrary involves delegation of rule-making power

43. AIR 1954 SC 465.

which constitutionally can be exercised by the administrative authority. In delegated legislation the legislature is required to lay down the broad policy or principles governing the statute and allow the delegated authority to frame other details of the legislation within the prescribed limits of the statute. In such kind of delegation the administrative authority is required to fill in the details of the legislation and ensure that the purpose of the legislation is fulfilled and the rights and obligations under the statute are properly implemented.

> The legislature cannot delegate its power to make a law, but it can make a law to delegate a power to determine some fact or state of things upon which the law makes or intends to make its own action depend. There are many things upon which wise and useful legislation must depend which cannot be known to the law making power, and must therefore be subject of enquiry and determination outside the hall of legislatures.[44]

Thus the legislature is required to put their minds to the future and ensure that the legislation shall meet the challenges of future contingencies which might appear in the course of implementation of law, hence the legislature has to confer different kinds of rule-making power to the executive authorities to overcome the various challenges and maintain the relevancy of the law. Some of the important types of delegated legislations have been classified below.

4.8.1 Power to Fill up the Details or Skeleton Legislation

The core function of delegated legislation is to perform *what is fictionally called as "power to fill up the details"*. In *Harishankar Bagla v. State of Madhya Pradesh*[45] the Court justifying the broad delegation of legislative powers to the executive authorities under the Essential Supplies Act and stated that *'the ambit and character of the Act is such that the details of that policy can only be worked out by delegating them to a subordinate authority within the framework of that policy'*. Thus after the legislative policy has been laid down by the legislature then an administrative of executive agency to whom the legislative power has been conferred under the statute shall *work out details within the framework of the legislative policy laid down in the plenary enactment.* The power to make delegated legislation requires that–

> [T]he delegate on whom such power is conferred has to act within the limitations of the authority conferred by the Act. It is equally well settled

44. As quoted from *Lockes Appeal* 72 Pa. 491; *Field v. Clark* 143 U.S. 649 in Hamdard Dawakhana Para 28.
45. AIR 1954 SC 465.

that, Rules made on matters permitted by the Act in order to supplement the Act and not to supplant the Act, cannot be held to be in violation of the Act. A delegate cannot override the Act either by exceeding the authority or by making provisions inconsistent with the Act.[46]

Sometime the power to fill up the details is also described as 'skeleton legislation'. The term skeleton legislation is generally used to 'denote the broad outlines of a particular scheme found in an Act of which details are to be filled in later by administrative orders of experts'.[47] In these legislations the legislature lays down the broad policy outlines and leaving the responsibility of filling out the body of the legislation with *flesh and blood* to other authorities.

4.8.2 Power of Inclusion and Exclusion

The legislature often confers power on the executive to bring individuals, institutions, bodies, services or commodities within the fold of a legislation or remove it. The Act may contain some of the subjects in a schedule annexed to it, but to bring in flexibility and ensure suitability of the legislation for all contingencies in the future the legislation delegates power to the executive authorities to include or exclude items from the schedule. Such delegated powers are described as power of inclusion and power of exclusion respectively.

> The aim of all legislatures is to project their minds as far as possible into the future, and to provide in terms as general as possible for all contingencies likely to arise in the application of the law. But it is not possible to provide specifically for all cases and, therefore, legislation from the very earliest times, and particularly in modern times, has taken the form of conditional legislation, leaving it to some specified authority to determine the circumstances in which the law shall be applied, or to what its operation shall be extended, or the particular class of parsons or goods to which it shall be applied.[48]

In *Edward Mills Co. Ltd v. State of Ajmer*[49] the Supreme Court analyzed the scope of the power of inclusion in light of the Minimum Wages Act, 1948. The Preamble to the legislation described the objective of the statute as fixing the minimum rates of wages in certain employments. The Schedule attached to the Act specified certain employments in respect of which the minimum wages of the employees were fixed. Section 27 of the Act authorized

---

46. *JK Industries Ltd. v. Union of India* (2007) 13 SCC 673.
47. *Prag Ice & Oil Mills v. Union of India*, (1978) 3 SCC 459.
48. *Baxter v. Ah Way* (8 C.L.R. 626) quoted in *Edward Mills Co. Ltd v. State of Ajmer* AIR 1955 SC 25.
49. AIR 1955 SC 25.

the appropriate government to add to the Schedule any other employment in respect of which it is of the opinion that minimum rates of wages should be fixed under the Act, after giving three months' notice of its intention to do. The Chief Commissioner of Ajmer after complying with the procedures under the statute declared that the employment in textile industry as part of the Schedule of the Act. The Court while dealing with the power of the executive authority to add to the list of employment recognized it as a delegated power which was not unwarranted or unconstitutional in nature. It observed–

> The legislative policy is apparent on the face of the present enactment. What it aims at is the statutory fixation of minimum wages with a view to obviate the chance of exploitation of labour. The Legislature undoubtedly intended to apply this Act not to all industries but to those industries only where by reason of unorganized labour or want of proper arrangements for effective regulation of wages or for other causes the wages of labourers in a particular industry were very low. It is with an eye to these facts that the list of trades has been drawn up in the schedule attached to the Act but the list is not an exhaustive one and it is the policy of the Legislature not to lay down at once and for all time to which industries the Act should be applied. Conditions of labour vary under different circumstances and from State to State and the expediency of including a particular trade or industry within the schedule depends upon a variety of facts which are by no means uniform and which can best be ascertained by the person who is placed in charge of the administration of a particular State. It is to carry out effectively the purpose of this enactment that power has been given to the "appropriate Government" to decide, with reference to local conditions, whether it is desirable that minimum wages should be fixed in regard to a particular trade or industry which is not already included in the list. We do not think that in enacting section 27 the Legislature has in any way stripped itself of its essential powers or assigned to the administrative authority anything but an accessory or subordinate power which was deemed necessary to carry out the purpose and the policy of the Act.

In contradistinction in the case of *Jalan Trading Co. v. Mill Mazdoor Union*[50] the Supreme Court was required to analyze the power of the Central Government to exempt certain establishments from the purview of the Payment of Bonus Act 1965 under Section 36 of the Act. The law was enacted to provide for payment of bonus to all employees drawing a salary not exceeding Rs. 1600. Payment of bonus was deemed to be a right of the employees to share in the surplus profits and was made enforceable through the machinery of the Industrial Disputes Act. But an exception was made for industries suffering from financial losses and under Section 36 authorised

50. AIR 1967 SC 691.

the appropriate government, having regard to the financial position and other relevant circumstances of any establishment or class of establishments, to exempt for such period as may be specified therein such establishment or class of establishments from all or any of the provisions of the Act. The Court held that by Section 36 the appropriate government has been invested with the power to exempt an establishment from the operation of the Act, provided the Government is of the opinion that having regard to the financial position and other relevant circumstances of the establishment, it would not be in the public interest to apply all or any of the provisions of the Act. The condition for the exercise of such power was to keep in view the public interest and to frame an opinion based on consideration of the financial position and other relevant circumstances. Thus the Parliament had clearly laid down the principles and had provided adequate guidance to the appropriate government in exercising the powers under Section 36. The section did not confer any excessive authority and was merely a conditional legislation.

4.8.3 Power of Removal of Difficulty Clause (*Henry VIII clause*)

The *removal of difficulty clause* is popularly referred to as the Henry VIII clause in the English Administrative law. The nick name was used *in scornful commemoration of the absolutist ways in which that English King got the "difficulties" in enforcing his autocratic will removed through the instrumentality of a servile Parliament.*[51] In 1539 the British Parliament gave power to the Crown with the Statute of Proclamation and empowered King Henry VIII the power to *create, amend or repeal legislation without having to look to Parliament.* The statute was repealed after his death in 1547. The term Henry VIII clause popularly refers to "a provision in a Bill which enables primary legislation to be amended or repealed by subordinate legislation with or without further parliamentary scrutiny".[52]

The legislature delegates their law making powers to the executive for the purposes of obtaining flexibility, expediency and experimentation. In the course of delegation the legislature sometimes enables the executive to make minor alterations or modifications in the legislation in the course of implementation of the statute to avoid the dilatory process of amendment made through the legislative process by inserting the 'removal of difficulty clause' in the parent statute.

51. *Transcore v. Union of India* MANU/SC/5319/2006.

52. Review of the first year's work of the House of Lord Select Committee on the Scrutiny of Delegated Powers, para 16 (October 1994).

This kind of delegation first appeared in England in the Local Government Act 1888 which empowered the minister with power to amend so as to bring the Act "into full operation". Subsequently it had been used in several legislations in England like the National Insurance Act 1911. This form of excessive ministerial power was greatly criticized by Lord Hewart in his book *The New Despotism* which compelled the appointment of the Donoughmore Committee in 1929 to examine and report on the whole issue of Ministerial powers. The Committee on Ministers' Powers in its report submitted in 1932 stated that the term was nicknamed with reference to the autocratic exercise of power by Henry VIII through the institutions of Parliament and is used to express *executive autocracy.* The Committee's Report criticized the *removal of difficulty clause* as *"as a temptation to slipshod work in the preparation of bills and recommended that such provisions should be used only where they were justified before Parliament on compelling grounds".*[53] The Committee recommended that all the delegated legislations should have clearly defined limits in the bill and the *Henry VIII clauses should be abandoned in all but the most exceptional cases* and should be valid for a maximum period of one year. The Committee reported–

> It cannot but be regarded as inconsistent with the principles of parliamentary government that the subordinate law-making authority should be given by the superior law-making authority power to amend a Statute which has been passed by the superior authority.... Even with safeguards,... it is clearly a power which in theory at any rate may be unscrupulously used.... If it does prove necessary in the public interest to amend an Act of Parliament,... and the matter is of sufficient political urgency, parliamentary time can be found possible to bring certain important and complicated legislative schemes into operation without such a power, relying upon the ordinary method of an amending Bill in Parliament to meet unexpected emergencies.... It is a standing temptation to Ministers and their subordinates either to be slipshod in the preparatory work before the Bill is introduced in Parliament or to attempt to seize for their own Departments the authority which properly belongs to Parliament.... It can only be essential for the limited purpose of bringing an Act into operation and it should accordingly be in most precise language restricted to those purely machinery arrangements vitally requisite for that purpose; and the clause should always contain a maximum limit of one year after which the powers would lapse... The use of the so-called "Henry VIII Clause".... should not be permitted by Parliament except upon special grounds stated in the Ministerial Memorandum attached to the Bill.[54]

Post 1932 based on the recommendations of the Committee the British Parliament has ceased to use the removal of difficulty clause in their

53. Cmd. 4060.
54. Cmd. 4060, p. 293-294.

legislations.[55] But in India this provision has been included in several legislations of post-independence era *as a practical necessity.*

The power of removal of difficulty clause has been generally used in statutes dealing with socio-economic welfare activities wherein the legislature is uncertain about the possible difficulties which are likely to crop up during the implementation of the laws, hence includes the removal clause to deal with minor difficulties arising during implementation of the law.

In the case of *Madave Upendra Sinai v. Union of India*[56] the Supreme Court while analyzing the power of the Central Government to remove difficulties under the Income Tax Act had highlighted the relevancy of such provisions in modern statutes and stated–

> To keep pace with the rapidly increasing responsibilities of a welfare democratic State, the Legislature has to turn out a plethora of hurried legislation, the volume of which is often matched with its complexity. Under conditions of extreme pressure, with heavy demands on the time of the Legislature and the endurance and skill of the draftsman, it is well-nigh impossible to foresee all the circumstances to deal with which a statute is enacted or to anticipate all the difficulties that might arise in its working due to peculiar local conditions or even a local law. This is particularly true when Parliament undertakes legislation which gives a new dimension to socio-economic activities of the State or extends the existing Indian laws to new territories or areas freshly merged in the Union of India. In order to obviate the necessity of approaching the Legislature for removal of every difficulty, howsoever trivial, encountered *in the enforcement* of a statute, by going through the time-consuming amendatory process, the legislature sometimes thinks it expedient to invest the Executive with a very limited power to make minor adaptations and peripheral adjustments in the statute, for making its implementation effective, without touching its substance.

The Supreme Court in the decision of *Jalan Trading Co. v. Mill Mazdoor Union*[57] negated the legality of Section 37(1) of the Payment of Bonus Act, 1965 which conferred power on the 'Central Government to make provision, not inconsistent with the *purpose of the Act,* for removal of difficulties or doubts in giving effect to the provisions of the Act'. Clause (2) further stated that the order of the Central Government issued under sub-section (1) is final. The Court struck down Section 37 on the ground that it authorized the Central Government to determine for itself what the purposes of the Act are and to make provisions for removal of doubts or difficulties as it was primarily a function to be performed by the legislature. It observed–

55. MANU/SC/0439/1986,Para 100.
56. MANU/SC/0436/1974, para 39.
57. AIR 1967 SC 691.

> If in giving effect to the provisions of the Act any doubt or difficulty arises, normally it is for the Legislature to remove that doubt or difficulty. Power to remove the doubt or difficulty by altering the provisions of the Act would in substance amount to exercise of legislative authority and that cannot be delegated to an executive authority. Sub-section (2) of Section 37 purports to make the order of the Central Government in such cases final accentuates the vice in sub-section (1), since by enacting that provision the Government is made the sole judge whether difficulty or doubt had arisen in giving effect to the provisions of the Act, whether it is necessary or expedient to remove the doubt or difficulty, and whether the provision enacted is not inconsistent with the provisions of the Act.

Thus Section 37 was invalidated on the ground that the Central Government was made the *sole judge* about whether any difficulty or doubt had arisen in giving effect to the Act, whether it was necessary or expedient to remove the doubt or difficulty, and whether the order made was inconsistent or not with the purposes of the Act.

In the subsequent case of *Gammon India Ltd. v. Union of India*[58] while dealing with the validity of the Contract Labour (Regulation and Abolition) Act, 1970 revisited the debate relating to the scope of removal of difficulty clause. Section 34 of the Act provided that 'if any difficulty arises in giving effect to the provisions of the Act, the Central Government may, by order, published in the Official Gazette, make such provisions not inconsistent with the provisions of the Act as appears to it to be necessary or expedient for removing the difficulty'. While analyzing the scope of Section 34 the Court distinguished the provision from Section 37 of the Payment of Bonus Act as which was held to be excessive delegation in the *Jalan Trading case* because the government was authorized to determine for itself what the purposes of the Act were and to make provisions for the removal of doubts and difficulties. On the contrary Section34 of the Contract Labour Act was only limited to giving effect to the provisions of the Act in case any difficulty arises in the implementation of the rules. The provision is integral for the *application of the internal functioning of the administration machinery.* In addition, Section 34 did not confer any finality to the act of the executive and was subjected to judicial review in case of any inconsistencies with the Act.

Professor S.P. Sathe commenting on the distinction drawn in the *Gammon India case* observed–

> These distinguishing features are hardly satisfying but the basic essence of this judgment is that it has over-ruled the majority decision in *Jalan*

58. AIR 1974 SC 960.

Trading case. Such decision is deemed correct because through the 'removal of difficulty' clause minor changes, which do not alter the policy should be allowed to be made.[59]

In *Madave Upendra Sinai v. Union of India*[60] the Court laid down the limits of 'difficulty' and the scope of power of the Central Government to supply a deficiency or *casus omissus* to remove such difficulties. It observed that the power of removal cannot be uncontrolled or unfettered and stated–

> It is strictly circumscribed, and its use is conditioned and restricted. The existence or arising of a "difficulty" is the sine qua non for the exercise of the power. If this condition precedent is not satisfied as an objective fact, the power under this Clause cannot be invoked at all. Again, the "difficulty" contemplated by the clause must be a difficulty arising *in giving effect to* the provisions of the Act and not a difficulty arising *aliunde*, or an extraneous difficulty. Further, the Central Government can exercise the power under the clause only to the extent it is necessary for applying or giving effect to the Act, etc., and no further. It may slightly tinker with the Act to round off angularities, and smoothen the joints or remove minor obscurities to make it workable, but it cannot change, disfigure or do violence to the basic structure and primary features of the Act. In no case, can it, under the guise of removing a difficulty, change the scheme and essential provisions of the Act.

By applying the above rationale the Supreme Court in the case of *Transcore v. Union of India*[61] upheld the legality of the Securitisation and Reconstruction of Financial Assets and Enforcement of Security Interest (Removal of Difficulties) Order, 2004 issued by the Central Government under Section 40(1) of the Securitisation and Reconstruction of Financial Assets and Enforcement of Security Interest Act, 2002 (NPA Act) and stated that the order was issued merely to *supply a deficiency, namely, levy of fees*. It was clarified that the 2004 Order did not alter the nature and scope of the NPA Act but merely filled in the deficiency.

Presently the power of removal of difficulty clause is being used in a limited capacity. The recently enacted The National Judicial Appointments Commission Act, 2014 has categorically stated that no order shall be issued under the power of removal of difficulty clause under S.14 of the Act after an expiry of five years from the date of commencement of the Act.

---

59. 7th Ed. 2010.

60. MANU/SC/0436/1974, para 40.

61. AIR 2007 SC 712, MANU/SC/5319/2006.

4.8.4 Power of By-passing

In *Harishankar Bagla v. State of Madhya Pradesh*[62] the constitutionality of Section 6 was challenged on the ground of excessive delegation. It was argued that Section 6 empowered the Central Government with the power of repeal. Section 6 of the Essential Supplies Act 1946 provided that 'any order made under Section 3 shall have effect notwithstanding anything inconsistent therewith contained in any enactment other than this Act or any instrument having effect by virtue of any enactment other than this Act'. The Supreme Court interpreted the provision as empowering the executive to bypass any other laws which might be inconsistent with the rules of the Essential Supplies Act without causing any repeal or amendment of those laws. It observed–

> Section 6 does not either expressly or by implication repeal any of the provisions of pre-existing laws; neither does it abrogate them. Those laws remain untouched and unaffected so far as the statute book is concerned. The repeal of a statute means as if the repealed statute was never on the statute book. It is wiped out from the statute book. The effect of Section 6 certainly is not to repeal any one of those laws or abrogate them. Its object is simply to by-pass them where they are inconsistent with the provisions of the Essential Supplies (Temporary Powers) Act, 1946 or the orders made thereunder. In other words, the orders made under Section 3 would be operative in regard to the essential commodity covered by the Textile Control Order wherever there is repugnancy in this Order with the existing laws and to that extent, the existing laws with regard to those commodities will not operate. By-passing a certain law does not necessarily amount to repeal or abrogation of that law. That law remains unrepealed but during the continuance of the order made under Section 3 it does not operate in that field for the time being. The ambit of its operation is thus limited without there being any repeal of any one of its provisions. Conceding, however, for the sake of argument that to the extent of a repugnancy between an order made under Section 3 and the provisions of an existing law, to the extent of the repugnancy, the existing law stands repealed by implication, it seems to us that the repeal is not by any Act of the delegate, but the repeal is by the legislative Act of Parliament itself. By enacting Section 6 Parliament itself has declared that an order made under Section 3 shall have effect notwithstanding any inconsistency in this order with any enactment other than this Act. This is not a declaration made by the delegate but the legislature itself has declared its will that way in Section 6. The abrogation or the implied repeal is by force of the legislative declaration contained in Section 6 and is not by force of the order made by the delegate under Section 3. The power of the delegate is only to make an order under Section 3. Once the delegate has made that order its power is exhausted. Section 6 then steps in wherein Parliament has declared that as

62. AIR 1954 SC 465.

> soon as such an order comes into being that will have effect notwithstanding any inconsistency therewith contained in any enactment other than this Act. Parliament being supreme, it certainly could make a law abrogating or repealing by implication provisions of any pre-existing law and no exception could be taken on the ground of excessive delegation to the Act of Parliament itself. There is no delegation involved in the provisions of Section 6 at all and that section could not be held to be unconstitutional on that ground.

Thus the power of delegation includes the power to by-pass other legislations. But Parliament, being the supreme law making agency, has the power to repeal or amend laws and make necessary provisions for the same within the provisions of the parent statute.

4.8.5 Power of Modification

A statute may confer power on the executive to modify the statute or any provisions contained in it. Conferring of such powers is deemed necessary to bring in flexibility and ensure proper application of the laws through necessary adjustments, but there is an equal need to ensure control over the exercise of such powers to prevent any abuse of such powers. In *In Re: Delhi Laws Act case*[63] the Supreme Court had upheld the delegation of the power of modification as a permissible form of delegated legislation. It held that an executive authority was authorized to modify either an existing or future laws but not any essential feature, including a change if policy. In the subsequent case of *Rajnarain Singh v. The Chairman, Patna Administration Committee.*[64] Supreme Court took the opportunity to further clarify the extent of power of modification. In this case while applying Section 104 of the Bihar and Orissa Municipality Act 1922 relating to imposition of taxes to the newly added territories of Patna village area the Court held that in applying the statute with necessary modification the executive authority could not change or modify the legislative policy behind the statute. Hence before imposition of tax the local authority was bound to comply with the rules relating to right of hearing and consultation as laid in the parent statute. Applying the legal principle laid in *In Re: Delhi Laws Act case* in the context of the present case, the court observed–

> Now the only difference between that case and this is that whereas in the former case the whole of an enactment, or a part of it could be extended, here, any section can be picked out. But to pick out a section is to apply a part of an Act, and to pick out a part is to effect a modification, and as the previous decision holds that a part of an Act can be extended, it follows

63. (1951) 2 SCR 747.
64. AIR 1954 SC 569 : (1955) 1 SCR 290.

that a section or sections can be picked out and applied, as in Burah's case (5 I.A. 178) where just that was done; also, for the same reason that the whole or a part of an Act can be modified; it follows that a section can also be modified. But even as the modification of the whole cannot be permitted to effect any essential change in the Act or an alteration in its policy, so also a modification of a part cannot be permitted to do that either. If that were not so, the law, as laid down in the previous decision, could be evaded by picking out parts on an Act only, with or without modification, in such a way as to effect an essential change in the Act as a whole. It follows that when a section of an Act is selected for application, whether it is modified or not, it must be done so as not to effect any change of policy, or any essential change in the Act regarded as a whole. Subject to that limitation we hold that section 3(1)(f) is intra vires, that is to say, we hold that any section or sections of the Bihar and Orissa Municipal Act of 1922 can be picked out and applied to "Patna" provided that does not effect any essential change in the Act or alter its policy.

4.9 DIFFERENTIATING BETWEEN RULES, REGULATIONS, BYE-LAWS AND ORDERS

The difference between the various nomenclatures used for identifying the different forms of delegated legislations is quite difficult.

The term statutory rules has been used to describe a subordinate legislation wherein the enabling statute has laid down the general policy of the legislature and has delegated to another authority the function of filing in the details of that policy. The regulation framed by such authority is described as statutory rules. The legislature generally grants such power to the executive.

When the legislature enables the creation of a local authority or a statutory Corporation and lays down its objective and purpose, and empowers such authority to make provisions for carrying into effect the various purposes for which the body was constituted, such regulations made by the local authority or the statutory corporation are referred to as bye-laws.[65] It generally refers to any order, rule or regulation made by any local authority or statutory corporation subordinate to the Parliament.[66]

Distinguishing between a statutory rule and bye-law it was observed in *Mulchand Gulabchand v. Mukund Shivram Bhide*–[67]

65. AIR 1968 Bom 156.
66. Odgers, Common Law (1927).
67. AIR 1952 Bom 296.

> Now, there is a clear distinction between statutory rules and bye-laws. Bye-laws are usually framed by corporations under their inherent powers in order to carry out the purposes of the corporation or they are framed by public authorities set up by Parliament and as it is left to the corporations or the public authorities to frame there bye-laws and carry out their purposes, the Courts have retained certain amount of control over the bye-laws considering their reasonableness. But statutory rules stand on entirely different footing, Parliament or Legislature, instead of incorporating the rules into the statute itself, ordinarily authorises Government to carry out the details of the policy laid down by the Legislature by framing the rules under the statute, and once the rules are framed, they are incorporated in the statute itself and become part of the statute, and the rules must be governed by the same principles as the statute itself.

The Committee on Ministers Power had differentiated between rules, regulations and orders.[68] Accordingly the term 'rules' should be used predominantly with reference to provisions relating to procedures, whereas the term 'order' should be used to describe executive acts and legal decisions. But writing on the futility to define and differentiate between the various nomenclatures used to describe delegated legislation, Wade and Forsyth writes that *"But the nomenclature in practice honours these distinctions nearly as much in the breach as in the observance. Untidy though the language is, it makes no legal difference".*[69]

4.10 CONTROL OF DELEGATED LEGISLATION

There are three principle mechanisms to control the administrative rule-making powers. They are a. Parliamentary control, b. Procedural control and c. Judicial control.

4.11 PARLIAMENTARY FROM OF CONTROL

Parliament is the primary controlling authority of the delegated legislation. Under the scheme of distribution of function the Parliament is the principal law making agency and have been entrusted with the task of policy formulation and laying the rules of conduct. The conditional or subordinate law making power which is entrusted to the administrative authorities have to be exercised in compliance with the policy objective and the norms laid down by the Parliament. The executive authorities act as the *agent* of the legislature and the legislature consequently should exercise control of the delegated legislations. A brief description of the parliamentary form of control

68. Cmd. 4060 (1932), 64.
69. Wade & Forsyth, Administrative Law, Oxford University Press, 10th Ed. (2009).

in UK and US will help us to evaluate the working of the legislative control mechanism in India.

4.11.1 United Kingdom

Due to the concept of parliamentary sovereignty in England the control exercised by the Parliament over the administrative rule making is elaborate and effective. The recommendations of the Donoughmore Committee on delegated legislations were adopted in 1946 under the prime-ministership of Clement Attlee the enactment of Statutory Instruments Act 1946 was framed to deal with 'statutory powers to make orders, rules, regulations and other subordinate legislations' and the procedure for parliamentary scrutiny. Some of the important provisions under the statute are–

(i) Statutory instruments

Laws are traditionally passed through the Parliament in the form of bills. The bills pass through the different stages to become Acts of Parliament. These Acts often confer powers on Ministers to make more detailed orders, rules or regulations by means of Statutory Instruments. The term Statutory Instruments (SI) refer to 'a form of legislation which allow the provisions of an Act of Parliament to be subsequently brought into force or altered without Parliament having to pass a new Act'. They are also popularly referred to as secondary, delegated or subordinate legislation. The SI are used to provide all the necessary details essential for working of the legislation, that would be considered too complex and elaborate to be included in the body of an Act. They are also used to amend, update or enforce an existing primary legislation. The SI are part of the law of the land and are subject to judicial review. The judiciary can question the authority of a minister under a parent statute when issuing a SI.

(ii) Drafting

The SI are drafted by the legal office of the Government Department concerned after holding consultations with interested bodies and parties. They are made in the name of the person who is authorized by the parent statute eg. a Minister or a Secretary of State. After drafting each SI is given a number in the SI series which runs from number 1 each calendar year eg. SI 2014/123

(iii) Preamble

Each SI is required to contain a preamble stating the authority or the source legislation and the person to whom the power of subordinate law-making is confirmed.

(iv) *Explanatory notes*

Every SI must carry an explanatory note which will explain the scope and purpose of the delegated legislation. These notes do not have any legal force.

(v) *Explanatory memoranda*

All SI which are required to comply with the parliamentary procedures are required to be accompanied with an Explanatory Memorandum. The memorandum is a short document which explains in plain English the purpose and objective of the SI. It clarifies if the SI is linked with other SIs or fulfills the requirements of the parent statute. The memorandum also includes information regarding the cost consideration of the measure and the detailed outcome of the public consultation exercise. The details of the memorandum are also available to the public through the Regulatory Impact Assessment. The memorandum is freely available to the public through the Office of Public Sector Information (OPSI) website.

(vi) *Parliamentary procedure*

The nature of the parliamentary procedure which is required to be followed by a SI is prescribed by the parent statute. Some SI are not required to be laid before the Parliament and are also not subject to any parliamentary procedure.[70] These SI are simple non-contentious in nature, for example Commencement Orders, and they become laws automatically on the date stated on them. There are some other SI which require to be merely laid down before the parliament but does not require any further parliamentary procedures to be followed.

The SI which are subject to parliamentary control are required to follow the procedures laid in the SI Act. The SI is laid before the parliament either in draft form or after the instrument has been made. Ordinarily the SI cannot be amended or adapted by either House of Parliament. Each House is simply required to express their intention to annul or pass the law, as the case may be. There are two types of procedures which may be followed in the Parliament based on the application of the negative resolution procedure or the positive resolution procedure.

The negative resolution procedure is the more common parliamentary procedure adopted for enacting the SI. By virtue of such resolution the instruments will become law unless there is an objection from any of the House. In case the SI is laid in draft form, it cannot be made into law if

---

70. The term 'laid' refers to the procedure of laying of a SI on the table of the House i.e. placing a copy of the Instrument with the Votes and Proceedings desk in the Journal Office.

the draft is disapproved within a 40 days period.[71] In case the instrument is laid after making, it will be subject to annulment if a motion to annul is passed within 40 days. In case the SI become law on the date stated on them but will be annulled if either House passes a motion calling for their annulment within a specified time. The time period is usually 40 days including the day on which it was laid before the parliament.

The affirmative resolution procedure is less common parliamentary procedure and is applicable for less than 10 percent of the SI as the procedure demands more stringent parliamentary control because the SI will only come into force or continue to remain in force after receiving the parliamentary approval.[72] The instruments will not become law unless they are approved by both houses of parliament. If the SI is laid in draft form, then it cannot be made unless the draft is approved by both the Houses. In case the instrument is laid after making it will not come into force unless and until it is approved. If the SI comes into immediate effect then it will not continue to be in force unless approved within the specified statutory period of 28 days or 40 days.

An appendix to the *Votes and Proceedings* of the House records the day on which the SI is laid before the Parliament.

(vii) Joint committee on statutory instruments

To aid the parliamentary examination of SI a joint committee of both houses is appointed to deliberate and scrutinize the different SI. The committee has the service of Counsel to the Speaker and the Lord Chairman of the Committees available for the purpose of deliberation. The committee may take oral or written evidence from the Government Department responsible for the drafting of the instrument for any information relating to the SI they are considering. The committee does not consider the merits of any SI. They are responsible for ensuring that the Minister's power is being carried out in accordance with the provisions of the enabling Act. The committee is required to report to the Houses on issues relating to–

(a) Whether the authority of the Act has been exceeded,

(b) Whether there is any unusual or unexpected use of powers,

(c) Whether the SI has been drafted defectively, or

(d) Whether the SI might require further explanation.

71. The term 'made' refers to SI which are signed by a Minister or another authorized person; in other words the instrument is not in draft.

72. The term 'coming into force' implies when the provisions in the Statutory Instrument take effect.

The reports of the deliberation of the Committee are printed as House of Commons and House of Lords papers and their publication is noted in the *Weekly Information Bulletin.*

(viii) Lord committee on the merits of statutory instruments

The committee was first appointed in 2003 and consists of 11 members. The committee works in complement with that of the Joint Committee on Statutory Instruments. It deals with issues relating to the policy implications of the SI. The terms of reference of the Merits Committee are wide ranging. Its primary task is to consider whether the special attention of the House should be drawn to a SI on any of the following grounds–

(a) That it is politically or legally important or gives rise to issues of public policy likely to be of interest to the House.

(b) That it is inappropriate in view of the changed circumstances since the passage of the parent Act;

(c) That it inappropriately implements EU legislations;

(d) That it imperfectly implements achieves its policy objectives.

The Committee meets on a weekly basis to ensure that the consideration of the negative instruments are undertaken within 40 days 'praying time' and to review the large number of pending of documents.

(ix) Debates on SI in the house of commons

In recent years there has been an increase of SI in the House of Commons thereby reducing the time available for the debate. Debates, normally on Motions to approve or annul instruments, may take place on the floor of the House usually late in the parliamentary day, or in the Delegated Legislation Committees. The duration of the debate in the House of Commons is for an hour and a half whereas in the House of Lords it is determined by the number of speakers.

(x) Delegated legislation committees

It was initially known as the Standing Committees on Statutory Instruments in 1973-74 to relieve the pressure of time. In 1995-96 it was renamed as Standing Committees on Delegated Legislation and in 2006-07 the name was changed to its present title of Delegated Legislation Committee. The Committee comprises of 17 members, but other Members may attend and speak during the meetings, however the right to vote is restricted to the original members of the Committee. The SI requiring affirmative resolution is automatically referred to the Committee. The SI requiring negative resolution is only referred to the DLC if a Minister puts a motion to the House of Commons, but if more than 20 members object to the Motion, then the SI cannot be placed before the Committee.

Reports of the Committee debate are published the next day by the Stationery Office. The SI which are subject to parliamentary approval appear in an Appendix to the daily *Votes and Proceedings* and a list of them, compiled by the Journal Office, with number of 'praying days' remaining, is issued each week. The information is also available on the Parliament Internet site or the House of Commons Information Office. Debates on the SI to be held in the following week are noted with other business in the appropriate sections of the *Weekly Information Bulletin*, depending on whether the debate is to be taken on the floor of the House or in the Standby Committee.

(xi) Publication and bibliography

All SI are required to be printed and put on sale by the Stationery Office. The Statutory Publications Office produces a numerical Table to statutory instruments together with an Index every two years and the general SI for each year are issued in a number of volumes for permanent record purposes. The Table indicates whether an Order is still in force and how it was amended or revoked. The Stationary Office issues monthly and annual Lists of SI, available on subscription. These include publishing details, the effect of each instrument on other legislation, details on its commencement and comprehensive subject indexing. In addition, all the materials are available on official website.

4.11.2 India

Under the Constitution of India it is the function of the legislature to legislate but if the power has been conferred to the executive authority to make delegated legislations, then it is not only the right of the legislature but also their duty as principal law making body to oversee the functions of their agents i.e. the executive and ensure that they act in accordance with the will of the Parliament. It is the responsibility of the legislature as the delegating authority to supervise and control the actual exercise of power by the executive authority and to prevent any objectionable, abusive and unwarranted exercise of such powers. Based on this theory, a system of legislative control and supervision has been formulated in India.

The legislative control over the delegated legislation is exercised at two stages. The first stage of control happens at the time of delegation of law making powers to the administrative agencies through the enabling Act. This stage is known as pre-enactment control. The second stage of control takes place after the delegated legislations have been framed under the provisions of the parent statute and are placed before the parliament under the laying down rules for parliamentary scrutiny. This stage is referred to as post-enactment control.

4.11.2.1 Pre-enactment control

The pre-enactment control is initiated at the time of drafting of the Bill of the parent statute. If the bill contains provisions relating to delegation of legislative powers then under the provisions of the Parliamentary Rules of Procedure and Conduct of Business then it is a prerequisite that such a Bill before the Parliament should be accompanied with the Statement of Objects and Reasons, the memorandum regarding delegation of legislative powers and the financial memorandum.[73] The Memorandum on Delegated Legislation is required to explain the purpose of such delegation of legislative powers and draw attention to their scope and specify whether the delegation is of a normal or exceptional character.[74] The rule is deemed to be fundamental in the context of parliamentary form of control because it is the first stage of control process. It enables the Parliament to have a direct control over the nature and scope of delegation. It provides the members of the parliament with the opportunity to discuss about the power of delegation in the House while debating over the Bill. Other opportunities include raising of specific questions at the time of Question Hour sessions, by moving a specific resolution in case the matter delegation of power is urgent and important and through vote on grant.

The pre-enactment control process of delegated legislation is often deemed ineffective because of inadequate time and lack of involvement. The political issues often take the time away from law making activities, depriving the nation from serious legislative debate. It has been observed by the Committee on Subordinate Legislation that inspite of the importance of this salutary rule, in reality it is a weak form of control process because the memorandum is often scrappily written and are not adequately informative. It has been suggested by the Committee that since this parliamentary rule is mandatory in nature it should be drafted in a proper manner which shall include the purpose and effect of delegation of legislative power to the executive authorities, the issues to be covered in the rule making power, the details of the subordinate agency to whom the law making power has to be granted and the manner of their exercises. At the time of drafting of the Bill, the concerned Ministry should draft the memorandum in a manner so as to draw the attention of the members of the parliament to clause on delegated legislation.

---

73. Rule 61 – Rules of Procedure and Conduct of Business in the Council of States (Rajya Sabha) 8th Ed. 2013.

74. Rule 65 – Rules of Procedure and Conduct of Business in the Council of States (Rajya Sabha) 8th Ed. 2013.

4.11.2.2 Post-enactment control

The second stage of control takes place through two processes – (i) Direct control through the laying down procedure and (ii) Indirect control by scrutiny of parliamentary committees.

4.11.2.2.1 Laying down procedure

After the subordinate legislation has been framed it is important that Parliament should have the opportunity to scrutinize the rules framed. The requirement to place the subordinate legislations before the Parliament is referred to as the 'laying down' procedure. Principally there are three different forms of laying down procedure involving three different legal consequences.

(i) Simple laying down – Under this procedure the rules and regulations immediately comes into force after their enactment and they are merely required to be placed before the Parliament for their information. There is no requirement for any further action to be taken by the Parliament. Ordinarily this form of laying down procedure is used in case of simple legislations like commencement orders.

(ii) Laying down subject to negative resolution – Under this form of laying down the rules come into effect immediately after they are framed, but they cease to continue or get annulled if within the specified period the Parliament passes a motion of annulment. This form of laying down is the most common of legislative practice.

(iii) Laying down subject to affirmative resolution – Under this form of laying down procedure the rules shall come into effect only after the Parliament passes a resolution of approval. In case of urgency the rules may immediately come into effect but unless approved by Parliament through the passing of affirmative resolution within a specified time, the rules shall cease to continue.

Speaking on the objective and purpose of laying down procedure the Supreme Court in *Atlas Cycle Industries Ltd. v. State of Haryana*[75] observed–

> Now, the policy and object underlying the provisions relating to laying the delegated legislation made by the subordinate law making authorities or orders passed by subordinate executive instrumentalities before both Houses of Parliament being to keep supervision and control over the aforesaid authorities and instrumentalities, the "laying clauses" assume different forms depending on the degree of control which the Legislature may like to exercise. As evident from the observations made at pp. 305 to 307 of the 7th Edn. of *Craies on*

75. AIR 1979 SC 1149.

Statute Law and noticed with approval in *Hukam Chand v. Union of India*[76] there are three kinds of laying which are generally used by the Legislature. These three kinds of laying are described and dealt with in Craies on Statute Law as under:

"(*i*) Laying without further procedure,

(*ii*) Laying subject to negative resolution,

(*iii*) Laying subject to affirmative resolution.

(*i*) *Simple laying.*—The most obvious example is in Section 10(2) of the 1946 Act. In earlier days, before the idea of laying in draft had been introduced, there was a provision for laying rules etc. for a period during which time they were not in operation and could be thrown out without ever having come into operation (compare Merchant Shipping Act, 1894, Section 417; Inebriates Act, 1898, Section 21) but this is not used now.

(*ii*) *Negative resolution.*—Instruments so laid have immediate operative effect but are subject to annulment within forty days without prejudice to a new instrument being made. The phraseology generally used is "subject to annulment in pursuance of a resolution of either House of Parliament". This is by far the commonest form of laying. It acts mostly as a deterrent and sometimes forces a Minister (in Sir Cecil Carr's phrase) to "buy off opposition" by promising some modification.

(*iii*) *Affirmative resolution.*—The phraseology here is normally no order shall be made unless a draft has been laid before Parliament and has been approved by a resolution of each House of Parliament. Normally, no time limit is fixed for obtaining approval — none is necessary because the Government will naturally take the earliest opportunity of bringing it up for approval — but Section 16(3) of the Housing (Financial and Miscellaneous Provisions) Act, 1946 did impose a limit of forty days. An old form (not much used nowadays) provided for an order to be made but not to become operative until a resolution of both Houses of Parliament had been obtained. This form was used in Section 10(4) of the Road Traffic Act, 1930 [cf. Road Traffic Act, 1960, Section 19(3)] .... The affirmative resolution procedure necessitates a debate in every case. This means that one object of delegation of legislation (viz. saving the time of Parliament) is to some extent defeated. The procedure therefore is sparingly used and is more or less reserved to cases where the order almost amounts to an Act, by effecting changes which approximate to true legislation (e.g. where the order is the meat of the matter, the enabling Act merely outlining the

76. (1972) 2 SCC 601.

general purpose) or where the order replaces local Acts or provisional orders and, most important of all, where the spending, etc. of public money is affected.

Sometimes where speedy or secret action is required (e.g. the imposition of import duties), the order is laid with immediate operation but has to be confirmed within a certain period [cf. Import Duties Act, 1958, Section 13(4)]. This process of acting first and getting approval after has also been adopted in the Emergency Powers Act, 1920 under which a state of emergency can be proclaimed and regulations made. The proclamation must be immediately communicated to Parliament and does not have effect for longer than a month; but it can be replaced by another proclamation. Any regulations made under the proclamation are to be laid before Parliament immediately and do not continue in force after the expiration of seven days from the time when they are so laid unless a resolution is passed by both Houses providing for their continuance".

In India there is no standard law relating to the laying down procedure and the administrative authorities are under legal obligation to place the subordinate legislations before the Parliament unless specifically provided in the enabling statute. In the absence of such clauses in the Parent statute the delegated legislations were not required to be placed before the Parliament.

The Committee on Subordinate Legislation has made a long standing demand for inclusion of a standard laying down clause in all statutes. It has largely recommended that every Act of Parliament should include the provision that delegated legislations should be placed before the Houses 'as soon as possible' for a uniform perform period of 30 days so that the parliamentarians may modify or amend them as necessary. Most Indian statutes in the early years of independence did not contain any provision relating to the laying down procedure. On the repeated recommendations of the Committee on Subordinate Legislation the Delegated Legislation Provisions (Amendment) Act 1983 was enacted to bring amendment to almost 50 Indian statutes by inserting the provision relating to laying before the Parliament or the State Legislation and providing for annulment or modification of the rules within a specified time period.

On the recommendation of the Committee at present a standard clause for laying down is included in most statutes. The standard clause states–

> Every rule made under this Act shall be laid, as soon as may be, after it is made before each House of Parliament, while it is in session, for a total period of 30 days which may be comprised in one session or in two or more successive sessions, and if, before the expiry of the session immediately

> following the session or the successive aforesaid, both Houses agree in making any modification in the rule should not be made, the rule shall thereafter have effect only in such modified form or be of no effect, as the case may be; so however, that any such modification or annulment shall be without prejudice to the validity of anything previously done under that rule.

4.11.2.2.2 Non-Compliance with Laying Down Procedure

Narendra Kumar v. Union of India[77] is the first case dealing with the issue of non-compliance with laying down procedure. The Non-ferrous Metal Control Order, 1958 framed under the Essential Commodities Act 1955 was challenged on the ground that the policy for grant of licenses under the Control Order were not officially published nor was it placed before the Parliament as required under Sections 3(5) and (6) respectively of the enabling statute. The Court held that the failure to publish the principles specified in the letter dated 18th April in the Official Gazette as well as lay them before the Parliament invalidates the principles as void. This view of the Court holding the laying down procedure as mandatory was subsequently challenged in several cases.

In *Jan Mohd. Noor Mohd. Bagban v. State of Gujarat* [78] the Court dealt with the issue of whether the rules framed by the Provincial Government in 1941 in exercise of the powers laid down under Section 26(1) of the Bombay Agricultural Produce Markets Act 1939 had any legal validity as they had not been laid before each House of the Provincial Legislature. Holding the laying down procedure as directory, the Supreme Court made the following observation–

> Finally, the validity of the rules framed under Bombay Act 22 of 1939 was canvassed. By Section 26(1) of the Bombay Act the State Government was authorised to make rules for the purpose of carrying out the provisions of the Act. It was provided by sub-section (5) that the rules made under Section 26 shall be laid before each of the Houses of the Provincial Legislature at the session thereof next following and shall be liable to be modified or rescinded by a resolution in which both Houses concur and such rules shall, after notification in the Official Gazette, be deemed to have been modified or rescinded accordingly. It was urged by the petitioner that the rules framed under Bombay Act 22 of 1939 were not placed before the Legislative Assembly or the Legislative Council at the first session and therefore they had no legal validity. The rules under Act 22 of 1939 were framed by the Provincial Government of Bombay in 1941. At that time there was no Legislature in session, the Legislature having been suspended during the emergency arising out of World War II. The session of the Bombay Legislative Assembly

77. AIR 1960 SC 430.
78. AIR 1966 SC 385 : (1966) 1 SCR 505.

was convened for the first time after 1941 on 20-5-1946 and that session was prorogued on 24-5-1946. The second session of the Bombay Legislative Assembly was convened on 15-7-1946 and that of the Bombay Legislative Council on 3-9-1946 and the rules were placed on the Assembly Table in the second session before the Legislative Assembly on 2-9-1946 and before the Legislative Council on 13-9-1946. Section 26(5) of Bombay Act 22 of 1939 does not prescribe that the rules acquired validity only from the date on which they were placed before the Houses of Legislature. The rules are valid from the date on which they are made under Section 26(1). It is true that the Legislature has prescribed that the rules shall be placed before the Houses of Legislature, but failure to place the rules before the Houses of Legislature does not affect the validity of the rules, merely because they have not been placed before the Houses of the Legislature. Granting that the provisions of sub-section (5) of Section 26 by reason of the failure to place the rules before the Houses of Legislature were violated, we are of the view that sub-section (5) of Section 26 having regard to the purposes for which it is made, and in the context in which it occurs, cannot be regarded as mandatory. The rules have been in operation since the year 1941 and by virtue of Section 64 of Gujarat Act 20 of 1964 they continue to remain in operation".

In *Atlas Cycle Industries Ltd. v. State of Haryana*[79] the Supreme Court revisited the issue of whether non-compliance of the laying down procedure under Sec. 3(6) of the Essential Commodities will invalidate a statutory regulation issued under the statute. It categorically observed–

Though sub-section (6) of Section 3 of the Act provides that every order made by the Central Government or by any officer or authority of the Central Government shall be laid before both Houses of Parliament as soon as may be after it is made, the important point to be considered in the absence of analogous statutes like the Statutory Instruments Act, 1946 and the Laying of Documents Before Parliament (Interpretation) Act, 1948 prescribing the conditions, the period and the legal effect of the laying of order before the Parliament is whether the provision is directory or mandatory.

.....

Now at p. 317 of the aforesaid Edition of *Craies on Statute Law*, the questions whether the direction to lay the rules before Parliament is mandatory or merely directory and whether laying is a condition precedent to their operation or may be neglected without prejudice to the effect of the rules are answered by saying that "each case must depend on its own circumstances or the wording of the statute under which the rules are made". In the instant case, it would be noticed that sub- section (6) of Section 3 of the Act merely provides that every order made under Section 3 by the Central Government or by any officer or authority of the Central Government shall be laid before

79. AIR 1979 SC 1149.

both Houses of Parliament, as soon as may be, after it is made. It does not provide that it shall be subject to the negative or the affirmative resolution by either House of Parliament. It also does not provide that it shall be open to the Parliament to approve or disapprove the order made under Section 3 of the Act. It does not even say that it shall be subject to any modification which either House of Parliament may in its wisdom think it necessary to provide. It does not even specify the period for which the order is to be laid before both Houses of Parliament nor does it provide any penalty for non-observance of or non-compliance with the direction as to the laying of the order before both Houses of Parliament. It would also be noticed that the requirement as to the laying of the order before both Houses of Parliament is not a condition precedent but subsequent to the making of the order. In other words, there is no prohibition to the making of the orders without the approval of both Houses of Parliament. In these circumstances, we are clearly of the view that the requirement as to laying contained in sub-section (6) of Section 3 of the Act falls within the first category i.e. "simple laying" and is directory not mandatory. We are fortified in this view by a catena of decisions, both English and Indian. In *Bailey v. Williamson*[80] where by Section 9 of the Parks Regulations Act, 1872 passed on June 27, 1872 "to protect the royal parks from injury, and to protect the public in the enjoyment of those royal parks and other royal possessions for the purpose of innocent recreation and exercise" it was provided that any rules made in pursuance of the first schedule to the Act shall be forthwith laid before both Houses of Parliament, if Parliament be sitting, or if not, then within three weeks after the beginning of the then next ensuing session of Parliament; and if any such rules shall be disapproved by either House of Parliament within one month of the laying, such rules, or such parts thereof as shall be disapproved shall not be enforced and rules for Hyde Park were made and published on September 30, 1872 when Parliament was not sitting and in November 18, 1872, the appellant was convicted under Section 4 of the Act for that he did unlawfully act in contravention of Regulation 8 contained in the first Schedule annexed thereto by delivering a public address not in accordance with the rules of the said Park but contrary to the Statute, and it was inter alia contended on his behalf that in the absence of distinct words in the statute stating that the rules would be operative in the interval from the time they were made to the time when Parliament should meet next or if Parliament was sitting then during the month during which Parliament had an opportunity of expressing its opinion upon them, no rule made as supplementing the schedule could be operative so as to render a person liable to be convicted for infraction thereof unless the same had been laid before the Parliament, it was held overruling the contention that the rules became effective from the time they were made and it could not be the intention of the Legislature that the laying of the rules before Parliament should be made a condition precedent to their acquiring validity and that they should not take effect until they are laid before and approved by Parliament. If the Legislature had intended the same

80. 1873 LR VIII QB 118.

thing as in Section 4, that the rules should not take effect until they had the sanction of the Parliament, it would have expressly said so by employing negative language.

The Court re-visited the *Narendra Kumar judgment* and distinguished it on the ground that in that case the Non-ferrous Metal Control Order, 1958 was held to be invalid fundamentally on the ground of non-publication in the Government Gazette, *it was only incidentally that a mention was made by the Court to the effect that the principles had not been laid before both Houses of Parliament.*

In *Bank of India v. O.P. Swarnakar*[81] the Supreme Court upheld the views expressed in *Atlas Cycle case* and held that the requirement of statutory rules to be placed before the legislature is merely directory and non-compliance of the same will not vitiate the legality of the rules framed. It was further clarified that an administrative scheme such as the Voluntary Retirement Schemes are contractual in nature and do not fall within the scope of statutory regulation, hence they are not required to be placed before the Parliament by the Central Government.

4.11.2.2.3 Indirect Control – Committees on Subordinate Legislation

The legislative control through the process of *laying down* of the subordinate legislations have been found to be ineffective because of factors like inadequate time availability of the Parliamentarians, hence like the Joint Committee on Statutory Instruments or the Lords Committee, in India each House of the Parliament has constituted a Committee on Subordinate Legislation. The primary function of these committees are '*to scrutinize and ensure whether powers to make rules, regulations, bye-laws, schemes or other statutory instruments conferred by the Constitution or delegated by Parliament have been properly exercised within such conferment or delegation*'.[82]

(a) Rajya sabha committee on subordinate legislation

The Committee shall scrutinize and report to the Rajya Sabha whether the powers to make rules, regulations, bye-laws, schemes or other statutory instruments conferred by the Constitution or delegated by Parliament have been properly within such conferment or delegation, as the case may be.[83] It was first constituted in 1964. The Committee consists of fifteen members who are nominated by the Chairman of the Rajya Sabha. A Chairman of the Committee is appointed by the Chairman from amongst the members of the

81. (2003) 2 SCC 721.
82. Rajya Sabha, Practice & Procedure Series – Committee on Subordinate Legislation.
83. Rule 204, Chapter XVII - Rules of Procedure and Conduct of Business in the Council of States (Rajya Sabha) 8th Ed. 2013.

Committee. The Committee shall have the power to require the attendance of persons or the production of papers or records for the discharge of its duties. Under Rule 209 after a rule, regulation, bye-law, scheme, order or other statutory instrument have been framed in pursuance of the Constitution or the legislative functions delegated by Parliament to a subordinate authority and which is required to be laid before Parliament, is so laid before the Council, the Committee shall, in particular consider–

(i) Whether the order is in accord with the provisions of the Constitution or the Act pursuant to which it is made;

(ii) Whether the order contains matter which is in the opinion of the Committee should more properly be dealt with in an Act of Parliament;

(iii) Whether the order contains imposition of taxation;

(iv) Whether the order directly or indirectly bars the jurisdiction of the court;

(v) Whether the order gives retrospective effect to any of the provisions in respect of which the Constitution or the Act does not expressly give any such power;

(vi) Whether the order involves expenditure from the Consolidated Fund of India or the public revenues;

(vii) Whether the order appears to make some unusual or unexpected use of the power conferred by the Constitution or the Act pursuant to which it is made;

(viii) Whether there appears to have been unjustifiable delay in its publication or laying the order before the Parliament; and

(ix) Whether for any reason the form or purport of the order calls for any elucidation.

The Committee is required to submit their report to the Council if it is of opinion that any statutory instruments or orders should be annulled wholly or in part, or should be amended in any respect and the reasons thereof.[84] They may also refer any other important matter relating to the statutory instruments to the Council. The report of the Committee shall be presented by the Chairman to the Council or by any other member in his absence.[85]

84. Rule 210 – Rules of Procedure and Conduct of Business in the Council of States (Rajya Sabha) 8th Ed. 2013.

85. Rule 211 – Rules of Procedure and Conduct of Business in the Council of States (Rajya Sabha) 8th Ed. 2013.

(b) Lok sabha committee on subordinate legislation

The Lok Sabha Committee on Subordinate Legislation has the primary responsibility to scrutinize and report to the House whether the powers to make regulations, rules, sub-rules, bye-laws etc., conferred by the Constitution or delegated by Parliament are being properly exercised within such delegation.[86] The Committee consists of not more than fifteen members nominated by the Speaker. A Minister is not a member of the committee. The term of office of the members is one year. After an order or statutory instrument is laid before the House, the Committee shall analyze and examine the delegated legislations on terms of the same issues which the Rajya Sabha Committee on Subordinate Legislation deals with.[87] The Committee shall submit its report to the House on whether the subordinate legislations should be annulled wholly or in part, or be amended and the reasons for the same.[88] They may also express their opinion on any other related matters which should be brought to the notice of the House. The Speaker has been empowered to issue directions on any matter relating to the regulation of procedures of the subordinate legislations either in the Committee or in the House.[89]

4.11.2.2.4 Recommendations of the Committee on Subordinate Legislation

The Committee in its 21st Report on "Non-Implementation of Oft-Repeated Recommendations of Committee on Subordinate Legislation, Lok Sabha by Various Ministries"[90] made several recommendations for ensuring that the Ministries should perform their statutory obligations and avoid being *casual and lackadaisical.* Some of the suggestions are–

(i) Framing of Rules–

Rules should be framed under the Act as soon as possible after the commencement of the Act and in no case this period should exceed six months.

If no rules are framed within a reasonable period after the commencement of the Act and the Committee will take up the matter with the Ministry concerned and report to the House the cases where it is felt that undue delay has occurred in framing the rules.

---

86. Rule 317, Chapter XXVI – Rules of Procedure and Conduct of Business in the Lok Sabha 15th Ed. 2014.
87. Rule 320, Chapter XXVI – Rules of Procedure and Conduct of Business in the Lok Sabha 15th Ed. 2014.
88. Rule 321, Chapter XXVI – Rules of Procedure and Conduct of Business in the Lok Sabha 15th Ed. 2014.
89. Rule 322, Chapter XXVI – Rules of Procedure and Conduct of Business in the Lok Sabha, 15th Ed. 2014.
90. Lok Sabha Secretariat, December 2011.

In case, a Ministry / Department finds that for any unavoidable reasons it is not possible for them to adhere to the prescribed time-limit (of six months to frame the rules) in an exceptional case they should at the expiration of six months from the commencement of the relevant Act, explain the reasons to the Committee and seek a specific extension of time from them.[91]

(ii) Laying of Orders

All the Ministries should ensure that all 'Orders' required to be laid before the House are so laid within a period of 15 days after their publication in the Gazette if the House is in session, and if the House is not in session, the 'Orders' should be laid on the Table of the House as soon as possible (but within 15 days) after the commencement of the following session.

The Committee would like the Ministries concerned to furnish them with the reasons explaining the delay caused in laying each such 'Order' on the Table of the House.

Whenever 'Order' are laid on the Table after an inordinate delay, an explanatory note giving the reasons for such delay should be appended to the 'Orders' when so laid.[92]

(iii) Delay in publication of the Draft Rules in final form

In cases where no objection / suggestion on the draft rules were forthcoming the final rules should be published within a period of 3 months and in cases where a large number of objections / suggestions were received, the gap should not be more than 6 months.

These recommendations and guidelines should be observed by the Ministry scrupulously in all such cases with a view to minimize the gap between the publication of draft rules and their final notification.[93]

(iv) Printing of Rules

The Committee desire that the Extraordinary Gazette which is the time bound publication and is used to publish urgent material must be printed and made available on the appointed date.[94]

(v) Giving Retrospective Effect to Rules

Normally all rules should be published before the date of their enforcement or they should be enforced from the date of their publication.

91. 5th Report (2nd LS) Para 34.
92. 6th Report (3rd LS) Para 38.
93. 24th Report (7th LS) Para 68.
94. 24th Report (10th LS) Para 2.11.

The Ministries / Departments should take appropriate steps to ensure the publication of rules before they come into force.

However, if in any particular case the rules have to be given retrospective effect in view of any unavoidable circumstances, a clarification should be given either by way of an explanation in the rules or in the form of foot-note to the relevant rules to the effect that no one will be adversely affected as a result of retrospective effect being given to such rules.[95]

(vi) Making Rules after Previous Publication

When the Acts give a right to the public to send their comments on certain draft rules, it is only reasonable that sufficient time should be given to them to study the draft rules and send their comments before they are finalized.

A period of not less than 30 clear days, exclusive of the time taken in publishing the draft rules in the Gazette and the dispatching the Gazette copies to various parts of the country, should be given to the public to send their comments on such draft rules.[96]

4.12 PROCEDURAL FROM OF CONTROL

Parliamentary form of control of delegated legislation is generally accepted as not a very effective form of control mechanism because of various factors like paucity of time, lack of expertise etc. Hence a general demand has been made that a procedural control mechanism should be developed which would impose constant vigilance over the delegated legislations and ensure that effective participation of the people in the law-making process takes place. It is often considered that adherence with procedural norms will facilitate in making more democratic subordinate legislations which would be more easily acceptable to the people at large. This form of control mechanism has been largely applied in the United States.

4.12.1 United States

Due to the application of the separation of power doctrine the Parliamentary form of control and the process of *laying down* has no application in the US. The judiciary has been entrusted with the task of controlling the administrative action and the Congress does not have any direct supervisory power over the functioning of the administrative authorities. Instead the control by Congress over the administrative process tends to be indirect

95. 2nd Report (4th LS) Para 10.
96. 6th Report (1st LS) Para 31.

by laying down procedures which needs to be complied with during the performance of their functions.

The Congress had enacted the Administrative Procedure Act, 1946 for prescribing the minimum procedural standards which administrative agencies must conform with in the course of their functioning. The Act was enacted during the period after the Great Depression and the Second World War when the power of the federal government increased manifold. President Roosevelt and the Democratic Congress had enacted several statutes which created a number of new federal agencies.

The federal agencies have been described as *unique governmental bodies* exercising powers characteristic of all three branches of government – judicial, legislative and executive. It was realized that existence of such administrative bodies are likely to threaten the core principles of *separation of powers* doctrine under the US constitution. To provide constitutional safeguards, the Administrative Procedure Act creates a framework for regulating the agencies and their unique functional roles.

The basic purposes of the Act is to–

(a) Require agencies to keep the public informed of their organization, procedures and rules;

(b) Provide for public participation in the rule making process;

(c) Establish uniform standards for the conduct of formal rule-making and adjudication;

(d) Define the scope of judicial review.

Section 553 of the Act has laid down the manner of administrative rule making.

(i) A general notice of the proposed rule-making has to be published in the Federal Register, unless the persons subject thereto are named and either personally served or otherwise have actual notice thereof in accordance with law.

(ii) The notice shall include–

 (a) A statement of the time, place and nature of public rule-making proceedings

 (b) Reference to the legal authority under which the rule is proposed, and

 (c) The terms or substance of the proposed rule or a description of the subjects and issues involved.

Exceptions- This rule is not applicable–

(i) Interpretation of rules, general statements of policy or rules of agency organization, procedure etc.

(ii) When it is deemed that the notice and public procedure are impracticable, unnecessary or contrary to the public interest.

(iii) Once notice has been issued, the agency shall give interested persons an opportunity to participate in the rule-making through submission of written data, views or arguments with or without opportunity for oral presentation.

After consideration of the relevant matter presented, the agency shall incorporate in the rules adopted a concise general statement of their basis and purpose.

(iv) The required publication or service of a substantive rule shall be made not less than 30 days before its effective date.

(v) Each agency shall give an interested person the right to petition for the issuance, amendment, or repeal of a rule.

Thus in the absence of any legislative control – an elaborate procedure regarding consultations and conferences with persons whose interests are likely to be affected have been laid down.

Along with the process of consultation in the rule-making process, lot of importance is also given to the procedures of publication. The maxim *Ignorance of law is no excuse* for violation of rules and regulations as to statutes has been adhered to hence a machinery for publication of rules and regulations is deemed essential. The Federal Register Act 1935 lays down the procedure for publication of federal rules and regulations. It provides for the establishment of the Federal Register as the official publication in which all federal rules, regulations, orders and other documents of 'general applicability and legal effect must be published. The Registrar is published every day from Monday to Friday. When sufficient number of rules has appeared, they are to be bound and indexed. In addition there is the need to publish the Code of Federal Regulations which is to be revised annually. The Code is divided into fifty subject matter titles. By publishing a regulation, the agency gives constructive notice to all about the application and enforcement of the rules. On the other hand if the agency fails to publish in the official register then the regulation will be only binding upon persons with actual knowledge of the rules, it shall not have application against the world at large.

The various procedural safeguards under the statute attempts to promote openness, fairness, participatory democracy and informed rule-making. These procedures ensure that the federal agencies are accountable to the common people.

4.12.2 India

In India in the absence of statutory provisions the administrative authorities are not bound to comply with any procedural norms, including notice and prior consultation with the interested parties. If the statute lays down certain procedures for the purposes of making the subordinate legislations, only in such circumstances can the administrative authorities be held accountable for compliance of such norms. But for the purpose of invalidating a delegated legislation on the ground of non-adherence to procedural norms a judicial order is necessary.

4.12.3 Mandatory and Directory Procedures

In *Atlas Cycle Industries Ltd. v. State of Haryana*[97] the Supreme Court has laid down the test of mandatory and directory provisions for the purpose of determining whether the non-compliance of a procedure will invalidate the subordinate legislations. It stated–

> It is well to remember at the outset that the use of the word 'shall' is not conclusive and decisive of the matter and the Court has to ascertain the true intention of the Legislature, which is the determining factor, and that must be done by looking carefully to the whole scope, nature and design of the statute. Reference in this connection may be made to the decision of this Court in *State of U.P. v. Manbodhan Lal Srivastava.*[98] Reference in this behalf may also be made with advantage to another decision of this Court in *State of Uttar Pradesh v. Babu Ram Upadhya*[99] where Subba Rao, J. (as he then was) after quoting with approval the passage occurring at pages 516 in Crawford "On the Construction of Statutes" as well as the passage occurring at p. 242 in *Craies on Statute Law*, 5th Edn., observed as follows:
>
> "The relevant rules of interpretation may be briefly stated thus: When a statute uses the word "shall", prima facie, it is mandatory, but the Court may ascertain the real intention of the Legislature by carefully attending to the whole scope of the statute. For ascertaining the real intention of the Legislature, the Court may consider, inter alia, the nature and the design of the statute, and the consequences which would follow from construing it one way or the other, the impact of other provisions whereby the necessity of complying with the provisions in question is avoided, the circumstances namely, that the statute provides for a contingency of the non-compliance with the provisions, the fact that the non-compliance with the provisions is or is not visited by some penalty, the serious or trivial consequences that flow therefrom, and, above all, whether the object of the legislation will be defeated or furthered".
>
> Thus two considerations for regarding a provision as directory are: (*1*) absence of any provision for the contingency of a particular provision not being complied with or followed, and (*2*) serious general inconvenience and prejudice that would

97. AIR 1979 SC 1149.
98. AIR 1957 SC 912.
99. AIR 1961 SC 751.

result to the general public if the act of the Government or an instrumentality is declared invalid for non-compliance with the particular provision.

In *Raza Buland Sugar Co. Ltd v. Municipal Board, Rampur*[1] the Supreme Court laid down the doctrine of 'substantial compliance' theory. Under the U.P. Municipalities Act 1916 the procedure for imposition of tax required the proposal for tax imposition was required to be 'published in a local paper published in Hindi and where there is no such local paper, in such manner as the State Government may, by general or special order, direct. In this case the Municipal Board of Rampur had published the resolution to impose water tax in Hindi language in a local Urdu newspaper. The appellant, a public limited company, aggrieved with the imposition of water taxes challenged order imposed on the ground of non-compliance with the mandatory provisions of publication. The Court discussed the scope of mandatory and directory provisions and observed–

> The question whether a particular provision of a statute which on the face of it appears mandatory, inasmuch as it uses the word "shall"-as in the present case-is merely directory cannot be resolved by laying down any general rule and depends upon the facts of each case and for that purpose the object of the statute in making the provision is the determining factor. The purpose for which the provision has been made and its nature, the intention of the legislature in making the provision, the serious general inconvenience or injustice to persons resulting from whether the provision is read one way or the other, the relation of the particular provision to other provisions dealing with the same subject and other considerations which may arise on the facts of a particular case including the language of the provision, have all to be taken into account in arriving at the conclusion whether a particular provision is mandatory or directory.

While dealing with the scope of publication the Court analyzed that the object of publication is to invite objections from the inhabitants of the municipality who will be required to pay the taxes so as to democratize the process and to provide a reasonable opportunity of being heard. If the provisions relating to publication are held to be directory then the elaborate procedure relating to ante-natal publicity and consultation under the statute would be meaningless and nugatory. Thus the requirement of publication is mandatory under the statute but the manner of publication will be deemed to be directory in nature. *So long as publication is made in substantial compliance with the manner provided in section 94(3) that would serve the purpose of the mandatory part of the section which provides for publication.* In this case the publication was made in a local Urdu paper,

1. AIR 1965 SC 895.

but that resolution was published in Hindi. Thus Section 94(3) substantially requires that the publication should be made in Hindi in a local newspaper, which had been fulfilled in the present case.

4.12.4 Forms of Procedural Control

There are primarily four main techniques of procedural control which are deemed essential for the successful implementation of the control mechanism. These are – drafting, ante-natal publicity, consultation and post-natal publicity.

4.12.4.1 Drafting

Proper drafting of delegated legislation is considered important in most jurisdictions because in the absence of proper drafting there is likelihood that the rules will be ambiguous or vague in nature which will be give rise to litigation in future. It is generally accepted that the rules should be simple, clear and unambiguous in nature, hence in England it is required that the rules should be drafted by legal experts working in the different ministries whereas in Australia the rules are sent to the Attorney-General for his opinion prior to its final notification.

4.12.4.2 Ante-natal publicity

Ante-natal publicity or pre-enactment publicity is the other technique which is often adopted to ensure people's participation in the law making process. This process is considered to be of great importance in US because members of business or trade organizations often engage in discussions relating to the framing of rules and regulations so that the views of the industry are taken into consideration by the administrative agency Under this procedure the rules are required to be first published in a draft form so as to give an opportunity to the people likely to be affected by such laws to have their say in the rules to be made. In India there are no specific laws dealing with ante-natal publicity, as it is in the US, hence the need to adopt such measures have to specified in the parent Act for the purpose of implementation. However if the parent Act has made provisions for ante-natal publicity, then the procedure as laid down in Section 23 of the General Clauses Act 1897 has to be applied–

(i) The authority having power to make the rule or bye-laws shall, before making them, publish a draft of the proposed rules or bye-laws for the information of person likely to be affected thereby.

(ii) The publication shall be made in such manner as that authority deems to be sufficient, or, if the condition with respect to previous publication so requires, in such manner as prescribed.

(iii) There shall be published with the draft a notice specifying a date on after which the draft will be taken into consideration.

(iv) The authority having power to make the rules or bye-rules, and where the rules or bye-laws are to be made with the sanction, approval or concurrence of another authority, that authority also, shall consider any objection or suggestion which may be received by the authority having power to make the rules or bye-laws from any person with respect to the draft before the date so specified.

(v) The publication in the Official gazette of a rule or bye-law purporting to have been made in exercise of a power to make rules or bye-laws after previous publication shall be conclusive proof that the rule or bye-law has been duly made.

Some of the shortcomings of this provision are that no time period has been specified for publication of the draft rule. The period may vary from 3 days to 6 months depending upon the statute, hence the Committee on Subordinate legislation has suggested that a minimum period of 30 days should be made a standard procedure for filing of objections and suggestions and in case of an urgent matter a press statement should be made informing the people about the publication of draft rules so that the public may send in their comments expeditiously. Also the Committee recommended that there should not be considerable time gap between the publication of the draft rules and the publication of the final rules.

4.12.4.3 Consultation

Ante-natal publicity is generally associated with another important procedural norm involving consultation. Consultation enables discussion with the people and interests which are likely to be affected by the rule-making process. This process is popularly referred to as the democratization of rule making process because it forces the subordinate rule-making to come out of the closed bureaucratic offices and take into consideration the views of the affected people. Unlike laws made by the Parliament which are a reflection of the demands of the common people as the members of the parliament are elected by the common people, delegated legislations framed by the executive will generally be substracted off such representations, hence consultation is an attempt to bridge that gap. Consultation also facilitates in bringing more legitimacy to the rules in the eyes of the common people and makes them more easily accept those rules by appreciating the ground realities.Like other procedural requirements,it is the parent Act which has to mandate the holding of consultation as part of the rule-making process.

Consultations can be of various kinds.

(i) A legislation specifically identifies a body to hold consultation with prior to the making of any rules or schemes. For example under the Banking Regulation Act, 1949 the Central Government is required to consult with the Reserve Bank of India on banking related matters.

(ii) Legislationimposes the obligation to consult with a statutory board constituted under a statute on all matters related to a specific subject matter as provided under a statute. For example, the Tea Board constituted under the Tea Act, 1953 is required to perform multifarious functions such as - Rendering financial and technical assistance for cultivation, manufacture and marketing of tea; Export Promotion; Aiding Research and Development activities for augmentation of tea production and improvement of tea quality; Extend financial assistance in a limited way to the plantation workers and their wards through labour welfare schemes; To encourage and assist both financially and technically the unorganised small growers sector; Collection and maintenance of Statistical data and publication and such other activities as are assigned from time to time by the Central Government.

(iii) Consultation with Administrative Bodies – A statute may provide for creation of different administrative bodies or committees to make recommendations to the Government for the purpose of making rules and regulations. Under the Mines Act 1952 the Central Government is required to constitute 'committees' for consideration of proposals for the purpose of making rules and regulations under the Act.Section 59 of the Act categorically lays down that no regulation or rule shall be made unless the draft has been referred to the Committee for their consideration.

(iv) Drafting of rules by affected parties – Keepingin view the safety issue the Mines Act has also made provisions requiring the affected parties to draft rules necessary to prevent accidents and submit it to the committee for consideration. Under Section 60 of the Act the owner, agent or manager of a mine can frame and submit to the Chief Inspector or Inspector a draft of such bye-laws governing the use of any particular machinery or the adoption of a particular method of working the mine as may be deemed necessary to prevent accidents and also to provide for the safety, convenience and discipline of the persons employed in the mine.

(v) Consultation with interested members of the public – Some legislation impose the obligation on the administrative authorities to hold consultations with the general public by publishing draft rules and inviting suggestions and comments from the interested public.

4.12.4.3.1 Non-compliance with Consultation and Legal Consequences

In *Rajnarain Singh v. The Chairman, Patna Administration Committee, Patna* the procedural requirement of consultation was considered to be an integral part of the enabling Act and the compliance of it was deemed mandatory. The imposition of tax without prior consultation with the affected people was held to be ultra vires to the parent statute. Similarly in *Banwarilal Agarwalla v. State of Bihar*[2] it was held that requirement of prior consultation with the Mining Board under Section 59 before framing of any rules and regulations under the Section 57 of the Mines Act 1952 was mandatory in nature. The Court elaborately analyzed the scope and purpose of the various provisions and observed–

> As has been recognised again and again by the courts, no general rule can be laid down for deciding whether any particular provision in a statute is mandatory, meaning thereby that non-observance thereof involves the consequence of invalidity or only directory, i.e., a direction the non-observance of which does not entail the consequence of invalidity, whatever other consequences may occur. But in each case the court has to decide the legislative intent. Did the legislature intend in making the statutory provisions that non-observance of this would entail invalidity or did it not? To decide this we have to consider not only the actual words used but also the scheme of the statute, the intended benefit to public of what is enjoined by the provisions and the material danger to the public by the contravention of the same. In the present case we have to determine therefore on a consideration of all these matters whether the legislature intended that the provisions as regards the reference to the Mines Board could be contravened only on pain of invalidity of the regulation. Looking at the language of the section, we find, the legislature, after saying in part of sub-section (3), that before any regulation is published, it "shall be" referred to every Mining Board which is, in the opinion of the Central Government concerned with the subject, and goes on to say in the latter part, that the regulation "shall not" be published until each Board has had a reasonable opportunity of reporting as to the expediency and suitability of the provisions.
>
> While it is true that language is only one of the many considerations which have to be taken into account in deciding whether a requirement is directory or mandatory, it is legitimate to note that the language used in this case is emphatic and appears to be designed to express an anxiety of the legislature that the publication of the regulation, which is condition precedent to the making of the regulations, should itself be subject to two conditions precedent-first, a reference to the Mining Boards concerned, and secondly, that sufficient opportunity to the Board to make a report as regards the expediency and suitability of the proposed regulations.

2. AIR 1961 SC 849.

The cause of this anxiety becomes patent, when one examines the matters on which regulations can be made. Even a cursory examination of the purposes set out in the 27 clauses of section 57 shows that most of them impinge heavily on the actual working of the mines. To mention only a few of these, viz., clause (c) under which regulations may be made for prescribing the duties of owners, agents and managers of mines and of persons acting under them; (g) for determining the circumstances in which and the conditions subject to which it shall be lawful for more mines than one to be under a single manager; (j) for prohibiting, restricting or regulating the employment of adolescents and women in mines; (k) for providing for the safety of the persons employed in a mine; (m) for providing for the safety of the roads and working places in mines; (n) for the inspection of workings and sealed off fire areas in a mine; (o) for providing for the ventilation of mines; (r) for providing for proper lighting of mines and regulating the use of safety lamps therein;-are sufficient to show that the very purpose of the Act may well be defeated unless suitable and practical regulations are framed to help the achievement of this purpose. Arbitrary and haphazard regulations without full consideration of their practicability and ultimate effect on the efficient working of the mines, would, apart from often defeating the purpose of the Act, affect injuriously the general economy of the country.

That, we are entitled to presume, is the reason behind the legislature's anxiety that Mining Boards should have an opportunity of examining regulations, and expressing their opinion before they are finalised. As has been already mentioned section 12 which deals with the formation of boards provides for representation thereupon of two persons nominated by owners of mines or their representatives and two persons to represent and interests of persons employed in mines, in addition to three persons representing the Government. The constitution is calculated to ensure that all aspects including on the one hand the need for securing the safety and welfare of labour and on the other hand practicability of the provisions proposed from the point of view of the likely expense and other considerations can be thoroughly examined. It is certainly to the public benefit that Boards thus constituted should have an opportunity of examining regulations proposed in the first place, by an administrative department of the government and of expressing their opinion. It is true that the law does not require concurrence of the board with the regulations proposed. It is reasonable to expect however that when a Board has expressed an opinion in favour of the rejection or modification of a proposed regulation, the department would not treat it lightly. But, even where the opinion expressed by the Board is not accepted the very fact that there has been such an examination by the Board, and a consequent re-examination by the department is likely to minimise the risks to public welfare.

But if the legislative requirement of prior consultation was considered to be directory in nature then the non-compliance of it will not invalidate the validity of the subordinate rules made under a statute. In *Hindustan Zinc*

Ltd. v. APSEB[3] the Supreme Court analyzed the role and functions of the State Electricity Consultative Council constituted under the Electricity (Supply) Act 1948. Under Sec. 16 of the Act the Council was comprised of members of the Electricity Board and representatives from the Electricity Generating Companies, local self-government, electricity supply industry, commerce, industry, transport, agriculture, labour employed in the electricity supply industry and consumers of electricity. The primary functions of the Council were to advise the Board and the Generating Companies on major questions of policies and schemes. On the issue of whether prior consultation of the Board with the Council was a mandatory requirement for revision of tariffs, the Court opining in the negative held that–

> The common premise for the purpose of this case that revision of tariffs by the Board is a question of policy may indicate that it would be open to the Consultative Council to advise the Board also on the question of revision of tariffs, and if such advice is given, then the Board must consider the same before taking the final decision. That, however, does not necessarily mean that where no such advice was taken from the Consultative Council or was rendered on account of the absence of any meeting of the Consultative Council during the relevant period, it would necessarily render invalid the revision of tariffs made by the Board. The consequence of non-compliance of Section 16 is not provided and the nature of function of the Consultative Council and the force of its advice being at the best only persuasive, it cannot be said that revision of tariffs without seeking the advice of the Consultative Council renders the revision of tariffs invalid.

4.12.4.3.2 Pre-legislative Consultation Policy

In light of growing importance of public participation in the law making process, recent attempts have been made to introduce pre-legislative consultation in the context of subordinate law making. The Committee of Secretaries (CoS) under the Chairmanship of Cabinet Secretary had decided on 10th January, 2014 to introduce the Pre-Legislative Consultation Policy with regards to Principal and Subordinate Legislations as framed under the different ministries. The legislative process would be mandatorily followed by every Ministry / Department of the Central Government before any legislative proposal or subordinate legislation is submitted to the Cabinet for its consideration and approval. This step was introduced to bring in transparency and create a better informed Government so as to resolve contentious and complex policies through the process of consensus.[4] The Manual for Parliamentary Procedures in the Government of India and the

---

3. (1991) 3 SCC 299.
4. Letter dated 5th February 2014 written by P.K. Malhotra, Secretary, Ministry of Law & Justice Legislative Department to the Secretaries of different ministries.

instructions on writing Cabinet Notes are being suitable modified to include these procedural rules.

The primary objective of such pre-consultative process is–

> While following this process, the Government sets out clearly the policy problem that is to be addressed through the provision of supportive evidence and analysis, the options that it has considered and the reasons for the choices the Government have made in bringing forward a legislation. The process also involves the study of social and financial costs, benefits and the key challenges that required to be settled before undertaking the legislation. Looking into all these aspects facilitate formation of perfect policy objectives which a Bill intends to achieve and improve the efficacy of any Act in its implementation.[5]

The pre-consultation procedures laid down are–[6]

1. Every Department / Ministry shall proactively publish the proposed legislations both on the internet as also through other means; the detailed modalities of such publication may be worked out by the Department / Ministry concerned.
2. The Department / Ministry concerned should publish / place in public domain the draft legislation or at least the information that may inter alia include brief justification for such legislation, essential elements of the legislation, its broad financial implications, and an estimated assessment of the impact of such legislation on environment, fundamental rights, lives and livelihoods of the concerned / affected people, etc. Such details may be kept in the public domain for a minimum period of thirty days for being proactively shared with the public in such manner as may be specified by the Department / Ministry concerned.
3. Where such legislation affect specific group of people, it may be documented and disclosed through print or electronic media or in such other manner, as may be considered necessary to give wider publicity to reach the affected people.
4. As a matter of practice, a provision regarding the previous publication of rules should be made in all new principal legislations.
5. Every draft legislation or rules, placed in public domain through pre-legislative process should be accompanied by an explanatory note explaining key legal provisions in a simple language.

---

5. Letter dated 5th February 2014 written by P.K. Malhotra, Secretary, Ministry of Law & Justice Legislative Department to the Secretaries of different ministries.
6. Decisions taken in the meeting of the Committee of Secretaries (CoS) held on 10th January, 2014 under the Chairmanship of Cabinet Secretary on the Pre-Legislative Consultation Policy (PLCP) (including principal and subordinate legislation).

6. The summary of feedback / comments received from the public / other stakeholders should also be placed on the website of the Department / Ministry concerned.
7. The Department / Ministry concerned might, in addition to placing the proposal in public domain, also hold consultations with all stakeholders. However, the degree of participation and mode of consultations may be decided by the Department / Ministry concerned and may vary according to the nature of the subject and the potential impact on those who will be affected by such legislation.
8. The Bill should be referred to the Ministry of Law and Justice for vetting after the pre-legislative consultation as well as inter-ministerial consultations are over. The Ministry of Law and Justice shall also, at the time of examination of the draft legislation or rules, ensure that the concerned Department / Ministry has compiled with the process of pre-legislative consultation.
9. The Department / Ministry concerned should include a brief summary of the feedback received from stakeholders (including Government Departments and the public) along with its response in the note for the Cabinet along with the draft legislation.
10. The summary of pre-legislative process should also be placed before the Department / Ministry concerned when the proposed legislation is brought to the Parliament and is referred to the Standing Committee.
11. It the Department / Ministry concerned is of the view that it is not feasible or desirable to hold pre-legislative consultation as detailed above, it may record the reasons in the note for the Cabinet.

4.12.4.4 Publication

The principle of 'ignorance of law is no excuse' makes it necessary for rules and regulations to be published by an official channel so that the laws are easily accessed by the common people. The term 'publication' refers "*to the act of publishing anything; offering it to public notice, or rendering it accessible to public scrutiny... an advising of the public; making known of something to them for a purpose*".[7] The need of publication of delegated legislation becomes important because when laws are being made through the legislative process adequate attention and publicity is conferred by the news media about the proposed bill. Discussions and debates on the floor of the Parliament in the course of law making provide necessary publicity to the enacted laws which make people aware about them. But delegated

7. *State of Madhya Pradesh v. Ram Ragubir Prasad Agarwal*, AIR 1979 SC 888.

legislations are generally made in the interiors of bureaucratic chambers which makes it difficult for the people to become aware about the rules and other subordinate legislations. In the absence of compulsory publication of delegated legislations through an official process it will be impossible for most of people to know about the existence of such laws which are integral part of the parent statute and will have equal bearing on their rights and liabilities. In the case of *B.K. Srinivasan v. State of Karnataka*[8] speaking on the importance of publication of delegated legislations Chinnappa Reddy J. observed–

> There can be no doubt about the proposition that where a law, whether Parliamentary or subordinate, demands compliance, those that are governed must be notified directly and reliably of the law and all changes and additions made to it by various processes. Whether law is viewed from the standpoint of the 'conscientious good man' seeking to abide by the law or from the standpoint of Justice Holmes's 'Unconscientious bad man' seeking to avoid the law, law must be known, that is to say, it must be so made that it can be known. We know that delegated or subordinate legislation is all pervasive and that there is hardly any field of activity where governance by delegated or subordinate legislative powers is not as important if not more important, than governance by Parliamentary legislation. But unlike Parliamentary Legislation which is publicly made, delegated or subordinate legislation is often made, unobtrusively in the chambers of a Minister, a Secretary to the Government or other official dignitary. It is, therefore, necessary that subordinate legislation, in order to take effect, must be published or promulgated in some suitable manner, whether such publication or promulgation is prescribed by the parent statute or not.[9]

The need of publication of delegated legislations has been recognized in most jurisdictions across the world. In England even though an Act of Parliament can become law from the day it receives the Royal assent, but Royal Proclamations (administrative orders) come into effect only when they published in the official gazette.[10] The Statutory Instruments Act makes it mandatory for subordinate legislations to be published, printed and sold for the use of common people in UK. Similarly in US the Federal Register Act makes it necessary for all rules and regulations to be published in the Federal Register for the common knowledge of all.

Unfortunately in India there is no substantive law relating to publication of rules and regulations in India. There is no general code laying down the rules

8. (1987) 1 SCR 1054, MANU/SC/0094/1987.
9. Para 18.
10. Crown Office Act 1877, Section 3 – Any royal proclamation shall be valid in law if published – a. As respects England, in the London Gazette; and b. As respects Scotland, in the Edinburgh Gazette; and c. As respects Ireland, in the Belfast Gazette.

of publication. The nature and scope of publication is generally determined by the parent statute and in the absence of any particular provision relating to publication the administrative authorities are required to publish them in the official gazette as per the Supreme Court decisions. Under Rule 319 of the Rules of Lok Sabha all regulation, rule, sub-rule, bye-law, order etc. framed in pursuance of the Constitution or the legislative functions delegated by Parliament to a subordinate authority, and which is required to be laid before the House shall be *numbered centrally and published in the Gazette immediately after it is promulgated.*[11]

4.12.4.4.1 Essential Part of Principles of Natural Justice

In the leading case of *Harla v. State of Rajasthan*[12] the Supreme Court recognized the importance of publication of rules in the governance of the country. In this case the appellant was convicted under the Jaipur Opium Act (JOA) and was fined Rs. 50 but it was subsequently found that the Act was never officially promulgated nor was it published in the official gazette. The Court held that Act as not a valid Act as no effort was ever made to make the law known to the public.

The Supreme Court made the following observations on the importance of publication in validating a legislation:

- If a law was not validly made then a mere inclusion of a clause subsequently stating that it shall come into force at an earlier date would be useless.
- The whole of an enactment needs to be published, publication of only one section would not validate the Act.
- It is against the principles of natural justice to permit the subjects of a State to be punished or penalized by laws they had no knowledge and of which they could not even with the exercise of reasonable diligence have acquired any knowledge.
- It is part of principles of natural justice that a law should be promulgated or published before it becomes operative.

In the words of Bose J.–

> Natural justice requires that before a law can become operative it must be promulgated or published. It must be broadcast in some recognisable way so that all men may know what it is, or, at the very least, there must be some special role or regulation or customary channel by or through which such knowledge can be acquired with the exercise of due and reasonable diligence. The thought that a decision reached in the secret recesses of a chamber

11. The Speaker may in consultation with the Leader of the House prescribe rules relating to numbering and publication of Orders.
12. AIR 1951 SC 467, MANU/SC/0014/1951.

> to which the public have no access and to which even their accredited representatives have no access and of which they can normally know nothing, can nevertheless affect their lives, liberty and property by the mere passing of a Resolution without anything more is abhorrent to civilised man. It shocks his conscience, In the absence therefore of any law, rule, regulation or custom, we hold that a law cannot come into being in this way, Promulgation or publication of some reasonable sort is essential.[13]

4.12.4.4.2 Official Gazette is the usual Mode of Publication

The important case on the topic of publication is the *State of Maharashtra v. M.H. George.*[14] A notification was issued by the RBI on August 25, 1948 by virtue of the power conferred in the Foreign Exchange Regulating Act stating that gold and gold articles could not be brought into India without permission from RBI. But a general permission was granted for bringing or sending gold for the purposes of transit to a place outside India. On November 24, 1962 the RBI published a notification dated November 8, 1962 providing that for transmit of gold to a place outside the territory of India it has to be disclosed as 'trans-shipment cargo, provided such articles are not removed from ship or conveyance except for the purpose of trans-shipment. The respondent, a German national, left Zurich by a Swiss Air plane on November 27, 1962 which touched Santa Cruz Airport the next day on its way to Manila. On being searched by the Customs Officers, he was found to carry 34 kg of gold in the jacket he was wearing. Till November 24, 1964 there was a general permission for a person to bring or send gold into India if it was for transit to a place outside the territory of India, but from that day it could not be done except on the condition that it was declared as a trans-shipment cargo. The respondent argued that when he boarded the plane on November 27 he could not have had the knowledge about the new condition imposed by the new notification. Under the earlier notification he did not commit any wrongful act as he was carrying the gold in person and was sitting in the plane. He further argued that the notification could come into effect only from the day it was brought to the notice of the persons who are likely to be affected by it, since it was published on November 24 in India, it was not possible for him t know about it on November 27 in Switzerland. The Supreme Court negated the argument of the Respondent and held that

- *Ignorance of law is no defence* implies that everyone in expected to know the law of the land. The maxim implies that persons should have knowledge or could have had knowledge if he was not negligent or if he had made proper enquiries about the provisions of law.

13. MANU/SC/0014/1951 Para 10.
14. AIR 1951 SC 467 : MANU/SC/0194/1964.

- There is no requirement for individually serving of notice a general notification made through the usual process would be adequate publication. It would suffice if publication takes place in a way whereby people can, if they are interested acquaint themselves with its content.
- A notification does not need to be published outside India. For an Indian law to operate and be effective in the territory where it operates, no publication outside the country is necessary
- The mode or form of publication is to be determined on the basis of statutory requirement. If such a provision is deemed to be mandatory then any failure to comply with those requirements make the notification invalid. But in the absence of any statutory requirement relating to publication it is necessary that it should be published in the usual mode i.e. by publication within the country in such media as generally adopted to notify to all the persons concerned in the making of rules.
- Publication in the Official Gazette is the ordinary method of bringing a rule or subordinate legislation to the notice of the persons concerned.
- The notification by RBI was published in the Official Gazette which is the usual mode of publication in India. The publication was made much before the Respondent landed in Bombay.
- There is no provision in the General Clauses Act as regards the time when a delegated legislation enacted under a statute comes into effect. It shall be determined on the basis of individual statutes. In the absence of any specific rule, there is bound to be ambiguity and uncertainty about the precise point of time when a law into effect. The RBI notification was deemed to come into effect on the date on which it came to the notice of the relevant public i.e. the next day after its publication. – November 25, 1962.

Official Gazette

The *Gazette of India (Bharat kaa Rajpatra)* is an authorized legal document published by the Government of India. It is published by the Department of Publication, Ministry of Urban Development and is authentic and accurate in content and strictly in accordance with Government policies and decisions. The publication is in accordance with the Government of India (Allocation of Business Rules) which are issued from time to time by the Cabinet Secretariat of the Republic of India. With the emergence of internet and development of e-governance online publication of the official gazette through *eGazette* (http://www.egazette.nic.in) has become a popular mode for accessing the weekly and extraordinary official gazettes of different ministries and departments. The object of publication in the Gazette is not only to provide information to the public but is also an official confirmation of the making of an order or rule. The same order or rule may be published in the newspapers, internet, broadcast on radio or television, but the version printed in the Gazette is deemed final. The date of publication in the Gazette is also taken into consideration to determine when a particular order or rule was made.

In the case of *ITC Bhadrachalam Paperboards v. Mandal Revenue Officer, A.P.*[15] highlighting the importance of publication in the Official Gazette the Supreme Court observed–

> The publication of an order or rule is the official irrefutable affirmation that a particular order or rule is made, is made on a particular day (where the order or rule takes effect from the date of its publication) and is made by a particular authority; it is also the official version of the order or rule. It is a common practice in courts to refer to the Gazette whenever there is a doubt about the language of, or punctuation in, an Act, Rule or Order. Section 83 of the Evidence Act says that the court shall presume the genuineness of the Gazette. Court will take judicial notice of what is published therein, unlike the publication in a newspaper, which has to be proved as a fact as provided in the Evidence Act. If a dispute arises with respect to the precise language or contents of a rule or order, and if such rule or order is not published in the Official Gazette, it would become necessary to refer to the original itself, involving a good amount of inconvenience, delay and unnecessary controversies. It is for this reason that very often enactments provide that Rules and/or Regulations and certain type of orders made thereunder shall be published in the Official Gazette. To call such a requirement as a dispensable one-directory requirement-is, in our opinion, unacceptable.[16]

In other cases like *Shambhu Nath Jha v. Kedar Prasad Sinha*[17] the Court have also held that publication in the Official Gazette is an imperitative requirement and cannot be dispensed with as it fulfills two fold objective of giving publicity to the notification and providing authenticity to the contents of that notification in case of any dispute with regard to its contents.

In the case of *B.K. Srinivasan v. State of Karnataka*[18] the Court categorically held that–

> [S]ubordinate legislation, in order to take effect, must be published or promulgated in some suitable manner, whether such publication or promulgation

15. (1996) 6 SCC 634 : MANU/SC/1292/1996.
16. Para 13.
17. 1973 CriLJ 453 : MANU/SC/0066/1972.
18. (1987) 1 SCR 1054 : MANU/SC/0094/1987.

> is prescribed by the parent statute or not. It will then take effect from the date of such publication or promulgation. Where the parent statute prescribes the mode of publication or promulgation that mode must be followed. Where the parent statute is silent, but the subordinate legislation itself prescribes the manner of publication, such a mode of publication may be sufficient, if reasonable. If the subordinate legislation does not prescribe the mode of publication or if the subordinate legislation prescribes a plainly unreasonable mode of publication, it will take effect only when it is published through the customarily recognised official channel, namely, the Official Gazette or some other reasonable mode of publication. There may be subordinate legislation which is concerned with a few individuals or is confined to small local areas. In such cases publication or promulgation by other means may be sufficient.[19]

In *Union of India v. M/s. Ganesh Das Bhojraj*[20] it was further reiterated that publication in the Official Gazette is the established practice for bringing a rule or subordinate legislation to the notice of the people. Individual service of notice to every member of the public about a general notification is not required and all interested persons can acquaint themselves with the contents of the notification published in the gazette.[21]

In the recent case of *Gulf Goans Hotels Co. Ltd. v. Union of India*[22] the Supreme Court was required to decide whether the various notifications relating to Coastal Regulation Zone could be deemed to be valid law. The Court by referring to the *Harla case* categorically held that since the guidelines issued by the Union of India were not published through the customarily recognized official channel they failed to satisfy the *essential and vital parameters/requirements of law* hence were not enforceable to the prejudice of the Appellants.

Not affect the merits of the case

An exception was made in the case of *Bangalore Woolen, Cotton and Silk Mills Co. Ltd. v. Commissioner, Bangalore Corporation*[23] wherein the octroi duty imposed on cotton and wool by the Bangalore Corporation was challenged on the ground that the procedure laid down in Section 98 of the City of Bangalore Municipal Corporation Act 1949 relating to publication

---

19. Id.
20. AIR 2000 SC 1102.
21. The Supreme Court overruled the earlier decision in *Collector of Central Excise v. New Tobacco Co.* AIR 1998 SC 668 : MANU/SC/0020/1998 wherein it was held that mere publication of the notification in the Official Gazette is not sufficient till the Gazette was made available to the people.
    Other relevant cases are *T. Narasimhulu v State of AP* MANU/SC/0374/2010.
22. 2014 (11) SCALE 83 : MANU/SC/0848/2014.
23. AIR 1962 SC 562 : MANU/SC/0093/1961.

of the resolution to impose octroi duty was not published in the Official Gazette. The five judge bench of the Supreme Court negated the argument that the defect of non-publication in the Official Gazette was fatal to the imposition of the tax. It referred to S. 38(1)(b) of the Act which provided that any act done or proceeding undertaken will not be questioned merely on the ground that a defect or irregularity in the conduct of such act or proceeding has taken place, so long as it does not affect the merits of the case and held that *"the resolution was published in the newspapers and was also communicated to those affected by it and thus it was well known. The failure to publish it in the Government Gazette did not affect the merits of its imposition".*[24]

This decision has been subsequently referred to in other cases like *B.K. Srinivasan v. State of Karnataka*[25] and *Kalyani Stores v. The State of Orissa.*[26]

4.12.4.4.3 Special Mode of Publication

There are many statutes which prescribe a special mode of publication of delegated legislations. In such cases the mode of publication of rules will be determined on the basis of whether such procedures are deemed to be mandatory or directory. The Supreme Court dealt with the issue in the leading case of *Govindlal Chaganlal Patel v. The Agricultural Produce Market Committee, Godhra.*[27] The appellant was arrested by the Inspector of the Godhra Agricultural Produce Market Committee on the ground of purchasing ginger without obtaining a license as required under the Gujarat Agricultural Produce Markets Act 1964. The principal contention of the appellant was that the notification whereby ginger was included was not promulgated or published as required under the Act hence the proceeding initiated was illegal. It was argued that the notification issued under Section 6(5) for including additional varieties of agricultural produce like ginger and onion was required to be published not only in the Official Gazette but also published in Gujarati in a local newspaper. The relevant provisions of the Act are–

> Section 5-The Director of Agricultural Marketing and Rural Finance may, by notification in the Official Gazette, declare his intention of regulating the purchase and sale of an agricultural produce and in such other manner as may be prescribed. Such notification is also required to be published in Gujarati language in a newspaper having circulation in the area and in such other manner as may be prescribed.

---

24. Id at Para 6.
25. MANU/SC/0094/1987.
26. MANU/SC/0223/1965.
27. AIR 1976 SC 263 : MANU/SC/0125/1975.

If any objection or suggestion is received by the Director within a month from the date of publication of the notification it shall be duly considered by the Director.

Section 6(1)-After the declaration is made in the manner specified in S.5 the Director may at any time by notification in the Official Gazette, declare the area specified or any portion thereof to be a market area for the purpose of the Act. A notification under this section is also required to be published in Gujarati in a newspaper having circulation in the said area and in such other manner as may be prescribed.

Section 6(5)-After the declaring in the manner specified in S.5 his intention and following the procedure thereon, the Director may at any time by notification in Official Gazette exclude any area from a market area or include therein and exclude from or add to the kinds of agricultural produce so specified any kind of agricultural produce.

Section 8-No person can operate in the market area or any part thereof except under and in accordance with the conditions of a license granted under the Act.

Chandrachud J. while delivering the decision observed that the concluding sentence of Section 6(1) says that a notification under 'this section' shall also be published in Gujarati in a newspaper having circulation in the particular area. The normal rule of construction of statutes requires that a provision should be given *its plain and natural meaning.* Hence it is not reasonable to assume that the legislature will be ignorant of the distinction between 'a section' of the statute and the 'sub-sections' of that section. Therefore, the requirement laid down by Section 6(1) that a notification under 'this section' shall also be published in Gujarati in a newspaper would govern any and every notification issued under any part of S.6, including the sub-sections of Section 6. If the legislature intended that the publication requirement was to govern notifications issued under Section 6(1) only, they would have specifically said so.

On the issue of whether it was mandatory for the Director to publish the notification in the local newspaper in addition to the publication in the Official Gazette the Court analyzed and interpreted the entire scheme of the Act as well as the relevant sections and held that–

> The object of these requirements is quite clear. The fresh notification can be issued only after considering the objections and suggestions which the Director receives within the specified time. In fact, the initial notification has to state expressly that the Director shall consider the objections and suggestions received by him within the stated period. Publication of the notification in the Official Gazette was evidently thought by the legislature not an adequate means of

> communicating the Director's intention to those who would be vitally affected by the proposed declaration and who would therefore be interested in offering their objections and suggestions. It is a matter of common knowledge that publication in a newspaper attracts greater public attention than publication in the Official Gazette. That is why the legislature has taken care to direct that the notification shall also be published in Gujarati in a newspaper. A violation of this requirement is likely to affect valuable rights of traders and agriculturists because in the absence of proper and adequate publicity, their right of trade and business shall have been hampered without affording to them an opportunity to offer objections and suggestions, an opportunity which the statute clearly deems so desirable. By Section 6(2), once an area is declared to be a market area, no place in the said area can be used for the purchase or sale of any agricultural produce specified in the notification except in accordance with the provisions of the Act. By Section 8 no person can operate in the market area or any part thereof except under and in accordance with the conditions of a licence granted under the Act. A violation of these provisions attracts penal consequences under Section 36 of the Act. It is therefore vital from the point of view of the citizens' right to carry on trade or business, no less than for the consideration that violation of the Act leads to penal consequences, that the notification must receive due publicity. As the statute itself has devised an adequate means of such publicity, there is no reason to permit a departure from that mode. There is something in the very nature of the duty imposed by Sections 5 and 6, something in the very object for which that duty is cast, that the duty must be performed.[28]

The Court concluded by observing that these rules *are vital and go to the root of the matter: they cannot be broken.* The provisions of the statute must be religiously implemented hence the publication in Gujarati language in a local newspaper is a mandatory requirement and must be strictly complied with.

Similarly in the case of *B.K. Srinivasan v. State of Karnataka*[29] it was held that publication of notices in the Official Gazette that the Outline Development Plan was available for inspection at the office of the Planning Authority was deemed to be sufficient compliance with the provisions of Mysore Town and Country Planning Act, 1961 even though the Plan and the Regulations themselves were never published in the Gazette. This defective is cured by the Omnibus Curative clause of Section 76J. The objective of such a clause is *to put beyond challenge defects of constitution of statutory bodies and defects of procedure which have not led to any substantial prejudice.* Non-publication of the Plan in the Official Gazette was a defect curable by Section 76J as the defect or the irregularity did not affect the merits of the case.

---

28. Supra note 27 at para 16.
29. MANU/SC/0094/1987.

4.13 JUDICIAL REVIEW OF DELEGATED LEGISLATION

In spite of the existence of the Parliamentary form of control, judicial form of control of delegated legislation is considered as an integral form of control mechanism. The fundamental justification for judicial control is based on the constitutional obligation of the courts to uphold the principles of *rule of law*. In a constitutionally governed state it is the essential function of the judiciary to ensure that the laws made by the Parliament are not *ultra vires* the Constitution and the delegated legislations enacted under a statute are within the ambit of both the parent statute and the constitution. In addition, Article 13(3)(a) of the Constitution has defined the term 'law' as *order, bye-laws, rules, regulations and notification* thereby clearly highlighting that not only by means of laws made by the legislatures but also through the subordinate executive laws, the State authorities should not attempt to take away or abridge the rights conferred by the Part III of the Constitution.

Judicial form of control is deemed to be a more effective form of control because the courts have the power to strike down a law if it is *ultra vires* to the parent statute or to the Constitution. The power of the judiciary is beyond the scope of mere recommendation and ensures the working of the delegated legislations in accordance with law at the stage of implementation. The scope of parliamentary control is generally restricted to pre-enactment control, i.e. at the stage of granting the power of law making to the executive authorities and the post-enactment control is limited to *laying down* of the rules before the parliament. The implementation of the procedural form of control is also entrusted to the judiciary who determine the legality of the subordinate law making process through the rules of procedural *ultra-vires.*

4.13.1 Judicial Control in UK and US

In England the paramount law making power has been granted to the Parliament. The Executive authorities do not have any inherent law making power in the absence of specific statutory grant of such powers. The administrative authorities can only make rules and regulations based on the provisions made by an Act of Parliament. The judiciary has adopted the test of *ultra vires* doctrine to uphold the validity of a delegated legislation by ensuring that it does not go beyond the scope of the parent Act. The Act of Parliament cannot be challenged in a court of law as they are immuned from judicial scrutiny, but no such immunity has been extended to the delegated legislations. The leading case in this regard is *Anisminic v. Foreign Compensation Committee*[30] wherein it was held that delegated legislations were amenable to judicial review. The Court observed–

> It is a well-established principle that a provision ousting the ordinary jurisdiction of the Court must be construed strictly—meaning, I think, that, if such a provision is reasonably capable of having two meanings, that meaning shall be taken which preserves the ordinary jurisdiction of the Court....
>
> It has sometimes been said that it is only where a tribunal acts without jurisdiction that its decision is a nullity. But in such cases the word "jurisdiction" has been used in a very wide sense, and I have come to the conclusion that it is better not to use the term except in the narrow and original sense of the tribunal being entitled to enter on the enquiry in question. But there are many cases where, although the tribunal had juris- diction to enter on the enquiry, it has done or failed to do something in the course of the enquiry which is of such a nature that its decision is a nullity. It may have given its decision in bad faith. It may have made a decision which it had no power to make. It may have failed in the course of the enquiry to comply with the requirements of natural justice. It may in perfect good faith have misconstrued the provisions giving it power to act so that it failed to deal with the question remitted to it and decided some question which was not remitted to it. It may have refused to take into account something which it was required to take into account. Or it may have based its decision on some matter which, under the provisions setting it up, it had no right to take into account.[31]

The judiciary's main task is to ensure that the *true intent* of the Act made by the Parliament is not modified by a subordinate administrative body.

In UK important constitutional statutes like the Bill of Rights 1688 can be repealed or amended by the Parliament like an ordinary statutes because the principles of Parliamentary sovereignty is inconsistent with the notions of constitutional limitations. But the judiciary in cases of delegated legislations have made them subject to judicial review and have ensured that the Fundamental Rights are not derogated or violated by the executive authorities unless expressly allowed by the Parliament. The judicial justification is based on the notion that Parliament will not sacrifice the fundamental rights of the people which act as checks and precautions on the Executive simply by implication. Extraordinary powers can be granted to a Minister only through express grant of such powers in the statute. In addition, the judiciary has adopted a number of principles to exercise their

30. (1969) 2AC 147.
31. Id. at p. 3-4.

power of judicial review such as unreasonableness, procedural errors, bad faith and wrong purpose etc.

Similarly in US the judiciary has large adopted the ultra vires test for upholding delegated legislation. In addition the courts have also applied the reasonable nexus theory i.e. there needs to be a rational relationship between particular regulations and the governing statute.[32]

4.13.2 Judicial Review in India

In *Ram Krishna Dalmia v. Justice S.R. Tendolkar*[33] the constitutional bench of five Judges of the Supreme Court after analyzing a series of earlier decisions laid down the scope and extent of the power of judicial review of legislations in India. The principles are–

(a) that a law may be constitutional even though it relates to a single individual if, on account of some special circumstances or reasons applicable to him and not applicable to others, that single individual may be treated as a class by himself;

(b) that there is always a presumption in favour of the constitutionality of an enactment and the burden is upon him who attacks it to show that there has been a clear transgression of the constitutional principles;

(c) that it must be presumed that the legislature understands and correctly appreciates the need of its own people, that its laws are directed to problems made manifest by experience and that its discriminations are based on adequate grounds;

(d) that the legislature is free to recognise degrees of harm and may confine its restrictions to those cases where the need is deemed to be the clearest;

(e) that in order to sustain the presumption of constitutionality the court may take into consideration matters of common knowledge, matters of common report, the history of the times and may assume every state of facts which can be conceived existing at the time of legislation; and

(f) that while good faith and knowledge of the existing conditions on the part of a legislature are to be presumed, if there is nothing on the face of the law or the surrounding circumstances brought to the notice of the court on which the classification may reasonably be regarded as based, the presumption of constitutionality cannot be carried to the extent of always holding that there must be some undisclosed and

32. *FCC v. American Broadcasting Co.*, 347 US 284 (1954).
33. 1959 SCR 279.

unknown reasons for subjecting certain individuals or corporations to hostile or discriminating legislation.

In light of the above principles the judicial review of delegated legislation has been classified in the following three categories

(i) The Parent Act is ultra vires the Constitution

(ii) The Delegated Legislation is ultra vires the Constitution

(iii) The Delegated Legislation is ultra vires the Parent Act

4.13.2.1 Parent act is ultra vires the constitution

If the parent statute or the enabling Act is in non-conformity with the Constitution then the different rules and regulations framed under such statute will also be deemed to be unconstitutional. The enabling statute will be deemed to be unconstitutional if it is in violation with the express or implied limits of the Constitution.

The express limits under the Constitution are those provisions which specifically set the limits on the powers of the state authorities such as no violation of the fundamental rights specified under Part III of the Constitution, strict adherence with the distribution of the legislative powers as specified under List I, II and III of the Seventh Schedule, no violation of the commerce clause under Article 301 of the Constitution, no retrospective effect of criminal legislation as provided under Article 20 etc. It is necessary that both the Parent statute as well as the delegated legislation should be in compliance with these express limits of the Constitution for the purpose of legal enforcement. In the leading case of *Chintaman Rao v. State of Madhya Pradesh*[34] the constitutionality of the order issued by the Deputy Commissioner under the provisions of the Central Provinces and Berar Regulation of Manufacture of Bidis (Agricultural Purposes) Act 1948 relating to forbidding of all persons residing the villages of Sagar district from engaging in the manufacture of bidis was challenged on the ground of the enabling statute being in violation of Article 19(1)(g) of the Constitution. Section 3 of the Act empowered the Deputy Commissioner to notify and fix a period as agricultural season with respect to certain specified villages. Section 4 provided that the 'Deputy Commissioner may, by general order which shall extend to such villages as he may specify, prohibit the manufacturer of bidis during the agricultural season. No person residing in a village specified in such order shall during the agricultural season engage himself in the manufacture of bidis, and no manufacturer shall during the said season employ any person for the manufacturer of bidis'. The Court upheld the contentions of the petitioners and observed–

34. AIR 1951 SC 118.

Unless it is shown that there is a reasonable relation of the provisions of the Act to the purpose in view, the right of freedom of occupation and business cannot be curtailed by it. The phrase "reasonable restriction" connotes that the limitation imposed on a person in enjoyment of the right should not be arbitrary or of an excessive nature, beyond what is required in the interests of the public. The word "reasonable" implies intelligent care and deliberation, that is, the choice of a course which reason dictates. Legislation which arbitrarily or excessively invades the right cannot be said to contain the quality of reasonableness and unless it strikes a proper balance between the freedom guaranteed in Article 19(1)(g) and the social control permitted by clause (6) of article 19, it must be held to be wanting in that quality.

Clause (6) in the concluding paragraph particularizes certain instances of the nature of the restrictions that were in the mind of the constitution-makers and which have the quality of reasonableness. They afford a guide to the interpretation of the clause and illustrate the extent and nature of the restrictions which according to the statute could be imposed on the freedom guaranteed in clause (g). The statute in substance and affect suspends altogether the right mentioned in Article 19(1)(g) during the agricultural seasons and such suspension may lead to such dislocation of the industry as to prove its ultimate ruin. The object of the statute is to provide measures for the supply of the adequate labour for agricultural purposes in bidi manufacturing areas of the Province and it could well be achieved by legislation restraining the employment of agricultural labour in the manufacture of bidis during the agricultural season. Even in point of time a restriction may well have been reasonable if it amounted to a regulation of the hours of work in the business. Such legislation though it would limit the field for recruiting persons for the manufacture of bidis and regulate the hours of the working of the industry, would not have amounted to a complete stoppage of the business of manufacture and might well have been within the ambit of clause (6). The effect of the provisions of the Act, however, has no reasonable relation to the object in view but is so drastic in scope that it goes much in excess of that object. Not only are the provisions of the statute in excess of the requirements of the case but the language employed prohibits a manufacturer of bidis from employing any person in his business, no matter wherever that person may be residing. In other words, a manufacturer of bidis residing in this area cannot import labour from neighbouring places in the district or province or from outside the province. Such a prohibition on the face of it is of an arbitrary nature inasmuch as it has no relation whatsoever to the object which the legislation seeks to achieve and as such cannot be said to be a reasonable restriction on the exercise of the right. Further the statute seeks to prohibit all persons residing in the notified villages during the agricultural season from engaging themselves in the manufacture of bidis. It cannot be denied that there would be a number of infirm and disabled persons, a number of children, old women and petty shop keepers residing in these villages who are incapable of being used for agricultural labour. All such persons are prohibited by law from engaging themselves in the manufacture of bidis; and are thus being deprived of earning their livelihood. It is a matter of common knowledge that there are certain classes of persons residing in every village who do not engage in agricultural operations. They and their womenfolk and children in their leisure hours supplement their income by engaging themselves in bidi business. There seems no reason for prohibiting them from carrying on this occupation. The statute as it stands, not only compels those who can be engaged in agricultural work from not taking to other avocations, but it also prohibits persons who have no connection or relation to agricultural operations from engaging in the business of bidi making and thus earning their livelihood. These provisions of the statute, in our opinion, cannot be said to amount to reasonable restrictions on the right of the applicants and that being so, the statute is not in conformity with the provisions of Part III of the Constitution. The law even to the extent that it could be said to authorize the imposition of restrictions in regard to agricultural labour cannot be held valid because the language employed is wide enough to cover restrictions both within and without the limits of constitutionally permissible legislative acting affecting the right. So long as the possibility of its being applied for purposes not sanctioned by the Constitution cannot be ruled out, it must be held to be wholly void.

Speaking on the scope of judicial review is was categorically observed that under the constitutional scheme of things the determination of reasonable restrictions imposed under a statute is not singularly in the domain of the legislature and cannot be considered as final or conclusive, but it is always subject to the supervision of the judiciary. *In the matter of fundamental rights, the Supreme Court watches and guards the rights guaranteed by the Constitution and in exercising its functions it has the power to set aside an Act of the Legislature of it is in violation of the freedoms guaranteed by the Constitution.* The Court struck down the orders issued by the Deputy Commissioner as void, inoperative and ineffective and held Sec. 4 of the Act as ultra vires to the Constitution.

The implied limits of the Constitution in the context of delegated legislation has been laid down the cases of *In Re: Delhi Laws Act case*[35] and *Harishankar Bagla v. State of Madhya Pradesh.*[36] wherein it was acknowledged that legislature can delegate the power of rule-making to a subordinate body after laying down the legislative policy and the general rules of conduct. In the case of *St. Johns Teachers Training Institute v. Regional Director, National Council for Teacher Education*[37] the Court applied the inherent policy of the statute to uphold the constitutionality of the delegated legislation.

35. [1951] 2 SCR 747.
36. AIR 1954 SC 465.
37. AIR 2003 SC 1533.

In this case the appellant being a Christian Minority Teacher Training Institute made an application to the Regional Director, National Council for Teacher Education Bangalore under the provisions of the National Council for Teacher Education Act 1993 for the purpose of seeking permission to start a course on Elementary Education Training. The application was rejected because it did not include the No Objection Certificate from the State Government as required under the Regulations. The appellants argued that by virtue of this regulation power to grant recognition has been conferred to the State Government which is wholly outside the purview of the Act. Under Section 14 of the Act 'every institution offering or intending to offer a course or training in teacher education... may for grant of recognition under the Act, make an application to the Regional Committee concerned in such form and in such manner as may be determined by the Regulations'. It is further provided that the Regional Committee should be satisfied with regard to various factors like adequate financial resources, accommodation, library, qualified staff, laboratory and other facilities required for proper functioning of the institution for a course or training in teacher education as may be laid down in the Regulations before grant of any recognition. Under Section 32 the National Council is empowered to frame regulations not inconsistent with the provisions of the Act to carry out the provisions of the Act. Accordingly the Council framed the regulation that 'every institution intending to offer a course or training in teacher education... shall submit application for recognition with a no objection certificate from the State Government in which the institution is located'.

The Court analyzed the scope of Section 4(3) and held that the requirement to submit NOC from the State Government was for the purpose of facilitating the Regional Committee in discharging their responsibilities and should not be deemed as delegation of power relating to grant of recognition. While holding the Regulations as valid and intra vires the Court observed–

> Sub-section (3) of Section 14 casts a duty upon the Regional Committee to be satisfied with regard to large number of matter before passing as order granting recognition to an institution which has moved an application for the said purpose. The factors mentioned in Sub-section (3) are that the institution has adequate financial resources, accommodation, library, qualified staff, laboratory and that it fulfils such other conditions required for proper functioning of the institution for a course or training in teacher education as may be laid down in the Regulations. As mentioned earlier there are only four Regional Committee in the whole country and, therefore, each Regional Committee has to deal with applications for grant of recognition from several States. It is therefore obvious that it will not only be difficult but almost impossible for the Regional Committee to itself obtain complete particulars and details of financial resources, accommodation, library, qualified staff, laboratory and other conditions of the institution which has moved an application for grant

of recognition. The institution may be located in the interior of the district in a far away State. The Regional Committee cannot perform such herculean task and it has to necessarily depend upon some other agency or body for obtaining necessary information. It is for this reason that the assistance of the State Government or Union Territory in which that institution is located is taken by the Regional Committee and this is achieved by making a provision in Regulations 5(e) and (f) that the application made by institution for grant of recognition has to be accompanied with a NOC from the concerned State or Union Territory. The impugned Regulations in fact facilitate the job of the Regional Committee in discharging their responsibilities.

Thus the power to make subordinate legislation is derived from the parent statute and it is essential that the delegate on whom such power has been conferred has to act within the limits of the authority specified under the Act and this referred to as the implied constitutional limits on the power of delegation of rule-making authority.

4.13.2.2 Delegated Legislation is Ultra Vires the Constitution

In the case of *Labh Chandra Reisurana v. State of Bihar*[38] the contentious issue before the Patna High Court was whether the Bihar Swetamber Jain Religious Trusts Rules 1955 framed under the provisions of Bihar Hindu Religious Trusts Act, 1950 was in accordance with constitutional provisions. It was argued that the constitution of the Bihar State Board of Swetamber Jain Religious Trust which was constituted under the Rules for the purpose of maintenance of the Pawapuri temples were in violation of the constitutionally protected religious freedom of the Swetamber Jain Community. Traditionally the concept of *Shree Sangh* referred to the entire community of Swetamber Jains living across India and this concept was modified by the rules when it provided that for the purpose of electing the five out of eleven members of the Board by Shree Sangh, the eligible electoral would be only those Swetamber Jains residing in Bihar and those residing outside the state of Bihar who had made a donation of Rupees 500 either to the Board or to the Swetamber Jain Religious Trust of Bihar during the last 10 years. The petitioners argued that the such a direction was discriminatory, unconstitutional and without jurisdiction. The Court held that by virtue of the rule making powers granted under the Parent Statute the State Government cannot make rules so as to limit the right of the members of the Shree Sangh to elect five members of the Board. Such rules will not only be inconsistent with the provisions of the statute but would also be in violation of the fundamental rights guaranteed under Articles 14 and 26 of the Constitution. The Court observed–

38. AIR 1969 Pat 209.

It is difficult to find out anything in the provisions of the Act to justify such a discrimination between persons professing Swetamber Jain faith residing in the State of Bihar and outside. There is no rational basis for it. The classification cannot be held to be reasonable. It is difficult to appreciate how merely because the Trust properties are situated in the State of Bihar and a Bihar State Board of Swetamber Jain Religious Trust is to be constituted under the Act, Swetamber Jains living in the State of Bihar have got a larger right as members of the Shree Sangh or a larger body of such persons can exercise their right of electing five members of the Board as members of the Shree Sangh and Swetamber Jains living outside the State of Bihar must get a limited right and not only limited, limited to an irrationally unreasonable extent. To illustrate my point, it is undisputed on the statements made in the various affidavits filed on behalf of the parties that the temples in question were established and constructed long time ago, in some cases centuries ago.

A donor from outside Bihar, who even would have contributed suppose a lac of rupees in construction of such a temple and who having not contributed five hundred rupees within the last ten years of the issuance of the instruction or preparation of the electoral roll will be de-barred from his right as a member of the Shree Sangh to exercise his vote in the matter of election of the five members of the Board under clause (c) of sub-section (2) of Section 8 of the Act.[39]

Thus the directions issued by the special officer, in exercise of the powers of the Board, were held to be ultra vires and completely void. The Court upheld the legality of the enabling statute but struck down the delegated legislation on the ground of infringement of express provisions of the constitution.

4.13.2.3 Delegated Legislation is Ultra Vires the Parent Act

Delegated legislations cannot be made to *supplant the provisions of the enabling Act but to supplement it* hence it cannot be ultra vires to the parent statute. The core function of delegated is to fill up the necessary details of the enabling statute and in this context the delegated legislation is deemed to subordinate, ancillary or conditional in nature. However many a times the delegated legislation becomes ultra vires the enabling statute. Some of the examples are–

4.13.2.3.1 Delegated Legislation is in Excess of the Power Conferred by the Enabling Act

In *Dwarka Nath v. Municipal Corporation*[40] the Supreme Court deliberated the issue of whether the rules relating to packing and labeling framed under the provisions of the Prevention of Food Adulteration Act were

39. Ibid at p. 213.
40. AIR 1971 SC 1844.

within the scope of the power conferred. By virtue of the rule making powers conferred to the Central Government under Sec. 23(1) the Central Government provided that on every label the name and business address of the manufacturer or importer or vendor or packer and the batch number or code number either in English or Hindi was to be specified, however in case of food package weighing not more than 60 grams such particulars need not be specified. The appellants who were in the business of manufacturing pure *desi ghee* were arrested for failing to adhere with the labelling requirements. The appellants argued that the rules relating to packing and labelling were outside the scope of law making powers. The Court analyzed the different provisions relating to the power of the Central Government to frame rules and concluded that under Sec. 23(1)(d) relating to 'restricting the packing and labelling of any article of food and the design of any such package or label with a view to preventing the public or the purchaser being deceived or misled as to the character, quality or quantity of the article' the power to frame rules relating to packing and labeling can be included within. It is not beyond the scope of rule-making power of the Central Government. Since the appellant had mentioned in the label their address as 'Mohan Ghee Laboratories, New Delhi – 5', they had substantially complied with the rules and regulations. The failure to mention the number of the premise, the locality or the area where the premise was situated would amount to technical breach and would not make the appellants liable for violation of the same.

Similarly in *T.B. Ibrahim v. Regional Transport Authority, Tanjore*[41] the primary issue before the Supreme Court was whether the amended Rule 268 of the Madras Vehicles Rule 1940 was within the scope of law making power under Section 68 of the enabling statute of Motor Vehicles Act, 1939.

Rule 268 stated that–

> In the case of public service vehicles (other than motor cabs) the transport authority may after consultation with such other authority as it may consider desirable, and after notice to the parties affected, fix or alter from time to time for good and proper reasons, the starting places and termini between which such vehicles shall be permitted to be used within its jurisdiction. A list of such places shall be supplied by such authority to every holder of a permit for such vehicles at the time of grant of or renewal of permits.
>
> When such places have been fixed every such vehicle shall start only from such places.

41. AIR 1953 SC 79.

The Court after analyzing the scope of rule making by the government under Section 68 stated that the government has got plenary power to make rules for the purpose of 'control of transport vehicles' and fixation or alteration of bus-stands is an inherent part of it. Secion 68(2)(r) has clearly contemplated three definite situations wherein the government may make rules – prohibiting the picking up or setting down of passengers – (i) At specified places, (ii) In specified areas, and (iii) At places other than duly notified stands or halting places. Thus the government has the power to prohibit a specified place from being used for picking up or settling down passengers and this will inevitably give rise to closing of a specified place for the purpose of picking up or settling down of passengers or exclusion of such a place.

> The expression "duly notified stands" is not defined in the Act, but it is reasonable to presume that a duly notified stand must be one which is notified by the Transport Authority and by none other.... Section 68, sub-section 2(r), involves both a general prohibition that the stand will cease to exist as well as a particular prohibition, namely that passengers shall not be picked up or set down at a specified point. The order passed by the Transport Authority properly construed falls within the ambit of section 68, sub-section 2(r). Rule 268 under which the order impeached was passed is a rule framed under the plenary rule-making power referred to in section 68, sub-section (1). Sub-section (2)(za) says that a rule may be made with respect to any other matter which is to be or may be prescribed. This shows the existence of residuary power vested in the rule-making authority. It follows therefore that rule 268 is within the scope of the powers conferred under section 68 of the Act.

The Court further stated that the power of the Transport Authority to regulate traffic control or impose restrictions as validly provided under the rule-making authority cannot be challenged as being void or as inconsistent with some provisions of a general law such as municipality laws. *By-law must not be repugnant to the statute or the general law. But by-laws and rules made under a rule-making power conferred by a statute do not stand on the same footing, as such rules are part and parcel of the statute itself.*[42]

In this case the court upheld the change of bus-stand by the Transport Authority and held that such change does not affect any legal right of the appellant, including Article 19(1)(g). The bus-stand as run by the appellant can be used for carrying passengers from the stand into the town and vice-versa, since the prohibition was only towards picking up and setting down of passengers to outward journeys. By reason of the shifting of the bus-stand the appellant may have been deprived of the income he used

42. As quoted in the judgment from Craies on Statute Law.

to enjoy but that cannot be the ground for claiming of infringement of fundamental rights.

In *Agricultural Market Committee v. Shalimar Chemicals Works Ltd*[43] the Supreme Court analysed whether Rule 74(2) framed by the State Government and Bye-law 24(5) framed by the Market Committee were within the scope of rule-making powers under the Andhra Pradesh (Agricultural Produce and Livestock) Markets Act, 1966. Section 12 of the Act provided for the levy of fees by the notified market committee. It stated–

> 12. *Levy of fees by the market committee.*—(1) The market committee shall levy fees on any notified agricultural produce, livestock or products of livestock purchased or sold in the notified market area [at such rate, not exceeding (two rupees) as may be specified in the bye-laws] for every hundred rupees of the aggregate amount for which the notified agricultural produce, livestock or products of livestock is purchased or sold, whether for cash or deferred payment or other valuable consideration.
>
> *Explanation I.*—For the purposes of this section, all notified agricultural produce, livestock or products of livestock taken out of a notified market area shall, unless the contrary is provided, be presumed to have been purchased or sold within such area.

The explanation I of Section 12 extended the scope of the purchase and sold by creating a legal fiction that any agricultural produce or livestock or products related to it if taken out of the market area will be presumed to have been purchased or sold for the purpose of levy of fees. This legal fiction was further extended by Rule 74(2) and Bye-law 24(5) which categorically provided that any weighing, measuring or counting of a notified agricultural produce, livestock or related products or taking it out of the notified market area would be deemed to have been purchased or sold within the notified market area. The Court negated the constitutionality of the delegated legislations as they were *ultra vires* to the provisions of the parent statute. The Court held–

> Explanation I to Section 12 creates a legal fiction and provides that if any notified agricultural produce is taken out of a notified market area, it shall be presumed to have been purchased or sold within such area. The presumption is a rebuttable presumption and can be shown to be not correct. The policy in enacting this provision is only to cover such transactions of sale and purchase for which direct evidence may not be available. Since a notified agricultural produce can be sold only within the notified market area, and, that too, by a trader having a licence issued to him by the committee, it is obvious that if such commodity is moved out of the notified area, it would mean either

43. AIR 1997 SC 2502.

that it has been sold or purchased. Otherwise, there would be no occasion to move such commodity out of the notified market area. The legal fiction was thus limited to the "moving" of the commodity from within the market area to a place outside the market area.

The Government to whom the power to make rules was given under Section 33 and the committee to whom power to make bye-laws was given under Section 34 widened the scope of "presumption" by providing further that if a notified agricultural produce is weighed, measured or counted within the notified area, it shall be deemed to have been sold or purchased in that area. The creation of legal fiction is thus beyond the legislative policy. Such legal fiction could be created only by the legislature and not by a delegate in exercise of the rule-making power. We are, therefore, in full agreement with the High Court that Rule 74(2) and Bye-law 24(5) are beyond the scope of the Act and, therefore, ultra vires. The reliance placed by the assessing authority as also by the appellate and revisional authority on these provisions was wholly misplaced and they are not justified in holding, merely on the basis of weighment of "copra" within the notified area committee that the transaction of sale took place in that market area.[44]

4.13.2.3.2 Delegated Legislation is in Conflict with the Parent Statute

In *State of Karnataka v. H. Ganesh Kamath*[45] the Supreme Court analysed the legality of a delegated legislation in the context of whether it was contrary to the provisions of the parent statute. Under the Motor Vehicles Act 1939 vehicles were classified into three categories based on the weight of the vehicle as heavy motor vehicle, medium motor vehicle and light motor vehicle. Section 7(7) dealing with grant of driving licenses provided that – The test of competence to drive shall be carried out in a vehicle of the type to which the application refers and, for the purposes of Part I of the test,- (a) a person who passes the test in driving a heavy motor vehicle shall be deemed also to have passed the test in driving any medium motor vehicle or light motor vehicle; (b) a person who passes the test in driving a medium motor vehicle shall be deemed also to have passed the test in driving any light motor vehicle.

In pursuance of the power of rule-making under Section 21 of the Act, the Karnataka government framed the Karnataka Motor Vehicles Rules 1963 which under Rule 5 (2) provided that no authorization to drive a heavy transport vehicle shall be granted unless the applicant satisfies the licensing authority that he has had at least three years' experience in driving any medium vehicle.

44. Id at para 27-28.
45. AIR 1983 SC 550.

The respondents in this after completion of their driving training had applied for a licence for driving heavy motor vehicles, but their applications were rejected by the licensing authority on the ground that the respondents did not satisfy the requirements of Rule 5(2) of the prior experience of three years in driving a medium vehicle. The Court after analysing the statutory provisions observed that Section 7(7) of the Act required competence in driving the vehicle in respect of which the applicant was interested in obtaining the driving licence. It further provided that a person who passed the test in driving such a vehicle would also be deemed to have passed the test in driving the medium or light motor vehicle. Thus under the statute for the purpose of passing the test of competence to drive a heavy motor vehicle a person is not required to possess any experience in driving a medium motor vehicle. In this context Rule 5(2) was held to be beyond the scope of the parent Act and was repugnant or contrary to the express provisions of the parent statute. The power of rule-making conferred under Section 21 *does not enable the rule-making authority to make a rule which travels beyond the Scope of the enabling Act or which is inconsistent there with or repugnant thereto.*

The Management of DTU v. BBL Hajelay[46] is another leading case dealing with the issue of application of delegated legislation was contrary to the provisions of the parent Act. Ved Prakash (Respondent no. 2)[47] was originally employed as a driver in the Delhi Road Transport Authority (DRTA). In 1958 the functions of the DRTA were taken over by the Delhi Municipal Corporation and the Delhi Municipal Corporation Act 1957 became the applicable statute and all the employees of DRTA became the employees of the Corporation. Under Section 92 of the Act the power of appointing municipal officers and other municipal employees, whether temporary or permanent, to posts carrying a minimum monthly salary (exclusive of allowances) of less than Rupees 350 shall vest in the General Manager (Transport). Hence Ved Prakash at the time of joining the Corporation was appointed by the General Manager.

Under Section 494 read with Section 504 the General Manager (Transport) is entitled by order to direct that any power conferred or any duty imposed on him by or under the Act shall be exercised and performed also by any municipal officer or other municipal employee specified in the other. In 1961 by an order issued the General Manager had delegated his power to the Asst. General Manager to appoint and consequently, to remove from service an employee in the category of Ved Prakash. Subsequently a disciplinary

46. AIR 1972 SC 2452.

47. Respondent no. 1 Hajelay was the Presiding Officer of the Labour Court where the proposed action for removal of Respondent no. 2 from service was submitted for approval.

enquiry was initiated by the Asst. General Manager (Transport) and he was removed from service by him in 1963. The Respondent no. 2 challenged the order of removal on the ground that the Asst. General Manager was not the competent authority to remove him from service under the provisions of the statute.

Section 95 of the Act dealing with disciplinary actions against municipal officers and employees provides that 'every municipal officer or other municipal employee shall be liable to have his increments or promotions withheld or to be censured, reduced in rank, compulsorily retired, removed or dismissed for any breach of any departmental regulations or of discipline or for carelessness, unfitness, neglect of duty or other misconduct by such authority as may be prescribed by regulations. Provided that no such officer or other employee as aforesaid shall be reduced in rank, compulsorily retired, removed or dismissed by any authority subordinate to that by which he was appointed'. The Court analysed the provision and observed that the Proviso to Section 95(1) gives protection to every officer and employee of the undertaking that he may not be removed or dismissed from service by an authority subordinate to that by which he was appointed. By the order in 1961 the functions of the General Manager (Transport) had been delegated to the Asst. General Manager with the consequence that *if after 1961 the Assistant General Manager makes the appointment of a driver like respondent No. 2, he would no doubt be entitled to remove him from service. But so far as respondent No. 2 is concerned his individual position will have to be determined with reference to the time when he was absorbed in Corporation Service. That was in January, 1958.... Respondent No. 2, at the time of his absorption in January, 1958 would be deemed to have been appointed Under Section 92(1)(b) which would mean that he was appointed by the General Manager (Transport). Being so appointed, no subordinate of his including the Assistant General Manager (Transport) would be entitled to remove him from service in view of Section 95(1) proviso.* Thus the Court negating the order of removal upheld that a protection which has been given to an employee by a statute cannot be nullified by rules and regulations authorized by the statute itself.

4.13.2.3.3 Delegated Legislation is in Conflict with the Procedures Laid Down in the Parent Act[48]

If the enabling statute has laid down certain rules and procedures for the purpose of enacting the delegated legislation then it is necessary that those procedural requirements should be adhered. In case of any breach or non-compliance with the procedures, then the courts shall apply the

48. Discussed in detail in Part.

mandatory and directory test as laid in the *Atlas cycle case* for invalidating the subordinate legislation. Non-compliance with the statutory procedures have been categorized as procedural *ultra vires.* After analysing the nature and scope of the enabling statute, including the procedural requirement if the provision is held to directory then the non-compliance of the procedure will not invalidate the rules framed thereunder as was held in *Hindustan Zinc case.* In case the procedures are held to be mandatory then rules should be framed after due compliance with the same as discussed in *Banwarilal Aggrawala.* In *Raza Buland Sugar* the Court further clarified that substantial compliance with the mandatory requirements of a provision will be sufficient to uphold the legality of a delegated legislation.

4.13.2.3.4 Delegated Legislation is Contrary to the Common Law Principle

In *Sophy Kelly v. State of Maharashtra*[49] the Bombay High Court referred to the common law principles to negate the Regulation 42 framed under the Maharashtra Secondary Education Boards Act 1965. The regulation was framed by the Maharashtra State Board of Secondary Education and provided that the eligibility of candidates for admission to the SSC Examination will be determined based on the candidates having from the head of his school a certificate as to his conduct, character and attendance at the school, but not a certificate regarding his academic progress. Under the rules it was deemed obligatory upon the Head Master of a school to forward the application of candidates irrespective of their progress. The writ petition filed by the various heads of the secondary schools challenged the regulations framed on the ground that the regulations were in violation of the internal autonomy of the educational institutions and violated the rights of the teacher to determine the academic progress of the candidates during the final year. The Court recognized that the contention of the petitioners is dependent on identifying their legal rights to withhold the applications of the candidates on the ground that their academic progress was unsatisfactory. The Court accepted the common law principle relating to *contract to educate* to uphold the rights of the school authorities. It observed–

> In Halbury's Laws of England, in the volume dealing with Education, the following portion appears under the heading "Common Law Right and Duties" and the sub-heading "The Contract to educate" (Halsbury, Third Edition, Volume 13, page 590, paragraphs 1241 and 1242):-
>
> "1241. Parents and school proprietors:- In schools which are not maintained by local education authorities the relations between the parent and the proprietor of the school are governed by the terms express or implied of the contract for the education of the child. Subject to the express terms of the contract,

49. AIR 1968 Bom 156.

there is an implied term that the proprietor shall continue to be responsible for the education of the child so long as the child's conduct does not warrant his expulsion from the school.

"1242. Position of schoolmasters:- The authority of a school master is, while it exits, the same as that of a parent. A parent, when he leaves his child with a schoolmaster, delegates to him all his own authority, so far as is necessary for the welfare of the child, and so far as necessary to maintain discipline with regard to the child committed to the teacher's care. The delegation is revocable, and in case of conflict the authority of the parent must prevail and he may have a habeas corpus if the master detains the child against his wish. The parent undertakes that the master shall be at liberty to enforce with regard to the child the rules of the school, or at all event such rules as are known to him and to which he has expressly or impliedly agreed. The master is bound to take such care of his pupils as a careful father would take of his children".

Applying these principles to the case before us, it seems clear that when a parent gets his child admitted to a secondary school he undertake that the Head Master shall be at liberty to enforce with regard to the child such rules of the school as are reasonably designed to promote the education of the child and to maintain discipline in the school. The main purpose of education in secondary schools is to prepare pupils for the S.S.C. Examination.... Since the main purpose of education in the secondary school is to prepare pupils for the S.S.C. Examination, it schools that a parent who gets his child admitted to secondary school undertakes that the Head Master shall be at liberty to enforce with regard to the child such rules of discipline as are reasonably designed to prepare him for that examination. Under the implied terms of the contract the Head Master is entitled to withhold promotion of a pupil from one standard to the next, if the pupil does not show satisfactory academic progress. The same right is exercised by Head Master in respect of pupils in the final standard by refusing to grant them leave to appear for the S.S.C. Examination unless satisfactory progress is made by them. Such a rule is obviously designed to promote habits of regular and diligent study in the pupils. The Head Masters claim the right to judge the academic progress and performance of their pupils before presenting them for the S.S.C. Examination, but that right results from the more basic rule enforced in the school that only those students will be presented for the S.S.C. Examination who have studies regularly in the course of the year and made adequate academic progress.

In this case the Court upheld the rights of the head of schools, which is contractual in nature and is binding upon the pupils and their guardians of not permitting the students to appear for the SSC Examination *if the Head Masters find that the pupils have failed to make adequate progress, and that this right is capable of being overridden by a valid regulation.* Thus the common law right could be overridden by a law passed by the legislature or if the legislature had authorised the Board to make a regulation to the same effect having a force of law.

4.13.2.3.5 Delegated Legislation is *Malafide*

The legislative intention behind a law is not questioned in a court of law. In *G. Nageshwara Rao v. A.P.S.R.T. Corporation*[50] the Supreme Court had categorically observed that a legislature can only make laws within its legislative competence, and that *"if, in fact, it has the power to make the law its motives in making the law are irrelevant"*. In *Srinivasan v. State of Kerala*[51] the Kerala High Court applied the same principles and held that when an attack of *malafide* is made against the exercise of legislative power or rule making power the power of the Court shall be restricted to examine only whether what has been done is within its competence. This view was reiterated by the Delhi High Court in *Madan Gopal Singh v. Union of India*[52] while dealing with issue of whether the subordinate legislation relating to change in service condition were malafide in nature it was categorically held that *since the legislative power of the Central Government to amend the Schedule was not disputed, there could be no question of any mala fides or the absence of good faith in the exercise of the said power.*

4.13.2.3.6 Delegated Legislation is Arbitrary or Unreasonableness

In *Indian Express Newspapers (Bombay) Pvt. Ltd. v. Union of India*[53] it was held that a subordinate legislation can be questioned on any ground on which the plenary legislation could be questioned. Accordingly a subordinate legislation can be questioned on the ground that it is unreasonable or manifestly arbitrary.

In *AIR India v. Nergesh Meerza*[54] the Court struck down Regulations 46 and 47 as arbitrary, unreasonable and discriminatory in nature. Regulation 46 which dealt with termination of service of air hostesses upon attaining 35 years of age or on marriage if it takes place within 4 years of service or on first pregnancy whichever occurs earlier. The Court struck down the condition of termination of service on first pregnancy as unconstitutional, void and violative of Article 14 because–

> This is a most unreasonable and arbitrary provision which shocks the conscience of the Court. The Regulation does not prohibit marriage after four years and if an AH after having fulfilled the first condition becomes pregnant, there

50. 1959 (Supp.) 1 S.C.R. 319.
51. A.I.R. 1968, Kerala 158.
52. 1969 SLR 576.
53. (1985) 1 SCC 641 : (1985) 2 SCR 287.
54. AIR 1981 SC 1829.

> is no reason why pregnancy should stand in the way of her continuing in service... the termination of the services of an AH under such circumstances is not only a callous and cruel act but an open insult to Indian womanhood the most sacrosanct and cherished institution. We are constrained to observe that such a course of action is extremely detestable and abhorrent to the notions of a civilised society. Apart from being grossly unethical, it smacks of a deep rooted sense of utter selfishness at the cost of all human values. Such a provision, therefore, is not only manifestly unreasonable and arbitrary but contains the quality of unfairness and exhibits naked despotism and is, therefore, clearly violative of Article 14 of the Constitution.

Regulation 47 was also held to be unconstitutional because it provided that the services of an employee, may at the option of the Managing Director, on the employee being found medically fit, be extended upto a period of ten years. It was clarified–

> The words 'at the option' are wide enough to allow the Managing Director to exercise his discretion in favour of one AH and not in favour of the other which may result in discrimination. The Regulation does not provide any guidelines, rules, or principles which may govern the exercise of the discretion by the Managing Directer. Similarly, there is also no provision in the Regulation requiring the authorities to give reason for refusing to extend the period of retirement of AHs. The provision does not even give any right of appeal to higher authorities against the order passed by the Managing Director. Under the provision, as it stands, the extension of the retirement of an AH is entirely at the mercy and sweet will of the Managing Director. The conferment of such a wide and uncontrolled power on the Managing Director is clearly violative of Article 14, as the provision suffers from the vice of excessive delegation of powers.

In *State of Maharashtra v. Chandrabhan Tale*[55] Supreme Court held that the second proviso to Rule 151(i)(ii)(b) of the Bombay Civil Service Rules was held to be void for violating Articles 14, 16 and 21 of the Constitution. The proviso provided for payment of subsistence allowance at the rate of Re. 1 per month to a government servant who was convicted by a competent court and sentenced to imprisonment and whose appeal against the conviction was pending. The Court described the award of subsistence allowance at the rate of Rupee 1 per month as *ludicrous*. The proviso was struck down on the ground of being unreasonable and illusory in nature and was contrary to the law making powers under Article 309 of the Constitution. In the words of Chinnappa Reddy J. "*It is mockery to say that subsistence allowance is awarded and to award Re. 1 per month*".

55. AIR 1983 SC 803.

SUMMATION

Delegated legislation is a modern day necessity. It is important that the exercise of such powers should be within the bounds of Constitution and should not be ultra vires to the parent statute. All efforts should be made to incorporate the pre-legislative consultation measures to ensure democratization of the rule making process so as to make more easily acceptable to the people at large.

V

Quasi-Judicial Functions and Principles of Natural Justice

LEARNING OBJECTIVES

After reading this chapter, you will be familiar with:

- Reasons for the growth of Administrative Adjudication
- Relationship between principles of natural justice and duty to act fairly
- Principles of Natural Justice
- Relationship between Principles of natural justice and Article 14
- Rule against Bias
- Types of Bias
  - Pecuniary Bias;
  - Personal Bias;
  - Departmental Bias;
  - Non-pecuniary interest
  - Inconsequential Bias
  - Institutional Bias
- Test of Biasness
- Non-compliance with the Rule against Bias
- Doctrine of Waiver
- Doctrine of Necessity
- Right of Fair Hearing
- Components of Fair Hearing
- Prejudice Test
  - Right of Notice;
  - Right of Hearing;
  - Right of Cross Examination;
  - Right to access and examine documents
  - Right of Oral Hearing
  - Right of Legal Representation
- Exception to the Right of Hearing
  - Statutory exception;
  - Emergency;
  - Legislative action;
  - No violation of legal rights
  - Useless formality theory
  - Confidentiality
  - Administrative necessity
- Reasoned Decision
- Non-compliance with principles of natural justice
- Summation

5.1 INTRODUCTION

The third category of administrative functions is known as the quasi-judicial functions.

Traditionally the judicial functions involved adjudicating disputes between two individuals or between the state and an individual. The Indian Constitution makes provision for a well ordered and well-regulated, hierarchical judicial system but the judiciary suffers from inherent limitations to meet the growing challenges of modern administration.

With the increase in state activities after the adoption of the welfare measures in the 20th century, the responsibilities of the different organs of the state have also increased manifold. The judiciary, like the legislature suffered from functional limitations because of the limited number of judicial officers in the country and their lack specialization to deal with complicated policy formulation and implementation. In addition, the existing judicial responsibilities relating to pending cases and ever increasing new litigation has overburdened the already the constrained judiciary. Hence it had become essential to transfer some of the dispute resolution functions to some of the administrative authorities. These bodies are required to deal with a variety of applications, claims and controversies.

5.2 REASONS FOR THE GROWTH OF ADMINISTRATIVE ADJUDICATION

(i) Expansion of state activities – With the adoption of various welfare programmes and public utility functions like health, education, planning, social security, transport agriculture, industrialization etc. it was impossible to carry out these programs and determining the legal questions involved therein with the assistance of the law courts because of their highly individualistic and ritualistic approach. Hence it was felt that the administrative decision making was the need of the day.

(ii) Litigation before a court of law is both time consuming and expensive, hence there was a need felt for an alternative system of adjudication which was informal, cheap and quick.

(iii) Creating new public welfare and utility standards outside the adversarial model of adjudication. E.g. Environmental cases needs to adopt a harmonious stand between protecting the environment and promoting economic development. Similarly industrial disputes have to balance the interests of the workers without compromising with economic well-being of the industries.

(iv) Need to adopt preventive measures – Courts generally provides remedies after the wrongful act has happened but many a times it is necessary to undertake preventive measures to prevent larger injury e.g. Traffic laws, food adulteration laws etc. Administrative agencies having adjudicating powers have the ability to prevent the commission of these acts.

(v) Administrative functioning depends on implementing executive policies in a fair, transparent and non-arbitrary manner. Grant of contracts, licensing etc. needs to be implemented based on administrative policies and not being dependent on adversarial adjudicatory process.

(vi) Large pendency in courts – The judiciary is already overburdened with pending litigations and any overburdening with additional litigations arising from intensive form of government will only add on to the pressure.

The administrative authorities while performing the dispute resolution functions are required to comply with the minimum threshold of judicial propriety and judicial norms. The administrative authorities are required to follow the procedures laid down in the statute and adhere to a minimum standard of judicial principles, including judicial independence while performing the quasi-judicial functions.

In the words of Forsyth and Wade–[1]

> A quasi-judicial function is an administrative function which the law requires to be exercised in some respects as if it were judicial. A typical example is a minister deciding whether or not to confirm a compulsory purchase order or to allow a planning appeal after a public inquiry. The decision itself is administrative, dictated by policy and expediency. But the procedure is subject to the principles of natural justice, which require the minister to act fairly towards the objectors and not (for example) to take fresh evidence without disclosing it to them. A quasi-judicial decision is therefore an administrative decision which is subject to some measure of judicial procedure.

In *Ranjit Thakur v. Union of India*[2] while dealing with the need to comply with the procedural safeguards provided in a statute the Court held that–

> The procedural safeguards contemplated in the Act must be considered in the context of and corresponding to the plenitude of the summary jurisdiction of the court-martial and the severity of the consequences that visit the person subject to that jurisdiction. The procedural safeguards should be commensurate with the sweep of the powers. The wider the power, the greater the need for

1. William Wade and Christopher Forsyth, Administrative Law, Oxford 2009 p. 34-35.
2. (1987) 4 SCC 611.

the restraint in its exercise and correspondingly, more liberal the construction of the procedural safeguards envisaged by the statute. The oft-quoted words of Frankfurter, J. in *Vitarelli v. Seaton*[3] are again worth recalling:

"...if dismissal from employment is based on a defined procedure, even though generous beyond the requirements that bind such agency, that procedure must be scrupulously observed.... This judicially evolved rule of administrative law is now firmly established and, if I may add, rightly so. He that takes the procedural sword shall perish with that sword."

"The history of liberty" said the same learned Judge "has largely been the history of observance of procedural safeguards"[4]

We are afraid, the non-compliance of the mandate of Section 130 is an infirmity which goes to the root of the jurisdiction and without more, vitiates the proceedings. Indeed it has been so held by this Court in *Prithi Pal Singh v. Union of India*[5] where Desai, J. referring to the purpose of Section 130 observed: "Whenever an objection is taken it has to be recorded. In order to ensure that anyone objected to does not participate in disposing of the objection. ...This is a mandatory requirement because the officer objected to cannot participate in the decision disposing of the objection. ...The provision conferring a right on the accused to object to a member of the court-martial sitting as a member and participating in the trial ensures that a charge of bias can be made and investigated against individual members composing the court-martial. This is pre-eminently a rational provision which goes a long way to ensure a fair trial."

The Court concluded that non-compliance with the procedural mandate laid down under the statute will render the proceedings of the summary court-martial as infirm in law.

5.3 VANISHING LINE OF DIFFERENCE BETWEEN QUASI-JUDICIAL FUNCTIONS AND PURE ADMINISTRATIVE ACTIONS: JOURNEY FROM PRINCIPLES OF NATURAL JUSTICE TO DUTY TO ACT FAIRLY

While performing quasi-judicial function the administrative authority is required to take decisions after hearing both the sides, whereas in the case of a pure administrative action there are no legal obligation to consider and weigh submissions and arguments or to collect any evidences. The grounds upon which the action is taken and the procedure for taking the action are left entirely to the discretion of the authority. The administrative decision is primarily taken on the ground of expediency and policy.

3. 359 US 535.
4. *McNobb v. US*, 318 US 332.
5. (1982) 3 SCC 140.

In quasi-judicial functions the administrative body has to follow certain principles of law while making the decisions. It is not essential to comply with laws like CPC and CrPC or other procedural laws but it is necessary to adhere to the principles of natural justice principles. Non-compliance with these principles will invalidate the decision made. Whereas in the case of discretionary actions it is the discretion of the authority which is the basis of the action and such discretion is primarily based on state policy and expedience.

In the early years the view of the law courts in England and India had been that administrative officers performing merely administrative functions which were not in the nature of judicial or quasi-judicial were not bound to comply with the principles of natural justice.[6] These principles were only applicable to the judicial and quasi-judicial authorities. But with passage of time the principles of natural justice became applicable to administrative proceedings.

One of the earliest English cases wherein principles of natural justice were applied was *Dr. Bonham's case.* Dr. Bonham was a doctor of Cambridge University and he started practicing in the City of London without license of the College of Physician, London. A complaint was made against him and the College of Physicians imposed fine and ordered for imprisonment. The statute under which the College acted provided that half of the fines imposed would go the king and rest to the College. Chief Justice Coke invalidating the order passed held that the Act of Parliament under which the action was taken was void because it made a man judge in his own cause, or was otherwise against common right and reason because the College had a financial interest in passing its own judgement. This case is a landmark decision because it is one of the very few cases where an Act of Parliament was subject to judicial review on grounds of violation of principles of natural justice as the doctrine of *sovereignty of the parliament* does not allow the judiciary to review laws made by the Parliament.

In the landmark case of *Cooper v. Wandsworth Board of Works*[7] the petitioner had built a house in Wandsworth without giving due notice to the local board of works and when the construction had reached the second storey, the board of works sent men one late evening and got the building demolished. Under the Metropolis Local Management Act of 1855 it was provided that no person shall put a building in London without giving 7 days' notice to the local board of works, and that if anyone did so, the Board might have the building demolished. The board did exactly what the

6. ***See*** *generally Franklin v. Minister of Town and Country Planning* (1947) 2 ALL ER 289; *Kishan Chand Arora v. Commissioner of Police, Calcutta,* AIR 1961 SC 705.
7. (1863) 14 CB (NS) 180:143 E.R. 414.

statue said the Board might do in exactly the same circumstances. The nature of the action taken was pure administrative in character and not quasi-judicial in nature, hence was not required to give notice or comply with principles of natural justice. Nevertheless the builder brought an action claiming damages for the injury caused to the building on the ground that the board had no power to act without giving him a notice an opportunity of being heard. The Court upheld the following proposition–

> I think the board ought to have given notice to the plaintiff, and to have allowed him to be heard. The default in sending notice to the board of the intention to build, is a default which may be explained. There may be a great many excuses for the apparent default. The party may have intended to conform to the law. He may have actually conformed to all the regulations which they would wish to impose, though by accident his notice may have miscarried; and, under those circumstances, if he explained how it stood, the proceeding to demolish, merely because they had ill-will against the party, is a power that the legislature never intended to confer. I cannot conceive any harm that could happen to the district board from hearing the party before they subjected him to a loss so serious as the demolition of his house; but I can conceive a great many advantages which might arise in the way of public order, in the way of doing substantial justice, and in the way of fulfilling the purposes of the statute, by the restriction which we put upon them, that they should hear the party before they inflict upon him such a heavy loss.
>
> ....
>
> I apprehend that a tribunal which is by law invested with power to affect the property of one of Her Majesty's subjects, is bound to give such subject an opportunity of being heard before it proceeds: and that that rule is of universal application, and founded upon the plainest principles of justice. Now, is the board in the present case such a tribunal? I apprehend it clearly is, whether we consider it with reference to the discretion which is vested in it, or whether we look at the analogy which exists between it and other recognised tribunals (and no one ever doubted that such tribunals are bound by the rules which a court of justice is bound by), or whether you look at it with reference the estimation in which it is held by the legislature, as appears from the language used in the statute.
>
> ......
>
> .....the board are wrong whether they acted judicially or ministerially. I conceive they acted judicially, because they had to determine the offence, and they had to apportion the punishment as well as the remedy. That being so, a long course of decisions, beginning with Dr. Bentley's case,[8] and ending with some very recent cases, establish that, although there are no positive

8. *The King v. The Chancellor, &c., of Cambridge*, 1 Stra. 557, 2 Ld. Raym. 1334, 8 Mod. 148, Fortescue, 202.

words in a statute requiring that the party shall be heard, yet the justice of the common law will supply the omission of the legislature.

Thus the Court justified that an administrative action which detrimentally affects the rights of the people should be preceded by adherence to the principles of natural justice. But subsequently the Court clarified that the action taken by Wandsworth Board of Works was judicial in nature, hence bound by the principles of natural justice. By classifying the action as judicial in nature, the Court continued with the distinction between judicial and administrative actions. An important consequence of this decision was the stretched extension of the administrative action as judicial action. Over a period of time for the purpose demanding the application of principles of natural justice *every administrative act was thus treated as 'judicial' if it adversely affected any person's rights or entailed a penalty.* But recognizing every administrative act as 'judicial', which has some impact on the rights of the people, virtually left no space for pure administrative action. As a method of differentiating between administrative action requiring judicial approach and those fundamentally administrative in character use of the epithet or title 'quasi-judicial' became popular for describing the administrative actions which are required to be exercised judicially and in accordance with principles of natural justice. The use of the term 'quasi-judicial' facilitated in the growth of fair administrative procedure.

In 1929 British government appointed a committee-The Committee on Ministers Powers[9] under the Chairmanship of Earl of Donoughmore to consider the law making and adjudicating powers of Ministers and their appointees. Differentiating between judicial and quasi-judicial decisions it was observed that a judicial decision 'disposes of the whole matter by a finding upon the facts in dispute and an application of the law of the land to the facts so found,' whereas quasi-judicial functions are performed by finding facts and applying administrative policy.

As a consequence a vast majority of the administrative actions which affected the rights or the legal position of the people came to be recognized as quasi-judicial in nature and subject to the principles of natural justice. Ultimately the terminological distinction between quasi-judicial action and administrative action was put to rest by Lord Loreburn in *Board of Education v. Rice*[10] when he categorically observed–

Comparatively recent statutes have extended, if they have not originated, the practice of imposing upon departments or officers of State the duty of deciding or determining questions of various kinds. In the present instance,

9. Cmd 4060 (1932).
10. [1911] AC 179.

> as in many others, what comes for determination is sometimes a matter to be settled by discretion, involving no law. It will, I suppose, usually be of an administrative kind; but sometimes it will involve matter of law as well as matter of fact, or even depend upon matter of law alone. In such cases the Board of Education will have to ascertain the law and also to ascertain the facts. I need not add that in doing either they must act in good faith and fairly listen to both sides, for that is a duty lying upon every one who decides anything. But I do not think they are bound to treat such a question as though it were a trial. They have no power to administer an oath, and need not examine witnesses. They can obtain information in any way they think best, always giving a fair opportunity to those who are parties in the controversy for correcting or contradicting any relevant statement prejudicial to their view. Provided this is done, there is no appeal from the determination of the Board under section 7, sub-section 3, of this Act. The Board have, of course, no jurisdiction to decide abstract questions of law, but only to determine actual concrete differences that may arise, and as they arise, between the managers and the local education authority. The Board is in the nature of the arbitral tribunal, and a Court of law has no jurisdiction to hear appeals from the determination either upon law or upon fact. But if the Court is satisfied either that the Board have not acted judicially in the way I have described, or have not determined the question which they are required by the Act to determine, then there is a remedy by mandamus and certiorari.

In this case the Board of Education had to determine a dispute between a body of school managers and the local education authority of Swansea, which had refused to pay teachers in church schools at the same rate as teachers in the authority's own schools. The Court quashed the decision of the Board as they failed to act judicially and complied with the principles of natural justice. Lord Loreburn in his observation had emphasized two pertinent points relating to observation of principles of natural justice by everyone who has the duty to decide anything and whose action may adversely affect the legal rights or liberties of other. In performance of these functions the administrative authorities are subject to judicial review.

The expanding scope of application of principles of natural justice suffered set back from 1914 to 1963 because of the growing executive dominance during the period of the two World Wars and the period of economic and social turmoil thereafter. The importance of principles of natural justice was revived in 1964 in the landmark decision of *Ridge v. Baldwin*.[11] In this case the appellant was the chief constable and was in police force for almost 33 years. He was arrested on October 25, 1957 for conspiring with senior members of his force to obstruct the course of justice. At a meeting of the Watch Committee it was resolved that he would be dismissed from

11. [1964] AC 40.

service. Under Section 191(4) of the Municipal Corporation Act 1882 'the watch committee or any two justices having jurisdiction in the borough, may at any time suspend or dismiss, any bourough constable whom they think negligent in the discharge of his duty, or otherwise unfit for the same.' The appellant challenged the order of dismissal on the ground of non-compliance with the principles of natural justice as no opportunity of being heard was provided to him before depriving him of his right to public office and denying him the statutory pension right which are proprietary in nature. Lord Reid upholding the application of principles of natural justice analyzes the nature, scope and importance of the principles and observed–

> The principle audi alteram partem goes back many centuries in our law and appears in a multitude of judgments of judges of the highest authority. In modern times opinions have sometimes been expressed to the effect that natural justice is so vague as to be practically meaningless. But I would regard these as tainted by the perennial fallacy that because something cannot be cut and dried or nicely weighed or measured therefore it does not exist. The idea of negligence is equally insusceptible of exact definition, but what a reasonable man would regard as fair procedure in particular circumstances and what he would regard as negligence in particular circumstances are equally capable of serving as tests in law, and natural justice as it has been interpreted in the courts is much more definite than that. It appears to me that one reason why the authorities on natural justice have been found difficult to reconcile is that insufficient attention has been paid to the great difference between various kinds of cases in which it has been sought to apply the principle. What a minister ought to do in considering objections to a scheme may be very different from what a watch committee ought to do in considering whether to dismiss a chief constable. So I shall deal first with cases of dismissal. These appear to fall into three classes: dismissal of a servant by his master, dismissal from an office held during pleasure, and dismissal from an office where there must be something against a man to warrant his dismissal. The law regarding master and servant is not in doubt. There cannot be specific performance of a contract of service, and the master can terminate the contract with his servant at any time and for any reason or for none. But if he does so in a manner not warranted by the contract he must pay damages for breach of contract. So the question in a pure case of master and servant does not at all depend on whether the master has heard the servant in his own defence: it depends on whether the facts emerging at the trial prove breach of contract. But this kind of case can resemble dismissal from an office where the body employing the man is under some statutory or other restriction as to the kind of contract which it can make with its servants, or the grounds on which it can dismiss them. The present case does not fall within this class because a chief constable is not the servant of the watch committee or indeed of anyone else. ....

So I come to the third class, which includes the present case. There I find an unbroken line of authority to the effect that an officer cannot lawfully be dismissed without first telling him what is alleged against him and hearing his defence or explanation. An early example is Bagg's Case,[12] though it is more properly deprivation of the privilege of being a burgess of Plymouth. Rex v. Gaskin[13] arose out of the dismissal of a parish clerk, and Lord Kenyon C.J. referred to audi alteram partem as one of the first principles of justice. *Reg. v. Smith*[14] was another case of dismissal of a parish clerk, and Lord Denman C.J. held that even personal knowledge of the offence was no substitute for hearing the officer: his explanation might disprove criminal motive or intent and bring forward other facts in mitigation, and in any event delaying to hear him would prevent yielding too hastily to first impressions. Ex parte Ramshay[15] is important. It dealt with the removal from office of a county court judge, and the form of the legislation which authorised the Lord Chancellor to act is hardly distinguishable from the form of section 191, which confers powers on the watch committee. The Lord Chancellor was empowered if he should think fit to remove on the ground of inability or misbehaviour, but Lord Campbell C.J. said[16] that this was "only on the implied condition prescribed by the principles of eternal justice." In *Osgood v. Nelson*[17] objection was taken to the way in which the Corporation of the City of London had removed the clerk to the Sheriff's Court, and Lord Hatherley L.C. said: "I apprehend, my Lords, that, as has been stated by the learned Baron who has delivered, in the name of the judges, their unanimous opinion, the Court of Queen's Bench has always considered that it has been open to that court, as in this case it appears to have considered, to correct any court, or tribunal, or body of men who may have a power of this description, a power of removing from office, if it should be found that such persons have disregarded any of the essentials of justice in the course of their inquiry, before making that removal, or if it should be found that in the place of reasonable cause those persons have acted obviously upon mere individual caprice."

........The question which was or ought to have been considered by the watch committee on March 7, 1958, was not a simple question whether or not the appellant should be dismissed. There were three possible courses open to the watch committee - reinstating the appellant as chief constable, dismissing him, or requiring him to resign. The difference between the latter two is that dismissal involved forfeiture of pension rights, whereas requiring him to resign did not. Indeed, it is now clear that the appellant's real interest in this appeal is to try to save his pension rights.

---

12. (1615) 11 Co.Rep. 93b.
13. (1799) 8 Term Rep. 209.
14. (1844) 5 Q.B. 614.
15. (1852) 18 Q.B. 173.
16. 18 Q.B. 173, 190.
17. (1872) L.R. 5. H.L. 636.

> It may be convenient at this point to deal with an argument that, even if as a general rule a watch committee must hear a constable in his own defence before dismissing him, this case was so clear that nothing that the appellant could have said could have made any difference. It is at least very doubtful whether that could be accepted as an excuse. But, even if it could, the respondents would, in my view, fail on the facts. It may well be that no reasonable body of men could have reinstated the appellant. But as between the other two courses open to the watch committee the case is not so clear. Certainly on the facts, as we know them, the watch committee could reasonably have decided to forfeit the appellant's pension rights, but I could not hold that they would have acted wrongly or wholly unreasonably if they had in the exercise of their discretion decided to take a more lenient course.

Thus in cases where a body is not merely required to declare what are the rights of the person but also decide how he should be treated it will be deemed to be performing a quasi-judicial function and it would be required to observe the essentials of the principles of natural justice. This rationale was followed in subsequent cases like *In re : H.K. (An Infant)*[18] wherein the validity of the action taken by an Immigration Officer came up for consideration. In the course of his judgment Lord Parker, C.J. observed thus:

> But at the same time, I myself think that even if an immigration officer is not in a judicial or quasi-judicial capacity, he must at any rate give the immigrant an opportunity of satisfying him of the matters in the sub-section, and for that purpose let the immigrant know what his immediate impression is so that the immigrant can disabuse him. That is not, as I see it, a question of acting or being required to act judicially, but of being required to act fairly. Good administration and an honest or bona fide decision must, as it seems to me, require not merely impartiality, nor merely bringing one's mind to bear on the problem, but acting fairly; and to the limited extent that the circumstances of any particular case allow, and within the legislative framework under which the administrator is working, only to that limited extent do the so-called rules of natural justice apply, which in a case such as this is merely a duty to act fairly. I appreciate that in saying that it may be said that one is going further than is permitted on the decided cases because heretofore at any rate the decisions of the courts do seem to have drawn a strict line in these matters according to whether there is or is not a duty to act judicially or quasi-judicially.

Post these decisions the applicable principle was that the powers of a purely administrative character were required to be exercised in a fair manner, implying that the action taken should be in accordance with the principles of natural justice. The gap between quasi-judicial functions and

18. [1967] 2 Q.B. 617.

administrative discretionary was ultimately merged in the opinion expressed by Lord Diplock in *R. v. Commission for Racial Equality*[19] when he laid down the principle that–

> Where an Act of Parliament confers upon an administrative body functions which involve its making decisions which affect to their detriment the rights of other persons or curtail their liberty do as they please, there is a presumption that Parliament intended that the administrative body should act fairly towards those persons who will be affected by their decisions.

Thus irrespective of the nature of administrative action, it has become obligatory for the authorities to act in a fair manner. The authority on one hand is bound to comply with the principles of natural justice in all cases wherein they have a duty to act judicially and also they will have a duty to act fairly whenever the actions affect the rights and interests of the people. The duty to act fairly implies to act in accordance with the principles of natural justice.

In India in the early case of *State of Orissa v. Dr. Binapani Dei*[20] the Supreme Court had emphasized the necessity to comply with norms of fair procedure and duty to act judicially by administrative authorities while dealing with issues of civil consequences as an integral part of rule of law.

> The rule that a party to whose prejudice an order is intended to be passed is entitled to a hearing applies alike to judicial tribunals and bodies of persons invested with authority to adjudicate upon matters involving civil consequences. It is one of the fundamental rules of our constitutional set-up that every citizen is protected against exercise of arbitrary authority by the State or its officers. Duty to act judicially would therefore arise from the very nature of the function intended to be performed; it need not be shown to be super-added. If there is power to decide and determine to the prejudice of a person, duty to act judicially is implicit in the exercise of such power. If the essentials of justice be ignored and an order to the prejudice of a person is made, the order is a nullity. That is a basic concept of the rule of law and importance thereof transcends the significance of a decision in any particular case.

In the case of *A.K. Kraipak v. Union of India*[21] one of the crucial question before the court was determining the nature of the function performed by the Selection Committee created under the All India Services Act for the purpose of selection of officers to the Indian Forest Service (IFS) was quasi-judicial or purely administrative in nature. The contention on behalf of the

19. [1982] AC 779.
20. AIR 1967 SC 1269 : (1967) 2 SCR 625.
21. AIR 1970 SC 150 : (1969) 2SCC 262.

appellants were that it was in the nature of quasi-judicial power because the language of Rule 4 in Regulation 5 prescribed that 'the selection should be made after *adjudging* the suitability of the officers belonging to the State service' which necessarily implies 'to judge or decide'. On the contrary the respondents argued that the function of the selection committee was statutory in nature and their duty was 'merely to select officers who in its opinion were suitable for being absorbed in the IFS' that is 'found worthy of selection'. The Court analyzing the nature and scope of the functions observed that *"The dividing line between an administrative power and a quasi-judicial power is quite thin and is being gradually obliterated. For determining whether a power is an administrative power or a quasi-judicial power one has to look to the nature of the power conferred, the person or persons on whom it is conferred, the framework of the law conferring that power, the consequences ensuing from the exercise of that power and the manner in which that power is expected to be exercised."*[22] On the issue of administrative accountability it was recognized that under the constitutionally governed rule of law it is essential that every instrumentalities of the State should act in a just and fair manner without being arbitrary and capricious. The procedural norms adhered by the judicial institutions for the purpose of ensuring probity, propriety and impartiality in actions should also be adopted by other administrative institutions when their actions will have an immediate or subsequent impact on the rights of the citizens.

> Under our Constitution the rule of law pervades over the entire field of administration. Every organ of the State under our Constitution is regulated and controlled by the rule of law. In a welfare State like ours it is inevitable that the jurisdiction of the administrative bodies is increasing at a rapid rate. The concept of rule of law would lose its vitality if the instrumentalities of the State are not charged with the duty of discharging their functions in a fair and just manner. The requirement of acting judicially in essence is nothing but a requirement to act justly and fairly and not arbitrarily or capriciously. The procedures which are considered inherent in the exercise of a judicial power are merely those which facilitate if not ensure a just and fair decision. In recent years the concept of quasi-judicial power has been undergoing a radical change. What was considered as an administrative power some years back is now being considered as a quasi-judicial power.[23]

Emphasizing the need for administrative accountability to prevent administrative despotism it is important that administrative actions are governed by the principles of natural justice. It categorically observed–

22. Ibid Para 13.
23. Ibid Para 13.

> With the increase of the power of the administrative bodies it has become necessary to provide guidelines for the just exercise of their power. To prevent the abuse of that power and to see that it does not become a new despotism, courts are gradually evolving the principles to be observed while exercising such powers. In matters like these, public good is not advanced by a rigid adherence to precedents. New problems call for new solutions. It is neither possible nor desirable to fix the limits of a quasi-judicial power.[24]

In *Maneka Gandhi v. Union of India*[25] the Supreme Court while dealing with the issue of whether principles of natural justice can be applicable in the exercise of an administrative discretionary when the statute has specifically excluded the application of fair hearing. It was categorically held that *the principle of reasonableness, which legally as well as philosophically, is an essential element of equality or non-arbitrariness pervades Article 14 like a brooding omnipresence and the procedure contemplated by Article 21 must answer the test of reasonableness in order to be in conformity with Article 14. It must be "right and just and fair" and not arbitrary, fanciful or oppressive; otherwise, it .would be no procedure at all and the requirement of Article 21 would not be satisfied.* Hence even when a statute is silent on the application of principles of natural justice the affected parties will be heard *yet the justice of the common law will supply the omission of the legislature.*

Speaking on the duty to act fairly as an integral part of natural justice it was observed–

> [T]he soul of natural justice is "fair-play in action" and that is why it has received the widest recognition throughout the democratic world. In the United States, the right to an administrative hearing is regarded as essential requirement of fundamental fairness. And in England too it has been held that **"fair-play in action"** demands that before any prejudicial or adverse action is taken against a person, he must be given an opportunity to be heard. The rule was stated by Lord Denning, MR in these terms in *Schmidt v. Secretary of State or Home Affairs*[26] — "where a public officer has power to deprive a person of his liberty or his property, the general principle is that it has not to be done without his being given an opportunity of being heard and of making representations on his own behalf". The same rule also prevails in other Commonwealth countries like Canada, Australia and New Zealand. It has even gained access to the United Nations (vide *American Journal of International Law,* Vol. 67, p. 479). Magarry, J., describes natural justice "as a distillate of due process of law" (vide *Fontaine v. Chastarton*[27]). It is

24. Id. Para 14.
25. AIR 1978 SC 597.
26. (1969) 2 Ch 149 : (1969) 1 All ER 904.
27. (1968) 112 Solicitor General 690.

the quintessence of the process of justice inspired and guided by **"fair-play in action".** If we look at the speeches of the various Law Lords in *Wiseman case*[28] it will be seen that each one of them asked the question "whether in the particular circumstances of the case, the Tribunal acted unfairly so that it could be said that their procedure did not match with what justice demanded", or, was the procedure adopted by the Tribunal "in all the circumstances unfair?" The test adopted by every Law Lord was whether the procedure followed was fair in all the circumstances and "fair-play in action" required that an opportunity should be given to the taxpayer "to see and reply to the counter-statement of the Commissioners" before reaching the conclusion that "there is a prima facie case against him". The inquiry must, therefore, always be: does fairness in action demand that an opportunity to be heard should be given to the person affected?

Now, if this be the test of applicability of the doctrine of natural justice, there can be no distinction between a quasi-judicial function and an administrative function for this purpose. The aim of both administrative inquiry as well as quasi-judicial inquiry is to arrive at a just decision and if a rule of natural justice is calculated to secure justice, or to put it negatively, to prevent miscarriage of justice, it is difficult to see why it should be applicable to quasi-judicial inquiry and not to administrative inquiry. It must logically apply to both. On what principle can distinction be made between one and the other? Can it be said that the requirement of "fair-play in action" is any the less in an administrative inquiry than in a quasi-judicial one? Sometimes an unjust decision in an administrative inquiry may have far more serious consequences than a decision in a quasi-judicial inquiry and hence the rules of natural justice must apply equally in an administrative inquiry which entails civil consequences. There was, however, a time in the early stages of the development of the doctrine of natural justice when the view prevailed that the rules of natural justice have application only to a quasi-judicial proceeding as distinguished from an administrative proceeding and the distinguishing feature of a quasi-judicial proceeding is that the authority concerned is required by the law under which it is functioning to act judicially. This requirement of a duty to act judicially in order to invest the function with a quasi-judicial character was spelt out from the following observation of Atkin, L.J. in *Rex v. Electricity Commissioners* [(1924) 1 KB 171 : (1923) All ER Rep 150], "wherever any body of persons having legal authority to determine questions affecting the rights of subjects, and having the duty to act judicially, act in excess of their legal authority, they are subject to the controlling jurisdiction of the King Bench Division ...". Lord Hewart, C.J., in *Rex v. Legislative Committee of the Church Assembly*[29] read this observation to mean that the duty to act judicially should be an additional requirement existing independently of the "authority to determine questions affecting the rights of subjects"— something super-added to it. This gloss placed by Lord Hewart, C.J., on the dictum

28. 1971 AC 297 : (1969) 3 All ER 275.
29. (1928) 1 KB 411.

of Lord Atkin, LJ., bedevilled the law for a considerable time and stultified the growth of the doctrine of natural justice. The Court was constrained in every case that came before it, to make a search for the duty to act judicially sometimes from tenuous material and sometimes in the services of the statute and this led to over subtlety and over-refinement resulting in confusion and uncertainty in the law. But this was plainly contrary to the earlier authorities and in the epoch-making decision of the House of Lords in *Ridge v. Baldwin*[30] which marks a turning point in the history of the development of the doctrine of natural justice, Lord Reid pointed out how the gloss of Lord Hewart, C.J., was based on a misunderstanding of the observations of Atkin, L.J., and it went counter to the law laid down in the earlier decisions of the Court. Lord Reid observed: "If Lord Hewart meant that it is never enough that a body has a duty to determine what the rights of an individual should be, but that there must always be something more to impose on it a duty to act judicially, then that appears to me impossible to reconcile with the earlier authorities". The learned Law Lord held that the duty to act judicially may arise from the very nature of the function intended to be performed and it need not be shown to be super-added. This decision broadened the area of application of the rules of natural justice and to borrow the words of Prof. Clark in his article on "*Natural Justice, Substance and Shadow*" in Public Law Journal, 1975, restored light to an area "benighted by the narrow conceptualism of the previous decade". This development in the law had its parallel in India in the *Associated Cement Companies Ltd. v. P.N. Sharma*[31] where this Court approvingly referred to the decision in *Ridge* v. *Baldwin*[32] and, later in *State of Orissa v. Dr Binapani Dei*[33] observed that: "If there is power to decide and determine to the prejudice of a person, duty to act judicially is implicit in the exercise of such power". This Court also pointed out in *A.K. Kraipak v. Union of India*[34] another historic decision in this branch of the law, that in recent years the concept of quasi-judicial power has been undergoing radical change and said:

"The dividing line between an administrative power and a quasi-judicial power is quite thin and is being gradually obliterated. For determining whether a power is an administrative power or a quasi-judicial power one has to look to the nature of the power conferred, the person or persons on whom it is conferred, the framework of the law conferring that power, the consequences ensuing from the exercise of that power and the manner in which that power is expected to be exercised."

The net effect of these and other decisions was that the duty to act judicially need not be super-added, but it may be spelt out from the nature of the

30. 1964 AC 40 : (1963) 2 All ER 66.
31. AIR 1965 SC 1595 : (1965) 2 SCR 366.
32. Supra note 30.
33. AIR 1967 SC 1269 : (1967) 2 SCR 625.
34. (1969) 2 SCC 262 : (1970) 1 SCR 457.

power conferred, the manner of exercising it and its impact on the rights of the person affected and where it is found to exist, the rules of natural justice would be attracted.

Thus in India no distinction is made between an administrative and a quasi-judicial proceeding for the purpose of application of the doctrine of natural justice. In case of non-compliance with the essential principles the aggrieved person can approach the court for issuance of writs of certiorari and prohibition against the quasi-judicial functions. At present the principles of natural justice are applicable to a wide range of administrative actions. The application of the principles of natural justice depends on the circumstances of each case, the nature of the inquiry, the subject-matter being dealt with etc. for the purpose of adhering to the standard of fairness.[35]

> The extent and application of the doctrine of natural justice cannot be imprisoned within the strait-jacket of a rigid formula. The application of the doctrine depends upon the nature of the jurisdiction conferred on the administrative authority, upon the character of the rights of the persons affected, the scheme and policy of the statute and other relevant circumstances disclosed in the particular case.[36]

5.4 PRINCIPLES OF NATURAL JUSTICE

The success of administrative adjudication is dependent on adopting a fair and transparent procedure. Adhering to the principles of natural justice holds the key to ensure an equitable adjudicatory process as it helps in achieving *justice that is simple and elementary, as distinct from justice that is complex, sophisticated and technical.*[37] The importance of the natural justice principles are generally traced to the biblical story of Adam and Eve in the Old Testament. After consuming the apple from the tree of knowledge in the Garden of Eden God had given both Adam and Eve an opportunity to explain their justification for violating the instruction of God. After hearing both of them God imposed proportionate punishments of suffering to Adam and Eve.

> "The objection for want of notice can never be got over. The laws of God and man both give the party an opportunity to make his defence, if he has any. I remember to have heard it observed by a very learned man, upon such an occasion, that even God himself did not pass sentence upon Adam before he was called upon to make his defence. 'Adam' (says God), 'where art thou?

35. *Russel v. Duke of Norfolk* (1949) 1 All ER 108.
36. *Union of India v. P.K. Roy* AIR 1968 SC 850.
37. *John v. Reese* [1969] 2 ALL ER 274.

Hast thou not eaten of the tree whereof I commanded thee that thou shouldest not eat?' And the same question was put to Eve also."[38]

Professor Wade in his book on Administrative Law has equated the importance of principles of natural justice as part of natural law. *The horizon of natural justice is constantly expanding.*[39]

The term 'natural justice' has described in different names by different judicial authorities.[40] For example it has been referred to as 'universal justice',[41] 'requirements of substantial justice',[42] 'substantial requirements of justice',[43] 'natural sense of what is right and wrong',[44] 'fundamental justice',[45] 'fair play in action',[46] 'a duty to act fairly',[47] 'a fair crack of the whip',[48] 'common fairness'[49] etc. Speaking on the different terminologies used for referring to the concept of natural justice Maugham, J., in *Maclean v. Workers Union*[50] observed–

> Eminent Judges have at times used the phrase 'the principles of natural justice'. The phrase is, of course, used only in a popular sense and must not be taken to mean that there is any justice natural among men. Among most savages there is no such thing as justice in the modern sense. In ancient days, a person wronged executed his own justice. Amongst our own ancestors, down to the thirteenth century, manifest felony, such as that of a manslayer taken with his weapon, or a thief with the stolen goods, might be punished by summary execution without any form of trial. Again every student has heard of compurgation and of ordeal; and it is hardly necessary to observe that (for example) a system of ordeal by water in which sinking was the sign of innocence and floating the sign of guilt, a system which lasted in this country for hundreds of years, has little to do with modern ideas of justice. It is unnecessary to give further illustrations. The truth is that justice is a very

38. Mr. Justice Fortescue, in *The King v. The Chancellor, &c., of Cambridge*, (*Dr. Bentley's case)* 1 Stra. 557, 2 Ld. Raym. 1334, 8 Mod. 148.
39. AIR 1970 SC 150 : (1969) 2SCC 262.
40. ***See*** generally (1985) 3 SCC 398.
41. *Drew v. Drew and Leburn* [1855) 2 Macq 1, 8.
42. *James Dunbar Smith v. Queen* (1877-78) 3 App Cas 614, 623 (PC).
43. *Arthur John Spackman v. Plumstead District Board of Works* [LR (1885) 10 App Cas 229.
44. *Vionet v. Barrett* [(1885) 55 LJ QB 39, 41.
45. *Hopkins v. Smethwick Local Board of Health* [LR (1890) 24 QBD 712.
46. *Ridge v. Baldwin* [LR (1963) I QB 539.
47. In *re H.K. (An Infant)* (1967) 1 All ER 226.
48. *Fairmount Investments Ltd. v. Secretary of State for the Environment* (1976) 2 All ER 865 (HL).
49. *Regina v. Secretary of State for Home Affairs, Ex parte Hosenball* (1977) 3 All ER 452.
50. LR (1929) I Ch 602 : 1929 WN 59 : 141 LT 83.

elaborate conception, the growth of many centuries of civilization; and even now the conception differs widely in countries usually described as civilized.

In *Rattan Lal Sharma v. Managing Committee, Dr. Hari Ram (Co-education) Higher Secondary School*[51] speaking on the importance of principles of natural justice Supreme Court observed *"In Administrative Law, rules of natural justice are foundational and fundamental concepts and law is now well settled that the principles of natural justice are part of the legal and judicial procedures."*

In *Maneka Gandhi v. Union of India*[52] the Supreme Court discussed the importance of natural in the field of administrative law–

Natural justice is a great humanising principle intended to invest law with fairness and to secure justice and over the years it has grown into a widely pervasive rule affecting large areas of administrative action. Lord Morris of Borth-y-Gest spoke of this rule in eloquent terms in his address before the Bentham Club:

"We can, I think, take pride in what has been done in recent periods and particularly in the field of administrative law by invoking and by applying these principles which we broadly classify under the designation of natural justice. Many testing problems as to their application yet re-remain to be solved. But I affirm that the area of administrative action is but one area in which the principles are to be deployed. Nor are they to be invoked only when procedural failures are shown. Does natural justice qualify to be described as a 'majestic' conception? I believe it does. Is it just a rhetorical but vague phrase which can be employed, when needed, to give a gloss of assurance? I believe that it is very much more. If it can be summarised as being fair-play in action—who could wish that it would ever be out of action? It denotes that the law is not only to be guided by reason and by logic but that its purpose will not be fulfilled; it lacks more exalted inspiration. [Current Legal Problems, 1973, Vol. 26, p. 16]"

And then again, in his speech in the House of Lords in *Wiseman v. Borneman*[53] the learned Law Lord said in words of inspired felicity:

"... that the conception of natural justice should at all stages guide those who discharge judicial functions is not merely an acceptable but is an essential part of the philosophy of the law. We often speak of the rules of natural justice. But there is nothing rigid or mechanical about them. What they comprehend has been analysed and described in many authorities. But any analysis must bring into relief rather their spirit and their inspiration than any precision of definition or precision as to application. We do not search for prescriptions

51. (1993) 4 SCC 10.
52. AIR 1978 SC 597.
53. 1971 AC 297 : (1969) 3 All ER 275.

which will lay down exactly what must, in various divergent situations, be done. The principles and procedures are to be applied which, in any particular situation or set of circumstances, are right and just and fair. Natural justice, it has been said, is only 'fair play in action'. Nor do we wait for directions from Parliament. The common law has abundant riches : there may we find what Byles, J., called 'the justice of the common law".[54]

The aim of the rules of natural justice is to secure justice or to put it negatively to prevent miscarriage of justice. These rules can operate only in areas not covered by any law validly made. In other words they do not supplant the law of the land but supplement it. The concept of natural justice has undergone a great deal of change in recent years. In the past it was thought that it included just two rules namely (1) no one shall be a judge in his own case (*Nemo debet esse judex propria causa*) and (2) no decision shall be given against a party without affording him a reasonable hearing (*audi alteram partem*). Very soon thereafter a third rule was envisaged and that is that quasi-judicial enquiries must be held in good faith, without bias and not arbitrarily or unreasonably. But in the course of years many more subsidiary rules came to be added to the rules of natural justice. Till very recently it was the opinion of the courts that unless the authority concerned was required by the law under which it functioned to act judicially there was no room for the application of the rules of natural justice. The validity of that limitation is now questioned. If the purpose of the rules of natural justice is to prevent miscarriage of justice one fails to see why those rules should be made inapplicable to administrative enquiries. Often times it is not easy to draw the line that demarcates administrative enquiries from quasi-judicial enquiries. Enquiries which were considered administrative at one time are now being considered as quasi-judicial in character. Arriving at a just decision is the aim of both quasi-judicial enquiries as well as administrative enquiries. An unjust decision in an administrative enquiry may have more far reaching effect than a decision in a quasi-judicial enquiry. As observed by this Court in *Suresh Koshy George v. The University of Kerala and Ors.*[55] the rules of natural justice are not embodied rules. These rules cannot be confined within a strait-jacket of a rigid formula.[56] What particular rule of natural justice should apply to a given case must depend to a great extent on the facts and circumstances of that case, the framework of the law under which the enquiry is held and the Constitution of the Tribunal or body of persons appointed for that purpose. Whenever a complaint is made before a court that some principle of natural justice had been contravened the court

54. Id. Para 9.
55. MANU/SC/0368/1968.
56. *Union of India v. P.K. Roy* AIR 1968 SC 850.

has to decide whether the observance of that rule was necessary for a just decision on the facts of that case.[57]

5.5 RELATIONSHIP BETWEEN PRINCIPLES OF NATURAL JUSTICE AND ARTICLE 14

In *Union of India v. Tulsiram Patel*[58] Supreme Court discussed the relationship between the principles of natural justice and Article 14 of the Constitution and observed–

> The principles of natural justice are not the creation of Article 14. Article 14 is not their begetter but their constitutional guardian. Principles of natural justice trace their ancestry to ancient civilizations and centuries long past. Until about two centuries ago the term "natural justice" was often used interchangeably with "natural law" and at times it is still so used. The expression "natural law" has been variously denned. In *Jowitt's Dictionary of English Law* (Second Edition, p. 1221) it is defined as "rules derived from God, reason or nature, as distinct from man-made law". *Black's Law Dictionary* (Fifth Edn., p. 925) states:
>
> "This expression, 'natural law', or *jus naturale*, was largely used in the philosophical speculations of the Roman jurists of the Antonine age, and was intended to denote a system of rules and principles for the guidance of human conduct which, independently of enacted law or of the systems peculiar to any one people, might be discovered by the rational intelligence of man, and would be found to grow out of and conform to his *nature*, meaning by that word his whole mental, moral, and physical constitution. The point of departure for this conception was the Stoic doctrine of a life ordered "according to nature", which in its turn rested upon the purely supposititious existence, in primitive times, of a 'state of nature'; that is, a condition of society in which men universally were governed solely by a rational and consistent obedience to the needs, impulses, and promptings of their true nature, such nature being as yet undefaced by dishonesty, falsehood, or indulgence of the baser passions. In ethics, it consists in practical universal judgments which man himself elicits. These express necessary and obligatory rules of human conduct which have been established by the author of human nature as essential to the divine purposes in the universe and have been promulgated by God solely through human reason."
>
> There are certain basic values which man has cherished throughout the ages. But man looked about him and found the ways of men to be cruel and unjust and so also their laws and customs He saw men flogged, tortured, mutilated, made slaves, and sentenced to row the galleys or to toil in the darkness of the mines or to fight in an arena with wild and hungry beasts of the jungle or

57. Id. Para 19.
58. (1985) 3 SCC 398.

to die in other ways a cruel, horrible and lingering death. He found judges to be venal and servile to those in power and the laws they administered to be capricious, changing with the whims of the ruler to suit his purpose. When, therefore, he found a system of law which did not so change, he praised it. Thus, the Old Testament in the Book of Esther (I, 19) speaks admiringly of the legal system of the Achaemenid dynasty (the First Persian Empire) in which "a royal commandment" was "written among the laws of the Persians and the Medes, that it be not altered". Man saw cities and towns sacked and pillaged, their populace dragged into captivity and condemned to slavery — the men to labour, the women and the girls to concubinage, and the young boys to be castrated into eunuchs — their only crime being that ruler had the misfortune to be defeated in battle and to lose one of his cities or towns to the enemy. Thus, there was neither hope nor help in man-made laws or man-established customs for they were one-sided and oppressive, intended to benefit armed might and monied power and to subjugate the downtrodden poor and the helpless needy. If there was any help to be found or any hope to be discovered, it was only in a law based on justice and reason which transcended the laws and customs of man, a law made by someone greater and mightier than those men who made these laws and established these customs. Such a person could only be a divine being and such a law could only be "natural law" or "the law of nature" meaning thereby "certain rules of conduct supposed to be so just that they are binding upon all mankind". It was not "the law of nature" in the sense of "the law of the jungle" where the lion devours the lamb and the tiger feeds upon the antelope because the lion is hungry and the tiger famished but a higher law of nature or "the natural law" where the lion and the lamb lie down together and the tiger frisks with the antelope.

Most, if not all, jurists are agreed that "reason" and "the nature of man" constitute the fountain-head of natural law but there is a considerable divergence of opinion amongst them as also amongst philosophers about the nature and meaning of that law and its relation to positive law. Among the ancient Greeks the Sophists, Aristotle in his treatises on "Logic" and "*Ethics*", and the Stoics developed different theories. The theory propounded by Aristotle in his "*Logic*" adhered substantially to the point of view of the Sophists, namely, that man is a natural creature but is also endowed with reason. Later, in his "*Ethics*", Aristotle came to distinguish between natural and legal or conventional justice and postulated that natural law had authority everywhere and was discoverable by the use of reason. The ancient Romans were not given to philosophical speculations or creative originality in Article They preferred to borrow these from the Greeks. The Romans were a hard-headed, practical race of conquerors, administrators and legislators. Roman jurists, therefore, used the concept of natural law, that is, *jus naturale* or *ius naturale* as the Romans wrote it because Roman alphabet had no letter 'J' or 'J' in it) to introduce into the body of law those parts of laws and customs of foreigners, that is, non-Roman people with whom they came in commercial contract or whom they subjugated. The rules which the Romans borrowed from these laws and customs were those which were capable of general application and they developed them into general legal principles, which came to form *jus gentium* or the law of nations. In doing so they acted upon the principle that any rule of law which was common to the nations (*gentes*) they knew of must be basically in consonance with reason and, therefore, fundamentally just. They applied *jus gentium* to those to whom *ius civile* (civil law) did not apply, that is, in cases between foreigners or between a Roman citizen and a foreigner. On this basic formulation that what was common to all known nations must be in consonance with reason and justice, the Roman jurists and Magistrates proceeded to the theory that any rule which instinctively commanded itself to the sense of justice and reason would be part of the *jus gentium*. The *jus gentium* of the Romans was different from what we call international law and should not be confused with it, for the scope of the *jus gentium* was much wider than our international law. Because of the theory of its identity with justice and reason, the term "*jus gentium*" came at times to be used for *aequitas*, that is, equity as understood by the Romans, which was the basis of praetorian law or the power of the praetors to grant remedies where none existed under the *jus civile*. In the Dark Ages the expression "natural law" acquired a theological base and the Fathers of the Church, particularly St. Ambrose, St. Augustine and St. Gregory, held the belief that it was the function of the Church to bring about the best possible approximation of human laws to Christian principles. As Europe emerged from the Dark Ages in about the ninth century, Christianity became substituted for reason as the supreme force in the universe; and this led to the development of a theory of law in which Christianity had the supreme spiritual and legal force and was superior to all other laws, with the Church as the authentic expositor of the law of nature. Gratian (Francisco Graziano) in the twelfth century in his "*Decretum*" or "*Concordia discordantium canonum*" considered the law of nature as part of the law of God. According to St. Thomas Aquinas (1226-74), natural law was derived from the law of God which was supreme and such of it as was intelligible to men was revealed through Church law as the incorporation of divine wisdom. Thus, according to this theory, natural law was that part of divine law which revealed itself in natural reason, and man as a reasonable being applied this part of divine law to human affairs. This theory, though it upheld the supreme authority of the Church, made some concession to the authority of the Emperor, that is, the Holy Roman Emperor. Dante in his "*De Monarchia*" championed the supremacy of the Holy Roman Empire as against the Church on the ground that the Emperor was the legitimate successor of the Roman people and was chosen by God to rule the world. The authority of the law of nature or natural law was repeatedly sought support from during the centuries which saw the struggle for supremacy between the Popes and the General Councils of the Church and between the Popes and the Emperors and later in the struggle between the Catholics and the Protestants. Both sides in these conflicts found in natural law the interpretation of scriptural texts which supported their respective views and were, therefore, according to them, the true interpretation. Bracton, in the thirteenth century, however, considered natural law as that which nature, that is, God, teaches to all animals, and though he tried to reconcile natural law with human law, he acknowledged the difficulty of doing so because he found rules of positive law which could hardly be so reconciled.[59]

.....

The principles of natural justice have thus come to be recognized as being a part of the guarantee contained in Article 14 because of the new and dynamic interpretation given by this Court to the concept of equality which is the subject-matter of that article. Shortly put, the syllogism runs thus: violation of a rule of natural justice results in arbitrariness which is the same as discrimination; where discrimination is the result of State action, it is a violation of Article 14: therefore, a violation of a principle of natural justice by a State action is a violation of Article 14. Article 14, however, is not the sole repository of the principles of natural justice. What it does is to guarantee that any law or State action violating them will be struck down. The principles of natural justice, however, apply not only to legislation and State action but also where any tribunal, authority or body of men, not coming within the definition of State in Article 12, is charged with the duty of deciding a matter. In such a case, the principles of natural justice require that it must decide such matter fairly and impartially.[60]

Traditionally there are two core principles of natural justice[61]–

(a) *Audi alteram partem* or Right of Hearing–

- No one should be condemned unheard.
- Hear the other side or both the sides must be heard
- There must be fairness on the part of the deciding authority

It implies that the judge must give parties of both the sides a reasonable opportunity to put their case before the judge and only thereafter the judge would impose a penalty on one party and vindicate the rights of the other party.

(b) *Nemo debet esse judex in propria causa* or Rule against Bias–

- No one shall be a judge in his own cause.
- No man can act as both at the one and the same time as part or a suitor and also as a judge.
- Deciding authority must be fairness on the part of the deciding authority.

It implies that in a dispute the judge should be an independent and neutral third party in order to ensure fairness in the adjudication process. These principles form the foundational basis of an adversarial legal system. The adversarial legal model is based on the core ideals that the litigating

59. Supra note 58.
60. Id. Para 95.
61. AIR 2011 SC 3711 : 2011 (6) SCALE 97.

parties shall put forth their legal arguments before a neutral third party judge who after hearing the legal and the factual arguments of both the sides and after perusing through the evidentiary materials will give his decision after applying his rationality and principles of law to the facts and issue of the case. Thus the adversarial model is essentially dependent on the two pillars of independent and neutral judge on one hand and providing hearing to both the sides on the other hand. The importance of these principles can be traced from ancient to modernity through the medieval period. In *Union of India v. Tulsiram Patel*[62] it was observed–

> How then have the principles of natural justice been interpreted in the courts and within what limits are they to be confined? Over the years by a process of judicial interpretation two rules have been evolved as representing the principles of natural justice in judicial process, including therein quasi-judicial and administrative processes. They constitute the basic elements of a fair hearing, having their roots in the innate sense of man for fair play and justice which is not the preserve of any particular race or country but is shared in common by all men. The first rule is "*nemo judex in causa sua*" or "*nemo debet esse judex in propria causa*" as stated in the *Earl of Derby*'s *case*[63] that is, "no man shall be a judge in his own cause". Coke used the form "*aliquis non debet esse judex in propria causa, quia non potest esse judex et pars*" (Co. Litt. 141-a), that is, "no man ought to be a judge in his own cause, because he cannot act as a judge and at the same time be a party". The form "*nemo potest esse simul actor et judex*", that is, "no one can be at once suitor and judge" is also at times used. The second rule—and that is the rule with which we are concerned in these appeals and writ petitions—is "audi alteram partem", that is, "hear the other side". At times and particularly in continental countries the form "*audietur et altera pars*" is used, meaning very much the same thing. A corollary has been deduced from the above two rules and particularly the audi alteram partem rule, namely, "*qui aliquid statuerit, parte inaudita altera aequum licet dixerit, hand aequum fecerit*", that is, "he who shall decide anything without the other side having been heard, although he may have said what is right, will not have done what is right" (**see** *Boswell case*[64]) or, in other words, as it is now expressed, "justice should not only be done but should manifestly be seen to be done".
>
> The above two rules and their corollary are neither new nor were they the discovery of English judges. They were recognized in many civilizations and over many centuries. Roman law recognized the need for a judge to be impartial and not to have a personal interest in the case before him (Digest V.I. 17) and Tacitus in his "*Dialogus*" referred to this principle. Under Roman law a judge who heard a cause in which he had an interest was liable as on a quasi-delict to the party prejudiced thereby (Justinian's Institutes IV, 5 pr.;

62. (1985) 3 SCC 398.
63. (1613) 12 Co Rep 114.
64. (1606) 6 Co Rep 48-b, 52-a.

as also Justinian's Codex III, 5, 1). Even the Kiganda tribesmen of Buganda have an old proverb which literally translated means "a monkey does not decide an affair of the forest" (**See** *Law and Justice in Buganda* by E.S. Haydon, p. 333). The requirement of hearing both sides before arriving at a decision was part of the judicial oath in Athens. It also formed the subject-matter of a proverb which was often referred to or quoted by Greek playwrights, as for instance, by Aritophanes in his comedy *The Wasps* and Euripides in his tragedies *Heracleidae* and *Andromache*, and by Greek orators, for instance, Demosthenes in his speech *De Corona.* Among the Romans, Seneca in his tragedy *Medea* referred to the injustice of coming to a decision without a full hearing. In fact, the corollary drawn in *Boswell case* is taken from a line in Seneca's *Medea.* In The Gospel according to St. John (vii, 51), Nicodemus asked the chief priests and the Pharisees, "Doth our law judge any man, before it hear him, and know what he doeth?" Even the proverbs and songs of African tribesmen, for instance, of the Lozi tribe in Barotseland refer to this rule (**See** *The Judicial Process Among the Barotse of Northern Rhodesia* by Max Gluckman, p. 102).

The above two rules and their corollary are neither new nor were they the discovery of English judges. They were recognized in many civilizations and over many centuries. Roman law recognized the need for a judge to be impartial and not to have a personal interest in the case before him (Digest V.I. 17) and Tacitus in his "*Dialogus*" referred to this principle. Under Roman law a judge who heard a cause in which he had an interest was liable as on a quasi-delict to the party prejudiced thereby (Justinian's Institutes IV, 5 pr.; as also Justinian's Codex III, 5, 1). Even the Kiganda tribesmen of Buganda have an old proverb which literally translated means "a monkey does not decide an affair of the forest" (**See** *Law and Justice in Buganda* by E.S. Haydon, p. 333). The requirement of hearing both sides before arriving at a decision was part of the judicial oath in Athens. It also formed the subject-matter of a proverb which was often referred to or quoted by Greek playwrights, as for instance, by Aritophanes in his comedy *The Wasps* and Euripides in his tragedies *Heracleidae* and *Andromache*, and by Greek orators, for instance, Demosthenes in his speech *De Corona.* Among the Romans, Seneca in his tragedy *Medea* referred to the injustice of coming to a decision without a full hearing. In fact, the corollary drawn in *Boswell case* is taken from a line in Seneca's *Medea.* In The Gospel according to St. John (vii, 51), Nicodemus asked the chief priests and the Pharisees, "Doth our law judge any man, before it hear him, and know what he doeth?" Even the proverbs and songs of African tribesmen, for instance, of the Lozi tribe in Barotseland refer to this rule (see *The Judicial Process Among the Barotse of Northern Rhodesia* by Max Gluckman, p. 102).[65]

In medieval England the sanctity of the principles of natural justice were so high that even Parliament was prohibited from violating the same. In

65. Ibid Para 84 - 86.

the famous case of *Dr. Bonham (1610)* Chief Justice Coke had observed that an Act of Parliament would be deemed void if it 'made a man judge in his own cause or was against common right and reason.'

In modern day the theory of natural justice has found its application in a new way. The principle of natural justice does not imply destroying any enacted law but as a means of fulfilling its true objective. It also helps in making better interpretation of laws. Courts generally presume that Parliament when it grants powers intends them to be exercised in a right and proper way. Since Parliament is very unlikely to make provision to the contrary it allows considerable scope for the courts to devise a set of canons of fair administrative procedure, suitable to the needs of the time. The courts have used the natural justice principles to develop a code of fair administrative procedure. The fundamental task of courts is to control the substance of what public authorities do by means of the rules relating to reasonableness, improper purpose etc. By applying the principles of natural justice they can control the procedure by which the public authorities act.

In modern day state the principles of natural justice have an important role to play in the numerous discretionary administrative power. The more the power of the State it is all the more essential that such powers are exercised in a procedurally fair manner. This is because it is deemed that continuous increase of State power can be tolerated by people if the procedure used in the exercise of such power is fair. The judiciary has developed new facets of principles of natural justice to comply with the norms of fairness and have applied them to judicial, quasi-judicial and administrative actions.[66]

The case of *A.R. Antulay v. R.S. Nayak*[67] is landmark case wherein the Supreme Court recognizing the importance of principles of natural justice invalidated an earlier order passed by themselves as the order was made contrary to the norms of fair procedure. In an earlier proceeding the Supreme Court had passed an order stating that the corruption charges made against the appellant under the provisions of the Prevention of Corruption Act will be heard by a Judge of the High Court on a day to day basis. These directions were issued without any pleadings or arguments and without giving any opportunity to the appellant to make his submissions. An appeal was made against such orders by the appellant on the ground that under Section 6 of the Prevention of Corruption Act the State Government is required to appoint Special Judges to deal with the specified offences under the Act, hence the Supreme Court by its power to transfer cases could have only transferred it to another Special Judge appointed under the Act and not to

66. *Justice P.D. Dinakaran v. Hon'ble Judges Inquiry Committee,* AIR 2011 SC 3711 : 2011 (6) SCALE 97.
67. AIR 1988 SC 1531.

the High Court. In addition, the order of the Supreme Court transferring the case to the High Court was not authorized by law and the Supreme Court did not have the power to confer jurisdiction – the power to create or enlarge jurisdiction is legislative in character and it is Parliament alone which has the power to confer a right of appeal or to take away a right of appeal. The appellant had claimed that the passing of such orders were in violation of Articles 14, 19 and 21 and also the principles of natural justice as the orders were passed without giving any opportunity of being heard. The various rights infringed by the order are–

(i) Right to be tried by Special Judge in accordance with the procedure established by law;
(ii) Right of revision to the High Court under Section 9 of CrPC;
(iii) Right of First appeal to the High Court; and
(iv) Right to move Supreme Court under Article 136 as a second appeal.

Upholding the contentions of the appellant the Supreme Court observed that–

> We are clearly of the opinion that the right of the appellant under Article 14 regarding equality before the law and equal protection of law in this case has been violated. The appellant has also a right not to be singled out for special treatment by a Special Court created for him alone. This right is implicit in the right to equality. See Anwar Ali Sarkar's case (supra).
>
> Here the appellant has a further right under Article 21 of the Constitution a right to trial by a Special Judge under Section 7(1) of the 1952 Act which is the procedure established by law made by the Parliament, and a further right to move the High Court by way of revision or first appeal under Section 9 of the said Act. He has also a right not to suffer any order passed behind his back by a Court in violation of the basic principles of natural justice. Directions having been given in this case as we have seen without hearing the appellant though it appears from the circumstances that the order was passed in the presence of the counsel for the appellant, these were bad.[68]
>
> ....
>
> The directions were in deprival of Constitutional rights and contrary to the express provisions of the Act of 1952. The directions were given in violation of the principles of natural justice. The directions were without precedent in the background of the Act of 1952. The directions definitely deprived the appellant of certain rights of appeal and revision and his rights under the Constitution.[69]

68. Ibid Para 57-58.
69. Id. Para 77.

The Court concluded by holding that *the principle of finality on which the Article proceeds applies to both judgments and orders made by the Supreme Court. But directions given per incuriam and in violation of certain constitutional limitations and in derogation of the principles of natural justice can always be remedied by the court ex debite justitiae.*

5.6 RULE AGAINST BIAS

The term bias refers to 'a predisposition to decide for or against one party, without proper regard to the true merits of the dispute'.[70] Speaking on the importance of rule against bias Lord Denning had made the famous observation *'justice must be rooted in confidence; and confidence is destroyed when right-minded people go away thinking: 'The judge was biased.'*

The traditional English law of rule against bias is based on three maxims–

(i) No one shall be a judge in his own cause;

(ii) Justice should not only be done, but manifestly and undoubtedly be seen to be done; and

(iii) Judges, like Caesar's wife should be above suspicion.

These principles form the basis of a fair and impartial judicial system. Article 14.1 of the International Covenant on Civil and Political Rights has insisted that 'everyone shall be entitled to a fair and public hearing by a competent independent and *impartial* tribunal established by law.' The term 'impartiality' has been explained by the UN Human Rights Committee as implying that *judges must not harbour preconceptions about the matter put before them, and ... they must not act in ways that promote the interests of one of the parties ... A trial flawed by the participation of a judge who, under domestic statutes, should have been disqualified cannot normally be considered to be fair or impartial within the meaning of Article 14.* The appearance of justice is an essential ingredient of *actuality of justice* because the foundation of a judicial system is based on *appearance of impartiality both to the public and to the community.*

In *Justice P.D. Dinakaran v. Hon'ble Judges Inquiry Committee*[71] explained these propositions in the following words–

> The first requirement of natural justice is that the Judge should be impartial and neutral and must be free from bias. He is supposed to be indifferent to the parties to the controversy. He cannot act as Judge of a cause in which

70. Secretary to *Government, Transport Department v. Munuswamy Mudaliar,* 1988 (Supp.) SCC 651.

71. AIR 2011 SC 3711 : 2011 (6) SCALE 97.

> he himself has some interest either pecuniary or otherwise as it affords the strongest proof against neutrality. He must be in a position to act judicially and to decide the matter objectively. A Judge must be of sterner stuff. His mental equipoise must always remain firm and undetected. He should not allow his personal prejudice to go into the decision-making. The object is not merely that the scales be held even; it is also that they may not appear to be inclined. If the Judge is subject to bias in favour of or against either party to the dispute or is in a position that a bias can be assumed, he is disqualified to act as a Judge, and the proceedings will be vitiated. This rule applies to the judicial and administrative authorities required to act judicially or quasi-judicially.[72]

The real question is not whether a person is biased or not. It is difficult to prove the state of mind of a person. There must be reasonable ground for believing that a person was likely to have been biased. Mere suspicion of bias is not sufficient. There must be reasonable likelihood of bias. The test of bias should be based into taken consideration of human probabilities and ordinary course of human conduct.

One of the earliest cases on the issue of bias was *A.K. Kraipak v. Union of India.*[73] Naquishbund one of the applicants was also appointed as a member of the selection board. Supreme Court negating the selection process held that '*it is against all canons of justice to make a man judge in his own cause'*. The Court categorically observed–

> It is true that he did not participate in the deliberations of the committee when his name was considered. But then the very fact that he was a member of the selection board must have had its own impact on the decision of the selection board. Further admittedly he participated in the deliberations of the selection board when the claims of his rivals particularly that of Basu was considered He was also party to the preparation of the list of selected candidates in order of preference. At every stage of this participation in the deliberations of the selection board there was a conflict between his interest and duty. Under those circumstances it is difficult to believe that he could have been impartial. The real question is not whether he was biased. It is difficult to prove the state of mind of a person. Therefore what we have to see is whether there is reasonable ground for believing that he was likely to have been biased.[74]

5.7 SUBTLE FORM OF BIAS

In *A.K. Kraipak v.Union of India*[75] an important question was whether there can be subtle bias. The members of the selection committee had asserted

72. Id. Para 25.
73. AIR 1970 SC 150 : (1969) 2SCC 262.
74. Id. Para 15.
75. AIR 1970 SC 150 : (1969) 2SCC 262.

that the presence of Naqishbund had not influenced their decision making. Supreme Court negated the argument and observed–

> In a group deliberation each member of the group is bound to influence the others, more so, if the member concerned is a person with special knowledge. His bias is likely to operate in a subtle manner. It is no wonder that the other members of the selection board are unaware of the extent to which his opinion influenced their conclusions. We are unable to accept the contention that in adjudging the suitability of the candidates the members of the board did not have any mutual discussion. It is not as if the records spoke of themselves. We are unable to believe that the members of selection board functioned like computers.[76]

5.8 TYPES OF BIAS

Bias can be of different nature. The different forms of bias have adopted different standards for disqualifying a person to act as a judge.

5.8.1 Pecuniary Bias

Pecuniary bias or interest, however small, disqualifies a person from acting as a judge.[77] Any form of financial or proprietary interest in the outcome of a case will be interpreted as sitting as a judge in his own cause and will be sufficient for his automatic disqualification.

In *The Queen v. Rand*[78] the core issue was whether two of the judges who were trustees of a hospital and a charitable society respectively, each of which had lent money to Bradford Corporation on bonds charging the corporate fund, were disqualified to act as judges in the case involving issuance of certificates in favour of the corporation for withdrawing water without authorization from the mill owners. Negating the contention Blackburn J laid down the test of pecuniary bias–

> ... There is no doubt that any direct pecuniary interest, however small, in the subject of inquiry, does disqualify a person from acting as a judge in the matter; and if by any possibility these gentlemen, though mere trustees, could have been liable to costs, or to other pecuniary loss or gain, in consequence of their being so, we should think the question different from what it is: for that might be held an interest. But the only way in which the facts could affect their impartiality, would be that they might have a tendency to favour those for whom they were trustees; and that is an objection not in the nature of interest, but of a challenge to the favour. Wherever there is a

76. Id Para 16.
77. AIR 2011 SC 3711 : 2011 (6) SCALE 97.
78. (1866) LR 1 (QBD) 230.

real likelihood that the judge would, from kindred or any other cause, have a bias in favour of one of the parties, it would be very wrong in him to act; and we are not to be understood to say, that where there is a real bias of this sort this Court would not interfere; but in the present case there is no ground for doubting that the justices acted perfectly *bona fide;* and the only question is, whether in strict law, under such circumstances, the certificate of such justices is void, as it would be if they had a pecuniary interest; and we think that *Reg. v. Dean of Rochester* (1) is an authority, that circumstances, from which a suspicion of favour may arise, do not produce the same effect as a pecuniary interest....

The concept of pecuniary bias is based on the core idea that any form of financial interest, including even a miniscule amount then it would vitiate the administrative action. In the *Halsbury's Laws of England*[79] it has been observed–

Disqualification for financial interest. There is a presumption that any direct financial interest, however small, in the matter in dispute disqualifies a person from adjudicating. Membership of a company, association or other organization which is financially interested may operate as a bar to adjudicating, as may a bare liability to casts where the decision itself will involve no pecuniary loss.

The leading case on pecuniary bias is *J. Mohapatra & Co. v. State of Orissa.*[80] In Orissa there was no statutory rule or regulation prescribing the method for selection of books for general reading to be kept in school and college libraries. The general practice was that the State Government would periodically issue administrative instructions in the form of Government Resolutions constituting committees and lay down procedures for selecting books. As per such instructions three committees were to be constituted – Assessment Sub-Committee, Distribution Sub-Committee and Purchase Committee. The procedure which was generally followed was that the Member-Secretary of the Purchase Committee through advertisements in newspaper called upon publishers and authors to submit books for consideration. The Assessment Sub-Committee then considered the books submitted and recommended a list of books which were deemed suitable for general reading by school and college students. Thereafter the Purchase Committee prepared the final list based on the recommendations of the Assessment Sub-Committee. The State Government had the discretion to reject a book from the list without assigning any reason and the decision of the State Government was final. This procedure was generally followed

79. Halsbury's Laws of England, Fourth Edition, Volume 1, para 68.
80. AIR 1984 SC 1572 , MANU/SC/0008/1984.

each year and there was very rarely any change in the composition of the members of the Committees. Some of the members of the Assessment Sub-Committees were themselves authors of books and some of the books written by them were selected and purchased. The selection of books in the years 1980, 1981 and 1982 were made in that particular fashion. In 1982 due to unprecedented floods and cyclones many schools and colleges, including their libraries were damaged. The Central Government thereupon granted an amount of Rs 45 lakhs for purchase of books for libraries. Since it was a time bound grant the State Government decided to purchase those books which were selected for the previous three years. This decision of the State Government was subsequently challenged through a writ petition before the High Court by the appellants who were book publishers. The Appellants claimed for quashing of the list of books selected for the years 1980, 1981 and 1982 on the ground of bias on the part of some of the members of the Assessment Sub-committee whose books were submitted for selection. The writ petition before the High Court was dismissed and an appeal was made to the Supreme Court. The Court upheld the claims of the appellants on the ground of pecuniary bias. Applying the rationale in the *A.K. Kraipak case* the Court observed that–

> [A] person who has written a book which is submitted for selection, either by himself or by his publisher, is interested in the matter of selection. Authors get their books published by publishers or may themselves publish them. In either case, they stand to benefit financially. In the first case, by getting royalty from publishers and in the second case, by making profits on the sale of books if the amount realized exceeds the cost of publication, or if the sales are not to that extent, by reducing the cost incurred in the publication of the book.... The amount of royalty depends on the agreement between the author and the publisher as also upon the sale price of the book. The fact, however, remains that by the books being selected and purchased for distribution to school and college libraries the sales of those books had gone up and correspondingly the royalty received by the author-members also went up and such author-members thus received financial benefit. It is no answer to say that an author-member is only one of the members of the Assessment Sub-Committee and that the ultimate decision rests with the State Government which may reject any book out of the list of approved books. A similar argument was rejected by this Court in *Kraipak's case.* The State Government would normally be guided by the list approved by the Assessment Sub-Committee. Further, to say that such author-member is only one of the members of the Assessment Sub-Committee is to overlook the fact that the author-member can subtly influence the minds of the other members against selecting books by other authors in preference to his own. It can also be that books by some of the other members may also have been submitted for selection and there can be between them a quid pro quo or, in other words, you see that my book is selected and in return I will

> do the same for you. In either case, when a book of an author-member comes up for consideration, the other members would feel themselves embarrassed in frankly discussing its merits. Such author-member may also be a person holding a high official position whom the other members may not want to displease. It can be that the other members may not be influenced by the fact that the book which they are considering for approval was written by one of their members. Whether they were so influenced or not is, however, a matter impossible to determine. It is not, therefore, the actual bias in favour of the author-member that is material but the possibility of such bias. All these considerations require that an author-member should not be a member of any such committee or sub-committee.
>
> ......
>
> Mere non-participation in the discussion by the member concerned or even his withdrawing from the deliberations of the committee while his or her book or books are being considered is not sufficient because the evil of quid pro quo cannot be eliminated by this. Members deliberating would bear in mind that the turn for selecting their books would also come and the concerned member who had not participated or had withdrawn would not then be favourably inclined to select their books"[81]

5.8.2 Non-pecuniary Interest

In *R. v. Bow Street Metropolitan Stipendiary Magistrate ex parte Pinochet Ugarte* the House of Lords applied the 'alter ego' theory as a ground for personal bias. In this review petition the ground for seeking quashing of the decision of the House of Lords on the ground of bias was whether the presence of Lord Hoffman as one of the Law Lords and who constituted the majority of the House of Lords, and who was also a director and chairperson of Amnesty International Charity Limited, was disqualified from being party in the proceedings of an appeal in which Amnesty International was granted leave to intervene. While dealing with the review petition Lord Browne-Wilkinson held that *there was no allegation that Lord Hoffman was in fact biased but the argument was that there was a real danger or reasonable apprehension or suspicion that Lord Hoffman might have been biased.* He clarified the rule against bias by observing–

> The fundamental principle is that a man may not be a judge in his own cause. This principle, as developed by the courts, has two very similar but not identical implications. First it may be applied literally: if a judge is in fact a party to the litigation or has a financial or proprietary interest in its outcome then he is indeed sitting as a judge in his own cause. In that case, the mere fact that he is a party to the action or has a financial or proprietary interest

81. Supra note 80.

in its outcome is sufficient to cause his automatic disqualification. The second application of the principle is where a judge is not a party to the suit and does not have a financial interest in its outcome, but in some other way his conduct or behaviour may give rise to a suspicion that he is not impartial, for example because of his friendship with a party. This second type of case is not strictly speaking an application of the principle that a man must not be judge in his own cause, since the judge will not normally be himself benefiting, but providing a benefit for another by failing to be impartial.

In my judgment, this case falls within the first category of case, viz. where the judge is disqualified because he is a judge in his own cause. In such a case, once it is shown that the judge is himself a party to the cause, or has a relevant interest in its subject matter, he is disqualified without any investigation into whether there was a likelihood or suspicion of bias. The mere fact of his interest is sufficient to disqualify him unless he has made sufficient disclosure: **See** Shetreet Judges on Trial (1976) p 303 and De Smith, Woolf and Jowell Judicial Review of Administrative Action (5th edn, 1995) p 525. I will call this 'automatic disqualification'.

xxx xxx xxx xxx

The importance of this point in the present case is this. Neither AI, nor AICL, have any financial interest in the outcome of this litigation. We are here confronted, as was Lord Hoffmann, with a novel situation where the outcome of the litigation did not lead to financial benefit to anyone. The interest of AI in the litigation was not financial; it was its interest in achieving the trial and possible conviction of Senator Pinochet for crimes against humanity.

By seeking to intervene in this appeal and being allowed so to intervene, in practice AI became a party to the appeal. Therefore if, in the circumstances, it is right to treat Lord Hoffmann as being the alter ego of AI and therefore a judge in his own cause, then he must have been automatically disqualified on the grounds that he was a party to the appeal. Alternatively, even if it be not right to say that Lord Hoffmann was a party to the appeal as such, the question then arises whether, in non-financial litigation, anything other than a financial or proprietary interest in the outcome is sufficient automatically to disqualify a man from sitting as judge in the cause.

Are the facts such as to require Lord Hoffmann to be treated as being himself a party to this appeal? The facts are striking and unusual. One of the parties to the appeal is an unincorporated association, AI. One of the constituent parts of that unincorporated association is AICL. AICL was established, for tax purposes, to carry out part of the functions of AI-those parts which were charitable-which had previously been carried on either by AI itself or by AIL. Lord Hoffmann is a director and chairman of AICL, which is wholly controlled by AI, since its members (who ultimately control it) are all the members of the international executive committee of AI. A large part of the work of AI is, as a matter of strict law, carried on by AICL which instructs AIL to do the work on its behalf. In reality, AI, AICL and AIL are a close-knit group carrying on the work of AI.

However, close as these links are, I do not think it would be right to identify Lord Hoffmann personally as being a party to the appeal. He is closely linked to AI but he is not in fact AI. Although this is an area in which legal technicality is particularly to be avoided, it cannot be ignored that Lord Hoffmann took no part in running AI. Lord Hoffmann, AICL and the executive committee of AI are in law separate people.

Then is this a case in which it can be said that Lord Hoffmann had an 'interest' which must lead to his automatic disqualification? Hitherto only pecuniary and proprietary interests have led to automatic disqualification. But, as I have indicated, this litigation is most unusual. It is not civil litigation but criminal litigation. Most unusually, by allowing AI to intervene, there is a party to a criminal cause or matter who is neither prosecutor nor accused. That party, AI, shares with the government of Spain and the CPS, not a financial interest but an interest to establish that there is no immunity for ex-heads of state in relation to crimes against humanity. The interest of these parties is to procure Senator Pinochet's extradition and trial-a non-pecuniary interest. So far as AICL is concerned, cl (c) of its memorandum provides that one of its objects is 'to procure the abolition of torture, extra-judicial execution and disappearance'. AI has, amongst other objects, the same objects. Although AICL, as a charity, cannot campaign to change the law, it is concerned by other means to procure the abolition of these crimes against humanity. In my opinion, therefore, AICL plainly had a non-pecuniary interest, to establish that Senator Pinochet was not immune.

That being the case, the question is whether in the very unusual circumstances of this case a non-pecuniary interest to achieve a particular result is sufficient to give rise to automatic disqualification and, if so, whether the fact that AICL had such an interest necessarily leads to the conclusion that Lord Hoffmann, as a director of AICL, was automatically disqualified from sitting on the appeal? My Lords, in my judgment, although the cases have all dealt with automatic disqualification on the grounds of pecuniary interest, there is no good reason in principle for so limiting automatic disqualification. The rationale of the whole rule is that a man cannot be a judge in his own cause. In civil litigation the matters in issue will normally have an economic impact; therefore a judge is automatically disqualified if he stands to make a financial gain as a consequence of his own decision of the case. But if, as in the present case, the matter at issue does not relate to money or economic advantage but is concerned with the promotion of the cause, the rationale disqualifying a judge applies just as much if the judge's decision will lead to the promotion of a cause in which the judge is involved together with one of the parties. Thus in my opinion if Lord Hoffmann had been a member of AI he would have been automatically disqualified because of his non-pecuniary interest in establishing that Senator Pinochet was not entitled to Immunity. Indeed, so much I understood to have been conceded by Mr Duffy.

> Can it make any difference that, instead of being a direct member of AI, Lord Hoffmann is a director of AICL, that is of a company which is wholly controlled by AI and is carrying on much of its work? Surely not. The substance of the matter is that AI, AIL and AICL are all various parts of an entity or movement working in different fields towards the same goals. If the absolute impartiality of the judiciary is to be maintained, there must be a rule which automatically" disqualifies a judge who is involved, whether personally or as a director of a company, in promoting the same causes in the same organisation as is a party to the suit. There is no room for fine distinctions if Lord Hewart CJ's famous dictum is to be observed: it is 'of fundamental importance that justice should not only be done, but should manifestly and undoubtedly be seen to be done.

Similar view was taken by the Indian Supreme Court in *Bhajan Lal, Chief Minister v. Jindal Strips Ltd.*[82] wherein it was recognized that *the decision-maker should have no interest by way of gain or detriment in the outcome of a proceeding. Interest may take many forms. It may be direct, it may be indirect, it may arise from a personal relationship or from a relationship with the subject-matter, from a close relationship or from a tenuous one. In the case of non-pecuniary bias, as alleged in the instant case, regard is to be had to the extent and nature of interest. Then alone, the judge will be disqualified.*

5.8.3 Personal Bias

The first essential principle of personal bias is that if the judge is a party to a litigation or is having some interest in the dispute then it will be deemed to be sitting as a judge in his own cause. In such a case the mere fact that of his presence will be sufficient to cause his automatic disqualification.

In the landmark case of *Rex v. Sussex Justices, Ex Parte McCarthy*[83] the core principle that justice should not only be done, but manifestly and undoubtedly be seen to be done as an integral part of rule against bias was laid down. In this case a collision had taken place between the applicant riding a motor cycle and another motorcycle driven by one Whitworth, wherein Whitworth and his wife suffered from serious injuries. In an accident claim for damages filed by Messrs Langham, Son & Douglas on behalf of Whitworth, the applicant's lawyer raised an objection to the imposition of fine on the ground that the deputy clerk of the justices hearing the case had retired with the judges after the hearing of the case. It was argued that the deputy clerk was a brother of Mr. F.G. Langham and was also a partner in the firm Langham, Son & Douglas and so was interested as a

82. (1994) 6 SCC 19.
83. (1924) 1 KB 256.

solicitor for Whitworth in the conviction of the applicant. It was further challenged on the ground that it was irregular for a deputy clerk to retire with the judges when they are deliberating over the decision. Quashing the conviction on the ground of bias Lord Hewart C.J. raised the question of *"The question therefore is not whether in this case the deputy clerk made any observation or offered any criticism which he might not properly have made or offered; the question is whether he was so related to the case in its civil aspect as to be unfit to act as clerk to the justices in the criminal matter."* He further observed:

> ...The answer to that question depends not upon what actually was done but upon what might appear to be done. Nothing is to be done which creates even a suspicion that there has been an improper interference with the course of justice. Speaking for myself, I accept the statements contained in the justices' affidavit, but they show very clearly that the deputy clerk was connected with the case in a capacity which made it right that he should scrupulously abstain from referring to the matter in any way, although he retired with the justices; in other words, his one position was such that he could not, if he had been required to do so, discharge the duties which his other position involved. His twofold position was a manifest contradiction. In those circumstances I am satisfied that this conviction must be quashed, unless it can be shown that the applicant or his solicitor was aware of the point that might be taken, refrained from taking it, and took his chance of an acquittal on the facts, and then, on a conviction being recorded, decided to take the point....

In *Meenglas Tea Estate v. Its Workmen*[84] Supreme Court reaffirmed the decision of the West Bengal Industrial Tribunal to re-instate the workmen who were dismissed by the appellant. On January 18, 1956 in an assault with the workmen the Manager and the two Assistant Managers were injured confrontation between the workmen and the managers of the tea estate. The company had initiated proceedings against some of the workers – they were first issued a notice of suspension and were then served with charge-sheet charging them with participation in the riot. After the enquiry the workmen were dismissed from service. On appeal to the Industrial Tribunal it was held that the enquiry was vitiated for failure to comply with the principles of natural justice. Supreme Court upheld the order of the tribunal and observed–

> It is an elementary principle that a person who is required to answer a charge must know not only the accusation but also the testimony by which the accusation is supported. He must be given a fair chance to hear the evidence in support of the charge and to put such relevant questions by way of cross-examination as he desires. Then he must be given a chance to rebut

84. AIR 1963 SC 1719.

> the evidence led against him. This is the barest requirement of an enquiry of this character and this requirement must be substantially fulfilled before the result of the enquiry can be accepted. A departure from this requirement in effect throws the burden upon the person charged to repel the charge without first making it out against him. In the present case neither was any witness examined nor was any statement made by any witness tendered in evidence. The enquiry, such as it was, was made by Mr. Marshall or Mr. Nichols who were not only in the position of judges but also of prosecutors and witnesses. There was no opportunity to the persons charged to cross-examine them and indeed they drew upon their own knowledge of the incident and instead cross-examined the persons charged. This was such a travesty of the principles of natural justice that the Tribunal was justified in rejecting the findings and asking the Company to prove the allegation against each workman de novo before it.

Rattan Lal Sharma v. Managing Committee, Dr. Hari Ram (Co-education) Higher Secondary School[85] is a land mark case on the issue of personal bias. The appellant was the Principal of the Higher Secondary School was suspended and charge-sheet was issued to him. One of the charge was that he had received Rupees 129.37 from Mr. Maru Ram on account of amalgamated fund but the same was not accounted for. The inquiry committee constituted by the school authorities constituted of three members including Mr. M. The appellant's objection to the inclusion of Mr Manu Ram was rejected. The inquiry committee found the appellant guilty of some of the charges including misappropriation of Rupees 129.37 wherein Manu Ram had himself appeared before the committee as a witness in support of the charge. Based on their report the Managing Committee dismissed the appellant from service which was confirmed by Deputy Commissioner in accordance with Section3(2) of the Punjab Aided (Schools Security of Service) Act, 1969. The appellant filed a writ petition before the High Court challenging the dismissal on the ground of bias. The division bench rejected the petition on the ground of waiver of rights, even though earlier the single judge of the High Court had allowed the petition on the ground that one who appeared as a witness was also a member of the inquiry committee. The Supreme Court upheld the decision of the single judge and held that the act of dismissal was vitiated on the ground of bias. Applying the test of real likelihood of bias the Court observed–

> In the facts of the case, there was not only a reasonable apprehension in the mind of the appellant about the bias of one of the members of the inquiry committee, namely, the said Shri Maru Ram but such apprehension became real when the said Shri Maru Ram appeared as a witness against the

85. (1993) 4 SCC 10.

appellant to prove the said charge and thereafter proceeded with the inquiry proceeding as a member of the inquiry committee to uphold the correctness of his deposition as a judge.

In *G.N.Nayak v. Goa University*[86] the Supreme Court was required to scrutinize the selection of the appellant as Professor of Marine Science in the University of Goa. The appointment of the appellant was challenged on several grounds, including bias. It was alleged that the selection of the appellant was vitiated on the ground of bias. The Head of the Department of Marine Science had prior to the interview for selection to the post of Professor had written a note to the Vice-Chancellor extolling the qualities of the appellant and requesting him to conduct the selection interview on a priority basis. Respondent no. 5 was also an applicant to the post of Professor challenged the selection process on the ground that the presence of the HOD as a member of the selection committee would vitiate the selection process as he had earlier praised the performance of the appellant. The Court in this case distinguished between preference and bias and observed–

> Bias may be generally defined as partiality or preference. It is true that any person or authority required to act in a judicial or quasi-judicial matter must act impartially. "If however, 'bias' and 'partiality' be defined to mean the total absence of preconceptions in the mind of the judge, then no one has ever had a fair trial and no one ever will. The human mind, even at infancy, is no blank piece of paper. We are born with predispositions and the processes of education, formal and informal, create attitudes which precede reasoning in particular instances and which, therefore, by definition, are prejudices".
>
> It is not every kind of bias which in law is taken to vitiate an act. It must be a prejudice which is not founded on reason, and actuated by self interest - whether pecuniary or personal. Because of this element of personal interest, bias is also seen as an extension of the principle of nature justice that no man should be a judge in his own cause. Being a state of mind, a bias is sometimes impossible to determine. Therefore, the Courts have evolved the principle that it is sufficient for a litigant to successfully impugn an action by establishing a reasonable possibility of bias or proving circumstances from which the operation of influences affecting a fair assessment of the merits of the case can be inferred.

It held that even though the HOD had praised the performance of the appellant but it will not amount to bias. *If a preference is rational and unaccompanied by consideration of personal interest, pecuniary or otherwise, it would not vitiate a decision.* It is a natural for the HOD to form an opinion about the abilities of the staffs who are working under

86. AIR 2002 SC 790.

him. In this context it was categorically observed that *if a senior officer expresses appreciation of the work of a junior in the Confidential Report, it would not amount to bias nor would it preclude that senior officer from being part of the Departmental Promotion Committee to consider such junior officer along with others for promotion.*

Similarly in *Hindustan Vanaspathi Ltd. v. AP State Electricity Board*[87] the Court held that existence of *lis* necessary for an allegation of bias. In this when the officers of the Electricity Board inspected the factory premises of the appellant and noticed pilferage of electricity, immediately electricity supply was disconnected and a provisional assessment of the loss was made at Rupees 61 lakhs. Under the provisions of the Electricity Act the Board initiated proceedings calling upon the appellant to file its objection to the provisional assessment. After the enquiry, the final assessment was fixed at Rupees 55 lakhs. The appellant filed a suit for declaration that the company was not liable to pay any amount as penal damages, for refund of the amount of Rupees 22.50 lakhs which were collected by the Board during the pendency of the assessment proceeding and for perpetual injunction restraining the defendants from disconnecting power supply. One of the principle points of argument was that Clause 39 was violative of the principles of natural justice as the rule enabled the officers of the Board to disconnect the service on a mere suspicion of malpractice and the consumer was required to pay 50% of the provisional assessment amount before electricity could be restored. It was further alleged that the officials of the Board suffered from bias as they were judge in their own cause. The Court negated the arguments of the appellants on the ground that the exercise of powers by the Board has been specifically laid down in the statute with the primary objective of preventing theft of electricity, hence the provisions are not arbitrary or unreasonable. On the issue of bias it was held that *"the principle 'Nemo Judex in Cause Sua' will not apply in this case as the officers have no personal lis with the consumers..... they are similar to Income Tax or Sales Tax Officials. There is nothing wrong in their adjudicating the matter especially when the consumers may be represented by an advocate and the formula for making provisional assessment is fixed in the clause itself."*

The case of *Andhra Pradesh State Road Transport Corporation v. Satyanarayana Transports*[88] is a landmark decision wherein the Supreme Court applied the ground of personal bias in invalidating an administrative action. In this case several appeals were filed challenging the nationalization of road transport order in the district of Guntur passed by the APSRT on several grounds. However the petition filed by one of the respondent

87. AIR 1998 SC 1715.
88. AIR 1965 SC 1303.

raised the issue of colourable exercise of power under the statute by the Minister in charge of Transport department. It was alleged that the Minister had a personal bias against Ramakotaiah because the latter had failed to comply with the wishes of the Minister and failed to pursue some of his friends in the Andhra Pradesh Congress Committee members to vote for the Minister in an election. Ramakotaiah tried but failed to convince his friends to vote for the Minister, this fact angered the Minister extremely who then told Ramakotaiah that *the consequences of his failure would be unpallatable to him.* In this angry frame of mind the Minister heard the objections relating to the proposed nationalization scheme and decided the matter against Ramakotaiah's company. The Court analyzing the plea of bias observed that–

> The position in law in regard to the plea of bias raised against the Minister is not in doubt. It is clear that when the Minister heard the objections to the proposed schemes under Section 68-D(2), he was dealing with the matter in a quasi-judicial manner and his inquiry had to conform to the principles of natural justice. It is an elementary rule of natural justice that a person who tries a cause should be able to deal with the matter before him objectively, fairly, and impartially. As has been observed in the *Jewitt's Dictionary of English Law*, "anything which tends or may be regarded as tending to cause such a person to decide a case otherwise than on evidence must be held to be biased". If a person has a pecuniary interest in the case brought before him, that is an obvious case of bias which disqualifies him to try the cause. If a person is hostile to a party whose cause he is called upon to try, that again would introduce the infirmity of bias and would disqualify him from trying the cause. In dealing with cases of bias, it is necessary to remember that "no one can act in a judicial capacity if his previous conduct gives ground for believing that he cannot act with an open mind". The broad principle which is universally accepted is that a person trying a cause even in quasi-judicial proceedings, must not only act fairly, but must be able to act above suspicion of unfairness. As was observed in *Franklin v. Minister of Town and Country Planning* [(1948) AC 87] "the use of the word 'bias' should be confined to it sphere. Its proper significance is to denote a departure from the standard of even-handed justice which the law requires from those who occupy judicial office or those who are commonly regarded as holding a quasi-judicial office, such as an arbitrator. The reason for this clearly is that having to adjudicate as between two or more parties, he must come to his adjudication with an independent mind without any inclination or bias towards one side or the other in disputed". That being the true position in law about personal bias, there would be no difficulty in holding that the Minister would be disqualified from hearing objections raised by the respective bus operators against the ten schemes if the material facts alleged by Ramakotaiah are held proved. It cannot be disputed that if the Minister had asked Ramakotaiah to help him in his election to the Election Committee of the Andhra Pradesh Congress

Committee and when he was told that Ramakotaiah was unable to help him, he threatened him with dire consequences, that clearly would introduce a serious infirmity in the impugned order which the Minister passed under Section 68-D(2)

......we cannot overlook the fact that if Ramakotaiah's allegations are held proved, that would inevitably create a serious infirmity in the impugned order, because then the impugned order would naturally become invalid inasmuch as it was passed by a person who by his bias had been disqualified from trying the cause. It is hardly necessary to emphasise that the elementary rule of natural justice that a person trying a cause, though in a quasi-judicial proceeding, should not suffer from a personal bias, is of such great significance that its application cannot be controlled by considerations which are confined to Ramakotaiah and would have no relevance in regard to the complaints raised by the respondents in challenging the validity of the impugned order.[89]

On the issue of evidences to prove the allegation of bias the Court held that–

It is not unlikely that a person who has lost his cause before a quasi-judicial tribunal, may feel frustrated and angry and may make allegations about bias in a casual or irresponsible way. It is not unknown that when suitors lose their causes either in courts or before quasi-judicial tribunals they are unable or unwilling to see the correctness of the verdict and are apt to attribute the said verdict to a bias in the mind of the Judge or the Tribunal. The transport business involves considerations of large financial profit and if an operator finds that the introduction of the scheme of nationalisation hits his trade or business very badly, he may in his frustration adopt the desperate course of making a serious allegation of bias against the Minister who sanctions the scheme of nationalisation. That is one aspect of the matter which cannot be overlooked in dealing with cases of this kind......

On the other hand, when very large discretionary powers are vested in the Minister to deal with the problem of introducing nationalisation of transport, it is not impossible that he may be subconsciously influenced by considerations of bias if such a bias is held proved against him. In a struggle for political power which was obviously going on between the two wings of the Council of Ministers in Andhra Pradesh at the relevant time, it is again not unlikely that everyone of the important members of the two groups would try his utmost to collect as much support as he could in the cause of his group. It is well known that when a person enters the arena of political elections, he cannot afford to stand on his own dignity or status and must stoop to conquer, and that means anyone who can bring votes assumes importance at the time of election contests. The evidence on the record clearly shows that the rivalry between the two opposing groups had reached such a stage that it would not be unreasonable to assume that canvassing for votes was proceeding apace on

89. Ibid Para 9-10.

a very large scale. That is the background in the light of which the relevant allegations made by the parties have to be judged.[90]

Thus the Supreme Court after reviewing all the evidences and unsatisfactory by the Minister upheld the order of the High Court on the ground that *once the bias was held proved, in law it followed that the order passed by the Minister was incompetent, because the presence of the bias in his mind disqualified him from hearing the objections against the proposed notified schemes.*

5.8.4 Inconsequential Bias

In the case of *Ramanand Prasad Singh v. Union of India*[91] while dealing with the appeal made against the order of the Central Administrative Tribunal which had set aside the selections made by the Selection Committee of the officers of the Bihar Administrative Service for promotion to the Indian Administrative Service the Supreme Court applied the doctrine of inconsequential bias. One of the factors for setting aside the order by CAT was the participation of one of the member of the Selection Committee whose brother was within the zone of consideration. It was held that since the brother was not selected by the Selection Committee the *selection of all other candidates cannot be held to be vitiated in any manner by this factor.*

5.8.5 Departmental Bias

Departmental bias is one of the grounds for invalidating an administrative action. It generally refers to situations where the deciding authority being part of the same department which has initiated the matter, hence there might be a predisposition to act in a particular manner to fulfill the functional priorities of the department. But generally such decisions are not deemed to be vitiated on the ground of bias because the very purpose for grant of such powers is to enable the adjudicating authority to decide in accordance with the policy of the department. The judiciary has adopted a stringent stand that so long the adjudicating authority is acting in accordance with the powers conferred in the statute, are in compliance with the procedural norms laid down in the statute and principles of fair hearing, the action taken will not be deemed to be bias unless a personal *lis* can be established between the parties.[92]

---

90. Id. Para 12 - 14.
91. (1996) 4 SCC 64.
92. AIR 1998 SC 1715.

The jurisprudential basis of the official bias was laid down in the case of in *Rex v. Sussex Justices Ex Parte McCarthy*[93] by Lord Hewart, C.J. when he stated *it is not merely of some importance but is of fundamental importance that justice should not only be done, but should manifestly and undoubtedly be seen to be done. The question therefore is not whether in this case the deputy clerk made any observation or offered any criticism which he might not properly have made or offered; the question is whether he was so related to the case in its civil aspects as to be unfit to act as clerk to the justices in the criminal matter. The answer to that question depends not upon what actually was done, but upon what might appear to be done.*

One of the leading cases on the issue is *Gullapalli Nageswara Rao v. Andhra Pradesh State Road Transport Corporation.*[94] The appellants were carrying on motor transport business for several years in Krishna district in Andhra Pradesh. Shri Guru Pershad, the General Manager of the State Transport Undertaking of the Andhra Pradesh Road Transport, had published a scheme for nationalization of motor transport in the Krishna district and invited objections to be filed against the proposed scheme. On December 26, 1957, the Secretary in charge of the Transport Department gave a personal hearing to the objectors and heard the representations made on behalf of the State Transport Undertaking. The entire material gathered by him was thereafter placed before the Chief Minister of the State in charge of transport who made the order approving the scheme. The approved scheme was then implemented by the Andhra Pradesh Road Transport Corporation. A writ petition under Article 32 of the Constitution was filed for quashing the scheme. One of the major points of argument was made on the ground of departmental or official bias as the hearing was given by the Secretary in charge of the Transport Department. Dealing with the issue the Court observed–

> [T]he fundamental principle of natural justice that in the case of quasi-judicial proceedings, the authority empowered to decide the dispute between opposing parties must be one without bias towards one side or other in the dispute. It is also a matter fundamental importance that a person interested in one party or the other should not, even formally, take part in the proceedings though in fact he does not influence the mind of the person, who finally decides the case. This is on the principle that justice should not only be done, but should manifestly and undoubtedly be seen to be done. The hearing given by the Secretary, Transport Department, certainly offends the said principle

93. [1924] 1 K.B. 256,.
94. (1959) SCR (Suppl.) 319.

of natural justice and the proceeding and the hearing given, in violation of that principle, are bad.

After the decision of the Supreme Court fresh notices were issued by the Government to all the objectors informing them that a personal hearing would be given by the Chief Minister on December 9, 1958, and they were further informed that they were at liberty to file further objections before November 30, 1958. The Chief Minister heard the representatives of the objectors and the Corporation and passed orders dated December 19, 1958, rejecting the objections filed and approving the scheme as originally published. The order approving the scheme was duly published by the Government in the Official Gazette on December 22, 1958 and thereafter the Authority passed orders rendering the transport permit given to Nageswara Rao as ineffective from December 24, 1958. Aggrieved with the passing of such order a writ petition was filed before the High Court for quashing of the same. In *Gullapalli Nageswara Rao v. State of Andhra Pradesh(II)*[95] an appeal was made to the Supreme Court challenging the order of nationalization of road transport issued by the State on the ground that the hearing given by Chief Minister was improper and being in charge of the transport department he was disqualified to hear the objections and decide based on the proposition laid in the *Gullapalli (I)* decision.

The Court applied the doctrine of official bias to determine the contentious issue of 'whether, when a statute confers a power on an authority and imposes a duty on it to be a Judge of its own cause or to decide a dispute in which it has an official bias, the doctrine of bias is qualified to the extent of the statutory authorization.' The Court referred to the principle laid down in the English case of *King v. Bath Compensation Authority*[96] wherein the House of Lords held that *no one can both be a party and a Judge in the same cause*–

> No doubt the statute contemplates the possibility of the licensing Justices appearing before the compensation authority and taking part in the argument; for it is provided by Section 19 sub-section 2, that the compensation authority shall give any person appearing to them to be interested in the question of the renewal of a licence, "including the licensing Justices," an opportunity of being heard. But the statute nowhere says that Justices who elect to appear as opponents of the renewal and take active steps (such as instructing a solicitor) to take their opposition affective, may nevertheless act as Judges in the dispute; and in the absence of a clear provision to that effect I think that the ordinary rule, that no one can be both party and Judge in the same cause, holds good.

95. AIR 1959 SC 1376 : (1960) 1 SCR 580.
96. 1926 AC 586.

This decision is considered as landmark in the field of official bias wherein it was categorically held that *unless the legislature clearly and expressly ordained to the contrary, the principles of natural justice cannot be violated.* In India a law made by the Parliament must also stand the scrutiny of the fundamental rights test as provided in Part III of the Constitution. By applying the same rationale the Supreme Court held that–

> In the instant case the relevant provisions of the Act do not sanction any dereliction of the principles of natural justice. Under the Act a statutory authority, called the Transport Undertaking, is created and specified statutory functions are conferred on it. The said Undertaking prepares a scheme providing for road transport service in relation to an area to be run or operated by the said Undertaking. Any person affected by the scheme is required to file objections before the State Government and the State Government, after receiving the objections and representations, gives a personal hearing to the objectors as well as to the Undertaking and approves or modifies the scheme as the case may be. The provisions of the Act, therefore, do not authorise the Government to initiate the scheme and thereafter constitute itself a Judge in its own cause. The entire scheme of the Act visualises, in case of conflict between the Undertaking and the operators of private buses, that the State Government should sit in judgment and resolve the conflict. The Act, therefore, does not authorise the State Government to act in derogation of the principles of natural justice.

In reference to the issue of whether the hearing given by the Chief Minister can be held to be vitiated on the ground of bias on the same rationale as the hearing given by the Secretary was held to be bad in the earlier case, the Court answered in the negative and observed–

> The argument that as this Court held in the previous stage of this litigation that the hearing given by the Secretary in charge of the Transport Department offended the principles of natural justice, we should hold, as a logical corollary to the same, that the same infirmity would attach to the Chief Minister. This argument has to be rejected on two grounds: firstly, for the reason that on the last occasion the appellants did not question the right of the Chief Minister to decide on the objections to the scheme, — and indeed they assumed his undoubted right to do so — but canvassed the validity of his order on the basis that the secretary, who was part of the Transport Department, gave the hearing and not the Chief Minister and, therefore, a party to the dispute was made a Judge of his own cause. If, as it is now contended, on the same reasoning the Chief Minister also would be disqualified from deciding the dispute, that point should have been raised at that stage: instead, a distinction was made between the Secretary of a Department and the Chief Minister, and the validity of the order of the Chief Minister was questioned on the basis of this distinction. This Court accepted that argument. Having obtained the

judgment of this Court on that basis, it could not be open to the appellants, at this stage, to reopen the closed controversy and take a contrary position. That apart, there are no merits in this contention.

The Court also drew a distinction between the functional role of a Minister as part of the Cabinet and that of a Secretary of a Department who is deemed to be part of the Department in contradistinction to a Minister in charge of a Department who is responsible for the disposal of the business of the Department. The Court observed–

> There is a clear distinction between the position of a Secretary of the Department and the Chief Minister of the State. Under the Constitution, the Governor is directed to act on the advice of the Ministers headed by the Chief Minister. In exercise of the powers conferred by clauses 2 and 3 of Article 166 of the Constitution the Governor of Madras made rules styled as "The Madras Government Business Rules and Secretariat Instructions", and Rule 9 thereof prescribes that without prejudice to the provisions of Rule 7, the Minister in charge of a department shall be primarily responsible for the disposal of the business pertaining to that department. The Governor of Andhra, in exercise of the powers under the Constitution, directed that until other provisions are made in this regard the business of the Government of Andhra shall be transacted in accordance with the said Rules. It is, therefore, manifest that under the Constitution and the Rules framed thereunder a Minister in charge of a department is primarily responsible for the disposal of the business pertaining to that department, but the ultimate responsibility for the advice is on the entire ministry. But the position of the Secretary of a department is different. Under the said Rules, the Secretary of a department is its head i.e., he is part of the department. There is an essential distinction between the functions of a Secretary and a Minister; the former is a part of the department and the latter is only primarily responsible for the disposal of the business pertaining to that department. On this distinction the previous judgment of this Court was based, for in that case, after pointing out the position of the Secretary in that Department, it was held that "though the formal orders were made by the Chief Minister, in effect and substance, the enquiry was conducted and personal hearing was given by one of the parties to the dispute itself". We cannot, therefore, accept the argument of the learned counsel that the Chief Minister is part of the department constituted as a statutory Undertaking under the Act.

Similarly in *Krishna Bus Service (P) Ltd. v. State of Haryana*[97] the Court applied the rationale of official bias to invalidate the appointment of the General Manager of Haryana Roadways as Deputy Superintendent of Police under the Motor Vehicles Act, 1939. The appellants who are in the business of motor transport had challenged the appointment made on the

97. (1985) 3 SCC 711.

ground of bias. It was the contention of the petitioners that the 'appointment of the General Manager, Haryana Roadways, who is himself responsible for the proper management of the activities of the Haryana Roadways and its prosperity and profitability and who is carrying on business in competition with other private operators as an officer who can exercise the powers of the Deputy Superintendent of Police under the Act is violative under Article 19(1)(*g*) of the Constitution and it is otherwise contrary to the object and spirit of the Act. It is further urged that the General Manager, Haryana Roadways would not be able to discharge his functions satisfactorily in the interests of the general public since he being himself under a duty to comply with the provisions of the Act and the rules made thereunder in respect of the motor vehicles of the Haryana Roadways cannot be expected to discharge the functions of checking, inspection, search and seizure regarding the motor vehicles belonging to the Haryana Roadways and to take appropriate steps to prosecute the officers of his own department who are not complying with the provisions of the Act. In a given case it is likely that the General Manager himself may have to be prosecuted for not complying with law.'

The Court upholding the contention of the petitioners observed–

> The powers of stopping the motor vehicles and the powers of inspection, search, seizure and detention exercised under the Act are serious restrictions on the fundamental right of the operators of motor vehicles guaranteed under Article 19(1)(*g*) of the Constitution. These powers can be considered as reasonable restrictions only when they are exercised properly in the interests of the general public. They should be reasonable both from the substantive as well as the procedural standpoint. Such powers should, therefore, be entrusted to a person who is expected to exercise them fairly and without bias. The General Manager of Haryana Roadways who is a rival in business to the private operators of motor vehicles in the State and is intimately connected with the running of motor vehicles cannot be expected to discharge his duties in a fair and reasonable manner. An unobstructed operation of the motor vehicles by private owners operating along the same route or routes would naturally affect the earnings of the Haryana Roadways. There is, therefore, every likelihood of his being over-zealous in discharging his duties of stopping a vehicle and in searching, seizing and detaining motor vehicles belonging to others and at the same time excessively lenient in the case of vehicles belonging to his own department. If in discharging his duties in the case of vehicles belonging to others he fails to give due regard to the interests of the owners thereof he would be violating their fundamental right to carry on business in a reasonable way. If he is too lenient in inspecting the vehicles belonging to his own department, the interests of the travelling public at large would be in peril. In both the cases there is a conflict between his duty on the one hand and his interest on the other. Moreover administration must be rooted in confidence and that confidence is destroyed when people begin to think

> that the officer concerned is biased. This is not a case which is governed by the rule of necessity. As it is, there are many other officers who are entrusted with the powers of the police officers under the Act. There was, therefore, no necessity to appoint the General Manager of Haryana Roadways also to exercise the said powers. We are, therefore, of the opinion that the appointment of the General Manager, Haryana Roadways who is directly responsible for running its motor vehicles as one of the officers who can exercise the powers of a Deputy Superintendent of Police under the Act imposes an unreasonable restriction on the fundamental right of the private motor vehicles operators and is therefore violative of Article 19(1)(*g*) of the Constitution. We however make it clear that the appointment of other officers of the State Government is not bad even though the Government is the owner of the vehicles as their connection with the running of the vehicles is too remote. The appointment of the General Manager as an officer who can exercise the powers of the Deputy Superintendent of Police under the Act is also not in the interests of the general public since the large number of motor vehicles owned by the Haryana Roadways would not be subject to inspection and checking by an independent agency. Can we expect a fair investigation by a police officer into a criminal case in which his own kith and kin are involved as the accused? The position is not different in this case. The Legislature could not have intended while enacting Section 133-A of the Act that a person who was himself directly responsible for the proper running of the motor vehicles according to law could be appointed as the inspecting and investigating officer by the State Government for the purpose of enforcing the Act.[1]

However in *K. Ashok Reddy v. Govt. of India*[2] the Supreme Court denied the contention of bias while dealing with the issue of transfer of judges and whether such transfers can be vitiated on grounds of bias. The Supreme Court upheld the norms of judicial integrity and negated the contention on the ground that when decisions are made *by the collective exercise of several Judges at the apex level on objective criterion on which the recommendation of the Chief Justice of India is based* it acts as *an inbuilt check against arbitrariness and bias.* Hence the scope of judicial review of transfer of Judges is very limited.

5.8.6 Institutional Bias

In the case of *Lalit Modi v. BCCI*[3] Supreme Court discussed the issue of institutional bias. The respondent had appointed a three-member Disciplinary Committee to look into various charges of misconduct when he was functioning as the Chairman of Indian Premier League (IPL). The petitioner

1. Ibid Para 10.
2. (1994) 2 SCC 303 : AIR 1994 SC 1207.
3. (2011) 10 SCC 106.

contended that the committee was not validly constituted as its members suffered from *institutional bias* as they were part of the Governing Council of BCCI. It was alleged that the *petitioner could not expect fair play from the members who have already been party to the decision to initiate the disciplinary action against the petitioner.* The Court negated the contention and laid down the rules relating to institutional bias. It observed–

> As far as the disciplinary actions by societies and associations are concerned, many of the societies under the Tamil Nadu Societies Registration Act and similar State Acts, are smaller societies. It is another matter that the first respondent society is a large body having large resources. If the members or the Managing Committee of a Society receive a complaint of any misconduct on the part of any of its office bearers, surely the subject is expected to be taken up in the General Body Meeting of the Society. These societies are expected to sort out the future course of action with respect to such allegations on their own on the basis of their internal disciplinary mechanism. Merely because all the members of a society have participated in the discussion concerning such allegation, the Society can't be expected to appoint an outsider to hold the disciplinary proceeding. It may not be financially possible as well for such small societies. That apart, only a prima facie opinion is formed in such meetings. Merely because a member has participated in such a meeting he cannot be accused of bias to disentitle him from being appointed on the Disciplinary Committee.......As held in M.P. Special Police Establishment, a mere apprehension of bias cannot be a ground for interference. There must exist a real danger of bias. And, following *T.P. Daver v. Lodge Victoria,*[4] though such domestic inquiries have undoubtedly to be fair, a member of a society cannot stretch the principle of fairness to the extent of demanding a tribunal consisting of outsiders, on the basis that the society members are biased against him.
>
> ......The Petitioner was alleging institutional bias against the members of the Committee, which was only on the basis of their participation in the meetings of the first Respondent society. In this way, institutional bias can be alleged against every member of the Governing Council of IPL and the General Body of the first Respondent which cannot be accepted. The Petitioner may have an apprehension, but it is not possible to say from the material on record that he was facing a real danger of bias.

5.9 TEST OF BIASNESS

The test of bias differs based on the ground of bias. In case of any direct pecuniary or proprietary interest in the subject matter of proceedings will give rise to automatic disqualification on the ground of bias.[5] On the issue

4. AIR 1963 SC 1144.
5. (1955) 1 QB 41.

of personal bias the English Courts have applied different tests ranging from real likelihood test to reasonable suspicion test and lastly to the real danger test.

In *Regina v. Camborne Justices Ex parte Pearce*[6] the Divisional Bench of Queen's Bench Division after analyzing several decisions held that *"real likelihood was the proper test, and that a real likelihood of bias had to be made to appear not only from the materials in fact ascertained by the party complaining, but from such further facts as he might readily have ascertained and easily verified in the course of his inquiries."* The test for disqualification is based on assessment of the facts by the court giving rise to a real likelihood of bias.

In *Metropolitan Properties Ltd. v. Lannon*[7] the Court applied the suspicion test and reasserted 'justice must be seen to be done' as the operative principle. It implies that 'no person should adjudicate in any way if it might reasonably be thought that he ought not to act because of some personal interest.'[8]

In *R. v. Gough*[9] the House of Lords had applied the 'real likelihood' test by using the expression 'real danger'. Explaining the principle Lord Goff observed–

> I think it unnecessary, in formulating the appropriate test, to require that the court should look at the matter through the eyes of a reasonable man, because the court in cases such as these personifies the reasonable man; and in any event the court has first to ascertain the relevant circumstances from the available evidence, knowledge of which would not necessarily be available to an observer in court at the relevant time. Finally, for the avoidance of doubt, I prefer to state the test in terms of real danger rather than real likelihood, to ensure that the court is thinking in terms of possibility rather than probability of bias. Accordingly, having ascertained the relevant circumstances, the court should ask itself whether, having regard to those circumstances, there was a real danger of bias on the part of the relevant member of the tribunal in question, in the sense that he might unfairly regard (or have unfairly regarded) with favour, or dis favour, the case of a party to the issue under consideration by him....

It was further asserted–

> In my opinion, if the circumstances of the case (as ascertained by the court), it appears that there was a real likelihood, in the sense of a real possibility,

6. Id. (1955) 1 QB 41.
7. (1969) 1 QB 577.
8. AIR 2011 SC 3711.
9. (1993) AC 646.

> of bias on the part of a justice or other member of an inferior tribunal, justice requires that the decision should not be allowed to stand. I am by no means persuaded that, in its original form, the real likelihood test required that any more rigorous criterion should be applied. Furthermore the test as so stated gives sufficient effect, in cases of apparent bias, to the principle that justice must manifestly be seen to be done, and it is unnecessary, in my opinion, to have recourse to a test based on mere suspicion, or even reasonable suspicion, for that purpose
>
> In conclusion, I wish to express my understanding of the law as follows. I think it possible, and desirable, that the same test should be applicable in all cases of apparent bias, whether concerned with justices or members of other inferior tribunals, or with jurors, or with arbitrators. Likewise I consider that, in cases concerned with jurors, the same test should be applied by a judge to whose attention the possibility of bias on the part of a juror has been drawn in the course of a trial, and by the Court of Appeal when it considers such a question on appeal.

In *re Medicaments and Related Classes of goods* the Court of Appeal laid down the ingredients of real danger of bias test. It explained–

> ...The court has first to ascertain all the circumstances which had a bearing on the suggestion that the judge was biased and then ask whether those circumstances would lead a fair-minded and informed observer to conclude that there was a real possibility, or a real danger, the two being the same, that the judge was biased; that the material circumstances included any explanation given by the impugned judge as to his knowledge or appreciation of those circumstances and where any such explanation was disputed the reviewing court did not have to rule whether the explanation should be accepted or rejected but rather had to decide whether the fair-minded observer would consider that there was a real danger of bias notwithstanding the explanation advanced that instead of determining whether R's statement was truthful the court should have considered what impression her conduct, including her explanation for it, would have had on a fair-minded observer; that such an observer would not have been convinced that all prospects of R working for the firm at some time in the future had been destroyed or that she might not still hope to work for them in due course; that, in those circumstances, the fair-minded observer would apprehend that there was a real danger that R would be unable to make an objective and impartial appraisal of the expert evidence placed before the court by the firm; and that, accordingly, R ought to have recused herself and the other members of the court should stand down.

Thus from the above analysis it can be concluded that the English courts are presently applying the real danger test for determining the scope of bias. But in several judgments the courts have clarified that the terminologies like real likelihood or real danger are being used in an inter-changeable manner with the essential ingredients of application being the same. However in other jurisdictions courts have insisted on the application of real suspicion or apprehension test for the purpose of upholding the dignity of the judicial office.

The Constitutional Court of South Africa in the case of *President of the Republic of South Africa v. South African Rugby Football Union*[10] had observed–

> ...The question is whether a reasonable, objective and informed person would on the correct facts reasonably apprehend that the judge has not or will not bring an impartial mind to bear on the adjudication of the case, that is a mind open to persuasion by the evidence and the submissions of counsel. The reasonableness of the apprehension must be assessed in the light of the oath of office taken by the judges to administer justice without fear or favour; and their ability to carry out that oath by reason of their training and experience. It must be assumed that they can disabuse their minds of any irrelevant personal beliefs or predispositions. They must take into account the fact that they have a duty to sit in any case in which they are not obliged to recuse themselves. At the same time, it must never be forgotten that an impartial judge is a fundamental prerequisite for a fair trial and a judicial officer should not hesitate to recuse herself or himself if there are reasonable grounds on the part of a litigant for apprehending that the judicial officer, for whatever reasons, was not or will not be impartial.

Similarly the High Court of Australia in the seven Judge Bench in *Johnson v. Johnson*[11] upheld the application of real suspicion or apprehension test in place of real likelihood test by arguing that–

> That test has been adopted, in preference to a differently expressed test that has been applied in England, for the reason that it gives due recognition to the fundamental principle that justice must both be done, and be seen to be done. It is based upon the need for public confidence in the administration of justice. "If fair-minded people reasonably apprehend or suspect that the tribunal has prejudged the case, they cannot have confidence in the decision." The hypothetical reasonable observer of the judge's conduct is postulated in order to emphasise that the test is objective, is founded in the need for public confidence in the judiciary, and is not based purely upon the assessment by some judges of the capacity or performance of their colleagues. At the same time, two things need to be remembered: the observer is taken to be reasonable; and the person being observed is "a professional judge whose training, tradition and oath or affirmation require [the judge] to discard the irrelevant, the immaterial and the prejudicial.

10. 1999 (4) SA 147.
11. (2000) 174 Aust LR 655.

In India the courts have generally applied the reasonable apprehension test to determine the likelihood of bias. In the landmark case of *Manak Lal v. Dr Prem Chand Singhvi*[12] it was observed that–

> If it is true that in judicial or quasi-judicial proceedings justice must not only be done but must appear to be done to the litigating public, it is equally true that when a lawyer is charged for professional misconduct and is given the privilege of being tried by a Tribunal of the Bar Council, the enquiry before the Tribunal must leave no room for a reasonable apprehension in the mind of the lawyer that the Tribunal may have been even indirectly influenced by any bias in the mind of any of the members of the Tribunal. In the present case, we have no hesitation in assuming that when Shri Chhangani agreed to work as the Chairman of the Tribunal, he did not remember that he had appeared against the appellant's clients in the criminal proceedings under Section 145. We are told that Shri Chhangani is a senior member of the Bar and was once Advocate-General of the High Court of Rajasthan. Besides he had not appeared in the case at all stages but had appeared only once as a senior counsel to argue the matter. It is, therefore, not at all unlikely that Shri Chhangani had no personal contact with the client Dr Prem Chand and may not have been aware of the fact that, in the case from which the present proceedings arose, he had appeared at any stage for Dr Prem Chand. We are, however, inclined to hold that this fact does not in any way affect the legal argument urged before us by Shri Daphtary. It is not Shri Daphtary's case that Shri Chhangani actually had a bias against the appellant and that the said bias was responsible for the final report made against the appellant. Indeed it is unnecessary for Shri Daphtary to advance such an argument. If Shri Chhangani was disqualified from working as a member of the Tribunal by reason of the fact that he had appeared for Dr Prem Chand in the criminal proceedings under Section 145 in question, then it would not be necessary for Shri Daphtary to prove that any prejudice in fact had been caused or that Shri Chhangani improperly influenced the final decision of the Tribunal. Actual proof of prejudice in such cases may make the appellant's case stronger but such proof is not necessary in order that the appellant should effectively raise the argument that the Tribunal was not properly constituted.

In some of the subsequent cases the judiciary applied the *real likelihood test* for determining whether a judicial or quasi-judicial decision was vitiated on the ground of bias. In *A.K. Kraipak* the issue was before the Court was *not whether he was biased. It is difficult to prove the state of mind of a person. Therefore what we have to see is whether there is reasonable ground for believing that he was likely to have been biased...'*

Similarly in *S. Parthasarthi v. State of AP.*[13] Mathew J applied the 'real likelihood test' and observed "We think that the reviewing authority

12. 1957 SCR 575 : AIR 1957 SC 425.
13. (1974) 3SCC 459.

must make a determination on the basis of the whole evidence before it, whether a reasonable man would in the circumstances infer that there is real likelihood of bias. The Court must look at the impression which other people have. This follows from the principle that justice must not only be done but seen to be done. If right minded persons would think that there is real likelihood of bias on the part of an inquiring officer, he must not conduct the enquiry; nevertheless, there must be a real likelihood of bias. Surmise or conjecture would not be enough. There must exist circumstances from which reasonable men would think it probable or likely that the inquiring officer will be prejudiced against the delinquent. The Court will not inquire whether he was really prejudiced. If a reasonable man would think on the basis of the existing circumstances that he is likely to be prejudiced, that is sufficient to quash the decision...."

In *Ranjit Thakur v. Union of India* [14]the court observed "a judgment which is the result of bias or want of impartiality is a nullity and the trial *coram non-judice'*. It clarified that 'the proper approach for the Judge is not to look at his own mind and ask himself, however honestly, "Am I biased?"; but to look at the mind of the party before him.'

In the recent case of *Justice P.D. Dinakaran v. Hon'ble Judges Inquiry Committee*[15] the court revisited the entire jurisprudence of rule against bias. In this case fifty members of the Rajya Sabha had submitted a motion for removal of the petitioner from the post of Chief Justice of Karnataka High Court under Article 217 read with Article 124(4) of the Constitution. As per the Judges (Inquiry) Act, 1968 the Chairman of the Rajya Sabha appointed a committee comprising Justice V.S. Sirpurkar, Justice A.R. Dave and Senior advocate P.P.Rao, however objection was raised against the inclusion of Shri P.P. Rao on the ground of personal bias. It was alleged that being the Vice-President of the Bar Association of India he had actively spoken against the elevation of the petitioner as a Judge and had also drafted a resolution in this regard. The Court after analyzing a plethora of cases on the issue of bias upheld the application of 'real likelihood test based on the threshold of *real danger of bias.* It observed–

> [N]o man can be a Judge in his own cause and justice should not only be done, but manifestly be seen to be done. Scales should not only be held even but it must not be seen to be inclined. A person having interest in the subject matter of cause is precluded from acting as a Judge. To disqualify a person from adjudicating on the ground of interest in the subject matter of lis, the test of real likelihood of the bias is to be applied. In other words, one has to enquire as to whether there is real danger of bias on the part of the person

14. (1987) 4 SCC 611.
15. AIR 2011 SC 3711 : 2011 (6) SCALE 97.

against whom such apprehension is expressed in the sense that he might favour or disfavour a party. In each case, the Court has to consider whether a fair minded and informed person, having considered all the facts would reasonably apprehend that the Judge would not act impartially. To put it differently, the test would be whether a reasonably intelligent man fully apprised of all the facts would have a serious apprehension of bias. In cases of non-pecuniary, the 'real likelihood' test has been preferred over the 'reasonable suspicion' test and the Courts have consistently held that in deciding the question of bias one has to take into consideration human probabilities and ordinary course of human conduct. We may add that real likelihood of bias should appear not only from the materials ascertained by the complaining party, but also from such other facts which it could have readily ascertained and easily verified by making reasonable inquiries.

After analyzing the facts of the case the Court concluded that the facts could give rise to a reasonable apprehension in the mind of an intelligent person that Shri P.P. Rao was likely to be biased. It observed–

A reasonable, objective and informed person may say that Respondent No. 3 would not have opposed elevation of the Petitioner if he was not satisfied that there was some substance in the allegations levelled against him. It is true that the Judges and lawyers are trained to be objective and have the capacity to decipher grain from the chaff, truth from the falsehood and we have no doubt that Respondent No. 3 possesses these qualities. We also agree with the Committee that objection by both sides perhaps "alone apart from anything else is sufficient to confirm his impartiality". However, the issue of bias of Respondent No. 3 has not to be seen from the view point of this Court or for that matter the Committee. It has to be seen from the angle of a reasonable, objective and informed person. What opinion he would form! It is his apprehension which is of paramount importance. From the facts narrated in the earlier part of the judgment it can be said that Petitioner's apprehension of likelihood of bias against Respondent No. 3 is reasonable and not fanciful, though, in fact, he may not be biased.

5.10 FACTORS FOR DETERMINATION OF APPARENT BIAS

In *Regina v. Camborne Justices Ex parte Pearce*[16] a warning was issued by the court about the need to exercise judicial restraint so that frequent allegations of bias should not become an hindrance in judicial or quasi-judicial functioning. It was observed–

The frequency with which allegations of bias have come before the courts in recent times seems to indicate that Lord Hewart's reminder in the Sussex

16. (1955) 1 QB 41.

Justices case that it "is of fundamental " importance that justice should not only be done, but should "manifestly and undoubtedly be seen to be done "is being urged as a warrant for quashing convictions or invalidating orders upon quite unsubstantial grounds and, indeed, in some cases upon the flimsiest pretexts of bias. Whilst indorsing and fully maintaining the integrity of the principle reasserted by Lord Hewart, this Court feels that the continued citation of it in cases to which it is not applicable may lead to the erroneous impression that it is more important that justice should appear to be done than that it should in fact be done."

In this context it becomes essential to adhere to the principles laid down in *Halsbury's Laws of* England[17] regarding the test of disqualification on the ground of apparent bias by justices, members of inferior tribunals, jurors or with arbitrators is to look into all the relevant circumstances which have a bearing on the suggestion that the judge or justice is biased and analyze if there is a real possibility of bias, in the sense that he might unfairly regard with favour, or disfavour, the case of a party to the issue under consideration by him.

5.11 NON-COMPLIANCE WITH THE RULE AGAINST BIAS

In *Ranjit Thakur v. Union of India*[18] the appellant was subjected to punishment for not commending well to the commanding officer (Respondent 4) of the regiment and subsequently he was further punished with rigorous imprisonment by Respondent 4 for making complaints to the higher officers of ill-treatment at the hands of Respondent 4. A writ petition was filed by the appellant challenging the proceedings of the court-martial and one of the grounds for challenge was bias as the Respondent 4 had participated and dominated in the conduct of the proceedings. The Court while dealing with the issue of alleged bias on the part of Respondent 4 observed–

> The test of real likelihood of bias is whether a reasonable person, in possession of relevant information, would have thought that bias was likely and is whether Respondent 4 was likely to be disposed to decide the matter only in a particular way.
>
> It is the essence of a judgment that it is made after due observance of the judicial process; that the court or tribunal passing it observes, at least the minimal requirements of natural justice; is composed of impartial persons acting fairly and without bias and in good faith. A judgment which is the result of bias or want of impartiality is a nullity and the trial "*coram non-judice*". (**See** *Vassiliades v. Vassiliades* [AIR 1945 PC 38 : 221 IC 603])

17. Vol. 29(2) 4th Edn. Reissue 2002, para 560 page 379.
18. (1987) 4 SCC 611.

> As to the tests of the likelihood of bias what is relevant is the reasonableness of the apprehension in that regard in the mind of the party. The proper approach for the Judge is not to look at his own mind and ask himself, however, honestly, "Am I biased?"; but to look at the mind of the party before him.
>
> ....
>
> Thus tested the conclusion becomes inescapable that, having regard to the antecedent events, the participation of Respondent 4 in the court-martial rendered the proceedings *coram non-judice.*

Thus a decision which is made in violation of the doctrine of bias will be deemed to be a nullity and the entire proceeding will be considered to be a legal proceeding without a judge, or without a proper jurisdiction. The meaning of the Latin phrase *coram non-judice* is not in the presence of a judge.

5.12 DOCTRINE OF WAIVER

The term waiver refers to 'an intentional relinquishment of a known right'. It is based on the maxim *Cuilibet licet renuntiare juri pro ce introducto* which implies 'everyone has a right to waive and to agree to waive the advantage of a law or rule made solely for the benefit and protection of the individual in his private capacity, which may be dispensed with without infringing any public right or public policy.'[19] The doctrine has been has used as point of defence to deny the application of the rule against bias.

Manak Lal v. Dr. Prem Chand[20] is the leading case on the application of the doctrine of waiver in charges. In this case the appellant was a practicing advocate and was charged with professional misconduct on account of making a forged document for obtaining a stay order in a case where the respondent was the other party. An inquiry committee was appointed by the High Court to look into the charges of professional misconduct and the committee was headed Shri Changanni. The committee found Manak Lal guilty of professional misconduct and recommended for removal of his name from the roll of advocates. Based on the recommendation the High Court removed the name of Manak Lal from the roll of advocates. On appeal one of the points of argument on behalf of appellant was on the ground of personal bias because Changanni in an earlier matter had filed a vakalatnama on behalf of Dr. Prem Chand, hence there was a reasonable apprehension of bias. The Court even though accepted the argument of bias, it was held to be not applicable because of the application of the doctrine of waiver. The Court observed–

19. *Dhirendra Nath Gorai v. Sudhir Chandra,* AIR 1964 SC 1300.
20. 1957 SCR 575: AIR 1957 SC 425.

The alleged bias in a member of the Tribunal does not render the proceedings invalid if it is shown that the objection against the presence of the member in question had not been taken by the party even though the party knew about the circumstances giving rise to the allegations about the alleged bias and was aware of his right to challenge the presence of the member in the Tribunal. It is true that waiver cannot always and in every case be inferred merely from the failure of the party to take the objection. Waiver can be inferred only if and after it is shown that the party knew about the relevant facts and was aware of his right to take the objection in question. As Sir John Romilly, M.R., has observed in *Vyvyan v. Vyvyan*[21] "waiver or acquiescence, like election, presupposes that the person to be bound is fully cognizant of his rights, and, that being so, he neglects to enforce them, or chooses one benefit instead of another, either, but not both, of which he might claim". If, in the present case, it appears that the appellant knew all the facts about the alleged disability of Shri Chhangani and was also aware that he could effectively request the learned Chief Justice to nominate some other member instead of Shri Chhangani and yet did not adopt that course, it may well be that he deliberately took a chance to obtain a report in his favour from the Tribunal and when he came to know that the report had gone against him he thought better of his rights and raised this point before the High Court for the first time. In other words, though the point of law raised by Shri Daphtary against the competence of the Tribunal be sound, it is still necessary for us to consider whether the appellant was precluded from raising this point before the High Court by waiver or acquiescence.

From the record it is clear that the appellant never raised this point before the Tribunal and the manner in which this point was raised by him even before the High Court is somewhat significant. The first ground of objection filed by the appellant against the Tribunal's report was that Shri Chhangani had pecuniary and personal interest in the complainant Dr Prem Chand. The learned Judges of the High Court have found that the allegations about the pecuniary interest of Shri Chhangani in the present proceedings are wholly unfounded and this finding has not been challenged before us by Shri Daphtary. The learned Judges of the High Court have also found that the objection was raised by the appellant before them only to obtain an order for a fresh enquiry and thus gain time. It may be conceded in favour of Shri Daphtary that the judgment of the High Court does not in terms find against the appellant on the ground of waiver though that no doubt appears to be the substance of their conclusion. We have, however, heard Shri Daphtary's case on the question of waiver and we have no hesitation in reaching the conclusion that the appellant waived his objection deliberately and cannot now be allowed to raise it. Shri Daphtary does not contend that at the material time the appellant did not remember the fact that Shri Chhangani had appeared for Dr Prem Chand in the criminal proceedings. Indeed such a plea cannot be raised by the appellant in view of the affidavit which the appellant sought to place before us in the

21. (1861) 30 Beav 65, 74 : 54 ER 813, 817.

present appeal. Under this affidavit, the appellant's case appears to be that, until he met his advocate Shri Murli Manohar for filing objections to the report of the Tribunal, the appellant did not know that Shri Chhangani was legally disqualified from acting as a member of the Tribunal. It is obvious that this ground necessarily implies that the appellant knew about the facts giving rise to the alleged disqualification of Shri Chhangani to act as a member of the Tribunal. In substance, the contention is that though the appellant knew that Shri Chhangani had appeared for Dr Prem Chand in the criminal proceedings in question, he was not aware that, in consequence, Shri Chhangani was disqualified to act as a member of the Tribunal. It is this limited aspect of the matter which is pressed before us by Shri Daphtary. Shri Daphtary contends and no doubt rightly that if we are satisfied that the appellant did not know about the true legal position in this matter and his rights arising therefrom, his failure to challenge the appointment of Shri Chhangani on the Tribunal would not raise an effective plea of waiver. However, in our opinion, it is very difficult to accept Shri Daphtary's argument that his client did not know the true legal position or his rights until he met Shri Murli Manohar. No doubt the appellant is a junior at the Bar but even so he can claim ten years' standing at the Bar. Besides, he had the assistance of a lawyer in defending him in the present proceedings and it appears extremely difficult to assume that neither the appellant nor his lawyer knew that the presence of Shri Chhangani in the Tribunal could be effectively challenged by them. We are disposed to think that even a layman, not familiar with legal technicalities and equitable principles on which this doctrine of disability has been based would have immediately apprehended that the lawyer who had appeared for Dr Prem Chand was authorised to sit in judgment over the conduct of the appellant and that might cause embarrassment to the appellant and might lead to prejudice against him. From a purely common sense point of view of a layman, the position was patently awkward, and so, the argument that the appellant was not conscious of his legal rights in this matter appears to us to be an after-thought. Since the appellant was driven to adopt this untenable position before the High Court in seeking to raise this point for the first time at that stage, we are not surprised that the High Court took the view that the plea had been taken late in order to gain time and to secure a fresh enquiry in the matter. Since we have no doubt that the appellant knew the material facts and must be deemed to have been conscious of his legal rights in that matter, his failure to take the present plea at the earlier stage of the proceedings creates an effective bar of waiver against him. It seems clear that the appellant wanted to take a chance to secure a favourable report from the Tribunal which was constituted and when he found that he was confronted with an unfavourable report, he adopted the device of raising the present technical point.

In the case of *Justice P.D. Dinakaran v. Hon'ble Judges Inquiry Committee*[22] the court applied the doctrine of waiver against the petitioner

22. AIR 2011 SC 3711 : 2011 (6) SCALE 97.

as he had waited for almost ten months after the nomination of Shri PP Rao as a member of the Committee and was knowingly using this defence as a dilatory tactic. As a member of the higher judiciary it could be presumed that the petitioner was always aware of his right to raise an objection. It was categorically held that *no Court can render assistance to the Petitioner in a petition filed with the sole object of delaying finalization of the inquiry.*

However in *Rattan Lal Sharma v. Managing Committee, Dr. Hari Ram (Co-education) Higher Secondary School*[23] the Court refused to apply the defense of waiver and laid down the important rule–

> Generally, a point not raised for the first time in the writ proceeding, more so when the interference in the writ jurisdiction which is equitable and discretionary is not of course a must as indicated by this Court in *A.M.Allison v. B.L. Sen* particularly when the plea sought to be raised for the first time in a writ proceeding requires investigation of facts. But if the plea though not specifically raised before the subordinate tribunals or the administrative and quasi-judicial bodies, is raised before the High Court in the writ proceeding for the first time and the plea goes to the root of the question and is based on admitted and uncontroverted facts and does not require any further investigation into a question of fact, the High Court is not only justified in entertaining the plea but in the anxiety to do justice which is the paramount consideration of the court, it is only desirable that a litigant should not be shut out from raising such plea which goes to the root of the *lis* involved.

5.13 DOCTRINE OF NECESSITY

The principles of natural justice are based on the notions of fairness hence they cannot be *cast in a rigid mould nor can they be put in a legal strait-jacket.* The rules can be adapted and modified by statutory provisions for the purpose of fulfilling the dual objective of administrative efficiency along with fairness. In *Union of India v. Col. J.N. Sinha*[24] the Court held that–

> [T]he aim of rules of natural justice is to secure justice or to put it negatively to prevent miscarriage of justice. These rules can operate only in areas not covered by any law validly made. In other words they do not supplant the law but supplement it." It is true that if a statutory provision can be read consistently with the principles of natural justice, the courts should do so because it must be presumed that the Legislatures and the statutory authorities intend to act in accordance with the principles of natural justice. But if on the other hand a statutory provision either specifically or by necessary implication excludes the application of any or all the principles of natural justice then the

23. (1993) 4 SCC 10.
24. (1970) 2 SCC 458 : (1971) 1 SCR 791.

court cannot ignore the mandate of the Legislature or the statutory authority and read into the concerned provision the principles of natural justice. Whether the exercise of a power conferred should be made in accordance with any of the principles of natural justice or not depends upon the express words of the provision conferring the power, the nature of the power conferred, the purpose for which it is conferred and the effect of the exercise of that power.

Similarly in *Swadeshi Cotton Mills v. Union of India*[25] it was clarified that–

> Where authority functions under a statute and the statute provides for the observance of the principles of natural justice in a particular manner, natural justice will have to be observed in that manner and in no other. No wider right than that provided by statute can be claimed nor can the right be narrowed. Where the statute is silent about the observance of the principles of natural justice, such statutory silence is taken to imply compliance with the principles of natural justice. *The implication of natural justice being presumptive it may be excluded by express words of statute or by necessary intendment. Where the conflict is between the public interest and the private interest, the presumption must necessarily be weak and may, therefore, be readily displaced.*"

Thus it can be summarized that the principles of natural justice can not only be modified *but in exceptional circumstances they can even be excluded.*

There is an exception to the general rule that no person shall be a judge in his bias, which is popularly known as the doctrine of necessity. Where doctrine of necessity is made applicable then the principles of natural justice would be excluded. Under this doctrine *"An adjudicator, who is subject to disqualification on the ground of bias or interest in the matter which has to decide, may be required to adjudicate if there is no other person who is competent or authorized to adjudicate or if a quorum cannot be formed without him or if no other competent tribunal can be constituted."*[26] It implies that in certain exceptional circumstances the administrative or quasi-judicial authorities can pass a legally valid decision, even when the circumstances of the case may give rise to an element of bias. The exception has been developed on the ground that the administration of justice will collapse in the absence of competent adjudicating authority. *The doctrine of necessity is a common law doctrine, and is applied to tide over the situations where there are difficulties. Law does not contemplate a vacuum, and a solution has to be found out rather than allowing the problem to*

25. [(1981) 1 SCC 664 : (1981) 2 SCR 533.
26. MANU/SC/0008/1984, para 13.

boil over.[27] This doctrine is applicable not only to judicial matters but also to quasi-judicial and administrative matters.

In the words of Prof. Wade–[28]

> But there are many cases where no substitution is possible, since no one else is empowered to act. Natural justice then has to give way to necessity; for otherwise there is no means of deciding and the machinery of justice or administration will break down..... In administrative cases the same exigency may arise. Where the statute empowers a particular minister or official to act, he will usually be the one and only person who can do so. There is then no way of escaping the responsibility, even if he is personally interested. Transfer of responsibility is, indeed, a recognised type of ultra vires. In one case it was unsuccessfully argued that the only minister competent to confirm a compulsory purchase order for land for an airport had disqualified himself by showing bias and that the local authority could only apply for a local Act of Parliament.

In the case of *J. Mohapatro* the Supreme Court did not apply the doctrine of necessity on the ground that the members of the Assessment Sub-Committee who were holding official positions like Secretary, Education Department or Director, Higher Education could be substituted by the State Government through Government Resolution and the other non-official author members should have resigned from the Committee on the ground of their interest in the matter.[29]

One of the leading cases underlying the principles of doctrine of necessity is *Ashok Kumar Yadav v. State of Haryana.*[30] In this case the selections made by the Haryana Public Service Commission (HPSC) to the Haryana Civil Service (Executive) were challenged on the ground of bias. It was alleged that the Chairman and some other members of the HPSC were related to some of the selected candidates hence some of the meritorious candidates who had secured high marks at the written examination were not selected during the viva voce test. The respondents argued that since the Commission was a constitutional authority it was not necessary for the concerned members to withdraw altogether from the interview but to abstain from participating when their relatives came to be interviewed. The Court highlighted the necessity to comply with the principles of fairness by every authority who is entrusted with the task of acting independently while arriving *at a fair and just decision between the rival claims of parties.* It applied the doctrine of necessity and made the following observation–

27. (2011) 10 SCC 106.
28. As quoted in *State of U.P. v. Sheo Shanker Lal Srivastava,* (2006) 3 SCC 276.
29. MANU/SC/0008/1984, para 13.
30. AIR 1987 SC 454.

> We must straightaway point out that A.K. Kraipak'a case is a landmark in the development of administrative law and it has contributed in a large measure to the strengthening of the rule of law in this country. We would not like to whittle down in the slightest measure the vital principle laid down in this decision which has nourished the roots of the rule of law and injected justice and fair play into legality. There can be no doubt that if a selection committee is constituted for the purpose of selecting candidates on merits and one of the members of the Selection Committee is closely related to a candidate appearing for the selection, it would not be enough for such member merely to withdraw from participation in the interview of the candidate related to him but he must withdraw altogether from the entire selection process and ask the authorities to nominate another person in his place on the selection committee, because other-wise all the selections made would be vitiated on account of reasonable likelihood of bias affecting the process of selection. But the situation here is a little different because the selection of candidates to the Haryana Civil Service (Executive) and allied services is being made not by any Selection Committee constituted for that purpose but it is being done by the Haryana Public Service f Commission which is a Commission set up under Article 316 of the Constitution. It is a Commission which consists of a Chairman and a specified member of members and is a Constitutional Authority. We do not think that the principle which requires that a member of a Selection Committee whose close relative is appearing for selection should decline to become a member of the selection committee or withdraw from it leaving it to the appointing authority to nominate another person in his place, need be applied in case of a Constitutional Authority like the Public Service Commission, whether Central or State. If a member of a Public Service Commission were to withdraw altogether from the selection process on the ground that a close relative of his is appearing for selection, no other person save a member can be substituted in his place. And it may sometimes happen that no other member is available to take the place of such member and the functioning of the Public Service Commission may be affected. When two or more members of a Public Service Commission are holding a viva voce examination, they are functioning not as individuals but as the Public Service Commission. Of course, we must make it clear that when a close relative of a member of a Public Service Commission is appearing for interview, such member must withdrew from participation in the interview of that candidate and must not take part in any discussion in regard to the merits of that candidate and even the marks or credits given to that candidate should not be disclosed to him.

By applying the above principle the Court held that the function of the Public Service Commission was not in violation of procedural fairness. It observed–

> Here in the present case it was common ground between the parties that Shri Raghubar Dayal Gaur did not participate at all in interviewing Trilok

Nath Sharma and likewise Shri R.C. Marya did not participate at all when Shakuntala Rani and Balbir Singh came to be interviewed and in fact, both of them retired from the room when the interviews of their respective relatives were held. Moreover, neither of them took any part in any discussion in regard to the merits of his relatives nor is there anything to show that the marks or credits obtained by their respective relatives at the interviews were disclosed to them. We are therefore of the view that there was no infirmity attaching to the selections made by the Haryana Public Service Commission on the ground that, though their close relative were appearing for the interview, Shri Raghubar Dayal Gaur and Shri R.C. Marya did not withdraw completely from the entire selection process. This ground urged on behalf of the petitioners must therefore be rejected.

In the leading case of *Election Commission of India v. Dr Subramaniam Swamy*[31] the Supreme Court had the opportunity to analyse the doctrine to the functioning of the constitutional body such as the Election Commission of India. In this case the disqualification of Ms. Jayalalitha to become a member of the Legislative Assembly had to be determined by the Election Commission. She raised an objection against Chief Election Commissioner on the ground of reasonable apprehension of bias on the ground of close and intimate relationship between the respondent and the CEC, apart from the fact that the wife of CEC was the lawyer of the respondent in different suit. The Court while dealing with the issue analysed the doctrine of necessity–

> It is well settled that the law permits certain things to be done as a matter of necessity which it would otherwise not countenance on the touchstone of judicial propriety. Stated differently, the doctrine of necessity makes it imperative for the authority to decide and considerations of judicial propriety must yield. It is often invoked in cases of bias where there is no other authority or Judge to decide the issue. If the doctrine of necessity is not allowed full play in certain unavoidable situations, it would impede the course of justice itself and the defaulting party would benefit therefrom. Take the case of a certain taxing statute which taxes certain perquisites allowed to Judges. If the validity of such a provision is challenged who but the members of the judiciary must decide it. If all the Judges are disqualified on the plea that striking down of such a legislation would benefit them, a stalemate situation may develop. In such cases the doctrine of necessity comes into play. If the choice is between allowing a biased person to act or to stifle the action altogether, the choice must fall in favour of the former as it is the only way to promote decision-making. In the present case also if the two Election Commissioners are able to reach a unanimous decision, there is no need for the Chief Election Commissioner to participate, if not the doctrine of necessity may have to be invoked.

31. (1996) 4 SCC 104.

Thus the Court concluded that–

> [T]he proper course to follow is that the Chief Election Commissioner should call a meeting of the Election Commission to adjudicate on the issue of disqualification of Ms J. Jayalalitha on the grounds alleged by Dr Swamy. After calling the meeting he should act as the Chairman but then he may recuse himself by announcing that he would not participate in the formation of opinion. If the two Election Commissioners reach a unanimous opinion, the Chief Election Commissioner will have the opinion communicated to the Governor. If the two Election Commissioners do not reach a unanimous decision in the matter of expressing their opinion on the issue referred to the Election Commission, it would be necessary for the Chief Election Commissioner to express his opinion on the doctrine of necessity. We think that in the special circumstances of this case this course of action would be the most appropriate one to follow because if the two Election Commissioners do not agree, we have no doubt that the doctrine of necessity would compel the Chief Election Commissioner to express his views so that the majority opinion could be communicated to the Governor to enable him to take a decision in accordance therewith as required by Article 192(1) of the Constitution.

5.14 RIGHT OF FAIR HEARING

Audi alteram partem is the second cardinal principles of natural justice which aims to protect an individual from administrative actions whenever his legal rights are jeopardized or adversely affected. It implies that 'no decision shall be given against a party without affording him a reasonable hearing'. The person concerned should be given a reasonable opportunity to defend his legal right. The primary objective of this procedural tool is to enable an administrative authority *to arrive at a just decision and it is calculated to act as a healthy check on abuse or misuse of power and hence its reach should not be narrowed and its applicability circumscribed.*[32]

In *Canara Bank v. Debasis Das*[33] the Supreme Court observed–

> Natural justice is another name for commonsense justice. Rules of natural justice are not codified canons. But they are principles ingrained into the conscience of man. Natural justice is the administration of justice in a commonsense liberal way. Justice is based substantially on natural ideals and human values. The administration of justice is to be freed from the narrow and restricted considerations which are usually associated with a formulated law involving linguistic technicalities and grammatical niceties. It is the substance of justice which has to determine its form.

32. (1978) 1 SCC 248.
33. AIR 2003 SC 2041: (2003) 4 SCC 557.

The expressions "natural justice" and "legal justice" do not present a water-tight classification. It is the substance of justice which is to be secured by both, and whenever legal justice fails to achieve this solemn purpose, natural justice is called in aid of legal justice. Natural justice relieves legal justice from unnecessary technicality, grammatical pedantry or logical prevarication. It supplies the omissions of a formulated law. As Lord Buckmaster said, no form or procedure should ever be permitted to exclude the presentation of a litigants' defence.

The adherence to principles of natural justice as recognized by all civilized States is of supreme importance when a quasi-judicial body embarks on determining disputes between the parties, or any administrative action involving civil consequences is in issue. These principles are well settled. The first and foremost principle is what is commonly known as *audi alteram partem* rule. It says that no one should be condemned unheard. Notice is the first limb of this principle. It must be precise and unambiguous. It should appraise the party determinatively the case he has to meet. Time given for the purpose should be adequate so as to enable him to make his representation. In the absence of a notice of the kind and such reasonable opportunity, the order passed becomes wholly vitiated. Thus, it is but essential that party should be put on notice of the case before any adverse order is passed against him. This is one of the most important principles of natural justice. It is after all an approved rule of fair play. The concept has gained significance and shades with time. When the historic document was made at (sic) in 1215, the first statutory recognition of this principle found its way into the "Magna Carta". The classic exposition of Sir Edward Coke of natural justice requires to "vocate interrogate and adjudicate'. In the celebrated case of *Cooper v. Wandsworth Board of Works*,[34] the principle was thus stated:

"Even God did not pass a sentence upon Adam, before he was called upon to make his defence. "Adam" says God, "where art thou has thou (sic) not eaten of the tree whereof I commanded thee that though should not eat".

Since then the principle has been chiselled, honed and refined, enriching its content. Judicial treatment has added light and luminosity to the concept, like polishing of a diamond.

Principles of natural justice are those rules which have been laid down by the Courts as being the minimum protection of the rights of the individual against the arbitrary procedure that may be adopted by a judicial, quasi-judicial and administrative authority while making an order affecting those rights. These rules are intended to prevent such authority from doing injustice.

In the case of *State of Orissa v. Dr. Binapani Dei*[35] the Supreme Court had for the first time emphasized the importance of fair procedures as an essential part of *justice.* While dealing with the issue of superannuation

34. 1963 (143) ER 414.
35. AIR 1967 SC 1269 (1967) 2 SCR 625.

based on re-fixation of date of birth of the respondent the Court held that when a person disputes the claim then it is necessary to inform him about the case, the available evidences and should provide him with a *fair opportunity of meeting that case before a decision adverse to him is taken.* Describing the importance and purpose of fair hearing it observed that–

> An order by the State to the prejudice of a person in derogation of his vested rights may be made only in accordance with the basic rules of justice and fair play. The deciding authority, it is true, is not in the position of a Judge called upon to decide an action between contesting parties, and strict compliance with the forms of judicial procedure may not be insisted upon. He is however under a duty to give the person against whom an enquiry is held an opportunity to set up his version or defence and an opportunity to correct or to controvert any evidence in the possession of the authority which is sought to be relied upon to his prejudice. For that purpose the person against whom an enquiry is held must be informed of the case he is called upon to meet, and the evidence in support thereof.

In *Bharat Swak Samaj v. Lt. Governor*[36] the land of the appellant was to be acquired by the Government of Delhi for the public purpose of creating Mehrauli Heritage Zone under the Land Acquisition Act. The order was challenged on the ground of improper invocation of urgency provision. Quashing the land acquisition order the Supreme Court held that the invocation of the urgency provision under Section 17(1) of the Act was *ex facie illegal* as well as arbitrary and unjustified. After referring to several judgments the Court highlighted the importance of *audi alteram partem* by recognizing that–

> [T]he acquisition of one's land is a serious matter and, except in the cases of real urgency, no person can be deprived of his property without being afforded an opportunity to file objections under Section 5-A(1) and without the sanction of law and without complying with the basics of natural justice. Section 5-A represents the statutory embodiment of the rule of audi alteram partem and unless there are compelling reasons, the State cannot invoke the urgency provision contained in Section 17(1) and dispense with the application of Section 5-A.[37]

It held that no material was produced by the respondents to show the need of execution on an emergency basis and concluded that the development of Mehrauli Heritage Zone was *not so urgent that it could not wait for the few month's time likely to be consumed in giving opportunity to the appellant to file objections under Section 5-A and holding of inquiry*

36. (2012) 12 SCC 675.
37. Ibid Para 11.

under Section 5-A(2). It further observed that the Lieutanant Governor of Delhi had not applied his mind regarding the issue of urgency and had mechanically invoked S.17(1) without giving due consideration to the grave consequences imposed on the person whose land is to be acquired.

5.15 COMPONENTS OF FAIR HEARING

The three important aspects of the doctrine of *audi alteram partem* are–

(a) The person against whom the proposed action is to be taken should be informed of the charges and through a notice should be intimated about the reasons and the nature and consequences of the proposed action.

(b) The person should be given an adequate opportunity to put forward his defence against the proposed action.

(c) The administrative authority should take the decision or action after duly considering the charges made, and the explanation and defences made by the affected person. The decision must be based on valid reasons.

The Court described the components of fair hearing in *Tulsiram Patel case*[38] as–

> [T]he audi alteram partem rule, in its fullest amplitude means that a person against whom an order to his prejudice may be passed should be informed of the allegations and charges against him, be given an opportunity of submitting his explanation thereto, have the right to know the evidence, both oral or documentary, by which the matter is proposed to be decided against him, and to inspect the documents which are relied upon for the purpose of being used against him, to have the witnesses who are to give evidence against him examined in his presence and have the right to cross-examine them, and to lead his own evidence, both oral and documentary, in his defence. The process of a fair hearing need not, however, conform to the judicial process in a Court of law, because judicial adjudication of causes involves a number of technical rules of procedure and evidence which are unnecessary and not required for the purpose of a fair hearing within the meaning of audi alteram partem rule in a quasi-judicial or administrative inquiry.[39]

Right of Fair Hearing comprises of several sub-set of rights which ensures that the administrative action does not prejudicially affect the rights of an individual. Some of the important rights are–

(i) Right of Notice

(ii) Right to access and examine documents

38. (1985) 3 SCC 398.

39. Id. Para 96.

(iii) Right to access enquiry reports
(iv) Right of Oral Hearing
(v) Right of Cross Examination
(vi) Right of Legal Representation

These rights are subject to statutory limitations and exceptions. The extent of application of these rights will be dependent upon the facts of each case, on the procedural norms laid down in the rules and regulations and to the extent of prejudice caused to the claimant in case of non-compliance. Speaking on the issue the Supreme Court in *Managing Director, ECIL Hyderbad v. B. Karunakar*[40] observed – *What particular rule of natural justice should apply to a given case must depend to a great extent on the facts and circumstances of that case, the framework of the law under which the inquiry is held and the Constitution of the tribunal or the body of persons appointed for that purpose. Whenever a complaint is made before a Court that some principle of natural justice has been contravened, the Court has to decide whether the observance of that rule was necessary for a just decision on the facts of that case. The rule that inquiry must be held in good faith and without bias and not arbitrarily or unreasonably is now included among the principles of natural justice.*

5.16 PREJUDICE TEST

Principles of natural justice have been developed with the objective of ensuring fairness in administrative action. But it is equally important to note that these principles should not become unnecessary road blocks in the way of administrative efficiency and functioning. In this context the Supreme Court has developed the prejudice test to determine the scope and extent of the application of the various components of fair hearing and whether non-compliance of any rules of fair hearing will invalidate the entire administrative action taken.

In *Chairman, Board of Mining Examination v. Ramjee*[41], the Supreme Court had observed that–

> Natural justice is not an unruly horse, no lurking land-mine, nor a judicial cure-all. If fairness is shown by the decision-maker to the man proceeded against, the form features and the fundamentals of such essential processual propriety being conditioned by the facts and circumstances of each situation, no breach of natural justice can be complained of. Unnatural expansion of natural justice, without reference to the administrative realities and other

40. AIR 1994 SC 1074 (1993) 4 SCC 727.
41. MANU/SC/0061/1977 as quoted in *Karunakar case* (AIR 1994 SC 1074).

> factors of a given case, can be exasperating. The Courts cannot look at law in the abstract or natural justice as a mere artifact. Nor can they fit into a rigid mould the concept of reasonable opportunity. If the totality of circumstances satisfies the Court that the party visited with adverse order has not suffered from denial of reasonable opportunity, the Court will decline to be punctilious or fanatical as if the rules of natural justice were sacred scriptures.

In *Canara Bank v. Debasis Das*[42] the Court concretized the theory of prejudice test and observed–

> Concept of natural justice has undergone a great deal of change in recent years. Rules of natural justice are not rules embodied always expressly in a statute or in rules framed thereunder. They may be implied from the nature of the duty to be performed under a statute. What particular rule of natural justice should be implied and what its context should be in a given case must depend to a great extent on the fact and circumstances of that case, the frame-work of the statute under which the enquiry is held. The old distinction between a judicial act and an administrative at has withered away. Even an administrative order which involves civil consequences must be consistent with the rules of natural justice. Expression 'civil consequences' encompasses infraction of not merely property or personal rights but of civil liberties, material deprivations, and non-pecuniary damages. In its wide umbrella comes everything that affects a citizen in his civil life.

It was further observed that if the appellant fails to show that any prejudice suffered, failure of justice has taken place or it is not in public interest to dismiss a petition, the Court may refuse to exercise jurisdiction – *Legal formulations cannot be divorced from the fact situation of the case.*

5.17 DISTINGUISHING BETWEEN SUBSTANTIVE AND MANDATORY PROVISION WITH DIRECTORY PROVISIONS

In *State Bank of Patiala v. S.K. Sharma*[43] the Supreme Court distinguished between mandatory and directory provisions and upheld the relevancy of the prejudice test based on the nature of the procedural non-compliance. In this case the respondent was working as a Manager in one of the branches of the appellant Bank. He was charged with temporary misappropriation of fund of one Jarnail Singh. The respondent had received the amount from Jarnail Singh but did not credit the amount into the concerned bank account even though he had issued a letter stating that the bank loan had been adjusted. The principle point of defence was that half an hour before the

42. AIR 2003 SC 2041 : (2003) 4 SCC 557.
43. AIR 1996 SC 1669 : (1996) 3 SCC 364.

commencement of the enquiry proceedings a list of documents and witness statements were provided to the respondent but the actual copies of the documents and the statements recorded during the preliminary enquiry were not supplied to him. He was asked to peruse, examine and take notes of the documents and statements. The respondent contended that non-furnishing of the documents and statements of the witnesses adversely affected his ability to properly defend himself and were in violation of Regulation of 68 (b) (iii) of the

Relevant portions of Regulation 68 are–

(*a*) The inquiring authority shall where the officer does not admit all or any of the articles of charge furnish to such officer a list of documents by which and a list of witnesses by whom, the articles of charge are proposed to be proved.

(*b*) The inquiring authority shall also record an order that the officer may for the purpose of preparing his defence:–

(*i*) inspect and take notes of the *documents listed* within five days of the order or within such further time not exceeding five days as the inquiring authority may allow;

(*ii*) submit a list of documents and witnesses that he wants for enquiry;

(*iii*) be supplied with *copies of statements of witnesses*, if any, recorded earlier and the inquiring authority shall furnish such copies *not later than three days before the commencement of the examination of the witnesses by the inquiring authority.*

(*iv*) give a notice within ten days of the order or within such further time not exceeding ten days as the inquiring authority may allow for the discovery of production of the documents referred to at (*ii*) above.

In violation of the requirement to provide documents prior to three days of the enquiry, the respondent was given the opportunity to examine the documents on the same day of the enquiry. The core issue before the Supreme Court was 'whether the failure to literally comply with sub-clause (*iii*) of clause (*b*) of Regulation 68 vitiates the enquiry altogether *or* whether it can be held in the circumstances that there has been a substantial compliance with the said sub-clause and that on that account, the enquiry and the punishment awarded cannot be said to have been vitiated.' In this case the Court laid down the theory of mandatory and directory procedures and held that–

> Sub-clause (*iii*) aforesaid is indisputably part of a regulation made in exercise of statutory authority. The sub-clause incorporates a facet of the principle of natural justice. It is designed to provide an adequate opportunity to the

delinquent officer to cross-examine the witnesses effectively and thereby defend himself properly. It is relevant to note in this behalf that neither the enquiry officers' report nor the judgment of the trial court, appellate court or High Court say that the respondent had protested at the relevant time that he was denied an adequate opportunity to cross-examine the witnesses effectively or to defend himself properly on account of non-supply of the statements of witnesses. The appellate court, on the contrary, has recorded that when he was advised to peruse, examine and take notes from the documents including the statements of witnesses (Kaur Singh and Balwant Singh), the only objection raised by the respondent was that "the documents marked Exhs. P-6, P-10 and P-11 were only photostat copies and not originals and should not be considered or marked exhibits. (Exhs. P-6, P-10 and P-11 are documents other than the statements of witnesses, i.e., of Kaur Singh and Balwant Singh.) Moreover, as pointed out above, the examination of witnesses began long after the expiry of three days from the day on which the respondent was advised to and he did peruse the documents and statements of witnesses. In the circumstances, it is possible to say that there has been a substantial compliance with the aforesaid sub-clause (*iii*) in the facts and circumstances of this case, though not a full compliance. This, in turn, raises the question whether each and every violation of rules or regulations governing the enquiry automatically vitiates the enquiry and the punishment awarded *or* whether the test of substantial compliance can be invoked in cases of such violation and whether the issue has to be examined from the point of view of prejudice. So far as the position obtaining under the Code of Civil Procedure and the Code of Criminal Procedure is concerned, there are specific provisions thereunder providing for such situation. There is Section 99 of the Code of Civil Procedure and Chapter 35 of the Code of Criminal Procedure. Section 99 CPC says:

"No decree shall be reversed or substantially varied, nor shall any case be remanded, in appeal on account of any misjoinder or non-joinder of parties or causes of action *or any error, defect or irregularity in any proceedings in the suit, not affecting the merits of the case or the jurisdiction of the Court.*"

Section 465(1) of the Criminal Procedure Code, which occurs in Chapter 35 similarly provides that:

"Subject to the provisions hereinbefore contained, no finding, sentence or order passed by a Court of competent jurisdiction shall be reversed or altered by a Court of appeal, confirmation or revision on account of any error, omission or irregularity in the complaint, summons, warrant, proclamation, order, judgment *or other proceedings before or during trial or in any inquiry or other proceedings under this Code*, or any error, or irregularity in any sanction for the prosecution, unless in the opinion of that Court, a failure of justice has in fact been occasioned thereby."

It is not brought to our notice that the State Bank of Patiala (Officers') Service Regulation contains provision corresponding to Section 99 CPC or Section 465 CrPC. Does it mean that any and every violation of the regulations renders

> the enquiry and the punishment void *or* whether the principle underlying Section 99 CPC and Section 465 CrPC is applicable in the case of disciplinary proceedings as well. In our opinion, the test in such cases should be one of prejudice, as would be later explained in this judgment. But this statement is subject to a rider. The regulations may contain certain substantive provisions, e.g., who is the competent authority to impose a particular punishment on a particular employee/officer. Such provisions must be strictly complied with. But there may be any number of procedural provisions which stand on a different footing. We must hasten to add that even among procedural provisions, there may be some provisions which are of a fundamental nature in the case of which the theory of substantial compliance may not be applicable. For example, take a case where a rule expressly provides that the delinquent officer/employee shall be given an opportunity to produce evidence/material in support of his case after the close of evidence of the other side. If no such opportunity is given at all in spite of a request therefor, it will be difficult to say that the enquiry is not vitiated. But in respect of many procedural provisions, it would be possible to apply the theory of substantial compliance or the test of prejudice, as the case may be. The position can be stated in the following words: (1) Regulations which are of a substantive nature have to be complied with and in case of such provisions, the theory of substantial compliance would not be available. (2) Even among procedural provisions, there may be some provisions of a fundamental nature which have to be complied with and in whose case, the theory of substantial compliance may not be available. (3) In respect of procedural provisions other than of a fundamental nature, the theory of substantial compliance would be available. In such cases, complaint/objection on this score have to be judged on the touchstone of *prejudice*, as explained later in this judgment. In other words, the test is: *all things taken together whether the delinquent officer/employee had or did not have a fair hearing.* We may clarify that which provision falls in which of the aforesaid categories is a matter to be decided in each case having regard to the nature and character of the relevant provision.

After analysis of the facts of the case and the behaviour of the respondent the Court concluded that the respondent had waived of his right to claim the procedural safeguards and since there was substantial compliance of the rules no prejudice was suffered by the respondent. *The respondent did not raise any objection during the enquiry that the non-furnishing of the copies of the statements is disabling him or has disabled him, as the case may be, from effectively cross-examining the witnesses or to defend himself.... no prejudice has resulted to the respondent on account of not furnishing him the copies of the statements of witnesses.*

5.18 RIGHT OF NOTICE

The right of notice is the first essential component of *audi alteram partem.* The term 'notice' originated from the Latin word *'notia'* implying 'being known'. The sending of notice marks the first step towards initiating an adjudication process and fulfils the objective of informing the other party and enabling him to prepare for the defence. Non-compliance with this essential rule is often considered as negating the application of principles of natural justice. Notice is considered as *sine quo non* of fair hearing.

A valid notice should contain information relating to time, place and nature of hearing; the legal authority before whom the hearing is to take place; description of the specific charges etc. The adequacy of a notice is to determined on the basis of whether sufficient information had been provided to the affected person so as to enable him to prepare for his defence effectively. In *State of Jammu and Kashmir v. Haji Wali Mohammed*[44] a notice of 24 hours were given by the Municipality for the purpose of demolition of a house in a dilapidated condition. The Supreme Court invalidating the action taken held that even though no time was fixed in the statute for determining the period of notice, it was necessary to grant a reasonable period of time.

Speaking on the importance of notice the Supreme Court made the following observation in *Olga Tellis v. Bombay Municipal Corporation*[45]-

> The proposition that notice need not be given of a proposed action because, there can possibly be no answer to it, is contrary to the well-recognised understanding of the real import of the rule of hearing. That proposition overlooks that justice must not only be done but must manifestly be seen to be done and confuses one for the other. The appearance of injustice is the denial of justice. It is the dialogue with the person likely to be affected by the proposed action which meets the requirement that justice must also be seen to be done. Procedural safeguards have their historical origins in the notion that conditions of personal freedom can be preserved only when there is some institutional check on arbitrary action on the part of public authorities [Kadish, 'Methodology and Criteria in Due Process Adjudication — A Survey and Criticism'[46]] . The right to be heard has two facets, intrinsic and instrumental. The intrinsic value of that right consists in the opportunity which it gives to individuals or groups, against whom decisions taken by public authorities operate, to participate in the processes by which those decisions are made, an opportunity that expresses their dignity as persons. [*Goldberg v. Kelly*[47] (right of the poor to participate in public processes).]
>
> Whatever its outcome, such a hearing represents a valued human interaction in which the affected person experiences at least the satisfaction of participating in the decision that vitally concerns her, and perhaps the separate satisfaction

44. (1972) 2 SCC 402.
45. AIR 1986 SC 180.
46. 66 Yale LJ 319, 340 (1957).
47. 397 US 254, 264-65 (1970).

> of receiving an explanation of why the decision is being made in a certain way. Both the right to be heard from, and the right to be told why, are analytically distinct from the right to secure a different outcome; these rights to interchange express the elementary idea that to be a *person*, rather than a *thing*, is at least to be consulted about what is done with one. Justice Frankfurter captured part of this sense of procedural justice when he wrote that the "validity and moral authority of a conclusion largely depend on the mode by which it was reached ....No better instrument has been devised for arriving at truth than to give a person in jeopardy of serious loss notice of the case against him and opportunity to meet it. Nor has a better way been found for generating the feeling, so important to a popular government, that justice has been done" [*Joint Anti-facist Refugee Committee* v. *McGrath*[48]]. At stake here is not just the much-acclaimed *appearance* of justice but, from a perspective that treats process as intrinsically significant, the very *essence* of justice [**See** American Constitutional Law by Laurence H. Tribe, Professor of Law, Harvard University[49]] .
>
> The instrumental facet of the right of hearing consists in the means which it affords of assuring that the public rules of conduct, which result in benefits and prejudices alike, are in fact accurately and consistently followed.
>
> It ensures that a challenged action accurately reflects the substantive rules applicable to such action; its point is less to assure *participation* than to use participation to assure *accuracy.*[50]

In the leading case of *S.L. Kapoor v. Jagmohan*[51] invalidated an administrative action on the ground of non-issuance of a show cause notice. The Court categorically held that *"In our view the principles of natural justice know of no exclusionary rule dependent on whether it would have made any difference if natural justice had been observed. The non-observance of natural justice is itself prejudice to any man and proof of prejudice independently of proof of denial of natural justice is unnecessary. It ill comes from a person who has denied justice that the person who has been denied justice is not prejudiced."*

The importance of right to notice was discussed by the Supreme Court in the leading case of *Olga Tellis v. Bombay Municipal Corporation.*[52] In this case the Court recognized the necessity to issue notice even when the statute specifically provided for taking an action without a notice. Under Section 314 (a) of the Bombay Municipal Corporation Act the Commissioner may, *without notice*, take steps for the removal of encroachments in or upon

48. 341 US 123, 171-72 (1951).
49. (1978 Edn., p. 503).
50. Id.
51. (1980) 4 SCC 379.
52. AIR 1986 SC 180.

any street, channel, drains, etc. One of the core issue before the Court was whether such a procedure can be considered to be legal, fair and reasonable. The Court upheld the legality of the provision by emphasizing that such powers could be exercised by the Commissioner without notice only in extraneous and urgent circumstances. The Court observed–

> Section 314 is in the nature of an enabling provision and not of a compulsive character. It enables the Commissioner, in appropriate cases, to dispense with previous notice to persons who are likely to be affected by the proposed action. It does not require and, cannot be read to mean that, in total disregard of the relevant circumstances pertaining to a given situation, the Commissioner must cause the removal of an encroachment without issuing previous notice. The primary rule of construction is that the language of the law must receive its plain and natural meaning. What Section 314 provides is that the Commissioner *may*, without notice, cause an encroachment to be removed. It does not command that the Commissioner shall, without notice, cause an encroachment to be removed. Putting it differently, Section 314 confers on the Commissioner the discretion to cause an encroachment to be removed with or without notice. That discretion has to be exercised in a reasonable manner so as to comply with the constitutional mandate that the procedure accompanying the performance of a public act must be fair and reasonable. We must lean in favour of this interpretation because it helps sustain the validity of the law. Reading Section 314 as containing a command not to issue notice before the removal of an encroachment will make the law invalid.
>
> It must further be presumed that, while vesting in the Commissioner the power to act without notice, the legislature intended that the power should be exercised sparingly and in cases of urgency which brook no delay. In all other cases, no departure from the audi alteram partem rule ("Hear the other side") could be presumed to have been intended. Section 314 is so designed as to exclude the principles of natural justice by way of exception and not as a general rule. There are situations which demand the exclusion of the rules of natural justice by reason of diverse factors like time, place, the apprehended danger and so on. The ordinary rule which regulates all procedure is that persons who are likely to be affected by the proposed action must be afforded an opportunity of being heard as to why that action should not be taken. The hearing may be given individually or collectively, depending upon the facts of each situation. A departure from this fundamental rule of natural justice may be presumed to have been intended by the legislature only in circumstances which warrant it. Such circumstances must be shown to exist, when so required, the burden being upon those who affirm their existence.[53]

In this case the Court recognized that the unauthorized pavement dwellers are also entitled to enjoy the benefits of fair hearing.

53. (1985) 3 SCC 545, para 44-45.

However if the aggrieved party had prior information about the proposed action to be taken and he had been adequate opportunity to make representation against such action, then the formal requirement of notice can be dispensed with on the ground of useless formality. In *Keshav Mills Co. Ltd v. Union of India*[54] the Government of India after complying with procedures laid down under the Industries (Development and Regulation) Act, 1951 decided to take over the management of the Keshav Mills for a period of five years because after due enquiry it was of the opinion that the factory was being managed in a manner which was detrimental to public interest. At the time of handing over the keys of the factory the appellants objected to the action taken by the Government on the ground of no prior notice being sent. The Court after analyzing the various facts of the case negated the requirement of a fresh notice and held that –

> [S]ince the appellants have received a fair treatment and also all reasonable opportunities to make out their own case before Government they cannot be allowed to make any grievance of the fact that they were not given a formal notice calling upon them to show cause why their undertaking should not be taken over or that they had not been furnished with a copy of the report. They had made all the representations that they could possibly have made against the proposed take-over. By no stretch of imagination, can it be said that the order for take-over took them by surprise. In fact Government gave them ample opportunity to reopen and run the mill on their own if they wanted to avoid the takeover. The blunt fact is that the appellants just did not have the necessary resources to do so. Insistence on a formal hearing in such circumstances is nothing but insistence on an empty formality.

5.19 RIGHT TO ACCESS AND EXAMINE DOCUMENTS

Access to documents on the basis of which charges have been made needs to be provided to the affected person so that he may be able to prepare for his defence properly and be able to refute the charges made.[55] In *Kashinath Dikshita v. Union of India*[56] a departmental enquiry was instituted against the appellant on some serious charges which were specified in the statement of allegations accompanying the chargesheet. He challenged the dismissal order on the ground of violation of principles of natural justice as he had not been given copies of all the statements made by witnesses at the preliminary inquiry nor were the copies of the document based on which the charges were levelled were provided to him. The disciplinary authority allowed

54. (1973) 1 SCC 380.
55. *State of Uttar Pradesh v. Saroj Kumar Sinha* (2010) 2 SCC 772.
56. (1986) 3 SCC 229.

him to inspect the copies of the statement and documents in question and make personal notes from it, but denied his request of taking the help of a stenographer. In totality there were about 38 witnesses who were examined and about 112 documents which were produced. Upholding the claim of denial of reasonable opportunity to defend himself the Court observed–

> When a government servant is facing a disciplinary proceeding, he is entitled to be afforded a reasonable opportunity to meet the charges against him in an effective manner. And no one facing a departmental enquiry can effectively meet the charges unless the copies of the relevant statements and documents to be used against him are made available to him. In the absence of such copies, how can the concerned employee prepare his defence, cross-examine the witnesses, and point out the inconsistencies with a view to show that the allegations are incredible? It is difficult to comprehend why the disciplinary authority assumed an intransigent posture and refused to furnish the copies notwithstanding the specific request made by the appellant in this behalf. Perhaps the disciplinary authority made it a prestige issue. If only the disciplinary authority had asked itself the question: "What is the harm in making available the material?" and weighed the pros and cons, the disciplinary authority could not reasonably have adopted such a rigid and adamant attitude. On the one hand there was the risk of the time and effort invested in the departmental enquiry being wasted if the courts came to the conclusion that failure to supply these materials would be tantamount to denial of reasonable opportunity to the appellant to defend himself. On the other hand by making available the copies of the documents and statements the disciplinary authority was not running any risk. There was nothing confidential or privileged in it. It is not even the case of the respondent that there was involved any consideration of security of State or privilege. No doubt the disciplinary authority gave an opportunity to the appellant to inspect the documents and take notes as mentioned earlier. But even in this connection the reasonable request of the appellant to have the relevant portions of the documents extracted with the help of his stenographer was refused. He was told to himself make such notes as he could.
>
> ……
>
> Be that as it may, even without going into minute details it is evident that the appellant was entitled to have an access to the documents and statements throughout the course of the inquiry. He would have needed these documents and statements in order to cross-examine the 38 witnesses who were produced at the inquiry to establish the charges against him. So also at the time of arguments, he would have needed the copies of the documents. So also he would have needed the copies of the documents to enable him to effectively cross-examine the witnesses with reference to the contents of the documents. It is obvious that he could not have done so if copies had not been made available to him. Taking an overall view of the matter we have no doubt in our mind that the appellant has been denied a reasonable opportunity of

exonerating himself. We do not consider it necessary to quote extensively from the authorities cited on behalf of the parties, beyond making passing reference to some of the citations, for, whether or not there has been a denial to afford a reasonable opportunity in the backdrop of this case must substantially depend upon the facts pertaining to this matter.[57]

In this case the Department had failed to establish that the appellant did not suffer from any prejudice due to non-suppliance of the documents. This view was reiterated by the Supreme Court in *State of U.P. v. Shatrughan Lal*[58] wherein the respondent argued that the dismissal order issued were illegal as the copies of the documents on the basis of which charge-sheet were prepared were not supplied to him nor were the copies of the statements recorded during the preliminary enquiry. In addition the records were not made available to him for inspection. Applying the test laid down in *Kashinath Dikshita case* the Court held that–

Preliminary enquiry which is conducted invariably on the back of the delinquent employee may often constitute the whole basis of the charge-sheet. Before a person is, therefore, called upon to submit his reply to the charge-sheet, he must, on a request made by him in that behalf, be supplied the copies of the statements of witnesses recorded during the preliminary enquiry particularly if those witnesses are proposed to be examined at the departmental trial. This principle was reiterated in *Kashinath Dikshita* v. *Union of India*[59] wherein it was also laid down that this lapse would vitiate the departmental proceedings unless it was shown and established as a fact that non-supply of copies of those documents had not caused any prejudice to the delinquent in his defence.

It was held that copies of the documents which were indicated in the charge-sheet to be relied upon as proof in support of the articles of charges were not supplied to the respondent nor was any offer made to him to inspect those documents, hence there was a failure to comply with the principles of natural justice. In addition the appellant had failed to establish that non-supply of the documents had not caused any prejudice to the respondent in defending himself.

Highlighting the importance of access to documents the Sagir Ahmad J. observed–

[O]ne of the principles of natural justice is that a person against whom an action is proposed to be taken has to be given an opportunity of hearing. This opportunity has to be an effective opportunity and not a mere pretence. In departmental proceedings where charge-sheet is issued and the documents which are proposed to be utilised against that person are indicated in the

57. Id Para 10 - 12.
58. (1998) 6 SCC 651.
59. (1986) 3 SCC 229.

charge-sheet but copies thereof are not supplied to him in spite of his request, and he is, at the same time, called upon to submit his reply, it cannot be said that an effective opportunity to defend was provided to him.[60]

5.20 RIGHT OF HEARING

Right of hearing is the most important component of fair hearing. Hearing provides an opportunity to the aggrieved person to make a representation against the proposed action to be taken and to rebut and refute any adverse charges made against him.

Right of hearing includes–

(i) Presentation of the arguments by written statements or oral submissions

(ii) Producing of witnesses and relevant evidences

(iii) Cross-examination of other witnesses giving evidences against him

(iv) Submission of the claims

In *Keshav Mills Co. Ltd v. Union of India*[61] the Court discussed the importance of right of hearing. The appellants had argued that the Government was bound to give them a hearing before finally deciding to take over the factory under Section 18A of the Act. Recognizing the far-reaching consequences of such actions on the rights of the company, its shareholders, its employees and all persons who have contractual dealings and transactions with that company the Court held that it is necessary to provide at *some stage a reasonable opportunity to the undertaking concerned for making suitable representations against the proposed take-over.* Determining the nature and extent of fair hearing the Court observed–

> The concept of natural justice cannot be put into a straight-jacket. It is futile, therefore, to look for definitions or standards of natural justice from various decisions and then try to apply them to the facts of any given case. The only essential point that has to be kept in mind in all cases is that the person concerned should have a reasonable opportunity of presenting his case and that the administrative authority concerned should act fairly, impartially and reasonably. Where administrative officers are concerned, the duty is not so much to act judicially as to act fairly. See, for instance, the observations of Lord Parker in *In re H.K. (an infant).*[62] It only means that such measure of natural justice should be applied as was described by Lord Reid in *Ridge* v. *Baldwin case* a "insusceptible of exact definition but what a reasonable man would regard as a fair procedure in particular circumstances". However, even

60. (1998) 6 SCC 651.
61. (1973) 1 SCC 380.
62. (1967) 2 QB 617.

the application of the concept of fair-play requires real flexibility. Everything will depend on the actual facts and circumstances of a case. As Tucker, L.J., observed in *Russell* v. *Duke of Norfolk* [63]: "The requirements of natural justice must depend on the circumstances of the case, the nature of the enquiry, the rules under which the tribunal is acting, the subject-matter that is being dealt with and so forth."

Applying the above rationale in the present case, the Court held that –

In the instant case, the Government of India came to hold the opinion that there was a substantial fall in the volume of production in respect of the Company's production of cotton textiles for which Government apparently found no justification having regard to the prevailing economic conditions. The Government was perfectly within its rights to appoint, under the terms of Section 15, an investigating body for the purpose of making full and complete investigation into the circumstances of the case. This is what the Government did and the appellants do not, as indeed they cannot, find fault with this action of the Government. It is the admitted case that for three years prior to 1969 the Company had been running into continual difficulties as a result of which the company suffered losses which amounted up to Rupees 57.76 lakhs. In fact the mill had to be closed by the end of 1968. It was only on May 31, 1969, that Government of India appointed the Investigating Committee to investigate into the affairs of the Company's mill. The appellants do not make any grievance against the Investigating Committee regarding the manner in which they carried out the investigation. It is admitted that the Committee gave to the Company a full opportunity of being heard and also an opportunity of adducing evidence. There can, therefore, be no complaint that up to this stage there was any failure to observe the rules of natural justice.

In January 1970, the report of the Investigating Committee was submitted to Government and, on the appellants' own showing, they knew that there was a likelihood of Government appointing a Controller under Section 18-A to take over the appellants' undertaking. There can be no question that the appellants were fully aware of the scope and amplitude of the investigation initiated by Government.

...... The terms of reference of the Committee would make it clear even to one not aware of the economic condition of the Company that the Government was genuinely concerned about its financial position. Even though the enquiry itself was ordered under the provisions of Section 15(*a*), the Committee and the Government had authority to treat the report as if it was also made under Section 15(*b*) of the Act.... Once an investigation has been validly made under Section 15 it was held sufficient to empower the Central Government to authorise a person to take over the management of an industrial undertaking irrespective of the nature or content of the opinion on which the investigation was initiated. In view of this decision it is not possible for the appellants

63. (1949) 1 All ER 109.

> to contend that they were not aware that as a result of the report of the Investigating Committee the Government could pass an order under Section 18-A(1)(*b*) and assume management or control of the Company's undertaking......
>
> All these circumstances leave us in no manner of doubt that the Company had full opportunities to make all possible representations before the Government against the proposed take-over of its mill under Section 18-A. In this connection it is significant that even after the writ petition had been filed before the Delhi High Court the Government of India had given the appellants at their own request one month's time to obtain the necessary funds to commence the working of the mill. Even then, they failed to do so.

On the issue of application of principles of natural justice it was held that adequate compliance had taken place because *the appellants were given a full hearing at the time of the investigation held by the Investigating Committee and were also given opportunities to adduce evidence...even after the Investigating Committee had submitted its report, the appellants were in constant communion with the Government and were in fact negotiating with Government for such help as might enable them to reopen the mill and to avoid a take-over of their undertaking by the Government.* Any additional opportunity of hearing would only have acted as an *empty formality.*

5.21 RIGHT OF ORAL HEARING

In departmental enquiries hearing generally takes place through written submissions. Oral hearing takes place in certain occasions depending upon the nature of the enquiry conducted, involvement of complicated facts, complicated legal and technical questions are involved etc. In the case of *S.L. Kapoor v. Jagmohan*[64] the Court held that oral hearing is not a necessity and the nature of the hearing has to be determined based on the nature of the proceeding as long as reasonable opportunity of representation is provided. An aggrieved person cannot demand oral hearing as a matter of right, unless the statute categorically provides for the same or the adjudicating authority determines that in the absence of oral hearing the concerned parties will not be in a position to adequately present their case.[65]

In *M.P. Industries Ltd. v. Union of India*[66] the Court categorically held that the aggrieved person is not entitled as of right to a personal hearing.

---

64. (1980) 4 SCC 379.
65. *State Bank of Patiala v. Mahendra Kumar Singhal* 1994 Supp (2) SCC 463.
66. (1966) 1 SCR 466 : AIR 1966 SC 671.

> It is no doubt a principle of natural justice that a quasi-judicial tribunal cannot make any decision adverse to a party without giving him an effective opportunity of meeting any relevant allegations against him.... no order shall be passed against any applicant unless he has been given an opportunity to make his representations against the comments, if any, received from the State Government or other authority. The said opportunity need not necessarily be by personal hearing. It can be by written representation. Whether the said opportunity should be by written representation or by personal hearing depends upon the facts of each case and ordinarily it is in the discretion of the tribunal. The facts of the present case disclose that a written representation would effectively meet the requirements of the principles of natural justice.

In the case of *State of Uttar Pradesh v. Maharaja Dharmander Prasad Singh*[67] controversy had arisen relating to lease of land by the Lucknow Development Authority to the respondent and the subsequent permission to develop the land by the respondent. Upholding the need for a personal/oral hearing the Supreme Court held that "On a matter of such importance where the stakes are heavy for the lessees who claim to have made large investments on the project and where a number of grounds require the determination of factual matters of some complexity, the statutory authority should, in the facts of this case, have afforded a personal hearing to the lessees."

5.22 RIGHT OF CROSS EXAMINATION

Right of cross-examination is an integral part of the right to rebut adverse evidences. It enables the aggrieved person to challenge the veracity of the various charges made against him and discredit all adverse evidences. It is an essential component of adversarial system of adjudication. But in administrative adjudication right of cross-examination cannot be demanded as a matter of right, it becomes generally applicable in those circumstances wherein fairness in adjudication would be adversely affected in the absence of such procedural norms. In cases where the proceedings have been based on written submissions in the form of affidavits cross-examination is generally not permitted. In the case of *State of Jammu and Kashmir v. Bakshi Gulam Mohammad*[68] a Commission of Inquiry was constituted to enquire into the various corruption charges made against the respondent, when he was the Prime Minister of the State of Jammu and Kashmir. Large number of affidavits were filed before the Commission, numbering to almost 400 witnesses and Bakshi Mohammad had made a request to cross-examine all the persons who had filed affidavits in support of the allegations made.

67. AIR 1989 SC 997 : (1989) 2 SCC 505.
68. 1966 Supp SCR 401 : AIR 1967 SC.

The Commission had refused to grant permission. The respondent filed a petition challenging the order of refusal on the ground of violation of the principles of natural justice for denying him the right to cross-examine. The Supreme Court upheld the order of the Commission in denying him the permission to cross-examine. It was held that the right of hearing did not per se include the right to cross-examine. *The right must depend upon the circumstances of each case and must also depend on the statute under which the allegations are being inquired into...... a person whose conduct comes up for inquiry by the Commission directly, has a right to cross-examine only those persons who give viva voce evidence before the Commission against him.*

The judiciary has consistently balanced the right to cross-examine with general fairness in the conduct of the proceedings. They have recognized the right mostly in cases of oral hearing, but exceptions have been made on grounds of confidentiality, physical security of the witnesses, practical difficulties etc. One of the leading cases where the right of cross-examination was denied was the case of *Hira Nath Mishra v. The Principal, Rajendra Medical College, Ranchi.*[69] In this case few male students from the respondent college had entered into the girls' hostel middle of the night and misbehaved with the female students staying therein. On complaint made the female students, the Principal had set up a committee to look into the incidents. The three-member Enquiry Committee had called individually each of the complainant students and recorded their statements. Thereafter they called the four male students explained them the charges and asked them to write down whatever they had to say. All the male students denied the charges made against them. The Committee after the enquiry came to an unanimous decision that the appellant students were guilty of the gross misconduct and deserved deterrent punishment. Based on the recommendation the Principal expelled all the students for a period of two calendar years. The order of the Principal was challenged in a writ petition on the ground of non-compliance with the principles of natural justice, particularly the right to cross-examine the witnesses. The Court upheld that enquiry procedure adopted by the College and held that in light of the sensitive nature of the case denial of right of cross-examination and refusal to disclose the names of the complainants were not in violation of the principles of natural justice. The Supreme Court observed that –

> [D]octrine of natural justice cannot be imprisoned within the strait-jacket of a rigid formula and its application depends upon several factors. In the present case the complaint made to the Principal related to an extremely serious

---

69. AIR 1973 SC 1260 : (1973) 1 SCC 805.

matter as it involved not merely internal discipline but the safety of the girl students living in the Hostel under the guardianship of the college authorities. These authorities were in loco parentis to all the students-male and female who were living in the Hostels and the responsibility towards the young girl students was greater because their guardians had entrusted them to their care by putting them in the Hostels attached to the college. The authorities could not possibly dismiss the matter as of small consequence because if they did, they would have encouraged the male student rowdies to increase their questionable activities which would, not only, have brought a bad name to the college but would have compelled the parents of the girl students to withdraw them from the Hostel and, perhaps, even stop their further education. The Principal was, therefore, under an obligation to make a suitable enquiry and punish the miscreants.

But how to go about it was a delicate matter. The Police could not be called in because if an investigation was started the female students out of sheer fright and harm to their reputation would not have cooperated with the police. Nor was an enquiry, as before a regular tribunal, feasible because the girls would not have ventured to make their statements in the presence of the miscreants because if they did, they would have most certainly exposed themselves to retaliation and harassment thereafter. The college authorities are in no position to protect the girl students outside the college precincts. Therefore, the authorities had to devise a just and reasonable plan of enquiry which, on the one hand, would not expose the individual girls to harassment by the male students and, on the other, secure reasonable opportunity to the accused to state their case.

Accordingly, an Enquiry Committee of three independent members of the staff was appointed. There is no suggestion whatsoever that the members of the Committee were anything but respectable and independent. The Committee called the girls privately and recorded their statements. Thereafter the students named by them were called. The complaint against them was explained to them. The written charge was handed over and they were asked to state whatever they had to state in writing. The Committee was not satisfied with the explanation given and thereafter made the report.

We think that under the circumstances of the case the requirements of natural justice were fulfilled. The learned Counsel for the respondents made available to us the report of the Committee just to show how meticulous the members of the Committee were to see that no injustice was done. We are informed that this report had also been made available to the learned Judges of the High Court who heard the case and it further appears that the counsel for the appellants before the High Court was also invited to have a look into the report, but he refused to do so. There was no question about the incident. The only question was of identity. The names had been specifically mentioned in the complaint and, not to leave anything to chance, the Committee obtained photographs of the four delinquents and mixed them up with 20 other photographs of students. The girls by and large identified these four students from the photographs. On the other hand, if as the appellants say, they were in their own Hostel at the time it would not have been difficult for them to produce necessary evidence apart from saying that they were innocent and they had not gone to the girls Hostel at all late at night. There was no evidence in that behalf. The Committee on a careful consideration of the material before them came to the conclusion that the three appellants and Upendra had taken part in the night raid on the girls Hostel. The report was confidentially sent to the Principal. The very reasons for which the girls were not examined in the presence of the appellants, prevailed on the authorities not to give a copy of the report to them. It would have been unwise to do so. Taking all the circumstances into account it is not possible to say that rules of natural justice had not been followed. In Board of Education v. Rice[70] Lord Loreburn laid down that in disposing of a question, which was the subject of an appeal to it, the Board of Education was under a duty to act in good faith, and to listen fairly to both sides, inasmuch as that was a duty which lay on everyone who decided anything. He did not think that the Board was bound to treat such a question as though it were a trial. The Board need not examine witnesses. It could, he thought, obtain information in any way it thought best, always giving a fair opportunity to those who were parties in the controversy to correct or contradict any relevant statement prejudicial to their view-More recently in Russell v. Duke of Norfolk[71] Tucker, L.J. observed: "There are, in my view, no words which are of universal application to every kind of inquiry and every kind of domestic tribunal. The requirements of natural justice must depend on the circumstances of the case, the nature of the inquiry the rules under which the tribunal is acting, the subject-matter that is being dealt with, and so forth. Accordingly, I do not derive much assistance from the definitions of natural justice which have been from time to time used, but, whatever standard is adopted, one essential is that the person concerned should have a reasonable opportunity of presenting his case." More recently in Byrne *v.* Kinematograph Renters Society Ltd.[72] Harman, J. observed "what, then, are the requirements of natural justice in a case of this kind? First, I think that the person accused should know the nature of the accusation made; secondly that he should be given an opportunity to state his case; and thirdly, of course, that the tribunal should act in good faith. I do not think that there really is anything more".

Rules of natural justice cannot remain the same applying to all conditions. We know of statutes in India like the Goonda Acts which permit evidence being collected behind the back of the goonda and the goonda being merely asked to represent against the main charges arising out of the evidence collected. Care is taken to see that the witnesses who gave statements would not be identified. In such cases there is no question of the witnesses being called and the goonda being given an opportunity to cross-examine the witnesses.

70. 1911 AC 179.
71. 1949 1 All ER 109 at p. 118.
72. 1958 2 All ER 579.

> The reason is obvious. No witness will come forward to give evidence in the presence of the goonda. However unsavoury the procedure may appear to a. judicial mind, these are facts of life which are to be faced. The girls who were molested that night would not have come forward to give evidence in any regular enquiry and if a strict enquiry like the one conducted in a court of law were to be imposed in such matters, the girls would have had to go under the constant fear of molestation by the male students who were capable of such indecencies. Under the circumstances the course followed by the Principal was a wise one. The Committee whose integrity could not be impeached, collected and sifted the evidence given by the girls. Thereafter the students definitely named by the girls were informed about the complaint against them and the charge. They were given an opportunity to state their case. We do not think that the facts and circumstances of this case require anything more to be done.

Right to access enquiry report

Enquiry report is an important document prepared by the investigating authority. Based on the enquiry report the competent officer makes the recommendation suggesting for an appropriate course of action. A copy of the report is required to be submitted to the delinquent officer so as to enable him to prepare for his defence before the disciplinary authority and make representation against the proposed action or order, including on the issue of quantum of punishment.

In the landmark case of *Managing Director, ECIL Hyderbad v. B. Karunakar*[73] the five Judge bench of the Supreme Court laid down the law relating to access to enquiry report and held that supply of enquiry report is a precondition before any action can be proposed to be taken by the administrative authorities. The Court looked into the issue of 'whether the report of the Inquiry Officer/authority who/which is appointed by the disciplinary authority to hold an inquiry into the charges against the delinquent employee, is required to be furnished to the employee to enable him to make proper representation to the disciplinary authority before such authority arrives at its own finding with regard to the guilt or otherwise of the employee and the punishment, if any, to be awarded to him.' The Court recognized that the supply of enquiry report is an essential part of the principles of natural justice. It observed–

> [F]indings recorded by the Inquiry Officer form an important material before the disciplinary authority which along with the evidence is taken into consideration by it to come to its conclusion. It is difficult to say in advance, to what extent the said findings including the punishment, if any, recommended in the report

73. AIR 1994 SC 1074 : (1993) 4 SCC 727.

would influence the disciplinary aulhority while drawing its conclusions. The findings further might have been recorded without considering the relevant evidence on record, or by misconstruing it or unsupported by it. If such a finding is to be one of the documents to be considered by the disciplinary authority, the principles of natural justice require that the employee should have a fair opportunity to meet, explain and controvert it before he is condemned. It is the negation of the tenets of justice and a denial of fair opportunity to the employee to consider the findings recorded by a third party like the Inquiry Officer without giving the employee an opportunity to reply to it. Although it is true that the disciplinary authority is supposed to arrive at its own findings on the basis of the evidence recorded in the inquiry, it is also equally true that the disciplinary authority takes into consideration the findings recorded by the Inquiry Officer along with the evidence on record. In the circumstances, the findings of the Inquiry Officer do constitute an important material before the disciplinary authority which is likely to influence its conclusions. If the Inquiry Officer were only to record the evidence and forward the same to the disciplinary authority, that would not constitute any additional material before the disciplinary authority of which the delinquent employee has no knowledge. However, when the Inquiry Officer goes further and records his findings, as stated above, which may or may not be based on the evidence on record or are contrary to the same or in ignorance of it, such findings are an additional material unknown to the employee but are taken into consideration by the disciplinary authority while arriving at its conclusions. Both the dictates of the reasonable opportunity as well as the principles of natural justice, therefore, require that before the disciplinary authority comes to its own conclusion, the delinquent employee should have an opportunity to reply to the Inquiry Officer's findings. The disciplinary authority is then required to consider the evidence, the report of the Inquiry Officer and the representation of the employee against it.

It will thus be seen that where the Inquiry Officer is other than the disciplinary authority, the disciplinary proceedings break into two stages. The first stage ends when the disciplinary authority arrives at its conclusion on the basis of the evidence, Inquiry Officer's report and the delinquent employee's reply to it. The second stage begins when the disciplinary authority decides to impose penalty on the basis of its conclusions. If the disciplinary authority decides to drop the disciplinary proceedings, the second stage is not even reached. The employee's right to receive the report is thus, a part of the reasonable opportunity of defending himself in the first stage of the inquiry. If this right is denied to him, he is in effect denied the right to defend himself and to prove his innocence in the disciplinary proceedings.

Relating to the supply of enquiry reports the Court laid down the following propositions–

(i) Since the denial of the report of the Inquiry Officer is a denial of reasonable opportunity and a breach of the principles of natural justice, it follows that the statutory rules if any, which deny the report to the employee are against the principles of natural justice and, therefore, invalid. The delinquent employee will, therefore be entitled to a copy of the report even if the statutory rules do not permit the furnishing of the report or are silent on the subject.

(ii) Whenever, therefore, the service rules contemplate an inquiry before a punishment is awarded, and when the Inquiry Officer is not the disciplinary authority the delinquent employee will have the right to receive the Inquiry Officer's report notwithstanding the nature of the punishment.

(iii) Since it is the right of the employee to have the report to defend himself effectively, and he would not known in advance whether the report is in his favour or against him, it will not be proper to construe his failure to ask for the report, as the waiver of his right. Whether, therefore, the employee asks for the report or not, the report has to be furnished to him.

(iv) right to make representation to the disciplinary authority against the findings recorded in the inquiry report is an integral part of the opportunity of defence against the charges and is a breach of principles of natural justice to deny the said right..... whenever the rules require an inquiry to be held, for inflicting the punishment in question, the delinquent employee should have the benefit of the report of the Inquiry Officer before the disciplinary authority records its findings on the charges levelled against him.

On the issue of the effect of non-compliance with the rules relating to submission of enquiry report the Court held that–

The answer to this question has to be relative to the punishment awarded. When the employee is dismissed or removed from service and the inquiry is set aside because the report is not furnished to him, in some cases the non-furnishing of the report may have prejudiced him gravely while in other cases it may have made no difference to the ultimate punishment awarded to him. Since to direct reinstatement of the employee with back-wages in all cases is to reduce the rules of justice is a mechanical ritual the theory of reasonable opportunity and the principles of natural justice have been evolved to uphold the rule of law and to assist the individual to vindicate his just rights. They are not incantations to be invoked nor rites to be performed on all and sundry occasions. Whether in fact, prejudice has been caused to the employee or not on account of the denial to him of the report, has to be considered on the facts and circumstances of each case. Where, therefore, even after the furnishing of the report, no different consequence would have followed, it would be perversion of justice to permit the employee to resume duty and to get all the consequential benefits. It amounts to rewarding the dishonest and the guilty and thus to stretching the concept of justice to illogical and exasperating limits. It amounts to an "unnatural expansion of natural justice" which in itself is antithetical to justice.

Hence, in all cases where the Inquiry Officer's report is not furnished to the delinquent employee in the disciplinary proceedings, the Courts and Tribunals should cause the copy of the report to be furnished to the aggrieved employee if he has not already secured it before coming to the Court / Tribunal, and give the employee an opportunity to show how his or her case was prejudiced because of the non-supply of the report. If after hearing the parties, The Court / Tribunal comes to the conclusion that the non-supply of the report would have made no difference to the ultimate findings and the punishment given, the Court / Tribunal should not interfere with the order of punishment the Courts / Tribunal should not mechanically set aside the order of punishment on the ground that the report was not furnished as is regrettably being done at present. The courts should avoid resorting to short-cuts. Since it is the Court / Tribunals which will apply their judicial mind to the question and give their reasons for setting aside or not setting aside the order of punishment, (and not any internal appellate of revisional authority), there would be neither a breach of the principles of natural justice nor a denial of the reasonable opportunity. It is only if the Court / Tribunal finds that the furnishing of the report would have made a difference to the result in the case that it should set aside the order of punishment. Where after following the above procedure, the Court / Tribunal sets aside the order of punishment, the proper relief that should be granted is to direct reinstatement of the employee with liberty to the authority / management to proceed with the inquiry, by placing the employee under suspension and continuing the inquiry from the stage of furnishing him with the report. The question whether the employee would be entitled to the back-wages and other benefits from the date of his dismissal to the date of his reinstatement if ultimately ordered, should invariably be left to be decided by the authority concerned according to law, after the culmination of the proceedings and depending on the final outcome. If the employee succeeds in the fresh inquiry and is directed to be reinstated, the authority should be at liberty to decide according to law how it will treat the period from the date of dismissal till the reinstatement and to what benefits, if any and the extent of the benefits, he will be entitled. The reinstatement made as a result of the setting aside of the inquiry for failure to furnish the report, should be treated as a reinstatement for the purpose of holding the fresh inquiry from the stage of furnishing the report and no more, where such fresh inquiry is held. That will also be the correct position in law.

In *S.K. Singh v. Central Bank of India*[74] the Court referred to the judgement of the Court in *Karunakar* decision and by applying the prejudice test and questioned the petitioner *as to what prejudice the petitioner had suffered for non-supply* of the enquiry report but since the petitioner was unable to explain the prejudice suffered the Supreme Court declined to interfere in the order made by the High Court and other lower courts and held that *no illegality* had taken place.

5.23 RIGHT OF LEGAL REPRESENTATION

Right of legal representation is an important ingredient of fair trial. In *M.H. Hoskot v. State of Maharashtra*[75] the Supreme Court had highlighted the importance of legal representation in judicial proceedings because of the complicated legal procedures which make it difficult even for an intelligent and educated person to understand the intricacies of law and make it difficult for him to make effective presentation of his before the court. It was observed that "*The other ingredient of fair procedure to a prisoner, who has to seek his liberation through the court process is lawyer's services. Judicial justice, with procedural intricacies, legal submissions and critical examination of evidence, leans upon professional expertise; and a failure of equal justice under the law is on the cards where such supportive skill is absent for one side. Our judicature, moulded by Anglo-American models and our judicial process, engineered by kindred legal technology, compel the collaboration of lawyer-power for steering the wheels of equal justice under the law.*"

In spite of the judicial recognition that the right to be advised by a legal counsel is part of fair procedure, but in administrative proceedings right of legal representation has often been considered as less essential. The arguments against the presence of lawyers have been generally in the nature of – tendency to formalize and complicate the proceedings, causing delay etc. However in certain cases the tribunals have permitted the presence of lawyers in cases where the aggrieved person may be illiterate, or where the case involves complicated and technical matters, or complicated legal issues, or if the case involves expert evidences etc. The judiciary has always looked into the question of fairness in dealing with the issue of involvement of lawyers, hence in exceptional circumstances the Courts have upheld the right of legal representation of the aggrieved party even when there has been express statutory prohibition.

74. (1996) 6 SCC 415.
75. AIR 1978 SC 1548.

Under Article 22(3) of the Constitution provides that in case of detention under the preventive detention laws the detenue may not be allowed to be defended by a legal practitioner of his choice before the advisory board. In *A.K. Roy v. Union of India*[76] the Supreme Court while dealing with the constitutionality of National Security Ordinance 1980 dealt with the constitutionality of A. 22(3) relating to right to consult and to be defended by a legal practitioner of one's choice. It held that–

> [A]ccording to the express intendment of the Constitution itself, no person who is detained under any law, which provides for preventive detention, can claim the right to consult a legal practitioner of his choice or to be defended by him. In view of this, it seems to us difficult to hold, by the application of abstract, general principles or on a priori considerations that the detenue has the right of being represented by a legal practitioner in the proceedings before the Advisory Board, Since the Constitution, as originally enacted, itself contemplates that such a right should not be made available to a detenue, it cannot be said that the denial of the said right is unfair, unjust or unreasonable.

Supreme Court clarified that the Constitution did not contemplate that the detaining authority or Government should have facility of appearing before board with aid of legal practitioner but detenue should be denied such facility. It would be deemed to be in violation of Article 14 if the detaining authority or government to appear with aid of legal practitioner, if the similar facility denied to detenue. Normally the detenue does not have the right to appear through legal practitioner in proceedings before Advisory Board but if the detaining authority appears with the help of legal practitioner, the same must be allowed to the detenue.

Similarly in the case of *Nandlal Bajaj v. State of Punjab*[77] Supreme Court while dealing with the issue of whether denial of legal assistance to a person detained under Section 3 of the Prevention of Blackmarketing and Maintenance of Supplies of Essential Commodities Act, 1980 was violative of Articles 14 and 21 of the Constitution when on the other hand the State was being represented by the District Attorney, Additional District Attorney, District Legal Advisor and one legal assistance before the Advisory Board held that–

> Under Article 22(3)(b) of the Constitution, the right to consult and be defended by a legal practitioner of his choice is denied to any person who is arrested or detained under any law providing for preventive detention. Sub-section (4) of Section 11 of the Act is undoubtedly in conformity with

76. AIR 1982 SC 710 : (1982) 1 SCC 271.
77. AIR 1981 SC 2041.

Article 22(3)(b) of the Constitution. Normally, lawyers have no place in the proceedings before the Advisory Board. The functions of the Advisory Board are purely consultative. It is an independent body constituted under Section 9 of the Act consisting of a sitting Judge as the Chairman and not less than two other members who may be sitting or retired judges of the High Court. It is expected that the Advisory Board would act in a fair and impartial manner in making a report whether or not there is, in its opinion, sufficient cause for the detention of a person. In coming to that conclusion, the Board has to make an objective determination on the question as to whether there was sufficient material on which the subjective satisfaction of the detaining authority could be based. Under Sub-section (1) of Section 11 of the Act, the Board is not only entitled to look into the record and see whether there was any material on which the order of detention could be passed under Section 3 of the Act, but may also call for such further information as it may deem necessary from the appropriate Government or from the person concerned and if, in any particular case, it considers essential to do so or if the person concerned desires to be heard, shall hear him in person. The Board is entitled to devise its own procedure.

It is the arbitrariness of the procedure adopted by the Advisory Board that vitiates the impugned order of detention. There is no denying the fact that while the Advisory Board disallowed the detenue's request for legal assistance, it allowed the detaining authority to be represented by counsel. It appears that the Advisory Board blindly applied the provisions of Sub-section (4) of Section 11 of the Act to the case of the detenue failing to appreciate that it could not allow legal assistance to the detaining authority and deny the same to the detenue. The Advisory Board is expected to act in a manner which is just and fair to both the parties. The report of the Board placed before us shows that the detenue exercised his right to recall some of the witnesses for the purpose of cross-examination. We are informed that the hearing before the Advisory Board went on for 4 to 5 days and there were as many as 11 witnesses cross-examined by the detenue. It cannot be, as is suggested by the counsel for the State, that the lawyers representing the State Government did not participate in the proceedings. On the contrary, the report itself shows that the Public Prosecutor was called upon to explain some aspects of the case. If the matter was so intricate, the Advisory Board should have ensured that both the parties had equal opportunity to place their respective cases. It appears that the dice was loaded against the detenu in that whereas he had to go without legal assistance, the State Government had the benefit of an array of lawyers.

In the case of *Devji Vallabhbhai Tandel v. Administrator of Goa, Daman and Diu*[78] it was clarified by the Court that denial of help of legal practitioners in matters of detention under the provisions of Conservation of Foreign Exchange and Presentation of Smuggling Act 1974 did not extend to

78. AIR 1982 SC 1029 : (1982) 2 SCC 222.

denying of the help of a 'friend'. The Court referred to the judicial opinion in *A.K. Roy case* on the issue of 'friend' that *the embargo on the appearance of legal practitioners should not be extended so as to prevent the detenue from being aided or assisted by a friend who, in truth and substance, is not a legal practitioner. Every person whose interests are adversely affected as a result of the proceedings which have a serious import, is entitled to be heard in those proceedings and be assisted by a friend...*[79]

The Court upheld the above view and further clarified that–

> [A] 'friend' who, in truth and substance, is a friend of the detenue may appear for the detenue but if such a 'friend' also happens to be a legal practitioner, he cannot, as of right, appear before the Advisory Board on behalf of the detenue.
>
> The same reasoning will apply to appearance by an 'agent'. In other words, if an 'agent' is in 'truth and substance' an agent, the detenue may appear through him. But if the 'agent' is a legal practitioner, appearance by him as of right will be barred. But a 'friend' or an 'agent' of the detenue who is essentially a comrade in the profession of the detenue for which he is detained, such a 'friend' or 'agent' will also be barred from appearance on behalf of the detenue.

5.24 EXCEPTION TO THE RIGHT OF HEARING - POST DECISIONAL HEARING

In recent times the principle of *audi alteram partem* has assumed definite meaning and connotation in law and are deemed to applicable when the rights and liberties of the citizens have been encroached or adversely affected by an administrative action. But the scope and extent of the application of the doctrine differs from case to case depending on statutory provisions and the nature of the administrative action taken. In certain exceptional circumstances the application of these principles can be excluded such as right to prior notice and an opportunity to be heard can be excluded when a prompt action needs to be taken or in circumstances wherein the entire administration may be paralyzed or made infructuous.

Maneka Gandhi v. Union of India[80] is the land mark decision laying down the jurisprudential premise for exception to the right of fair hearing. In this case the petitioner was the holder of a valid passport. On July 4, 1977 she received a letter dated July 2, 1977 from the Regional Passport Officer, Delhi intimating to her that in the public interest it has been decided by the Government of India to impound her passport under Section 10(3)

79. Id Para 94.
80. (1978) 1 SCC 248.

(*c*) of the Passport Act and required her to surrender the passport within seven days from the date of receipt of the letter. Thereafter the petitioner immediately addressed a letter to the Regional Passport Officer requesting him to furnish a copy of the statement of reasons for making the order as required under Section 10(5). Subsequently the Ministry of External Affairs wrote back a letter stating that the Government has decided "in the interest of the general public" not to furnish her a copy of the statement of reasons for the making of the order. Section 10(5) enabled the passport authority impounding or revoking a passport or travel document or varying or cancelling an endorsement made upon it to "record in writing a brief statement of the reasons for making such order and furnish to the holder of the passport or travel document on demand a copy of the same unless, in any case, the passport authority is of the opinion that it will not be in the interests of the sovereignty and integrity of India, the security of India, friendly relations of India with any foreign country or in the interests of the general public to furnish such a copy." The principle point of argument of the petitioner was that the procedure prescribed in the Passports Act would be deemed to an unfair and unjust procedure as it provided for impounding of a passport without affording reasonable opportunity to the holder of the passport to be heard in defence. Impounding the passport is a serious matter as it prevented her from exercising her constitutional right to go abroad and *such a drastic consequence cannot in fairness be visited without observing the principle of audi alteram partem.* On the other hand the Government of India argued that in light of the peculiarity of the circumstances and the very nature of the administrative action involved in impounding the passport "the *audi alteram partem* rule must be held to be excluded, because if notice were to be given to the holder of the passport and reasonable opportunity afforded to him to show cause why his passport should not be impounded, he might immediately, on the strength of the passport, make good his exit from the country and the object of impounding the passport would be frustrated. The argument was that if the *audi alteram partem* rule were applied, its effect would be to stultify the power of impounding the passport and it would defeat and paralyse the administration of the law and hence the *audi alteram partem* rule cannot in fairness be applied while exercising the power to impound a passport."

Recognizing the principle of exclusion of principles of natural justice in certain circumstances to uphold the notions of fair-play in administrative action, the Court by referring to the legal principles laid down by Prof. de Smith held that in certain circumstances fairness demands non-application of any rigid principles of natural justice. Bhagwati J. observed–

[S]tatement of the law in *S.A. de Smith's Judicial Review of Administrative Action,* 2nd Edn., where the learned author says at p. 174 that "in administrative law a prima facie right to prior notice and opportunity to be heard may be held to be excluded by implication...... where an obligation to give notice and opportunity to be heard would obstruct the taking of prompt action, especially action of a preventive or remedial nature". Now, it is true that since the right to prior notice and opportunity of hearing arises only by implication from the duty to act fairly, or to use the words of Lord Morris of Borth-y-Gest, from "fair-play in action", it may equally be excluded where, having regard to the nature of the action to be taken, its object and purpose and the scheme of the relevant statutory provision, fairness in action does not demand its implication and even warrants its exclusion. There are certain well recognised exceptions to the *audi alteram partem* rule established by judicial decisions and they are summarised by S.A. de Smith in *Judicial Review of Administrative Action*, 2nd Edn., p. 168 to 179. If we analyse these exceptions a little closely, it will be apparent that they do not in any way militate against the principle which requires fair-play in administrative action. The word "exception" is really a misnomer because in these exclusionary cases, the *audi alteram partem* rule is held inapplicable not by way of an exception to "fair-play in action", but because nothing unfair can be inferred by not affording an opportunity to present or meet a case. The *audi alteram partem* rule is intended to inject justice into the law and it cannot be applied to defeat the ends of justice, or to make the law "lifeless, absurd, stultifying, self-defeating or plainly contrary to the common sense of the situation". Since the life of the law is not logic but experience and every legal proposition must, in the ultimate analysis, be tested on the touchstone of pragmatic realism, the *audi alteram partem* rule would, by the experiential test, be excluded, if importing the right to be heard has the effect of paralysing the administrative process or the need for promptitude or the urgency of the situation so demands. But at the same time it must be remembered that this is a rule of vital importance in the field of administrative law and it must not be jettisoned save in very exceptional circumstances where compulsive necessity so demands. It is a wholesome rule designed to secure the rule of law and the court should not be too ready to eschew it in its application to a given case. True it is that in questions of this kind a fanatical or doctrinaire approach should be avoided, but that does not mean that merely because the traditional methodology of a formalised hearing may have the effect of stultifying the exercise of the statutory power, the *audi alteram partem* should be wholly excluded. The court must make every effort to salvage this cardinal rule to the maximum extent permissible in a given case. It must not be forgotten that "natural justice is pragmatically flexible and is amenable to capsulation under the compulsive pressure of circumstances". The *audi alteram partem* rule is not cast in a rigid mould and judicial decisions establish that it may suffer situational modifications. The core of it must, however, remain, namely, that the person affected must have a reasonable opportunity of being heard and the hearing must be a genuine hearing and not an empty public relations exercise. That is why Tucker, L.J., emphasised in *Russel v. Duke of Norfolk* [(1949) 1 All

ER 109] that "whatever standard of natural justice is adopted, one essential is that the person concerned should have a reasonable opportunity of presenting his case". What opportunity may be regarded as reasonable would necessarily depend on the practical necessities of the situation. It may be a sophisticated full-fledged hearing or it may be a hearing which is very brief and minimal : it may be a hearing prior to the decision or it may even be a post-decisional remedial hearing. The *audi alteram partem* rule is sufficiently flexible to permit modifications and variations to suit the exigencies of myriad kinds of situations which may arise. This circumstantial flexibility of the *audi alteram partem* rule was emphasised by Lord Reid in *Wiseman* v. *Borneman* [1971 AC 297 : (1969) 3 All ER 275] when he said that he would be "sorry to see this fundamental general principle degenerate into a series of hard and fast rules" and Lord Hailsham, L.C., also observed in *Pearlberg v. Varty* [(1971) 1 Weekly Law Reports 728] that the courts "have taken in increasingly sophisticated view of what is required in individual cases". It would not, therefore, be right to conclude that the *audi alteram partem* rule is excluded merely because the power to impound a passport might be frustrated, if prior notice and hearing were to be given to the person concerned before impounding his passport The Passport Authority may proceed to impound the passport without giving any prior opportunity to the person concerned to be heard, but as soon as the order impounding the passport is made, an opportunity of hearing, remedial in aim, should be given to him so that he may present his case and controvert that of the Passport Authority and point out why his passport should not be impounded and the order impounding it recalled. This should not only be possible but also quite appropriate, because the reasons for impounding the passport are required to be supplied by the Passport Authority after the making of the order and the person affected would, therefore, be in a position to make a representation setting forth his case and plead for setting aside the action impounding his passport. A fair opportunity of being heard following immediately upon the order impounding the passport would satisfy the mandate of natural justice and a provision requiring giving of such opportunity to the person concerned can and should be read by implication in the Passports Act, 1967. If such a provision were held to be incorporated in the Passports Act, 1967 by necessary implication, as we hold it must be, the procedure prescribed by the Act for impounding a passport would be right, fair and just and it would not suffer from the vice of arbitrariness or unreasonableness. We must, therefore, hold that the procedure "established" by the Passports Act, 1967 for impounding a passport is in conformity with the requirement of Article 21 and does not fall foul of that article.[81]

Based on the above legal rationale the Court held that impounding of passport without assigning any reasons and not providing the petitioner any opportunity of being heard amounted to violation of the principles of natural justice, but the Court accepted the suggestion made by the government

81. Id. Para 14.

to give an opportunity of being heard to the petitioner expeditiously and in accordance with law. It was held that in the given circumstances such procedural adherence will remove all vices from the administrative order and will be deemed to be in compliance with the norms of *audi alteram partem*. Some of the other leading cases wherein the Supreme Court upheld the application of post-decisional hearing are *Mohinder Singh Gill v. Chief Election Commissioner*[82] and *Union of India v. Tulsiram Patel.*[83]

But the practice of post decisional hearing is acceptable only in rare occasions wherein the very purpose of the administrative action will be lost by complying with pre-decisional hearing. This was reiterated by the Supreme Court in the case of *K.I. Shephard v. Union of India*[84] wherein the Court refused to accept the government's plea of post-decisional hearing to be provided to those bank employees whose services were terminated after the amalgamation of the three private banks of Hindustan Commercial Bank, Bank of Cochin and Lakshmi Commercial Bank with Punjab National Bank, Canara Bank and State Bank of India respectively. The argument of the excluded employees were that at the time of submission of the draft schemes there were no mention of the names of any employee whose service would be terminated nor were they provided any opportunity of being heard before their names were excluded – the action of the State was vitiated on the ground failure to act fairly. Upholding the arguments of the appellants the Court observed–

> Natural justice has various facets and acting fairly is one of them. RBI which monitored the three amalgamations was required to act fairly in the facts of the case. The situation necessitated a participatory enquiry in regard to the excluded employees. Since the decision to exclude them from service under the transferee banks is grounded upon a set of facts the correctness whereof they deny, if an opportunity to know the allegations and to have their say had been afforded, they could have no grievance on this score. The action deprives them of their livelihood and brings adverse civil consequences and could obviously not be taken on the ipse dixit of RBI officers without verification effects. It is quite possible that a manoeuvring officer of the banking company adversely disposed of towards a particular employee of such bank could make a report against such employee and have him excluded from further service under the transferee bank. The possibility of exclusion on the basis of some mistake such as to identity cannot also be ruled out. There is all the more apprehension of this type as the process has to be completed quickly and very often the records of a large number of employees have to be scrutinised. We are of the view that rules of natural justice apply to administrative action and in

82. Supra note 80.
83. (1985) 3 SCC 398.
84. AIR 1988 SC 686.

> the instant cases the decision to exclude a section of the employees without complying with requirement of natural justice was bad.
>
> ....
>
> For the reasons we have indicated, there is no justification to think of a post-decisional hearing. On the other hand the normal rule should apply. It was also contended on behalf of the respondents that the excluded employees could now represent and their cases could be examined. We do not think that would meet the ends of justice. They have already been thrown out of employment and having been deprived of livelihood they must be facing serious difficulties. There is no justification to throw them out of employment and then give them an opportunity of representation when the requirement is that they should have the opportunity referred to above as a condition precedent to action. It is common experience that once a decision has been taken, there is a tendency to uphold it and a representation may not really yield any fruitful purpose.

This view was reiterated by the Supreme Court in *H.L. Trehan v. Union of India*[85] wherein it was observed that *"the post-decisional opportunity of hearing does not subserve the rules of natural justice. The authority who embarks upon a post-decisional hearing will naturally proceed with a closed mind and there is hardly any chance of getting a proper consideration of the representation at such a post-decisional opportunity.....once a decision has been taken, there is a tendency to uphold it and a representation may not yield any fruitful purpose. Thus, even if any hearing was given to the employees of CORIL after the issuance of the impugned circular, that would not be any compliance with the rules of natural justice or avoid the mischief of arbitrariness as contemplated by Article 14 of the Constitution."*[86]

Other exceptions are-

5.24.1 Statutory Exception

Principles of natural justice are always subject to the express provisions of the statute. They act as supplements to the prescribed procedures identified by the legislature. Hence if the statute in unequivocal terms, deny the application of principles of natural justice, then the same will not be applicable. In *Charan Lal Sahu v. Union of India*[87] it was held that no principles of natural justice will be applicable in the face of clear provisions of the statute.

85. (1989) 1 SCC 764.
86. Ibid Para 12 - 13.
87. MANU/SC/0285/1990.

5.24.2 Useless Formality Theory

The very objective behind conferring of the principles of natural justice is to ensure fairness in the administrative process and to prevent arbitrary or abusive exercises of power. But these procedural norms cannot be allowed to become road blocks in the performance of administrative actions. Hence the Court may deny the performance of a particular procedural norm if it is found to be of no effective purpose or utility in terms of creating more efficiency. Where grant of opportunity in terms of principles of natural justice do not improve the situation 'useless formality theory' has been used as a point of defence.[88] In *Keshav Mills case* the Supreme Court denied the need to send additional notice to the appellants on the ground of 'useless formality theory'.

5.24.3 Emergency

Emergency circumstance often necessitates the conduct of administrative action on an expeditious note. In such circumstances strict compliance with all the procedural rules might cause delay and defeat the very objective of the administrative action taken, hence in such circumstances the authorities might be justified in taking all necessary actions without complying with the prior norms of principles of natural justice. For example in the face of natural calamities or accidents the administrative officers might be forced to take actions such as breaking open of house or demolition of dilapidated house without providing prior notice or hearing.

5.24.4 Confidentiality

Maintenance of confidentiality becomes necessary in certain extraneous situations and in those circumstances the authorities might be justified in non-complying with the norms of fair hearing. In *Hiranath Mishra case* the Court upheld confidentiality as a valid ground for maintaining the physical security and safety of the girl students and denying the delinquent male students from accessing the enquiry report or conducting cross examination.

In *Malak Singh v. State of Punjab and Haryana*[89] the Supreme Court recognized that surveillance for the purpose of prevention of crime can be a ground for denying principles of natural justice. The Court observed–

> Prevention of crime is one of the prime purposes of the constitution of a police force. The preamble to the Police Act, 1861 says: "Whereas it is expedient to reorganise the police and to make it a more efficient instrument for *the*

88. *Canara Bank v. Debasis Das* AIR 2003 SC 2041: (2003) 4 SCC 557.
89. (1981) 1 SCC 420.

prevention and detection of crime." Section 23 of the Police Act prescribes it as the duty of police officers "to collect and communicate intelligence affecting the public peace; to prevent the commission of offences and public nuisances". In connection with these duties it will be necessary to keep discreet surveillance over reputed bad characters, habitual offenders and other potential offenders. Organised crime cannot be successfully fought without close watch of suspects. But, surveillance may be intrusive and it may so seriously encroach on the privacy of a citizen as to infringe his fundamental right to personal liberty guaranteed by Article 21 of the Constitution and the freedom of movement guaranteed by Article 19(1)(*d*). That cannot be permitted. This is recognised by the Punjab Police Rules themselves. Rule 23.7, which prescribes the mode of surveillance, permits the close watch over the movements of the person under surveillance but without any illegal interference. Permissible surveillance is only to the extent of a close watch over the movements of the person under surveillance and no more. So long as surveillance is for the purpose of preventing crime and is confined to the limits prescribed by Rule 23.7 we do not think a person whose name is included in the surveillance register can have a genuine cause for complaint. We may notice here that interference in accordance with law and for the prevention of disorder and crime is an exception recognised even by European Convention of Human Rights to the right to respect for a person's private and family life. Article 8 of the Convention reads as follows:

"(*1*) Everyone's right to respect for his private and family life, his home and his correspondence shall be recognised.

(*2*) There shall be no interference by a public authority with the exercise of this right, except such as is in accordance with law and is necessary in a democratic society in the interests of national security, public safety, for the prevention of disorder and crime or for the protection of health or morals."

5.24.5 Legislative Action

Under the classification of administrative action, the administrative authorities performing rule making functions or legislative actions are not bound by the principles of natural justice. In *Cynamide Industries case* it was held that in the absence of specific statutory provisions relating to consultation or prior notice, the administrative authorities are not required to provide an interested party with the opportunity of being heard. The administrative authorities steps into the shoes of the legislatures while performing the rule making functions, and the manner and performance of the functions are similarly determined.

5.24.6 Administrative Necessity

Grant of powers to the administrative authorities is with the core purpose of ensuring efficiency in the functioning of various activities without compromising with fairness. But, if the very objective of administrative action gets defeated due to strict adherence with principles of natural justice, then efficiency demands that principles of natural justice may be suitably modified to fulfil the needs of administrative necessity. In *Director of School Education v. O. Karuppa Thevan*[90] the Supreme Court held that an employee is not required to be given a hearing before his transfer transfer when the authorities make the transfer for the exigencies of administration. Similarly in *Maneka Gandhi case* the Court developed the notions of post-decisional hearing as a necessary balance between administrative necessity and fairness.

5.24.7 No Violation of Legal Rights

The core purpose of principles of natural justice is to ensure that the administrative authorities act in a fair manner when the action proposed to be taken is likely to affect the rights and liberties of a person. The rule against bias and right of fair hearing have been developed to uphold the common law principles of fair adjudication. In the absence of any violation of legal right or non-determination of legal rights or liabilities, the principles of natural justice does not have any application.

5.25 REASONED DECISION

Speaking order or reasoned decision is considered as the third limb of the principles of natural justice. Giving of reasoned orders are considered as essential so as to understand the rationale behind the making of the administrative orders. On one hand citing of reasons gives satisfaction to the aggrieved party to know about the purpose and objective of the order passed whereas on the other hand it enables the review authority or the appellate authority to understand the thinking process behind making of the decision. The authorities would be left guessing about the approach of the inquiry officer, his conclusion and his finding. Absence of reasons in the order issued will be presumed to be an attempt to *decline a peep into the working of their minds.* Such orders will be considered to be passed in *sub silence.*[91]

In *Maneka Gandhi v. Union of India*[92] the Court discussed the importance of providing reasons while interpreting Section 10(5) of the Passport Act which enabled the passport authority to impound or revoke a passport or

90. 1994 Supp (2) SCC 666.

91. *A.L. Kalra v. Project and Equipment Corporation of India Limited* AOR 1984 SC 1361.

92. (1978) 1 SCC 248.

travel document by recording in writing a brief statement of the reasons for making such order. It emphasised that–

The necessity of giving reasons has obviously been introduced in sub-section (5) so that it may act as a healthy check against abuse or misuse of power. If the reasons given are not relevant and there is no nexus between the reasons and the ground on which the passport has been impounded, it would be open to the holder of the passport to challenge the order impounding it in a court of law and if the court is satisfied that the reasons are extraneous or irrelevant, the court would strike down the order. This liability to be exposed to judicial scrutiny would by itself act as a safeguard against improper or mala fide exercise of power. The court would, therefore, be very slow to accept, without close scrutiny, the claim of the passport authority that it would not be in the interests of the general public to disclose the reasons. The passport authority would have to satisfy the court by placing proper material that the giving of reasons would be clearly and indubitably against the interests of the general public and if the court is not so satisfied, the court may require the passport authority to disclose the reasons, subject to any valid and lawful claim for privilege which may be set up on behalf of the Government.

In a plethora of cases the judiciary has remitted back an order or declined to uphold an order on the ground of absence of speaking orders or reasoned decisions. In *Omar Usman Chamadia v. Abdul*[93] speaking on the issue the Supreme Court observed–

> In the recent past, we had several occasions to notice that the High Courts by recording the concessions shown by the counsel in the criminal proceedings refrain from assigning any reason even in orders by which it reverses the orders of the lower courts. In our opinion, this is not proper if such orders are appealable, be it on the ground of concession shown by the learned counsel appearing for the parties or on the ground that assigning of elaborate reasons might prejudice the future trial before the lower courts. The High Court should not, unless for very good reasons, desist from indicating the grounds on which their orders are based because when the matters are brought up in appeal, the court of appeal has every reason to know the basis on which the impugned order has been made. It may be that while concurring with the lower courts' order, it may not be necessary for the said appellate court to assign reasons but that is not so while reversing such orders of the lower courts. It may be convenient for the said court to pass orders without indicating the grounds or basis but it certainly is not convenient for the court of appeal while considering the correctness of such impugned orders. The reasons need not be very detailed or elaborate, lest it may cause prejudice to the cause of the parties, but must be sufficiently indicative of the process of reasoning leading to the passing of

93. (2004) 13 SCC 234.

> the impugned order. The need for delivering a reasoned order is a requirement of law which has to be complied with in all appealable orders. This Court in a somewhat similar situation has deprecated the practice of non-speaking orders in the case of *State of Punjab v. Jagdev Singh Talwandi.*[94] That was a case where the High Court in a detention order while allowing the challenge to the detention order directed the release of the detenue before it could give a reasoned order. Even such a practice was deprecated by a Constitution Bench of this Court. Whereas in the instant case it is a final order reversing the order of the learned Sessions Judge wherein the High Court thought it is not necessary to give the reasons on the ground that the counsel appearing for the parties did not press for a reasoned order. Consequently, when the matter was taken up for hearing, we had no benefit of the reasons which persuaded the High Court to pass the impugned order. Hence, we have proceeded to decide the appeal on merit based on the material available on record and the arguments addressed before us, from which we have come to the conclusion that the impugned order ought to be set aside. Though a prayer was made on behalf of the first respondent that the matter be remanded to the High Court to facilitate it to pass a reasoned order, on facts of this case, we think it proper to decide the issue before us ourselves without prolonging the proceeding any further by remanding it to the High Court. But we do record our disapproval of the practice followed by the High Court reflected in the impugned order and hope the same will not be repeated.

In the case of *National Insurance Company Ltd. v. Bharat Bhushan*[95] the Supreme Court concluded that "the High Court had disposed of the appeal without applying its mind and without passing a speaking and reasoned order. That being the position, only on this ground the matter is remitted back to the High Court for fresh disposal in accordance with law. It is expected that this time, the High Court shall decide the same by passing a speaking and a reasoned order." In *Kolkata Municipal Corpn. v. Chhater Singh Baid*[96] the Supreme Court set aside the order passed by the Division bench of the High Court on the ground of modifying or varying the order of the Single Judge without giving any reasons and restored back the order of the Single Judge. Similarly in *Union of India v. Essel Mining & Industries Ltd.*[97] while reviewing the decision of the High Court, the Supreme Court observed–

> We find that though the High Court referred to various statutes relating to the mining activities e.g. the Mining Act, etc. it did not indicate any reason as to why it was of the view that the authority issuing the notification lacked

94. (1984) 1 SCC 596 : AIR 1984 SC 444.
95. (2008) 11 SCC 112.
96. (2005) 12 SCC 196.
97. (2005) 6 SCC 675.

statutory power to issue the notification. Though the judgment runs to several pages, after noticing the rival submissions, the High Court in a very cryptic manner, disposed of the writ petition coming to the aforesaid view. It is not the number of pages in a judgment which is relevant. It is on the other hand, the sufficiency of reasons indicated to justify the conclusions. We may only add here that paras 28 and 29 of the judgment which are supposed to contain the conclusions are not only confusing, but also make little sense. They, to quote the immortal words of Lord Sumner in *R. v. Nat Bell Liquors Ltd.*[1] "speak only with the inscrutable face of a sphinx". It is "unspeaking order" as classically described by Lord Cairns, IC in *Overseers of the Poor of Walsall Overseers v. London & NWR Co.*[2]

5.26 NON-COMPLIANCE WITH PRINCIPLES OF NATURAL JUSTICE

Different statutes and rules made thereunder contain provisions relating to disciplinary enquiries. Most of these procedures are nothing but elaboration of the principles of natural justice and their several facets. *It is a case of codification of the several facets of rule of audi alteram partem or the rule against bias.*[3] A relevant question arises that if a decision arrived at is in violation of some principles of natural justice or any of such rules then whether such decision should be considered as void or in some cases it will be treated as not void. The judicial opinion in this regard has been quite at variance.

In *Ridge v. Baldwin*[4] on failure to provide a right of hearing to the chief constable and dismissing him without a notice or proper enquiry was held to be in violation of principle of natural justice. Lord Reid holding the violation to be fundamental in nature held that *a decision given without regard to the principles of natural justice is void..... The body with the power to decide cannot lawfully proceed to make a decision until it has afforded to the person affected a proper opportunity to state his case.* But in other English cases such as *Malloch v. Aberdeen Corpn*[5] and *R. v. Secy. of State for Transport, ex p Gwent County Council*[6] the judges have applied the prejudice test to determine the issue of non-compliance with the principles of natural justice.

1. (1922) 2 AC 128 : 127 LT 437 (PC).
2. (1878) 4 AC 30 : 39 LT 453 (HL).
3. (1996) 3 SCC 364.
4. 1964 AC 40 : (1963) 2 All ER 66.
5. (1971) 2 All ER 1278.
6. (1987) 1 All ER 161, CA.

Similarly in India there has been divergence of opinion on the issue. In *State of U.P. v. Mohd. Nooh*[7] S.R. Das C.J. speaking for the Constitution Bench observed that–

> If an inferior court or tribunal of first instance acts wholly without jurisdiction or patently in excess of jurisdiction or manifestly conducts the proceedings before it in a manner which is contrary to the rules of natural justice and all accepted rules of procedure *and which offends the superior court's sense of fair play* the superior court may, we think, quite properly exercise its power to issue the prerogative writ of certiorari to correct the error of the court or tribunal of first instance, even if an appeal to another inferior court or tribunal was available and recourse was not had to it or if recourse was had to it, it confirmed what ex facie was a nullity for reasons aforementioned."

In *Jankinath Sarangi v. State of Orissa,*[8] Hidayatullah, C.J. on non-compliance with the principles of natural justice applied the test of gross violation and held that–

> From this material it is argued that the principles of natural justice were violated because the right of the appellant to have his own evidence recorded was denied to him and further that the material which was gathered behind his back was used in determining his guilt...... There is no doubt that if the principles of natural justice are violated and there is a gross case this Court would interfere by striking down the order of dismissal; but there are cases and cases. *We have to look to what actual prejudice has been caused to a person by the supposed denial to him of a particular right....* Anyway the questions which were put to the witnesses were recorded and sent to the Chief Engineer and his replies were received. No doubt the replies were not put in the hands of the appellant but he saw them at the time when he was making the representations and curiously enough he used those replies in his defence. In other words, they were not collected behind his back and could be used to his advantage and he had an opportunity of so using them in his defence. We do not think that any prejudice was caused to the appellant in his case by not examining the two retired Superintending Engineers whom he had cited or any one of them."

In *Hira Nath Mishra v. Principal, Rajendra Medical College*[9] the denial of opportunity to cross-examine the girl students who made the complaint was held to be not a violation of natural justice. Similarly in *Maneka Gandhi v. Union of India* denial of pre-decisional hearing was not considered as violation of fair hearing. But in *Chintapalli Agency Taluk Arrack Sales*

7. 1958 SCR 595 : AIR 1958 SC 86.
8. (1969) 3 SCC 392.
9. (1973) 1 SCC 805.

Coop. Society Ltd. v. Secy. (Food and Agriculture) Govt. of A.P.[10] the Court held the action void on the ground of total denial of principles of natural justice. In *S.L. Kapoor v. Jagmohan*[11] on the issue of an administrative action without providing a notice the Court also observed that–

> In our view the principles of natural justice know of no exclusionary rule dependent on whether it would have made any difference if natural justice had been observed. The non-observance of natural justice is itself prejudice to any man and proof of prejudice independently of proof of denial of natural justice is unnecessary. It ill comes from a person who has denied justice that the person who has been denied justice is not prejudiced. As we said earlier where on the admitted or indisputable facts only one conclusion is possible and under the law only one penalty is permissible, the court may not issue its writ to compel the observance of natural justice, not because it is not necessary to observe natural justice but because courts do not issue futile writs. We do not agree with the contrary view taken by the Delhi High Court in the judgment under appeal."

In *K.L. Tripathi v. State Bank of India*[12] Supreme Court analysed the issue of whether violation of each and every facet of principles of natural justice has the effect of vitiating the enquiry and observed–

> The basic concept is fair play in action administrative, judicial or quasi-judicial. The concept of fair play in action must depend upon the particular lis, if there be any, between the parties. If the credibility of a person who has testified or given some information is in doubt, or if the version or the statement of the person who has testified, is, in dispute, right of cross-examination must inevitably form part of fair play in action but where there is no lis regarding the facts but certain explanation of the circumstances there is no requirement of cross-examination to be fulfilled to justify fair play in action. When on the question of facts there was no dispute, no real prejudice has been caused to a party aggrieved by an order, by absence of any formal opportunity of cross-examination per se does not invalidate or vitiate the decision arrived at fairly. This is more so when the party against whom an order has been passed does not dispute the facts and does not demand to test the veracity of the version of the credibility of the statement.
>
> The party who does not want to controvert the veracity of the evidence from record or testimony gathered behind his back cannot expect to succeed in any subsequent demand that there was no opportunity of cross-examination specially when it was not asked for and there was no dispute about the veracity of the statements. Where there is no dispute as to the facts, or the weight to be attached on disputed facts but only an explanation to the acts,

10. (1977) 4 SCC 337 : AIR 1977 SC 2313.
11. (1980) 4 SCC 379 : (1981) 1 SCR 746.
12. (1984) 1 SCC 43.

> absence of opportunity to cross-examination does not create any prejudice in such cases.
>
> The principles of natural justice will, therefore, depend upon the facts and circumstances of each particular case. We have set out hereinbefore the actual facts and circumstances of the case. The appellant was associated with the preliminary investigation that was conducted against him. He does not deny or dispute that. Information and materials undoubtedly were gathered not in his presence but whatever information was there and gathered namely, the versions of the persons, the particular entries which required examination were shown to him. He was conveyed the information given and his explanation was asked for. He participated in that investigation. He gave his explanation but he did not dispute any of the facts nor did he ask for any opportunity to call any evidence to rebut these facts.

The Court after applying the above principle held that the enquiry conducted and the punishment imposed without conferring the right of cross-examination will not be deemed to be vitiated.

In *Managing Director, ECIL v. B. Karunakar*[13] the Constitution Bench held that even though non-furnishing of enquiry report amounted to denial of natural justice but setting aside of the punishment imposed on that ground will not be the appropriate action. In every such case a copy of the report should be provided to the delinquent officer and the court should interfere only when it is satisfied that there has been a failure of fair process.

Ultimately the Supreme Court summarized the legal position in the case of *State Bank of Patiala v. S.K. Sharma*[14] wherein it held that–

> [P]rinciples of natural justice cannot be reduced to any hard and fast formulae. As said in *Russell v. Duke of Norfolk*[15] way back in 1949, these principles cannot be put in a strait-jacket. Their applicability depends upon the context and the facts and circumstances of each case. (**See** *Mohinder Singh Gill v. Chief Election Commr.*[16]) The objective is to ensure a fair hearing, a fair deal, to the person whose rights are going to be affected. (**See** *A.K. Roy v. Union of India*[17] and *Swadeshi Cotton Mills v. Union of India.*[18]) As pointed out by this Court in *A.K. Kraipak v. Union of India,*[19] the dividing line between quasi-judicial function and administrative function (affecting the rights of a party) has become quite thin and almost indistinguishable — a fact also emphasised by House of Lords in *Council of Civil Service Unions*

13. (1993) 4 SCC 727.
14. (1996) 3 SCC 364, para 28 - 33.
15. (1949) 1 All ER 109.
16. (1978) 1 SCC 405.
17. (1982) 1 SCC 271.
18. (1981) 1 SCC 664.
19. (1969) 2 SCC 262.

v. *Minister for the Civil Service*[20] where the principles of natural justice and a fair hearing were treated as synonymous. Whichever the case, it is from the standpoint of fair hearing — applying the test of prejudice, as it may be called — that any and every complaint of violation of the rule of audi alteram partem should be examined. Indeed, there may be situations where observance of the requirement of prior notice/hearing may defeat the very proceeding — which may result in grave prejudice to public interest. It is for this reason that the rule of post-decisional hearing as a sufficient compliance with natural justice was evolved in some of the cases, e.g., *Liberty Oil Mills v. Union of India.*[21] There may also be cases where the public interest or the interests of the security of State or other similar considerations may make it inadvisable to observe the rule of audi alteram partem altogether [as in the case of situations contemplated by clauses (*b*) and (*c*) of the proviso to Article 311(2)] or to disclose the material on which a particular action is being taken. There may indeed be any number of varying situations which it is not possible for anyone to foresee. In our respectful opinion, the principles emerging from the decided cases can be stated in the following terms in relation to the disciplinary orders and enquiries: a distinction ought to be made between violation of the principle of natural justice, audi alteram partem, as such *and* violation of a facet of the said principle. In other words, distinction is between "no notice"/"no hearing" and "no *adequate* hearing" or to put it in different words, "no opportunity" and "no *adequate* opportunity". To illustrate — take a case where the person is dismissed from service without hearing him altogether (as in *Ridge v. Baldwin*).[22] It would be a case falling under the first category and the order of dismissal would be *invalid* — or void, if one chooses to use that expression (*Calvin v. Carr*).[23] But where the person is dismissed from service, say, without supplying him a copy of the enquiry officer's report (*Managing Director, ECIL v. B. Karunakar*[24]) or without affording him a due opportunity of cross-examining a witness (*K.L. Tripathi*[25]) it would be a case falling in the latter category — violation of a facet of the said rule of natural justice — in which case, the validity of the order has to be tested on the touchstone of prejudice, i.e., whether, all in all, the person concerned did or did not have a fair hearing. It would not be correct — in the light of the above decisions to say that for any and every violation of a facet of natural justice or of a rule incorporating such facet, the order passed is altogether void and ought to be set aside without further enquiry. In our opinion, the approach and test adopted in *B. Karunakar* should govern all cases where the complaint is not that there was no hearing (no notice, no opportunity and no hearing) but one of not affording a *proper hearing* (i.e., adequate or a full hearing) *or* of violation of a procedural rule

20. (1984) 3 All ER 935.
21. (1984) 3 SCC 465.
22. 1964 AC 40.
23. 1980 AC 574.
24. (1993) 4 SCC 727.
25. (1984) 1 SCC 43.

or requirement governing the enquiry; the complaint should be examined on the touchstone of prejudice as aforesaid.

The matter can be looked at from the angle of justice or of natural justice also. The object of the principles of natural justice — which are now understood as synonymous with the obligation to provide a fair hearing[26] — is to ensure that justice is done, that there is no failure of justice and that every person whose rights are going to be affected by the proposed action gets a fair hearing. The said objective can be tested with reference to sub-clause (*iii*) concerned here. It says that copies of statements of witnesses should be furnished to the delinquent officer "not later than three days before the commencement of the examination of the witnesses by the inquiring authority". Now take a case — not the one before us — where the copies of statements are supplied only two days before the commencement of examination of witnesses instead of three days. The delinquent officer does not object; he does not say that two days are not sufficient for him to prepare himself for cross-examining the witnesses. The enquiry is concluded and he is punished. Is the entire enquiry and the punishment awarded to be set aside on the only ground that instead of three days before, the statements were supplied only two days before the commencement of the examination of witnesses? It is suggested by the appellate court that sub-clause (*iii*) is mandatory since it uses the expression 'shall'. Merely because the word 'shall' is used, it is not possible to agree that it is mandatory. We shall, however, assume it to be so for the purpose of this discussion. But then even a mandatory requirement can be waived by the person concerned if such mandatory provision is conceived in his interest and not in public interest, vide *Dhirendra Nath Gorai v. Sudhir Chandra Ghosh*[27] Subba Rao, J., speaking for the Court, held:

"Where the court acts without inherent jurisdiction, a party affected cannot by waiver confer jurisdiction on it, which it has not. Where such jurisdiction is not wanting, a directory provision can obviously be waived. But a mandatory provision can only be waived if it is not conceived in the public interests, but in the interests of the party that waives it. In the present case the executing court had inherent jurisdiction to sell the property. We have assumed that Section 35 of the Act is a mandatory provision. If so, the question is whether the said provision is conceived in the interests of the public or in the interests of the person affected by the non-observance of the provision. It is true that many provisions of the Act were conceived in the interests of the public, but the same cannot be said of Section 35 of the Act, which is really intended to protect the interests of a judgment-debtor and to see that a larger extent of his property than is necessary to discharge the debt is not sold. Many situations may be visualized when the judgment-debtor does not seek to take advantage of the benefit conferred on him under Section 35 of the Act."

26. **See** the discussion of this aspect at p. 515 of Wade: Administrative Law (7th Edn.). In particular, he refers to the speech of Lord Scarman in *CCSU v. Minister for the Civil Service* where he used both these concepts as signifying the same thing.

27. (1964) 6 SCR 1001 : AIR 1964 SC 1300.

....

Now, coming back to the illustration given by us in the preceding para, would setting aside the punishment and the entire enquiry on the ground of aforesaid violation of sub-clause (*iii*) be in the interests of justice *or* would it be its negation? In our respectful opinion, it would be the latter. Justice means justice between both the parties. The interests of justice equally demand that the guilty should be punished and that technicalities and irregularities which do not occasion failure of justice are not allowed to defeat the ends of justice. Principles of natural justice are but the means to achieve the ends of justice. They cannot be perverted to achieve the very opposite end. That would be a counter-productive exercise.

The Court laid down the following legal proposition on the issue –

(1) An order passed imposing a punishment on an employee consequent upon a disciplinary/departmental enquiry in violation of the rules/regulations/statutory provisions governing such enquiries should not be set aside automatically. The Court or the Tribunal should enquire whether (*a*) the provision violated is of a substantive nature or (*b*) whether it is procedural in character.

(2) A substantive provision has *normally* to be complied with as explained hereinbefore and the theory of substantial compliance or the test of prejudice would not be applicable in such a case.

(3) In the case of violation of a procedural provision, the position is this: procedural provisions are generally meant for affording a reasonable and adequate opportunity to the delinquent officer/employee. They are, generally speaking, conceived in his interest. Violation of any and every procedural provision cannot be said to automatically vitiate the enquiry held or order passed. Except cases falling under — "no notice", "no opportunity" and "no hearing" categories, the complaint of violation of procedural provision should be examined from the point of view of prejudice, viz., whether such violation has prejudiced the delinquent officer/employee in defending himself properly and effectively. If it is found that he has been so prejudiced, appropriate orders have to be made to repair and remedy the prejudice including setting aside the enquiry and/or the order of punishment. If no prejudice is established to have resulted therefrom, it is obvious, no interference is called for. In this connection, it may be remembered that there may be certain procedural provisions which are of a fundamental character, whose violation is by itself proof of prejudice. The Court may not insist on proof of prejudice in such cases. As explained in the body of the judgment, take a case where there is a provision expressly providing that after the evidence of the employer/government is over, the employee shall be given an opportunity to lead defence in his evidence, and in a given case, the enquiry officer does not give that opportunity in spite of the delinquent officer/employee asking for it. The prejudice is self-evident. No proof of prejudice as such need be called for in such a case. To repeat, the test is one of prejudice, i.e., whether the person has received a fair hearing

considering all things. Now, this very aspect can *also* be looked at from the point of view of directory and mandatory provisions, if one is so inclined. The principle stated under (4) herein below is only another way of looking at the same aspect as is dealt with herein and not a different or distinct principle.

(4)(*a*) In the case of a procedural provision which is not of a mandatory character, the complaint of violation has to be examined from the standpoint of substantial compliance. Be that as it may, the order passed in violation of such a provision can be set aside only where such violation has occasioned prejudice to the delinquent employee.

(*b*) In the case of violation of a procedural provision, which is of a mandatory character, it has to be ascertained whether the provision is conceived in the interest of the person proceeded against or in public interest. If it is found to be the former, then it must be seen whether the delinquent officer has waived the said requirement, either expressly or by his conduct. If he is found to have waived it, then the order of punishment cannot be set aside on the ground of the said violation. If, on the other hand, it is found that the delinquent officer/employee has not waived it *or* that the provision could not be waived by him, then the Court or Tribunal should make appropriate directions (include the setting aside of the order of punishment), keeping in mind the approach adopted by the Constitution Bench in *B. Karunakar* . The ultimate test is always the same, viz., test of prejudice or the test of fair hearing, as it may be called.

(5) Where the enquiry is not governed by any rules/regulations/statutory provisions and the only obligation is to observe the principles of natural justice — or, for that matter, wherever such principles are held to be implied by the very nature and impact of the order/action — the Court or the Tribunal should make a distinction between a total violation of natural justice (rule of *audi alteram partem*) and violation of a facet of the said rule, as explained in the body of the judgment. In other words, a distinction must be made between "no opportunity" and no *adequate* opportunity, i.e., between "no notice"/"no hearing" and "no fair hearing". (*a*) In the case of former, the order passed would undoubtedly be invalid (one may call it 'void' or a nullity if one chooses to). In such cases, normally, liberty will be reserved for the Authority to take proceedings afresh according to law, i.e., in accordance with the said rule (*audi alteram partem*). (*b*) But in the latter case, the effect of violation (of a facet of the rule of *audi alteram partem*) has to be examined from the standpoint of prejudice; in other words, what the Court or Tribunal has to see is whether in the totality of the circumstances, the delinquent officer / employee did or did not have a fair hearing and the orders to be made shall depend upon the answer to the said query. [It is made clear that this principle (No. 5) does not apply in the case of rule against bias, the test in which behalf are laid down elsewhere.]

(6) While applying the rule of *audi alteram partem* (the primary principle of natural justice) the Court / Tribunal / Authority must always bear in mind the ultimate and overriding objective underlying the said rule, viz., to ensure

a fair hearing and to ensure that there is no failure of justice. It is this objective which should guide them in applying the rule to varying situations that arise before them.

(7) There may be situations where the interests of State or public interest may call for a curtailing of the rule of *audi alteram partem*. In such situations, the Court may have to balance public / State interest with the requirement of natural justice and arrive at an appropriate decision.

SUMMATION

It has been a long drawn endeavour of the judiciary to include the values of fairness in administrative actions. Application of the principles of natural justice or the duty to act fairly should be made an integral part of all administrative and quasi-judicial actions so that the rights and liberties of the people are never restricted or infringed without due process of law. The following words of Ranganath Misra J. should act as the guiding principle–

> Fair play is a part of the public policy and is a guarantee for justice to citizens. In our system of Rule of Law every social agency conferred with power is required to act fairly so that social action would be just and there would be furtherance of the well-being of citizens. The rules of natural justice have developed with the growth of civilisation and the content thereof is often considered as a proper measure of the level of civilisation and Rule of Law prevailing in the community. Man within the social frame has struggled for centuries to bring into the community the concept of fairness and it has taken scores of years for the rules of natural justice to conceptually enter into the field of social activities.[28]

28. *K.I. Shephard v. Union of India*, AIR 1988 SC 686.

VI

Administrative Discretion and Principles of Judicial Review

LEARNING OBJECTIVES

After reading this chapter, you will be familiar with:

- Nature, objective and purpose of Discretionary powers
- Purpose and objective for Control of Discretionary power
- Duty of the Court to Control the exercise of Discretionary power
- Scope of Judicial Review of Administrative Action
- Judicial Control over Exercise of Discretionary Powers
  - Failure to Exercise Discretion or Abdication of Power
  - No Exercise of Discretion
  - Usurption of Power by a Superior Authority
  - Acting Mechanically
  - Outside the Scope of the Statutory Provisions
  - Irrelevant Considerations
  - Malafide Exercise of Power
  - Colourable Exercise of Power
- Principles of Judicial Review
  - Doctrine of Proportionality
  - Doctrine of Legitimate Expectation
  - Doctrine of Promissory Estoppel
  - Grant of Largess
  - Doctrine of Public Accountability

6.1 INTRODUCTION

The core administrative function is described as implementation of the laws framed by the legislature. Unlike the legislative and judicial functions performed by the legislature and judiciary respectively, the scope of administrative function is wide and undefined. The executive is required to undertake all tasks necessary for the proper implementation of the laws and bringing them into effect. The Supreme Court in the *Ram Jawaya Kapoor case* had described the executive function as 'residuary functions' referring to all the remaining functions which the administrative authorities are required to perform after subtracting the law making functions and the judicial functions.

Pure administrative function involves the implementation of the laws made by the Parliament, including the various rules and regulations made thereunder. The pure administrative functions involve discretionary functions as well as ministerial actions. Ministerial functions are generally described as those functions which an authority has a duty to do and is required to do in a particular manner.[1] On the contrary in pure administrative discretionary functions it is the discretion of the authority which is the basis of the action and such discretion is primarily based on state policy, expedience and individual wisdom. In case of discretionary functions the administrative authority has the power to act or choose not to act, act in one particular manner or in another manner. The term discretion is generally described as the power to decide or make a choice based on one's own judgment.

Discretionary power is generally accompanied by the word 'may' and often phrases such as *if he is of the opinion, if he is satisfied or if he has reasonable grounds to believe* confers discretionary powers to an officer. The purpose of conferring such powers is to enable the administrative officer to exercise his individual judgment while implementing a particular provision of law. The legislature has imposed the responsibility on such officers to act based on their knowledge, skills, experiences and wisdom. Grant of discretionary power is a modern day necessity. In *State of Punjab v. Khan Chand*[2] the Supreme Court while discussing the importance of grant of discretionary power to the administrative authorities observed *"Considering the complex nature of problems which have to be faced by a modern State, it is but inevitable that the matter of details should be left to the authorities acting under an enactment. Discretion has, therefore, to be given to the authorities concerned for the exercise of the powers vested in them under an enactment"*.

6.2 NEED TO CONTROL EXERCISE OF DISCRETIONARY POWER

There is a thin gap between exercise of discretionary power and arbitrary exercise of power. Dicey in his rule of law proposition had advocated for

1. Discussed elaborately in Chapter III.
2. (1974) 1 SCC 549.

absence of discretionary power in the hands of administrative officers based on the rationality that personal discretion of individual officers would give rise to arbitrary exercise of power and would discrimination and inequality in the actual application of the land. Modern scholars like Prof. Goodhart has advocated that instead of negating discretionary exercise of power more emphasis should be placed on imposing inherent limits on the exercise of powers so as to avoid discriminatory and arbitrary exercise of power. In this context the judiciary has played an instrumental role in imposing legal restraints on the exercise of discretionary powers by requiring that the legislature should lay down the necessary policy guidelines and essential rules of conduct at the time of conferring of discretionary powers. In the exercise of actual powers the judiciary has always exercised their power of review to ensure that the process and purpose of exercise of power is always in accordance with law, constitutional principles and legislative intent.

In *Maneka Gandhi v. Union of India*[3] emphasized the application of constitutional provisions of Articles 14 and 21 in exercise of discretionary power and stated that–

> Article 14 strikes at arbitrariness in State action and ensures fairness and equality of treatment. The principle of reasonableness, which legally as well as philosophically, is an essential element of equality or non-arbitrariness pervades Article 14 like a brooding omnipresence and the procedure contemplated by Article 21 must answer the test of reasonableness in order to be in conformity with Article 14. It must be "right and just and fair" and not arbitrary, fanciful or oppressive; otherwise, it. would be no procedure at all and the requirement of Article 21 would not be satisfied.[4]

In *State of Punjab v. Khan Chand*[5] the Supreme Court highlighted the need to control the exercise of discretionary power. It emphasized–

> [T]he vesting of discretion in authorities in the exercise of power under an enactment does not by itself entail contravention of Article 14. What is objectionable is the conferment of arbitrary and uncontrolled discretion without any guidelines whats oever with regard to the exercise of that discretion. Considering the complex nature of problems which have to be faced by a modern State, it is but inevitable that the matter of details should be left to the authorities acting under an enactment. Discretion has, therefore, to be given to the authorities concerned for the exercise of the powers vested in them under an enactment. The enactment must, however, prescribe the guidelines for the furtherance of the objects of the enactment and it is within the framework of those guidelines that the authorities can use their discretion

3. (1978) 1 SCC 248.
4. (1978) 1 SCC 248, Ibid at Para 7.
5. (1974) 1 SCC 549.

in the exercise of the powers conferred upon them. Discretion which is absolute, uncontrolled and without any guidelines in the exercise of the powers can easily degenerate into arbitrariness. When individuals act according to their sweet will, there is bound to be an element of "pick and choose" according to the notion of the individuals. If a Legislature bestows such untrammelled discretion on the authorities acting under an enactment, it abdicates its essential function for such discretion is bound to result in discrimination which is the negation and antithesis of the ideal of equality before law as enshrined in Article 14 of the Constitution. It is the absence of any principle or policy for the guidance of the authority concerned in the exercise of discretion which vitiates an enactment and makes it vulnerable to the attack on the ground of violation of Article 14. It is no answer to the above that the executive officers are presumed to be reasonable men who do not stand to gain in the abuse of their power and can be trusted to use "discretion" with discretion. As mentioned on p. 3 of *Parliamentary Supervision of Delegated Legislation* by John E. Kersell, 1960 Edn.

"The point is, however, that no one ought to be trusted with power without restraint. Power can be of an encroaching nature, and its encroachments are usually for the sake of what are sincerely believed to be good, and indeed necessary, objectives. Throughout history the most terrible form of tyranny has been, the forcing on human beings of what someone believes to be good for them. The imposition of controls on the use of delegated legislative authority, therefore, does not imply a deep suspicion of malevolent intentions. Human nature, being what it is, has to be protected against itself, and where power is concerned the very existence of the possibility of restraint, as we shall see, is a safeguard against abuses in which ends may be used to justify means and the good in intent becomes the evil in effect."

6.3 IMPLICIT PRESUMPTION OF *'PUBLIC PURPOSE'*

In *State of Punjab v. Khan Chand*[6] Matthew J. had made the argument that even if a legislative provision did not include phrases such as 'public purpose', 'public interest' or 'public good', there should always be a presumption made that *"Courts and parties all assume that the Legislature always wants protection of the public interest, to serve public cause and do things for public good or to exercise powers for public purpose and always intends that administrators act justly and reasonably whether the Legislature says so in the statute or not [***see*** Kenneth Culp Davis, "Administrative Law Treatise", (1958) Vol. I, p. 87]. Every legislative body must be presumed to favour the true, the good and above all the public interest and public good and whether it says so or not is of absolutely no consequence".*[7]

6. (1974) 1 SCC 549.
7. (1974) 1 SCC 549, Ibid at para 23.

But the majority opinion negated the argument and categorically held that *"The words "for a public purpose" do not find a mention in Section 2 and it is, in our opinion, impermissible to construe that Section in such a way as if those words were a part of that Section. To read those words in the Section, even though those words are not there, would for all intents and purposes amount to judicial legislation".*[8] Thus it is necessary that the statute must lay down the policy and the conditions for exercise of power before conferring of discretionary power to administrative officers.

6.4 DUTY OF THE COURT TO CONTROL THE EXERCISE OF DISCRETIONARY POWER

Speaking on the duty of the Court to control arbitrary exercise of discretionary power, Khanna J. in *Khan Chand* observed–

> It would be wrong to assume that there is an element of judicial arrogance in the act of the Courts in striking down an enactment. The Constitution has assigned to the Courts the function of determining as to whether the laws made by the Legislature are in conformity with the provisions of the Constitution. In adjudicating the constitutional validity of statutes, the Courts discharge an obligation which has been imposed upon them by the Constitution. The Courts would be shirking their responsibility if they hesitate to declare the provisions of a statute to be unconstitutional, even though those provisions are found to be violative of the Articles of the Constitution. Articles 32 and 226 are an integral part of the Constitution and provide remedies for enforcement of fundamental rights and other rights conferred by the Constitution. Hesitation or refusal on the part of the Courts to declare the provisions of an enactment to be unconstitutional, even though they are found to infringe the Constitution because of any notion of judicial humility would in a large number of cases have the effect of taking away or in any case eroding the remedy provided to the aggrieved parties by the Constitution. Abnegation in matters affecting one's own interest may sometimes be commendable but abnegation in a matter where power is conferred to protect the interest of others against measures which are violative of the Constitution is fraught with serious consequences. It is as much the duty of the Courts to declare a provision of an enactment to be unconstitutional if it contravenes any Article of the Constitution as it is theirs to uphold its validity in case it is found to suffer from no such infirmity.

The judicial control should be more stringent if the administrative action will detrimentally impact a fundamental right. Distinguishing the scope of exercise of discretionary power with reference to a fundamental right and a

8. (1974) 1 SCC 549, Id at para 11.

statutory right, the Supreme Court in *Pannalal Binjraj v. Union of India*[9] held that–

> There is a broad distinction between discretion which has to be exercised with regard to a fundamental right guaranteed by the Constitution and some other right which is given by the statute. If the statute deals with a right which is not fundamental in character the statute can take it away but a fundamental right the statute cannot take away. Where, for example, a discretion is given in the matter of issuing licences for carrying on trade, profession or business or where restrictions are imposed on freedom of speech, etc. by the imposition of censorship, the discretion must be controlled by clear rules so as to come within the category of reasonable restrictions. Discretion of that nature must be differentiated from discretion in respect of matters not involving Fundamental Rights such as transfer of cases. An inconvenience resulting from a change of place or venue occurs when any case is transferred from one place to another but it is not open to a party to say that a fundamental right has been infringed by such transfer. In other words, the discretion vested has to be looked at from two points of view viz. (*1*) does it admit of the possibility of any real and substantial discrimination, and (*2*) does it impinge on a fundamental right guaranteed by the Constitution? Article 14 can be invoked only when both these conditions are satisfied.

This view was reiterated by the Supreme Court while dealing with the constitutionality of Section 2 of the East Punjab Movable Property (Requisitioning) Act, 1947 in *State of Punjab v. Khan Chand.*[10]

6.5 SCOPE OF JUDICIAL REVIEW OF ADMINISTRATIVE ACTION

The courts have the inherent power of judicial review. In the case of *Union of India v. Cynamide India Ltd*[11] the court had observed that the court had the power to enquire whether the administrative authorities had taken into consideration relevant factors and had excluded all irrelevant factors out of consideration while fixing the prices of essential drugs. The authority should take into consideration the legislative policy and the prescribed factors while performing the administrative task. The judiciary shall not delve into the question further. Thus the task of the judiciary is more of 'supervisory' than corrective in nature wherein the Court particularly looks into the process of decision making rather than merit of the decision itself.

9. (1957) 1 SCR 233.
10. (1974) 1 SCC 549.
11. AIR 1987 SC 1802 : MANU/SC/0076/1987.

Courts can issue writ of quo-warranto in case of discretionary functions but the writ of mandamus is not generally issued. It can be issued only if the authority has undertaken an obligation in pursuance of a rule or regulation.

Judicial control over discretionary power is divided into two stages. The first stage commences at the time of grant of discretionary powers by the legislature to the administrative authorities and the second stage takes place at the stage of actual exercise of discretionary powers.

6.5.1 Grant of Discretion to the Administrative Authorities

One of the first cases to deal with the issue of constitutionality of discretionary power is *State of West Bengal v. Anwar Ali Sarkar.*[12] The State of West Bengal had enacted the West Bengal Special Courts Act 1950. Anwar Ali Sarkar and 49 co-accused's were arrested for committing several acts of brutalities in the course of their raid in a factory in West Bengal. They were tried before the Special Judge under the Special Courts Act. They challenged the trial conducted on the ground of violation of Article 14 as the legislation made discrimination between persons similarly situated and for conferring wide discretion to the State Government under Section 5 of the Act. The Preamble to the statute stated – "Whereas it is expedient to provide for the speedier trial of certain offences". Section 5 provided – "A Special Court shall try such offences or classes of offences or cases or classes of cases as the State Government may, by general or special order in writing direct".

Holding Section 5(1) as unconstitutional Mukherjee J. observed–

> [T]he language of Section 5(1) is perfectly clear and free from any ambiguity. It vests an unrestricted discretion in the State Government to direct any cases or classes of cases to be tried by the Special Court in accordance with the procedure laid down in the Act. It is not stated that it is only when speedier trial is necessary that the discretion should be exercised. In the second place, assuming that the preamble throws any light upon the interpretation of the section, I am definitely of opinion that the necessity of a speedier trial is too vague, uncertain and elusive a criterion to form a rational basis for the discriminations made. The necessity for speedier trial may be the object which the legislature had in view or it may be the occasion for making the enactment. In a sense quick disposal is a thing which is desirable in all legal proceedings. The word used here is "speedier" which is a comparative term and as there may be degrees of speediness, the word undoubtedly introduces an uncertain and variable element. But the question is: how is this necessity of speedier trial to be determined? Not by reference to the nature of the offences or the

12. AIR 1952 SC 75.

circumstances under which or the area in which they are committed, nor even by reference to any peculiarities or antecedents of the offenders themselves, but the selection is left to the absolute and unfettered discretion of the executive government with nothing in the law to guide or control its action. This is not a reasonable classification at all but an arbitrary selection. A line is drawn artificially between two classes of cases. On one side of the line are grouped those cases which the State Government chooses to assign to the Special Court; on the other side stand the rest which the State Government does not think fit and proper to touch. It has been observed in many cases by the Supreme Court of America that the fact that some sort of classification has been attempted at will not relieve a statute from the reach of the equality clause. "It must appear not only that a classification has been made but also that it is based upon some reasonable ground — some difference which bears a just and proper relation to the attempted classification [165 US 150]". The question in each case would be whether the characteristics of the class are such as to provide a rational justification for the differences introduced? Judged by this test, the answer in the present case should be in the negative; for the difference in the treatment rests here solely on arbitrary selection by the State Government. It is true that the presumption should always be that the legislature understands and correctly appreciates the needs of its own people and that its discriminations are based on adequate grounds [Middleton *v. Taxes Power & Light Co.*[13]]; but as was said by Mr Justice Brewer in *Gulf Colorado etc. Company v. Ellis*[14] "to carry the presumption to the extent of holding that there must be some undisclosed and unknown reason for subjecting certain individuals or corporations to hostile and discriminatory legislation is to make the protection clauses of the Fourteenth Amendment a mere rope of sand".

In *State of Punjab v. Khan Chand*[15] the constitutionality of Section 2 of the East Punjab Movable Property (Requisitioning) Act, 1947 was challenged on the ground of conferring arbitrary powers and for being violative of Article 14 of the Constitution. In this case the Tata Mercedes Benz Truck of the respondent was requisitioned by the District Magistrate of Rohtak for the purposes of carrying road materials for famine work under the provisions of the Act. The respondent filed a writ petition under Article 226 challenging the validity of the order and declaration of Section 2 of the Act as unconstitutional.

Sec 2 of the Act provided that–

(1) The State Government, if it considers necessary or expedient so to do, may by order in writing requisition any movable property and

13. 249 US 152.
14. 165 US 150.
15. (1974) 1 SCC 549.

may make such further orders as may be necessary or expedient in connection with the requisitioning:

Provided that no property used for the purpose of religious worship and no aircraft or anything forming part of an aircraft or connected with the operation, repair or maintenance of aircraft, shall be requisitioned.

(2) Where the State Government makes any order under sub-section (1), it may use or deal with the property in such manner as may appear to it to be expedient.

Holding Section 2 as unconstitutional and violative of Article 14 the Court held that–

> The relevant provisions of the Act have been reproduced above and from a perusal thereof we find that the Act confers uncontrolled power on the State Government or the officers authorised by it to requisition any movable property. The only property excluded from the purview of the Act is one used for the purpose of religious worship or an aircraft or anything forming part of an aircraft or connected with the operation, repair or maintenance of aircraft. No guidelines have been laid down in the Act regarding the object or the purpose for which the State Government or the officers authorised by it may consider it necessary or expedient to requisition a movable property. It is not even the requirement of the Act that the authority requisitioning movable property should specify in the order the purpose for which it has become necessary or expedient to requisition that property. There is no provision in the Act that the power of requisitioning movable property can be exercised under the Act only for a public purpose nor is there any provision that powers under the Act can be exercised only in an emergency or in some special contingency. It is open under the provisions of the Act for an officer authorised under the Act to requisition movable property for any purpose whatsoever. For example, it would be permissible under the provisions of the Act for the District Magistrate, who is an officer authorised under the Act, to requisition the furniture of anyone within the district for use in the office of the District Magistrate. Likewise, it would be permissible for the District Magistrate to requisition any private car which may have caught his fancy for his own use. It is not necessary to go into the question as to whether the District Magistrate would ever use his powers under the Act for such purposes. Suffice it to say that there is nothing in the provisions of the Act which makes it impermissible for a District Magistrate to requisition movable property for any purpose whatsoever for which he considers it necessary or expedient to do so.
>
> The power conferred under the Act can be exercised not only by the State Government but also by the officers to whom it may be delegated by the State Government. There is nothing in the Act that the officer to whom the powers under the Act can be delegated must not be below a particular rank. The result is that the powers of requisitioning a movable property, which are of a most comprehensive nature, can be conferred even upon a petty

> officer. No suitable machinery is also provided in the Act for determining the compensation payable to the owner of the movable property nor does the Act contain any guiding principles for determining the amount of compensation. According to Section 4 of the Act, the compensation to be paid shall be such "as the State Government may determine".
>
> The drastic and unusual features of the Act which have been pointed out above highlight the fact that the Act confers arbitrary powers for requisitioning of movable property upon the authorities under the Act and that no guidelines whatsoever have been prescribed for the exercise of the powers of requisitioning. The total absence of guidelines for the exercise of power of requisitioning of movable property, in our opinion, vitiates Section 2 of the Act. Arbitrariness and the power to discriminate are writ large on the face of the said provision of the Act and, in our opinion, that provision falls within the mischief which Article 14 of the Constitution is designed to prevent.

In *Himat Lal K. Shah v. Commissioner of Police*[16] the Supreme Court looked into the constitutionality of the Rule 7 of the Rules for Processions and Public Meetings framed by the Commissioner of Police, Ahmedabad under the Bombay Police Act 1951. The Bombay Police Act empowered the Commissioner and the District Magistrate with the power to make rules in order to prevent the obstruction, inconvenience, annoyance, risk, danger due to any processions or assemblies.

> Sec. 33 of the Act provided (1)— The Commissioner and the District Magistrate, in areas under their respective charges or any part thereof may make, alter or rescind rules or orders not inconsistent with this Act for;
>
> * * *
>
> (*n*) licensing, controlling or, in order to prevent the obstruction, inconvenience, annoyance, risk, danger or damage of the residents or passengers in the vicinity, prohibiting the playing of music, the beating of drums, tom-toms or other instruments and blowing or sounding of horns or other noisy instruments in or near streets or public places;
>
> (*o*) regulating the conduct of and behaviour or action of persons constituting assemblies and processions on or along the streets and prescribing in the case of processions, the routes by which, the order in which and the times at which the same may pass;
>
> (*y*) prescribing the procedure in accordance with which any licence or permission sought to be obtained or required under this Act should be applied for and fixing the fees to be charged for any such licence or permission

In exercise of such power, the Commissioner of Police, Ahmedabad framed Rule 7 – "No public meeting with or without loudspeaker, shall be held

16. AIR 1973 SC 87 : (1973) 1 SCC 227.

on the public street within the jurisdiction of the Commissionerate of the Police, Ahmedabad City unless the necessary permission in writing has been obtained from the officer authorised by the Commissioner of Police". On an application made by the appellant that Section 33 of the Parent statute and Rule 7 suffered from the vice of arbitrariness and were in violation of Article 19 (1)(b) and (d) of the Constitution.

The Court upheld the constitutionality of Sec. 33 on the rationality that–

> Under Section 33(*o*) no rule could be prescribed prohibiting all meetings or processions. The section proceeds on the basis that the public has a right to hold assemblies and processions on and along streets though it is necessary to regulate the conduct and behaviour or action of persons constituting such assemblies or processions in order to safeguard the rights of citizens and in order to preserve public order. The word "regulate", according to Shorter Oxford Dictionary, means, "to control, govern, or direct by rule or regulation; to subject to guidance or restrictions". The impugned Rules do not prohibit the holding of meetings but only prescribe that permission should be taken although it is not stated on what grounds permission could be refused. We shall deal with this aspect a little later".[17]

However on the issue of whether Rule 7 is within the scope of constitutional limits, it was categorically held that *"Rule 7 does not give any guidance to the officer authorised by the Commissioner of Police as to the circumstances in which he can refuse permission to hold a public meeting. Prima facie, to give an arbitrary discretion to an officer is an unreasonable restriction".* The Court struck down Rule 7 on the ground of arbitrariness.

The Indian judiciary has consciously reviewed the legislative provisions so as to ensure that the grant of discretionary is always circumscribed with necessary policy guidelines and avoid all possible arbitrary exercise of powers.

6.5.2 Judicial Control over Exercise of Discretionary Powers

The second stage of control commences at the stage of exercise of discretionary power by the administrative officer. The judiciary has fundamentally relied on Article 14 to strike down an arbitrary exercise of power. Under the traditional scheme of separation of functions theory the power and responsibility to implement laws is within the exclusive domain of the administration and it has been accepted that the legislature at the time of enacting the laws had reposed their faith on the executive to use their practical understandings and

17. Ibid at Para 15.

experiences for the purpose of implementation and execution of laws. In the absence of specific legislations dealing with judicial review of administrative actions, the judiciary has relied on constitutional provisions and principles to develop various administrative law principles to regulate the exercise of discretionary exercise of powers.

One of the leading English cases dealing with the judicial control over exercise of discretionary powers is *Associated Provincial Picture Houses Ltd. v. Wednesbury Corporation.*[18] In this case the plaintiffs who were proprietors of a cinematograph theatre in Wednesbury challenged the order issued by the Wednesbury Corporation under the provisions of the Sunday Entertainments Act, 1932. Before the enactment opening of cinematograph theatres on Sundays were deemed illegal but Section 1(1) of the statute provided that – "The authority having power, in any area to which this section extends, to grant licenses under the Cinematograph Act, 1909, may, notwithstanding anything in any enactment relating to Sunday observance, allow places in that area licensed under the said Act to be opened and used on Sundays for the purpose of cinematograph entertainments, subject to such conditions as the authority think fit to impose". Based on the power conferred the Wednesbury Corporation imposed the restriction on the issuance of license that 'No children under the age of 15 years shall be admitted to any entertainment, whether accompanied by an adult or not.'

Speaking on the scope of judicial review Lord Greene made the observation–

> The courts can only interfere with an act of an executive authority if it be shown that the authority have contravened the law. It is for those who assert that the local authority have contravened the law to establish that proposition. On the face of it, a condition of this kind is perfectly lawful. It is not to be assumed prima facie that responsible bodies like local authorities will exceed their powers, and the court, whenever it is alleged that the local authority have contravened the law, must not substitute itself for the local authority. It is only concerned with seeing whether or not the proposition is made good. When an executive discretion is entrusted by Parliament to a local authority, what purports to be an exercise of that discretion can only be challenged in the courts in a very limited class of case. It must always be remembered that the court is not a court of appeal. The law recognises certain principles on which the discretion must be exercised, but within the four corners of those principles the discretion is an absolute one and cannot be questioned in any court of law.

On the exercise of discretionary power by administrative authorities it was observed that–

18. [1948] 1 KB 223.

> The exercise of such a discretion must be a real exercise of the discretion. If, in the statute conferring the discretion, there is to be found, expressly or by implication, matters to which the authority exercising the discretion ought to have regard, then, in exercising the discretion, they must have regard to those matters. Conversely, if the nature of the subject-matter and the general interpretation of the Act make it clear that certain matters would not be germane [relevant] to the matter in question, they must disregard those matters.
>
> Expressions have been used in cases where the powers of local authorities came to be considered relating to the sort of thing that may give rise to interference by the court. Bad faith, dishonesty-those, of course, stand by themselves-unreasonableness, attention given to extraneous circumstances, disregard of public policy, and things like that have all been referred to as being matters which are relevant for consideration.

In this case *unreasonability* was recognized as a separate ground for review of administrative actions. Traditionally the word 'unreasonable' has been used to describe proper exercise of discretionary power by consideration of relevant matters and excluding irrelevant matters, improper exercise of discretion etc. In the case the court created the doctrine of unreasonability based on the proposition that *no sensible person could ever dream that it lay within the powers of the authority.* Summarizing the scope of judicial review it was held that–

> [T]he court is entitled to investigate the action of the local authority with a view to seeing whether it has taken into account matters which it ought not to take into account, or, conversely, has refused to take into account or neglected to take into account matters which it ought to take into account. Once that question is answered in favour of the local authority, it may still be possible to say that the local authority, nevertheless, have come to a conclusion so unreasonable that no reasonable authority could ever have come to it. In such a case, again, I think the court can interfere. The power of the court to interfere in each case is not that of an appellate authority to override a decision of the local authority, but is that of a judicial authority which is concerned, and concerned only, to see whether the local authority have contravened the law by acting in excess of the powers which Parliament has confided in it.

Upholding the restrictions imposed by the local authority the Court clarified that *nobody, at this time of day, can say that the well-being and the physical and moral health of children are not matters which a local authority, in exercising its powers, can properly have in mind when those questions are germane to what it has to consider.*

It further observed–

> It is perfectly clear that the local authority are entrusted by Parliament with the decision on a matter in which the knowledge and experience of the authority can best be trusted to be of value. The subject-matter with which the condition deals is one relevant for its consideration. It has considered it and come to a decision on it. Theoretically it is true to say—and in practice it may operate in some cases—that, if a decision on a competent matter is so unreasonable that no reasonable authority could ever have come to it, then the courts can interfere. That, I think, is right, but that would require overwhelming proof, and in this case the facts do not come anywhere near such a thing. Counsel in the end agreed that his proposition that the decision of the local authority can be upset if it is proved to be unreasonable, really meant that it must be proved to be unreasonable in the sense, not that it is what the court considers unreasonable, but that it is what the court considers is a decision that no reasonable body could have come to, which is a different thing altogether. The court may very well have different views from those of a local authority on matters of high public policy of this kind. Some courts might think that no children ought to be admitted on Sundays at all, some courts might think the reverse. All over the country, I have no doubt, on a thing of that sort honest and sincere people hold different views. The effect of the legislation is not to set up the court as an arbiter of the correctness of one view over another. It is the local authority who are put in that position and, provided they act, as they have acted here, within the four corners of their jurisdiction, the court, in my opinion, cannot interfere.

Lord Diplock in *Council of Civil Services Union v. Minister for the Civil Service* further advanced the principles of judicial control of administrative actions. He summarized the scope of judicial review in the following words–

> Judicial review provides the means by which judicial control of administrative action is exercised. The subject matter of every judicial review is a decision made by some person (or body of persons) whom I will call the 'decision-maker' or else a refusal by him to make a decision.
>
> To qualify as a subject for judicial review the decision must have consequences which affect some person (or body of persons) other than the decision-maker, although it may affect him too. It must affect such other person either (a) by altering rights or obligations of that person which are enforceable by or against him in private law or (b) by depriving him of some benefit or advantage which either (i) he has in the past been permitted by the decision-maker to enjoy and which he can legitimately expect to be permitted to continue to do until there has been communicated to him some rational ground for withdrawing it on which he has been given an opportunity to comment or (ii) he has received assurance from the decision-maker will not be withdrawn without giving him first an opportunity of advancing reasons for contending that they should not be withdrawn....

> For a decision to be susceptible to judicial review the decision-maker must be empowered by public law (and not merely, as in arbitration, by agreement between private parties) to make decisions that, if validly made, will lead to administrative action or abstention from action by an authority endowed by law with executive powers, which have one or other of the consequences mentioned in the preceding paragraph. The ultimate source of the decision-making power is nearly always nowadays a statute or subordinate legislation made under the statute; but in the absence of any statute regulating the subject matter of the decision the source of the decision-making power may still be the common law itself, i.e that part of the common law that is given by lawyers the label of 'the prerogative'. Where this is the source of decision-making power, the power is confined to executive officers of central as distinct from local government and in constitutional practice is generally exercised by those holding ministerial rank.

Lord Diplock classified under three heads the grounds on which administrative action is subject to control by judicial review – illegality, irrationality and procedural impropriety. He also recognized the possibility of principles of proportionality being considered as new ground of judicial review in the future.

Illegality as a ground of judicial review implies that the "decision-maker must understand correctly the law that regulates his decision-making power and must give effect to it. Whether he has or not is par excellence a justiciable question to be decided, in the event of dispute, by those persons, the judges, by whom the judicial power of the state is exercisable".

Irrationality refers to the concept of Wednesbury unreasonableness. "It applies to a decision which is so outrageous in its defiance of logic or of accepted moral standards that no sensible person who had applied his mind to the question to be decided could have arrived at it. Whether a decision falls within this category is a question that judges by their training and experience should be well equipped to answer, or else there would be something badly wrong with our judicial system".

Procedural impropriety refers to not only the failure to observe basic rules of natural justice but also "failure to act with procedural fairness towards the person who will be affected by the decison. This is because susceptibility to judicial review under this head covers also failure by an administrative tribunal to observe procedural rules that are expressly laid down in the legislative instrument by which its jurisdiction is conferred, even where such failure does not involve any denial of natural justice".

Thus the judicial review of administrative action through the various principles of administrative law has become an essential part of administrative accountability.

6.8 EXERCISE OF DISCRETIONARY POWER-SOME ILLUSTRATIONS

6.8.1 Failure to Exercise Discretion or Abdication of Power

In the leading case of *Purtabpore Co. Ltd. v. Cane Commissioner of Bihar*[19] Supreme Court analyzes the failure of the Cane Commissioner to perform his statutory duty independently and acting under the dictates of the Chief Minister. The appellants were in the business of sugar manufacturing from 1903. Though their mills were located in UP but they used to procure raw sugarcane from some 208 villages in neighbouring Bihar for more than 30 years. In 1962 with the establishment of the New Siwan Mills in Bihar the supply of sugarcane from these villages were stopped for a period of time. In 1964 a meeting was held between the Cane Commissioners of Bihar and UP and deal was made whereby it was agreed that the 208 villages in Bihar would be reserved for the appellants and sugarcane from some villages in UP would be supplied to the New Siwan Mills. But this settlement was not agreeable to them and they pressurized the Bihar Chief Minister to change the order. The Cane Commissioner of Bihar was firm in his decision that there was no justification for disturbing the reservation made in favour of the appellants, but the Chief Minister who was personally interested in the matter compelled the Cane Commissioner to pass an order on November 14, 1967 under the provisions of Sugar Cane (Control) Order, 1966 whereby 99 villages were reserved exclusively for the New Siwan Mills and the rest for the appellants. The appellants challenged the orders issued by the Cane Commissioner of Bihar on the ground that he had practically abdicated his statutory functions and had mechanically implemented the directions of the Chief Minister. The Court held–

> [W]e are of the opinion that the impugned orders though purported to have been made by the Cane Commissioner were in fact made by the Chief Minister and hence they are invalid. We have earlier seen that the Cane Commissioner was definitely of the view that the reservation made in favour of the appellant should not be disturbed but the Chief Minister did not agree with that view. It is clear from the documents before us that the Chief Minister directed the Cane Commissioner to divide the reserved area into two portions and allot one portion to the 5th respondent. In pursuance of that direction, the Cane Commissioner prepared two lists "Ka" and "Kha". Under the orders of the Chief Minister, the villages contained in list "Ka" were allotted to the appellant and in list "Kha" to the 5th respondent. The Cane Commissioner merely carried out the orders of the Chief Minister. It is true that the impugned orders were issued in the name of the Cane Commissioner. He merely obeyed

19. AIR 1970 SC 1896 : (1969) 1 SCC 308.

the directions issued to him by the Chief Minister. We are unable to agree with the contention of Shri Chagla that though the Cane Commissioner was initially of the view that the reservation made in favour of the appellant should not be disturbed, he changed his opinion after discussion with the Chief Minister. From the material before us, the only conclusion possible is that the Chief Minister imposed his opinion on the Cane Commissioner. The power exercisable by the Cane Commissioner under Clause 6(1) is a statutory power. He alone could have exercised that power. While exercising that power he cannot abdicate his responsibility in favour of anyone — not even in favour of the State Government or the Chief Minister. It was not proper for the Chief Minister to have interfered with the functions of the Cane Commissioner. In this case what has happened is that the power of the Cane Commissioner has been exercised by the Chief Minister, an authority not recognised by clause (6) read with clause (11) but the responsibility for making those orders was asked to be taken by the Cane Commissioner.

The executive officers entrusted with statutory discretions may in some cases be obliged to take into account considerations of public policy and in some context the policy of a Minister or the Government as a whole when it is a relevant factor in weighing the policy but this will not absolve them from their duty to exercise their personal judgment in individual cases unless explicit statutory provision has been made for them to be given binding instructions by a superior.

6.8.2 No Exercise of Discretion

In the landmark case of *Commissioner of Police, Bombay v. Gordhandas Bhanji*[20] the Supreme Court was faced with the issue of whether the Government of Bombay had the authority to grant, refuse, suspend or cancel licenses issued by the Commissioner of Police for erection of building for public amusements. In this case the respondent, Gordhandas Bhanji, wanted to build a cinema house on a plot of land at Andheri and made due application to the Commissioner of Police. Subsequently the Commissioner granted permission by a letter dated 14/16th of July 1947. In the contents of the letter there was *no suggestion that his will was overborne or that there was dishonesty or fraud in what he did. In the absence of that, he was entitled to take into consideration the advice thus tendered to him by a public body set up for this express purpose, and he was entitled in the bona fide exercise of his discretion to accept that advice and act upon it even though he would have acted differently if this important factor had not been present to his mind when he reached a decision.*

20. AIR 1952 SC 16.

Later on the Commissioner wrote to the respondent on the 19/20th September, 1947, and directed him 'not to proceed with the construction of the cinema pending Government orders'. Thereafter on the 27/30th September, 1947, the Commissioner sent a communication to the respondent stating 'I am directed by Government to inform you that the permission to erect a cinema at the above site granted to you under this office letter... dated the 16th July, 1947, is hereby cancelled'. Aggrieved with the cancellation order, the respondent challenged the legality of the order issued on the ground of non-exercise of discretion by the Commissioner and acting under the dictates of the government.

The Supreme Court while dealing with the issue of whether the cancellation by the Commissioner was on his own volition or he *merely acted as a post office in forwarding orders issued by some other authority* categorically held that *"We have no hesitation on reaching the conclusion that this is not an order of cancellation by the Commissioner but merely intimation by him of an order passed and made by another authority, namely the Government of Bombay"*.

On the issue of subsequent submission of affidavit by the Commissioner stating that the order of cancellation was actually made by him and not by the Government, the Court rejected the argument and held that–

> We are clear that public orders, publicly made, in exercise of a statutory authority cannot be construed in the light of explanations subsequently given by the officer making the order of what he meant, or of what was in his mind, or what he intended to do. Public orders made by public authorities are meant to have public effect and are intended to affect the actings and conduct of those to whom they are addressed and must be construed objectively with reference to the language used in the order itself.

6.8.3 Usurption of Power by a Superior Authority

In the case of *State of Punjab v. Hari Krishan Sharma*[21] the Supreme Court analyzed the concepts of failure to exercise discretionary power by an administrative officer and abdication of power. The Punjab Cinemas (Regulation) Act, 1952 was enacted to regulate exhibitions by means of cinematographs in Punjab. Under Section 3 of the statute no person could give an exhibition, by means of a cinematograph other than in a place licensed under the Act and in accordance with the conditions and restrictions imposed by such licence. Sec. 4 empowers the District Magistrate as the licensing authority. Section 5(3) provides that any person aggrieved by the decision of the licensing authority refusing to grant a licence under the

21. AIR 1966 SC 1081 : (1966) 2SCR 982.

Act may appeal to the Government. Section 5(4) further authorises the Government to issue directions to licensees generally or to any licensee in particular for the purpose specified by it. Sec. 8 further empowers the State Government or the licensing authority to suspend, cancel or revoke a licence granted under Section 5.

On April 24, 1957, the State Government had issued instructions under Section 5(4) with regard to grant of licences and required that all requests for the grant of permission for opening all new permanent cinemas should be referred to the State Government for orders. It was further specified that all applications should be accompanied with particulars such as population of the town where the permanent cinema is proposed to be constructed; whether there are any permanent cinema already in existence in the town, and if so, how many; whether the applicant / applicants has / have been taking any part in any activity undermining the security of the State; and whether the financial position of the applicant / applicants is sound.

The respondent had made an application under the statute for grant of license for construction of a cinema hall. Based on the order issued by the Government the application of the respondent was forwarded to the State Government. The application was rejected on the ground that it was reported by the police that the respondent had been arrested in connection with "Save Hindi Agitation" and was discharged on tendering apology and that he also did not pay any income tax. License was granted to another applicant Sultan Singh and that probably was the reason for the application of the respondent to be rejected. Aggrieved with the decision of the State Government, the respondent challenged the order issued primarily on the ground that the under the provisions of the statute the State Government was not authorized to deal with the applications for issuance of licenses.

After analysing the provisions of the statute the Supreme Court upheld the order of the High Court and made the following observations–

> The question which we have to decide in the present appeal lies within a very narrow compass. What Appellant 1 has done is to require the licensing authority to forward to it all applications received for grant of licences, and it has assumed power and authority to deal with the said applications on the merits for itself in the first instance. Is Appellant 1 justified in assuming jurisdiction which has been conferred on the licensing authority by Section 5(1) and (2) of the Act? It is plain that Section 5(1) and (2) have conferred jurisdiction on the licensing authority to deal with applications for licences, and either grant them or reject them. In other words, the scheme of the statute is that when an application for licence is made, it has to be considered by the licensing authority and dealt with under Section 5(1) and (2) of the Act. Section 5(3) provides for an appeal to Appellant 1 where the licensing authority has refused to grant a licence; and this provision clearly shows that

Appellant 1 is constituted into an Appellate Authority in cases where an application for licence is rejected by the licensing authority. The course adopted by Appellant 1 in requiring all applications for licences to be forwarded to it for disposal, has really converted the Appellate Authority into the original authority itself, because Section 5(3) clearly allows an appeal to be preferred by a person who is aggrieved by the rejection of his application for a licence by the licensing authority.

..... It is true that Section 5(2) provides that the licensing authority may grant licences subject to the provisions of Section 5(1) and subject to the control of the Government; and it may be conceded that the control of the Government subject to which the licensing authority has to function while exercising its power under Section 5(1) and (2) is very wide; but however wide this control may be, it cannot justify Appellant 1 to completely oust the licensing authority and itself usurp his functions. The legislature contemplates a licensing authority as distinct from the Government. It no doubt recognises that the licensing authority has to act under the control of the Government; but it is the licensing authority which has to act and not the Government itself. The result of the instructions issued by Appellant 1 is to change the statutory provision of Section 5(2) and obliterate the licensing authority from the Statute-book altogether. That, in our opinion, is not justified by the provision as to the control of Government prescribed by Section 5(2).

The control of Government contemplated by Section 5(2) may justify the issue of general instructions or directions which may be legitimate for the purpose of the Act, and these instructions and directions may necessarily guide the licensing authority in dealing with applications for licences. The said control may, therefore, take the form of the issuance of general directions and instructions which are legitimate and reasonable for the purpose of the Act. The said control may also involve the exercise of revisional power after an order has been passed by the licensing authority. It is true that Section 5(2), in terms, does not refer to the revisional power of the Government; but having regard to the scheme of the section, it may not be unreasonable to hold that if the Government is satisfied that in a given case, licence has been granted unreasonably, or contrary to the provisions of Section 5(1), or contrary to the general instructions legitimately issued by it, it may *suo moto* exercise its power to correct the said order by exercising its power of control. In other words, in the context in which the control of the Government has been provided for by Section 5(2), it would be permissible to hold that the said control can be exercised generally before applications for licences are granted, or particularly by correcting individual orders if they are found to be erroneous, but in any case, Government has to function either as an Appellate Authority or as a revisional authority, for that is the result of Section 5(2) and (3). Government cannot assume for itself the powers of the licensing authority which have been specifically provided for by Section 5(1) and (2) of the Act. To hold that the control of the Government contemplated by Section 5(2) would justify their taking away the entire jurisdiction and authority from the licensing authority, is to permit the Government by means of its executive power to change the statutory provision in a substantial manner; and that position clearly is not sustainable.

The scheme of the Act clearly indicates that there are two authorities which are expected to function under the Act — the licensing authority, as well as the Government. Section 8 is an illustration in point. It empowers the State Government or the licensing authority to suspend, cancel or revoke a licence on the grounds specified by it; and that shows that if a licence is granted by the licensing authority, it has the power to suspend, cancel or revoke such a licence just as Government has a similar power to take action in respect of the licence already granted. We are, therefore, satisfied that the High Court was right in coming to the conclusion that Appellant 1 had no authority or power to require all applications for licences made under the provisions of the Act to be forwarded to it, and to deal with them itself in the first instance. Section 5 clearly requires that such applications must be dealt with by the licensing authorities in their respective areas in the first instance, and if they are granted, they may be revised by Government under Section 5(2); and if they are rejected, parties aggrieved by the said orders of rejection may prefer appeals under Section 5(3) of the Act. The basic fact in the scheme of the Act is that it is the licensing authority which is solely given the power to deal with such applications in the first instance, and this basic position cannot be changed by Government by issuing any executive orders, or by making rules under Section 9 of the Act.

6.8.4 Acting Mechanically

In *Nandlal Khodidas Barot v. Bar Council of Gujarat*[22] the Supreme Court highlighted the importance of individual application of mind when an administrative authority has been conferred with discretionary power under the statute. Under Section 35(1) of the Advocates Act, 1961 "Where on receipt of a complaint or otherwise a State Bar Council has reason to believe that any advocate on its roll has been guilty of professional or other misconduct, it shall refer the case for disposal to its Disciplinary Committee". In this case the Gujarat State Bar Council had received several complaints of misconduct against advocates enrolled with the Bar and had referred the complaints to the Disciplinary Committee of the Bar Council by passing a resolution stating - "Resolved that the following complaints be and are hereby referred to the disciplinary committee of the Bar Council". The names of the advocates and the complaints in which they were concerned were listed.

In the earlier case of *Bar Council of Maharashtra v. M.V. Dabholkar (I)*[23] the Court had laid down the objective and purpose of Section 35(1) as–

22. 1980 Supp (1) SCC 318 : AIR 1981 SC 477.
23. (1975) 2 SCC 702.

> It is apparent that a State Bar Council not only receives a complaint but is required to apply its mind to find out whether there is any reason to believe that any advocate has been guilty of professional or other misconduct. The Bar Council of a State acts on that reasoned belief...
>
> ... The Bar Council acts as the sentinel of professional code of conduct and is vitally interested in the rights and privileges of the advocates as well as the purity and dignity of the profession.
>
> ... the function of the Bar Council in entertaining complaints against advocates is when the Bar Council has reasonable belief that there is a prima facie case of misconduct that a disciplinary committee is entrusted with such inquiry..."

Applying the same rationale the Court in this case held that *Nothing appears from the record of the case to suggest that before referring the complaint against the appellant to the Disciplinary Committee, the State Bar Council applied its mind to the allegations made in the complaint and found that there was a prima facie case to go before the Disciplinary Committee.*

Interpreting the scope of requirement of 'reason to believe' the Court applied the *Dabholkar test*[24] of *"The requirement of 'reason to believe' cannot be converted into a formalised procedural road-block, it being essentially a barrier against frivolous enquiries. It is implicit in the resolution of the Bar Council, when it says that it has considered the complaint and decided to refer the matter to the Disciplinary Committee, that it had reason to believe, as prescribed by the statute"*. In the present case the Court concluded that the Resolution of the State Bar Council had failed to specify that the complaints were considered and there were prima facie cases for referring them to the Disciplinary Committee, hence the proceedings before the disciplinary committee were considered to be invalid.

6.8.5 Outside the Scope of the Statutory Provisions

In *Jaswant Singh v. State of Punjab*[25] the appellant was prosecuted for receiving illegal gratification under Section 5(1)(a) of the Prevention of Corruption Act 1947 and the charge against him was in the following terms:

"That, you, Jaswant Singh, while employed as a Patwari, Fatehpur Rajputan habitually accepted or obtained for yourself illegal gratification and that you received in the sum of Rs 50 on 19-3-1953 at Subzi Mandi Amritsar from Pal Singh PW as a reward for forwarding the application Es.

---

24. (1976) 2 SCC 291.
25. AIR 1958 SC 124.

P.A. with your recommendation for helping Santa Singh father of Pal Singh in the allotment of Ahata No. 10 situate at village Fatehpur Rajputan and thereby committed an offence of Criminal misconduct in the discharge of your duty mentioned in Section 5(1)(*a*) of the Prevention of Corruption Act, 1947, punishable under sub-section (2) of Section 5 of the aforesaid Act and within my cognizance".

The appellant challenged the prosecution on the ground that he was being charged for a much graver offence of habitually accepting bribes under Section 5(1)(a) whereas the specific charge against the appellant was a single charge of accepting illegal gratification of Rs 50 from Pal Singh. It was argued that- "Section 5(1)(*a*) relates to a case of a public servant if he habitually accepts illegal gratification and Section 5(1)(*d*) if he obtains for himself any valuable thing or pecuniary advantage. The contention comes to this that as the sanction was only for receiving Rs 50 as illegal gratification from Pal Singh and therefore an offence under Section 5(l)(*d*) the prosecution, the change and conviction should have been under that provision and had that been so there would have been no defect in the jurisdiction of the court trying the case nor any defect in the conviction but as the appellant was tried under the charge of being a habitual receiver of bribes and the sanction was only for one single act of receiving illegal gratification the trial was wholly void as it was a trial by a court without jurisdiction".

The Supreme Court emphasised that *"The sanction under the Act is not intended to be nor is an automatic formality and it is essential that the provisions in regard to sanction should be observed with complete strictness. The object of the provision for sanctions is that the authority giving the sanction should be able to consider for itself the evidence before it comes to a conclusion that the prosecution in the circumstances be sanctioned or forbidden".* Hence in the present case it was concluded that based on the facts the sanction was obtained relating to the receiving of illegal gratification from Pal Singh and therefore the appellant could only be validly tried for that offence under Section 5(1)(d).

6.8.6 Irrelevant Considerations

In the case of *Indian Nut Products v. Union of India*[26] the Supreme Court analyzes the ground of improper exercise of discretionary powers by taking into consideration irrelevant factors and leaving aside relevant factors. In this case the owners and occupiers of cashew-factories filed the petition challenging the validity of the order issued by the Government of Kerala in exercise of the powers conferred on them under Section 3(1)(c) of the Kerala Cashew Factories (Acquisition) Act, 1974. The Government had given notice

26. (1994) 4 SCC 269.

to the petitioners stating their intention to take action under Section 3(1) and directed the petitioners to file objections, if any. The specific ground provided in the notice was – "It has been reported by the authorised officer that your factory is lying closed and that there is no possibility of it to start functioning within a period of ten days or in the immediate future. Government are, therefore, of opinion that the said situation will lead to a large scale unemployment, other than by way of lay off or retrenchment, of the workers of the Cashew factory". After complying with the norms of hearing an order dated 6.7.1988 was issued by the Government stating that the factories of the petitioners are being transferred and vested in the Government. The petitioners filed a writ petition challenging the acquisition order on the ground that the action taken was contrary to the provisions of the parent statute and were *colourable exercise of statutory powers with oblique motives.*

The Court analyzed the objective of the legislation and the scope of Section 3(1). Section 3(1) dealing with the Order of acquisition provides that- (1) The Government may, if they are satisfied- (a) that the occupier of a cashew factory does not conform to the provisions of law relating to safety, conditions of service of fixation and payment of wages to the workers of the factory; or (b) that raw cashew nuts allotted to a cashew factory by the Cashew Corporation 'of India are not being processed in the factory to which allotment has been made or that such nuts are being transferred to any other cashew factory; or (c) that there has been large scale unemployment, other than by way of lay off or retrenchment of the workers of a cashew factory, by order published in the Gazette, declare that that cashew factory shall stand transferred to, and vest in, the Government: Provided that before making a declaration under this sub-section in respect of a cashew factory, the Government shall give the occupier of the factory and the owner of the factory, where he is not the occupier, a notice of their intention to take action under this sub-section and the grounds therefor and consider the objections that may be preferred in pursuance of such notice.

The Court identified the primary objective of the legislation was 'to acquire cashew factories in the public interest, in order to prevent large scale unemployment of workers in the cashew industry and to provide employment to such workers who have been rendered unemployed.' Analyzing the action of the State Government it observed–

> It is well-settled that if a statute requires an authority to exercise power, when such authority is satisfied that conditions exist for exercise of that power, the satisfaction has to be based on the existence of grounds mentioned in the statute. The grounds must be made out on the basis of the relevant material. If the existence of the conditions required for the exercise of the power is challenged, the courts are entitled to examine whether those conditions existed

when the order was made. A person aggrieved by such action can question the satisfaction by showing that it was wholly based on irrelevant grounds and hence amounted to no satisfaction at all. In other words, the existence of the circumstances in question is open to judicial review.

It cannot be disputed that serious consequences follow on the basis of the order passed by the Government on grounds mentioned in Clauses (a), (b) and (c). Hence it is all the more necessary that the Government furnishes the full particulars on the basis of which the Government claims to be satisfied that there is a case for taking over the factory. As already pointed out above there is not even an assertion in the notice that there has been any unemployment much less large scale unemployment. The ground simply says that the Government was of the opinion that the closure of the factory "will lead to a large scale unemployment". We are of the view, that in the facts and circumstances of the present case, the notice issued to the petitioners with the so-called grounds was not in accordance with the requirement of the provisions of Sub-section (1) of Section 3 of the Act. The notices issued to different petitioners are, therefore, declared to be null and void. Consequent thereto, the order dated 6.7.1988 is also quashed.

6.8.7 Malafide Exercise of Power

Pratap Singh v. State of Punjab[27] is the leading case of mala fide exercise of discretionary power. The appellant was a Civil Surgeon in the employment of Punjab Government and had been given leave preparatory to retirement. Subsequently, in June 1961 the State Government issued orders revoking the leave granted to the appellant and recalling him to duty. Simultaneously a departmental inquiry was instituted against him and pending the inquiry he was placed under suspension. The orders issued within the scope of the power of the State Government under Article 310(1) because "members of a Civil Service of a State hold office during the pleasure of the Governor". The appellant challenged the legality of the orders issued primarily on the ground of mala fide exercise of power. The appellant asserted that at the instance of the Chief Minister of Punjab the hostile orders were issued and alleged that the Chief Minister was personally hostile to him and these actions were taken to wreck personal vengeance against him. Based on the principle laid down by Lord Denning said in *Lazarus Estates, Ltd. v. Beasley*[28] that "No judgment of a court, no order of a Minister, can be allowed to stand if it has been obtained by fraud" Supreme Court analyzed whether the order issued by the Chief Minister was vitiated on the ground of mala fide interest. It was further emphasized that–

27. AIR 1964 SC 72.
28. [1956] 1 All E.R. 341.

> Doubtless, he who seeks to invalidate or nullify any act or order must establish the charge of bad faith, an abuse or a misuse by Government of its powers. While the indirect motive or purpose, or bad faith or personal ill-will is not to be held established except on clear proof thereof, it is obviously difficult to establish the state of a man's mind, for that it what the appellant has to establish in this case, though this may sometimes be done (**See** *Edgington v. Fitzmaurice* ([1855] 29 C.D. 459.)). The difficulty is not lessened when one has to establish that a person in the position of a minister apparently acting on the legitimate exercise of power has, in fact, been acting mala fide in the sense of pursuing an illegitimate aim. We must, however, demur to the suggestion that mala fide in the sense of improper motive should be established only by direct evidence that is that it must be discernible from the order impugned or must be shown from the notings in the file which preceded the order. If bad faith would vitiate the order, the same can, in our opinion, be deduced as a reasonable and inescapable inference from proved facts.

Speaking on the limited role of judicial review on exercise of discretionary powers the Supreme Court clarified that–

> [T]he Court is not an appellate forum where the correctness of an order of Government could be canvassed and, indeed, it has no jurisdiction to substitute its own view as to the necessity or desirability of initiating disciplinary proceedings, for the entirety of the power, jurisdiction and discretion in that regard is vested by law in the Government. The only question which could be considered by the Court is whether the authority vested with the power has paid attention to or taken into account circumstances, events or matters wholly extraneous to the purpose for which the power was vested, or whether the proceedings have been initiated mala fide for satisfying a private or personal grudge of the authority against the officer. If the act is in excess of the power granted or is an abuse or misuse of power, the matter is capable of interference and rectification by the Court. In such an event the fact that the authority concerned denies the charge of mala fides, or asserts the absence of oblique motives or of its having taken into consideration improper or irrelevant matter does not preclude the Court from enquiring into the truth of the allegations made against the authority and affording appropriate reliefs to the party aggrieved by such illegality or abuse of power in the event of the allegations being made out.

In light of the seriousness of the various allegations made in the present case against the Chief Minister and his family the Court exercised judicial restraint and objectively tried to analyze the various facts and evidences placed before them. Ayyangar J. emphasized–

> Before entering on a discussion of the question whether the appellant has established that the action of Government was vitiated by mala fides, we consider it pertinent to make a few preliminary observation. In considering

> the evidence we have kept in view the high position which the Chief Minister holds in the State and are conscious of the fact that charges of a personal nature made against such a dignitary are not to be lightly accepted. We have also borne in mind that charges of personal hostility are easily and very often made by persons who are subjected to penal or quasi penal proceedings against those who initiate them, and have therefore made full allowance for these factors, and we have examined and weighed the evidence with anxious care. We would only add that the fact that two of our brethren feel differently on this matter has heightened our responsibility and in the care to be bestowed in appreciating the evidence. The Constitution enshrines and guarantees the rule of law and Article 226 is designed to ensure that each and every authority in the State, including the Government, acts bona fide and within the limits of its power and we consider that when a Court is satisfied that there is an abuse or misuse of power and its jurisdiction is invoked, it is incumbent on the Court to afford justice to the individual. It is with these considerations in mind that we approach the facts of this case.

After analyzing the different facts alleged by the appellant based on various evidences, the Court concluded that the charges had been satisfactorily proved and held that "the dominant motive which induced the Government to take action against the appellant was not to take disciplinary proceedings against him for misconduct which it bona fide believed he had committed, but to wreak vengeance on him for incurring his wrath and for the discredit that he had brought on the Chief Minister by the allegations that he had made in the article which appeared in the Blitz in its issue dated January 15, 1961 followed by the communication to the same newspapers by the appellant's wife, in which these allegations were affirmed and in large part we have found to be true". The impugned orders were held to be vitiated by mala fides and were set aside because *they were motivated by an improper purpose which was outside that for which the power or discretion was conferred on Government.*

6.8.8 Colourable Exercise of Power

In *Lal Kamal Das v. State of West Bengal*[29] the petitioner was detained under the Maintenance of Internal Security Act 1971 so as to prevent him from acting in any manner prejudicial to the maintenance of supplies and services essential to the community. The petitioner was previously arrested and was in jail for committing an act of theft under the Indian Penal Code. No witnesses were produced, hence he was about to be released. The detention order was made while the petitioner was already in jail. The contention of the petitioner was that the power of detention was exercised

29. AIR 1975 SC 753.

out of fear and not of necessity. The Court, after analysing the facts of the case and the evidences placed by the state authorities, made the following observation–

> The striking feature of this case is that the petitioner has been preventively detained for committing an offence of simple theft for which he could be dealt with under the ordinary penal law. He was arrested by the police in connection with that theft and forwarded to a Judicial Magistrate. The impugned order was passed when the petitioner was in jail custody. While it is true that in theory, an order of preventive detention can be validly passed against a person in jail custody on the same facts on which he is being prosecuted, such an order is often vulnerable to the charge that it has been passed as a colourable exercise of jurisdiction. The reason is that the scheme of Section 3 of the Act postulates that the person against whom the detention order is made has freedom to act in a prejudicial manner. In such cases, therefore, in response to *rule nisi* the respondent State must disclose full facts showing how in spite of the detenu being in jail, it was reasonably possible to apprehend that he was likely to act in the same prejudicial manner in future. All the circumstances showing inter alia that the jail custody of the detenue was not going to be long and why he was or was about to be discharged by the court must be set out.
>
> .....
>
> It may be remembered that the power under Section 3 of the Act can be exercised only if the detaining authority, on the basis of the past prejudicial conduct of the detenue is *satisfied* about the probability of the latter acting similarly in future. This means the past activity of the detenue on the basis of which such a prognosis is made, must be reasonably suggestive of a repetitive tendency or inclination on the part of the detenue to act likewise in future. A simple, solitary incident of theft, such is the one in the present case, without anything more, is hardly suggestive of such a tendency. Here, it is not alleged that the commission of theft was accompanied by violence or show of force. Nor is it alleged that it was committed openly or in a daring fashion by overawing or overcoming resistance from any quarter, whatever. The theft was committed stealthily before 6 a.m. presumably under cover of night. Nor is it clear from the grounds that a large number of persons were concerned in this theft. All that is alleged is that the petitioner and his associates committed this theft. The number of the "associates" has not been indicated. Since the petitioner or any of his "associates" was not arrested on the scene of occurrence, the chief witness against him would be only the police officer who arrested him and recovered the stolen property, if any, from him. We therefore, find it impossible to accept the fanciful plea set up in the counter for not following up the prosecution of the petitioner in court.

The Court asserted that the power of detention was exercised *in a casual, "care-free" and colourable manner.*

In *Mahesh Chandra v. U.P. Financial Corpn.*[30] it was further clarified that–

> Every wide power, the exercise of which has far-reaching repercussion, has inherent limitation on it. It should be exercised to effectuate the purpose of the Act. In legislations enacted for general benefit and common good the responsibility is far graver. It demands purposeful approach. The exercise of discretion should be objective. Test of reasonableness is more strict. The public functionaries should be duty conscious rather than power charged. Its actions and decisions which touch the common man have to be tested on the touchstone of fairness and justice. That which is not fair and just is unreasonable. And what is unreasonable is arbitrary. An arbitrary action is ultra vires. It does not become bona fide and in good faith merely because no personal gain or benefit to the person exercising discretion should be established. An action is mala fide if it is contrary to the purpose for which it was authorised to be exercised. Dishonesty in discharge of duty vitiates the action without anything more. An action is bad even without proof of motive of dishonesty, if the authority is found to have acted contrary to reason. Power under Section 29 of the Act to take possession of a defaulting unit and transfer it by sale requires the authority to act cautiously, honestly, fairly and reasonably.

The exercise of discretionary power is required to be in accordance with the provisions of the parent statute and must be exercised in a just, fair and reasonable manner. The scope of judicial review is limited and is restricted to review the manner of performance of the discretionary power or the process by the administrative action is undertaken. Based on the various principles derived from the plethora of case laws it is essential that the administrative authority must apply its own mind, taken into consideration all relevant factors, should not act mechanically and act in good faith.

6.9 PRINCIPLES OF JUDICIAL REVIEW

The judiciary with the objective of creating accountability in the exercise of discretionary power or in performance of administrative actions has developed certain judicial principles to bring in predictability and certainty in government actions and for avoiding arbitrariness. Some of the important judicial principles have been discussed in brief.

6.9.1 Doctrine of Proportionality

The doctrine of proportionality as a ground of judicial review was derived from the European Court of Justice and applied by the English Courts in

30. (1993) 2 SCC 279.

implementing the Human Rights Act 1998. The doctrine in its application is similar to the *Wednesbury unreasonableness.* It proposes to review the nature of the administrative action taken on the touchstone of whether the action taken was really required and also whether the action was within the possible courses of action which could be reasonably taken under the provisions of law. Doctrine of proportionality justifies the courts to exercise their power of judicial review so as to ensure that the administrative action is not unreasonable or totally disproportionate to the objective sought to be achieved – *you must not use a steam hammer to crack a nut if a nut cracker would do.*[31]

In England the doctrine of proportionality has been largely applied through a three-pronged test as laid down in *de Freitas v. Permanent Secretary of Ministry of Agriculture*[32] requiring into whether "(1) the legislative objective is sufficiently important to justify limiting a fundamental right, (2) the measures designed to meet the objective are rationally connected to it, and (3) the means used to impair the right or freedom are no more than is necessary to accomplish the objective".

In India the doctrine of proportionality has been largely used by the courts to review the orders passed by the administrative authorities to find out if they are *disproportionate, excessive or unreasonable.* The test adopted by the judiciary is to apply the reasonable man theory and to analyse whether the action was so outrageous that no reasonable man could have taken such decision or it is beyond all moral standards and logical reasoning or it is too excessive in light of the action taken. Fundamentally the test applicable in India is that of *Wednesbury standard* of judicial review. In *V. Ramana v. A.P. SRTC*[33] the Supreme Court after referring to a large number of cases on the applicability of the doctrine of proportionality, held that–

> The common thread running through in all these decisions is that the court should not interfere with the administrator's decision unless it was illogical or suffers from procedural impropriety or was shocking to the conscience of the court, in the sense that it was in defiance of logic or moral standards. In view of what has been stated in *Wednesbury case* the court would not go into the correctness of the choice made by the administrator open to him and the court should not substitute its decision for that of the administrator. The scope of judicial review is limited to the deficiency in decision-making process and not the decision.

31. *Lord Diplock in R v. Goldsmith* (1983) 1 WLR 151.
32. [1999] 1 AC 69.
33. (2005) 7 SCC 338.

In *State of U.P. v. Sheo Shanker Lal Srivastava*[34] the Supreme Court emphatically asserted that "*It is now well settled that principles of law that the High Court or the Tribunal in exercise of its power of judicial review would not normally interfere with the quantum of punishment. Doctrine of proportionality can be invoked only under certain situations. It is now well settled that the High Court shall be very slow in interfering with the quantum of punishment, unless it is found to be shocking to one's conscience*". In some of the recent judgments like *Moni Shankar v. Union of India*[35] the Supreme Court has further re-emphasised that in quasi-judicial proceedings in departmental enquiries even after compliance with all the procedural requirements if on evidence it is found that the test of the doctrine of proportionality has not been satisfied, then the judicial authorities will be within their power to interfere. It is further asserted that *doctrine of unreasonableness is giving way to the doctrine of proportionality.*

In the leading case of *Coimbatore District Central Coop. Bank v. Employees Assn*[36] the Supreme Court had laid the nature, scope and application of the doctrine of proportionality. It was stated–

> With the rapid growth of administrative law and the need and necessity to control possible abuse of discretionary powers by various administrative authorities, certain principles have been evolved by courts. If an action taken by any authority is contrary to law, improper, irrational or otherwise unreasonable, a court of law can interfere with such action by exercising power of judicial review. One of such modes of exercising power, known to law is the "doctrine of proportionality".
>
> "Proportionality" is a principle where the court is concerned with the process, method or manner in which the decision-maker has ordered his priorities, reached a conclusion or arrived at a decision. The very essence of decision-making consists in the attribution of relative importance to the factors and considerations in the case. The doctrine of proportionality thus steps in focus true nature of exercise—the elaboration of a rule of permissible priorities.
>
> De Smith states that "proportionality" involves "balancing test" and "necessity test". Whereas the former (balancing test) permits scrutiny of excessive onerous penalties or infringement of rights or interests and a manifest imbalance of relevant considerations, the latter (necessity test) requires infringement of human rights to the least restrictive alternative.[37]

34. (2006) 3 SCC 276.
35. (2008) 3 SCC 484.
36. (2007) 4 SCC 669.
37. *Judicial Review of Administrative Action* (1995), pp. 601-05, para 13.085; *see also* Wade & Forsyth: *Administrative Law* (2005), p. 366.

In *Halsbury's Laws of England*[38] it is stated:

"The court will quash exercise of discretionary powers in which there is no reasonable relationship between the objective which is sought to be achieved and the means used to that end, or where punishments imposed by administrative bodies or inferior courts are wholly out of proportion to the relevant misconduct. The principle of proportionality is well established in European law, and will be applied by English courts where European law is enforceable in the domestic courts. The principle of proportionality is still at a stage of development in English law; lack of proportionality is not usually treated as a separate ground for review in English law, but is regarded as one indication of manifest unreasonableness".

The doctrine has its genesis in the field of administrative law. The Government and its departments, in administering the affairs of the country, are expected to honour their statements of policy or intention and treat the citizens with full personal consideration without abuse of discretion. There can be no "pick and choose", selective applicability of the government norms or unfairness, arbitrariness or unreasonableness. It is not permissible to use a "sledgehammer to crack a nut". As has been said many a time; "where paring knife suffices, battle axe is precluded".

Prior to the recognition of the doctrine of proportionality in the *Council of Civil Service Union v. Minister for Civil Service*[39] India had given effective recognition to the inherent principles of the doctrine. In the case of *Hind Construction & Engg Co. Ltd. v. Workmen*[40] few workers who were absent from duty on a particular day thinking it to be a holiday were dismissed from service. Supreme Court held that "*It is impossible to think that any other reasonable employer would have imposed the extreme punishment of dismissal on its entire permanent staff in this manner.* It was further observed that the punishment imposed on the workmen *not only severe and out of proportion to the fault, but one which, in our judgment, no reasonable employer would have imposed.* The Court asserted that in the circumstance the workers should have been warned and fined and the absence treated as leave without pay. Similarly while holding the termination of service of an employee as disproportionate in *Federation of Indian Chambers of Commerce and Industry v. Workmen*[41] the Court made the observation that *"[T]he Federation had made a mountain out of a mole hill and made a trivial matter into one involving loss of its prestige and reputation".*

38. (4th Edn.), Reissue, Vol. 1(1), pp. 144-45, para 78.
39. [1985] A.C. 374.
40. AIR 1965 SC 917 : (1965) 2 SCR 85.
41. (1972) 1 SCC 40 : AIR 1972 SC 763.

In *Jaswant Singh v. Pepsu Roadways Transport Corporation*[42] the Supreme Court applied the doctrine of proportionality to modify the order passed by an administrative authority. In this case the appellant was a driver employed with the respondent was found to have consumed liquor while on duty. A disciplinary proceeding was initiated against him and he was dismissed from service. The Labour Court looking into the case held that in the 'circumstances of the case the punishment of dismissal from service is rather on the heavier side and therefore, he directed reinstatement of the appellant in service denying back wages.' On appeal before the Supreme Court it was observed that–

> ... a driver of a passenger bus or for that matter any mechanically propelled vehicle cannot and should not consume intoxicating liquor while on duty because that endangers the safety not only of those in the vehicle but of those using the roads also. However, looking to the conduct of the appellant it appears to be his first offence and the Labour Court in exercise of its jurisdiction under Section 11A of the Industrial Disputes Act was of the opinion that in the facts of the case punishment of dismissal was rather heavy and was not called for and therefore, reduced the punishment. But the reduction was to a level namely mere refusal of back wages, which would be inadequate punishment in the facts of this case... In our opinion to keep the appellant within the bounds of well-disciplined conduct a further punishment is also called for and should be imposed so that our humanistic approach may not induce him to repeat his intemperate performance. Accordingly, we direct that the appellant should not be given three increments in the time scale in which he would be reinstated, for the next three years. For all other benefits he will be treated as continuing in service.

In the leading case of *Ranjit Thakur v. Union of India*[43] when an army officer did not obey the lawful command of his superior officer by not eating food offered to him the punishments of one year rigorous imprisonment, dismissal from service and a declaration that he would be deemed unfit for all future employment were held to disproportionate in nature by the Supreme Court. It was observed that – "Judicial review generally speaking, is not directed against a decision, but is directed against the "decision making process". The question of the choice and quantum of punishment is within the jurisdiction and discretion of the court martial. But the sentence has to suit the offence and the offender. It should not be vindictive or unduly harsh. It should not be so disproportionate to the offence as to shock the conscience and amount in itself to conclusive evidence of bias. The doctrine of proportionality, as part of the concept of judicial review, would ensure

42. AIR 1984 SC 355 : (1984) 1 SCC 35.
43. (1987) 4 SCC 611 : 1988 SCC (L&S) 1.

that even on an aspect which is, otherwise, within the exclusive province of the court martial, if the decision of the court even as to sentence is an outrageous defiance of logic, then the sentence would not be immune from correction. Irrationality and perversity are recognised grounds of judicial review".

One of the other important cases where the doctrine of proportionality was used by the judiciary is *Shambhu Ram Yadav v. Hanuman Das Khatry.*[44] In this case the respondent while appearing as a counsel in a suit pending before a civil court wrote a letter to his client stating that he has been informed by another of his client that the judge concerned in the case accepts bribe and he has obtained several favourable orders from him. It was further stated that unless the client had alternative means of influencing the judge, the client should send Rupees 10,000/ so that necessary payment could be made to the judge. A complaint was made before the Bar Council of Rajasthan and a disciplinary proceeding was initiated against him. After the enquiry the State Bar Council held the action to be a case of misconduct which adversely affected the interest of the litigating public and the legal profession and suspended him from practice for 2 years. On appeal to the Bar Council of India the punishment was enhanced and the name of the respondent was directed to be struck off from the roll of advocates and debarred him permanently. On a review petition filed before the BCI the punishment of debarment was substituted with one reprimanding him in light of his old age and his previously unblemished character. But Supreme Court struck down the changed order issued by the review committee as all the reasons and facts on the basis of which the order were reviewed had all been considered by the earlier Disciplinary Committee of the BCI. The Court held that the power of review does not empower the Disciplinary Committee to modify the earlier order made by another Disciplinary Committee by taking a different view on the same set of facts. It was further held that in light of the serious nature of misconduct, public interest and high standards of morality the order of permanent debarment was necessary.
The Court observed–

> The respondent was indeed guilty of a serious misconduct by writing to his client the letter as aforesaid. Members of the legal profession are officers of the court. Besides courts, they also owe a duty to the society which has a vital public interest in the due administration of justice. The said public interest is required to be protected by those on whom the power has been entrusted to take disciplinary action. The disciplinary bodies are guardians of the due administration of justice. They have requisite power and rather a duty while supervising the conduct of the members of the legal profession, to

44. AIR 2001 SC 2509 : (2001) 6 SCC 1.

inflict appropriate penalty when members are found to be guilty of misconduct. Considering the nature of the misconduct, the penalty of permanent debarment had been imposed on the respondent which without any valid ground has been modified in exercise of power of review. It is the duty of the Bar Councils to ensure that lawyers adhere to the required standards and on failure, to take appropriate action against them. The credibility of a Council including its disciplinary body in respect of any profession whether it is law, medicine, accountancy or any other vocation depends upon how they deal with cases of delinquency involving serious misconduct which has a tendency to erode the credibility and reputation of the said profession. The punishment, of course, has to be commensurate with the gravity of the misconduct.

In the case of *LIC v. R. Suresh*[45] the respondent was appointed as a Development Officer in the LIC. Subsequently a departmental proceeding was initiated against him on five specific charges. After the enquiry, the enquiry officer found him guilty of the first four charges relating issuing a policy in the name of a dead person by relying on the statements of the agent and for not personally verifying the same, but exonerated him of the fifth one relating to forgery. The respondent was dismissed from service by the disciplinary authority by an order dated 19-4-1989. The respondent challenged the dismissal order on the ground that he did not intentionally commit any wrongful act and was only guilty of negligence. The respondent had relied on the opinion expressed in *Union of India v. J. Ahmed*[46] that negligence by itself may not be held to be a misconduct wherein the Court had stated- "It is, however, difficult to believe that lack of efficiency or attainment of highest standards in discharge of duty attached to public office would ipso facto constitute misconduct. There may be negligence in performance of duty and a lapse in performance of duty or error of judgment in evaluating the developing situation may be negligence in discharge of duty but would not constitute misconduct unless the consequences directly attributable to negligence would be such as to be irreparable or the resultant damage would be so heavy that the degree of culpability would be very high. An error can be indicative of negligence and the degree of culpability may indicate the grossness of the negligence. Carelessness can often be productive of more harm than deliberate wickedness or malevolence". The Supreme Court held that while exercising jurisdiction regard must be made by keeping all relevant factors in mind including, the nature of the misconducts alleged, the conduct of the parties, the manner in which the enquiry proceeding had been conducted etc. It was further stated that if a misconduct was committed with an intention then it deserves the

45. (2008) 11 SCC 319.
46. (1979) 2 SCC 286.

maximum punishment. Hence each case must be decided on its own facts, and if necessary the doctrine of proportionality may also be invoked. In this case the Court applying the doctrine of proportionality recognized that there was no quantum of loss and the respondent was out of job for more than 20 years and in that process he had already suffered a lot.

In the case of *M.P. Gangadharan v. State of Kerala*[47] the Supreme Court recognized the doctrine of proportionality as a ground of judicial review and used the doctrine to determine the suitability of the shifting of a Family Court. The Court held that–

> The constitutional requirement for judging the question of reasonableness and fairness on the part of the statutory authority must be considered having regard to the factual matrix obtaining in each case. It cannot be put in a straitjacket formula. It must be considered keeping in view the doctrine of flexibility. Before an action is struck down, the court must be satisfied that a case has been made out for exercise of power of judicial review. We are not unmindful of the development of the law that from the doctrine of Wednesbury unreasonableness, the court is leaning towards the doctrine of proportionality. But in a case of this nature, the doctrine of proportionality must also be applied having regard to the purport and object for which the Act was enacted.

Thus the Court by applying the substantive aspect of the doctrine of proportionality held that *while constituting a Family Court the State must provide for all requisite infrastructure so as to meet the objects for which the Family Courts are required to be established. A court should not be established only because it is provided for under the Act. The State must be alive to the situation that it has a duty to see that the dispute resolution fora are provided with adequate infrastructure.*

6.9.2 Doctrine of Legitimate Expectation

The doctrine of legitimate expectation is a significant effort on the part of the judiciary to make the state accountable or answerable for its various policies and actions. When the state authorities make a sudden change in the policy of the state or deviates from its past practices or goes back on its announced policies, which adversely affects the interests of common people then the judiciary may hold the state authorities liable for violating the legitimate expectation of the people. The doctrine has been developed to provide a relief to the people when their interests but they are unable to demand for a relief on the basis of violation of their legal rights. The doctrine has been included within the domain of public law so as to bring about

47. (2006) 6 SCC 162.

predictability and certainty in government actions and to avoid arbitrary changes in government policies. In the words of Supreme Court – *Principle of natural justice will apply in cases where there is some right which is likely to be affected by an act of administration. Good administration, however, demands observance of doctrine of reasonableness in other situations also where the citizens may legitimately expect to be treated fairly. Doctrine of legitimate expectation has been developed in the context of principles of natural justice.*[48] In Indian jurisprudence the doctrine has been deemed to be an integral part of Article 14 so as to ensure that the citizens are dealt in a non-arbitrary manner.[49]

In Halsbury's Laws of England the doctrine of legitimate expectation has been explained as–

> A person may have a legitimate expectation of being treated in a certain way by an administrative authority even though he has no legal right in private law to receive such treatment. The expectation may arise either from a representation or promise made by the authority, including an implied representation, or from consistent past practice. The existence of a legitimate expectation may have a number of different consequences; it may give locus standi to seek leave to apply for judicial review; it may mean that the authority ought not to act so as to defeat the expectation without some overriding reason of public policy to justify its doing so; or it may mean that, if the authority proposes to defeat a person's legitimate expectation, it must afford him an opportunity to make representations on the matter. The courts also distinguish, for example in licensing cases, between original applications, applications to renew and revocations; a party who has been granted a licence may have a legitimate expectation that it will be renewed unless there is some good reason not to do so, and may therefore be entitled to greater procedural protection than a mere applicant for a grant.[50]

Prof. Clive Lewis in his book *Judicial Remedies in Public Law* has defined the scope of the doctrine of legitimate expectation as–

> *Decisions affecting legitimate expectations*— In the public law field, individuals may not have strictly enforceable rights but they may have legitimate expectations. Such expectations may stem either from a promise or a representation made by a public body, or from a previous practice of a public body. The promise of a hearing before a decision is taken may give rise to a legitimate expectation that a hearing will be given. A past practice of consulting before a decision is taken may give rise to an expectation of consultation before any future decision is taken. A promise to confer, or past

48. *Ashoka Smokeless Coal India (P) Ltd. v. Union of India*, (2007) 2 SCC 640.
49. *State of W.B. v. Niranjan Singha*, (2001) 2 SCC 326.
50. Halsbury's Laws of England, 4th Ed. Vol. 1(1) 151.

> practice of conferring a substantive benefit, may give rise to an expectation that the individual will be given a hearing before a decision is taken not to confer the benefit. The actual enjoyment of a benefit may create a legitimate expectation that the benefit will not be removed without the individual being given a hearing. On occasions, individuals seek to enforce the promise or expectation itself, by claiming that the substantive benefit be conferred. Decisions affecting such legitimate expectations are subject to judicial review.[51]

This doctrine was introduced in the branch of administrative law by Lord Denning in the leading case of *Schmidt v. Secretary of State for Home Affairs.*[52] It was observed that an administrative body is bound to give a person an opportunity of being heard if his right, interest or legitimate expectation were adversely impacted by an administrative action. In this case a petition was filed by some foreign students who had come to study Scientology at the Hubbard College of Scientology against the Home Secretary for not extending their stay permits to complete their studies. It was alleged that the refusal to grant extension was invalid, done for an unauthorized purpose and failed to comply with the norms of fair procedure. The policy of the Home Affairs was to allow aliens to enter the country to pursue full time study at a recognized educational establishment and on the basis of which permission was given to the plaintiffs to enter the country. Subsequently there was a change of policy and the Minister of Health issued a statement to the House of Commons declaring Scientology as an objectionable practice and all necessary steps should be taken to curb its growth, including denial of extensions to foreign students who had already come to UK to study Scientology. Based on the new policy the applications of the plaintiffs were rejected by the Department of Home Affairs. Dealing with the issue of whether the action of the Minister was an authorized action, the Court held that under common law *no alien has any right to enter this country except by leave of the Crown: and the Crown can refuse leave without giving any reason.* Interpreting the provisions of the Alien Order, 1953 the Court observed that the "*Secretary of State has ample power either to refuse admission to an alien or to grant him leave to enter for a limited period, or to refuse to extend his stay... the Minister can exercise his power for any purpose which he considers to be for the public good or to be in the interests of the people of this country. There is not the slightest ground for thinking that the Minister exercised his power here for any unauthorised purpose or with any ulterior motive*". On the issue of whether the Home Secretary was under a duty to act fairly,

51. As quoted in *Madras City Wine Merchants' Assn. v. State of T.N.*, (1994) 5 SCC 509.
52. (1969) 1 All ER 904.

the Court emphasized the need to not act in an arbitrary manner or in an unfair manner. In this case it was held that held that the purpose of the Minister's action was disclosed in the statement submitted before the House of Commons.

The doctrine was further conceptually developed by Lord Fraser in A-G of Hong Kong *v.* Ng Yuen Shiu.[53] In this case the applicant was an illegal immigrant from China and had entered into Hong Kong in 1967. After a change in immigration policy, the Director of Immigration was given the power to pass removal orders against such people and repatriate them. On petitioning the Governor a senior immigration officer had made the announcement that each illegal entrant would be interviewed and his case "treated on its merits". After being questioned by an immigration officer, the applicant was detained and the Director of Immigration passed a removal order against him without giving him a reasonable opportunity of making a representation as to why he should not be removed. The core issue in the appeal was whether the applicant can claim for a right of fair hearing before a decision adversely affecting his interests are made by a public official based on the concept of 'legitimate expectation' of being accorded such a hearing. The Court held that "the expectations may be based upon some statement or undertaking by, or on behalf of, the public authority which has the duty of making the decision, if the authority has, through its officers, acted in a way that would make it unfair or inconsistent with good administration for him to be denied such an inquiry".

Applying the principles of legitimate expectation in favour of an alien it was held that–

> The justification for it is primarily that, when a public authority has promised to follow a certain procedure, it is in the interest of good administration that it should act fairly and should implement its promise, so long as implementation does not interfere with its statutory duty. The principle is also justified by the further consideration that, when the promise was made, the authority must have considered that it would be assisted in discharging its duty fairly by any representations from interested parties and as a general rule that is correct. In the opinion of their Lordships the principle that a public authority is bound by its undertakings as to the procedure it will follow, provided they do not conflict with its duty, is applicable to the undertaking given by the Government of Hong Kong to the applicant, along with other illegal immigrants from Macau, in the announcement outside the Government House on October 28, that each case would be considered on its merits.

53. (1983) 2 All ER 346.

Their Lordships quashed the order of removal made by the Director against the applicant and passed the order of conducting a fair inquiry wherein the applicant should be given an opportunity *to make such representations as he may see fit as to why he should not be removed.*

In the leading case of *Council of Civil Service Union v. Minister for Civil Service*[54] the House of Lords had categorically recognized legitimate expectation as valid ground for judicial review of administrative action and had observed that *even where a person claiming some benefit or privilege has no legal right to it, as a matter of private law, he may have a legitimate expectation of receiving the benefit or privilege, and, if so, the courts will protect his expectation by judicial review as a matter of public law.... Legitimate, or reasonable, expectation may arise either from an express promise given on behalf of a public authority or from the existence of a regular practice which the claimant can reasonably expect to continue.* It generally relates *to a benefit or privilege to which the claimant has no right in private law, and it may even be to one which conflicts with his private law rights.*

Lord Diplock described the application of the doctrine in the following words–

> To qualify as a subject for judicial review the decision must have consequences which affect some person (or body of persons) other than the decision-maker, although it may affect him too. It must affect such other person either (a) by altering rights or obligations of that person which are enforceable by or against him in private law or (b) by depriving him of some benefit or advantage which either (i) he has in the past been permitted by the decision-maker to enjoy and which he can legitimately expect to be permitted to continue to do until there has been communicated to him some rational ground for withdrawing it on which he has been given an opportunity to comment or (ii) he has received assurance from the decision-maker will not be withdrawn without giving him first an opportunity of advancing reasons for contending that they should not be withdrawn.

Lord Diplock categorically justified the usage of the term 'legitimate expectation' in preference of reasonable expectation so as to indicate *that it has consequences to which effect will be given in public law, whereas an expectation or hope that some benefit or advantage would continue to be enjoyed, although it might well be entertained by a 'reasonable' man, would not necessarily have such consequences.* Lord Roskill in the same judgment had also stated that in recent times the terms reasonable

54. (1985) A.C. 374.

expectation and legitimate expectation are being treated synonymously but is preferable to use the adjective of 'legitimate'.

In case of breach of legitimate expectation the ground of judicial review is limited to determining whether procedural norms were adhered to by the administrative authorities at the time of taking the administrative decisions. The applicable procedural norms are to be determined based on the nature of the *subject matter of the decision, the executive functions of the decision-maker and the particular circumstances in which the decision came to be made... the prima facie rule of 'procedural propriety' in public law, applicable to a case of legitimate expectations that a benefit ought not to be withdrawn until the reason for its proposed withdrawal has been communicated to the person who has theretofore enjoyed that benefit and that person has been given an opportunity to comment on the reason.*[55] Thus the procedural obligation applicable in cases of legitimate expectation is associated with the concept of 'right to be heard' and may involve procedural expectations like expectation of prior consultation, expectation of being allowed to time to make representations etc. The doctrine does not give rise to any enforceable right but it fundamentally helps in testing the action taken by the government authority whether arbitrary or relevant.[56]

In recent years the doctrine has been expanded to include claim for substantive rights. Lord Woolf in *R. v. North and East Devon Health Authority, ex p Coughlan*[57] had stated that "where the court considers that a lawful promise or practice has induced a legitimate expectation of a *benefit which is substantive*, not simply procedural, authority now establishes that here too the court will in a proper case decide whether to frustrate the expectation is so unfair that to take a new and different course will amount to an abuse of power. Here, once the legitimacy of the expectation is established, the court will have the task of weighing the requirements of fairness against any overriding interest relied upon for the change of policy". Subsequently in *R. v. Secy. of State for the Home Deptt. ex p Hindley* the English Courts have clubbed the substantive and procedural part of legitimate expectation and emphasized that in all cases of legitimate expectation the court should fundamentally look into three practical questions i.e. what has the public authority, whether by practice or by promise, committed itself; the second is whether the authority has acted or proposes to act unlawfully in relation to its commitment; the third is what the court should do and thereafter fundamentally determine *whether the reneging by an authority on its promise was 'so unfair as to amount to an abuse of power'.*

55. Ibid Lord Diplock in CCSU.
56. *State of W.B. v. Niranjan Singha*, (2001) 2 SCC 326.
57. (2000) 3 All ER 850 (CA).

6.9.2.1 Indian jurisprudence

In the leading case of *Union of India v. Hindustan Development Corpn.*[58] K. Jayachandra Reddy J. took the effort to explain the meaning and scope of the doctrine of legitimate expectation and addressed crucial questions in the nature of- Who is the expectant and what is the nature of the expectation? When does such an expectation become a legitimate one and what is the foundation for the same? What are the duties of the administrative authorities while taking a decision in cases attracting the doctrine of legitimate expectation. It was observed–

> Time is a three-fold present: the present as we experience it, the past as a present memory and future as a present expectation. For legal purposes, the expectation cannot be the same as anticipation. It is different from a wish, a desire or a hope nor can it amount to a claim or demand on the ground of a right. However earnest and sincere a wish, a desire or a hope may be and however confidently one may look to them to be fulfilled, they by themselves cannot amount to an assertable expectation and a mere disappointment does not attract legal consequences. A pious hope even leading to a moral obligation cannot amount to a legitimate expectation. The legitimacy of an expectation can be inferred only if it is founded on the sanction of law or custom or an established procedure followed in regular and natural sequence. Again it is distinguishable from a genuine expectation. Such expectation should be justifiably legitimate and protectable. Every such legitimate expectation does not by itself fructify into a right and therefore it does not amount to a right in the conventional sense.
>
> It has to be noticed that the concept of legitimate expectation in administrative law has now, undoubtedly, gained sufficient importance. It is stated that "legitimate expectation" is the latest recruit to a long list of concepts fashioned by the courts for the review of administrative action and this creation takes its place beside such principles as the rules of natural justice, unreasonableness, the fiduciary duty of local authorities and "in future, perhaps, the principle of proportionality". A passage in *Administrative Law*, Sixth Edition by H.W.R. Wade page 424 reads thus:
>
> "*These are revealing decisions. They show that the courts now expect Government departments to honour their published statements or else to treat the citizen with the fullest personal consideration. Unfairness in the form of unreasonableness here comes close to unfairness in the form of violation of natural justice, and the doctrine of legitimate expectation can operate in both contexts. It is obvious, furthermore, that* this principle of substantive, as opposed to procedural, fairness may undermine some of the established rules about estoppel and misleading advice, which tend to operate unfairly. Lord Scarman has stated emphatically that unfairness in the

58. (1993) 3 SCC 499.

purported exercise of a power can amount to an abuse or excess of power, and this seems likely to develop into an important general doctrine".

Another passage at page 522 in the above book reads thus:

"*It was in fact for the purpose of restricting the right to be heard that 'legitimate expectation' was introduced into the law. It made its first appearance in a case where* alien students of 'scientology' were refused extension of their entry permits as an act of policy by the Home Secretary, who had announced that no discretionary benefits would be granted to this sect. The court of appeal held that they had no legitimate expectation of extension beyond the permitted time, and so no right to a hearing, though revocation of their permits within that time would have been contrary to legitimate expectation. Official statements of policy, therefore, may cancel legitimate expectation, just as they may create it, as seen above. In a different context, where car-hire drivers had habitually offended against airport byelaws, with many convictions and unpaid fines, it was held that they had no legitimate expectation of being heard before being banned by the airport authority.

There is some ambiguity in the dicta about legitimate expectation, which may mean either expectation of a fair hearing or expectation of the licence or other benefit which is being sought. But the result is the same in either case; absence of legitimate *expectation will absolve the public authority from affording a hearing*".

.....

On examination of some of these important decisions it is generally agreed that legitimate expectation gives the applicant sufficient locus standi for judicial review and that the doctrine of legitimate expectation is to be confined mostly to right of a fair hearing before a decision which results in negativing a promise or withdrawing an undertaking is taken. The doctrine does not give scope to claim relief straightaway from the administrative authorities as no crystallised right as such is involved. The protection of such legitimate expectation does not require the fulfilment of the expectation where an overriding public interest requires otherwise. In other words where a person's legitimate expectation is not fulfilled by taking a particular decision then decision-maker should justify the denial of such expectation by showing some overriding public interest. Therefore even if substantive protection of such expectation is contemplated that does not grant an absolute right to a particular person. It simply ensures the circumstances in which that expectation may be denied or restricted. A case of legitimate expectation would arise when a body by representation or by past practice aroused expectation which it would be within its powers to fulfil. The protection is limited to that extent and a judicial review can be within those limits. But as discussed above a person who bases his claim on the doctrine of legitimate expectation, in the first instance, must satisfy that there is a foundation and thus has locus standi to make such a claim. In considering the same several factors which give rise to such legitimate expectation must be present. The decision taken by the authority must be found to be arbitrary, unreasonable and not taken in public interest. If it is a question of policy, even by way of change of old policy, the courts cannot interfere with a decision. In a given case whether there are such facts and circumstances giving rise to a legitimate expectation, it would primarily be a question of fact. If these tests are satisfied and if the court is satisfied that a case of legitimate expectation is made out then the next question would be whether failure to give an opportunity of hearing before the decision affecting such legitimate expectation is taken, has resulted in failure of justice and whether on that ground the decision should be quashed. If that be so then what should be the relief is again a matter which depends on several factors.

We find in *Attorney General for New South Wales case*[59] that the entire case-law on the doctrine of legitimate expectation has been considered. We also find that on an elaborate and erudite discussion it is held that the courts' jurisdiction to interfere is very much limited and much less in granting any relief in a claim based purely on the ground of 'legitimate expectation'. In *Public Law and Politics* edited by Carol Harlow, we find an article by Gabriele Ganz in which the learned author after examining the views expressed in the cases decided by eminent judges to whom we have referred to above, concluded thus:

"The confusion and uncertainty at the heart of the concept stems from its origin. It has grown from two separate roots, natural justice or fairness and estoppel, but the stems have become entwined to such an extent that it is impossible to disentangle them. This makes it very difficult to predict how the hybrid will develop in future. This could be regarded as giving the concept a healthy flexibility, for the intention behind it is benign; it has been fashioned to protect the individual against administrative action which is against his interest. On the other hand, the uncertainty of the concept has led to conflicting decisions and conflicting interpretations in the same decision".

However, it is generally accepted and also clear that legitimate expectation being less than right operates in the field of public and not private law and that to some extent such legitimate expectation ought to be protected though not guaranteed.

Legitimate expectations may come in various forms and owe their existence to different kind of circumstances and it is not possible to give an exhaustive list in the context of vast and fast expansion of the governmental activities. They shift and change so fast that the start of our list would be obsolete before we reached the middle. By and large they arise in cases of promotions which are in normal course expected, though not guaranteed by way of a statutory right, in cases of contracts, distribution of largess by the Government and in somewhat similar situations. For instance discretionary grant of licences, permits or the like, carry with it a reasonable expectation, though not a

59. (1990) 64 Aust LJR 327.

legal right to renewal or non-revocation, but to summarily disappoint that expectation may be seen as unfair without the expectant person being heard. But there again the court has to see whether it was done as a policy or in the public interest either by way of G.O., rule or by way of a legislation. If that be so, a decision denying a legitimate expectation based on such grounds does not qualify for interference unless in a given case, the decision or action taken amounts to an abuse of power. Therefore the limitation is extremely confined and if the according of natural justice does not condition the exercise of the power, the concept of legitimate expectation can have no role to play and the court must not usurp the discretion of the public authority which is empowered to take the decisions under law and the court is expected to apply an objective standard which leaves to the deciding authority the full range of choice which the legislature is presumed to have intended. Even in a case where the decision is left entirely to the discretion of the deciding authority without any such legal bounds and if the decision is taken fairly and objectively, the court will not interfere on the ground of procedural fairness to a person whose interest based on legitimate expectation might be affected. For instance if an authority who has full discretion to grant a licence prefers an existing licence holder to a new applicant, the decision cannot be interfered with on the ground of legitimate expectation entertained by the new applicant applying the principles of natural justice. It can therefore be seen that legitimate expectation can at the most be one of the grounds which may give rise to judicial review but the granting of relief is very much limited. It would thus appear that there are stronger reasons as to why the legitimate expectation should not be substantively protected than the reasons as to why it should be protected. In other words such a legal obligation exists whenever the case supporting the same in terms of legal principles of different sorts, is stronger than the case against it. As observed in *Attorney General for New South Wales case* [(1990) 64 Aust LJR 327]: "To strike down the exercise of administrative power solely on the ground of avoiding the disappointment of the legitimate expectations of an individual would be to set the courts adrift on a featureless sea of pragmatism. Moreover, the notion of a legitimate expectation (falling short of a legal right) is too nebulous to form a basis for invalidating the exercise of a power when its exercise otherwise accords with law". If a denial of legitimate expectation in a given case amounts to denial of right guaranteed or is arbitrary, discriminatory, unfair or biased, gross abuse of power or violation of principles of natural justice, the same can be questioned on the well-known grounds attracting Article 14 but a claim based on mere legitimate expectation without anything more cannot ipso facto give a right to invoke these principles. It can be one of the grounds to consider but the court must lift the veil and see whether the decision is violative of these principles warranting interference. It depends very much on the facts and the recognised general principles of administrative law applicable to such facts and the concept of legitimate expectation which is the latest recruit to a long list of concepts fashioned by the courts for the review of administrative action, must be restricted to the general legal limitations applicable and binding the manner of the future exercise of administrative power in a particular case. It follows that the concept of legitimate expectation is "not the key which unlocks the treasury of natural justice and it ought not to unlock the gates which shuts the court out of review on the merits", particularly when the element of speculation and uncertainty is inherent in that very concept. As cautioned in *Attorney General for New South Wales case*[60] the courts should restrain themselves and restrict such claims duly to the legal limitations. It is a well-meant caution. Otherwise a resourceful litigant having vested interests in contracts, licences etc. can successfully indulge in getting welfare activities mandated by directive principles thwarted to further his own interests. The caution, particularly in the changing scenario, becomes all the more important.[61]

Food Corporation of India v. Kamdhenu Cattle Feed Industries[62] is one of the first Indian cases to apply the doctrine of legitimate expectation. In this case the appellant had invited tenders for sale of stocks of damaged foodgrain. After the submission of the tenders, the appellant was not satisfied with the adequacy of bid amount, hence rejected all the applications and invited all the applicants to participate for individual negotiations. The respondent was the highest bidder as per the tender process and they refused to participate in the subsequent negotiations. After the negotiations the offer prices were much higher and on that basis the contract was entered into by the appellant. The respondent challenged the action on the ground of arbitrariness and stated that the appellant could not grant a contract by rejecting the tender process and were bound to give the contract to the highest tender. The Supreme Court upheld the action of the appellant and observed–

> In contractual sphere as in all other State actions, the State and all its instrumentalities have to conform to Article 14 of the Constitution of which non-arbitrariness is a significant facet. There is no unfettered discretion in public law: A public authority possesses powers only to use them for public good. This imposes the duty to act fairly and to adopt a procedure which is 'fairplay in action'. Due observance of this obligation as a part of good administration raises a reasonable or legitimate expectation in every citizen to be treated fairly in his interaction with the State and its instrumentalities, with this element forming a necessary component of the decision-making process in all State actions. To satisfy this requirement of non-arbitrariness in a State action, it is, therefore, necessary to consider and give due weight to the reasonable or legitimate expectations of the persons likely to be affected by the decision or else that unfairness in the exercise of the power may amount to an abuse or excess of power apart from affecting the bona fides of the decision in a given case. The decision so made would be exposed to

60. (1990) 64 Aust LJR 327.
61. (1993) 3 SCC 499, pp. 540-549.
62. (1993) 1 SCC 71.

challenge on the ground of arbitrariness. Rule of law does not completely eliminate discretion in the exercise of power, as it is unrealistic, but provides for control of its exercise by judicial review.

The mere reasonable or legitimate expectation of a citizen, in such a situation, may not by itself be a distinct enforceable right, but failure to consider and give due weight to it may render the decision arbitrary, and this is how the requirement of due consideration of a legitimate expectation forms part of the principle of non-arbitrariness, a necessary concomitant of the rule of law. Every legitimate expectation is a relevant factor requiring due consideration in a fair decision-making process. Whether the expectation of the claimant is reasonable or legitimate in the context is a question of fact in each case. Whenever the question arises, it is to be determined not according to the claimant's perception but in larger public interest wherein other more important considerations may outweigh what would otherwise have been the legitimate expectation of the claimant. A bona fide decision of the public authority reached in this manner would satisfy the requirement of non-arbitrariness and withstand judicial scrutiny. The doctrine of legitimate expectation gets assimilated in the rule of law and operates in our legal system in this manner and to this extent.

In the case of *Madras City Wine Merchants' Assn. v. State of T.N*[63] the members of the appellant association had been granted licenses to carry on business of Indian made foreign spirits (IMFS). Subsequently they were given license to set up bar adjoining to the liquor shops for which higher license fee were collected. The license holders had made major investments in acquiring adjacent properties and for setting up the bar. The setting up of the bar had caused major public outcry and had given rise to law and order problem. The Government repealed the Bar Rules framed under the Tamil Nadu Prohibition Act. 1937 and thereby the bar licenses of the appellants were not renewed. One of the major legal arguments made on behalf of the appellants was based on the doctrine of legitimate expectation. The Court revisited the various judicial opinions relating to the doctrine and reiterated the principles of legitimate expectation as held in *Union of India v. Hindustan Development Corporation*[64] and asserted the doctrine shall become applicable – "(*a*) if there is an express promise given by a public authority; or (*b*) because of the existence of a regular practice which the claimant can reasonably expect to continue; and (*c*) Such an expectation must be reasonable. However, if there is a change in policy or in public interest the position is altered by a rule or legislation, no question of legitimate expectation would arise".[65] But in cases of delegated

63. (1994) 5 SCC 509.
64. (1993) 3 SCC 499.
65. (1994) 5 SCC 509, Para 48.

legislation the doctrine has no application and can only arise in the field of administrative decisions. It was emphasized that *"if the plea of legitimate expectation relates to procedural fairness there is no possibility whatever of invoking the doctrine as against the legislation"*. In the absence of any specific promise or right renewal the government is within their prerogative to change their policy and the principle of non-arbitrariness does not apply to a change in legislative policy.

In the case of *Navjyoti Co-Group Housing Society v. Union of India*[66] the Supreme Court applied the doctrine of legitimate expectation while dealing with the sudden change of policy in determining seniority of registered Cooperative Group Housing Societies by the Delhi Development Authority (DDA). The DDA had earlier followed the practice of making land allotment based on the 'first come first serve' basis wherein the seniority was determined on the basis of serial number and date of registration of societies with the Registrar of Cooperative Societies but subsequently it changed the policy and held that the seniority will be on the basis of when the papers of the Society were found to be in order and approved by the office of the Registrar. This change of policy was challenged not only on the ground of unreasonableness and arbitrariness but also on violation of the legitimate expectation of the people. The Court held that *"the doctrine of 'legitimate expectation' imposes in essence a duty on public authority to act fairly by taking into consideration all relevant factors relating to such 'legitimate expectation'. Within the conspectus of fair dealing in case of 'legitimate expectation', the reasonable opportunities to make representation by the parties likely to be affected by any change of consistent past policy, come in. We have not been shown any compelling reasons taken into consideration by the Central Government to make a departure from the existing policy of allotment with reference to seniority in Registration by introducing a new guideline"*. The Court further emphasized that before introducing or making any change in the guidelines or procedures to be followed for allotment an opportunity to make representations against the proposed changes should be given to the affected people by way of a public notice. However in *Bajaj Hindustan Ltd. v. Sir Shadi Lal Enterprises Ltd.*[67] the Court has categorically clarified that the doctrine has limited application in restricting the power of policy formulation by the state. *When the Government is satisfied that change in the policy was necessary in the public interest it would be entitled to revise the policy and lay down a new policy.*[68]

66. AIR 1993 SC 155.
67. (2011) 1 SCC 640.
68. (2011) 1 SCC 640, Id at para 41.

In *Southern Petrochemical Industries Co. Ltd. v. Electricity Inspector & ETIO*[69] expanded the scope of the doctrine and recognized the legitimate expectation of substantive benefit. Ordinarily the principle will not be applicable in the face of legislative provisions but if the legislature has itself allowed the parties to take benefit of their existing rights with reference to the repeal and saving clauses contained in the statute then the same shall also apply. It was observed–

> Legitimate expectation is now considered to be a part of the principles of natural justice. If by reason of the existing state of affairs, a party is given to understand that the other party shall not take away the benefit without complying with the principles of natural justice, the said doctrine would be applicable. The legislature, indisputably, has the power to legislate but where the law itself recognises existing right and did not take away the same expressly or by necessary implication, the principles of legitimate expectation of a substantive benefit may be held to be applicable.

In *Mahabir Auto Stores v. Indian Oil Corporation*[70] the issue was whether continuous past practice can give rise to legitimate expectation and can create a legal obligation. The appellant company had been receiving all kinds of lubricants from the respondent for the past 18 years acted as a Lube Distributor of the respondent corporation in Northern India but there was no formal distributorship contract between the appellant and the respondent. Subsequently there was a change of policy in the respondent corporation and supply of lubricants were stopped to those companies which were merely re-sellers, traders and those who did not have any written contracts with the company. Based on this new policy supply of lubricants to the appellant company were stopped. The appellant company challenged the action of the respondents and one of the arguments were based on the doctrine of promissory estoppel. The Supreme Court while dealing with the various contentions recognized that IOC was an instrumentality of the State under Article 12 of the Constitution and in exercise of their powers are bound by the norms of rationality and non-arbitrariness - Every action of the State executive authority must be subject to rule of law and must be informed by reason. So, whatever be the activity of the public authority, in such monopoly or semi-monopoly dealings, it should meet the test of Article 14 of the Constitution. If a Governmental action even in the matters of entering or not entering into contracts, fails to satisfy the test of reasonableness, the same would be unreasonable... rule of reason and rule against arbitrariness and discrimination, rules of fair play and natural justice are part of the rule

69. (2007) 5 SCC 447.
70. AIR 1990 SC 1031.

of law applicable in situation or action by State instrumentality in dealing with citizens in a situation like the present one. Even though the rights of the citizens are in the nature of contractual rights, the manner, the method and motive of a decision of entering or not entering into a contract, are subject to judicial review on the touchstone of relevance and reasonableness, fair play, natural justice, equality and non-discrimination in the type of the transactions and nature of the dealing as in the present case.

After considering the particular facts and circumstances of the case as well as the long period of association between the parties the Court held that–

> [D]ecision of the State/public authority under Article 298 of the Constitution, is an administrative decision and can be impeached on the ground that the decision is arbitrary or violative of Article 14 of the Constitution of India on any of the grounds available in public law field. It appears to us that in respect of Corporation like IOC when without informing the parties concerned, as in the case of the appellant firm herein on alleged change of policy and on that basis action to seek to bring to an end the course of transaction over 18 years involving large amounts of money is not fair action, especially in view of the monopolistic nature of the power of the respondent in this field. Therefore, it is necessary to reiterate that even in the field of public law, the relevant persons concerned or to be affected, should be taken into confidence. Whether and in what circumstances that confidence should be taken into consideration cannot be laid down on any straight jacket basis. It depends on the nature of the right involved and nature of the power sought to be exercised in a particular situation. It is true that there is discrimination between power and right but whether the State or the instrumentality of a State has the right to function in public field or private field is a matter which, -in our opinion, depends upon the facts and circumstances of the situation, but such exercise of power cannot be dealt with by the State or the instrumentality of the State without informing and taking into confidence, the party whose rights and powers affected or sought to be affected, into confidence. In such situations most often people feel aggrieved by exclusion of knowledge if not being taken into confidence.
>
> Such transaction should continue as an administrative decision with the organ of the State. It may be contractual or statutory but in a situation of transaction between the parties for nearly two decades, such procedure should be followed which will be reasonable, fair and just, that is, the process which normally be accepted to be followed by an organ of the State and that process must be conscious and all those affected should be taken into confidence.

The Court directed that the respondent company should consider the afresh the submissions of the appellant regarding the nature of the contractual relation as well as the whether they would fall within the scope of distributorship under the new policy after taking the appellant firm into confidence.

In *State of Haryana v. Jagdish*[71] the Supreme Court reiterated the principle that consistent past practice by the State could furnish the ground of legitimate expectation. In this case the respondent had already served 15 years of imprisonment and was eligible for being considered under the remission policy of the state. The Court emphasised that – "The State authority is under an obligation to at least exercise its discretion in relation to an honest expectation perceived by the convict, at the time of his conviction that his case for premature release would be considered after serving the sentence, prescribed in the short-sentencing policy existing on that date. The State has to exercise its power of remission also keeping in view any such benefit to be construed liberally in favour of a convict which may depend upon case to case and for that purpose, in our opinion, it should relate to a policy which, in the instant case, was in favour of the respondent. In case a liberal policy prevails on the date of consideration of the case of a "lifer" for premature release, he should be given benefit thereof".

In *Chandrakala Trivedi v. State of Rajasthan*[72] the appellant was provisionally selected for appointment to the post of teacher but subsequently she received a letter from the Rajasthan Public Service Commission informing her that provisional selection has been cancelled as the appellant did not pass the Higher Secondary / Senior Secondary Examination after passing the Secondary Examination. The appellant argued that at the time when she passed the Secondary Examination, it was permissible for a candidate passing the Secondary Examination to get admission in the higher classes with a preparatory course. Based on it she had completed her graduation from Indira Gandhi Open University and then got her BEd degree as well as MA degree on a regular basis from Maharishi Dayanand Saraswati University, Ajmer, Rajasthan. Hence it was argued that the appellant had satisfied the criteria of the required qualification for appointment to the post in question. Applying the doctrine of legitimate expectation relating to substantive benefits the Supreme Court held that *after a person is provisionally selected, a certain degree of reasonable expectation of the selection being continued also comes into existence.* The Court ordered that the appellant should be considered for provisional appointment and the same should not be cancelled based on the special facts and circumstances of the case.

71. (2010) 4 SCC 216.
72. (2012) 3 SCC 129.

In *Ashoka Smokeless Coal India (P) Ltd. v. Union of India*[73] the Supreme Court had to look into the issue whether the doctrine of legitimate expectation will be applicable in case of unlawful representation i.e. the representation is ultra vires the power of the local authority. In such cases even though exercise of such powers has been held to be illegal, it has been generally accepted by the English Courts that it would be unjust to allow the administration to take advantage of their own wrong. However the European Court of Human Rights awarded damages as it found on facts that the action was not against public interest nor did it affect the statutory duties of the authority.[74] In this case while dealing with the issue of sale of coal by electronic auction (e-auction) the Supreme Court advocated for the *doctrine of balancing* so as to ensure that the principles of legitimate expectation would be *extended to all cases where the unlawful action was not adverse to public interest.*

In the case of *Monnet Ispat & Energy Ltd. v. Union of India*[75] the Supreme Court summarized the essential principles of the doctrine of legitimate expectation as–

(1) The doctrine of legitimate expectation can be invoked as a substantive and enforceable right.

(2) The doctrine of legitimate expectation is founded on the principle of reasonableness and fairness. The doctrine arises out of principles of natural justice and there are parallels between the doctrine of legitimate expectation and promissory estoppel.

(3) Where the decision of an authority is founded in public interest as per executive policy or law, the court would be reluctant to interfere with such decision by invoking the doctrine of legitimate expectation. The legitimate expectation doctrine cannot be invoked to fetter changes in administrative policy if it is in the public interest to do so.

(4) The legitimate expectation is different from anticipation and an anticipation cannot amount to an assertable expectation. Such expectation should be justifiable, legitimate and protectable.

(5) The protection of legitimate expectation does not require the fulfilment of the expectation where an overriding public interest requires otherwise. In other words, personal benefit must give way to public interest and the doctrine of legitimate expectation would not be invoked which could block public interest for private benefit.

73. (2007) 2 SCC 640.
74. *Stretch v. U.K.* (2004) 38 EHRR 12.
75. (2012) 11 SCC 1, para 188.

6.9.3 Doctrine of Promissory Estoppel

The doctrine of promissory estoppel has been incorporated by the judiciary within the domain of public law to hold the administration accountable to the people for the promises made by it in the course of running of the state affairs. The doctrine has referred by various names such as 'promissory estoppel', 'equitable estoppel', 'quasi estoppel' and 'new estoppel'. This doctrine has been fundamentally ingrained within the norms of equity and fairness so as to ensure that someone who acts or alters his position based on the promises made by the state authorities in their official capacity is not made to suffer by subsequent rescinding of the promise i.e. *where a promise is made by a person knowing that it would be acted on by the person to whom it is made and in fact it is so acted on and it is inequitable to allow the party making the promise to go back upon it.*[76] The principle has been evolved under the principles of equity to avoid injustice. Describing the potential importance of this doctrine Bhagwati J. had described it as a doctrine which *is potentially so fruitful and pregnant with such vast possibilities for growth that traditional lawyers are alarmed lest it might upset existing doctrines which are looked upon almost reverentially and which have held the field for a long number of years.*[77]

The doctrine originally developed within the realm of equity *to mitigate the rigours of strict law.* In the early case of *Hughes v. Metropolitan Railway Co*[78] Lord Cairn had described the applicable principle as–

> It is the first principle upon which all Courts of Equity proceed, that if parties who have entered into definite and distinct terms involving certain legal results... afterwards by their own act or with then own consent enter upon a course of negotiation which has the effect of leading one of the parties to suppose that the strict rights arising under the contract will not be enforced, or will be kept in suspense, or held in abeyance, the person who otherwise might have enforced those rights will not be allowed to enforce them where it would be inequitable having regard to the dealings which have thus taken place between the parties.

The doctrine was developed in modern times by Lord Denning in the celebrated case of *Central London Property Trust Ltd. v. High Trees House Ltd.*[79] In this case the plaintiffs had leased a number of flats to the respondents for a period of 99 years at a rent of £2500. Early in 1940 because of the war the defendants were unable to find tenants, hence at

76. (1979) 2 SCC 409.
77. Id.
78. (1877) 2 A.C. 439.
79. (1956) 1 All. E.R. 256 : 1947 KS 130.

their request the plaintiffs reduced the rent to £1250 from the beginning of the term. By 1945 with the improvement in the economic conditions the plaintiffs claimed the full rent from the middle of that year. The claim of the plaintiff was upheld because the court held that the period for which the rent was claimed was outside the scope of representation, but Denning in his opinion held that the plaintiffs could not be allowed to act inconsistent with the promises based on which the defendants had acted. In the words of Lord Denning *cases in which a promise was made which was intended to create legal relations and which, to the knowledge of the person making the promise, was going to be acted on by the person to whom it was made, and which was in fact so acted on. In such cases the courts have said that the promise must be honoured.* The doctrine as formulated by him was *"that a promise intended to be binding, intended to be acted on and in fact acted, on, is binding so far as its terms properly apply".*

Union of India v. Anglo-Afghan Agencies[80] is one of the earliest cases wherein the Supreme Court applied the doctrine of promissory estoppel. The Textile Commissioner published on October 10, 1962, a scheme called the Export Promotion Scheme providing incentives to exporters of woollen goods to Afghanistan. The scheme stated that – "It has been decided that the manufacturers-exporters and merchants-exporters of the above woollen textiles and woollen goods will be entitled to import raw materials, namely, raw wool, wool tops, shoddy, man-made fibres and tops, permissible types of dyes and chemicals and machinery and machinery parts and spare parts for woollen industry for a total amount equal to 100% of the f.o.b. value of the exports". Based on the incentives provided in the export scheme the respondents, a firm dealing in woollen goods at Amritsar exported to Afghanistan woollen goods of the f.o.b. value of Rs. 5,03,471. Contrary to the provisions of the scheme the Deputy Director in the office of the Textile Commissioner, Bombay issued to the respondents an Import Entitlement Certificate for Rs. 1,99,459 only/-. All representations made by the respondents to the Textile Commissioner for grant of Import Entitlement Certificate for the full f.o.b. value of the goods exported failed to produce any response. A writ petition was filed by the respondents for issuance of an order directing the Government to issue a license of the value of the remaining amount. Their principle point of argument was that the schemes were statutory in nature and created an obligation on the Textile Commissioner to uphold the promise made unless after due investigation it was found that there was over-invoicing of the goods exported whereas the argument of the Union of India was that the Export Promotion Scheme was administrative in character and was in the nature of mere administrative

80. (1968) 2 SCR 366 : AIR 1968 SC 718.

instruction issued by the Union Government to the Textile Commissioner and it created no rights in the public generally or in the exporters who exported their goods in pursuance of the Scheme. These schemes did not impose any obligations on the Government to issue the import certificates.

The Court refused to accept the defence of executive necessity on behalf of the Government and categorically held the State liable for the promises made. The Court observed that–

> We are unable to accede to the contention that the executive necessity releases the Government from honouring its solemn promises relying on which citizens have acted to their detriment. Under our constitutional set-up no person may be deprived of his right or liberty except in due course of and by authority of law: if a member of the executive seeks to deprive a citizen of his right or the liberty otherwise than in exercise of power derived from the law-common or statute-the Courts will be competent to and indeed would be to bound to, protect the rights of the aggrieved citizen.
>
> .....
>
> Under our jurisprudence the Government is not exempt from liability to carry out the representation made by it as to its future conduct and it cannot on some undefined and undisclosed ground of necessity or expediency fail to carry out the promise solemnly made by it, nor claim to be the judge of its own obligation to the citizen on an ex parte appraisement of the circumstances in which the obligation has arisen.

On the specific issue of whether the State can be made liable to uphold a contractual obligation in the absence of a formal contract as required under Article 299. It was asserted by the Court that the claims of the respondents were not arising out a breach of a formal contract but the grievance was arising out of the failure of the Textile Commissioner to carry out the terms of the scheme. The claims of the respondents were based on the principles of equity as the respondents acted on the representations made by the government and altered their position. Before independence this legal principle was largely applied by the judiciary in several cases, including the case of *Municipal Corporation of the City of Bombay v. The Secretary of State for India in Council331*[81] wherein the Bombay High Court had held *that even though there is no formal contract as required by the statute, the Government may be bound by a representation made by it.* In this case the Bombay High Court had also differentiated the principle of estoppel as applied in public law from other branches of law. It distinguished it from the evidentiary rules specified under Section 115 of the Evidence Act and stated

81. I.L.R. 29 Bom. 580.

that the doctrine was formulated as a rule of equity and In this case the Supreme Court differentiated the principle of estoppel as applied in public law from other branches of law. It distinguished it from the evidentiary rules specified under Section 115 of the Evidence Act and stated that the doctrine was formulated as a rule of equity and takes its origin from the jurisdiction assumed by Courts of Equity to intervene in the case of, or to prevent fraud. In this case the Supreme Court differentiated the principle of estoppel as applied in public law from other branches of law. It distinguished it from the evidentiary rules specified under Section 115 of the Evidence Act and stated that the doctrine was formulated as a *rule of equity* and *takes its origin from the jurisdiction assumed by Courts of Equity to intervene in the case of, or to prevent fraud.* The Supreme Court after referring to various judgments and principles of law concluded that it is legitimate demand of *a party who has acted on a representation made by the Government to claim that the Government shall be bound to carry out the promise made by it, even though the promise is not recorded in the form of a formal contract as required by the Constitution.*

The decision in the *Anglo-Afghan case* was instrumental in giving rise to the doctrine of promissory estoppel in the Indian legal landscape. The Supreme Court followed the same rationale and formally laid down the jurisprudential propositions of the doctrine in the land mark case of *Motilal Padampat Sugar Mills Co. Ltd. v. State of Uttar Pradesh.*[82] In this case the appellants who were engaged in the business of manufacture and sale of sugar read a news item on October 10, 1968 in the National Herald stating that the 'State of Uttar Pradesh had decided to give exemption from sales tax for a period of three years under Section 4A of the U.P. Sales Tax Act to all new industrial units in the State with a view to enabling them to come on firm footing in developing stage'. The news was based on a statement made by the then Secretary in the Industries Department of the Government. After reading the news item the appellants sent a letter to the Director of Industries inquiring whether the sales tax holidays will be applicable if a hydro-genation plant for manufacture of Vanaspati were set up. A reply was sent by the Director confirming that "there will be no sales tax for three years on the finished product of your proposed Vanaspati factory from the date it gets power connection for commencing production". In addition the appellants met with the Chief Secretary to the Government who was also the Advisor to the Governor and re-confirmed the issue of tax exemption. An exemption letter was issued by the Chief Secretary based on which the appellants entered into agreements with financial institutions and went on to set up the Vanaspati plant. However after the setting up

82. AIR 1979 SC 621 : (1979) 2 SCC 409.

of the Vanaspati factory by the appellant, the Government had second thoughts about the grant of exemption and by a letter dated 20th January 1970 granted partial concession in Sales Tax to the appellant and ultimately by a news item dated 12th August 1970 the Government decided to rescind totally from its earlier decision and withdrew all concessions in the rates of Sales Tax granted to new Vanaspati plants. The appellants filed a petition challenging the rescinding order of the government and asking for a writ directing the government to uphold their earlier decision of providing sales tax exemption for a period of three years. The principle point of argument of the appellant was based on the doctrine of promissory estoppel as the Chief Secretary had given unequivocal assurance about the sales tax exemption based on which the appellant had altered their position and had set up the Vanaspati factory.

Before analyzing the legal issues of the case the Court laid down the nature, scope and extent of the doctrine of promissory estoppel. Laying down the *true principle of promissory estoppel* the Court observed–

> Where one party has by his words or conduct made to the other a clear and unequivocal promise which is intended to create legal relations or affect a legal relationship to arise in the future, knowing or intending that it would be acted upon by the other party to whom the promise is made and it is in fact so acted upon by the other party, the promise would be binding on the party making it and he would not be entitled to go back upon it, if it would be inequitable to allow him to do so having regard to the dealings which have taken place between the parties, and this would be so irrespective whether there is any pre-existing relationship between the parties or not.
>
> ......
>
> The law may, therefore, now be taken to be settled as a result of this decision, that where the Government makes a promise knowing or intending that it would be acted on by the promisee and, in fact, the promisee, acting in reliance on it, alters his position, the Government would be held bound by the promise and the promise would be enforceable against the Government at the instance of the promisee, notwithstanding that there is no consideration for the promise and the promise is not recorded in the form of a formal contract as required by Article 299 of the Constitution. It is elementary that in a republic governed by the rule of law, no one, howsoever high or low, is above the law. Everyone is subject to the law as fully and completely as any other and the Government is no exception. It is indeed the pride of constitutional democracy and rule of law that the Government stands on the same footing as a private individual so far as the obligation of the law is concerned: the former is equally bound as the latter. It is indeed difficult to see on what principle can a Government, committed to the rule of law, claim immunity from the doctrine of promissory estoppel. Can the Government say that it is under no

obligation to act in a manner that is fair and just or that it is not bound by considerations of "honesty and good faith"? Why should the Government not be held to a high "standard of rectangular rectitude while dealing with its citizens"? There was a time when the doctrine of executive necessity was regarded as sufficient justification for the Government to repudiate even its contractual obligations; but, let it be said to the eternal glory of this Court, this doctrine was emphatically negatived in the *Indo-Afghan Agencies case* and the supremacy of the rule of law was established. It was laid down by this Court that the Government cannot claim to be immune from the applicability of the rule of promissory estoppel and repudiate a promise made by it on the ground that such promise may fetter its future executive action. If the Government does not want its freedom of executive action to be hampered or restricted, the Government need not make a promise knowing or intending that it would be acted on by the promisee and the promisee would alter his position relying upon it. But if the Government makes such a promise and the promisee acts in reliance upon it and alters his position, there is no reason why the Government should not be compelled to make good such promise like any other private individual. The law cannot acquire legitimacy and gain social acceptance unless it accords with the moral values of the society and the constant endeavour of the Courts and the legislature, must, therefore, be to close the gap between law and morality and bring about as near an approximation between the two as possible. The doctrine of promissory estoppel is a significant judicial contribution in that direction. But it is necessary to point out that since the doctrine of promissory estoppel is an equitable doctrine, it must yield when the equity so requires. If it can be shown by the Government that having regard to the facts as they have transpired, it would be inequitable to hold the Government to the promise made by it, the Court would not raise an equity in favour of the promisee and enforce the promise against the Government. The doctrine of promissory estoppel would be displaced in such a case because, on the facts, equity would not require that the Government should be held bound by the promise made by it. When the Government is able to show that in view of the facts as have transpired since the making of the promise, public interest would be prejudiced if the Government were required to carry out the promise, the Court would have to balance the public interest in the Government carrying out a promise made to a citizen which has induced the citizen to act upon it and alter his position and the public interest likely to suffer if the promise were required to be carried out by the Government and determine which way the equity lies. It would not be enough for the Government just to say that public interest requires that the Government should not be compelled to carry out the promise or that the public interest would suffer if the Government were required to honour it. The Government cannot, as Shah, J., pointed out in the *Indo-Afghan Agencies case*, claim to be exempt from the liability to carry out the promise "on some indefinite and undisclosed ground of necessity or expediency", nor can the Government claim to be the sole Judge of its liability and repudiate it "on an ex parte appraisement of the circumstances". If the Government wants to resist the liability, it will have to disclose to the Court what are the facts and circumstances on account of which the Government claims to be exempt from the liability and it would be for the Court to decide whether those facts and circumstances are such as to render it inequitable to enforce the liability against the Government. Mere claim of change of policy would not be sufficient to exonerate the Government from the liability: the Government would have to show what precisely is the changed policy and also its reason and justification so that the Court can judge for itself which way the public interest lies and what the equity of the case demands. It is only if the Court is satisfied, on proper and adequate material placed by the Government, that overriding public interest requires that the Government should not be held bound by the promise but should be free to act unfettered by it, that the Court would refuse to enforce the promise against the Government. The Court would not act on the mere ipse dixit of the Government, for it is the Court which has to decide and not the Government whether the Government should be held exempt from liability. This is the essence of the rule of law. The burden would be upon the Government to show that the public interest in the Government acting otherwise than in accordance with the promise is so overwhelming that it would be inequitable to hold the Government bound by the promise and the Court would insist on a highly rigorous standard of proof in the discharge of this burden. But even where there is no such overriding public interest, it may still be competent to the Government to resile from the promise "on giving reasonable notice, which need not be a formal notice, giving the promisee a reasonable opportunity of resuming his position" provided of course it is possible for the promisee to restore status quo ante. If, however, the promisee cannot resume his position, the promise would become final and irrevocable. Vide *Emmanuel Avodeji Ajaye v. Briscoe* [(1964) 3 All ER 556 : (1964) 1 WLR 1326].[83]

The Court held the State Government liable because the Chief Secretary had clearly stated that the Vanaspati factory of the appellant would be entitled to sales tax exemption for a period of three years from the date of commencement of production. The representation made by the Chief Secretary was on behalf of the Government and it shall be binding on them. On the specific contention of the State that since the appellant did not suffer from any loss the doctrine of promissory estoppel will have no application, the Court negated the contention and held that it is not necessary *in order to attract the applicability of the doctrine of promissory estoppel, that the promisee, acting in reliance on the promise, should suffer any detriment. What is necessary is only that the promisee should have altered his position in reliance on the promise.... The alteration of position need not involve any detriment to the promisee. If detriment were a necessary element, there would be no need for the doctrine of promissory estoppel because, in that event, in quite a few cases, the detriment would form the*

83. Supra note 82 at Para 24.

consideration and the promise would be binding as a contract. The Court further clarified that *if by detriment we mean injustice to the promisee which would result if the promisor were to recede from his promise, then detriment would certainly come in as a necessary ingredient. The detriment in such a case is not some prejudice suffered by the promisee by acting on the promise, but the prejudice which would be caused to the promisee, if the promisor were allowed to go back on the promise.* Thus the Court concluded that *in order to invoke the doctrine of promissory estoppel it is enough to show that the promisee has, acting in reliance on the promise, altered his position and it is not necessary for him to further show that he has acted to his detriment.*

The essential norms of the doctrine of promissory estoppel were reiterated by the Court in the case of *Union of India v. Godfrey Philips India Ltd*[84] wherein the Court overruled the decision of the *Jit Ram v. State of Haryana*[85] which had held that the doctrine of promissory estoppel is not available against the exercise of executive functions of the State and the State cannot be prevented from exercising its functions under the law and upheld the law laid down in the *Motilal Sugar Mills case.* The Court in this case had to deal with the issue of whether the Central Board of Excise and Customs were bound by the rule of promissory estoppel as regards the exemption order issued by them for the period between May 24, 1976 and November 2, 1982 relating to the payment of excise duty on the cost of corrugated fibre board containers used for packing the cigarettes. The Court upholding the contention of the respondents relating to the applicability of the doctrine of promissory estoppel held that–

> [T]he doctrine of promissory estoppel is well established in the administrative law of India. It represents a principle evolved by equity to avoid injustice and, though commonly named promissory estoppel, it is neither in the realm of contract nor in the realm of estoppel. The basis of this doctrine is the interposition of equity which has always, true to its form, stepped in to mitigate the rigour of strict law.... The true principle of promissory estoppel is that where one party has by his word or conduct made to the other a clear and unequivocal promise or representation which is intended to create legal relations or effect a legal relationship to arise in the future, knowing or intending that it would be acted upon by the other party to whom the promise or representation is made and it is in fact so acted upon by the other party, the promise or representation would be binding on the party making it and he would not be entitled to go back upon it, if it would be inequitable to allow him to do so, having regard to the dealings which have taken place between the parties. It has often been said in England that the doctrine of

84. (1985) 4 SCC 369.
85. (1981) 1 SCC 11 : AIR 1980 SC 1285.

> promissory estoppel cannot itself be the basis of an action: it can only be a shield and not a sword: but the law in India has gone far ahead of the narrow position adopted in England and as a result of the decision of this Court in *Motilal Padampat Sugar Mills v. State of U.P.* [(1979) 2 SCC 409 : 1979 SCC (Tax) 144 : (1979) 2 SCR 641] it is now well settled that the doctrine of promissory estoppel is not limited in its application only to defence but it can also found a cause of action. The decision of this Court in *Motilal Sugar Mills case* [(1979) 2 SCC 409 : 1979 SCC (Tax) 144 : (1979) 2 SCR 641] contains an exhaustive discussion of the doctrine of promissory estoppel and we find ourselves wholly in agreement with the various parameters of this doctrine outlined in that decision.
>
> ......
>
> There can therefore be no doubt that the doctrine of promissory estoppel is applicable against the Government in the exercise of its governmental, public or executive functions and the doctrine of executive necessity or freedom of future executive action cannot be invoked to defeat the applicability of the doctrine of promissory estoppel.

In some recent cases the doctrine of promissory estoppel has been used in conjunction with the doctrine of legitimate expectation because there are parallels between these two doctrines as they are both founded on the concept of fairness and arise out of natural justice.[86] In the case of *Southern Petrochemical Industries Co. Ltd. v. Electricity Inspector & ETIO*[87] an argument was made by some of the petitioners that the various exemptions given to certain classes of consumers under the Tamil Nadu Electricity Duty Act, 1939 and the Tamil Nadu Electricity (Taxation on Consumption) Act, 1962 should be continued after the repeal of these legislations and enactment of the new Tamil Nadu Tax on Consumption or Sale of Electricity Act 2003. One of the principle points of argument was based on the application of the doctrine of promissory estoppel. Upholding the argument the Court held that–

> The doctrine of promissory estoppel would undoubtedly be applicable where an entrepreneur alters his position pursuant to or in furtherance of the promise made by a State to grant inter alia exemption from payment of taxes or charges on the basis of the current tariff. Such a policy decision on the part of the State shall not only be expressed by reason of notifications issued under the statutory provisions but also under the executive instructions. The appellants had undoubtedly been enjoying the benefit of (*sic* exemption from) payment of tax in respect of sale / consumption of electrical energy in relation to the cogenerating power plants.

86. *Monnet Ispat & Energy Ltd. v. Union of India*, (2012) 11 SCC 1, para 183.
87. (2007) 5 SCC 447.

......

> In view of the application of doctrine of promissory estoppel in the case of the appellants, their right is not destroyed and in that view of the matter although the scheme under the impugned Act is different from the 1939 Act and the 1962 Act and furthermore in view of the phraseology used in Section 20(1) of the 2003 Act, right of the appellants cannot be said to have been destroyed. The legislature in fact has acknowledged that right to be existing in the appellants.

In the case of *Monnet Ispat and Energy v. Union of India*[88] the mining proposals made in favour of the appellants were subsequently withdrawn by the Union Government at the request of the State Government and against such withdrawal a writ petition was filed by the appellants. The appellants argued on the principles of promissory estoppel and legitimate expectation. The Supreme Court after analyzing held that the State Government could not be held bound by its commitments, assurances and representations because the recommendation for the withdrawal was made in the larger public interest. In this case, after analyzing the major judicial decisions on the doctrine of promissory estoppel, the Court laid the essential principles which shall act as a guide to determine the applicability of promissory estoppel. The principles are–

(1) Where one party has by his words or conduct made to the other a clear and unequivocal promise which is intended to create legal relations or affect a legal relationship to arise in the future, knowing or intending that it would be acted upon by the other party to whom the promise is made and it is, in fact, so acted upon by the other party, the promise would be binding on the party making it and he would not be entitled to go back upon it, if it would be inequitable to allow him to do so having regard to the dealings which have taken place between the parties, and this would be so irrespective of whether there is any pre-existing relationship between the parties or not.

(2) The doctrine of promissory estoppel may be applied against the Government where the interest of justice, morality and common fairness dictate such a course. The doctrine is applicable against the State even in its governmental, public or sovereign capacity where it is necessary to prevent fraud or manifest injustice. However, the Government or even a private party under the doctrine of promissory estoppel cannot be asked to do an act prohibited in law. The nature and function which the Government discharges is not very relevant. The Government is subject to the rule of promissory estoppel and if

88. JT 2012 (7) SC 50.

the essential ingredients of this doctrine are satisfied, the Government can be compelled to carry out the promise made by it.

(3) The doctrine of promissory estoppel is not limited in its application only to defence but it can also furnish a cause of action. In other words, the doctrine of promissory estoppel can by itself be the basis of action.

(4) For invocation of the doctrine of promissory estoppel, it is necessary for the promisee to show that by acting on promise made by the other party, he altered his position. The alteration of position by the promisee is a sine qua non for the applicability of the doctrine. However, it is not necessary for him to prove any damage, detriment or prejudice because of alteration of such promise.

(5) In no case, the doctrine of promissory estoppel can be pressed into aid to compel the Government or a public authority to carry out a representation or promise which is contrary to law or which was outside the authority or power of the officer of the Government or of the public authority to make. No promise can be enforced which is statutorily prohibited or is against public policy.

(6) It is necessary for invocation of the doctrine of promissory estoppel that a clear, sound and positive foundation is laid in the petition. Bald assertions, averments or allegations without any supporting material are not sufficient to press into aid the doctrine of promissory estoppel.

(7) The doctrine of promissory estoppel cannot be invoked in abstract. When it is sought to be invoked, the court must consider all aspects including the result sought to be achieved and the public good at large. The fundamental principle of equity must forever be present to the mind of the court. Absence of it must not hold the Government or the public authority to its promise, assurance or representation.

Thus the core essence of the doctrine can be expressed as *"that the Government ought to set a high standard in its dealings and relationships with citizens and the word of a duly authorised Government agent, acting within the scope of his authority, ought to be as good as a Government bond".*[89] In India the doctrine has been used to create a cause of action to the person to whom the promise was made and the same cannot be limited by imposing the requirement of consideration or the defence of executive necessity, or overriding public interest without justiciable reasons. In addition the doctrine is not applicable against the legislature in the exercise of its legislative functions nor can it be used to enforce a statutory prohibition. The doctrine cannot also be used to compel the government or a public authority

89. Supra note 88 at Para 18.

to do something contrary to the provisions of law or which is outside the scope and power of the authority.[90] In *Godfrey Philips case* the court had re-asserted that "*the doctrine of promissory estoppel being an equitable doctrine, it must yield when the equity so requires; if it can be shown by the Government or public authority that having regard to the facts as they have transpired, it would be inequitable to hold the Government or public authority to the promise or representation made by it, the Court would not raise an equity in favour of the person to whom the promise or representation is made and enforce the promise or representation against the Government or public authority. The doctrine of promissory estoppel would be displaced in such a case, because on the facts, equity would not require that the Government or public authority should be held bound by the promise or representation made by it*".

6.9.4 Grant of Largess

Traditionally the term largess referred to conferring of some gifts or prizes by the king or the nobility. In a modern day democracy the term has assumed significance from the perspective of conferring of some exclusive contracts, quota, allotment, benefits etc. by the State to a private individual. These contracts, allotments or benefits provides monopoly power to the private individual to derive economic gains by using the state resources or natural resources to the exclusion of others. In the landmark case of *R.D. Shetty v. International Airport Authority of India*[91] the Supreme Court discussed the concept of grant of largess from the public law perspective and the need to adhere to the norms of fairness, transparency and accountability. It was observed–

> To-day the Government, is a welfare State, is the regulator and dispenser of special services and provider of a large number of benefits, including jobs contracts, licences, quotas, mineral rights etc. The Government pours forth wealth, money, benefits, services, contracts, quotas and licences. The valuables dispensed by Government take many forms, but they all share one characteristic. They are steadily taking the place of traditional forms of wealth. These valuables which derive from relationships to Government are of many kinds. They comprise social security benefits, cash grants for political sufferers and the whole scheme of State and local welfare. Then again, thousands of people are employed in the State and the Central Governments and local authorities. Licences are required before one can engage in many kinds of business or work. The power of giving licences means power to withhold them and this gives control to the Government or to the agents of

90. *State of Bihar v. Project Uchcha Vidya, Sikshak Sangh* (2006) 2 SCC 545.

91. AIR 1979 SC 1628 : (1979) 3 SCC 489.

Government on the lives of many people. Many individuals and many more businesses enjoy largess in the form of Government contracts. These contracts often resemble subsidies. It is virtually impossible to lose money on them and many enterprises are set up primarily to do business with Government. Government owns and controls hundreds of acres of public land valuable for mining and other purposes. These resources are available for utilisation by private corporations and individuals by way of lease or licence. All these mean growth in the Government largess and with the increasing magnitude and range of governmental functions as we move closer to a welfare State, more and more of our wealth consists of these new forms. Some of these forms of wealth may be in the nature of legal rights but the large majority of them are in the nature of privileges. But on that account, can it be said that they do not enjoy any legal protection? Can they be regarded as gratuity furnished by the State so that the State may withhold, grant or revoke it at its pleasure? Is the position of the Government in this respect the same as that of a private giver? We do not think so. The law has not been slow to recognise the importance of this new kind of wealth and the need to protect individual interest in it and with that end in view, it has developed new forms of protection. Some interests in Government largess, formerly regarded as privileges, have been recognised as rights while others have been given legal protection not only by forging procedural safeguards but also by confining/structuring and checking Government discretion in the matter of grant of such largess. The discretion of the Government has been held to be not unlimited in that the Government cannot give or withhold largess in its arbitrary discretion or at its sweet will. It is insisted, as pointed out by Prof. Reich in an especially stimulating article on "The New Property" in 73 Yale Law Journal 733, "that Government action be based on standards that are not arbitrary or unauthorised". "The Government cannot be permitted to say that it will give jobs or enter into contracts or issue quotas or licences only in favour of those having grey hair or belonging to a particular political party or professing a particular religious faith. The Government is still the Government when it acts in the matter of granting largess and it cannot act arbitrarily. It does not stand in the same position as a private individual.

In the grant of such largess the Government cannot act freely as an individual and select the recipients at its own free will. *Whatever its activity, the Government is still the Government and will be subject to restraints, inherent in its position in a democratic society. A democratic Government cannot lay down arbitrary and capricious standards for the choice of persons with whom alone it will deal.*[92] These principles are equally applicable for the various instrumentalities of the state as identified under Article 12 of the Constitution as well as the administrative agencies. Speaking on the same the Court observed–

92. *V. Punnan Thomas v. State of Kerala* AIR 1969 Ker 81.

[I]t is obvious that the Government which represents the executive authority of the State, may act through the instrumentality or agency of natural persons or it may employ the instrumentality or agency of juridical persons to carry out its functions. In the early days, when the Government had limited functions, it could operate effectively through natural persons constituting its civil service and they were found adequate to discharge governmental functions, which were of traditional vintage. But as the tasks of the Government multiplied with the advent of the welfare State, it began to be increasingly felt that the framework of civil service was not sufficient to handle the new tasks which were often of specialised and highly technical character. The inadequacy of the civil service to deal with these new problems came to be realised and it became necessary to force a new instrumentality or administrative device for handling these new problems. It was in these circumstances and with a view to supplying this administrative need that the public corporation came into being as the third arm of the Government. As early as 1819 the Supreme Court of the United States in *Mac Cullough v. Maryland* 4 Wheat 315 held that the Congress has power to charter corporations as incidental to or in aid of governmental functions and, as pointed out by Mathew, J., in *Sukhdev v. Bhagat Ram* (supra) such federal corporations would ex-hypothesi be agencies of the Government. In Great Britain too, the policy of public administration through separate corporations was gradually evolved and the conduct of basic industries through giant corporations has now become a permanent feature of public life. So far as India is concerned, the genesis of the emergence, of corporations as instrumentalities or agencies of Government is to be found in the Government of India Resolution on Industrial Policy dated 6th April, 1948 where it was stated inter alia that "management of State enterprises will as a rule be through the medium of public corporation under the statutory control of the Central Government who will assume such powers as may be necessary to ensure this". It was in pursuance of the policy envisaged in this and subsequent resolutions on Industrial Policy that corporations were created by Government for setting up and management of public enterprises and carrying out other public functions. Ordinarily these functions could have been carried out by Government departmentally through its service personnel, but the instrumentality or agency of the corporations was resorted to in these cases having regard to the nature of the task to be performed. The corporations acting as instrumentality or agency of Government would obviously be subject to the same limitations in the field of constitutional and administrative law as Government itself, though in the eye of the law, they would be distinct and independent legal entities. If Government acting through its officers is subject to certain constitutional and public law limitations, it must follow a fortiori that Government acting through the instrumentality or agency of corporations should equally be subject to the same limitations.

....

Now, obviously where a corporation is an instrumentality or agency of Government, it would, in the exercise of its power or discretion, be subject

> to the same constitutional or public law limitations as Government. The rule inhibiting arbitrary action by Government which we have discussed above must apply equally where such corporation is dealing with the public, whether by way of giving jobs or entering into contracts or otherwise, and it cannot act arbitrarily and enter into relationship with any person it likes at its sweet will, but its action must be in conformity with some principle which meets the test of reason and relevance.

In India the core principles of grant of largess has been developed by the judiciary from the principles and values of equality embodied in Article 14 of the Constitution.

> Article 14 strikes at arbitrariness in State action and ensures fairness and equality of treatment. It requires that State action must not be arbitrary but must be based on some rational and relevant principle which is non-discriminatory: it must not be guided by any extraneous or irrelevant considerations, because that would be denial of equality. The principle of reasonableness and rationality which is legally as well as philosophically an essential element of equality or non-arbitrariness is protected by Article 14 and it must characterise every State action, whether it be under authority of law or in exercise of executive power without making of law. The State cannot, therefore act arbitrarily in entering into relationship, contractual or otherwise with a third party, but its action must conform to some standard or norm which is rational and non-discriminatory.... The State has the right to trade. The State has there the duty to observe equality. An ordinary individual can choose not to deal with any person. The Government cannot choose to exclude persons by discrimination. The order of black-listing has the effect of depriving a person of equality of opportunity in the matter of public contract. A person who is on the approved list is unable to enter into advantageous relations with the Government because of the order of blacklisting.... A citizen has a right to claim equal treatment to enter into a contract which may be proper, necessary and essential to his lawful calling.... It is true that neither the petitioner nor the respondent has any right to enter into a contract but they are entitled to equal treatment with others who offer tender or quotations for the purchase of the goods". It must, therefore follow as a necessary corollary from the principle of equality enshrined in Article 14 that though the State is entitled to refuse to enter into relationship with any one, yet if it does so, it cannot arbitrarily choose any person it likes for entering into "such relationship and discriminate between persons similarly circumstanced, but it must act in conformity with some standard or principle which meets the test of reasonableness and non-discrimination and any departure from such standard or principle would be invalid unless it can be supported or justified on some rational and non-discriminatory ground.

In the *R.D. Shetty case* Supreme Court held that the International Airport Authority of India (Respondent no. 1) being a 'state' is bound to comply with the norms of equality and fairness. Negating the grant of contract to Respondent no. 2, the Court laid down the proposition that–

> [B]oth having regard to the constitutional mandate of Article 14 as also the judicially evolved rule of administrative law, the 1st respondent was not entitled to act arbitrarily in accepting the tender of the 4th respondents, but was bound to conform to the standard or norm laid down in paragraph 1 of the notice inviting tenders which required that only a person running a registered IInd Class hotel or restaurant and having at least 5 years' experience as such should be eligible to tender. It was not the contention of the appellant that this standard or norm prescribed by the 1st respondent was discriminatory having no just or reasonable relation to the object of inviting tenders namely, to award the contract to a sufficiently experienced person who would be able to run efficiently a IInd class restaurant at the airport. Admittedly the standard or norm was reasonable and non-discriminatory and once such a standard or norm for running a IInd Class restaurant should be awarded was laid down, the 1st respondent was not entitled to depart from it and to award the contract to the 4th respondents who did not satisfy the condition of eligibility prescribed by the standard or norm. If there was no acceptable tender from a person who satisfied the condition of eligibility, the 1st respondent could have rejected the tenders and invited fresh tenders on the basis of a less stringent standard or norm, but it could not depart from the standard or norm prescribed by it and arbitrarily accept the tender of the 4th respondents. When the 1st respondent entertained the tender of the 4th respondents even though they did not have 5 years' experience of running a IInd Class restaurant or hotel, denied equality of opportunity to others similarly situate in the matter of tendering for the contract. There might have been many other persons, in fact the appellant himself claimed to be one such person, who did not have 5 years' experience of running a IInd Class restaurant, but who were otherwise competent to run such a restaurant and they might also have competed with the 4th respondents for obtaining the contract, but they were precluded from doing so by the condition of eligibility requiring five years' experience. The action of the 1st respondent in accepting the tender of the 4th respondents, even though they did not satisfy the prescribed condition of eligibility, was clearly discriminatory, since it excluded other person similarly situate from tendering for the contract and it was plainly arbitrary and without reason The acceptance of the tender of the 4th respondents was, in the circumstances invalid as being violative of the equality clause of the Constitution as also of the rule of administrative law inhibiting arbitrary action.

This was reiterated in the case of *Sachidanand Pandey v. State of West Bengal*[93] wherein it was observed that–

> State-owned or public-owned property is not to be dealt with at the absolute discretion of the executive. Certain precepts and principles have to be observed.

93. (1987) 2 SCC 295.

Public interest is the paramount consideration. One of the methods of securing the public interest, when it is considered necessary to dispose of a property, is to sell the property by public auction or by inviting tenders. Though that is the ordinary rule, it is not an invariable rule. There may be situations where there are compelling reasons necessitating departure from the rule but then the reasons for the departure must be rational and should not be suggestive of discrimination. Appearance of public justice is as important as doing justice. Nothing should be done which gives an appearance of bias, jobbery or nepotism".

In *Akhil Bharatiya Upbhokta Congress v. State of M.P.*[94] while examining the legality of the allocation of 20 acres of land by the Government of Madhya Pradesh to an institute in the name of Kushabhau Thakre, Supreme Court observed–

What needs to be emphasised is that the State and / or its agencies / instrumentalities cannot give largesse to any person according to the sweet will and whims of the political entities and / or officers of the State. Every action / decision of the State and / or its agencies / instrumentalities to give largesse or confer benefit must be founded on a sound, transparent, discernible and well-defined policy, which shall be made known to the public by publication in the Official Gazette and other recognised modes of publicity and such policy must be implemented / executed by adopting a non-discriminatory and non-arbitrary method irrespective of the class or category of persons proposed to be benefited by the policy. The distribution of largesse like allotment of land, grant of quota, permit licence, etc. by the State and its agencies / instrumentalities should always be done in a fair and equitable manner and the element of favouritism or nepotism shall not influence the exercise of discretion, if any, conferred upon the particular functionary or officer of the State.

In some of the recent judgments relating to allocation of natural resources the doctrine of largess has been read with the public trust doctrine to ensure the applicability of norms of fairness and propriety in resource allocation. In the case of *Centre for Public Interest Litigation v. Union of India*[95] discussed the concept of natural resources and the necessary obligations arising from exploitation of such resources. It observed–

[E]ven though there is no universally accepted definition of natural resources, they are generally understood as elements having intrinsic utility to mankind. They may be renewable or non-renewable. They are thought of as the individual elements of the natural environment that provide economic and social services to human society and are considered valuable in their relatively unmodified,

94. (2011) 5 SCC 29.
95. AIR 2013 SC 3725 :(2012) 3 SCC 1.

natural, form. A natural resource's value rests in the amount of the material available and the demand for it. The latter is determined by its usefulness to production. Natural resources belong to the people but the State legally owns them on behalf of its people and from that point of view natural resources are considered as national assets, more so because the State benefits immensely from their value. The State is empowered to distribute natural resources. However, as they constitute public property / national asset, while distributing natural resources, the State is bound to act in consonance with the principles of equality and public trust and ensure that no action is taken which may be detrimental to public interest. Like any other State action, constitutionalism must be reflected at every stage of the distribution of natural resources. In Article 39(b) of the Constitution it has been provided that the ownership and control of the material resources of the community should be so distributed so as to best sub-serve the common good, but no comprehensive legislation has been enacted to generally define natural resources and a framework for their protection. of course, environment laws enacted by Parliament and State legislatures deal with specific natural resources, i.e., Forest, Air, Water, Costal Zones, etc.

The ownership regime relating to natural resources can also be ascertained from international conventions and customary international law, common law and national constitutions. In international law, it rests upon the concept of sovereignty and seeks to respect the principle of permanent sovereignty (of peoples and nations) over (their) natural resources as asserted in the 17th Session of the United Nations General Assemble and then affirmed as a customary international norm by the International Court of Justice in the case opposing the Democratic Republic of Congo to Uganda. Common Law recognizes States as having the authority to protect natural resources insofar as the resources are within the interests of the general public. The State is deemed to have a proprietary interest in natural resources and must act as guardian and trustee in relation to the same. Constitutions across the world focus on establishing natural resources as owned by, and for the benefit of, the country. In most instances where constitutions specifically address ownership of natural resources, the Sovereign State, or, as it is more commonly expressed, 'the people', is designated as the owner of the natural resource.

....

In India, the Courts have given an expansive interpretation to the concept of natural resources and have from time to time issued directions, by relying upon the provisions contained in Articles 38, 39, 48, 48A and 51A(g), for protection and proper allocation / distribution of natural resources and have repeatedly insisted on compliance of the constitutional principles in the process of distribution, transfer and alienation to private persons.

The doctrine of public trust initially originated in the case of *Illinois Central Railroad Company v. People of the State of Illinois*[1] which was made part of the Indian jurisprudence in the leading case of *M.C. Mehta v. Kamal Nath.*[2] In the subsequent case of *Jamshed Hormusji Wadia v. Board of Trustee, Port of Mumbai*[3] the Court held that *"the State's actions and the actions of its agencies/instrumentalities must be for the public good, achieving the objects for which they exist and should not be arbitrary or capricious. In the field of contracts, the State and its instrumentalities should design their activities in a manner which would ensure competition and not discrimination. They can augment their resources but the object should be to serve the public cause and to do public good by resorting to fair and reasonable methods".* The Indian judiciary has largely referred to the classic article of Professor Joseph L. Sax *The Public Trust Doctrine in Natural Resources Law: Effective Judicial Intervention* to formulate *a practical and philosophical premise and legal tool for protecting* public rights and for protecting and managing resources, ecological values or objects held in trust. In the case of *Formento Resorts and Hotels Limited v. Minguel Martins*[4] the Court made the observation–

> The public trust doctrine enjoins upon the Government to protect the resources for the enjoyment of the general public rather than to permit their use for private ownership or commercial purposes. This doctrine puts an implicit embargo on the right of the State to transfer public properties to private party if such transfer affects public interest, mandates affirmative State action for effective management of natural resources and empowers the citizens to question ineffective management thereof.
>
> The heart of the public trust doctrine is that it imposes limits and obligations upon government agencies and their administrators on behalf of all the people and especially future generations. For example, renewable and non-renewable resources, associated uses, ecological values or objects in which the public has a special interest (i.e. public lands, waters, etc.) are held subject to the duty of the State not to impair such resources, uses or values, even if private interests are involved. The same obligations apply to managers of forests, monuments, parks, the public domain and other public assets. Professor Joseph L. Sax in his classic article, "The Public Trust Doctrine in Natural Resources Law: Effective Judicial Intervention" (1970), indicates that the public trust doctrine, of all concepts known to law, constitutes the best practical and philosophical premise and legal tool for protecting public rights and for protecting and managing resources, ecological values or objects held in trust.

1. 146 U.S. 387 (1892).
2. (1997) 1 SCC 388.
3. (2002) 3 SCC 214.
4. (2009) 3 SCC 571.

> The public trust doctrine is a tool for exerting long-established public rights over short-term public rights and private gain. Today every person exercising his or her right to use the air, water, or land and associated natural ecosystems has the obligation to secure for the rest of us the right to live or otherwise use that same resource or property for the long-term and enjoyment by future generations. To say it another way, a landowner or lessee and a water right holder has an obligation to use such resources in a manner as not to impair or diminish the people's rights and the people's long-term interest in that property or resource, including down slope lands, waters and resources.

Similarly in the *2G Spectrum case*[5] Supreme Court speaking on the allocation of natural resources such as spectrum waves observed–

> As natural resources are public goods, the doctrine of equality, which emerges from the concepts of justice and fairness, must guide the State in determining the actual mechanism for distribution of natural resources. In this regard, the doctrine of equality has two aspects: first, it regulates the rights and obligations of the State vis-a-vis its people and demands that the people be granted equitable access to natural resources and/or its products and that they are adequately compensated for the transfer of the resource to the private domain; and second, it regulates the rights and obligations of the State vis-a-vis private parties seeking to acquire/use the resource and demands that the procedure adopted for distribution is just, non-arbitrary and transparent and that it does not discriminate between similarly placed private parties.
>
> ....
>
> State is the legal owner of the natural resources as a trustee of the people and although it is empowered to distribute the same, the process of distribution must be guided by the constitutional principles including the doctrine of equality and larger public good.

However in *Mahesh Chandra v. U.P. Financial Corpn.*[6] it was emphasized that in government actions a balance between accountability and autonomy should be struck so that efficiency in government functions are not affected. The Court laid down the test of reasonableness as an yardstick to strike the balance. It observed–

> Bureaucracy feels that accountability is an impediment to efficient discharge of the duty. Accountability is no more and no less than, the concept of accountability of a private concern to their shareholders. There is a distinction between prying into details of day-to-day administration and of the legitimate actions or resultant consequences thereof. To enthuse efficiency

5. *Centre for Public Interest Litigation v. Union of India* AIR 2013 SC 3725 : (2012) 3 SCC 1.
6. (1993) 2 SCC 279.

into administration, a balance between accountability and autonomy of action of management in public enterprises should be carefully maintained. Over-emphasis on either would impinge upon public efficiency. But undermining the accountability would give immunity or carte blanche power to deal with the public property or of the debtor at whim or vagary. Whether the public authority acted bona fide and in the best interest as prudent owner in the given facts would do, be gauged from impugned action and attending circumstances. The authority should justify the action assailed on the touchstone of justness, fairness, reasonableness and as a reasonable prudent owner.

6.9.5 Doctrine of Public Accountability

The doctrine of public accountability has been developed by the judiciary based on the concept of *public trust*. The theory is based on the proposition that the exercise of power by the administrative officers is for the ultimate benefit of the public at large and the officer's act as the trustee of the people for all the acts done by them in their official capacity. Traditionally the doctrine of public trust has been used to assert the ownership of the natural resources by a Sovereign State. Presently the doctrine has been largely used by the judiciary in their efforts to tackle corruption in public life. The doctrine was initially developed in the landmark case of *Attorney General of Hong Kong v. Reid*[7] wherein Lord Templeman used the concept of 'constructive trustee' to hold that the dishonest officer who accepts a bribe shall hold the bribe as a constructive trustee for the beneficiary. In this case Mr. Reid had joined the legal service of the Hong Kong Government as the King's Counsel. He was corrupt and often accepted bribes, subsequently he was convicted under the Prevention of Bribery Ordinance and sentenced to eight years' imprisonment along with fine of Laying down the proposition of 'constructive trustee' Lord Templeman had observed that "any benefit obtained by a fiduciary through a breach of duty belongs in equity to the beneficiary. It is held that a gift accepted by a person in a fiduciary position as an incentive for his breach of duty constituted a bribe and, although in law it belonged to the fiduciary, in equity he not only became a debtor for the amount of the bribe to the person to whom the duty was owed but he also held the bribe and any property acquired therewith on constructive trust for that person. It is held further that if the value of the property representing the bribe depreciated the fiduciary had to pay to the injured person the difference between that value and the initial amount of the bribe, and if the property increased in value the fiduciary was not entitled to retain the excess since equity would not allow him to make any profit

7. (1993) 3 WLR 1143.

from his breach of duty".[8] Recognizing that taking of bribe by a public official is a violation of the public trust reposed on him, the Privy Council categorically observed–

> A bribe is a gift accepted by a fiduciary as an inducement to him to betray his trust. A secret benefit, which may or may not constitute a bribe is a benefit which the fiduciary derives from trust property or obtains from knowledge which he acquires in the course of acting as a fiduciary.... Bribery is an evil practice which threatens the foundations of any civilised society.... Where bribes are accepted by a trustee, servant, agent or other fiduciary, loss and damage are caused to the beneficiaries, master of principal whose interests have been betrayed.... When a bribe is offered and accepted in money or in kind, the money or property constituting the bribe belongs in law to the recipient. Money paid to the false fiduciary belongs to him. The legal estate in freehold property conveyed to the false fiduciary by way or bribe vests in him. Equity however which acts in personam insists that it is unconscionable for a fiduciary to obtain and retain a benefit in breach of duty. The provider of a bribe cannot recover it because he committed a criminal offence when he paid the bribe. The false fiduciary who received the bribe in breach of duty must pay and account for the bribe to the person to whom that duty was owed. In the present case, as soon as Mr. Reid received a bribe in breach of the duties he owed to the Government of Hong Kong, he became a debtor in equity to the Crown for the amount of that bribe.... As soon as the bribe was received, whether in cash or in kind, the false fiduciary held the bribe on a constructive trust for the person injured.... If the property representing the bribe exceeds the original bribe in value, the fiduciary cannot retain the benefit of the increase in value which he obtained solely as a result of his breach of duty.... When a bribe is accepted by a fiduciary in breach of his duty then he holds that bribe in trust for the person to whom the duty was owed. If the property representing the bribe decreases in value the fiduciary must pay the difference between that value and the initial amount of the bribe because he should not have accepted the bribe or incurred the risk of loss. If the property increases in value, the fiduciary is not entitled to any surplus in excess of the initial value of the bribe because he is not allowed by any means to make a profit out of a breach of duty.

The Supreme Court had applied the same doctrine against private bodies in the case of *Delhi Development Authority v. Skipper Construction Company*[9] and made strong arguments for enacting *a law providing for forfeiture of properties acquired by holders of 'public office" (including the offices/posts in the public sector corporations) by indulging in corrupt and illegal acts and deals, is a crying necessity in the present state of our society.... Such a law has become an absolute necessity, if the*

8. As quoted in AIR 1996 SC 2005.
9. AIR 1996 SC 2005.

canker of corruption is not to prove the death knell of this nation. For the purpose of doing justice the Court applied the principles of public trust doctrine under Article 142 of the Constitution and held that- *The fiduciary relationship may not exist in the present case nor is it a case of a holder of public office, yet if it is found that someone has acquired properties by defrauding the people and if it is found that the persons defrauded should be restored to the position in which they would have been but for the said fraud, the court can make all necessary orders. This is what equity means and in India the courts are not only courts of law but also courts of equity.* In this case the Court held that along with the directors of Skipper Constructions some of the top officials of the DDA were equally liable for defrauding the public.

In the case of *Union of India v. Sushil Kumar Modi*[10] (Bihar Fodder Scam case) the Supreme Court emphasizing the role and purpose of judicial intervention in matters of corruption by public functionaries observed–

> It has to be borne in mind that the purpose of these proceedings is essentially to ensure performance of the statutory duty by the CBI and the other government agencies in accordance with law for the proper implementation of the rule of law. To achieve this object a fair, honest and expeditious investigation into every reasonable accusation against each and every person reasonably suspected of involvement in the alleged offences has to be made strictly in accordance with law. The duty of the Court in such proceedings is, therefore, to ensure that the CBI and other government agencies do their duty and do so strictly in conformity with law. In these proceedings, the Court is not required to go into the merits of the accusation or even to express any opinion thereon, which is a matter for consideration by the competent court in which the charge-sheet is filed and the accused have to face trial. It is, therefore, necessary that not even an observation relating to the merits of the accusation is made by the Court in these proceedings lest in prejudice the accused at the trial. The nature of these proceedings may be described as that of "continuing mandamus" to require performance of its duty by the CBI and the other government agencies concerned. The agencies concerned must bear in mind and, if needed, be reminded of the caution administered by Lord Denning in this behalf in R. *v.* Metropolitan Police Commr., [1968] 1 All ER 763/(1968) 2 QB 118. Indicating the duty of the Commissioner of Police, Lord Denning stated thus: (All ER p. 769)

> "I have no hesitation, however in holding that, like every constable in the land, he should be, and is, independent of the executive. He is not subject to the orders of the Secretary of State,... I hold it to be the duly of the Commissioner of Police, as it is of every chief constable, to enforce the law of

10. MANU/SC/1167/1997.

> the land. He must take steps so to post his men that crimes may be detected; and that honest citizens may go about their affairs in peace. He must decide whether or not suspected persons are to be prosecuted; and if need be, bring the prosecution or see that it is brought; but in all these things he is not the servant of anyone, save of the law itself. No Minister of the Crown can tell him that he must, or must not, keep observation on this place or that; or that he must, or must not prosecute this man or that one. Nor can any police authority tell him so. The responsibility for law enforcement lies on him. He is answerable to the law and to the law alone".

The case of *Vineet Narain v. Union of India*[11] has been a watershed in the development of the public accountability doctrine in India. Following the decision in the *Sushil Kumar Modi case* the Supreme Court exercising its power of judicial review under Article 32 highlighted the functional importance of the Central Bureau of Investigation (CBI) and emphasized the need of probity in public life. In this case the Court looked into the issue of insulating the CBI and other investigating agencies from other extraneous influences and to develop a procedure within the discipline of law for the conduct of fair and unbiased inquiry. Failure of the CBI to investigate the details of the two diaries of the Jain brothers in the *Havala* scam compelled the judiciary to devise legal measures based on the rule of law principles to ensure fair and impartial conduct of investigation by these agencies. The Court in this case took up the responsibility to monitor the investigations so that the independence of the investigating agencies were maintained without compromising with the rights of the accused to a full and fair trail. It was deemed necessary to direct the CBI not to submit their progress reports to the superior political executive but to submit them to a monitoring court-*the task of the monitoring court would end the moment a charge-sheet was filed in respect of a particular investigation and that the ordinary processes of the law would then take over.* The innovative judicial procedure has been described as 'continuing mandamus'. Such order was issued because the Supreme Court realized that *merely issuance of a mandamus directing the agencies to perform their task would be futile and, therefore, it was decided to issue directions from time to time and keep the matter pending requiring the agencies to report the progress of investigation so that monitoring by the court could ensure continuance of the investigation.* In this case the Court also recommended for bringing structural changes in the functioning of the CBI so as to make them foremost independent investigating agency of the country.

11. AIR 1998 SC 889 : (1998) 1 SCC 226.

In the *2G Spectrum case*[12] the Supreme Court while dealing with the issue of allocation of 2G spectrum licenses highlighted the need to fight for clean governance and promote accountability of the constitutional institutions. *In re Natural Resources Allocation*[13] the Constitution Bench held that *"Common good" is the sole guiding factor under Article 39(b) for distribution of natural resources. It is the touchstone of testing whether any policy subserves the "common good" and if it does, irrespective of the means adopted, it is clearly in accordance with the principle enshrined in Article 39(b).* The same principle was reiterated in the case of *Manhor Lal Sharma v. The Principal Secretary.*[14]

SUMMATION

Exercise of discretionary power in accordance with the constitutional norms and provisions of the statute holds the key to efficient working of the administration. The various principles relating to judicial review of administrative actions have been developed with the sole objective of creating an administration governed by the goals of accountability, good governance and citizen-centric administration.

12. Centre for Public Interest Litigation *v.* Union of India AIR 2013 SC 3725; (2012) 3 SCC 1.
13. (2012) 10 SCC 1.
14. 2014 (9) SCALE 693.

VII Tribunalization in India

LEARNING OBJECTIVES

After reading this chapter, you will be familiar with:

- Nature, scope and meaning of Tribunals
- Difference between courts and Tribunals
- Justification for Constitution of Tribunals
- 42nd Constitutional Amendment: Articles 323A and 323B
- Constitutionality of Tribunals
- Objective behind enactment of the Administrative Tribunals Act, 1985
- Judicial Opinions post *L. Chandra Kumar case*-from *R. Gandhi* to *Madras Bar Association*

7.1 INTRODUCTION

The term tribunal broadly refers to a judgment seat; a court of justice; board or committee appointed to adjudicate on claims of a particular kind. It is generally acknowledged that *all tribunals are not courts, though all courts are Tribunals.* Tribunal refers to an adjudicating body, which may include a court or body which has been vested with judicial functions and powers, and allows it to adjudicate on matters that affects the rights of the citizens. However in the ordinary context tribunals are distinguished from courts and primarily refer to the adjudicating bodies other than the ordinary courts of law. In performance of their judicial functions the tribunals are not required to strictly comply with procedural rules but are bound by the principles of natural justice.

7.2 DIFFERENCE BETWEEN COURTS AND TRIBUNALS

Courts are adjudicating bodies which have been established by the state for administration of justice. The term 'administration of justice' implies 'exercise of juridical power of the state to maintain and uphold rights and to punish wrongs'. When a legal right of an individual is violated or infringed, then the aggrieved party can approach the courts for redressal of their grievance. It is the responsibility of the courts to restore the *vinculum juris* in case of any infringement or violation of any right or causing of injury.[1] The courts are recognised as instrumentalities of the States and are conferred with the judicial powers of the state. The powers of the judiciary are derived from the Constitution or from any other Act of Legislature constituting those authorities. Some of the essential characteristic feature of courts are – they are permanent bodies whose numbers are fixed and can try any suit or other causes within their jurisdiction.

On the other hand tribunals are administrative bodies and are a consequence of the multifarious activities of the state. In *Associated Cement Companies Ltd. v. P.N. Sharma*[2] the functional role of the tribunals were explained as–

> In every State there are administrative bodies or authorities which are required to deal with matters within their jurisdiction in an administrative manner and their decisions are described as administrative decisions. In reaching their administrative decisions, administrative bodies can and often do take into consideration questions of policy. It is not unlikely that even in this process of reaching administrative decisions, the administrative bodies or authorities are required to act fairly and objectively and would in many cases have to follow the principles of natural justice; but the authority to reach decisions conferred on such administrative bodies is clearly distinct and separate from the judicial power conferred on courts, and the decisions pronounced by administrative bodies are similarly distinct and separate in character from judicial decisions pronounced by courts.

The Indian Constitution has recognized both courts and tribunals as separate entities. In Articles 136 and 227 it refers to courts and tribunals separately. The Constitution refers to the Courts of Civil Judicature as Courts and Tribunals refer to the 'bodies of men who are appointed to decide controversies arising under certain special laws'. Thus Tribunals deal with certain special matters whereas all other matters generally go before the ordinary courts. The corollary of this proposition is that *the courts perform all the judicial functions of the State except those that are excluded by all from their jurisdiction.*

Some of the important cases wherein the difference between court and tribunal were discussed are–

1. *Harinagar Sugar Mills Ltd. v. Shyam Sundar Jhunjhunwala* (1962) 2 SCR 339.
2. AIR 1965 SC 1595 : (1965) 2 SCR 366.

In *Harinagar Sugar Mills Ltd. v. Shyam Sundar Jhunjhunwala*,[3] Hidayatullah, J. had elaborately explained the difference between the courts and the tribunals as–

> All tribunals are not courts, though all courts are tribunals. The word 'courts' is used to designate those tribunals which are set up in an organised State for the administration of justice. By administration of justice is meant the exercise of judicial power of the State to maintain and uphold rights and to punish 'wrongs'. Whenever there is an infringement of a right or an injury, the courts are there to restore the *vinculum juris*, which is disturbed.
>
> ...
>
> When rights are infringed or invaded, the aggrieved party can go and commence a querela before the ordinary civil courts. These courts which are instrumentalities of Government, are invested with the judicial power of the State, and their authority is derived from the Constitution or some Act of legislature constituting them. Their number is ordinarily fixed and they are ordinarily permanent, and can try any suit or cause within their jurisdiction. Their numbers may be increased or decreased, but they are almost always permanent and go under the compendious name of 'courts of civil judicature'. There can thus be no doubt that the Central Government does not come within this class.
>
> With the growth of civilisation and the problems of modern life, a large number of administrative tribunals have come into existence. These tribunals have the authority of law to pronounce upon valuable rights; they act in a judicial manner and even on evidence on oath, but they are not part of the ordinary courts of Civil Judicature. They share the exercise of the judicial power of the State, but they are brought into existence to implement some administrative policy or to determine controversies arising out of some administrative law. They are very similar to courts, but are not courts. When the Constitution speaks of 'courts' in Articles 136, 227 or 228 or in Articles 233 to 237 or in the Lists, it contemplates courts of civil judicature but not tribunals other than such courts. This is the reason for using both the expressions in Articles 136 and 227.
>
> By 'courts' is meant courts of civil judicature and by 'tribunals', those bodies of men who are appointed to decide controversies arising under certain special laws. Among the powers of the State is included the power to decide such controversies. This is undoubtedly one of the attributes of the State, and is aptly called the judicial power of the State. In the exercise of this power, a clear division is thus noticeable. *Broadly speaking, certain special matters go before tribunals, and the residue goes before the ordinary courts of civil judicature. Their procedures may differ, but the functions are not essentially different.* What distinguishes them has never been successfully established...
>
> In my opinion, a court in the strict sense is a tribunal which is a part of the ordinary hierarchy of courts of civil judicature maintained by the State

3. AIR 1961 SC 1669: (1962) 2 SCR 339.

under its constitution to exercise the judicial power of the State. *These courts perform all the judicial functions of the State except those that are excluded by law from their jurisdiction.* The word 'judicial', be it noted, is itself capable of two meanings. They were admirably stated by Lopes, L.J. in *Royal Aquarium and Summer and Winter Garden Society Ltd. v. Parkinson* [(1892) 1 QB 431 (CA)], in these words: (QB p. 452)

'... The word "judicial" has two meanings. It may refer to the discharge of duties exercisable by a Judge or by Justices in court, or to administrative duties which need not be performed in court, but in respect of which it is necessary to bring to bear a judicial mind—that is, a mind to determine what is fair and just in respect of the matters under consideration'.

That an officer is required to decide matters before him 'judicially' in the second sense does not make him a court or even a tribunal, because that only establishes that he is following a standard of conduct, and is free from bias or interest.

Courts and tribunals act 'judicially' in both senses, and in the term 'court' are included the ordinary and permanent tribunals and in the term 'tribunal' are included all others, which are not so included.

In *Union of India v. R. Gandhi*[4] the Supreme Court highlighted the difference between Courts and Tribunals as–

The term 'Courts' refers to places where justice is administered or refers to Judges who exercise judicial functions. Courts are established by the state for administration of justice that is for exercise of the judicial power of the state to maintain and uphold the rights, to punish wrongs and to adjudicate upon disputes. Tribunals on the other hand are special alternative institutional mechanisms, usually brought into existence by or under a statute to decide disputes arising with reference to that particular statute, or to determine controversies arising out of any administrative law. Courts refer to Civil Courts, Criminal Courts and High Courts. Tribunals can be either private Tribunals (Arbitral Tribunals), or Tribunals constituted under the Constitution (Speaker or the Chairman acting under Para 6(1) of the Tenth Schedule) or Tribunals authorized by the Constitution (Administrative Tribunals under Article 323A and Tribunals for other matters under Article 323B or Statutory Tribunals which are created under a statute (Motor Accident Claims Tribunal, Debt Recovery Tribunals and consumer fora). Some Tribunals are manned exclusively by Judicial Officers (Rent Tribunals, Motor Accidents Claims Tribunal, Labour Courts and Industrial Tribunals). Other statutory Tribunals have Judicial and Technical Members (Administrative Tribunals, TDSAT, Competition Appellate Tribunal, Consumer fora, Cyber Appellate Tribunal, etc).

The Court further laid down the essential points of difference as–

4. (2010) 11 SCC 1.

(*i*) Courts are established by the State and are entrusted with the State's inherent judicial power for administration of justice in general. Tribunals are established under a statute to adjudicate upon disputes arising under the said statute, or disputes of a specified nature. Therefore, all courts are tribunals. But all tribunals are not courts.

(*ii*) Courts are exclusively manned by Judges. Tribunals can have a Judge as the sole member, or can have a combination of a judicial member and a technical member who is an "expert" in the field to which the tribunal relates. Some highly specialised fact-finding tribunals may have only technical members, but they are rare and are exceptions.

(*iii*) While courts are governed by detailed statutory procedural rules, in particular the Code of Civil Procedure and the Evidence Act, requiring an elaborate procedure in decision making, tribunals generally regulate their own procedure applying the provisions of the Code of Civil Procedure only where it is required, and without being restricted by the strict rules of the Evidence Act.

7.3 JUSTIFICATION FOR CONSTITUTION OF TRIBUNALS

Tribunalization in India had structurally emerged about twenty years ago. The 42nd Amendment to the Constitution introduced Part XIV-A which included Articles 323-A and 323-B providing for constitution of tribunals dealing with administrative service issues and other matters. Some of the justifications for constitution of tribunals as separate body of adjudication other than ordinary courts have been described as–

(i) Elaborate procedural rules and highly technical evidence laws brings rigidity and formalism in the judicial process.

(ii) The extended rules relating to appeals, revisions and reviews as well as other rules of fair procedures causes major delay in the disposal of cases.

(iii) Litigation is prolonged process involving many years for the final disposal of the case.

(iv) Huge pendency forces the judges to expeditiously deal with complicated issues to the dissatisfaction of the parties.

(v) Tribunals on the other hand are free from the shackles of procedural laws and evidence law, and can provide quick, easy and speedy justice in a "cost affordable" and "user friendly" manner.

(vi) Tribunals generally consist of a judicial member and a technical member. *The judicial member will act as a bulwark against apprehensions of bias and will ensure compliance with the basic principles of natural justice such as fair hearing and reasoned orders. The judicial member would also ensure impartiality, fairness and reasonableness in consideration. The presence of a technical member ensures*

> *the availability of expertise and experience related to the field of adjudication for which the special Tribunal is created, thereby improving the quality of adjudication and decision making.*[5]

In De Smith's *Judicial Review* the advantages of tribunals in comparison to an ordinary courts have been stated as–

> In the design of an administrative justice system, a tribunal may be preferred to an ordinary court because its members have specialised knowledge of the subject-matter, because it will be more informal in its trappings and procedure, because it may be better at finding facts, applying flexible standards and exercising discretionary powers, and because it may be cheaper, more accessible and more expeditious than the High Court. Many of the decisions given to tribunals concern the merits of cases with relatively little legal content, and in such cases a tribunal, usually consisting of a legally qualified tribunal Judge and two lay members, may be preferred to a court. Indeed dissatisfaction with the overtechnical and allegedly unsympathetic approach of the courts towards social welfare legislation led to a transfer of functions to special tribunals; the Workmen's Compensation Acts were administered by the ordinary courts, but the National Insurance (Industrial Injuries) scheme was applied by tribunals. It is, however, unrealistic to imagine that technicalities and difficult legal issues can somehow be avoided by entrusting the administration of complex legislation to tribunals rather than the courts.[6]

7.4 42ND CONSTITUTIONAL AMENDMENT: ARTICLES 323A AND 323B

Part XIV-A

Tribunals

323-A. *Administrative tribunals.*—(1) Parliament may, by law, provide for the adjudication or trial by administrative tribunals of disputes and complaints with respect to recruitment and conditions of service of persons appointed to public services and posts in connection with the affairs of the Union or of any State or of any local or other authority within the territory of India or under the control of the Government of India or of any corporation owned or controlled by the Government.

323-B. *Tribunals for other matters.*—(1) The appropriate Legislature may, by law, provide for the adjudication or trial by tribunals of any disputes, complaints, or offences with respect to all or any of the matters specified in clause (2) with respect to which such Legislature has power to make laws.

5. *Union of India v. R. Gandhi* (2010) 11 SCC 1, para 59.
6. De Smith's Judicial Review, Sweet & Maxwell, 6th Ed. 2007.

(2) A law made under clause (1) may—	(2) The matters referred to in clause (1) are the following, namely—
(*a*) provide for the establishment of an administrative tribunal for the Union and a separate administrative tribunal for each State or for two or more States;	(*a*) levy, assessment, collection and enforcement of any tax;
(*b*) specify the jurisdiction, powers (including the power to punish for contempt) and authority which may be exercised by each of the said tribunals;	(*b*) foreign exchange, import and export across customs frontiers;
(*c*) provide for the procedure (including provisions as to limitation and rules of evidence) to be followed by the said tribunals;	(*c*) industrial and labour disputes;
(*d*) *exclude the jurisdiction of all courts, except the jurisdiction of the Supreme Court under Article 136, with respect to the disputes or complaints referred to in clause (1)*;	(*d*) land reforms by way of acquisition by the State of any estate as defined in Article 31-A or of any rights therein or the extinguishment or modification of any such rights or by way of ceiling on agricultural land or in any other way;
(*e*) provide for the transfer to each such administrative tribunal of any cases pending before any court or other authority immediately before the establishment of such tribunal as would have been within the jurisdiction of such tribunal if the causes of action on which such suits or proceedings are based had arisen after such establishment;	(*e*) ceiling on urban property;

(*f*) repeal or amend any order made by the President under clause (3) of Article 371-D;	(*f*) elections to either House of Parliament or the House or either House of the Legislature of a State, but excluding the matters referred to in Article 329 and Article 329-A;
(*g*) contain such supplemental, incidental and consequential provisions (including provisions as to fees) as Parliament may deem necessary for the effective functioning of, and for the speedy disposal of cases by, and the enforcement of the orders of, such tribunals.	(*g*) production, procurement, supply and distribution of foodstuffs (including edible oilseeds and oils) and such other goods as the President may, by public notification, declare to be essential goods for the purpose of this article and control of prices of such goods;
	(*h*) offences against laws with respect to any of the matters specified in sub-clauses (*a*) to (*g*) and fees in respect of any of those matters;
	(*i*) any matter incidental to any of the matters specified in sub-clauses (*a*) to (*h*).
(3) The provisions of this article shall have effect notwithstanding anything in any other provision of this Constitution or in any other law for the time being in force.	(3) A law made under clause (1) may—
	(*a*) provide for the establish-ment of a hierarchy of tribunals;
	(*b*) specify the jurisdiction, powers (including the power to punish for contempt) and authority which may be exercised by each of the said tribunals;
	(*c*) provide for the procedure (including provisions as to limitation and rules of evidence) to be followed by the said tribunals;

(*c*) *exclude the jurisdiction of all courts except the jurisdiction of the Supreme Court under Article 136 with respect to all or any of the matters falling within the jurisdiction of the said tribunals;*

(*d*) provide for the transfer to each such tribunal of any cases pending before any court or any other authority immediately before the establishment of such tribunal as would have been within the jurisdiction of such tribunal if the causes of action on which such suits or proceedings are based had arisen after such establishment;

(*f*) contain such supplemental, incidental and consequential provisions (including provisions as to fees) as the appropriate Legislature may deem necessary for the effective functioning of, and for the speedy disposal of cases by, and the enforcement of the orders of, such tribunals.

(4) The provisions of this article shall have effect notwithstanding anything in any other provision of this Constitution or in any other law for the time being in force.

Explanation.—In this article, "appropriate Legislature", in relation to any matter, means Parliament or, as the case may be, a State Legislature competent to make laws with respect to such matter in accordance with the provisions of Part XI.

Articles 323-A and 323-B were introduced in the Constitution as Part XIV A by the Constitution (42nd Amendment) Act, 1976. Tribunals as adjudicating bodies had been recognized in the Constitution under Articles 136 and 227. The introduction of Articles 323-A and 323-B was done with the primary objective of excluding the jurisdiction of the High Courts under Articles 226 and 227, except the jurisdiction of the Supreme Court under Article 136 and for creating an effective alternative institutional mechanism or authority for judicial review.[7] The purpose for establishing tribunals to the exclusion of the jurisdiction of the High Courts was done to reduce the pendency and lower the burden of case load. Speaking on the objective behind enacting Articles 323-A and 323-B, the Supreme Court in the case of *S. P. Sampath Kumar v. Union of India*[8] observed–

> In these thirty-six years following the enforcement of the Constitution, not only has India's population been more than doubled but also the number of litigations before the courts including the High Courts has greatly increased. As the pendency in the High Courts increased and soon became the pressing problem of backlog, the nation's attention came to be bestowed on this aspect. Ways and means to relieve the High Courts of the load began to engage the attention of the government at the Centre as also in the various States. As early as 1969, a Committee was set up by the Central Government under the chairmanship of Mr Justice Shah of this Court to make recommendations suggesting ways and means for effective, expeditious and satisfactory disposal of matters relating to service disputes of government servants as it was found that a sizeable portion of pending litigations related to this category. The Committee recommended the setting up of an independent Tribunal to handle the pending cases before this Court and the High Courts. While this report was still engaging the attention of government, the Administrative Reforms Commission also took note of the situation and recommended the setting up of Civil Services Tribunals to deal with appeals of Government servants against disciplinary action. In certain States, Tribunals of this type came into existence and started functioning. But the Central Government looked into the matter further as it transpired that the major chunk of service

7. ***See*** generally (2014) 10 SCC 1, para 44.
8. (1987) 1 SCC 124 : AIR 1987 SC 386.

litigations related to matters other than disciplinary action. In May 1976, a Conference of Chief Secretaries of the States discussed this problem. Then came the Forty-second Amendment of the Constitution bringing in Article 323-A which authorised Parliament to provide by law "for the adjudication or trial by Administrative Tribunals of disputes and complaints with respect to recruitment and conditions of service of persons appointed to public services and posts in connection with the affairs of the Union or of any State or of any local or other authority within the territory of India or under the control of the Government of India or of any Corporation owned or controlled by the Government". As already stated this article envisaged exclusion of the jurisdiction of all courts, except the jurisdiction of the Supreme Court under Article 136, with respect to the disputes or complaints referred to in clause (1). Though the Constitution now contained the enabling power, no immediate steps were taken to set up any Tribunal as contemplated by Article 323-A. A Constitution Bench of this Court in *K.K. Dutta v. Union of India* [(1980) 4 SCC 38 : 1980 SCC (L&S) 485 : AIR 1980 SC 2056 : (1980) 3 SCR 811] observed: [SCC p. 39, para 1 : SCC (L & S) p. 486].

7.5 CONSTITUTIONALITY OF TRIBUNALS

The Supreme Court has in series of judicial decisions has upheld the legislative competence of the Parliament and the State Legislatures to vest judicial powers in a tribunal in exclusion of an ordinary court.

S. P. Sampath Kumar v. Union of India[9] was the first case wherein the constitutionality validity of Article 323A as introduced by the Constitution (42nd Amendment) Act, 1976 was challenged on the ground of whether the exclusion of the jurisdiction of the High Court under Articles 226 and 227 of the Constitution in service matters specified in Section 28 of the Administrative Tribunals Act, 1985 and the vesting of exclusive jurisdiction in such service matters in the Administrative Tribunal, subject to an exception in favour of the jurisdiction of the Supreme Court under Articles 32 and 136, is unconstitutional and void. Upholding the power of the Parliament to alternative authorities without compromising with the power of judicial review of the Supreme Court, Justice Bhagwati observed–

> [J]udicial review is a basic and essential feature of the Constitution and it cannot be abrogated without affecting the basic structure of the Constitution and it is equally clear from the same decision that though judicial review cannot be altogether abrogated by Parliament by amending the Constitution in exercise of its constituent power, Parliament can certainly, without in any way violating the basic structure doctrine, set up effective alternative institutional mechanisms or arrangements for judicial review. The basic and essential feature of judicial review cannot be dispensed with but it would

9. (1987) 1 SCC 124 : AIR 1987 SC 386.

be within the competence of Parliament to amend the Constitution so as to substitute in place of the High Court, another alternative institutional mechanism or arrangement for judicial review, provided it is no less efficacious than the High Court. Then, instead of the High Court, it would be another institutional mechanism or authority which would be exercising the power of judicial review with a view to enforcing the constitutional limitations and maintaining the rule of law. Therefore, if any constitutional amendment made by Parliament takes away from the High Court the power of judicial review in any particular area and vests it in any other institutional mechanism or authority, it would not be violative of the basic structure doctrine, so long as the essential condition is fulfilled, namely, that the alternative institutional mechanism or authority set up by the parliamentary amendment is no less effective than the High Court.

...... If this constitutional amendment were to permit a law made under clause (1) of Article 323-A to exclude the jurisdiction of the High Court under Articles 226 and 227 without setting up an effective alternative institutional mechanism or arrangement for judicial review, it would be violative of the basic structure doctrine and hence outside the constituent power of Parliament. It must, therefore, be read as implicit in this constitutional amendment that the law excluding the jurisdiction of the High Court under Articles 226 and 227 permissible under it must not leave a void but it must set up another *effective* institutional mechanism or authority and vest the power of judicial review in it. Consequently, the impugned Act excluding the jurisdiction of the High Court under Articles 226 and 227 in respect of service matters and vesting such jurisdiction in the Administrative Tribunal can pass the test of constitutionality as being within the ambit and coverage of clause (2)(*d*) of Article 323-A, only if it can be shown that the Administrative Tribunal set up under the impugned Act is equally efficacious as the High Court, so far as the power of judicial review over service matters is concerned.

Speaking on the same Justice Ranganatha Mishra observed–

[E]xclusion of the jurisdiction of the High Court does not totally bar judicial review. This Court in *Minerva Mills case*[10] did point out that "effective alternative institutional mechanisms or arrangements for judicial review" can be made by Parliament. Thus it is possible to set up an alternative institution in place of the High Court for providing judicial review. The debates and deliberations spread over almost two decades for exploring ways and means for relieving the High Courts of the load of backlog of cases and for assuring quick settlement of service disputes in the interest of the public servants as also the country cannot be lost sight of while considering this aspect. It has not been disputed before us — and perhaps could not have been — that the Tribunal under the scheme of the Act would take over a part of the existing backlog and a share of the normal load of the High Courts. The Tribunal has been contemplated as a substitute and not as supplemental to the High Court in the

10. (1980) 4 SCC 38.

scheme of administration of justice. To provide the Tribunal as an additional forum from where parties could go to the High Court would certainly have been a retrograde step considering the situation and circumstances to meet which the innovation has been brought about. Thus barring of the jurisdiction of the High Court can indeed not be a valid ground of attack.

7.6 OBJECTIVE BEHIND ENACTMENT OF THE ADMINISTRATIVE TRIBUNALS ACT, 1985

After the inclusion of the constitutional provisions relating to tribunals, it took another ten years for the enactment of the Administrative Tribunals Act, 1985. Highlighting the need of a service tribunal the Supreme Court in *K.K. Dutta v. Union of India*[11] had observed that–

> There are few other litigative areas than disputes between members of various services inter se, where the principle that public policy requires that all litigation must have an end can apply with greater force. Public servants ought not to be driven or required to dissipate their time and energy in courtroom battles. Thereby their attention is diverted from public to private affairs and their inter se disputes affect their sense of oneness without which no institution can function effectively. The constitution of Service Tribunals by State Governments with an apex Tribunal at the Centre, which, in the generality of cases, should be the final arbiter of controversies relating to conditions of service, including the vexed question of seniority, may save the courts from the avalanche of writ petitions and appeals in service matters. The proceedings of such Tribunals can have the merit of informality and if they will not be tied down to strict rules of evidence, they might be able to produce solutions which will satisfy many...."

Ultimately in January 1985 the Parliament enacted the law relating to service tribunals which came into effect on November 1, 1985. The Statement of Objects and Reasons of the Act specifying the purpose behind the enactment was that a large number of cases relating to service matters were pending before various courts and it was expected that "the setting up of such Administrative Tribunals to deal exclusively with service matters would go a long way in not only reducing the burden of the various courts and thereby giving them more time to deal with other cases expeditiously but would also provide to the persons covered by the Administrative Tribunals speedy relief in respect of their grievances".

Immediately after coming into effect the constitutionality of various provisions relating to the composition of tribunals and mode of appointment

11. AIR 1980 SC 2056.

of the Chairperson and other members were challenged before the Supreme Court in the *Sampath Kumar case.*[12]

(i) Effective as the High Court

One of the important issues deliberated by the Court was whether the Tribunals could effectively substitute the role and functioning of the High Court. The functioning of the Administrative Tribunal should be such *as to inspire confidence in the public mind that it is a highly competent and expert mechanism with judicial approach and objectivity.* Speaking on the same issue Justice Ranganatha Mishra stated–

> What, however, has to be kept in view is that the Tribunal should be a real substitute for the High Court — not only in form and *de jure* but in content and de facto. As was pointed out in *Minerva Mills*[13] the alternative arrangement has to be effective and efficient as also capable of upholding the constitutional limitations. Article 16 of the Constitution guarantees equality of opportunity in matters of public employment. Article 15 bars discrimination on grounds of religion, race, caste, sex or place of birth. The touchstone of equality enshrined in Article 14 is the greatest of guarantees for the citizen. Centring around these articles in the Constitution a service jurisprudence has already grown in this country. Under Sections 14 and 15 of the Act all the powers of the courts except those of this Court in regard to matters specified therein vest in the Tribunal — either Central or State. Thus the Tribunal is the substitute of the High Court and is entitled to exercise the powers thereof.
>
> The High Courts have been functioning over a century and a quarter and until the Federal Court was established under the Government of India Act, 1935, used to be the highest courts within their respective jurisdictions subject to an appeal to the Privy Council in a limited category of cases. In this long period of about six scores of years, the High Courts have played their role effectively, efficiently as also satisfactorily. The litigant in this country has seasoned himself to look up to the High Court as the unfailing protector of his person, property and honour. The institution has served its purpose very well and the common man has thus come to repose great confidence therein. Disciplined, independent and trained Judges well versed in law and working with all openness in an unattached and objective manner have ensured dispensation of justice over the years. Aggrieved people approach the court — the social mechanism to act as the arbiter — not under legal obligation but under the belief and faith that justice shall be done to them and the State's authorities would implement the decision of the court. It is, therefore, of paramount importance that the substitute institution — the Tribunal — must be a worthy successor of the High Court in all respects. That is exactly what

12. (1987) 1 SCC 124 : AIR 1987 SC 386.
13. (1980) 3 SCC 625.

this Court intended to convey when it spoke of an alternative mechanism in *Minerva Mills case.*

(ii) Need of Legal Knowledge and Expertise and Presence of Judicial Members

In *Sampath Kumar* Supreme Court had categorically recognized that if the jurisdiction of the High Court under Articles 226 and 227 of the Constitution had to be removed and entrusted to the Administrative Tribunal then for the purpose of adjudicating issues involving interpretation and applicability of Articles 14, 15, 16 and 311 it is necessary to determine them through judicial approach based on expert knowledge in constitutional and administrative law. Hence it is necessary that the members of the tribunal should have same modicum of legal training and judicial experience. Therefore the Court had emphasised the need to have one judicial member and one administrative member at every Bench of the Administrative Tribunal and *there should be no preponderance of administrative members on any Bench.* It was also emphasised that 'the Chairman of the Administrative Tribunal should be or should have been a Judge of a High Court' because *substituting the Chief Justice of a High Court by a Chairman of the Administrative Tribunal who has merely held the post of a Secretary to the government and who has no legal or judicial experience would not only fail to inspire confidence in the public mind but would also render the Administrative Tribunal a much less effective and efficacious mechanism than the High Court. We cannot afford to forget that it is the High Court which is being supplanted by the Administrative Tribunal and it must be so manned as to inspire confidence in the public mind that it is a highly competent and expert mechanism with judicial approach and objectivity.*[14]

(iii) Need of Expert Members

In light of the peculiarity in the functioning of government services and to bring in efficiency to deal with policy related issues the court had recognized the presence of an administrative member in the tribunal.

(iv) Manner of Appointment of the Members

Emphasizing the need to have an independent selection procedure for the appointment of Chairman and other members of the Tribunal Supreme Court held that–

14. (1987) 1 SCC 124, Para 6.

[S]o far as the appointment of Chairman, Vice-Chairmen and administrative members is concerned, the sole and exclusive power to make such appointment is conferred on the government under the impugned Act. There is no obligation cast on the government to consult the Chief Justice of India or to follow any particular selection procedure in this behalf. The result is that it is left to the absolute unfettered discretion of the government to appoint such person or persons as it likes as Chairman, Vice-Chairman and administrative members of the Administrative Tribunal. Now it may be noted that almost all cases in regard to service matters which come before the Administrative Tribunal would be against the Government or any of its officers and it would not at all be conducive to judicial independence to leave unfettered and unrestricted discretion in the executive to appoint the Chairman, Vice-Chairmen and administrative members, if a judicial member or an administrative member is looking forward to promotion as Vice-Chairman or Chairman, he would have to depend on the goodwill and favourable stance of the executive and that would be likely to affect the independence and impartiality of the members of the Tribunal. The same would be the position vis-à-vis promotion to the office of Chairman of the Administrative Tribunal. The administrative members would also be likely to carry a sense of obligation to the executive for having been appointed members of the Administrative Tribunal and that would have a tendency to impair the independence and objectivity of the members of the Tribunal. There can be no doubt that the power of appointment and promotion vested in the executive can have prejudicial effect on the independence of the Chairman, Vice-Chairmen and members of the Administrative Tribunal, if such power is absolute and unfettered. If the members have to look to the executive for advancement, it may tend, directly or indirectly, to influence their decision-making process particularly since the government would be a litigant in most of the cases coming before the Administrative Tribunal and it is the action of the Government which would be challenged in such cases. That is the reason why in case of appointment of High Court Judges, the power of appointment vested in the executive is not an absolute unfettered power but it is hedged in by a wholesome check and safeguard and the President cannot make an appointment of a High Court Judge without consultation with the Chief Justice of the High Court and the Chief Justice of India and a healthy convention has grown up that no appointment would be made by the government which is not approved by the Chief Justice of India. This check or safeguard is totally absent in the case of appointment of the Chairman, Vice-Chairmen and administrative members of the Administrative Tribunal and the possibility cannot be ruled out — indeed the litigating public would certainly carry a feeling — that the decision-making process of the Chairman, Vice-Chairmen and members of the Administrative Tribunal might be likely to be affected by reason of dependence on the executive for appointment and promotion. It can no longer be disputed that total insulation of the judiciary from all forms of interference from the coordinate branches of government is a basic essential feature of the Constitution. The Constitution-makers have made anxious provision to secure total independence of the judiciary from executive pressure or influence. Obviously, therefore, if the Administrative Tribunal is created in

> substitution of the High Court and the jurisdiction of the High Court under Articles 226 and 227 is taken away and vested in the Administrative Tribunal, the same independence from possibility of executive pressure or influence must also be ensured to the Chairman, Vice-Chairmen and members of the Administrative Tribunal. Or else the Administrative Tribunal would cease to be an equally effective and efficacious substitute for the High Court and the provisions of the impugned Act would be rendered invalid. I am, therefore, of the view that the appointment of Chairman, Vice-Chairmen and administrative members should be made by the concerned government only after consultation with the Chief Justice of India and such consultation must be meaningful and effective and ordinarily the recommendation of the Chief Justice of India must be accepted unless there are cogent reasons, in which event the reasons must be disclosed to the Chief Justice of India and his response must be invited to such reasons. There is also another alternative which may be adopted by the Government for making appointments of Chairman, Vice-Chairmen and members and that may be by setting up a High Powered Selection Committee headed by the Chief Justice of India or a sitting Judge of the Supreme Court or concerned High Court nominated by the Chief Justice of India. Both these modes of appointment will ensure selection of proper and competent persons to man the Administrative Tribunal and give it prestige and reputation which would inspire confidence in the public mind in regard to the competence, objectivity and impartiality of those manning the Administrative Tribunal. If either of these two modes of appointment is adopted, it would save the impugned Act from invalidation. Otherwise, it will be outside the scope of the power conferred on Parliament under Article 323-A. I would, however, hasten to add that this judgment will operate only prospectively and will not invalidate appointments already made to the Administrative Tribunal. But if any appointments of Vice-Chairmen or administrative members are to be made hereafter, the same shall be made by the Government in accordance with either of the aforesaid two modes of appointment.

The primary objective in dealing with the above legal issues was that the Tribunals should *become an institution in which the parties could repose faith and trust.*

L. Chandra Kumar case– Review of the *Sampath Kumar* decision

The introduction of Articles 323-A and 323-B gave rise to large scale creation of tribunals to deals with matters involving different branches of law. Along with the Central Administrative Tribunal, State Administrative Tribunals were constituted in eight States and also under Article 323-B other tribunals such as the Customs, Excise and Gold Control (Appellate) Tribunal, Tamil Nadu Taxation Special Tribunal, West Bengal Taxation Tribunal, Rajasthan Taxation Tribunal, Tamil Nadu Land Reforms Special Appellate Tribunal etc. had been created.

After 10 years of the passing of *Sampath Kumar judgment* it became crucial for the Supreme Court to review the working of the tribunals (Articles 323-A and 323-B) in India generally and the *Sampath Kumar decision* in particular because of several legal issues and challenges raised in various cases pending before the different High Courts involving working of the tribunals.

In *R.K. Jain v. Union of India*[15] Ahmadi, J. had categorically observed–

> [T]he time is ripe for taking stock of the working of the various tribunals set up in the country after the insertion of Articles 323-A and 323-B in the Constitution. A sound justice delivery system is a sine qua non for the efficient governance of a country wedded to the rule of law. An independent and impartial justice delivery system in which the litigating public has faith and confidence alone can deliver the goods. After the incorporation of these two articles, Acts have been enacted whereunder tribunals have been constituted for dispensation of justice. Sufficient time has passed and experience gained in these last few years for taking stock of the situation with a view to finding out if they have served the purpose and objectives for which they were constituted. Complaints have been heard in regard to the functioning of other tribunals as well and it is time that a body like the Law Commission of India has a comprehensive look-in with a view to suggesting measures for their improved functioning. That body can also suggest changes in the different statutes and evolve a model on the basis whereof tribunals may be constituted or reconstituted with a view to ensuring greater independence. An intensive and extensive study needs to be undertaken by the Law Commission in regard to the constitution of tribunals under various statutes with a view to ensuring their independence so that the public confidence in such tribunals may increase and the quality of their performance may improve. We strongly recommend to the Law Commission of India to undertake such an exercise on priority basis. A copy of this judgment may be forwarded by the Registrar of this Court to the Member-Secretary of the Commission for immediate action".[16]

A seven-judge bench of the Supreme Court was constituted to review the *Sampath Kumar decision* in the case of *L. Chandra Kumar v. Union of India.*[17] The Court clubbed the various issues raised under three broad heads–

> (1) Whether the power conferred upon Parliament or the State Legislatures under Article 323-A and Article 323-B, to totally exclude the jurisdiction of 'all courts', except that of the Supreme Court under Article 136 runs counter to the power of judicial review conferred on the High Courts under Articles 226/227 and on the Supreme Court under Article 32 of the Constitution?

15. (1993) 4 SCC 119.
16. (1993) 4 SCC 119, Id, Para 8.
17. (1997) 3 SCC 261 : AIR 1997 SC 1125.

(2) Whether the Tribunals, constituted either under Article 323-A or under Article 323-B of the Constitution, possess the competence to test the constitutional validity of a statutory provision / rule?

(3) Whether these Tribunals, as they are functioning at present, can be said to be effective substitutes for the High Courts in discharging the power of judicial review? If not, what are the changes required to make them conform to their founding objectives?

The Supreme Court while dealing with the above issues were aware about the practical challenges and difficulties which was necessary for the introduction of the provisions relating to tribunals in the Constitution.

> We are conscious of the fact that when a Constitution Bench of this Court in *Sampath Kumar case* adopted the theory of alternative institutional mechanisms, it was attempting to remedy an alarming practical situation and the approach selected by it appeared to be most appropriate to meet the exigencies of the time. Nearly a decade later, we are now in a position to review the theoretical and practical results that have arisen as a consequence of the adoption of such an approach.

After elaborate analysis of the functioning of the tribunals and the jurisprudential foundations of the power of judicial review of the higher judiciary the Supreme Court made the following points–

(1) The power of judicial review over legislative action vested in the High Courts under Article 226 and in Supreme Court under Article 32 of the Constitution is an integral and essential feature of the Constitution, constituting part of its basic structure.

(2) Ordinarily the power of High Courts and the Supreme Court to test the constitutional validity of legislations can never be ousted or excluded.

(3) Power vested in the High Courts to exercise judicial superintendence over the decisions of all courts and tribunals within their respective jurisdictions is also part of the basic structure of the Constitution.

(4) Though the subordinate judiciary or Tribunals created under ordinary legislations cannot exercise the power of judicial review of legislative action to the exclusion of the High Courts and the Supreme Court, there is no constitutional prohibition against their performing a supplemental — as opposed to a substitutional — role in this respect. Such a situation is contemplated under clause (3) of Article 32 of the Constitution.

(5) If the power under Article 32 of the Constitution, which has been described as the "heart" and "soul" of the Constitution, can be

additionally conferred upon "any other court", there is no reason why the same situation cannot subsist in respect of the jurisdiction conferred upon the High Courts under Article 226 of the Constitution. So long as the jurisdiction of the High Courts under Articles 226/227 and that of this Court under Article 32 is retained, there is no reason why the power to test the validity of legislations against the provisions of the Constitution cannot be conferred upon Administrative Tribunals created under the Act or upon Tribunals created under Article 323-B of the Constitution.

(6) Both Parliament and the State Legislatures possess legislative competence to effect changes in the original jurisdiction of the Supreme Court and the High Courts. This power is available to Parliament under Entries 77, 78, 79 and 95 of List I and to the State Legislatures under Entry 65 of List II; Entry 46 of List III can also be availed of both by Parliament and the State Legislatures for this purpose.

(7) All decisions of Tribunals, whether created pursuant to Article 323-A or Article 323-B of the Constitution, will be subject to the High Court's writ jurisdiction under Articles 226/227 of the Constitution, before a Division Bench of the High Court within whose territorial jurisdiction the particular Tribunal falls.

(8) No appeal from the decision of a Tribunal will directly lie before the Supreme Court under Article 136 of the Constitution; but instead, the aggrieved party will be entitled to move the High Court under Articles 226/227 of the Constitution and from the decision of the Division Bench of the High Court the aggrieved party could move this Court under Article 136 of the Constitution.

(9) Where a question involving the interpretation of a statutory provision or rule in relation to the Constitution arises for the consideration of a Single Member Bench of the Administrative Tribunal, the proviso to Section 5(6) will automatically apply and the Chairman or the Member concerned shall refer the matter to a Bench consisting of at least two Members, one of whom must be a Judicial Member. This will ensure that questions involving the vires of a statutory provision or rule will never arise for adjudication before a Single Member Bench or a Bench which does not consist of a Judicial Member.

(10) Setting up of these Tribunals is founded on the premise that specialist bodies comprising both trained administrators and those with judicial experience would, by virtue of their specialised knowledge, be better equipped to dispense speedy and efficient justice. It was expected that a judicious mix of Judicial Members and those with grassroot experience would best serve this purpose. To hold that the Tribunal

should consist only of Judicial Members would attack the primary basis of the theory pursuant to which they have been constituted.

(11) The Selection Committee shall be headed by a Judge of the Supreme Court, nominated by the Chief Justice of India, the Committee would take care to ensure that Administrative Members are chosen from amongst those who have some background to deal with such cases.

(12) Until a wholly independent agency for the administration of all such Tribunals can be set up, it is desirable that all such Tribunals should be, as far as possible, under a single nodal ministry which will be in a position to oversee the working of these Tribunals. For a number of reasons that Ministry should appropriately be the Ministry of Law. It would be open for the Ministry, in its turn, to appoint an independent supervisory body to oversee the working of the Tribunals. This will ensure that if the President or Chairperson of the Tribunal is for some reason unable to take sufficient interest in the working of the Tribunal, the entire system will not languish and the ultimate consumer of justice will not suffer.

In the words of Supreme Court the jurisdictional powers of the Tribunal can be summarized as–

> The Tribunals are competent to hear matters where the vires of statutory provisions are questioned. However, in discharging this duty, they cannot act as substitutes for the High Courts and the Supreme Court which have, under our constitutional set-up, been specifically entrusted with such an obligation. Their function in this respect is only supplementary and all such decisions of the Tribunals will be subject to scrutiny before a Division Bench of the respective High Courts. The Tribunals will consequently also have the power to test the vires of subordinate legislations and rules. However, this power of the Tribunals will be subject to one important exception. The Tribunals shall not entertain any question regarding the vires of their parent statutes following the settled principle that a Tribunal which is a creature of an Act cannot declare that very Act to be unconstitutional. In such cases alone, the High Court concerned may be approached directly. All other decisions of these Tribunals, rendered in cases that they are specifically empowered to adjudicate upon by virtue of their parent statutes, will also be subject to scrutiny before a Division Bench of their respective High Courts. We may add that the Tribunals will, however, continue to act as the only courts of first instance in respect of the areas of law for which they have been constituted. By this, we mean that it will not be open for litigants to directly approach the High Courts even in cases where they question the vires of statutory legislations (except, as mentioned, where the legislation which creates the particular Tribunal is challenged) by overlooking the jurisdiction of the Tribunal concerned.
>
> ......

Clause 2(*d*) of Article 323-A and clause 3(*d*) of Article 323-B, to the extent they exclude the jurisdiction of the High Courts and the Supreme Court under Articles 226/227 and 32 of the Constitution, are unconstitutional. Section 28 of the Act and the "exclusion of jurisdiction" clauses in all other legislations enacted under the aegis of Articles 323-A and 323-B would, to the same extent, be unconstitutional. The jurisdiction conferred upon the High Courts under Articles 226/227 and upon the Supreme Court under Article 32 of the Constitution is a part of the inviolable basic structure of our Constitution. While this jurisdiction cannot be ousted, other courts and Tribunals may perform a supplemental role in discharging the powers conferred by Articles 226/227 and 32 of the Constitution. The Tribunals created under Article 323-A and Article 323-B of the Constitution are possessed of the competence to test the constitutional validity of statutory provisions and rules. All decisions of these Tribunals will, however, be subject to scrutiny before a Division Bench of the High Court within whose jurisdiction the Tribunal concerned falls. The Tribunals will, nevertheless, continue to act like courts of first instance in respect of the areas of law for which they have been constituted. It will not, therefore, be open for litigants to directly approach the High Courts even in cases where they question the vires of statutory legislations (except where the legislation which creates the particular Tribunal is challenged) by overlooking the jurisdiction of the Tribunal concerned. Section 5(6) of the Act is valid and constitutional and is to be interpreted in the manner we have indicated.

7.7 JUDICIAL OPINIONS POST *L. CHANDRA KUMAR* CASE-FROM *R. GANDHI* TO *MADRAS BAR ASSOCIATION*

R. Gandhi case

In *Union of India v. R. Gandhi*[18] the constitutionality of the National Company Law Tribunal (NCLT) and National Company Law Appellate Tribunal (NCLAT) was challenged before the Madras High Court and which went on appeal to the Supreme Court. The principle objectives behind establishment of NCLT and NCLAT are to–

(*i*) reduce the pendency of cases and reduce the period of winding-up process from 20 to 25 years to about two years;

(*ii*) avoid multiplicity of litigation before various fora (the High Courts and the quasi-judicial authorities like CLB, BIFR and AAIFR)[19] as all can be heard and decided by NCLT;

(*iii*) the appeals will be streamlined with an appeal provided against the order of NCLT to an Appellate Tribunal (NCLAT) exclusively dedicated to matters

18. (2010) 11 SCC 1.
19. CLB – Company Law Board, BIFR – Board for Industrial and Financial Reconstruction and AAIFR – Appellate Authority for Industrial and Financial Reconstruction.

arising from NCLT, with a further appeal to the Supreme Court only on points of law, thereby reducing the delay in appeals; and

(*iv*) with the pending cases before the Company Law Board and all winding-up cases pending before the High Courts being transferred to NCLT, the burden on the High Courts will be reduced and BIFR and AAIFR could be abolished.

Speaking on the necessity to ensure the independence of the tribunals so as to uphold public confidence in the adjudicating process the Court observed–

Independent judicial tribunals for determination of the rights of citizens, and for adjudication of the disputes and complaints of the citizens, is a necessary concomitant of the rule of law. The rule of law has several facets, one of which is that disputes of citizens will be decided by Judges who are independent and impartial; and that disputes as to legality of acts of the Government will be decided by Judges who are independent of the executive. Another facet of the rule of law is equality before law. The essence of the equality is that it must be capable of being enforced and adjudicated by an independent judicial forum. Judicial independence and separation of judicial power from the executive are part of the common law traditions implicit in a Constitution like ours which is based on the Westminster model.

The fundamental right to equality before law and equal protection of laws guaranteed by Article 14 of the Constitution, clearly includes a right to have the person's rights, adjudicated by a forum which exercises judicial power in an impartial and independent manner, consistent with the recognised principles of adjudication. Therefore wherever access to courts to enforce such rights is sought to be abridged, altered, modified or substituted by directing him to approach an alternative forum, such legislative Act is open to challenge if it violates the right to adjudication by an independent forum. Therefore, though the challenge by MBA is on the ground of violation of principles forming part of the basic structure, they are relatable to one or more of the express provisions of the Constitution which gave rise to such principles. Though the validity of the provisions of a legislative Act cannot be challenged on the ground it violates the basic structure of the Constitution, it can be challenged as violative of constitutional provisions which enshrine the principles of the rule of law, separation of powers and independence of the judiciary.[20]

After analysing the various judicial opinions on creation of tribunals and their effective, the Court in *R. Gandhi* summed up the essential principles of tribunalization as–

(a) A legislature can enact a law transferring the jurisdiction exercised by courts in regard to any specified subject (other than those which are vested in courts by express provisions of the Constitution) to any tribunal.

20. (2010) 11 SCC 1, Para 101-102.

(b) All courts are tribunals. Any tribunal to which any existing jurisdiction of courts is transferred should also be a judicial tribunal. This means that such tribunal should have as members, persons of a rank, capacity and status as nearly as possible equal to the rank, status and capacity of the court which was till then dealing with such matters and the members of the tribunal should have the independence and security of tenure associated with judicial tribunals.

(c) Whenever there is need for "tribunals", there is no presumption that there should be technical members in the tribunals. When any jurisdiction is shifted from courts to tribunals, on the ground of pendency and delay in courts, and the jurisdiction so transferred does not involve any technical aspects requiring the assistance of experts, the tribunals should normally have only judicial members. Only where the exercise of jurisdiction involves inquiry and decisions into technical or special aspects, where presence of technical members will be useful and necessary, tribunals should have technical members. Indiscriminate appointment of technical members in all tribunals will dilute and adversely affect the independence of the judiciary.

(d) The legislature can reorganise the jurisdictions of judicial tribunals. For example, it can provide that a specified category of cases tried by a higher court can be tried by a lower court or vice versa (a standard example is the variation of pecuniary limits of the courts). Similarly while constituting tribunals, the legislature can prescribe the qualifications / eligibility criteria. The same is however subject to judicial review. If the court in exercise of judicial review is of the view that such tribunalisation would adversely affect the independence of the judiciary or the standards of the judiciary, the court may interfere to preserve the independence and standards of the judiciary. Such an exercise will be part of the checks and balances measures to maintain the separation of powers and to prevent any encroachment, intentional or unintentional, by either the legislature or by the executive.

One of the important issue which was analysed by the court in detail was the selection and manner of appointment of expert or technical members. The Court particularly dealt with the issue of 'whether judicial functions can be transferred to tribunals manned by persons who are not suitable or qualified or competent to discharge such judicial powers or whose independence is suspect' and made the following observations–

(i) On 'judicial members':

We have already held that the legislature has the competence to transfer any particular jurisdiction from courts to tribunals provided it is understood that the tribunals exercise judicial power and the persons who are appointed as President / Chairperson / Members are of a standard which is reasonably approximate to the standards of mainstream judicial functioning. On the other hand, if a tribunal is packed with members who are drawn from the civil services and who continue to be employees of different Ministries or government departments by maintaining lien over their respective posts, it would amount to transferring judicial functions to the executive which would go against the doctrine of separation of powers and independence of the judiciary.

The legislature is presumed not to legislate contrary to the rule of law and therefore know that where disputes are to be adjudicated by a judicial body other than courts, its standards should approximately be the same as to what is expected of mainstream judiciary. The rule of law can be meaningful only if there is an independent and impartial judiciary to render justice. An independent judiciary can exist only when persons with competence, ability and independence with impeccable character man the judicial institutions. When the legislature proposes to substitute a tribunal in place of the High Court to exercise the jurisdiction which the High Court is exercising, it goes without saying that the standards expected from the judicial members of the Tribunal and standards applied for appointing such members, should be as nearly as possible as applicable to the High Court Judges, which are apart from a basic degree in Law, rich experience in the practice of law, independent outlook, integrity, character and good reputation. It is also implied that only men of standing who have special expertise in the field to which the Tribunal relates, will be eligible for appointment as technical members. Therefore, only persons with a judicial background, that is, those who have been or are Judges of the High Court and lawyers with the prescribed experience, who are eligible for appointment as High Court Judges, can be considered for appointment as judicial members.[21]

(ii) On 'technical members':

A lifetime of experience in administration may make a member of the civil services a good and able administrator, but not a necessarily good, able and impartial adjudicator with a judicial temperament capable of rendering decisions which have to: (*i*) inform the parties about the reasons for the decision; (*ii*) demonstrate fairness and correctness of the decision and absence of arbitrariness; and (*iii*) ensure that justice is not only done, but also seem to be done.

As far as technical members are concerned, the officer should be of at least Secretary level officer with known competence and integrity. Reducing the standards, or qualifications for appointment will result in loss of confidence in the tribunals. We hasten to add that our intention is not to say that the persons of Joint Secretary level are not competent. Even persons of Under-Secretary level may be competent to discharge the functions. There may be brilliant and competent people even working as Section Officers or Upper

21. (2010) 11 SCC 1, Ibid at Para 107-108.

Division Clerks but that does not mean that they can be appointed as members. Competence is different from experience, maturity and status required for the post. As, for example, for the post of a Judge of the High Court, 10 years' practice as an advocate is prescribed. There may be advocates who even with 4 or 5 years' experience, may be more brilliant than advocates with 10 years' standing. Still, it is not competence alone but various other factors which make a person suitable. Therefore, when the legislature substitutes the Judges of the High Court with the Members of the Tribunal, the standards applicable should be as nearly as equal in the case of High Court Judges. That means only Secretary level officers (that is those who were Secretaries or Additional Secretaries) with specialised knowledge and skills can be appointed as technical members of the tribunal.[22]

Showing grave concerns with the falling standards of the tribunals in performing their judicial functions the Court laid the following important guidelines to improve the overall functions of the tribunals–

(i) Only Judges and advocates can be considered for appointment as judicial members of the Tribunal. Only High Court Judges, or Judges who have served in the rank of a District Judge for at least five years or a person who has practised as a lawyer for ten years can be considered for appointment as a judicial member. Persons who have held a Group A or equivalent post under the Central or State Government with experience in the Indian Company Law Service (Legal Branch) and the Indian Legal Service (Grade I) cannot be considered for appointment as judicial members as provided in sub-sections (2)(c) and (d) of Section 10-FD. The expertise in Company Law Service or the Indian Legal Service will at best enable them to be considered for appointment as technical members.

(ii) As NCLT takes over the functions of the High Court, the members should as nearly as possible have the same position and status as High Court Judges. This can be achieved, not by giving the salary and perks of a High Court Judge to the members, but by ensuring that persons who are as nearly equal in rank, experience or competence to High Court Judges are appointed as members. Therefore, only officers who are holding the ranks of Secretaries or Additional Secretaries alone can be considered for appointment as technical members of the National Company Law Tribunal. Clauses (c) and (d) of sub-section (2) and clauses (a) and (b) of sub-section (3) of Section 10-FD which provide for persons with 15 years experience in Group A post or persons holding the post of Joint Secretary or equivalent post in the Central or the State Government, being qualified for appointment as Members of Tribunal, are invalid.

---

22. Id at Para 109-110.

(iii) A "technical member" presupposes an experience in the field to which the Tribunal relates. A member of the Indian Company Law Service who has worked with Accounts Branch or officers in other departments who might have incidentally dealt with some aspect of company law cannot be considered as "experts" qualified to be appointed as technical members. Therefore clauses (a) and (b) of sub-section (3) are not valid.

(iv) The first part of clause (f) of sub-section (3) providing that any person having special knowledge or professional experience of 20 years in science, technology, economics, banking, industry could be considered to be persons with expertise in company law, for being appointed as technical members in the Company Law Tribunal, is invalid.

(v) Persons having ability, integrity, standing and special knowledge and professional experience of not less than fifteen years in industrial finance, industrial management, industrial reconstruction, investment and accountancy, may however be considered as persons having expertise in rehabilitation / revival of companies and therefore, eligible for being considered for appointment as technical members.

(vi) In regard to category of persons referred in clause (g) of sub-section (3) at least five years' experience should be specified.

(vii) Only clauses (c), (d), (e), (g), (h), and the latter part of clause (f) in sub-section (3) of Section 10-FD and officers of civil services of the rank of the Secretary or Additional Secretary in the Indian Company Law Service and the Indian Legal Service can be considered for purposes of appointment as technical members of the Tribunal.

(viii) Instead of a five-member Selection Committee with the Chief Justice of India (or his nominee) as Chairperson and two Secretaries from the Ministry of Finance and Company Affairs and the Secretary in the Ministry of Labour and the Secretary in the Ministry of Law and Justice as members mentioned in Section 10-FX, the Selection Committee should broadly be on the following lines:

   (a) Chief Justice of India or his nominee—Chairperson (with a casting vote);

   (b) A Senior Judge of the Supreme Court or Chief Justice of High Court—Member;

   (c) Secretary in the Ministry of Finance and Company Affairs—Member; and

   (d) Secretary in the Ministry of Law and Justice—Member.

(ix) The term of office of three years shall be changed to a term of seven or five years subject to eligibility for appointment for one more term.

This is because considerable time is required to achieve expertise in the field concerned. A term of three years is very short and by the time the members achieve the required knowledge, expertise and efficiency, one term will be over. Further the said term of three years with the retirement age of 65 years is perceived as having been tailor-made for persons who have retired or shortly to retire and encourages these Tribunals to be treated as post-retirement havens. If these Tribunals are to function effectively and efficiently they should be able to attract younger members who will have a reasonable period of service.

(x) The second proviso to Section 10-FE enabling the President and members to retain lien with their parent cadre / ministry / department while holding office as President or Members will not be conducive for the independence of members. Any person appointed as member should be prepared to totally disassociate himself from the executive. The lien cannot therefore exceed a period of one year.

(xi) To maintain independence and security in service, sub-section (3) of Section 10-FJ and Section 10-FV should provide that suspension of the President / Chairman or member of a Tribunal can be only with the concurrence of the Chief Justice of India.

(xii) The administrative support for all Tribunals should be from the Ministry of Law and Justice. Neither the Tribunals nor their members shall seek or be provided with facilities from the respective sponsoring or parent Ministries or Department concerned.

(xiii) Two-member Benches of the Tribunal should always have a judicial member. Whenever any larger or special Benches are constituted, the number of technical members shall not exceed the judicial members.

The Supreme Court upheld the constitutionality of NCLT and NCLAT in exercising the powers and jurisdiction of the High Court subject to the necessary changes to be made in the Companies Act 1952 as amended in 2002, through suitable amendments. It is important to note that the above principles as laid down in *R. Gandhi* with reference to the functioning of the NCLT and NCLAT are equally applicable for the effective functioning of other tribunals as has been recognized in the case of *Shamnad Basheer v. Union of India.*[23]

Madras bar association

In *Madras Bar Association v. Union of India*[24] the constitutional validity of National Tax Tribunal Act, 2005 was considered. The National Tax Tribunal (NTT) was constituted as a quasi-judicial appellate tribunal and had been

23. 2015 SCC Online Mad 299.

24. (2014) 10 SCC 1 : 2014 (11) SCALE 166.

vested with the power of adjudicating appeals arising from the orders of the Appellate Tribunals constituted under the Income Tax Act, Customs Act, 1962 and the Central Excise Act, 1944. Prior to the enactment of this legislation the appellate jurisdiction was conferred on the High Courts. The principle point of argument on behalf of the petitioners was that the powers and functions of the High Court cannot be substituted by an extra-judicial body, such as NTT. In addition it was argued that the essential characteristics of a judicial body i.e. independence and fairness was absent in the functioning of NTT.

While dealing with the above issues, the Supreme Court reiterated the importance and necessity of tribunals in spite of certain shortcomings in the working of the tribunals-*That the various Tribunals have not performed up to expectations is a self-evident and widely acknowledged truth. However, to draw an inference that their unsatisfactory performance points to their being founded on a fundamentally unsound principle would not be correct. The reasons for which the Tribunals were constituted still persist; indeed, those reasons have become even more pronounced in our times.* The need of the day is to adopt strict measures to improve the standard of functioning of the tribunals so that they can *stand up to constitutional scrutiny.*

The Supreme Court identified the following core issues and answered them accordingly–

On the legislative power to transfer judicial functions performed by courts to tribunals the Court observed–

> The Constitution regulates the manner of governance in substantially minute detail. It is the fountainhead distributing power for such governance. The Constitution vests the power of legislation at the Centre, with the Lok Sabha and the Rajya Sabha, and in the States with the State Legislative Assemblies (and in some States, the State Legislative Councils, as well). The instant legislative power is regulated by "Part XI" of the Constitution.... This Court has repeatedly held that an amendment to the provisions of the Constitution would not be sustainable if it violated the "basic structure" of the Constitution, even though the amendment had been carried out by following the procedure contemplated under "Part XI" of the Constitution. This leads to the determination that the "basic structure" is inviolable. In our view, the same would apply to all other legislations (other than amendments to the Constitution) as well, even though the legislation had been enacted by following the prescribed procedure, and was within the domain of the enacting legislature, any infringement to the "basic structure" would be unacceptable.
>
> .....

.... in every new Constitution, which makes separate provisions for the legislature, the executive and the judiciary, it is taken as acknowledged / conceded that the basic principle of "separation of powers" would apply. And that the three wings of governance would operate in their assigned domain / province. The power of discharging judicial functions which was exercised by members of the higher judiciary at the time when the Constitution came into force should ordinarily remain with the court, which exercised the said jurisdiction at the time of promulgation of the new Constitution. But the judicial power could be allowed to be exercised by an analogous / similar court / tribunal with a different name. However, by virtue of the constitutional convention while constituting the analogous court / tribunal it will have to be ensured that the appointment and security of tenure of Judges of that court would be the same as of the court sought to be substituted.

On the need to appoint judicial members and restrictions on appointment of technical members it was observed–

....that the members of NTT would most definitely be confronted with the legal issues emerging out of Family law, Hindu law, Mohammedan law, Company law, law of Partnership, law related to Territoriality, law related to Trusts and Societies, Contract law, law relating to Transfer of Property, law relating to Intellectual Property, Interpretation of Statutes, and other miscellaneous provisions of law, from time to time. NTT besides the aforesaid statutes, will not only have to interpret the provisions of the three statutes, out of which the appeals will be heard by it, but will also have to examine a challenge to the vires of statutory amendments made in the said provisions from time to time. They will also have to determine in some cases whether the provisions relied upon had a prospective or retrospective applicability.

On the constitutional validity of Sections 5, 6, 7, 8 and 13 of the NTT Act it was observed that–

Section 5–

Even though we have expressed the view, that it is open to Parliament to substitute the appellate jurisdiction vested in the jurisdictional High Courts and constitute courts / tribunals to exercise the said jurisdiction, we are of the view, that while vesting jurisdiction in an alternative court/tribunal, it is imperative for the legislature to ensure that redress should be available with the same convenience and expediency as it was prior to the introduction of the newly created court / tribunal. Thus viewed, the mandate incorporated in Section 5(2) of the NTT Act to the effect that the sittings of NTT would ordinarily be conducted in the National Capital Territory of Delhi, would render the remedy inefficacious, and thus unacceptable in law. The instant aspect of the matter was considered by this Court with reference to the Administrative Tribunals Act, 1985 in *S.P. Sampath Kumar case* [*S.P. Sampath Kumar v. Union of India*, (1987) 1 SCC 124 : (1987) 2 ATC 82] and *L. Chandra Kumar case*

[*L. Chandra Kumar v. Union of India*, (1997) 3 SCC 261 : 1997 SCC (L&S) 577] , wherein it was held that permanent Benches needed to be established at the seat of every jurisdictional High Court. And if that was not possible, at least a Circuit Bench required to be established at every place where an aggrieved party could avail of his remedy. The position on the above issue is no different in the present controversy. For the above reason, Section 5(2) of the NTT Act is in clear breach of the law declared by this Court".[25]

Section 6–

Court has declared the position in this behalf in *L. Chandra Kumar case* and in *Union of India v. Madras Bar Assn. case*, that Technical Members could be appointed to the tribunals, where technical expertise is essential for disposal of matters, and not otherwise. It has also been held that where the adjudicatory process transferred to a tribunal does not involve any specialised skill, knowledge or expertise, a provision for appointment of non-Judicial Members (in addition to, or in substitution of Judicial Members), would constitute a clear case of delusion and encroachment upon the "independence of judiciary", and the "rule of law". It is difficult to appreciate how Accountant Members and Technical Members would handle complicated questions of law relating to tax matters, and also questions of law on a variety of subjects (unconnected to tax), in exercise of the jurisdiction vested with NTT. That in our view would be a tall order. An arduous and intimidating asking. Since the Chairperson / Members of NTT will be required to determine "substantial questions of law", arising out of decisions of the Appellate Tribunals, it is difficult to appreciate how an individual, well-versed only in accounts, would be able to discharge such functions. Likewise, it is also difficult for us to understand how Technical Members, who may not even possess the qualification of law, or may have no experience at all in the practice of law, would be able to deal with "substantial questions of law", for which alone, NTT has been constituted.

We have already noticed hereinabove from data placed on record by the learned counsel for the petitioners that NTT would be confronted with disputes arising out of Family law, Hindu law, Mohammedan law, Company law, law of Partnership, law relating to Territoriality, law relating to Trusts and Societies, Contract law, law relating to Transfer of Property, law relating to Intellectual Property, Interpretation of Statutes / Rules, and other miscellaneous provisions of law. Besides the above, the Members of NTT will regularly have to interpret the provisions of the Income Tax Act, the Customs Act and the Excise Act. We are of the considered opinion that only a person possessing professional qualification in law with substantial experience in the practice of law will be in a position to handle the onerous responsibilities which a Chairperson and Members of NTT will have to shoulder.

25. Supra note 24 at Para 123.

There seems to be no doubt, whatsoever, that the Members of a court / tribunal to which adjudicatory functions are transferred must be manned by Judges / members whose stature and qualifications are commensurate to the court from which the adjudicatory process has been transferred. This position is recognised the world over..... Constitutions on the Westminster model. The Indian Constitution is one such constitution. The position has been clearly recorded while interpreting Constitutions framed on the above model, namely, that even though the legislature can transfer judicial power from a traditional court to an analogous court / tribunal with a different name, the court / tribunal to which such power is transferred should be possessed of the same salient characteristics, standards and parameters, as the court the power whereof was being transferred. It is not possible for us to accept that Accountant Members and Technical Members have the stature and qualification possessed by the Judges of High Courts.[26]

Section 7–

It should not have been forgotten that under the provisions of the Administrative Tribunals Act, 1985, which came up for consideration in *L. Chandra Kumar case*, the Tribunals constituted under the said Act, are to act like courts of first instance. All decisions of the Tribunal are amenable to challenge under Articles 226 / 227 of the Constitution before a Division Bench of the jurisdictional High Court. In such circumstances it is apparent, that tribunals under the Administrative Tribunals Act, 1985, were subservient to the jurisdictional High Courts. The manner of selection, as suggested in *L. Chandra Kumar case* cannot therefore be adopted for a tribunal of the nature as NTT. Herein the acknowledged position is that NTT has been constituted as a replacement of High Courts. NTT is, therefore, in the real sense a tribunal substituting the High Courts. The manner of appointment of Chairperson / Members to NTT will have to be by the same procedure (or by a similar procedure) to that which is prevalent for appointment of the Judges of High Courts. Insofar as the instant aspect of the matter is concerned, the above proposition was declared by this Court in *Union of India v. Madras Bar Assn.*[27] , wherein it was held that the stature of the Members who would constitute the tribunal, would depend on the jurisdiction which was being transferred to the tribunal. Accordingly, if the jurisdiction of the High Courts is being transferred to NTT, the stature of the Members of the tribunal had to be akin to that of the Judges of High Courts. So also the conditions of service of its Chairperson / Members, and the manner of their appointment and removal, including transfers. Including, the tenure of their appointments.

Section 7 cannot even otherwise be considered to be constitutionally valid, since it includes in the process of selection and appointment of the Chairperson and Members of NTT, Secretaries of Departments of the Central Government.

26. Ibid at Para 126-128.
27. (2010) 11 SCC 1.

In this behalf, it would also be pertinent to mention that the interests of the Central Government would be represented on one side in every litigation before NTT. It is not possible to accept a party to a litigation can participate in the selection process whereby the Chairperson and Members of the adjudicatory body are selected. This would also be violative of the recognised constitutional convention recorded by Lord Diplock in *Hinds case*[28], namely, that it would make a mockery of the Constitution, if the legislature could transfer the jurisdiction previously exercisable by holders of judicial offices to holders of a new court / tribunal (to which some different name was attached) and to provide that persons holding the new judicial offices should not be appointed in the manner and on the terms prescribed for appointment of members of the judicature. For all the reasons recorded hereinabove, we hereby declare Section 7 of the NTT Act, as unconstitutional.[29]

Section 8–

Insofar as the validity of Section 8 of the NTT Act is concerned, it clearly emerges from a perusal thereof that a Chairperson / Member is appointed to NTT, in the first instance, for a duration of 5 years. Such Chairperson / Member is eligible for reappointment for a further period of 5 years.... a provision for reappointment would itself have the effect of undermining the independence of the Chairperson / Members of NTT. Every Chairperson / Member appointed to NTT would be constrained to decide matters in a manner that would ensure his reappointment in terms of Section 8 of the NTT Act. His decisions may or may not be based on his independent understanding. We are satisfied that the above provision would undermine the independence and fairness of the Chairperson and Members of NTT. Since NTT has been vested with jurisdiction which earlier lay with the High Courts, in all matters of appointment, and extension of tenure, must be shielded from executive involvement. The reasons for our instant conclusions are exactly the same as have been expressed by us while dealing with Section 5 of the NTT Act. We therefore hold that Section 8 of the NTT Act is unconstitutional.

Thus the Court concluded that the Sections 5, 6, 7, 8 and 13 were illegal and unconstitutional based on the recognized constitutional conventions as developed in different nations on the Westminister model and the parameters laid down by the Supreme Court.

Nariman J. dissenting in the rationale but concurring on the decision made a distinction between the present case and the decision in *R. Gandhi case.* In the latter case the core issue was that one specialised tribunal replaced another specialised tribunal (The Company Law Board) at the original stage. He asserted that in that case when the jurisdiction of the High Courts were taken away and transferred to tribunals, the power of the High Court

28. *Hinds v. R.*, 1977 AC 195.

29. Supra note 24 Para 130-131.

were merely being supplanted at the original and first appellate stage so far as the company 'jurisdiction' is concerned and questions of fact had to be determined afresh at the first appellate stage also. In the present case the legal position is entirely different as the power of the High Court was being *supplanted by a tribunal which would be deciding only substantial questions of law.*

The Court summarized the legal position of tribunalization in India as–

(i) Parliament has the power to enact legislation and to vest adjudicatory functions earlier vested in the High Court with an alternative court / tribunal. Exercise of such power by Parliament would not per se violate the "basic structure" of the Constitution.

(ii) Recognised constitutional conventions pertaining to the Westminster model do not debar the legislating authority from enacting legislation to vest adjudicatory functions earlier vested in a superior court with an alternative court / tribunal. Exercise of such power by Parliament would per se not violate any constitutional convention.

(iii) The "basic structure" of the Constitution will stand violated if while enacting legislation pertaining to transfer of judicial power, Parliament does not ensure that the newly created court / tribunal conforms with the salient characteristics and standards of the court sought to be substituted.

(iv) Constitutional conventions pertaining to the Constitutions styled on the Westminster model will also stand breached, if while enacting legislation, pertaining to transfer of judicial power, conventions and salient characteristics of the court sought to be replaced are not incorporated in the court / tribunal sought to be created.

Company Secretaries are held ineligible for representing a party to an appeal before NTT.

Examined on the touchstone of Conclusions (*iii*) and (*iv*) Sections 5, 6, 7, 8 and 13 of the NTT Act, are held to be unconstitutional. Since the aforesaid provisions constitute the edifice of the NTT Act, and without these provisions the remaining provisions are rendered ineffective and inconsequential, the entire enactment is declared unconstitutional.

VIII

Independent Regulatory Authorities – Emerging Challenges

LEARNING OBJECTIVES

After reading this chapter, you will be familiar with:

- Nature, scope and meaning of IRAs
- Objective behind creation of IRAs
- Brief description of few leading IRAs
    - Telecom Regulatory Authority of India
    - Electricity Regulatory Commission
    - Insurance Regulatory and Development Authority of India
- Challenges faced by IRAs
- Application of the principles of Administrative Law for the purpose of regulating IRAs
- Scope of Judicial Review and Appeal

8.1 INTRODUCTION

In a modern State governed by a democratic constitution the functions of the Government are manifold. The Indian Constitution imposes responsibility on the Government to perform various social and economic activities to ensure the well-being of the citizens. This increase in governmental functions is accompanied with more power and discretion in the hands of the executive branch of the Government, its various instrumentalities and agencies. The administration in India has assumed many responsibilities and powers to fulfil the socio-economic and welfare goals of the State. This role of the State has been further reshaped in the post-liberal era. Emergence of the regulatory authorities to deal with specific areas of economic development and governance is a feature of post liberalization administrative process.

Since 1990s there has been a paradigm shift in the functioning of the state with regards to economic and financial matters of the country. The pro-active role of the state has given way to the more *market-friendly process in the economy.* The role of the state has been translated to act as a mechanism to rectify or modify the several imperfections existing in the efficient functioning of the market-based economy. Direct state intervention was replaced with a regulatory role with the specific task of putting in place a proper *market regulatory system.* Market liberalization has given rise to new types of organizations referred to as the 'independent regulatory authorities.' The primary function of these regulatory authorities is to ensure simplification, transparency and expediency in the conduct of business. The regulation of public utility services like telecommunications, electricity which were previously within the exclusive domain of the government have been liberalized and made subject to private competition, and these sectors are being regulated by the independent authorities. At present a large number of market regulatory agencies such as the Competition Commission and sectoral regulators like the Telecom Regulatory Authority of India (TRAI), Electricity Commission etc. have been set up to promote *a predictable regulatory environment and participatory decision making.* These regulators have been entrusted with the functions of – balancing the conflicting interests, promoting fair competition, facilitating investments, democratizing decision-making process and ensuring the overall development of the sector etc.

8.2 BRIEF DESCRIPTION OF FEW INDEPENDENT REGULATORS AUTHORITIES

8.2.1 Telecom Regularity Authority of India (TRAI)

Telecommunication service was a public utility service and was considered to be of great strategic importance in promoting socio-economic progress in the country. There were large varieties of telecommunication services having immense potential for ensuring the economic growth of the country. It was conscious realization of the State that the future of national growth was largely dependent on the way in which the telecom infrastructure is developed in the country so as to promote the processing and transmission of information without barriers. With this realization the Finance Minister in February 1993 in the budget speech announced the intention of the Government to encourage private sector involvement and participation in telecom to supplement efforts of Department of Telecommunications (DOT) especially in creation of internationally competitive industry. On 13-5-1994 National Telecom policy was announced which was placed in Parliament with the aim to supplement the effort of the DOT in providing telecommunications services.

Highlighting the objective of National Telecom Policy the Supreme Court in *Delhi Science Forum v. Union of India*[1] observed–

> The special aspect about telecommunications is interconnectivity which is known as "any to any requirement". Because of the economic growth and commercial changes in different parts of the world, need for inter-connectivity means that communication systems have to be compatible with each other and have to be actually interconnected. Because of this, there is a demand even in developing countries to have communication system of international standards. Even after several decades of invention of the telephone system, in almost all countries telecommunications was the subject of monopoly supplied with the public network operator normally being the State-owned Corporation or Government Department. Then it was not thought due to different considerations that such right could be granted to the private sector denuding the right of monopoly of the Government to maintain and run the system of telecommunications. The developed countries first took decision in respect of privatisation of Telecom which amounted to giving up the claim of exclusive privilege over such system and this led to the transition from monopoly to a duopoly policy in many countries. India, although a developing country also faced a challenge in this sector. By and large it was realised that this sector needed acceleration because of the adoption of liberalised economic policy for the economic growth of the country. It appears that the policy-makers were faced with the implications for public welfare vis-à-vis the sector being capital intensive. How the network is well maintained so as it reaches the largest number of people at a price to be paid by such users which can be held as reasonable? This issue was also interrelated with the defence and national security of the nation. Different committees and bodies constituted from time to time examined the Telecom policy which could be adopted by the nation from different aspects and angles.

Under the policy it was deemed necessary to create an independent regulatory authority to deal with different aspect of telecommunication services in India. It was advocated that the setting of an independent Telecom Regulatory Authority of India would be in line with similar initiatives made by other leading countries of the world as part of their effort to privatize the telecommunication services. In the United Kingdom under the Telecommunications Act, 1984 a Regulatory Authority had been constituted to ensure that the telecommunications services were made available throughout the country and to supervise all matters connected therewith. The functional role of such authority was to promote the interests of the consumers, purchasers and other users of telecommunication services by regulating the price charged, quality of the services provided etc. and also to promote effective competition between the different players engaged

1. (1996) 2 SCC 405.

in providing telecommunication services in UK. In United States the Federal Communication Commission was created as a primary federal regulator of the Communication industry by the Communication Act, 1934. There are six bureaus working under the Federal Communication Commission dealing with different aspects of telecommunication services, including decisions and policies of the FCC. In Canada the Telecommunication Act 1993 provides for creation of regulatory authorities to deal with different aspects of implementation and supervision of the telecommunication services. Similar sectoral regulatory authority had been set up in other countries including Australia, France and Japan.

In India the Telecom Regulatory Authority of India Act 1996 was enacted with the objective of establishing the Telecom Regulatory Authority of India (TRAI) to regulate the telecommunication services and for dealing with all matters connected therewith or incidental thereto. TRAI consists of a Chairperson and Members. Notwithstanding anything contained in the Indian Telegraph Act, 1885, the primary functions of TRAI are to ensure technical compatibility and effective interrelationship between different service providers, to ensure compliance of licence conditions by all service providers, to facilitate competition and promote efficiency in the operation of telecommunication services, to protect the interest of the consumers of the telecommunication services, to levy fees at such rates and in respect of such services as may be determined by regulations. Thus the core function of independent TRAI is to supervise the functioning of different telecom service providers and their activities.

Emphasizing the functional role of TRAI, the Supreme Court in *Delhi Science Forum v. Union of India*[2] observed–

> The new Telecom policy is not only a commercial venture of the Central Government, but the object of the policy is also to improve the service so that the said service should reach the common man and should be within his reach. The different licensees should not be left to implement the said Telecom policy according to their perception. It has rightly been urged that while implementing the Telecom policy the security aspect cannot be overlooked. The existence of a Telecom Regulatory Authority with the appropriate powers is essential for introduction of plurality in the Telecom sector. The National Telecom Policy is a historic departure from the practice followed during the past century. Since the private sector will have to contribute more to the development of the telecom network than DoT / MTNL in the next few years, the role of an independent Telecom Regulatory Authority with appropriate powers need not be impressed, which can harness the individual appetite for private gains, for social ends. The Central Government and the Telecom

2. (1996) 2 SCC 405.

Regulatory Authority have not to behave like sleeping trustees, but have to function as active trustees for the public good.[3]

8.2.2 Electricity Regulatory Commission

The Indian Electricity Act, 1910 was enacted for the purpose of generation, transmission and supply of electricity. The 1948 Act was framed with the objective of rationalizing the provisions relating to supply of electricity and to take measures conducive to electrical development. The Electricity Act, 2003 was introduced for the purpose of "generation, transmission, distribution, trading and use of electricity and generally for taking measures conducive to development of electricity industry, promoting competition therein, protecting interest of consumers and supply of electricity to all areas, rationalization of electricity tariff, ensuring transparent policies regarding subsidies, promotion of efficient and environmentally benign policies, constitution of Central Electricity Authority, Regulatory Commissions and establishment of Appellate Tribunal and for matters connected therewith or incidental thereto." The Electricity Commission under the statute has been constituted as a *high power expert committee with autonomous authority and is expected to function independently.*[4] The primary function of the Commission is to promote competition, efficiency and economy in the activities of the electricity industries in the country. The Mission statements of the Commission are–

> "The Commission intends to promote competition, efficiency and economy in bulk power markets, improve the quality of supply, promote investments and advise government on the removal of institutional barriers to bridge the demand supply gap and thus foster the interests of consumers. In pursuit of these objectives the Commission aims to–
>
> (i) Improve the operations and management of the regional transmission systems through Indian Electricity Grid Code (IEGC), Availability Based Tariff (ABT), etc.
>
> (ii) Formulate an efficient tariff setting mechanism, which ensures speedy and time bound disposal of tariff petitions, promotes competition, economy and efficiency in the pricing of bulk power and transmission services and ensures least cost investments.
>
> (iii) Facilitate open access in inter-state transmission
>
> (iv) Facilitate inter-state trading
>
> (v) Promote development of power market
>
> (vi) Improve access to information for all stakeholders.

3. Id at Para 31.
4. *W.B. Electricity Regulatory Commission v. CESC Ltd.*, (2002) 8 SCC 715.

(vii) Facilitate technological and institutional changes required for the development of competitive markets in bulk power and transmission services."[5]

(viii) Advise on the removal of barriers to entry and exit for capital and management, within the limits of environmental, safety and security concerns and the existing legislative requirements, as the first step to the creation of competitive markets.

8.2.3 Insurance Regulatory and Development Authority of India

The Insurance Regulatory Development Authority Act, 1999 was enacted for the purpose of establishing an independent regulatory authority for regulating the insurance sector in India. Traditionally with the passing of the General Insurance Business (Nationalization) Act 1972 the insurance business was nationalized in India. Life Insurance Corporation was the singular insurance provider in the country dealing with the life insurance sector. Based on the recommendations made by the R.N. Malhotra Committee the IRDA was constituted as an autonomous body to regulate and develop the insurance industry. The 1999 enactment private players were allowed entry into the insurance sector. The Insurance Regulatory and Development Authority of India (IRDAI) was constituted in 2000 and its primary objective is *'to protect the interests of the policy holders, to regulate, promote and ensure orderly growth of the insurance industry and for matters connected therewith or incidental thereto.'*[6] The IRDA has the power to make regulations relating to insurers, insurance intermediaries, surveyors and third party administrators for the purpose of smooth functioning of the insurance sector. It is also required to protect the interest of the policy holders. The Mission Statement of the Authority is as follows–

(1) To protect the interest of and secure fair treatment to policyholders;

(2) To bring about speedy and orderly growth of the insurance industry (including annuity and superannuation payments), for the benefit of the common man, and to provide long term funds for accelerating growth of the economy;

(3) To set, promote, monitor and enforce high standards of integrity, financial soundness, fair dealing and competence of those it regulates;

(4) To ensure speedy settlement of genuine claims, to prevent insurance frauds and other malpractices and put in place effective grievance redressal machinery;

5. http://www.cercind.gov.in/Mission.html.
6. https://www.irda.gov.in/Defaulthome.aspx?page=H1.

(5) To promote fairness, transparency and orderly conduct in financial markets dealing with insurance and build a reliable management information system to enforce high standards of financial soundness amongst market players;

(6) To take action where such standards are inadequate or ineffectively enforced;

(7) To bring about optimum amount of self-regulation in day-to-day working of the industry consistent with the requirements of prudential regulation.

In *United India Insurance Co. Ltd. v. Manubhai Dharmasinhbhai Gajera*[7] the Court made the following observation–

> The functions of the insurance companies are governed by statute. A contract of insurance, therefore, must subserve the statutory provisions. It must indisputably be construed having regard to the larger public policy and public interest guiding nationalisation of the insurance companies.
>
> Insurance sector is regulated. The provisions of the Insurance Act are applicable to all insurance companies irrespective of the fact as to whether they are in public sector or private sector. When a business is regulated, all concerned would be governed thereby.
>
> It is one thing to say that the terms and conditions of a contract are statutory in nature but it is another thing to say that the statute governs or controls the business itself. It is the latter which is applicable to the fact of the case.
>
> Two things are apparent. One, the Central Government has come out with a new economic policy. The monopoly status has been taken away from General Insurance Corporation of India and its subsidiaries. The insurance companies are required to compete with others in the field, but the same may not necessarily mean that despite the statutory interdicts the public sector insurance companies must have a level playing field with the private insurance companies.
>
> We have, despite the new economic policy of the Centre, no option but to proceed on the assumption that the public sector insurance companies being State have a different role to play. It is not to say that as a matter of policy, statutory or otherwise, the insurance companies are bound to regulate all contracts of insurance having the statement of directive principles in mind but there cannot be any doubt whatsoever that fairness or reasonableness on the part of the insurance companies must appear in all of its dealings.
>
> The Authority wants the insurance companies to offer a fair deal and all the terms and conditions of their offer must be transparent. There should not be any hidden agenda. Even they should not take recourse to "ticketing contract". When, however, the terms of the new product or revised product

7. (2008) 10 SCC 404.

require the approval of the Authority, prima facie, the same would mean that they are fair and reasonable. The action on the part of the Authority is not in question. Regulations, guidelines and circulars are binding on the insurance companies. [**See** *State of Kerala v. Kurian Abraham (P) Ltd.*[8]]

8.3 PRESENT CHALLENGES

In the present context the different regulatory authorities are faced with the challenge of performing their functions of formulation and implementation of policies, including resolution of any disputes by complying with the norms of fairness, efficiency, accountability and transparency. According to several studies the regulatory authorities in India function in an unregulated environment with the absence of adequate accountability and supervisory mechanisms, lack of functional clarity between the different sectoral regulators, absence of proper selection and appointing procedures, inadequate organizational structure etc.

The report of the World Bank and the International Finance Corporation titled "Doing Business 2012: Doing business in a very Transparent World" has ranked India at a low of 132 amongst a sample of 183 countries. The report took a discouraging view of the existing regulatory framework and highlighted the shortcomings which are hindering the economic progress of the country. As a response to this report the Government of India appointed the Damodaran Committee for Reforming the Regulatory Environment for Doing Business in India (2013) to study the Indian regulatory environment and make suitable recommendations. The Committee in its report had observed *"Before setting up a new regulatory organization, adequate thought should go into the need for such an organization and the ability to man it appropriately and vest it with functional autonomy."* It had identified a number of factors which are affecting the functioning of the regulatory authorities such as – plethora of Central and State government laws and regulations governing the functioning of the regulatory authorities and dealing with the conduct of business in India; absence of adequate functional mandate of the different sectoral regulators; absence of transparency and autonomy in appointment procedures; lack of procedural uniformity in the policy making process; absence of a regulatory review committee, lack of self-evaluation procedures and norms of accountability etc. In addition the Indian regulators are faced with issues like lack of jurisdictional clarity between the line ministry and the regulatory authorities, inconsistencies in the functioning procedures and core policy goals of the different sectoral regulators, absence of financial autonomy, inadequacy in the parliamentary control mechanism,

8. (2008) 3 SCC 582.

excessive proliferation of tribunals etc. Thus the regulatory environment in India is faced with several challenges due to lack of financial, organizational and decisional autonomy and the same should be resolved by maintaining a judicious balance between autonomy, accountability and transparency. Some of the major challenges are–

(i) Jurisdictional Conflict between the Line Ministry and the Regulatory Authorities

There have been incidents of conflict on policy issues between the DOT and TRAI on matters relating to tariff fixation or between the Ministry of Power and the ERCs regarding the scope of their functions. It is necessary to charter out a proper demarcation of power, functions and responsibilities between the line ministry and the regulatory authorities as well as establish the relationship status between the two.

(ii) Inconsistencies in the Functioning Approaches and Policy Goals of Different Sectors

The different regulators dealing with various sectors have been conferred with different policy goals and functional domain which may conflict with the functioning of other regulators. The scope of functioning of ERCs is wide and deals with issues relating to investment and growth, advise the government on policy matters as well as adjudicate on sectoral competition issues like abuse of market dominance etc. which conflict with the functioning of the CCI. It is necessary to bring clarity into the functional scope of different regulators and achieve unanimity in terms of powers and authorities enjoyed by the different regulators.

(iii) Ambiguity in the Meaning of 'Policy Directives'

Under the parliamentary scheme of things the executive along with the legislature has the task of framing policies. But the regulatory authorities need to be granted necessary autonomy for the purpose of performing their functions. The ministries should not try to unnecessary intervene in the functions of the regulators by issuing policy directive. The relationship between the different executive authorities needs to be established to maintain administrative efficiency.

(iv) Appointment of Experts and Competent Professionals

There have been many criticisms against the appointment procedures of the members of these regulatory authorities. Appointment of former judges and retired bureaucrats in place of professionals has adversely affected the functioning of these bodies and affected their credibility.[9]

(v) Financial Autonomy

The regulators should be granted financial autonomy to reduce their dependence on the ministries and ensure functional autonomy. The IRDA and SEBI have been allowed to raise revenue by sharing a part of the license fee, similar provisions should be made for other regulators as well.

(vi) Accountability

There is no established mechanism to ensure the accountability of the regulatory authorities. Efforts should be made to set up proper mechanisms of regulatory accountability.

(vii) Parliamentary Control

Some of the authorities are required to submit their annual report to the Parliament. Parliament does not have much time to conduct in depth analysis. The parliamentary control is *ex post* analysis. Alternative mechanisms need to be established to evaluate the functioning of these bodies.

8.4 APPLICATION OF THE PRINCIPLES OF ADMINISTRATIVE LAW FOR THE PURPOSE OF REGULATING IRAS

Maintaining a judicious balance between autonomy and accountability is the key to ensure the effective working of the IRAs. It is necessary to grant autonomy to the regulatory authorities to implement the policy of the state within the identified parameters and at the same time the regulators should be made accountable for their actions The application of the principles of Administrative law and the process of judicial review holds a crucial key in regulating and maintaining functional autonomy of the regulatory authorities on one hand and abiding by the norms of accountability on the other hand.

(i) Excessive Delegation of Rule-making Power

The rule-making powers granted to the regulatory authorities are bound by the principles of constitutionality of delegated legislations. In the case of *Global Energy Limited v. Central Electricity Regulatory Commission*[10] the

9. CUTS International, Regulatory Autonomy and Accountability, Issues for Parliamentarians, January 2005.

10. (2009) 15 SCC 570.

constitutionality of the Central Electricity Regulatory Commission (Procedure, Terms and Conditions for Grant of Trading License and Other Related Matters) Regulations, 2004 were challenged by the appellants on the ground of excessive delegation. The Court applied the 'essential legislative function' test to hold since Regulation 6-A created substantive right, obligations and disabilities which were not contemplated in the parent statute i.e. Electricity Act 2003, they were held to ultra vires to the Constitution as well as the parent statute. It was further clarified that the general rule-making power "for carrying out the purpose of the Act" cannot be the basis of creating substantive rights, obligations and disabilities. The Court equated such exercise of rule-making by the Commission as *Henry VIII clause.*

(ii) Exercise of Discretionary Powers

In exercise of discretionary power the regulatory bodies are bound by the principles of fairness and reasonableness. In *Delhi Science Forum v. Union of India*[11] it was held that the Central Government while exercising its statutory power of granting licences for establishment, maintenance and working of telecommunications has a fiduciary duty as well. The regulatory authorities are bound to adhere to the norms laid down by courts for exercise of a statutory discretion. *It cannot be exercised in a manner which can be held to be unlawful and which is now known in administrative law as Wednesbury principle, stated in Associated Provincial Picture Houses Ltd. v. Wednesbury Corpn.*[12] *The aforesaid principle is attracted where it is shown that an authority exercising the discretion has taken a decision which is devoid of any plausible justification and any authority having reasonable persons could not have taken the said decision.* Even if the statutes do not expressly lay down the specific conditions for the exercise of discretionary power, the authorities will be bound by the observation made by Lord Diplock in the case of *Bromley LBC v.* Greater London Council[13] it was said by - "Powers to direct or approve the general level and structure of fares to be charged by the LTE for the carriage of passengers on its transport system, although unqualified by any express words in the Act, may nonetheless be subject to implied limitations when expressed to be exercisable by a local authority such as the GLC...."

The IRAs are required to exercise their powers in a manner to fulfil the objective of public welfare and interest of the nation.

11. (1996) 2 SCC 405.
12. (1947) 2 All ER 680 : (1948) 1 KB 223.
13. (1982) 1 All ER 129 : (1982) 2 WLR 62 : (1983) 1 AC 768.

(iii) Grant of Licence

If a statute confers power on a IRA to grant licences then the authority is bound to comply with the norms of fairness, reasonableness and non-arbitrariness. In *Global Energy Ltd. v. Central Electricity Regulatory Commission*[14] it was held that "When a disqualification is provided, it is to operate at the threshold in respect of the players in the field of trading in electricity. When, however, a regulatory statute is sought to be enforced, the power of the authority to impose restrictions and conditions must be construed having regard to the purpose and object it seeks to achieve. Dealing in any manner with generation, distribution and supply and trading in electrical energy is vital for the economy of the country. The private players who are permitted or who are granted licence in this behalf may have to satisfy the conditions imposed. No doubt, such conditions must be reasonable. Concededly, the doctrine of proportionality may have to be invoked."

(iv) Compliance with Principles of Natural Justice

The regulatory authorities, like other forms of administrative bodies, are bound by the principles of natural justice in performance of quasi-judicial functions. In *Union of India v. Tata Teleservices (Maharashtra) Ltd.*[15] it was held that the TDSAT was bound to frame their procedural rules based on the principles of natural justice.

(v) Allocation of Natural Resources

In the leading case of *Centre for Public Interest Litigation v. Union of India*[16] the Supreme Court was extremely critical of the criteria adopted for the allocation of 2G spectrum and the pricing methodology. It was highlighted that TRAI had failed to perform their functions in accordance with the objectives of the National Telecom Policy 1999.

> To say the least, the entire approach adopted by TRAI was lopsided and contrary to the decision taken by the Council of Ministers and its recommendations became a handle for the then Minister of Communications and Information Technology and the officers of DoT who virtually gifted away the important national asset at throw-away prices by wilfully ignoring the concerns raised from various quarters including the Prime Minister, Ministry of Finance and also some of its own officers. This becomes clear from the fact that soon after obtaining the licences, some of the beneficiaries offloaded their

14. (2009) 15 SCC 570, para 38.
15. (2007) 7 SCC 517.
16. (2012) 3 SCC 1.

> stakes to others in the name of transfer of equity or infusion of fresh capital by foreign companies, and thereby made huge profits. We have no doubt that if the method of auction had been adopted for grant of licence which could be the only rational transparent method for distribution of national wealth, the nation would have been enriched by many thousand crores.[17]

It was emphatically emphasised that–

> While it cannot be denied that TRAI is an expert body assigned with important functions under the 1997 Act, it cannot make recommendations overlooking the basic constitutional postulates and established principles and thereby deny the people from participating in the distribution of national wealth and benefit a handful of persons. Therefore, even though the scope of judicial review in such matters is extremely limited, as pointed out in *Delhi Science Forum v. Union of India* [(1996) 2 SCC 405] and a large number of other judgments relied upon by the learned counsel for the respondents, keeping in view the facts which have been brought to the notice of the Court that the mechanism evolved by TRAI for allocation of spectrum and the methodology adopted by the then Minister of Communications and Information Technology and the officers of DoT for grant of UAS licences may have caused huge loss to the nation, we have no hesitation to record a finding that the recommendations made by TRAI were flawed in many respects and implementation thereof by DoT resulted in gross violation of the objective of the NTP, 1999 and the decision taken by the Council of Ministers on 31-10-2003.[18]

(vi) Relationship between IRA and the Ministry

Speaking on the relationship between TRAI, as the regulatory body for the telecommunications sector in India and the Government of India, the Supreme Court in *Avishek Goenka v. Union of India*[19] held that the ministry had responsibility to issue guidelines and frame regulations and conditions of licence, in consultation with TRAI, to ensure coordination, standardisation and compliance with the regulations, as well as protecting the security interests of the country.

> In terms of Section 11 of the Telecom Regulatory Authority of India Act, 1997 it is a statutory obligation upon TRAI to recommend a regulatory regime which will serve the purpose of development, facilitate competition and promote efficiency, while taking due precautions in regard to safety of the people at large and various other aspects of subscriber verification. Similarly, DoT is responsible for discharging its functions and duties as, ultimately, it is the responsibility of the Government to provide for the safety of its citizens. TRAI

17. Id. Para 91.
18. Supra note 16 Para 92.
19. (2012) 5 SCC 275.

has to regulate the interests of telecom service providers and subscribers, so as to permit and ensure orderly growth of telecom sector. The Government of India and TRAI, both, have to attain this delicate balance of interests by providing relevant instructions or guidelines in a timely manner and ensuring their implementation in accordance with law.[20]

IRAs are expert bodies and their primary function is to make recommendation to the Government on various crucial issues relating to the development and proper functioning of the sectors. In *Avishek Goenka v. Union of India*[21] it was observed that–

> If one examines the powers and functions of TRAI, as postulated under Section 11 of the Act, it is clear that TRAI would not only recommend, to DoT, the terms and conditions upon which a licence is granted to a service provider but has to also ensure compliance with the same and may recommend revocation of licence in the event of non-compliance with the regulations. It has to perform very objectively one of its main functions i.e. to facilitate competition and promote efficiency in the operation of the telecommunication services, so as to facilitate growth in such services. It is expected of this regulatory authority to monitor the quality of service and even conduct periodical survey to ensure proper implementation.

In *Cellular Operators Assn. of India v. Union of India*[22] it was clarified that TRAI's recommendations have to be given weightage because TRAI was a specialised body and if the Central Government rejected the recommendation of TRAI, it has to be based on logical and concrete reasoning.

(vii) Resolving Conflict between IRA and the Ministry

The judiciary has recognized that under the statutory schemes there are multiple authorities dealing with the efficient working and growth of a sectoral area. In case of conflict between these authorities on policy issues and other administrative instructions it is important that the various authorities should resolve the crisis through mutual discussions and deliberations. In *Avishek Goenka v. Union of India*[23] the Court held that–

> [T]here are certain points on which there is a difference of opinion between DoT and TRAI. This limited divergence is required to be resolved by further clarification and issuance of more specific instructions.....Proper deliberation between the stakeholders possessed of technical know-how can resolve such issues usefully and effectively.

20. Id.
21. (2012) 5 SCC 275.
22. (2003) 3 SCC 186.
23. Supra note 21.

> The abovementioned points of divergence between TRAI and DoT are matters which will have serious ramifications not only vis-à-vis the regulatory authorities and the licensees but also on the subscribers and the entire country. These aspects demand serious deliberation at the hands of the technical experts. It will not be appropriate for this Court to examine these technical aspects, as such matters are better left in the domain of the statutory or expert bodies created for that purpose.

8.5 LIMITED SCOPE OF JUDICIAL REVIEW

In *Avishek Goenka v. Union of India*[24] it was clarified by the Court in unequivocal terms that in dealing with policy matters of extremely technical nature the IRAs should be considered as expert authorities and the judiciary should restrain themselves from acting as an appellate authority in determining the merits of the policies.

> The concept of "regulatory regime" has to be understood and applied by the courts, within the framework of law, but not by substituting their own views, for the views of the expert bodies like an appellate court. The regulatory regime is expected to fully regulate and control activities in all spheres to which the particular law relates.
>
> We have clearly stated that it is not for this Court to examine the merit or otherwise of such policy and regulatory matters which have been determined by expert bodies having possessing requisite technical know-how and are statutory in nature. However, the Court would step in and direct the technical bodies to consider the matter in accordance with law, while ensuring that public interest is safeguarded and arbitrary decisions do not prevail.[25]
>
> .....
>
> Some divergence on certain specific issues of the regulatory regime has been projected in the instructions and comments filed by TRAI and DoT. They need to be resolved but, in absence of any technical know-how or expertise being available with this Court, it will not be appropriate to decide, by a judicial dictum, as to which of the views expressed by these high-powered bodies would be more beneficial to the regulatory regime and will prove more effective in advancing the public interest. Essentially this should be left to be clarified and the disputes be resolved by the expert bodies themselves.
>
> It is a settled canon of law that in a regulatory regime, the terms and conditions imposed thereunder should be unambiguous and certain. It is expected that the authorities concerned would enforce the regulatory regime with exactitude. Therefore, it is not only desirable but also imperative that

24. Ibid.
25. Id. Para 21-22.

TRAI and DoT seriously cogitate on the issues where divergence has been expressed between them and bring unanimity in the terms and conditions of licences which would form an integral part of the instructions dated 14-3-2011.[26]

The Court recommended for the constitution of a Joint Expert Committee consisting of two experts from TRAI and two experts from DoT to be chaired by the Secretary, Ministry of Communications and Information Technology, Government of India to discuss and resolve the various conflicting issues.

8.6 APPEAL TO THE HIGHER JUDICIARY

The appellate power of the higher judiciary as provided under the specific statutes is unlimited. But the judiciary exercises self-restraint in exercising their power in light of the functional expertise of the different IRAs. In *W.B. Electricity Regulatory Commission v. CESC Ltd*[27] while dealing with the power of appeal to the High Court the Supreme Court held that *the appellate power of the High Court statutorily is not hedged in by any restriction, but in our opinion, the High Court merely because it has unrestricted appellate power, should not interfere with the considered order of the Commission unless it is satisfied that the order of the Commission is perverse, not based on evidence or on misreading of evidence, keeping in mind the fact that the Commission is an expert body.* Similarly in *Cellular Operators Assn. of India v. Union of India*[28] it was held that an appeal under Section 18 of the TRAI Act before the Supreme Court has to be confined to only substantial questions of law which arise out of the order of the Tribunal.

SUMMATION

Independent Regulatory Authorities are a phenomenon of the 21st century and a consequence of the regulatory functions of the state. In order to ensure the efficiency of these bodies in performing their function it is necessary to confer them with necessary autonomy but at the same it is important to ensure that these bodies are bound by the norms of administrative accountability so that they effectively fulfill their statutory obligations.

26. Id.
27. (2002) 8 SCC 715.
28. (2003) 3 SCC 186.

IX Civil Servants: Doctrine of Pleasure and Constitutional Safeguards

LEARNING OBJECTIVES

After reading this chapter, you will be familiar with:

- Nature, scope and meaning of Civil Servants in India
- Appointment, Terms and Conditions of Service in British India
- Constitutional provisions relating to Appointment and Tenure of Service
- Interface between Articles 309, 310 and 311
- Analysis of the *Tulsiram* Patel case
- Analysis of some recent judgments

9.1 INTRODUCTION

Civil Servants in India

The Constitution of India has not defined the term 'civil servants', except for the reference made in Entry 70 of List I and Entry 41 of List II of the Seventh Schedule of the Constitution. One of the important challenges for the judiciary has been to identify who are the civil servants for the purpose of application of the constitutional safeguards. The Supreme Court in *Union of India v. Tulsiram Patel*[1] has described Civil servants as *persons who are members of a civil service of the Union of India or an all-India service or a civil service of a State or who hold a civil post under the Union or a State, occupy in law a special position.*[2]

The employment of civil servants is not governed by the ordinary laws of master and servant relationship. The traditional 'contract of service' which

1. (1985) 3 SCC 398 : AIR 1985 SC 1416.
2. Id.

generally governs terms of employment does not have any application for the civil servants. The nature and character of service of the civil servants in India have been modelled on the British system and is fundamentally governed by the 'doctrine of pleasure'. In England the appointment of the civil servants are made at the pleasure of the Crown which is referred to as *durante hem placito* ("during good pleasure" or "during the pleasure of the appointor") and not under the concept of *dum bene se gesserit* (during good conduct).

The Supreme Court in several of its decisions have described and analyzed the concept of the doctrine of pleasure.

In the leading case of *Union of India v. Tulsiram Patel*[3] the Court referred to the doctrine of pleasure and observed–

> When a person holds office during the pleasure of the Crown, his appointment can be terminated at any time without assigning cause. The exercise of pleasure by the Crown can, however, be restricted by legislation enacted by Parliament because in the United Kingdom Parliament is sovereign and has the right to make or unmake any law whatever and all that a court of law can do with an Act passed by Parliament is to interpret its meaning but not to set it aside or declare it void. Blackstone in his *Commentaries* has thus described the unlimited legislative authority of Parliament (1 Bl., Comm. pp. 160, 161):
>
> "It has sovereign and uncontrollable authority in the making, confirming, enlarging, restraining, abrogating, repealing, reviving, and expounding of laws, concerning matters of all possible denominations, ecclesiastical or temporal, civil, military, maritime, or criminal: this being the place where that absolute despotic power, which must in all governments reside somewhere, is entrusted by the constitution of these kingdoms. All mischiefs and grievances, operations and remedies, that transcend the ordinary course of the laws, are within the reach of this extraordinary tribunal. It can regulate or new-model the succession to the Crown; as was done in the reign of Henry VIII, and William III. It can alter the established religion of the land; as was done in a variety of instances, in the reigns of king Henry VIII and his three children. It can change and create afresh even the constitution of the kingdom and of parliaments themselves; as was done by the act of union, and the several statutes for triennial and septennial elections. It can, in short, do everything that is not naturally impossible; and therefore some have not scrupled to call its power, by a figure rather too bold, the omnipotence of Parliament. True it is, that what the Parliament do, no authority upon earth can undo."

In the leading case of *Moti Ram Deka v. G.M., North East Frontier Rly,*[4] *Subba Rao J. observed "Under the English law, all servants of the*

3. Supra note 1 Id.
4. (1964) 5 SCR 683 : AIR 1964 SC 600.

Crown hold office during the pleasure of the Crown. The right to dismiss at pleasure is an implied term in every contract of employment under the Crown. This doctrine is not based upon any prerogative of the Crown but on public policy. If the terms of appointment definitely prescribe a tenure for good behaviour or expressly provide for a power to determine for a cause, such an implication of a power to dismiss at pleasure is excluded, and an Act of Parliament can abrogate or amend the said doctrine of public policy in the same way as it can do in respect of any other part of common law.[5] In recent times years the terms of service for civil servants in England have improved with enactment of statutes which has enabled the civil servants to bring legal actions in case of unfair dismissal or sue for breach of conditions of service. But the civil servant cannot insist on continuing his service because his employment his based on the pleasure of the Crown and he can merely demand for damages.

In *B.P. Singhal v. Union of India*[6] the Supreme Court had elaborately discussed the application and object of the doctrine of pleasure and observed–

> There is a distinction between the doctrine of pleasure as it existed in a feudal set-up and the doctrine of pleasure in a democracy governed by the rule of law. In a nineteenth century feudal set-up unfettered power and discretion of the Crown was not an alien concept. However, in a democracy governed by the rule of law, where arbitrariness in any form is eschewed, no Government or authority has the right to do what it pleases. The doctrine of pleasure does not mean a licence to act arbitrarily, capriciously or whimsically. It is presumed that discretionary powers conferred in absolute and unfettered terms on any public authority will necessarily and obviously be exercised reasonably and for the public good.
>
> ***
>
> The doctrine of pleasure as originally envisaged in England was a prerogative power which was unfettered. It meant that the holder of an office under pleasure could be removed at any time, without notice, without assigning cause, and without there being a need for any cause. But where the rule of law prevails, there is nothing like unfettered discretion or unaccountable action. The degree of need for reason may vary. The degree of scrutiny during judicial review may vary. But the need for reason exists. As a result when the Constitution of India provides that some offices will be held during the pleasure of the President, without any express limitations or restrictions, it should however necessarily be read as being subject to the 'fundamentals of constitutionalism'. Therefore in a constitutional set-up, when an office is held during the pleasure of any authority, and if no limitations or restrictions are

5. Id at para 64 (1964) 5 SCR 683, Para 64.
6. (2010) 6 SCC 331.

placed on the 'at pleasure' doctrine, it means that the holder of the office can be removed by the authority at whose pleasure he holds office, at any time, without notice and without assigning any cause.

The doctrine of pleasure, however, is not a licence to act with unfettered discretion to act arbitrarily, whimsically, or capriciously. It does not dispense with the need for a cause for withdrawal of the pleasure. In other words, 'at pleasure' doctrine enables the removal of a person holding office at the pleasure of an authority, summarily, without any obligation to give any notice or hearing to the person removed, and without any obligation to assign any reasons or disclose any cause for the removal, or withdrawal of pleasure. The withdrawal of pleasure cannot be at the sweet will, whim and fancy of the authority, but can only be for valid reasons."[7]

In the recent decision of *Union of India v. S.P. Sharma*[8] Supreme Court further recognized *the "pleasure doctrine" is a constitutional necessity, for the reasons that the difficulty in dismissing those servants whose continuance in office is detrimental to the State would, in case necessity arises to prove some offence to the satisfaction of the court, be such as to seriously impede the working of public service.*[9] But it also clarified that *illegality, irrationality and procedural non-compliance are grounds on which judicial review is permissible.*[10]

9.2 APPOINTMENT, TERMS AND CONDITIONS OF SERVICE IN BRITISH INDIA

The modern day emergence of civil servants in India fundamentally owes its origin to the East India Company and the British rule. The crown as well as the company had the power to appoint a person and also could remove or dismiss them at their own pleasure. Subsequently by the end of nineteenth century a well-structured civil service had developed in India who were referred to as 'civil service of the Crown in India' and they were governed by such conditions of service relating to methods of recruitment, pay and allowances, disciplinary rules etc. as determined by the executive. The Government of India Act, 1919 for the first time dealt with the issue of tenure of service by the introduction of Section 96-B which provided that–

Section 96-B(1) - *Subject to the provisions of this Act and of rules made thereunder*, every person in the civil service of the Crown in India *holds*

7. Ibid paras 22 & 33-34.
8. (2014) 6 SCC 351.
9. Id. at Para 66.
10. Id at Para 67.

> *office during His Majesty's pleasure*, and may be employed in any manner required by a proper authority within the scope of his duty but no person in that service may be dismissed by any authority subordinate to that by which he was appointed, and the Secretary of State in Council may (except so far as he may provide by rules to the contrary) reinstate any person in that service who has been dismissed.
>
> If any such person appointed by the Secretary of State in Council thinks himself wronged by an order of an official superior in a governor's province, and on due application made to that superior does not receive the redress to which he may consider himself entitled, he may, without prejudice to any other right of redress, complain to the governor of the province in order to obtain justice, and the governor is hereby directed to examine such complaint and require such action to be taken thereon as may appear to him to be just and equitable.

Thus for the first time the service conditions of the civil servants categorically stated that *every person in the civil service of the Crown in India held office "during His Majesty's pleasure"*. But there were three major safeguards provided within the provision —

(*1*) a civil servant could not be dismissed by any authority subordinate to that by which he was appointed;

(*2*) the Secretary of State in Council had the power, unless he provided to the contrary in the rules, to reinstate any person in service who had been dismissed; and

(*3*) if a civil servant appointed by the Secretary of State in Council thought himself wronged by an order of an official superior in a Governor's Province and on due application made to that superior did not receive the redress to which he considered himself entitled, he could, without prejudice to any other right of redress, complain to the Governor of the Province in order to obtain justice and the Governor had to examine such complaint and require such action to be taken thereon as might appear to him to be just and equitable.

Similar provisions were made in Section 240 of the Government of India Act 1935 which provided –

> Section 240. Tenure of office of persons employed in civil capacities in India.— (1) Except as expressly provided by this Act, every person who is a member of a civil service of the Grown in India, or holds any civil post under the Crown in India, holds office during His Majesty's pleasure.
>
> (2) No such person as aforesaid shall be dismissed from the service of His Majesty by any authority subordinate to that by which he was appointed.

(3) No such person as aforesaid shall be dismissed or reduced in rank until he has been given a reasonable opportunity of showing cause against the action proposed to be taken in regard to him:

Provided that this sub-section shall not apply—

(a) where a person is dismissed or reduced in rank on the ground of conduct which has led to his conviction on a criminal charge; or

(b) where an authority empowered to dismiss a person or reduce him in rank is satisfied that for some reason, to be recorded by that authority in writing, it is not reasonably practicable to give to that person an opportunity of showing cause.

(4) Notwithstanding that a person holding a civil post under the Crown in India holds office during His Majesty's pleasure, any contract under which a person, not being a member of a civil service of the Crown in India, is appointed under this Act to hold such a post may, if the Governor-General, or, as the case may be, the Governor, deems it necessary in order to secure the services of a person having special qualifications, provide for the payment to him of compensation, if before the expiration of an agreed period that post is abolished or he is, for reasons not connected with any misconduct on his part, required to vacate that post."

Thus in comparison to the 1919 Act, the provision under the 1935 Act provided for greater safeguards to the civil servants in the application of the doctrine of pleasure. These safeguards are –

(i) A person could not be dismissed from service by any authority subordinate to that by which he was appointed, and

(ii) A person could not be dismissed or reduced in rank until he had been given a reasonable opportunity of showing cause against the action proposed to be taken in regard to him.

Exception to the right of hearing are - (*a*) where a civil servant was dismissed or reduced in rank on ground of conduct which had led to his conviction on a criminal charge, and (*b*) where an authority empowered to dismiss him or reduce him in rank was satisfied that for some reason, to be recorded by that authority in writing, it was not reasonably practicable to give to that person an opportunity of showing cause.

9.3 CONSTITUTIONAL PROVISIONS RELATING TO APPOINTMENT AND TENURE OF SERVICE

Post-independence similar provisions relating to the manner of recruitment and removal from service were incorporated in the Constitution of India. The three relevant provisions in the Constitution are – Articles 309, 310 and 311. The three constitutional provisions lays down the procedural norms and safeguards for dismissal, removal or reduction in rank of a government servant or for imposition of any other penalty but the specific grounds for removal, dismissal or reduction in ranks are dealt with the various services laws and rules made under Article 309.

In *Govt. of A.P. v. N. Ramanaiah*[11] the Supreme Court observed that *"the elaborate provisions in Part XIV relating to services under the Union and the States indicate the importance which the framers of our Constitution attached to the civil service. The trinity of Articles 309, 310 and 311 deal with the services regulating recruitment, and conditions of service of persons appointed to public services and posts in connection with the affairs of the Union or any of the State."*

Article 309–

> *Recruitment and conditions of service of persons serving the Union or a State.*—Subject to the provisions of this Constitution, Acts of the appropriate Legislature may regulate the recruitment, and conditions of service of persons appointed, to public services and posts in connection with the affairs of the Union or of any State:
>
> Provided that it shall be competent for the President or such person as he may direct in the case of services and posts in connection with the affairs of the Union, and for the Governor of a State or such person as he may direct in the case of services and posts in connection with the affairs of the State, to make rules regulating the recruitment, and the conditions of service of persons appointed, to such services and posts until provision in that behalf is made by or under an Act of the appropriate Legislature under this article, and any rules so made shall have effect subject to the provisions of any such Act.

Article 309 provides that subject to the provisions of the Constitution, the legislatures can make rules for the recruitment, conditions of service and other related issues for persons appointed to the various public services under the Union or the State. But the rules made under Article309 have to be read with the provisions of Article 310. In *Moti Ram Deka v. G.M., North East Frontier Rly*[12] the Supreme Court categorically observed that –

> [T]he proviso to Article 309 makes it clear that it would be competent for the President or such person as he may direct in the case of services and posts in connection with the affairs of the Union, and for the Governor of a State or such person as he may direct in the case of services and posts in connection with the affairs of the State, to make rules regulating the recruitment, and prescribing the conditions of service of persons respectively

11. (2009) 7 SCC 165, para 13.
12. (1964) 5 SCR 683 : AIR 1964 SC 600.

appointed to services and posts under the Union or the State. The pleasure of the President or the Governor mentioned in Article 310(1) can thus be exercised by such person as the President or the Governor may respectively direct in that behalf, and the pleasure thus exercised has to be exercised in accordance with the rules made in that behalf. These rules, and indeed, the exercise of the powers conferred on the delegate must be subject to Article 310, and so, Article 309 cannot impair or affect the pleasure of the President or the Governor therein specified."

Article 310–

> *Tenure of office of persons serving the Union or a State.*—(1) Except as expressly provided by this Constitution, every person who is a member of a defence service or of a civil service of the Union or of an all-India service or holds any post connected with defence or any civil post under the Union holds office during the pleasure of the President, and every person who is a member of a civil service of a State or holds any civil post under a State holds office during the pleasure of the Governor of the State.
>
> (2) Notwithstanding that a person holding a civil post under the Union or a State holds office during the pleasure of the President or, as the case may be, of the Governor of the State, any contract under which a person, not being a member of a defence service or of an all-India service or of a civil service of the Union or a State, is appointed under this Constitution to hold such a post may, if the President or the Governor, as the case may be, deems it necessary in order to secure the services of a person having special qualifications, provide for the payment to him of compensation, if before the expiration of an agreed period that post is abolished or he is, for reasons not connected with any misconduct on his part, required to vacate that post.

Article 310(1) has incorporated the doctrine of pleasure in the appointment and tenure of service for civil servants in India by specifying that all members of the civil service holds office during the pleasure of the President or the Governor as the case may be. But it has categorically excluded those appointments from its scope which have been specifically provided for in the text of the Constitution such as the Judges of the Supreme Court and High Court,[13] Auditor- General of India,[14] Chairman and Members of the Public Service Commission,[15] Chief Election Commissioner and other Election Commissioners[16] etc.

Article 310(2) deals with cases of persons who have been appointed under a contract and it also provides that in case of person having special

13. Article 124, 217 and 218.
14. Article 148.
15. Article 317.
16. Article 324.

qualification whose service may be sought by the state then the President or Governor may appoint him under a special contract, and such a contract may further specify for payment of compensation if before the expiration of the agreed period the post is abolished or for any other reasons, not amounting to misconduct, he may be required to vacate the post.

Article 311–

> *Dismissal, removal or reduction in rank of persons employed in civil capacities under the Union or a State.*—(1) No person who is a member of a civil service of the Union or an all-India service or a civil service of a State or holds a civil post under the Union or a State shall be dismissed or removed by an authority subordinate to that by which he was appointed.
>
> (2) No such person as aforesaid shall be dismissed or removed or reduced in rank except after an inquiry in which he has been informed of the charges against him and given a reasonable opportunity of being heard in respect of those charges:
>
> Provided that where it is proposed after such inquiry, to impose upon him any such penalty, such penalty may be imposed on the basis of the evidence adduced during such inquiry and it shall not be necessary to give such person any opportunity of making representation on the penalty proposed:
>
> Provided further that this clause shall not apply—
>
> (*a*) where a person is dismissed or removed or reduced in rank on the ground of conduct which has led to his conviction on a criminal charge; or
>
> (*b*) where the authority empowered to dismiss or remove a person or to reduce him in rank is satisfied that for some reason, to be recorded by that authority in writing, it is not reasonably practicable to hold such inquiry; or
>
> (*c*) where the President or the Governor, as the case may be, is satisfied that in the interest of the security of the State it is not expedient to hold such inquiry.
>
> (3) If, in respect of any such person as aforesaid, a question arises whether it is reasonably practicable to hold such inquiry as is referred to in clause (2), the decision thereon of the authority empowered to dismiss or remove such person or to reduce him in rank shall be final.

Article 311 confers certain safeguards to persons employed in services under the Union of India or a State. These safeguards are – (1) A person cannot be dismissed or removed by an authority subordinate to that by which he was appointed, and (2) A person cannot be dismissed, removed or reduced in rank except after an inquiry in which he has been informed of the charges against him and given a reasonable opportunity of being heard in respect of those charges. However these safeguards are not available to a person when he is dismissed, removed or reduced in rank in any of the three situations – (a) on the ground of conduct which has led to his conviction on a criminal charge; (b) when the authority empowered to impose any of these penalties is satisfied that for some reason, to be recorded by that authority in writing, it is not reasonably practicable to hold such inquiry; and (*c*) where the President or the Governor of a State, as the case may be, is satisfied that in the interest of the security of the State it is not expedient to hold such inquiry. Therefore the application of the doctrine of pleasure has received constitutional recognition in India and is subject to the express provisions of the Constitution. The Supreme Court in *Moti Ram Deka v. G.M., North East Frontier Rly*[17] had categorically observed that *the rule-making authority under Article 309 cannot be validly exercised so as to curtail or affect the rights guaranteed to public servants under Article 311(2).* While dealing with the issue of whether the benefit of pension is subject to the protection of Article 311(2) the Court emphasized that –

> Article 311(2) is intended to afford a sense of security to public servants who are substantively appointed to a permanent post and one of the principal benefits which they are entitled to expect is the benefit of pension after rendering public service for the period prescribed by the Rules. It would, we think, not be legitimate to contend that the right to earn a pension to which a servant substantively appointed to a permanent post is entitled can be curtailed by Rules framed under Article 309 so as to make the said right either ineffective or illusory. Once the scope of Article 311(1) and (2) is duly determined, it must be held that no rule framed under Article 309 can trespass on the rights guaranteed by Article 311. This position is of basic importance and must be borne in mind in dealing with the controversy in the present appeals.

In *Govt. of A.P. v. N. Ramanaiah*[18] the Court speaking on the importance of Article 311(2) holds that–

> Every person who is a member of civil service of a State or holds any civil post under a State holds office during the pleasure of the Governor. Article 311(2) qualifies the pleasure of the President or the Governor, and the pleasure cannot be exercised if a government servant's service is to be terminated as a punishment for misconduct. In such a case, Article 311(2) mandates that a reasonable opportunity of being heard in respect of the charges must be given to the government servant. Any order inflicting the punishment of dismissal, removal without giving the opportunities as is required by Article 311(2) would be null and void as violative of an express constitutional requirement.

17. (1964) 5 SCR 683 : AIR 1964 SC 600.
18. (2009) 7 SCC 165, para 13.

9.4 INTERFACE BETWEEN ARTICLES 309, 310 AND 311

In *Union of India v. S.P. Sharma*[19] the Supreme Court analysed the scope and inter-relationship of the three constitutional provisions and observed–

> Article 309 empowers the appropriate legislature to regulate the recruitment and conditions of services of persons appointed in public services and posts in connection with the affairs of the Union or the State. But Article 309 is subject to the provisions of the Constitution. Hence, the rules and regulations made relating to the conditions of service are subject to Articles 310 and 311 of the Constitution. The proviso to Article 309 confers powers upon the President in case of services and posts in connection with the affairs of the Union and upon the Governor of a State in connection with the services and the conditions of services of the persons appointed. The service conditions shall be regulated according to such rules. Posts connected with the affairs of the State to make rules regulating the recruitment.
>
> Article 310 provides that every person, who is a member of the defence service or of a civil service of the Union or all-India service, or any civil or defence force shall hold such posts during the pleasure of the President. Similarly, every person who is a member of the civil services of a State or holds any civil post under a State, holds office during the pleasure of the Governor of the State. It is worth to mention here that the opening words of Article 310 "Except as expressly provided by this Constitution" make it clear that a government servant holds the office during the pleasure of the President or the Governor except as expressly provided by the Constitution.
>
> From a bare perusal of the provisions contained in Article 311 of the Constitution, it is manifestly clear that clauses (1) and (2) of Article 311 impose restrictions upon the exercise of power by the President or the Governor of the State of his pleasure under Article 310(1) of the Constitution. Article 311 makes it clear that any person who is a member of civil services of the Union or the State or holds civil posts under the Union or a State shall not be removed or dismissed from service by an authority subordinate to that by which he was appointed. Further, clause (2) of Article 311 mandates that such removal or dismissal or reduction in rank of the members of the civil services of the Union or the State shall be only after giving reasonable opportunity of hearing in respect of the charges levelled against him. However, proviso to Article 311(2) makes it clear that this clause shall not apply inter alia where the President or the Governor, as the case may be, is satisfied that in the interest of the security of the State it is not expedient to hold such enquiry.
>
> The expression "*except as otherwise provided in the Constitution*" as contained in Article 310(1) means this article is subject only to the express

19. (2014) 6 SCC 351.

provision made in the Constitution. No provision in the statute can curtail the provisions of Article 310 of the Constitution.[20]

(i) Distinction between Temporary and Permanent Employee

Article 311 makes no distinction between permanent and temporary posts, and the constitutional protection is applicable to all government servants irrespective of the nature of the employment.

(ii) Nature of Penalties

Primarily there are two classes of penalties in service jurisprudence - minor penalties and major penalties. Examples of minor penalties are censure, withholding of promotion and withholding of increments of pay whereas some of the major penalties are dismissal or removal from service, compulsory retirement and reduction in rank. The fundamental difference between these two categories of penalties are that in case of minor penalties the tenure of service of a government servant is not adversely affected whereas the major penalties brings an end to the tenure of service of a government employee.

The protection afforded by Article 311(2) is with specific reference to the imposition of three major penalties contemplated by Service Rules such as dismissal, removal or reduction in rank. Hence in case of termination of services on notice of a specified period, or on payment of salary for the said period, and if in exercise of the power thus conferred on the employer, the services of a temporary or probationary servant are terminated, it may not necessarily amount to removal. In all such cases if it is shown that the termination of services is no more than discharge *simplicitor* effected by virtue of the contract or the relevant rules the provisions of Article 311(2) will not be applicable. But if the termination of a temporary servant's service is on account of a penalty imposed on him or punitive action taken against him, then such termination would amount to removal and the procedural safeguards provided under Article 311(2) would be attracted. Similarly in cases of reduction in rank of an officiating servant the provisions of Article 311(2) would be applicable.[21]

(iii) Compulsory Retirement vis-à-vis Termination of Service

In cases of compulsory retirement the constitutional protections under Article311 (2) are not be applicable because the act of compulsory retirement

20. Ibid (2014) 6 SCC 351, Paras 61-64.
21. **See** generally (1964) 5 SCR 683 : AIR 1964 SC 600.

is does not come within the scope of the term 'removal' under Article 311(2).

In *Moti Ram Deka v. G.M., North East Frontier Rly*[22] the Supreme Court while dealing with the issue of determining the nature of the right which a permanent servant observed–

> "A person who substantively holds a permanent post has a right to continue in service, subject, of course, to the rule of superannuation and the rule as to compulsory retirement. If for any other reason that right is invaded and he is asked to leave his service, the termination of his service must inevitably mean the defeat of his right to continue in service and as such, it is in the nature of a penalty and amounts to removal. In other words, termination of the services of a permanent servant otherwise than on the ground of superannuation or compulsory retirement, must per se amount to his removal, and so, if by Rule 148(3) or Rule 149(3) such a termination is brought about, the Rule clearly contravenes Article 311(2) and must be held to be invalid."[23]

It was further held that "Even if a person is holding a post which does not carry any pension, he has a right to continue in service until he reaches the age of superannuation and the said right is a very valuable right That is why the invasion of this right must inevitably mean that the termination of his service is, in substance, and in law, removal from service."[24] Thus if the civil servant has got a "right to continue in the post, then, unless the contract of employment or the Rules provide to the contrary, his services cannot be terminated otherwise than for misconduct, negligence, inefficiency or other good and sufficient cause. A termination of the service of such a servant on such grounds must be a punishment and, therefore, a dismissal or removal within Article 311, for it operates as a forfeiture of his right and he is visited with the evil consequences of loss of pay and allowances".

(iv) Subordinate Authority

The Supreme Court in *Govt. of A.P. v. N. Ramanaiah*[25] clarified that *Article 311(1) does not command that the dismissal must be by the very same authority who made the appointment or by its direct superior. The dismissal can be either by the appointing authority or by any other authority to which the appointing authority is subordinate. The dismissal of a civil servant must comply with the procedure laid down in Article 311.* It was further observed that–

22. (1964) 5 SCR 683 : AIR 1964 SC 600.
23. Id Para 26.
24. Id Para 29.
25. (2009) 7 SCC 165, para 15.

The Constitution being the transcendental law, the rule-making authority by making Rule 14(2) took care to see that constitutional guarantee enshrined in Article 311(1) of the Constitution which was available to the government servant was protected. That the construction placed by us on the expression "subordinate" is in consonance with the meaning and import of the word "subordinate" occurring in Article 311(1) of the Constitution is apparent from many a decisions of this Court. We shall refer to some of them. In our considered opinion there is nothing in the Constitution which debars the Government from exercising the powers of appointing authority to dismiss a government servant from service. These Rules cannot be read as implying that dismissal must be by the very authority who made the appointment or by his immediate superior.[26]"

9.5 ANALYSIS OF THE *TULSIRAM PATEL CASE*

In *Union of India v. Tulsiram Patel*[27] writ petitions were filed by several government servants who were either dismissed or removed from service without holding any inquiry. They were not assigned any reasons, not informed of the charges made against them nor were they given any opportunity of being heard before their removal or dismissal from service as the actions were taken under one or the other three clauses of the second proviso to Article 311(2). The Court while analyzing the different constitutional provisions made an in depth study of the application of the doctrine of pleasure.

On the application of doctrine of pleasure it was observed –

Ministers frame policies and Legislatures enact laws and lay down the mode in which such policies are to be carried out and the object of the legislation achieved. In many cases, in a Welfare State such as ours, such policies and statutes are intended to bring about socio-economic reforms and the uplift of the poor and disadvantaged classes. From the nature of things the task of efficiently and effectively implementing these policies and enactments, however, rests with the civil services. The public is, therefore, vitally interested in the efficiency and integrity of such services. Government servants are after all paid from the public exchequer to which everyone contributes either by way of direct or indirect taxes. Those who are paid by the public and are charged with public administration for public good must, therefore, in their turn bring to the discharge of their duties a sense of responsibility. The efficiency of public administration does not depend only upon the top echelons of these services. It depends as much upon all the other members of such services, even on those in the most subordinate posts. For instance, railways do not run because of the members of the Railway Board or the General Managers

26. (2009) 7 SCC 165, para 23.
27. (1985) 3 SCC 398.

> of different railways or the heads of different departments of the railway administration. They run also because of engine-drivers, firemen, signalmen, booking clerks and those holding hundred other similar posts. Similarly, it is not the administrative heads who alone can see to the proper functioning of the post and telegraph service. For a service to run efficiently there must, therefore, be a collective sense of responsibility. But for a government servant to discharge his duties faithfully and conscientiously, he must have a feeling of security of tenure. Under our Constitution, this is provided for by the Acts and rules made under Article 309 as also by the safeguards in respect of the punishments of dismissal, removal or reduction in rank provided in clauses (1) and (2) of Article 311. It is, however, as much in public interest and for public good that government servants who are inefficient, dishonest or corrupt or have become a security risk should not continue in service and that the protection afforded to them by the Acts and rules made under Article 309 and by Article 311 be not abused by them to the detriment of public interest and public good. When a situation as envisaged in one of the three clauses of the second proviso to clause (2) of Article 311 arises and the relevant clause is properly applied and the disciplinary inquiry dispensed with, the concerned government servant cannot be heard to complain that he is deprived of his livelihood. The livelihood of an individual is a matter of great concern to him and his family but his livelihood is a matter of his private interest and where such livelihood is provided by the public exchequer and the taking away of such livelihood is in the public interest and for public good, the former must yield to the latter. These consequences follow not because the pleasure doctrine is a special prerogative of the British Crown which has been inherited by India and transposed into our Constitution adapted to suit the constitutional set-up of our Republic but because public policy requires, public interest needs and public good demands that there should be such a doctrine.
>
> It is thus clear that the pleasure doctrine embodied in Article 310(1), the protection afforded to civil servants by clauses (1) and (2) of Article 311 and the withdrawal of the protection under clause (2) of Article 311 by the second proviso thereto are all provided in the Constitution on the ground of public policy and in the public interest and are for public good.[28]

On the relationship between the three Articles 309, 310 and 311 the Court observed that the *three articles are interlinked and form an integrated whole. There is an organic and thematic unity running through them* –

> These articles occur in Chapter I of Part XIV of the Constitution. Part XIV is entitled "Services under the Union and. the States" and Chapter I thereof is entitled "Services". While Article 309 deals with the recruitment and conditions of service of persons appointed to the public services and posts in connection with the affairs of the Union or a State, Article 310 deals with the tenure of office of members of the defence services and of civil services of the

28. Ibid Para 44-45.

Union and the States and Article 311 provides certain safeguards to persons employed in civil capacities under the Union or a State but not to members of the defence services. The first thing which is required to be noticed about Article 309 is that it itself makes no provision for recruitment or conditions of service of government servants but confers power upon the appropriate Legislature to make laws and upon the President and the Governor of a State to make rules in respect of these matters. The passing of these Acts and the framing of these rules are, however, made "*Subject* to the provisions of this Constitution". This phrase which precedes and qualifies the power conferred by Article 309 is significantly different from the qualifying phrase in Article 310(1) which is "*Except as expressly provided* by this Constitution".[29]

....

Clauses (1) and (2) of Article 311 impose restrictions upon the exercise by the President or the Governor of a State of his pleasure under Article 310(1). These are express provisions with respect to termination of service by dismissal or removal as also with respect to reduction in rank of a civil servant and thus come within the ambit of the expression "Except as expressly provided by this Constitution" qualifying Article 310(1). Article 311 is thus an exception to Article 310 and was described in *Parshotam Lal Dhingra v. Union of India*[30] as operating as a proviso to Article 310(1) though set out in a separate article. Article 309 is, however, not such an exception. It does not lay down any express provision which would derogate from the amplitude of the exercise of pleasure under Article 310(1). It merely confers upon the appropriate Legislature or executive the power to make laws and frame rules but this power is made subject to the provisions of the Constitution. Thus, Article 309 is subject to Article 310(1) and any provision restricting the exercise of the pleasure of the President or Governor in an Act or rule made or framed under Article 309 not being an express provision of the Constitution, cannot fall within the expression "Except as expressly provided by this Constitution" occurring in Article 310(1) and would be in conflict with Article 310(1) and must be held to be unconstitutional. Clauses (1) and (2) of Article 311 expressly restrict the manner in which a government servant can be dismissed, removed or reduced in rank and unless an Act made or rule framed under Article 309 also conforms to these restrictions, it would be void. The restriction placed by clauses (1) and (2) of Article 311 are two: (*1*) with respect to the authority empowered to dismiss or remove a government servant provided for in clause (1) of Article 311; and (*2*) with respect to the procedure for dismissal, removal or reduction in rank of a government servant provided for in clause (2). The second proviso to Article 311(2), which is the central point of controversy in these appeals and writ petitions, lifts the restriction imposed by Article 311(2) in the cases specified in the three clauses of that proviso.[31]

29. Supra note 27 Para 47.
30. AIR 1959 SC 36.
31. Supra note 27 Para 54.

On the issue of whether the term 'pleasure of the President or the Governor' has to be literally implemented the Court held that–

> The position, therefore, is that the pleasure of the President or the Governor is not required to be exercised by either of them personally, and that is indeed obvious from the language of Article 311. Under clause (1) of that article a government servant cannot be dismissed or removed by an authority subordinate to that by which he was appointed. The question of an authority equal or superior in rank to the appointing authority cannot arise if the power to dismiss or remove is to be exercised by the President or the Governor personally. Clause (*b*) of the second proviso to Article 311 equally makes this clear when the power to dispense with an inquiry is conferred by it upon the authority empowered to dismiss, remove or reduce in rank a government servant in a case where such authority is satisfied that for some reason, to be recorded by that authority in writing, it is not reasonably practicable to hold such inquiry, because if it was the personal satisfaction of the President or the Governor, the question of the satisfaction of any authority empowered to dismiss or remove or reduce in rank a government servant would not arise. Thus, though under Article 310(1) the tenure of a government servant is at the pleasure of the President or the Governor, the exercise of such pleasure can be either by the President or the Governor acting with the aid and on the advice of the Council of Ministers or by the authority specified in Acts made under Article 309 or in rules made under such Acts or made under the proviso to Article 309; and in the case of clause (*c*) of the second proviso to Article 311(2), the inquiry is to be dispensed with not on the personal satisfaction of the President or the Governor but on his satisfaction arrived at with the aid and on the advice of the Council of Ministers.[32]

On the application of principles of natural justice and right of fair hearing under Article 311–

> Clause (2) of Article 311 gives a constitutional mandate to the principles of natural justice and the audi alteram partem rule by providing that a person employed in a civil capacity under the Union or a State shall not be dismissed or removed from service or reduced in rank until after an inquiry in which he has been informed of the charges against him and has been given a reasonable opportunity of being heard in respect of those charges. To this extent, the pleasure doctrine enacted in Article 310(1) is abridged because Article 311(2) is an express provision of the Constitution. This safeguard provided for a government servant by clause (2) of Article 311 is, however, taken away when the second proviso to that clause becomes applicable. The safeguard provided by clause (1) of Article 311, however, remains intact and continues to be available to the government servant. The second proviso to Article 311(2) becomes applicable in the three cases mentioned in clauses (*a*) to (*c*) of that proviso. These cases are:

32. Id. Para 59.

"(*a*) where a person is dismissed or removed or reduced in rank on the ground of conduct which has led to his conviction on a criminal charge; or

(*b*) where the authority empowered to dismiss or remove a person or to reduce him in rank is satisfied that for some reason, to be recorded by that authority in writing, it is not reasonably practicable to hold such inquiry; or

(c) where the President or the Governor, as the case may be, is satisfied that in the interest of the security of the State it is not expedient to hold such inquiry."[33]

.....

On the issue of exclusion of the right to be heard under Article 311(2) the Court observed–

The language of the second proviso is plain and unambiguous. The keywords in the second proviso are "this clause shall not apply". By "this clause" is meant clause (2). As clause (2) requires an inquiry to be held against a government servant, the only meaning attributable to these words is that this inquiry shall not be held. There is no scope for any ambiguity in these words and there is no reason to give them any meaning different from the plain and ordinary meaning which they bear. The resultant effect of these words is that when a situation envisaged in any of the three clauses of the proviso arises and that clause becomes applicable, the safeguard provided to a government servant by clause (2) is taken away. As pointed out earlier, this provision is as much in public interest and for public good and a matter of public policy as the pleasure doctrine and the safeguards with respect to security of tenure contained in clauses (1) and (2) of Article 311.

Before, however, any clause of the second proviso can come into play the condition laid down in it must be satisfied. The condition for the application of each of these clauses is different. In the case of clause (*a*) a government servant must be guilty of conduct deserving the penalty of dismissal, removal or reduction in rank which conduct has led to him being convicted on a criminal charge. In the case of clause (*b*) the disciplinary authority must be satisfied that it is not reasonably practicable to hold an inquiry. In the case of clause (*c*) the President or the Governor of a State, as the case may be, must be, satisfied that in the interest of the security of the State, it is not expedient to hold an inquiry. When these conditions can be said to be fulfilled will be discussed later while dealing separately with each of the three clauses. The paramount thing, however, to bear in mind is that the second proviso will apply only where the conduct of a government servant is such as he deserves the punishment of dismissal, removal or reduction in rank. If the conduct is such as to deserve a punishment different from those mentioned above, the second proviso cannot come into play at all, because Article 311(2) is itself confined only to these three penalties. Therefore, before denying a government

33. Ibid Para 60.

servant his constitutional right to an inquiry, the first consideration would be whether the conduct of the concerned government servant is such as justifies the penalty of dismissal, removal or reduction in rank. Once that conclusion is reached and the condition specified in the relevant clause of the second proviso is satisfied, that proviso becomes applicable and the government servant is not entitled to an inquiry. The extent to which a government servant can be denied his right to an inquiry formed the subject-matter of considerable debate at the Bar and we, therefore, now turn to the question whether under the second proviso to Article 311(2) even though the inquiry is dispensed with, some opportunity at least should not be afforded to the government servant so that he is not left wholly without protection. As most of the arguments on this part of the case were common to all the three clauses of the second proviso, it will be convenient at this stage to deal at one place with all the arguments on this part of the case, leaving aside to be separately dealt with the other arguments pertaining only to a particular clause of the second proviso.[34]

****

The position which emerges from the above discussion is that the keywords of the second proviso govern each and every clause of that proviso and leave no scope for any kind of opportunity to be given to a government servant. The phrase "this clause *shall* not apply" is mandatory and not directory. It is in the nature of a constitutional prohibitory injunction restraining the disciplinary authority from holding an inquiry under Article 311(2) or from giving any kind of opportunity to the concerned government servant. There is thus no scope for introducing into the second proviso some kind of inquiry or opportunity by a process of inference or implication. The maxim "*expressum facit cessare tacitum*" ("when there is express mention of certain things, then anything not mentioned is excluded") applies to the case. As pointed out by this Court in *B. Shankara Rao Badami* v. *State of Mysore*[35] this well-known maxim is a principle of logic and common sense and not merely a technical rule of construction. The second proviso expressly mentions that clause (2) shall not apply where one of the clauses of that proviso becomes applicable. This express mention excludes everything that clause (2) contains and there can be no scope for once again introducing the opportunities provided by clause (2) or any one of them into the second proviso. In *Atkinson v. United States of America Government*[36] Lord Reid said:

"It is now well recognised that the court has power to expand procedure laid down by statute if that is necessary to prevent infringement of natural justice and is not plainly contrary to the intention of Parliament."

Here, however, the attempt is not merely to do something contrary to the intention of 'Parliament', that is, in our case, the Constituent Assembly, but to

34. Supra note 27.
35. (1969) 1 SCC 1.
36. LR 1971 AC 197.

do something contrary to an express prohibition contained in the Constitution. The conclusion which flows from the express language of the second proviso is inevitable and there is no escape from it. It may appear harsh but, as mentioned earlier, the second proviso has been inserted in the Constitution as a matter of public policy and in public interest and for public good just as the pleasure doctrine and the safeguards for a government servant provided in clauses (1) and (2) of Article 311 have been. It is in public interest and for public good that a government servant who has been convicted of a grave and serious offence or one rendering him unfit to continue in office should be summarily dismissed or removed from service instead of being allowed to continue in it at public expense and to public detriment. It is equally in public interest and for public good that where his offence is such that he should not be permitted to continue to hold the same rank, that he should be reduced in rank. Equally, where a public servant by himself or in concert with others has brought about a situation in which it is not reasonably practicable to hold an inquiry and his conduct is such as to justify his dismissal, removal or reduction in rank, both public interest and public good demand that such penalty should forthwith and summarily be imposed upon him; and similarly, where in the interest of the security of the State it is not expedient to hold an inquiry, it is in the public interest and for public good that where one of the three punishments of dismissal, removal or reduction in rank is called for, it should be summarily imposed upon the concerned government servant. It was argued that in a case falling under clause (*b*) or (*c*), a government servant ought to be placed under suspension until the situation improves or the danger to the security of the State has passed, as the case may be, and it becomes possible to hold an inquiry. This argument overlooks the fact that suspension involves the payment at least of subsistence allowance and such allowance is paid at public expense, and that neither public interest would be benefited nor public good served by placing such government servant under suspension because it may take a considerable time for the situation to improve or the danger to be over. Much as this may seem harsh and oppressive to a government servant, this Court must not forget that the object underlying the second proviso is public policy, public interest and public good and the Court must, therefore, repel the temptation to be carried away by feelings of commiseration and sympathy for those government servants who have been dismissed, removed or reduced in rank by applying the second proviso. Sympathy and commiseration cannot be allowed to outweigh considerations of public policy, concern for public interest, regard for public good and the peremptory dictate of a constitutional prohibition. The Court must bear in mind that the second proviso has been in the Constitution since it was originally enacted. It was not blindly or slavishly copied from Section 240(3) of the Government of India Act, 1935. Article 311 was Article 282-B of the draft Constitution of India and the draft Article 282-B was discussed and a considerable debate took place on it in the Constituent Assembly (see the *Official Report of the Constituent Assembly Debates*, Vol. IX, pp. 1099 to 1116). The greater part of this debate centred upon the proviso to clause (2) of the draft Article 282-B, which is now the second proviso to Article 311. Further, the Court should also bear in mind that clause (*c*) of the second proviso and clause (3) of Article 311 did not feature in Section 240 of the Government of India Act, 1935, but were new provisions consciously introduced by the Constituent Assembly in Article 311. Those who formed the Constituent Assembly were not the advocates of a despotic or dictatorial form of government. They were the persons who enacted into our Constitution the Chapter on Fundamental Rights. The majority of them had fought for freedom and had suffered imprisonment in the cause of liberty and they, therefore, were not likely to introduce into our Constitution any provision from the earlier Government of India Acts which had been intended purely for the benefit of a foreign imperialistic power. After all, it is not as if a government servant is without any remedy when the second proviso has been applied to him. There are two remedies open to him, namely, departmental appeal and judicial review.[37]

On the application of *audi alteram partem* the Court adopted the interpretative principle laid down in *Khem Chand v. Union of India*[38] wherein it was stated–

It is true that the provision does not, in terms, refer to different stages at which opportunity is to be given to the officer concerned. All that it says is that the government servant must be given a reasonable opportunity of showing cause against the action proposed to be taken in regard to him. He must not only be given an opportunity but such opportunity must be a reasonable one. In order that the opportunity to show cause against the proposed action may be regarded as a reasonable one, it is quite obviously necessary that the government servant should have the opportunity, to say, if that be his case, that he has not been guilty of any misconduct to merit any punishment at all and also that the particular punishment proposed to be given is much more drastic and severe than he deserves. Both these pleas have a direct bearing on the question of punishment and may well be put forward in showing cause against the proposed punishment. If this is the correct meaning of the clause, as we think it is, what consequences follow? If it is open to the government servant under this provision to contend, if that be the fact, that he is not guilty of any misconduct then how can he take that plea unless he is told what misconduct is alleged against him? If the opportunity to show cause is to be a reasonable one it is clear that he should be informed about the charge or charges levelled against him and the evidence by which it is sought to be established, for it is only then that he will be able to put forward his defence. If the purpose of this provision is to give the government servant an opportunity to exonerate himself from the charge and if this opportunity is to be a reasonable one he should be allowed to show that the evidence against him is not worthy of credence or consideration and that he can only do if he is given a chance to cross-examine the witnesses called against him and to examine himself or any other witness in support of his defence. All this

37. Supra note 27.

38. AIR 1958 SC 300 : 1958 SCR 1080.

appears to us to be implicit in the language used in the clause, but this does not exhaust his rights. In addition to showing that he has not been guilty of any misconduct so as to merit any punishment, it is reasonable that he should also have an opportunity to contend that the charges proved against him do not necessarily require the particular punishment proposed to be meted out to him. He may say, for instance, that although he has been guilty of some misconduct it is not of such a character as to merit the extreme punishment of dismissal or even of removal or reduction in rank and that any of the lesser punishments ought to be sufficient in his case.

To summarise: the reasonable opportunity envisaged by the provision under consideration includes:

(*a*) an opportunity to deny his guilt and establish his innocence, which he can only do if he is told what the charges levelled against him are and the allegations on which such charges are based;

(*b*) an opportunity to defend himself by cross-examining the witnesses produced against him and by examining himself or any other witnesses in support of his defence; and finally

(*c*) an opportunity to make his representation as to why the proposed punishment should not be inflicted on him, which he can only do if the competent authority, after the inquiry is over and after applying his mind to the gravity or otherwise of the charges proved against the government servant tentatively proposes to inflict one of the three punishments and communicates the same to the government servant.

In short the substance of the protection provided by rules, like Rule 55 referred to above, was bodily lifted out of the rules and together with an additional opportunity embodied in Section 240(3) of the Government of India Act, 1935 so as to give a statutory protection to the government servants and has now been incorporated in Article 311(2) so as to convert the protection into a constitutional safeguard.

It was further held–

....If we look at clause (2) of Article 311 in the light of what is stated above, it will be apparent that that clause is merely an express statement of the audi alteram partem rule which is implicitly made part of the guarantee contained in Article 14 as a result of the interpretation placed upon that article by recent decisions of this Court. Clause (2) of Article 311 requires that before a government servant is dismissed, removed or reduced in rank, an inquiry must be held in which he is informed of the charges against him and given a reasonable opportunity of being heard in respect of those charges. The nature of the hearing to be given to a government servant under clause (2) of Article 311 has been elaborately set out by this Court in *Khem Chand case* in the passages from the judgment extracted above. Though that case related to the original clause (2) of Article 311, the same applies to the present clause (2) of Article 311 except for the fact that now a government servant has no right to make any representation against the penalty proposed to be imposed upon him but, as pointed out earlier, in the case of *Suresh Koshy George* v. *University of Kerala*[39] such an opportunity is not the requirement of the principles of natural justice and as held in *Associated Cement Companies Ltd.* v. *T.C. Shrivastava*[40] neither the ordinary law of the land nor industrial law requires such an opportunity to be given. The opportunity of showing cause against the proposed penalty was only the result of the interpretation placed by the Judicial Committee of the Privy Council in *Lall case*[41] upon Section 240(3) of the Government of India Act, 1935, which was accepted by this Court in *Khem Chand case*. If, therefore, an inquiry held against a government servant under clause (2) of Article 311 is unfair or biased or has been conducted in such a manner as not to give him a fair or reasonable opportunity to defend himself, undoubtedly, the principles of natural justice would be violated, but in such a case the order of dismissal, removal or reduction in rank would be held to be bad as contravening the express provisions of clause (2) of Article 311 and there will be no scope for having recourse to Article 14 for the purpose of invalidating it.

Upholding the exceptions to the rule of *audi alteram partem* in Article 311(2) the Court held–

If legislation and the necessities of a situation can exclude the principles of natural justice including the audi alteram partem rule, a fortiori so can a provision of the Constitution, for a constitutional provision has a far greater and all-pervading sanctity than a statutory provision. In the present case, clause (2) of Article 311 is expressly excluded by the opening words of the second proviso and particularly its keywords "this clause shall not apply". As pointed out above, clause (2) of Article 311 embodies in express words the audi alteram partem rule. This principle of natural justice having been expressly excluded by a constitutional provision, namely, the second proviso to clause (2) of Article 311, there is no scope for reintroducing it by a side-door to provide once again the same inquiry which the constitutional provision has expressly prohibited. Where a clause of the second proviso is applied on an extraneous ground or a ground having no relation to the situation envisaged in that clause, the action in so applying it would be mala fide, and, therefore, void. In such a case the invalidating factor may be referable to Article 14. This is, however, the only scope which Article 14 can have in relation to the second proviso, but to hold that once the second proviso is properly applied and clause (2) of Article 311 excluded. Article 14 will step in to take the place of clause (2) would be to nullify the effect of the opening words of the second proviso and thus frustrate the intention of the makers of the Constitution.

39. AIR 1969 SC 198.
40. 1984 Supp SCC 87.
41. AIR 1948 PC 121.

The second proviso is based on public policy and is in public interest and for public good and the Constitution-makers who inserted it in Article 311(2) were the best persons to decide whether such an exclusionary provision should be there and the situations in which this provision should apply.

9.6 SOME RECENT JUDGMENTS

In *Union of India v. S.P. Sharma*[42] the Supreme Court looked into the scope of judicial review and held that that *the power of pleasure exercised by the President in terminating the services of the respondents does not suffer from any illegality, bias or mala fides, nor is based on any other extraneous ground, and the same cannot be challenged on the ground that it is a camouflage.* It further observed–

> There is no dispute that the order of termination passed against the Army personnel in exercise of the "pleasure doctrine", is subject to judicial review, but while exercising judicial review, this Court cannot substitute its own conclusion on the basis of materials on record. The Court exercising the power of judicial review has certain limitations, particularly in cases of this nature. The safety and security of the nation is above all/everything. When the President in exercise of his constitutional power terminates the services of the Army officers, whose tenure of services are at the pleasure of the President and such termination is based on materials on record, then this Court in exercise of powers of judicial review should be slow in interfering with such pleasure of the President exercising constitutional power. In a constitutional set-up, when office is held during the pleasure of the President, it means that the officer can be removed by the authority on whose pleasure he holds office without assigning any reason. The authority is not obliged to assign any reason or disclose any cause for the removal.[43]

In this case while dealing with the termination of service of two army officers on ground of espionage the Court applied the doctrine of pleasure to hold that a government servant holds the office during the pleasure of the President or the Governor, except as otherwise provided in the Constitution, and a right of hearing can be denied in the interest of the security of the state.

In *Ajit Kumar v. State of Jharkhand*[44] the Appellant was working as a subordinate judge and an order was issued by the Governor removing him from service on the basis of a resolution of the Full Court of the High Court of Jharkhand recommending his removal from service. The removal order was on ground of non-application of mind in passing the order under

42. (2014) 6 SCC 351.
43. Id.
44. (2011) 11 SCC 458.

proviso (b) Article 311(2) and for non-compliance with the principles of natural justice. It was argued by the State that 'the Full Court, after considering the confidential report and the report of the Inspecting Judge, resolved that the appellant can be recommended for removal from the service, without any enquiry as it was felt that it was not practicable in the interest of the institution to hold an inquiry since it may lead to the question of validity of several judgments rendered by him. Consequently, the Full Court recommended for invocation of proviso (*b*) to Article 311(2) of the Constitution of India to dispense with the inquiry as against the appellant to remove him from service, following which the Governor while exercising his power issued the impugned order of removal of the appellant from the service which was under challenge in the writ petition before the High Court.'

The Supreme Court deliberated the constitutional scheme of Article 309, 310 and 311 and observed–

> Within the scheme of the Constitution of India, provisions relating to public service may be found in Articles 309, 310 and 311. It is important to note that these provisions (namely, Articles 310 and 311) afford protection to public servants from being dismissed, removed or reduced in rank without holding a proper inquiry or giving a hearing.
>
> Article 311 provides for the protection to public servants against punitive action being taken against them by an authority subordinate to one who appointed them. Exceptions to Article 311 have been provided in clauses (*a*), (*b*) and (*c*) (*sic* of the second proviso) to clause (2) of Article 311 itself, which provide that the said article shall not apply to such employees who have been punished for conviction in a criminal case, where inquiry is not practicable to be held for reasons to be recorded in writing or where the President or the Governor as the case may be is satisfied that such an inquiry is not to be held in the interest of the security of the State.
>
> In order to appreciate the power to be exercised under Article 311 of the Constitution of India, it would be appropriate to look at Article 310 of the Constitution of India. Under the doctrine of pleasure, which has been recognised under our constitutional framework, all civil posts under the Government are held at the pleasure of the Government under which they are held and are terminable at its will. The aforesaid power is what the doctrine of pleasure defines, which was recognised in the United Kingdom and also received the constitutional sanction under our Constitution in the light of Article 310 of the Constitution of India. However, it is to be noticed that in India the same is subject to other provisions of the Constitution which include the restrictions imposed by Article 310(2) and Articles 311(1) and (2). Therefore, under the Indian constitutional framework, dismissal of civil servants must comply with the procedure laid down in Article 311 and Article 310(1) cannot be invoked independently with the object of justifying a contravention of Article 311(2).

> There is an exception provided by way of incorporation of Article 311(2) with sub-clauses (*a*), (*b*) and (*c*). No such enquiry is required to be conducted for the purposes of dismissal, removal or reduction in rank of persons when the same related to dismissal on the ground of conviction or where it is not practicable to hold an enquiry for the reasons to be recorded in writing by that authority empowered to dismiss or remove a person or reduce him in rank or it is not practicable to hold an enquiry for the security of the State. These three exceptions are well recognised for dispensing with an enquiry, which is required to be conducted under Article 311 of the Constitution of India when the authority takes a decision for dismissal or removal or reduction in rank in writing. In other words, although there is a pleasure doctrine, however, the same cannot be said to be absolute and the same is subject to the conditions that when a government servant is to be dismissed or removed from service or he is reduced in rank, a departmental enquiry is required to be conducted to enquire into his misconduct and only after holding such an enquiry and in the course of such enquiry if he is found guilty then only a person can be removed or dismissed from service or reduced in rank.
>
> As stated herein such constitutional provision for holding an enquiry as set out under Article 311 of the Constitution of India could also be dispensed with under the exceptions provided to Article 311(2) of the Constitution where clause (*a*) relates to a case where upon a conviction of a person by a criminal court on certain charges he could be removed from service without holding an enquiry. Similarly, under clause (*c*) an enquiry to be held against the government employee could be dispensed with if it is not possible to hold such an enquiry in the interest of the security of the State. Sub-clause (*b*) on the other hand provides that such an enquiry could be dispensed with by the authority concerned, after recording reasons, for which it is not practicable to hold an enquiry. The aforesaid power is an absolute power of the disciplinary authority who after following the procedure laid down therein could resort to such extraordinary power provided it follows the preconditions laid down therein meaningfully and effectively.[45]

In this case the Court concluded that in light of the facts of the case there was no necessity to hold an enquiry or to provide him with an opportunity of hearing. The invocation of Article 311(2)(*b*) of the Constitution was properly exercised within the parameters of the provisions.

CONCLUSION

Civil Servants are bulwark of our nation and the progress of the nation is dependent on the efficient working of these administrative officers. At present the civil service is faced with various internal of challenges of inefficiency, corruption, maladministration etc. hence it is important that a judicious balance between the doctrine of pleasure and the constitutional safeguards

45. Supra note 44.

are achieved so as to ensure that the corrupt and inefficient gets weeded out and the interest of the best officers are protected against political whims and fancies. In the words of Supreme Court in *Moti Ram Deka case*[46]-

> At this stage, we ought to add that in a modern democratic State the efficiency and incorruptibility of public administration is of such importance that it is essential to afford to civil servants adequate protection against capricious action from their superior authority. If a permanent civil servant is guilty of misconduct, he should no doubt be proceeded against promptly under the relevant disciplinary rules, subject, of course, to the safeguard prescribed by Article 311(2); but in regard to honest, straightforward and efficient permanent civil servants, it is of utmost importance even from the point of view of the State that they should enjoy a sense of security which alone can make them independent and truly efficient. In our opinion, the sword of Damocles hanging over the heads of permanent railway servants in the form of Rule 148(3) or Rule 149(3) would inevitably create a sense of insecurity in the minds of such servants and would invest appropriate authorities with very wide powers which may conceivably be abused.

46. (1964) 5 SCR 683, para 28.

[illegible] the [illegible] and [illegible] would be [illegible] [illegible] [illegible] [illegible] [illegible] [illegible] [illegible] [illegible] [illegible]

[illegible] [illegible] [illegible] [illegible] [illegible] the [illegible] over these [illegible] [illegible] [illegible] in the [illegible] [illegible] [illegible] Rule [illegible] would [illegible] [illegible] [illegible] [illegible] [illegible] [illegible] [illegible] [illegible] [illegible] [illegible] [illegible] [illegible] [illegible] which may [illegible] [illegible].

X Judicial Remedies

LEARNING OBJECTIVES

After reading this chapter, you will be familiar with:

- Purpose and objective of Public Law Remedy or Writ jurisdiction
- Authorities against whom writs can be issued
- Persons who can apply for writs
- Nature and purpose of Public Interest Litigation (PIL)
- Abuse of process of Court and consequent legal action
- Understanding about the scope and application of different writs
- Purpose and objective of Statutory Remedies or Private Law Remedies
    - Injunction
    - Declaratory action

10.1 INTRODUCTION

Judicial remedies are one of the most effective forms of control mechanism over administrative actions. The Supreme Court and the High Courts have been conferred with the power of judicial review under Articles 32, 136 and 226 of the Indian Constitution to ensure that the rights of the common people are not adversely affected without due process of law. The doctrine of separation of powers had advocated that the distribution of powers between the three organs of the state should be done in a manner so that none of the three organs could exercise a position of dominance over the two organs. Articles 32 and 226 have been included in the Constitution with the primary purpose of fulfilling the goals of checks and balances with reference to the functions of the other two organs so as to ensure that they do not abuse their powers and they act within the scope of the powers conferred to them under the Constitution.

In the words of famous political philosopher Alexander Hamilton[1]

Whoever attentively considers the different departments of power must perceive, that, in a government in which they are separated from each other, the judiciary, from the nature of its functions, will always be the least dangerous to the political rights of the Constitution; because it will be least in a capacity to annoy or injure them. The Executive not only dispenses the honors, but holds the sword of the community. The legislature not only commands the purse, but prescribes the rules by which the duties and rights of every citizen are to be regulated. The judiciary, on the contrary, has no influence over either the sword or the purse; no direction either of the strength or of the wealth of the society; and can take no active resolution whatever. It may truly be said to have neither FORCE nor WILL, but merely judgment; and must ultimately depend upon the aid of the executive arm even for the efficacy of its judgments.

This simple view of the matter suggests several important consequences. It proves incontestably, that the judiciary is beyond comparison the weakest of the three departments of power, that it can never attack with success either of the other two; and that all possible care is requisite to enable it to defend itself against their attacks. It equally proves, that though individual oppression may now and then proceed from the courts of justice, the general liberty of the people can never be endangered from that quarter, I mean so long as the judiciary remains truly distinct from both the legislature and the Executive. For I agree, that "there is no liberty, if the power of judging be not separated from the legislative and executive powers. And it proves, in the last place, that as liberty can have nothing to fear from the judiciary alone, but would have everything to fear from its union with either of the other departments; that as all the effects of such a union must ensue from a dependence of the former on the latter, notwithstanding a nominal and apparent separation; that as, from the natural feebleness of the judiciary, it is in continual jeopardy of being overpowered, awed, or influenced by its co-ordinate branches; and that as nothing can contribute so much to its firmness and independence as permanency in office, this quality may therefore be justly regarded as an indispensable ingredient in its constitution, and, in a great measure, as the citadel of the public justice and the public security.[2]

In *Kesavananda Bharati v. State of Kerala*[3] emphasizing the importance of power of judicial review J.M. Shelat and A.N. Grover, JJ had observed that "*Judicial review is undertaken by the courts "not out of any desire to tilt at legislative authority in a crusader's spirit, but in discharge of a duty plainly laid down upon them by the Constitution".* In *Minerva Mills*

1. Federalist Paper No. 78.
2. The passage was quoted by Rohinton Fali Nariman J. in *Madras Bar Association v. Union of India* (2014) 10 SCC 1.
3. (1973) 4 SCC 225.

Ltd. v. Union of India[4] the power of judicial review was recognized as a basic and essential feature of the Constitution and no law passed by Parliament in exercise of its constituent power could abrogate or limit its scope.

In *S.P. Sampath Kumar v. Union of India*[5] the Court discussed the concept of judicial review in the context of regulating administrative actions and the power of the executive. It was held that–

> It is a fundamental principle of our constitutional scheme that every organ of the State, every authority under the Constitution, derives its power from the Constitution and has to act within the limits of such power. It is a limited government which we have under the Constitution and both the executive and the legislature have to act within the limits of the power conferred upon them under the Constitution. Now a question may arise as to what are the powers of the executive and whether the executive has acted within the scope of its power. Such a question obviously cannot be left to the executive to decide and for two very good reasons. First the decision of the question would depend upon the interpretation of the Constitution and the laws and this would pre-eminently be a matter fit to be decided by the judiciary, because it is the judiciary which alone would be possessed of expertise in this field and secondly, the constitutional and legal protection afforded to the citizen would become illusory, if it were left to the executive to determine the legality of its own action. So also if the legislature makes a law and a dispute arises whether in making the law, the legislature has acted outside the area of its legislative competence or the law is violative of the fundamental rights or of any other provisions of the Constitution, its resolution cannot, for the same reasons, be left to the determination of the legislature. The Constitution has, therefore created an independent machinery for resolving these disputes and this independent machinery is the judiciary which is vested with the power of judicial review to determine the legality of executive action and the validity of legislation passed by the legislature. The judiciary is constituted the ultimate interpreter of the Constitution and to it is assigned the delicate task of determining what is the extent and scope of the power conferred on each branch of government, what are the limits on the exercise of such power under the Constitution and whether any action of any branch transgresses such limits. It is also a basic principle of the rule of law which permeates every provision of the Constitution and which forms its very core and essence that the exercise of power by the executive or any other authority must not only be conditioned by the Constitution but also be in accordance with law and it is the judiciary which has to ensure that the law is observed and there is compliance with the requirements of law on the part of the executive and other authorities. This function is discharged by the judiciary by exercise of the power of judicial review which is a most potent weapon in the hands of the judiciary for maintenance of the rule of law. The power of judicial review

4. (1980) 3 SCC 625.
5. (1987) 1 SCC 124.

is an integral part of our constitutional system and without it, there will be no government of laws and the rule of law would become a teasing illusion and a promise of unreality.[6]

10.2 PUBLIC LAW REMEDY/WRIT JURISDICTION

Public law remedies are exercised by the Supreme Court and the High Court under the provisions of Articles 32 and 226. These provisions confer the power writ jurisdiction to the Supreme Court and High Court respectively. In addition, Articles 136 and 227 enable the higher judiciary to exercise control over the functioning of all the lower courts, tribunals and other quasi-judicial bodies.

Article 32 - Remedies for enforcement of rights conferred by this Part

(a) The right to move the Supreme Court by appropriate proceedings for the enforcement of the rights conferred by this Part is guaranteed

(b) The Supreme Court shall have power to issue directions or orders or writs, including writs in the nature of habeas corpus, mandamus, prohibition, quo warranto and certiorari, whichever may be appropriate, for the enforcement of any of the rights conferred by this Part

(c) Without prejudice to the powers conferred on the Supreme Court by clause (1) and (2), Parliament may by law empower any other court to exercise within the local limits of its jurisdiction all or any of the powers exercisable by the Supreme Court under clause (2)

(d) The right guaranteed by this article shall not be suspended except as otherwise provided for by this Constitution

The primary objective of Article 32 is protection of fundamental rights. It provides a quick and guaranteed remedy in case of violation of fundamental rights. A person can directly go the Supreme Court under Article 32 for vindication of his fundamental right without requiring to approach any of the lower courts. Article 32 is a fundamental right itself and hence cannot be curtailed or restricted through legislative effort. The provision can only be invoked when the administrative action is in violation of a fundamental right. Highlighting the relevance of Article 32 in Constitution Y.V. Chandrachud C.J. observed–

> The jurisdiction conferred on the Supreme Court by Article 32 is an important and integral part of the basic structure of the Constitution because it is meaningless to confer fundamental rights without providing an effective remedy for their enforcement, if and when they are violated. A right without a remedy is a legal conundrum of a most grotesque kind. While the draft Article 25,

6. Ibid at para 8.

which corresponds to Article 32, was being discussed in the Constituent Assembly, Dr Ambedkar made a meaningful observation by saying:

"If I was asked to name any particular article in this Constitution as the most important — an article without which this Constitution would be a nullity — I could not refer to any other article except this one. It is the very soul of the Constitution and the very heart of it and I am glad that the House has realised its importance."[7]

But though the right guaranteed by Article 32 is one of the highly cherished rights conferred by the Constitution, the purpose for which that right can be enforced is stated in the very Article which confers that right. The violation of a fundamental right is the sine qua non of the exercise of the right conferred by Article 32.[8]

In the case of *Charanjit Lal Chowdhury v. Union of India*[9] the Supreme Court discussed the nature, scope and applicability of Article 32 of the Constitution. It observed–

Article 32(1) of the Constitution guarantees to everybody the right to move this Court, by appropriate proceeding, for enforcement of the fundamental rights which are enumerated in Part III of the Constitution. Clause (2) of the article lays down that the Supreme Court shall have the power to issue directions or orders or writs including writs in the nature of habeas corpus, mandamus, prohibition, quo warranto and certiorari whichever may be appropriate for the enforcement of any of the rights conferred by this part.

Thus anybody who complains of infraction of any of the fundamental rights guaranteed by the Constitution is at liberty to move the Supreme Court for the enforcement of such rights and this court has been given the power to make orders and issue directions or writs similar in nature to the prerogative writs of English law as might be considered appropriate in particular cases. The fundamental rights guaranteed by the Constitution are available not merely to individual citizens but to corporate bodies as well except where the language of the provision or the nature of the right compels the inference that they are applicable only to natural persons. An incorporated company, therefore, can come up to this court for enforcement of its fundamental rights and so may the individual shareholders to enforce their own; but it would not be open to an individual shareholder to complain of an Act which affects the fundamental rights of the company except to the extent that it constitutes an infraction of his own rights as well. This follows logically from the rule of law that a corporation has a distinct legal personality of its own with rights and capacities, duties and obligations separate from those of its individual

7. Constituent Assembly Debates, December 9, 1948, Vol. VII, p. 953.
8. (1981) 1 SCC 568.
9. 1950 SCR 869 : AIR 1951 SC 41.

> members. As the rights are different and inhere in different legal entities, it is not competent to one person to seek to enforce the rights of another except where the law permits him to do so. A well-known illustration of such exception is furnished by the procedure that is sanctioned in an application for a writ of habeas corpus. Not only the man who is imprisoned or detained in confinement but any person, provided he is not an absolute stranger, can institute proceedings to obtain a writ of habeas corpus for the purpose of liberating another from an illegal imprisonment.
>
> .... Article 32, as its provisions show, is not directly concerned with the determination of constitutional validity of particular legislative enactments. What it aims at is the enforcing of fundamental rights guaranteed by the Constitution, no matter whether the necessity for such enforcement arises out of an action of the executive or of the legislature. To make out a case under this article, it is incumbent upon the petitioner to establish not merely that the law complained of is beyond the competence of the particular legislature as not being covered by any of the items in the legislative lists, but that it affects or invades his fundamental rights guaranteed by the Constitution, of which he could seek enforcement by an appropriate writ or order. The rights that could be enforced under Article 32 must ordinarily be the rights of the petitioner himself who complains of infraction of such rights and approaches the court for relief.[10]

In *Ujjam Bai v. State of Uttar Pradesh*[11] it was held that the jurisdiction of Article 32 can be exercised for the enforcement of fundamental rights in three category of cases - (*1*) where action is taken under a statute which is ultra vires the Constitution; (*2*) where the statute is intra vires but the action taken is without jurisdiction; and (*3*) where the action taken is procedurally ultra vires as where a quasi-judicial authority under an obligation to act judicially passes an order in violation of the principles of natural justice.

The power of judicial review of the Supreme Court is further extended by Article 136 of the Constitution. Article 136 confers residuary or reserved power of judicial review in the area of public law which enables the Supreme Court in its discretion to grant 'special leave to appeal from any judgment, decree, determination, sentence or order in any cause or matter passed or made by any court or tribunal.' Thus Article136 does not confer a right of appeal on any person but it confers a discretionary power on the Supreme Court to interfere in suitable cases for the purpose of advancing the cause of justice. In addition Article 142 empowers the Supreme Court to pass any order necessary for doing complete justice in any matter or cause pending before it.

---

10. Ibid at para 44-45.
11. (1963) 1 SCR 778.

Article 226 - Power of High Courts to issue certain writs

(1) Notwithstanding anything in Article 32 every High Court shall have powers, throughout the territories in relation to which it exercise jurisdiction, to issue to any person or authority, including in appropriate cases, any Government, within those territories directions, orders or writs, including writs in the nature of habeas corpus, mandamus, prohibitions, quo warranto and certiorari, or any of them, for the enforcement of any of the rights conferred by Part III and for any other purpose

(2) The power conferred by clause (1) to issue directions, orders or writs to any Government, authority or person may also be exercised by any High Court exercising jurisdiction in relation to the territories within which the cause of action, wholly or in part, arises for the exercise of such power, notwithstanding that the seat of such Government or authority or the residence of such person is not within those territories

(3) Where any party against whom an interim order, whether by way of injunction or stay or in any other manner, is made on, or in any proceedings relating to, a petition under clause (1), without

(a) furnishing to such party copies of such petition and all documents in support of the plea for such interim order; and

(b) giving such party an opportunity of being heard, makes an application to the High Court for the vacation of such order and furnishes a copy of such application to the party in whose favour such order has been made or the counsel of such party, the High Court shall dispose of the application within a period of two weeks from the date on which it is received or from the date on which the copy of such application is so furnished, whichever is later, or where the High Court is closed on the last day of that period, before the expiry of the next day afterwards on which the High Court is open; and if the application is not so disposed of, the interim order shall, on the expiry of that period, or, as the case may be, the expiry of the aid next day, stand vacated

(4) The power conferred on a High Court by this article shall not be in derogation of the power conferred on the Supreme court by clause (2) of Article 32

The powers of the High Courts under Article 226 are wider than those of the Supreme Court.[12] The jurisdiction can be exercised to invoke not only violation of fundamental rights but also other legal rights. Hence in matters

12. *Naresh Shridhar Mirajkar v. State of Maharashtra* (1966) 3 SCR 744 : AIR 1967 SC 1.

relating to violation of fundamental rights an action can be taken under Article 32 as well as Article 226 whereas in violation of other rights, the jurisdiction under Article 226 alone can be exercise. Ordinarily if there are efficacious and alternative remedies available, then the Courts may refuse to exercise of their writ jurisdiction unless other remedial measures have been exhausted. However in cases of violation of fundamental rights, or breach of principles of natural justice, or where the exercise of administrative power was outside the scope or contrary to the provisions of the parent statute the doctrine of exhaustion of remedies will not be applicable. In *State of Orissa v. Madan Gopal Rungta*[13] speaking on the nature and scope of Article 226 the Court observed –

> The language of the Article shows that the issuing of writs or directions by the Court is not founded only on its decision that a right of the aggrieved party under Part III of the Constitution (Fundamental Rights) has been infringed. It can also issue writs or give similar directions for any other purpose. The concluding words of article 226 have to be read in the context of what precedes the same. Therefore the existence of the right is the foundation of the exercise of jurisdiction of the Court under this Article.

In addition Article 227 invests the High Court with the power of superintendence over all courts and tribunals within its jurisdiction. The power exercised by the Court is both administrative and judicial in nature. The power of superintendence includes the power to exercise judicial review over the orders passed and actions taken all lower courts and tribunals. The scope of judicial review includes the power to interfere in cases of acting beyond its jurisdiction, erroneous assumption of jurisdiction, refusal to exercise jurisdiction, arbitrary or capricious exercise of power, error apparent on the face of the record, patent error of procedure or arriving at a decision based on material evidences resulting in manifest injustices etc.

10.3 AUTHORITIES AGAINST WHOM WRITS CAN BE ISSUED

Writs can be issued against the State. Judiciary has made all attempts to widen the application of writs against all authorities exercising authoritative power of the state. In the words of Mathew J. *"The governing power wherever located must be subject to the fundamental constitutional limitations."*[14]

Under Article 12 of the Constitution the term 'State' includes–

(i) Government and Parliament of India,

13. 1952 SCR 28 : AIR 1952 SC 12.

14. *Sukhdev Singh v. Bhagatram*, AIR 1975 SC 1331.

(ii) Government and legislature of each of the State,

(iii) Local authorities and

(iv) Other authorities within the territory of India or under the control of the Government of India.

The term Government includes both executive and administrative bodies of the state such as Union Government, State Government, President, Governors, Government Departments Regulatory Authorities etc.

The term 'local authority' includes 'municipal corporations, improvement trusts, district boards, mining settlement authorities and other local authorities for the purpose of local self government or village administration.'[15]

The judiciary has given a wide interpretation to the term 'other authorities'. It has applied the test of whether a body is an instrumentality or agency of the government for the purpose of being categorised as 'state' under Article 12.[16] Accordingly bodies which been created and incorporated under the provisions of a statute and government incorporated bodies or statutory bodies are labelled as 'state'. Other categories include government companies, cooperative bodies, registered societies, universities etc.

10.4 WHO CAN APPLY FOR WRITS

Any aggrieved person can apply for issuance of writs when his fundamental rights have been violated. A petition for a writ of habeas corpus can be filed by any person whereas traditionally for a writ of certiorari, prohibition and mandamus a petition by an aggrieved person or a person whose rights are in jeopardy have been encouraged by the Courts. The narrow concept of *locus standi* was liberalized by the Supreme Court in the case of *Fertilizer Corporation Kamgar Union v. Union of India.*[17] Krishna Iyer J. made the observation –

> If a citizen is no more than a wayfarer or officious intervener without any interest or concern beyond what belongs to any one of the 660 million people of this country, the door of the court will not be ajar for him. But, if he belongs to an organisation which has special interest in the subject-matter, if he has some concern deeper than that of a busybody, he cannot be told off at the gates, although whether the issue raised by him is justiciable may still remain to be considered. I, therefore, take the view that the present petition would clearly have been permissible under Article 226. [Black: The Right to Be Heard, New Zealand LJ, No 4, 1977, p 66]

15. As included in Schedule VII, List II, Entry 5.
16. *Ajay Hasia v. Khalid Mujid*, (1981) 1 SCC 722.
17. AIR 1981 SC 344.

In *Kishore Samrite v. State of U.P*[18] it was further clarified that–

> [a] person who brings a petition even for invocation of a fundamental right must be a person having some direct or indirect interest in the outcome of the petition on his behalf or on behalf of some person under a disability and/or unable to have access to the justice system for patent reasons. Still, such a person must act bona fide and without abusing the process of law. Where a person is a stranger/unknown to the parties and has no interest in the outcome of the litigation, he can hardly claim locus standi to file such petition. There could be cases where a public-spirited person bona fide brings petition in relation to violation of fundamental rights, particularly in habeas corpus petitions, but even in such cases, the person should have some demonstrable interest or relationship to the involved persons, personally or for the benefit of the public at large, in a PIL. But in all such cases, it is essential that the petitioner must exhibit bona fides, by truthful and cautious exercise of such right. The courts would be expected to examine such requirement at the threshold of the litigation in order to prevent abuse of process of court.

10.5 PUBLIC INTEREST LITIGATION

Public Interest Litigation (PIL) is a judicial strategy to provide justice to those individuals whose fundamental rights have been violated or infringed but due to their socio-economic backwardness they are unable to appear before the judicial authorities for vindication of their rights. The objective of PIL is widen the concept of *locus standi* and allow a *pro bono publico* petition to be filed on matters of public interest or behalf of those aggrieved individuals who are not able to reach the doorsteps of the courts. The genesis of PIL arises from the oath which the judicial officers take at the time of holding the office that they shall always strive to uphold and defend the Constitution. The objective of PIL is to provide justice to the deprived sections of the society. In *Veena Sethi v. State of Bihar*[19] Supreme Court recognized that *it is the solemn duty of this Court to protect and uphold the basic human rights of the weaker sections of the society* and by means of the public interest litigation the judiciary is trying to discharge their noble obligation.

In *S.P. Gupta v. Union of India*[20] Bhagwati, J. speaking on the issue of *locus standi* observed:

> Any member of the public having sufficient interest can maintain an action for judicial redress for public injury arising from breach of public duty or from violation of some provision of the Constitution or the law and seek enforcement of such public duty and observance of such constitutional or legal provision.

18. (2013) 2 SCC 398.
19. (1982) 2 SCC 583.
20. MANU/SC/0080/1981.

> The rule of law constitutes the core of our Constitution and it is the essence of the rule of law that the exercise of the power by the State whether it be the Legislature or the Executive or any other authority should be within the constitutional limitations and if any practice is adopted by the Executive which is inflagrant and systematic violation of its constitutional limitations, petitioner No. 1 as a member of the public would have sufficient interest to challenge such practice by filing a writ petition and it would be the constitutional duty of this Court to entertain the writ petition and adjudicate upon the validity of such practice. We must therefore reject the preliminary contention raised on behalf of the respondents challenging the locus of the petitioners to maintain these writ petitions.

In *Vishwanath Chaturvedi v. Union of India*[21] it was clarified that "the test which one has to apply to decide the maintainability of the PIL concerns sufficiency of the petitioner's interest. In our view, it is wrong in law for the Court to judge the petitioner's interest without looking into the subject matter of his complaint and if the petitioner shows failure of public duty, the Court would be in error in dismissing the PIL."

10.6 ABUSE OF PROCESS OF COURT

In the case of *Kishore Samrite v. State of U.P.*[22] the Supreme Court discussed the unwanted practice of abuse of processes of court and laid certain important principles to deal with the same. *Access jurisprudence requires courts to deal with the legitimate litigation whatever be its form but decline to exercise jurisdiction, if such litigation is an abuse of process of court.* The principles are –

1. Courts have, over the centuries, frowned upon litigants who, with intent to deceive and mislead the courts, initiated proceedings without full disclosure of facts and came to the courts with "unclean hands". Courts have held that such litigants are neither entitled to be heard on the merits of the case nor are entitled to any relief.
2. The people, who approach the court for relief on an ex parte statement, are under a contract with the court that they would state the whole case fully and fairly to the court and where the litigant has broken such faith, the discretion of the court cannot be exercised in favour of such a litigant.
3. The obligation to approach the court with clean hands is an absolute obligation and has repeatedly been reiterated by this Court.

21. (2007) 4 SCC 380.
22. (2013) 2 SCC 398.

4. Quests for personal gains have become so intense that those involved in litigation do not hesitate to take shelter of falsehood and misrepresent and suppress facts in the court proceedings. Materialism, opportunism and malicious intent have overshadowed the old ethos of litigative values for small gains.
5. A litigant who attempts to pollute the stream of justice or who touches the pure fountain of justice with tainted hands is not entitled to any relief, interim or final.
6. The court must ensure that its process is not abused and in order to prevent abuse of process of court, it would be justified even in insisting on furnishing of security and in cases of serious abuse, the court would be duty-bound to impose heavy costs.
7. Wherever a public interest is invoked, the court must examine the petition carefully to ensure that there is genuine public interest involved. The stream of justice should not be allowed to be polluted by unscrupulous litigants.
8. The court, especially the Supreme Court, has to maintain the strictest vigilance over the abuse of process of court and ordinarily meddlesome bystanders should not be granted "visa". Many societal pollutants create new problems of unredressed grievances and the court should endure to take cases where the justice of the lis well justifies it.

10.7 TYPES OF WRITS

The public law remedies are generally exercised by the issuance of writs. There are five kinds of writs – habeas corpus, certiorari, prohibition, quo-warranto and mandamus.

(i) Writ of Habeas Corpus

The Latin term 'habeas corpus' implies 'you must have the body'. It is used primarily to secure the release of person who has been detained illegally. It is fundamental protector of our right to liberty and freedom. Under Article 22 a person arrested is required to be presented before the Magistrate within 24 hours of arrest. The writ of habeas corpus can issued against any person, including both public official and private individuals since the objective is to prevent unlawful detention of any person. In recent years the scope of application of the writ has been widened to include relief against custodial torture and inhuman treatment.[23]

---

23. *Sunil Batra v. Delhi Administration*, AIR 1978 SC 1675.

In the leading case *Kanu Sanyal v. Distt. Magistrate*[24] the petitioner filed a writ petition under Article 32 challenging the legality of his detention right from the time of its inception and praying that he may be set free by issue of a writ of habeas corpus. The Court held that *the earliest date with reference to which the legality of detention may be examined is the date of filing of the application for habeas corpus and the Court is not concerned with a date prior to the initiation of the proceedings for a writ of habeas corpus.* On the issue of whether in a writ petition of habeas corpus it was necessary to produce the person, the Court negated the judgment on the ground that *the Court was competent to dispense with the production of the body of the person detained while issuing rule nisi, and the rule nisi could be heard without requiring the body of the person detained to be brought before the Court.*

(ii) Writ of Certiorari

The term 'certiorari' is derived from the Latin word *certiorari* which means to inform. The writ is generally used to quash judicial or quasi-judicial actions which are improper, contrary to the provisions of law or has errors on the face of the record. It has been used to invalidate actions when the authority lacks necessary jurisdiction, has acted in excess of jurisdiction, has committed fraud or has abused the power conferred. The writ has also been used if the administrative authority has acted contrary or in violation of the principles of natural justice.

In *T.C. Basappa v. T. Nagappa*[25] describing the objective of the writ of certiorari as to supervise the functioning of lower judicial and quasi-judicial authorities the Supreme Court has observed–

> The control which is exercised through it over judicial or quasi-judicial tribunals or bodies is not in an appellate but supervisory capacity. In granting a writ of certiorari, the superior court does not exercise the powers of an Appellate Tribunal. It does not review or reweigh the evidence upon which the determination of the inferior tribunal purports to be based. It demolishes the order which it considers to be without jurisdiction or palpably erroneous but does not substitute its own views for those of the inferior tribunal. The supervision of the superior Court exercised through writs of certiorari goes to two points, one is the area of inferior jurisdiction and the qualifications and conditions of its exercise; the other is the observance of law in the course of its exercise. Certiorari may lie and is generally granted when a court has acted without or in excess of its jurisdiction. The want of jurisdiction may arise from the nature of the subject-matter of the proceeding or from the absence of

24. (1974) 4 SCC 141.
25. (1955) 1 SCR 250.

some preliminary proceeding or the court itself may not be legally constituted or suffer from certain disability by reason of extraneous circumstances. When the jurisdiction of the court depends upon the existence of some collateral fact, it is well settled that the court cannot by way of a wrong decision of the fact give its jurisdiction which it would not otherwise possess."

Some of the illustrative cases are –

In *Venkateswaran v. Wadhwani*[26] the writ of certiorari was issued for denial of principles of natural justice. In this case the Deputy Commissioner had confiscated an essential commodity without complying with the principles of natural justice.

(iii) Writ of Prohibition

Writ of prohibition is a judicial order issued by the higher judiciary such as the Supreme Court or the High Court to any constitutional, statutory and other administrative bodies so as to prohibit or prevent such bodies from continuing to proceed in a matter wherein the authority lacks jurisdiction or acts in excess of jurisdiction. It is also issued to prohibit the authority from acting contrary to the principles of natural justice or in contravention to a provision of law.

There is much commonality between certiorari and prohibition in matters of scope and application but the distinction lies at the stage in which the writs can be issued. The writ of prohibition is issued to prohibit or forbid the authority from continuing with the proceedings whereas certiorari is issued after the proceedings have been terminated so as to quash the final decision taken. The two writs can also be sometimes issued simultaneously so as to quash the decision on one hand and to prohibit the authority from continuing with the matter in future.

(iv) Writ of Mandamus

'Mandamus' is a Latin word which implies 'we command'. The writ is issued for enforcement of statutory duties or to compel a person holding a public office to do or forbear from doing something which is incumbent upon him to do or forbear from doing under the provisions of any law.[27] It is issued by a superior court to compel the performance of such duties or forbearance by a lower court or authority, including a government official. The functional objective of the writ is to keep the public authorities within the limits of their jurisdiction while exercising the functions. Mandamus can only be issued in the performance of mandatory functions and not that of optional

26. AIR 1961 SC 1506.
27. *State of Bihar v. Chandradip Rai*, AIR 1981 SC 2071.

or discretionary functions. It is necessary that the person seeking the writ should prove that *he has a legally protected and judicially enforceable right.*[28] The writ of mandamus can be issued on all grounds on which the writs of certiorari and prohibition can be issued. In exercise of the power to issue the writ, the court does not sit as a court of appeal and does not look into the correctness or merits of the action taken by the authority. However the Court would be reluctant to issue a *meaningless writ* which would be of no effect to the person seeking the relief.[29]

The essential ingredients of mandamus are –

(a) There must be a statutory or public duty and obligation

(b) There must be a specific demand and refusal

(c) There must be a clear right to enforce the duty

(d) The right must be subsisting on the date of the petition.

In *Union of India v. S.B. Vohra*[30] the nature, scope and importance of the writ of mandamus was discussed–

> Mandamus literally means a command. The essence of mandamus in England was that it was a royal command issued by the King's Bench (now Queen's Bench) directing performance of a public legal duty. A writ of mandamus is issued in favour of a person who establishes a legal right in himself. A writ of mandamus is issued against a person who has a legal duty to perform but has failed and/or neglected to do so. Such a legal duty emanates from either in discharge of a public duty or by operation of law. The writ of mandamus is of a most extensive remedial nature. The object of mandamus is to prevent disorder from a failure of justice and is required to be granted in all cases where law has established no specific remedy and whether justice despite demanded has not been granted.

In *Comptroller and Auditor General of India* v. *K.S. Jagannathan*[31] the Court clarified the scope of application of the writ in discretionary matters. It was held that–

> There is thus no doubt that the High Courts in India exercising their jurisdiction under Article 226 have the power to issue a writ of mandamus or a writ in the nature of mandamus or to pass orders and give necessary directions where the Government or a public authority has failed to exercise or has wrongly exercised the discretion conferred upon it by a statute or a rule or a policy decision of the Government or has exercised such discretion mala fide or on irrelevant considerations or by ignoring the relevant considerations

28. *Shabi Construction Co. v. City & Industrial Development Corpn.*, (1995) 4 SCC 301.
29. *K.N. Guruswamy v. State of Mysore*, (1955) 1 SCR 305.
30. (2004) 2 SCC 150.
31. (1986) 2 SCC 679.

and materials or in such a manner as to frustrate the object of conferring such discretion or the policy for implementing which such discretion has been conferred. *In all such cases and in any other fit and proper case a High Court can, in the exercise of its jurisdiction under Article 226, issue a writ of mandamus or a writ in the nature of mandamus or pass orders and give directions to compel the performance in a proper and lawful manner of the discretion conferred upon the Government or a public authority, and in a proper case, in order to prevent injustice resulting to the parties concerned, the court may itself pass an order or give directions which the Government or the public authority should have passed or given had it properly and lawfully exercised its discretion.*"

Analysing the meaning and scope of statutory duty, the Court in *Mansukhlal Vithaldas Chauhan v. State of Gujarat*[32] held that–

> Mandamus which is a discretionary remedy under Article 226 of the Constitution is requested to be issued, inter alia, to compel performance of public duties which may be administrative, ministerial or statutory in nature. Statutory duty may be either directory or mandatory. Statutory duties, if they are intended to be mandatory in character, are indicated by the use of the words 'shall' or 'must'. But this is not conclusive as 'shall' and 'must' have, sometimes, been interpreted as 'may'. What is determinative of the nature of duty, whether it is obligatory, mandatory or directory, is the scheme of the statute in which the 'duty' has been set out. Even if the 'duty' is not set out clearly and specifically in the statute, it may be implied as correlative to a 'right'.
>
> In the performance of this duty, if the authority in whom the discretion is vested under the statute, does not act independently and passes an order under the instructions and orders of another authority, the Court would intervene in the matter, quash the order and issue a mandamus to that authority to exercise its own discretion."

In *National Textile Corpn. Ltd. v. Haribox Swalram*[33] it was held that the writ of mandamus has no application in a business contract where there are no statutory right or duty. The Court held that–

> It is well settled that in order that a mandamus be issued to compel the authorities to do something, it must be shown that there is a statute which imposes a legal duty and the aggrieved party has a legal right under the statute to enforce its performance. The present is a case of pure and simple business contract. The writ petitioners have no statutory right nor is any statutory duty cast upon the appellants whose performance may be legally enforced. No writ of mandamus can, therefore, be issued as prayed by the writ petitioners.

32. (1997) 7 SCC 622.
33. (2004) 9 SCC 786.

(v) Writ of Quo-Warranto

The term 'quo warranto' implies 'by what warrant or authority'. A writ of quo warranto can be issued when the holder of a public office has been appointed in violation of constitutional or statutory provisions.[34] The writ can be issued by the higher judiciary to question the holder of public office as to under what right he claims to hold the title to the office and on failure to do so, such unauthorized person can be ousted or removed from such office.

The essential ingredients for issuance of quo-warranto are –

(a) Office must be a public office

(b) Public office must be permanent in nature

(c) Person must be in actual possession of the office

(d) Office must be held in contravention of statutory provisions

In *N. Kannadasan v. Ajoy Khose*[35] Supreme Court analysed the applicability of the writ of quo warranto. The writ shall become applicable–

> (*A*) in the event the holder of a public office was not eligible for appointment;
>
> (*B*) processual machinery relating to consultation was not fully complied.
>
> The writ of quo warranto proceedings affords a judicial remedy by which any person who holds an independent substantive public office is called upon to show by what right he holds the same so that his title to it may be duly determined and in the event it is found that the holder has no title he would be directed to be removed from the said office by a judicial order. The proceedings not only give a weapon to control the executive from making appointments to public office against law but also tend to protect the public from being deprived of public office to which it has a right. It is indisputably a high prerogative writ which was reserved for the use of the Crown. The width and ambit of the writ, however, in the course of practice, have widened and it is permissible to pray for issuance of a writ in the nature of quo warranto.
>
> In *Corpus Juris Secundum* [74 C.J.S. Quo Warranto § 14], "Quo Warranto" is defined as under: "Quo warranto, or a proceeding in the nature thereof, is a proper and appropriate remedy to test the right or title to an office, and to remove or oust an incumbent.
>
> It is prosecuted by the State against a person who unlawfully usurps, intrudes, or holds a public office. The relator must establish that the office is being unlawfully held and exercised by the respondent, and that relator is entitled to the office."
>
> In *Law Lexicon* by J.J.S. Wharton, Esq., 1987, "Quo Warranto" has been defined as under:

34. *N. Kannadasan v. Ajoy Khose*, (2009) 7 SCC 1.
35. Id.

"QUO WARRANTO, a writ issuable out of the Queen's Bench, in the nature of a writ of right, for the Crown, against him who claims or usurps any office, franchise, or liberty, to enquire by what authority he supports his claim, in order to determine the right. It lies also in case of non-user, or long neglect of a franchise, or misuser or abuse of it; being a writ commanding the defendant to show by what warrant he exercises such a franchise having never had any grant of it, or having forfeited it by neglect or abuse."

Thus the writ of quo warranto is issued when the appointment is contrary to the statutory rules.[36] In *Duryodhan Sahu (Dr.) v. Jitendra Kumar Mishra*[37] it was clarified that it is not for the court to embark upon an investigation of its own to ascertain the qualifications of the person concerned.

10.8 STATUTORY REMEDIES OR PRIVATE LAW REMEDIES

Other than the availability of writ remedies, there are judicial remedies available before the ordinary courts of the land through the ordinary process of law to regulate administrative exercise of power. These ordinary remedies are also referred to as private law remedies. Private law remedies are cheaper and more easily accessible. The applicability of the scope of private law remedies are much broader keeping in view they allow for production of evidences and witnesses.

The private law remedies are primarily exercised through three ways – Injunction, Declaratory action and Suit for Damages.

10.9 INJUNCTION

By grant of injunction a public authority can be compelled to do a thing which the law requires them to do or to refrain from doing something which is considered to be illegal. Injunction can be issued against both administrative and quasi-judicial bodies. The grant of injunction is governed by Sections 36 to 42 of the Specific Relief Act, 1963

Injunction is classified into three categories – temporary, perpetual and mandatory.

Section 36 of the Act provides for grant of injunction at the discretion of the court. The temporary and perpetual injunctions are considered as preventive in nature.

36. *High Court of Gujarat v. Gujarat Kishan Mazdoor Panchayat*, (2003) 4 SCC 712 : 2003 SCC (L&S) 565 and *R.K. Jain v. Union of India*, (1993) 4 SCC 119.
37. (1998) 7 SCC 273.

Section 37(1) provides that temporary injunctions are to continue until a specific time, or until further order of the court, and it may be granted at any stage of the suit. The application of temporary injunctions is made under the provisions of Code of Civil Procedure, 1908. Such injunctions are granted at the insistence of the applicant on the ground that irreparable damages or losses will be caused to him during the pendency of the proceeding. The primary objective of temporary injunction is to maintain status quo. It aims to lessen the risk of irreparable injury and prevent injustice which cannot be compensated by money or other means.[38]

A perpetual injunction can be granted under Section 37(2) of the Act which provides that the injunction can be granted by a decree made after hearing both the sides and determination of the merits of the suit. Such an injunction can be granted to the plaintiff to prevent the breach of an obligation existing in his favor, whether expressly or by implication.[39] In case the defendant invades or threatens to invade the plaintiff's right to property or enjoyment of such property, the court is empowered to grant a perpetual injunction.[40] In the following cases the court may grant perpetual injunction, namely–

(a) where the defendant is trustee of the property for the plaintiff;

(b) where there exists no standard for ascertaining the actual damage caused, or likely to be caused, by the invasion;

(c) where the invasion is such that compensation in money would not afford adequate relief;

(d) where the injunction is necessary to prevent a multiplicity of judicial proceedings.

Under Section 39 of the Act mandatory injunction can be granted in order to prevent the breach of an obligation by compelling the performance of certain acts which the court is capable of enforcing. It is within the discretion of the court to grant injunction to prevent the breach of the complaint made and to compel the performance of the requisite act.[41]

In a suit for perpetual injunction or grant of mandatory injunction the plaintiff may make a specific claim for award of damages either in addition to or in substitution of such injunction. However no such relief of damages may be granted if the plaint does not make a specific claim for the award of the same, but the court has the discretion to allow the plaintiff to amend the plaint to include terms of such claim at any later stage of the

38. *Hindustan Petroleum Corporation Ltd. v. Sriman Narayan*, (2002) 5 SCC 760.

39. Section 38 (1) of the Specific Relief Act.

40. Section 38 (3).

41. Section 39.

proceedings.[42] In case of dismissal of a suit for preventing the breach of an obligation existing in favour of the plaintiff, will also act as a bar to his right to sue for damages for such breach under Section 40(3).

There are certain grounds on which grant of injunction may be refused. Under Sec. 41 injunction may be refused on the following grounds –

(a) to restrain any person from prosecuting a judicial proceeding pending at the institution of the suit in which the injunction is sought, unless such restraint is necessary to prevent a multiplicity of proceedings;

(b) to restrain any person from instituting or prosecuting any proceeding in a court not subordinate to that from which the injunction is sought;

(c) to restrain any person from applying to any legislative body;

(d) to restrain any person from instituting or prosecuting any proceeding in a criminal matter;

(e) to prevent the breach of a contract the performance of which would not be specifically enforced;

(f) to prevent, on the ground of nuisance, an act of which it is not reasonably clear that it will be a nuisance;

(g) to prevent a continuing breach in which the plaintiff has acquiesced;

(h) when equally efficacious relief can certainly be obtained by any other usual mode of proceeding except in case of breach of trust;

(i) when the conduct of the plaintiff or his agents has been such as to disentitle him to the assistance of the court;

(j) when the plaintiff has no personal interest in the matter.

In *State of Haryana v. State of Punjab*[43] the Supreme Court differentiated between the different forms of injunction and observed–

> [T]he general law relating to injunctions is contained in Section 36 to Section 42 of the Specific Relief Act, 1963. Although these provisions may not limit the powers of this Court under Article 131, nevertheless, they provide valuable guidelines as to the nature of this form of equitable relief. An injunction may be permanent (perpetual) or temporary [Specific Relief Act, 1963, Section 36.]. A permanent injunction is final and conclusive of the facts in the context of which the injunction is granted. A temporary injunction by contrast is granted on a prima facie view of the facts and, as the word "temporary" itself indicates, is an interim order pending a final adjudication of the rights of the parties. This distinction is not to be confused with the distinction between a prohibitory or preventive injunction on the one hand and a mandatory injunction on the other. In the first case a party is prevented from doing a particular thing or continuing with a particular action [*Ibid*, Section 38.]. A mandatory injunction

42. Section 40.

43. (2004) 12 SCC 673.

on the other hand commands an act to be done and is provided for under Section 39 of the Specific Relief Act, 1963 which reads:

39. *Mandatory injunctions.*—When, to prevent the breach of an obligation, it is necessary to compel the performance of certain acts which the court is capable of enforcing, the court may in its discretion grant an injunction to prevent the breach complained of, and also to compel performance of the requisite acts."

This command may direct the restoration of status quo ante or may direct the performance of a positive act altering the existing state of things [*Kerr on Injunctions*, 6th Edn., p. 40]. A mandatory injunction like a preventive injunction may be temporary or final.

10.10 DECLARATORY ACTION

Declaratory action is a form of private law remedy wherein the court declares the legal rights of the parties. It is described as a form of judicial remedy which determines the rights and obligations of the public authorities and private person without any additional coercive or obligatory directions. Sections 34 and 35 of the Specific Relief Act contains the legal provisions relating to declaration of status and rights.

Section 34 provides that any person entitled to any legal character or any right to a property may institute a suit against such person denying or interested to deny his title to such character or right and the court may in its discretion make therein a declaration that he is so entitled to such a right, and the plaintiff need not in such suit ask for any further relief. If the plaintiff is entitled to any consequential relief it is necessary that the plaintiff must make a specific claim for it. A declaration so made is binding only on the parties to the suit or any persons claiming through them respectively.

The conditions for granting declaratory relief are –

(i) The person must be entitled to a legal character or to a right to any property. Examples include right to official position, sex, marital status, legitimacy, nationality, profession etc.

(ii) There must be some danger of denial of such right or character.

(iii) Plaintiff must specifically seek for further relief, if he is entitled for it.

In addition to the above, a suit for damages is also a remedy available under the law. In case a person has been wronged by an action of an administrative authority and he suffers an injury, then a suit for damages can be filed in the ordinary civil courts of first instance. The procedural rules laid down in the Civil Procedure Code will be applicable.

SUMMATION

Judicial control of administrative action forms the pillar for regulating administrative action. Ordinary citizens are largely dependent on the judiciary for vindication of their legal right in case of infringement by administrative action. The public law remedies form the primary means for ensuring the protection of legal rights of the citizens. The writ remedies are considered to be more potent and expeditious from the citizen's perspective, hence they are more popular. On the contrary the private law remedies have immense potential to provide effective legal remedies against administrative abuse of power at a much lower cost, but due to various factors such as complicated procedural rules, time consuming nature of the proceedings etc. the popularization of the administrative action has been hindered.

XI

Major Initiatives in Promoting Good Governance

LEARNING OBJECTIVES

After reading this chapter, you will be familiar with:

- Major initiatives in promoting Good Governance in Society
- Brief understanding of few investing and inquiry agencies in promoting accountability and transparency
  - Central Bureau of Investigation (CBI)
  - Commissions of Inquiry
- Brief understanding of few institutions promoting good governance and accountability
  - Comptroller and Auditor General
  - Central Vigilance Commission
  - Lokpal and Lokayukta
- Brief understanding of few Citizen-Centric Initiatives
  - Citizen Charters and Timely Delivery of Goods and Services
  - E-governance

11.1 PART I - INVESTIGATION AND INQUIRY

11.1.1 Introduction

In this last chapter an effort has been made to highlight the working of some principal institutions as well as some major initiatives undertaken in recent times to fulfil the goals of good governance in India. The chapter has been divided into three parts – Part I deals with institutions involved in investigating and inquiring on matters relating to corruption and governance, Part II deals with institutions promoting accountability in public life and

Part III deals with some major government initiatives undertaken in recent years to promote good governance and citizen-centric administration.

In the first part of the topic relating to implementation of Good Governance Initiatives a brief discussion about the two important institutions for conducting investigation and inquiry – Central Bureau of Investigation and Commissions of Inquiry have been undertaken. These institutions have been primary pillars for upholders transparency and accountability in public life.

11.1.2 Central Bureau of Investigation (CBI)

The Central Bureau of Investigation is the premier investigating agency of the country. It was set up as a Special Police Establishment body to meet the challenges of growing incidents of bribery and corruption in government officials. It was set up under the provisions of Delhi Special Police Establishment (DSPE) Act 1946. CBI is merely a change of name from the Delhi Special Police Establishment.[1] The superintendence of DSPE was originally exercised by the Home Department but after the enactment of the Central Vigilance Commission Act, 2003 the superintendence of DSPE relating to offences under the Prevention of Corruption Act, 1988 vests with the CVC. Under Section 2 the jurisdiction of DSPE was to investigate offences in the Union Territories only. But under Section 5 of the Act, the Central Government has been empowered to extend the powers and jurisdiction of Delhi Police Establishment to investigate an offence beyond the territorial limits of Delhi and by virtue of Section 6 the powers and jurisdiction can be extended to any other State with the consent of the Government of that State. The constitutionality of CBI had been upheld by the Supreme Court in *Advance Insurance Co. v. Gurudasma,*[2] *State of West Bengal v. Committee for Protection of Democratic Rights, West Bengal*[3] and *M.C Mehta (Taj Corridor Scam) v. Union of India.*[4] In *Navendra Kumar v. Union of India*[5] the constitutionality of CBI was challenged before the Gauhati High Court and the Court upheld the contention on the ground that the CBI was not constituted under the provisions of the DSPE Act and established through an executive order. At present the Supreme Court has imposed a stay on the operation of the Gauhati High Court order.

With passage of time a growing need to establish a Central Police Agency was considered essential to deal with cases other than that of bribery

1. (2014) 1 Gau LR 529.
2. (1970) 1 SCC 633.
3. (2010) 3 SCC 571.
4. (2007) 1 SCC 110.
5. (2014) 1 Gau LR 529.

and corruption, such as relating to violation of Central fiscal laws, major economic offences, financial frauds involving departments, public joint stock companies, passport frauds, crimes on the high seas, crimes on the Airlines and serious crimes committed by organised gangs and professional criminals. As a consequence the following divisions of CBI were set up[6]–

(1) Anti-Corruption Division – It is responsible for collection of intelligence with regard to corruption, maintaining liaison with various Departments through their Vigilance Officers, enquiries into complaints about bribery and corruption, investigation and prosecution of offences pertaining to bribery and corruption and tasks relating to preventive aspects of corruption. The Anti-Corruption Division investigates cases against public servants under the control of the Central Government, public servants in Public Sector Undertakings under the control of Central Government and cases against the public servants working under State Govt. entrusted to the CBI by the State Governments and serious departmental irregularities committed by the above mentioned public servants.

(2) Economic Offences Division – It investigates financial crimes, bank frauds, money laundering, illegal money market operations, graft in Public Sector Undertakings and Banks.

(3) Special Crimes Division – It handles all cases of economic offences and all cases of conventional nature such as offences relating to internal security, espionage, sabotage, narcotics and psychotropic substances, antiquities, murders, dacoities / robberies, cheating, criminal breach of trust, forgeries, dowry deaths, suspicious deaths and other IPC offences as well as offences under other laws notified under the DSPE Act. It is also responsible for investigation of interstate and international rackets, large-scale frauds affecting the property or revenue of the Government and crimes of national importance.

(4) Directorate of Prosecution – It was established in pursuance of the orders of Supreme Court in Vineet Narain case. The Directorate tenders legal advice in CBI cases, besides conducting prosecution in CBI cases. The Directorate also attends to matters relating to legal matters raised in the IGPs / DGPs conference, matters relating to interpretation of laws, appointment of special counsels, statutory rules and regulations and amendments thereof, preparation of notes on Legal matters for publication in CBI Gazette etc.

(5) Administration Division – It looks after all matters relating to personnel, establishment and accounts of all the Divisions of the CBI and is headed by an officer of the rank of Joint Director / IG.

---

6. CBI – Information Available at : http://cbi.nic.in/aboutus/div.php.

(6) Policy & Coordination Division It deals with all matters relating to policy, procedure, organisation, vigilance & security in the CBI, correspondence and liaison with Ministries and implementation of Special Programmes for vigilance and anti-corruption, etc.

(7) Technical Advisory Units – It provide expert guidance and assistance in banking, taxation, engineering and foreign trading / foreign exchange matters during enquiries and investigations taken up by the CBI. The technical advisory units are:

 (1) Banking Company Law / Insurance Advisory Unit.

 (2) Engineering Advisory Unit (Civil / Electrical matters).

 (3) Taxation Advisory Unit (Direct / Indirect Tax matters).

 (4) Foreign trading / Foreign Exchange Advisory Unit.

(8) Central Forensic Science Laboratory

At present the CBI has *evolved from an anti-corruption agency with capability, credibility and legal mandate to investigate and prosecute offences anywhere in India.* It has been entrusted to deal with offences under 69 existing Central and 18 State Acts, 231 offences under the Indian Penal Code have been notified to be tried under Section 3 of the DSPE Act by the Central Government. The following broad categories of offences are handled by the CBI–

(1) Cases of corruption and fraud committed by public servants of all Central Govt. Departments, Central Public Sector Undertakings and Central Financial Institutions.

(2) Economic crimes, including bank frauds, financial frauds, Import Export & Foreign Exchange violations, large-scale smuggling of narcotics, antiques, cultural property and smuggling of other contraband items etc.

(3) Special Crimes, such as cases of terrorism, bomb blasts, sensational homicides, kidnapping for ransom and crimes committed by the mafia/ the underworld.

In *Vineet Narain v. Union of India*[7] recognizing the important role which the CBI plays in conducting crucial investigation the need for the insulation of these agencies from any extraneous influence was emphasised by the Supreme Court. It was instructed that *the Central Government shall take all measures necessary to ensure that the CBI functions effectively and efficiently and is viewed as a non-partisan agency.*

In *Centre for Public Interest Litigation v. Union of India*[8] it was emphasised by the Supreme Court the need *to protect and preserve the*

7. AIR 1998 SC 889 : (1998) 1 SCC 226.

8. (2015) 2 SCC 362.

sanctity and the fair name of the institution including the reputation of the Office of the Director of CBI. The Court directed that 'the CBI Director Shri Ranjit Sinha should not interfere in investigation and prosecution of the case relating to the 2G Spectrum allocation being carried out by CBI, and to recuse himself from the case'.

In *Manohar Lal Sharma v. Principal Secy.*[9] dealing with the question of the nature of procedural norms applicable to the CBI, the Court held that–

> Once jurisdiction is conferred on CBI to investigate the offence by virtue of notification under Section 3 of the DSPE Act or CBI takes up investigation in relation to the crime which is otherwise within the jurisdiction of the State police on the direction of the constitutional court, the exercise of the power of investigation by CBI is regulated by the Code and the guidelines are provided in the CBI (Crime) Manual... A proper investigation into crime is one of the essentials of the criminal justice system and an integral facet of rule of law. The investigation by the police under the Code has to be fair, impartial and uninfluenced by external influences. Where investigation into crime is handled by CBI under the DSPE Act, the same principles apply and CBI as an investigating agency is supposed to discharge its responsibility with competence, promptness, fairness and uninfluenced and unhindered by external influences.

11.1.3 Commissions of Inquiry

In India the Commissions of Inquiry are constituted under the Commissions of Inquiry Act, 1952.

The commissions of inquiry are a hybrid of the judicial and administrative limb of the State. Their primary function is to act as fact-finding bodies which reports its findings to the government appointing it for the purpose of their knowledge, information and guidance. They are deemed to be a tool in the hands of the government for collection of information on matters of public importance. The Law Commission of India in its 24th Report (1962) on the Commissions of Inquiry Act, 1952 highlighted the genesis of the legislation as–

> The Commission of Inquiry Act, 1952 was enacted after due consultation with State Governments to facilitate the setting up of commissions with requisite powers to inquire into and report on any matter of public importance. Government realized, on the basis of its previous experience, that the expedient of promoting special legislation for setting up a commission of inquiry each time the need for it arose involved a tardy process which more often than

9. (2014) 2 SCC 532.

> not ended in the withdrawal of the proposals for inquiry. On the other hand Government felt convinced of the utility of such inquiries as a means of arriving at a proper appraisal of matters of public importance and of infusing the confidence of the public in its administration and conduct. As the necessity for such inquiries was bound to be recurring one, it was felt advantageous to have an enactment generalizing the powers which commissions of inquiry may exercise and leaving it to the Government to constitute a Commission as and when necessary.[10]

In *Jagannath v. State of Orissa*[11] the object of the statute was highlighted as–

> The purpose of the enquiry is stated in the preamble to the notification which states that "the matters aforesaid regarding the aforesaid persons should be enquired into through a Commission of Inquiry so that facts may be found which alone will facilitate rectification and prevention of recurrence of such lapses and securing the ends of justice and establishing a moral public order in future". In other words, the object of the enquiry to be made by the Commission appointed under Section 3 of the Act was to take appropriate legislative or administrative measures to maintain the purity and integrity of political administration in the State.

The important features of the legislation are–

(1) Appropriate Government on its own motion or on a resolution passed by the Legislature can appoint a commission for making an inquiry into a definite matter of public importance.
(2) Commission is conferred with the powers of Civil Court for summoning and enforcing attendance of any person, requisitioning documents, receiving any public document, issuing commission for the examination of any witness or documents etc.
(3) Nature of functioning of the Commission is investigatory and inquisitorial.
(4) No statements made by a person before a Commission can be used against him in any civil or criminal proceeding.
(5) Deemed to be quasi-judicial body and bound by principles of natural justice
(6) Commission acts as advisor to the government and makes recommendations to the government for future of action.
(7) Even if the recommendations are not be acceptable to the government, but the publicity of the recommendation have great social and administrative relevance.

10. 24th Law Commission Report, p. 1.
11. (1968) 3 SCR 789, para 11.

Highlighting the importance of the recommendations the Supreme Court in *Ram Krishna Dalmia v. Justice S.R. Tendolkar*[12]

> The whole purpose of setting up of a Commission of Inquiry consisting of experts will be frustrated and the elaborate process of inquiry will be deprived of its utility if the opinion and the advice of the expert body as to the measures and the situation disclosed calls for cannot be placed before the government for consideration notwithstanding that doing so cannot be to the prejudice of anybody because it has no force of its own. In our view the recommendations of a Commission of Inquiry are of great importance to the government in order to enable it to make up its mind as to what legislative or administrative measures should be adopted to eradicate the evil found or to implement the beneficial objects it has in view. From this point of view, there can be no objection even to the Commission of Inquiry recommending the imposition of some form of punishment which will, in its opinion, be sufficiently deterrent to delinquents in future. But seeing that the Commission of Inquiry has no judicial powers and its report will purely be recommendatory and not effective proprio vigore...

In *Kehar Singh v. State*[13] it was further clarified that *the statement made by any person before the Commission of Inquiry under Section 6 of the Act is wholly inadmissible in evidence in any future proceedings civil or criminal.*

Speaking on the nature of proceeding followed by the Inquiry Commissions the Court was observed that–

> The Commission under our Act is given the power to regulate its own procedure and also to decide whether to sit in camera or in public. A Commission appointed under the Act does not decide any dispute. There are no parties before the Commission. There is no lis. The Commission is not a court except for a limited purpose. The procedure of the Commission is inquisitorial rather than accusatorial. The Commission more often may have to give assurance to persons giving evidence before it that their statements will not be used in any subsequent proceedings except for perjury. Without such an assurance, the persons may not come forward to give statements. If persons have got lurking fear that their statements given before the Commission are likely to be used against them or utilised for productive use on them in any other proceeding, they may be reluctant to expose themselves before the Commission. Then the Commission would not be able to perform its task. The Commission would not be able to reach the nuggets of truth from the obscure horizon. The purpose for which the Commission is constituted may be defeated.[14]

12. AIR 1958 SC 538.
13. (1988) 3 SCC 609.
14. Id (1988) 3 SCC 609, para 237.

In *Sanjiv Kumar v. State of Haryana*[15] an important issue was deliberated by the Court about whether the Commission of Inquiry can be entrusted to conduct inquiries in criminal matters assisted by a special investigating task force. Negating the same the Court highlighted some of the short comings of the commissions of inquiry–

> The flaw with Commissions of Inquiry, as revealed by experience, is that they do not have enough teeth and for their functioning they have to depend on the State's assistance. Commissions of Inquiry remain pending for unreasonable lengths of time. The reports submitted do not bind the State and in spite of transparency and public hearings which the Commissions often hold, at times with fanfare, the reports hardly serve any purpose. By the time the reports are submitted the public memory has already fainted and people are not any more bothered about the results. It is in the discretion of the State to take or not to take any action on the report submitted by the Commission of Inquiry and the experience is that the follow-up action depends more on political considerations rather than for public good.
>
> We feel, Commissions of Inquiry are more suited for inquiring into such matters of public importance where the purpose is to find out the truth so as to learn lessons for the future and devise policies or frame legislation to avoid recurrence of lapses. Such Commissions do not suitably serve the object of punishing the guilty.

11.1.4 Present Significance

In the present context the importance of Commissions of Inquiry can be justified in the context of fulfilling the goals of people's right to know and be informed about major events of public importance under Article 19(1)(a) of the Constitution. By conducting public inquiry into major socio-economic and political matters it helps to promote transparency and good governance in public life. All efforts should be made to ensure that the independence of the institution is protected and it does not become a tool of political vendetta in the hands of political establishments.

11.2 PART II - INSTITUTIONS PROMOTING GOOD GOVERNANCE AND ACCOUNTABILITY

In the second part of the topic relating to implementation of Good Governance Initiatives a brief discussion about the three important institutions of – Comptroller and Auditor General of India (CAG), Central Vigilance Commission (CVC) and Lokpal and Lokayukta have been done. These

15. (2005) 5 SCC 517, para 13.

institutions in recent years have been acting as crusaders towards promoting accountability, transparency and rule of law in society.

Comptroller and Auditor-General of India (CAG)

11.2.1 Introduction

CAG is the *supreme audit institution* of India.[16] It is created under the Constitution of India as the 'auditor of India' and is neither part of the legislature nor executive. Globally the role of government auditors in recent years has undergone significant changes.[17] It is recognized that the primary functions of these institutions are beyond the traditional accounting tasks and include program evaluations, policy analyses, and offering legal opinions and decisions on a wide range of government programs and activities.[18] The functional objectives of these institutions are to *promote accountability, transparency and good governance through high quality auditing and accounting and provide independent assurance to our stakeholders, the Legislature, the Executive and the Public, that public funds are being used efficiently and for the intended purpose.*[19] From merely questioning whether the government funds were being spent appropriately, these institutions whether the various government schemes and programmes are in compliance with constitutional goals and needs of the society. These institutions have become flag bearers of transparency and accountability in government activities. Recognizing the importance of CAG it has held that "functioning of the Government is controlled by the government, laws of the land, legislature and the CAG".[20] It has the power to examine the *propriety, legality and validity* of all the government expenditures.

The UN General Assembly had passed a resolution in 2012 for the purpose 'promoting the efficiency, accountability, effectiveness and transparency of public administration by strengthening supreme audit institutions'.[21] It emphasised the importance of the SAIs in promoting national development objectives as well as internationally agreed development goals.[22]

16. The Comptroller and Auditor General is known as the Supreme Audit Institution in international parlance.
17. In US the name of General Accounting Office has been changed to *Government Accountability Office.*
18. David M. Walker, GAO Answers the Question: What's in a Name?, Available at :http://www.saiindia.gov.in/english/home/about_us/mandate/Excerpts/excerpts-mandate.pdf.
19. Comptroller and Auditor General of India, available at http://www.saiindia.gov.in/english/index.html.
20. *S. Subramniam Balaji v. State of Tamil Nadu* (2013) 9 SCC 659
21. UN General Assembly Resolution – A/Res/66/209.
22. Id.

11.2.2.1 CAG - historical background

The office of the CAG was established for the first time in the year 1858 when the British Crown proclaimed their authority to govern the British India from the East India Company.[23] The office was designated as Accountant General to Government of India and was responsible for maintaining the accounts of the Indian Empire as well as performing audit. In 1884 the designation was changed to Comptroller and Auditor General of Accounts. By the Government of India Act, 1935 several changes were introduced in the functioning of the CAG to ensure his functional independence. Firstly the CAG was to be appointed by the King of England, secondly he could be removed from office 'in like manner and on the like grounds as a judge of the Federal Court', and thirdly on vacating office he could not hold any other office under the Crown in India.

11.2.2.2 Constitutional authority

Articel 148 of the Constitution provides for the appointment of the Comptroller and Auditor-General of India for the purpose of auditing all receipts and expenditure of the Government of India and the state governments, including those bodies and authorities which have been substantially financed by the government.[24] In *Association of Unified Tele Services Providers v. Union of India*[25] the Supreme Court categorically observed that "Duties and powers conferred by the Constitution on the CAG under Article 149 cannot be taken away by the Parliament, being the basic structure of our Constitution, like Parliamentary democracy, independence of judiciary, rule of law, judicial review, unity and integrity of the country, secular and federal character of the Constitution, and so on".

CAG is also the external auditor of Government-owned corporations and conducts supplementary audit of government companies, i.e. any non-banking / non-insurance companies wherein the state and the Union governments have an equity share of at least 51 percent or they are subsidiary companies of existing government companies.

CAG is the head of the Indian Audit and Accounts Department, which comprises of officers of the Indian Audit and Accounts Service.

The Constitution has not prescribed any qualifications for the appointment to the post of CAG, but traditionally it has been held by a civil servant. On the issue of whether the CAG should be selected from amongst Chartered

23. **See** generally 'History of CAG', Available at : http://www.saiindia.gov.in/english/home/about_us/history/1990-2007/Vol_1/chap_1.pdf.
24. *S. Subramniam Balaji v. State of Tamil Nadu*, (2013) 9 SCC 659.
25. Judgment delivered on April 17, 2014.

Accountants, a member of the drafting committee of the Constitution Shri T.T. Krishnamachari had observed, *"[A]ctually the man who is an Auditor General is not an Accountant per se. He has a number of other duties to perform and in so functioning, he has got to have a knowledge of the entire administration and I think the present method of appointment of Auditors General in India is perhaps the best."*[26] In the case of *N. Gopalaswami v. Union of India*[27] it was reiterated that the appointment procedure laid down under Article 148(1) only stipulates that the CAG will be appointed by the President by warrant under his hand and seal on the aid and advice of the Council of Ministers headed by the Prime Minister. "There is no prescribed criteria as to what qualifications a person must possess before he is considered for the post of the CAG.... Of course, the person being considered for the position of the CAG must have a comprehensive knowledge of the entire administration".[28] It was further clarified that the since the *constitutional post of a CAG is an integrity institution the incumbent must have the qualities of competence and integrity.*[29]

11.2.2.3 Status and power

CAG is ranked 9th in the Indian order of precedence and enjoys the status of a judge of the Supreme Court. He is appointed by the President of India on the recommendation of the Prime Minister. On appointment he takes the oath of upholding the Constitution and other laws of India and safeguard the interests of the public exchequer[30] His function is often described as *'the guardian of the purse and that he should see that not farthing of it is spent without the authority of the Parliament'.*

The salary and other service conditions are determined by the Parliament through the Comptroller and Auditor-General's (Duties, Power and Conditions of Service) Act, 1971. The statute entitles the CAG to enjoy salary equivalent to the salary of a judge of the Supreme Court. His salary is charged on the Consolidated Fund of India.[31] The statute also provides for security of tenure and independence in office by ensuring the salary, his legal rights, retirement benefits etc. cannot be varied to his detriment after his appointment.[32] In addition, the CAG can be only removed from office in a manner and on

26. The Comptroller & Auditor General of India – A Thematic History 1990-2007 Vol-1 p. 10.
27. WP(C) 4653/2013 Judgment delivered on 13.08.2014.
28. *N. Gopalaswami v. Union of India*, Id at Para 46.
29. *N. Gopalaswami v. Union of India*, Id at Para 46.
30. Constitution of India, Third Schedule, Part IV.
31. Article 148 (6).
32. Article 148 (3).

grounds similar to a judge of the Supreme Court. After he ceases to be in office he becomes ineligible to hold office either under the Government of India or under any of the state government.[33]

Speaking on the importance of CAG in modern day governance and the need to uphold the dignity and the independence of the office Dr. Ambedkar had observed, "Personally speaking for myself, I am of the opinion that this dignitary or officer is probably the most important officer in the Constitution of India... and his duties, I submit, are far more important than the duties even of the judiciary – he should be certainly as independent as the Judiciary".[34]

11.2.2.4 Functions

The CAG is required to perform such duties and exercise such powers as prescribed by the Parliament.[35] Post-independence there existed four field offices within the Audit Department namely Civil, P&T, Railway and Defence Services audit offices. The department was faced with severe human resource as well as financial crisis in face of the growing responsibilities. The functions and the activities of CAG increased manifold with twin development of centralized planning system under the Five Year Plans and the growth of the public sector enterprises. In recent years the creation of the Panchayati Raj Institutions and the process of economic liberalization had further increased their responsibilities.

The Comptroller and Auditor-General's (Duties, Power and Conditions of Service) Act, 1971 lays down the duties and powers of CAG. The primary function is to conduct audit of government accounts and audit all expenditures of the Union and the state government, whether incurred in India or outside. The duties and function includes compiling the accounts of any particular service or departments the Union and of each State or the accounts of any particular class or character.[36] The accounts of the government are required to be maintained in the form as prescribed by the CAG.[37] It has to ensure that the rules and procedures framed for the purpose of effective check on the assessment, collection and proper allocation of revenue are being strictly adhered.[38] In *Arvind Gupta v. Union of India*[39] it was reiterated that the function of CAG should be analysed from the

33. Article 148 (4).
34. The Comptroller & Auditor General of India – A Thematic History 1990-2007 Vol-1 p. 11.
35. Article 149.
36. CAG Act S. 10.
37. Article 150.
38. *Arun Kumar Agarwal v. Union of India*, (2013) 7 SCC 1.
39. (2013) 1 SCC 393.

perspective of ensuring efficiency and effectiveness of government functions and resources utilization.

Some of the duties of CAG[40] are–

(i) To audit all expenditure from the Consolidated Fund of India and of each State and Union Territory and to ascertain whether the moneys shown in the accounts as having been disbursed were legally available for and applicable to the service or purpose to which they have been applied or charged and whether the expenditure conforms to the authority which governs it;

(ii) To audit all transactions of the Union and the States relating to Contingency Funds and Public Accounts;

(iii) To audit all trading, manufacturing, profit and loss accounts and balance-sheets and other subsidiary accounts kept in any department of the Union or of a State, and in each case to report on the expenditure, transactions or accounts so audited by him;

(iv) To audit receipts and expenditure of bodies or authorities substantially financed from Union or State Revenues;

(v) To audit the accounts of Government companies and corporations;

(vi) To audit the accounts of any other bodies and authorities as requested by the President or the Governor of a State.

Other function includes auditing of accounts of stores and stocks kept in any government office or department[41]; auditing of all receipts which are payable into the Consolidated Fund of India and of each State and also to ensure that all rules and procedures designed to secure an effective check on the assessment, collection and proper allocation of revenue are duly complied with[42] etc.

The CAG has been entrusted with the power to inspect any office of accounts, require the submission of any accounts, books, papers or any other documents for the purpose

11.2.2.5 CAG Reports

The reports of the CAG are relating to the accounts of the Union are required to be submitted to the President, who shall cause them to be laid before both Houses of Parliament and those relating to the States will be submitted to the Governor for the purpose of being placed before the state legislature.[43] In *Arun Kumar Agarwal v. Union of India*[44] the Court

40. **See** generally Sections 13, 14, 15, 19 and 20.
41. Section 15.
42. Section 16.
43. Article 151.
44. (2013) 7 SCC 1.

emphasized that by placing the reports in the Parliament, the CAG facilitates the accountability of the Executive to the Parliament on financial issues and thereby upholds the principles of parliamentary democracy.

In recent years the various reports of the CAG dealing with Commonwealth games, allocation of 2G Spectrum, coal mines have assumed great significance as they have been instrumental in exposing corruption and consequently loss to the government exchequer.

11.2.2.6 Power to audit private corporations

In the case of *Association of Unified Tele Services Providers v. Union of India*[45] the Supreme Court had to deal with the crucial question regarding whether CAG can exercise the authority to conduct audit of private corporations such as the tele-service providers when they deal with natural resources belonging to the nation. It categorically held that it is the responsibility of the CAG to ensure that all the rules and procedures are properly adhered by the Government as well as the private service providers when they deal with important natural resources of the nation. It observed–

> [W]hen the executive deals with the natural resources, like spectrum, which belongs to the people of this country, Parliament should know how the nation's wealth has been dealt with by the executive and even by the UAS Licence holders and the quantum of the Revenue generated out of the use of the spectrum and whether the same has been properly assessed, collected and accounted for by the Union and the UAS Licence holders. When nation's wealth, like spectrum, is being dealt with either by the Union, State or its instrumentalities or even the private parties, like service providers, they are accountable to the people and to the Parliament. Parliamentary democracy also envisages, inter alia, the accountability of the Council of Ministers to the Legislature.
>
> ......
>
> While examining the scope of Article 149, read with Section 16 of 1971 Act, let us not forget that we are dealing with a natural resource which belongs to the peoples of this country, and hence we have to give a purposive interpretation to Article 149 read with Section 16 of 1971 Act and Rule 5(i)(ii) of 2002 Rules.
>
> ....
>
> Parliament has an obligation to ascertain whether the entire receipts by way of licence fee, spectrum charges, have been realized by the Union of India and credited to the Consolidated Fund of India (CFI). Article 266 says, all the public moneys received by or on behalf of the Government of India shall be

45. CA NO. 4591 OF 2014 Judgment delivered on April 17, 2014.

credited to CFI. CAG can carry out examination into the economy, efficacy and effectiveness with which the Union of India has used its resources, and whether it has realized the entire licencee fee, spectrum charges and also whether the Union of India has correctly carried out the audit under Clauses 22.5 and 22.6 of UAS Licence Agreement. CAG's examination of the accounts of the Service Providers in a Revenue Sharing Contract is extremely important to ascertain whether there is an unlawful gain to the Service Provider and an unlawful loss to the Union of India, because the revenue generated out of that has to be credited to the Consolidated Fund of India. The subject matter, with which we are concerned, as already indicated, is "spectrum", a natural resource, which belongs to the people, therefore, people of this country, through Parliament should know how its natural resources have been dealt with by the Union, State or its instrumentalities or even by UAS licence holders. Instances are not rare, where even the Executive, at times, acts hand in glove with licence holders, who deal with the natural resources, hence, necessity of proper parliamentary control over the resources. We have to understand the scope of Article 149 of the Constitution, Section 16 of 1971 Act and Rule 5 of TRAI Rules 2002, in that perspective.

Post liberalization the role and function of the state has undergone changes. Privatization and private-public partnership models have become the norm for economic activities as well as executing major infrastructure projects. Under the present scheme of things almost 65 percent of government spending does not come under the scrutiny of the CAG. The judiciary has recognized the growing importance of CAG as an important social audit and accountability institution and has categorically held that the role and responsibility of CAG should accommodate the changing demands of the day and should function in a way so as to ascertain that the citizens and the Union of India receives their due share from exploitation of national wealth and resources and that the unscrupulous and corrupt practices of some individuals do not give rise to windfall gains to few. It is important that all efforts should be made to enable the CAG to act as an *integrity institution* by enabling it to work in an independent and professional manner. Thus it has become necessary to amend the Audit Act 1971 to bring all private-public partnerships (PPPs), Panchayati Raj Institutions and societies getting government funds within the jurisdiction of CAG.

11.2.2 Central Vigilance Commission

On the basis of recommendations made by the Committee on Prevention of Corruption, popularly known as the Santhanam Committee[46], the Central Vigilance Commission (CVC) was set up by the Government of India in 1964 to aid and advise the Central Government agencies in the field of

46. Committee chaired by Shri K. Santhanam.

vigilance. As a consequence of the judgment of the Supreme Court in *Vineet Narain v. Union of India*[47], through the Central Vigilance Commission Act, 2003 the institution was conferred with statutory status. It is the *apex vigilance institution* in charge of monitoring all vigilance activity of the Central Government organizations in 'planning, executing, reviewing and reforming their vigilance work'.[48] It acts as a vigilance authority over the administration of different Ministries and other organizations of the Central Government. The Commission functions through administrative set up, guidelines and manuals.

Under the CVC Act the commission is a multi-member body consisting of a Central Vigilance Commissioner and not more than two Vigilance Commissioners (members). The total sanctioned strength of the Commission is 296 officials. All government departments and organizations under the Commission's jurisdiction has vigilance units headed by Chief Vigilance Officers (CVO). The CVOs are considered as an extended arm of the Commission.

The primary function of CVC is to advise the Central Government on all matters pertaining to the maintenance of integrity in administration. It has its own Secretariat, Chief Technical Examiners' Wing (CTE) and a wing of Commissioners for Departmental Inquiries (CDI).

The CTE is concerned with the technical wing of the CVC and is headed by two Engineers of the rank of Chief Engineers (designated as Chief Technical Examiners) and is supported by a group of engineering staff. The primary functions of CTE are–

- Technical audit of construction works of Governmental organisations from a vigilance angle;
- Investigation of specific cases of complaints relating to construction works;
- Extension of assistance to CBI in their investigations involving technical matters and for evaluation of properties in Delhi; and
- Tendering of advice / assistance to the Commission and Chief Vigilance Officers in vigilance cases involving technical matters.

The CDI comprises of fourteen Commissioners for Department Inquiries whose primary function is to act as Inquiry Officers and conduct oral inquiries in departmental proceedings initiated against public servants. Under Section14 of the CVC Act an annual report is required to be submitted to the President of India highlighting the work done by the Commission during the year.

47. (1998) 1 SCC 226.
48. Abailable at : http://cvc.gov.in/cvc_back.htm (last visited 20/11/15).

(i) Vigilance Activities

Under the CVC Act 2003 the Commission is empowered to call for reports, returns, statements from all Ministries / Departments / Corporation / Central Undertakings so as to enable it exercise general check and supervision over their vigilance and anti-corruption work. The CVOs of different organizations are required to submit quarterly progress reports to the Commission.

(ii) Dealing with Anti-Corruption Matters

CVC exercises superintendence over the working of the Delhi Special Police Establishment (CBI), which is the principal investigating agency of the Central Government in anti-corruption matters, in all matters relating to investigation of offences under the Prevention of Corruption Act, 1988. By a government resolution on 'Public Interest Disclosure and Protection of Informer' the CVC has been authorized as the Designated Agency to receive all written complaints dealing with corruption or misuse of office and make necessary recommendation for appropriate action.[49] In 2014 the Commission tendered advices in 5867 cases involving major and minor penalty proceedings.[50] It recommended grant for sanction of prosecution in 93 cases and against 133 public servants in the year 2014.[51]

The CVC had also provided special assistance to the Supreme Court in the 2G Spectrum cases and the coal block allocation matters. Under the Lokpal and Lokayuktas Act, 2013 the CVC has been empowered to conduct preliminary inquiry into complaints referred by the Lokpal. The Act also provides for constitution of a Directorate of Inquiry to be constituted within the CVC.

(iii) Integrity Pack

One of the pioneering initiatives of the Commission was to promote transparency, equity and competitiveness in public procurements through the Integrity Pact (IP). In 2007 the Commission implemented the concept of IP in respect of all major government procurements wherein 'an agreement is made between the prospective vendors/bidders and the buyer committing the persons / officials of both the parties not to exercise any corrupt influence on any aspect of the contract.'[52] Under the Standard Operating Procedure for implementation of IP a panel of Independent External Monitors is required to be appointed for reviewing independently

49. GOI Resolution dated April 2004.
50. CVC Annual Report 2014.
51. Id.
52. CVC Office Order No. 41/12/07 dated 04.12.2007.

and objectively the compliance of IP. Application of the IP is mandatory for all Ministries / Departments / Organizations and as part of it nearly 100 Ministries / Departments / Organizations have appointed Independent External Monitors. It has been advocating for the use of e-procurement technologies for procurements / contracts so as to ensure transparency in government procurements and better project management.

(iv) Guidelines for Intensive Examination of Public Procurement and Other Contracts 2014

The Commission has recently come out with a detailed guideline on various public procurement contracts such as work contracts, purchase of goods, hiring of services etc. These guidelines are required to be treated as 'Standard Operating Procedure' in public procurement matters.

11.2.3 Lokpal and Lokayukta

The first Administrative Reforms Commission had recommended the setting up of the institution of Lok Pal. The ARC headed by Shri Moraji Desai had submitted a report on 'Problems of Redressal of Citizen's Grievances' in 1966. The report recommended for the creation of the two institutions of Lokpal and Lokayukta to deal with citizen's redress. The Lok Pal as an institution was supposed to act as a *watchdog over the integrity of Ministers and the Members of Parliament.* Subsequently the Lok Pal Bill was introduced several times in Parliament but it failed to be enacted into law.

Based on the recommendation of the first Administrative Reforms Commission *Lokayukta* was constituted in many States to investigate allegations or grievances arising out of the conduct of public servants including political executives, legislators, officers of the State Government, local bodies, public enterprises and other instrumentalities of Government. It investigates into allegations of corruption and mal-administration in public offices and tries to redress public grievances. Maharashtra was the first state to introduce Lokayukta through the Maharashtra Lokayukta and Upa-Lokayuktas Act 1971. There are about 19 states which have introduced Lokayukta. There are no Lokayukta in Arunachal Pradesh, Jammu and Kashmir, Manipur, Meghalaya, Mizoram, Nagaland, Sikkim, Tamil Nadu, Tripura and West Bengal. A Lokayukta is generally a former High Court Chief Justice or a Supreme Court judge. A citizen can make a complaint directly to the Lokayukta against any public servant or elected representatives. The Lokayukta can also initiate suo-motu inquiry into the conduct of public servants. The institution of Lokayukta in Karnataka is considered as one of the most effective bodies. Santosh Hegde, former Lokayukta of Karnataka had uncovered one of the biggest mining scams of the country and which lead to the imprisonment of the then Chief Minister Yeddyurappa.

In 2013 after major public outcry and large scale demonstrations by eminent anti-corruption activist Shri Anna Hazare, the Parliament enacted 'The Lokpal and Lokayukta Act, 2013. The law was enacted with the objective 'to provide for the establishment of the institution of Lokpal to inquire into allegations of corruption against certain public functionaries and for matters connecting them.' Some of the major features of the Act are–

(i) Act is applicable to States if they give consent to its application

(ii) Act excludes public servants who are covered under the Army Act, 1950; the Air Force Act, 1950; the Navy Act, 1957 and the Coast Guard, 1978.

(iii) Lokpal shall consist of a Chairperson and such number of Members not exceeding eight.

(vi) Appointment of a Director of Inquiry and a Director of Prosecution.

(v) Director of Inquiry shall be for the in charge of the Inquiry Wing constituted for the purpose of conducting preliminary inquiry into any offence alleged to have been committed by a public servant punishable under the Prevention of Corruption Act, 1988.

(vi) Director of Prosecution shall be for the in charge of the Prosecution Wing constituted for the purpose of prosecution of public servant in relation to any complaint by the Lokpal under the Act.

(vii) Inquiry can be conducted in an allegation of corruption made against a Prime Minister, Ministers, Members of Parliament, Groups A, B, C and D officers and officials of Central Government, and officers, directors and managers of corporations and bodies established by an Act of Parliament or wholly or partly financed by the Central Government or controlled by it.

(viii) Every public servant shall make a declaration of his assets and liabilities as well as those of his spouse and dependent children.

(ix) An inquiry against the PM can be initiated if it has been approved by a $2/3^{rd}$ majority of the full bench of the Lokpal

(x) Investigations are to be completed within a period of 6 months. An extension of 6 months at a time may be granted for reasons to be recorded in writing.

(xi) Lokpal shall send a copy of the investigation report to the Competent Authority (Lok Sabha – PM, Speaker or Chairman as the case may be.) The Competent Authority shall table the report in the House.

(xii) Lokpal has the power to make recommendations for transfer or suspension of public servants connected with allegation of corruption

(xiii) Special Courts to be constituted by the Central Government to hear and decide the cases arising out of the Prevention of Corruption Act, 1988 or under this Act.

(xiv) If the Special Court makes an assessment of losses caused to the public exchequer by a convicted public servant, then it may order for recovery of such losses from the public servant so convicted.

(xv) Similar provisions have made for appointment of Lokayukta at the State.

Inspite of the enactment of the Lokpal Act the Lokpal is yet to be constituted. The legislation is a positive step towards fighting corruption and all efforts should be made to bring the institution into force at the earliest.

11.3 PART III - CITIZEN-CENTRIC INITIATIVES

In the third part of the topic a brief discussion about three recent major initiatives for promoting citizen-centric model of governance have been done – Right to Information, Citizen's Charter and Timely Delivery of Service, and e-Governance. The focus of these initiatives has been to place citizens and their needs at the centre-stage of governance and national policies.

Right to Information

> True democracy cannot exist unless all citizens have a right to participate in the affairs of the polity of the country. The right to participate in the affairs of the country is meaningless unless the citizens are well-informed on all sides of the issues, in respect of which they are called upon to express their views. One-sided information, disinformation, misinformation and non-information all equally create an uninformed citizenry which makes democracy a farce when medium of information is monopolised either by a partisan central authority or by private individuals or oligarchic organisations. This is particularly so in a country like ours where about 65% of the population is illiterate and hardly 1½% of the population has an access to the print media which is not subject to pre-censorship.[53]

Right to information is equated with right to know and is considered to be an integral part of free speech. It is internationally recognized as part of human right and incorporated in the basic human rights documents such as the Universal Declaration of Human Rights, the International Covenant on Civil and Political Rights and the International Covenant on Economic, Social and Cultural Rights.

---

53. *Ministry of Information and Broadcasting, Govt. of India v. Cricket Assn. of Bengal,* (1995) 2 SCC 161, para 82.

Right to Information Act 2005 was enacted to promote transparency and accountability in administration.[54] The statute empowers the citizens to seek information from a Public Authority. Public disclosure of information is likely to give people an idea about the working of the Government and thereby make its functionaries more accountable and responsible.

> The basic object of the Right to Information Act is to empower the citizens, promote transparency and accountability in the working of the Government, contain corruption, and make our democracy work for the people in real sense. It goes without saying that an informed citizen is better equipped to keep necessary vigil on the instruments of governance and make the government more accountable to the governed. The Act is a big step towards making the citizens informed about the activities of the Government.[55]

In *Namit Sharma v. Union of India*[56] the Court observed that–

> Ours is a constitutional democracy and it is axiomatic that citizens have the right to know about the affairs of the Government which, having been elected by them, seeks to formulate some policies of governance aimed at their welfare. However, like any other freedom, this freedom also has limitations.
>
> It is a settled proposition that the right to freedom of speech and expression enshrined under Article 19(1)(*a*) of the Constitution of India encompasses the right to impart and receive information. The right to information has been stated to be one of the important facets of proper governance. With the passage of time, this concept has not only developed in the field of law, but also has attained new dimensions in its application. This Court while highlighting the need for the society and its entitlement to know has observed that public interest is better served by effective application of the right to information. This freedom has been accepted in one form or the other in various parts of the world.

RTI Act has been a major step towards creating an accountable, transparent, corruption-free and citizen-centric administration. This objective was highlighted in the *Namit Sharma case* wherein it was observed–

> The right to information was harnessed as a tool for promoting development; the strengthening the democratic governance and effective delivery of socio-economic services. Acquisition of information and knowledge and its application have intense and pervasive impact on the process of taking informed decision, resulting in overall productivity gains. It is also said that information and knowledge are critical for realising all human aspirations such as improvement in the quality of life. Sharing of information, for instance, about the new techniques

54. Abailable at : http://www.righttoinformation.gov.in/rticorner/studybypwc/Executive%20 Summary.pdf.
55. Abailable at : http://www.righttoinformation.gov.in/Id.
56. Id.

of farming, health care facilities, hazards of environmental degradation, opportunities for learning and earning, legal remedies for combating gender bias, etc. have over time made significant contributions to the well-being of poor people. It is also felt that this right and the laws relating thereto empower every citizen to take charge of his life and make proper choices on the basis of freely available information for effective participation in economic and political activities.[57]

Salient features of the statute are–

1. To secure access to information which are under the control of public authorities
2. To constitute a Central Information Commission and State Information Commissions
3. Obligation of Public Authorities to make suo motu disclosure of certain vital information
4. Citizen can make an application to the Information Officer for acquiring information.
5. On failure to receive information within a specified period then appeal may be made to the first Appellate Authority
6. Central Information Commission and State Information Commissions to act as quasi-judicial bodies

The basic tenets of the statute have been implemented, but it is faced with major challenges in the form of administrative apathy, compulsive behaviour among officers to deny or delay disclosure of information and lack of physical security to RTI seekers which needs to be overcome to fulfil the true goals of RTI. Efforts should be made to improve RTI awareness among the common citizens so that people realize the advantages of the legal right to information.

11.3.1 Citizen Charters and Timely Delivery of Goods and Services

Indian Constitution guarantees to its citizens *justice – social, economic and political* through a welfare economic model. The State has undertaken to provide a number of important services like issuance of passports, driving licenses, voters ID card, Aadhar cards etc. But even after 67 years of independence public delivery of essential services have been in pitiable conditions with factors like inordinate delays, corruption, bureaucratic insensitivity, red tapism, bribery which forced citizens to undergo difficult and unpleasant experiences while accessing these services. The process of

57. (2013) 1 SCC 745, para 23.

governance suffered from lack of transparency, accountability, responsiveness, ineffective grievance redressal mechanism and absence of a centralized monitoring system. These factors resulted in apathy among the citizens, break down of public service systems, loss of revenue for the state exchequer and a general unrest in society.[58] One of the ways by which efforts were made by the State to provide quality and timely delivery of public services was by promoting the concept of *citizen's charter.*

> Citizens' Charter is based on the premise that the Citizen is "King" and government organizations exist not to rule but to serve the citizens. Citizens' Charters are merely reflections of this principle. In order to ensure that both the service provider as well as citizens realize that public agencies are meant to provide service, each organization should spell out the services it has to perform and then specify the standards/norms for these services. Once this is done then the organisation can be held to account if the service standards are not met. Government of India commenced the exercise to formulate Citizens' Charters in 1996.[59]

Citizen's charters are described as 'an instrument which seeks to make an organization transparent, accountable and citizen friendly....is basically a set of commitments made by an organization regarding the standards of service which it delivers.'[60]

The Second Administrative Reforms Committee in its Fourth Report on 'Ethics in Governance' had highlighted that 'in order to make Charters an effective tool for holding public servants accountable, the Charters should clearly spell out the remedy/penalty/ compensation in case there is a default in meeting the standards spelt out in the Charter.'

The ARC Seven Step Model for Citizen Centricity[61] is–

(a) Define all services which you provide and identify your clients.
(b) Set standards and norms for each service
(c) Develop capability to meet the set standards
(d) Performs to achieve the standards
(e) Monitor performance against the set standards
(f) Evaluate the impact through an independent mechanism
(g) Continuous improvement based on monitoring and evaluation of results

58. SAKALA – Citizen Centric Service Delivery Model, Government of Karnataka.
59. Second Administrative Reforms Commission – 12th Report on 'Citizen Centric Administration – The Heart of Governance'.
60. Id.
61. Second Administrative Reforms Commission – 12th Report on 'Citizen Centric Administration – The Heart of Governance'.

As a principle initiative of the Ministry of Administrative Reforms and Public Grievances all Central Government Ministries / Department / Organizations have brought out their own Citizen's Charter and to ensure the effective implementation of the same Nodal Officers have also been appointed in various Ministries / Department / Organizations. By adhering to the concept of Citizen's Charter a commitment is made by the Organization towards *standard, quality and time frame of service delivery, grievance redress mechanism, transparency and accountability.*[62]

In order to achieve the objective of citizen centric administration a Bill was placed before the Lok Sabha on 'The Right of Citizens for Time Bound Delivery of Goods and Services and Redressal of the Grievance Bill, 2011'. The important features of the Bill are –

- Creation of a mechanism to ensure timely delivery of goods and services to citizens.
- Every public authority is required to publish a citizen's charter stating in detail the goods and services to be provided and their timelines for delivery within six months of the commencement of the Act.
- A complaint may be made regarding any grievance related to: (a) citizens charter; (b) functioning of a public authority; or (c) violation of a law, policy or scheme.
- Need to establish a grievance redressal mechanism which shall redress all grievances within 30 working days.
- Need to appoint a Central and State Public Grievance Redressal Commissions.
- A penalty of up to Rs. 50,000 may be levied upon the responsible officer or the Grievance Redressal Officer for failure to render services.

The Bill failed to become a law and was allowed to be lapsed, but in light of the importance of such legislations efforts are being made to bring forth before the Parliament a fresh Right of Citizens Bill. But based on the recommendation of the Administrative Reforms Commission different state governments have included the concept of citizen's charters in the course of performance of their administrative functions.

11.3.1.1 Karnataka sakala services

One of the first states to incorporate the concept of citizen's charter and create a statutory obligation for timely delivery of essential services was Karnataka. Former Chief Minister of Karnataka Shri Sadananda Gowda during his *Janatha Darshan* realized that a significant part of citizens

62. Government of India – Citizen's Charters, Abailable at : http://goicharters.nic.in/chartermain.htm (last visited 6/11/15).

grievances were relating to failure to receive essential services on a time bound manner from the Government. Absence of an adequate grievance redressal mechanism further aggravated the situation. It was then proposed for the creation of "a citizen friendly governance with time bound service guarantee". This facilitated the enactment of the Karnataka Guarantee of Services to Citizens Act, 2011 which was subsequently renamed by the citizens to Karnataka Sakala Services Act, 2011. The term *sakala* in Kannada implies 'in time or good time'. The primary motto of this legislation is *No More Delays...We Deliver in Time... else the hammer of justice strikes on the defaulters.*[63] The core objective of this Act is to provide guarantee of essential services to the citizens within a stipulated time limit and to create a grievance redressal mechanism for effective implementation of the service delivery goals.

The legislation was implemented in April 2012. In a span of two years the Sakala services has been expanded to 47 Government Departments and Institutions and includes 478 government services of which 150 services have been made online. Some of the important departments included are the home, revenue, local authority, rural development and panchayat raj, food and civil supplies, women and child welfare, education, health and family welfare, labour and transport department. According to official sources more than 44 million citizens requests have been delivered on time and the disposal rate is 96.55% till 2013 which indicates significant rate of success. The primary objective of this legislation is to create citizens charters and establish an internal administrative grievance redressal mechanism to deal with issues relating public services and avoid unnecessary government litigation. In facilitation of this objective the statute has imposed a bar on the jurisdiction of the civil courts in respect of matters which the competent officer or appellate authority under the statute is empowered to deal.

The enactment of such statutes have brought in considerable amount of transparency, accountability, reduced corruption and undue delay. It has also empowered the citizens to hold the defaulting officers liable for their acts.

11.3.2 E-governance

The growth of Information and Communication Technology had multifarious impact on the lives of common people, including in the process of governance. Digital technology has provided for cheaper and quicker means of communication; better storage, exchange and processing of information; and enabled superior data analysis for better decision-making.[64] From citizen

63. SAKALA – Citizen Centric Service Delivery Model, Government of Karnataka.

64. Government of India, Information Technology Action Plan: IT for all Indians by 2008.

perspective digital technology has facilitated in providing timely delivery of services in a transparent and hassle free manner. In promoting the goals of a citizen-centric administration digital technology has one of the most vital roles to play in India.

The term e-governance is described as 'usage of information and communication technology at the different levels pertaining to that of the government, for the purposes of carrying out government functions such as that of the delivery of information as well as services of the government, interchange among business undertakings as well as the interchange of information among the various agencies of that of the government.'[65]

National e-Governance Mission

The National e-Governance Plan of Indian Government had sought to lay the foundation and provide the impetus for long-term growth of e-Governance within the country. The objective of the mission was to "Make all Government services accessible to the common man in his locality, through common service delivery outlets and ensure efficiency, transparency & reliability of such services at affordable costs to realise the basic needs of the common man."[66]

As part of the initial efforts to promote e-governance attempts were made to improve the quality of government services to citizens by initiating Government to Citizen (G2C) programs such as computerization of land records, online registration of applications, redressal of public grievances, setting up of computer kiosks in rural areas, payment of taxes through online etc.

e-Governance Projects

- FRIENDS (Kerala) - To provide one-stop, front-end, IT enabled payment counter facility for citizens for making payments for bills originating from government entities.
- Gyandoot (Madhya Pradesh) - To provide useful information and services to people in rural areas and act as an interface between the district administration and rural people.
- bhoomi (Karnataka) - Computerisation of land records; allowing access to land records, updation of land records etc.
- eSeva (Andhra Pradesh) - To provide G2C and B2C services to citizens including online payments, issue of certificates, permits etc.

65. S. Kumar Dwivedi and Ajay Kumar Bharti, E-Governance in India – Problems and Acceptability, Journal of Theoretical and Applied Information Technology (2005).
66. National e-Governance, Abailable at : http://india.gov.in/e-governance/national-e-governance-plan.

- Lokvani (Uttar Pradesh) - To provide information and services to citizens of the district, especially those related to land records and grievance redressal.

e-Gov Services available to citizens online–

(a) e-Tourist visa – It provides information about e-Tourist visa service of Government of India.

(b) IRCTC services – It explains the services offered by IRCTC

(c) Pragati platform – Information relating to e-transparency and e-accountability.

(d) e-Transportation - Links to access the E-Transportation services.

(e) Know your Employee Provident Fund balance through online – Provide details regarding various online services related to Employees Provident Fund.

(f) e-Postal & Telecom Services - Describes various online services of postal and telecom departments.

(g) All about Aadhar - Covers all information related to Aadhaar or Unique Identification Number for individuals in India.

(h) e-Citizen Services - Tips and links to access online services for applying Aadhaar card, PAN card etc.

(i) e-India Information - Provides the political and geographical details of India.

(j) e-Educational services - Information about access to important educational materials / books, exam results, student loans for higher education and educational institutions of India.

11.3.2.1 Digital India

Recently in 2015 the Government of India has launched their flagship programme titled Digital India initiative to ensure that most government services are made available to the citizens electronically and all efforts are made to improve online infrastructure and internet connectivity. The vision of the programme *is to transform India into a digitally empowered society and knowledge economy.*[67] The three key vision areas are –

(i) Digital Infrastructure as a Core Utility to Every Citizen

  (a) Availability of high speed internet as a core utility for delivery of services to citizens

  (b) Cradle to grave digital identity that is unique, lifelong, online and authenticable to every citizen

67. Abailable at : http://digitalindia.gov.in/content/vision-and-vision-areas.

   (c) Mobile phone & bank account enabling citizen participation in digital & financial space
   (d) Easy access to a Common Service Centre
   (e) Shareable private space on a public cloud
   (f) Safe and secure cyber-space

(ii) Governance and Services on Demand
   (a) Seamlessly integrated services across departments or jurisdictions
   (b) Availability of services in real time from online & mobile platforms
   (c) All citizen entitlements to be portable and available on the cloud
   (d) Digitally transformed services for improving ease of doing business
   (e) Making financial transactions electronic & cashless
   (f) Leveraging Geospatial Information Systems (GIS) for decision support systems & development

(iii) Digital Empowerment of Citizens.
   (a) Universal digital literacy
   (b) Universally accessible digital resources
   (c) Availability of digital resources / services in Indian languages
   (d) Collaborative digital platforms for participative governance
   (e) Citizens not required to physically submit Govt. documents / certificates

SUMMATION

More and more involvement of the citizens in matters of governance and policy making is necessary to fulfil the goals of good governance. The crawling steps taken towards promoting citizen-centric governance should be pushed with much more vigour so that India can boast of empowered and enlightened citizenry.